Communications
in Computer and Information Science   1380

Editorial Board Members

Joaquim Filipe ⓘ
   Polytechnic Institute of Setúbal, Setúbal, Portugal
Ashish Ghosh
   Indian Statistical Institute, Kolkata, India
Raquel Oliveira Prates ⓘ
   Federal University of Minas Gerais (UFMG), Belo Horizonte, Brazil
Lizhu Zhou
   Tsinghua University, Beijing, China

More information about this series at http://www.springer.com/series/7899

K. C. Santosh · Bharti Gawali (Eds.)

Recent Trends in Image Processing and Pattern Recognition

Third International Conference, RTIP2R 2020
Aurangabad, India, January 3–4, 2020
Revised Selected Papers, Part I

 Springer

Editors
K. C. Santosh 🆔
University of South Dakota
Vermillion, SD, USA

Bharti Gawali
Dr. Babasaheb Ambedkar
Marathwada University
Aurangabad, India

ISSN 1865-0929   ISSN 1865-0937 (electronic)
Communications in Computer and Information Science
ISBN 978-981-16-0506-2   ISBN 978-981-16-0507-9 (eBook)
https://doi.org/10.1007/978-981-16-0507-9

This Springer imprint is published by the registered company Springer Nature Singapore Pte Ltd.
The registered company address is: 152 Beach Road, #21-01/04 Gateway East, Singapore 189721, Singapore

Preface

It is our great pleasure to introduce the collection of research papers in the Communications in Computer and Information Science (CCIS) Springer series from the third Biennial International Conference on Recent Trends in Image Processing and Pattern Recognition (RTIP2R). The RTIP2R conference event took place at Dr. B.A.M. University, Aurangabad, Maharashtra, India, during January 03–04, 2020, in collaboration with the Department of Computer Science, University of South Dakota (USA). Further, as in 2018, the conference had a very successful workshop titled Pattern Analysis and Machine Intelligence (PAMI), with more than 100 participants.

As announced in the call for papers, RTIP2R attracted current and/or recent research on image processing, pattern recognition, and computer vision with several different applications, such as document understanding, biometrics, medical imaging, and image analysis in agriculture. Altogether, we received 329 submissions and accepted 106 papers for conference presentations. Unlike in the past, conference chairs' reports were also considered to decide on publication. Based on thorough review reports, the conference chairs decided to move forward with 78 papers for publication. As a result, the acceptance rate was 23.70%. As before, we followed a double-blind submission policy and therefore the review process was extremely solid. On average, for a conference presentation, there were at least two reviews per paper except the few that had desk rejections. We also made the authors aware of plagiarism and rejected some of them even after conference presentations.

In brief, the event was found to be a great platform bringing together research scientists, academics, and industry practitioners. Following those review reports, we categorized the papers into five different tracks: a) computer vision and applications; b) data science and machine learning; c) image analysis and recognition; d) healthcare informatics and medical imaging; e) image and signal processing in agriculture.

The conference event (with more than 150 participants) was full of new ideas, including those presented by the primary keynote speaker Prof. Umapada Pal, Indian Statistical Institute (ISI), Kolkata, India.

October 2020

K. C. Santosh
Bharti Gawali

Organization

Conference website: rtip2r-conference.org

Patron

Pramod Yeole (Hon'sble Vice Chancellor)	Dr. B A M Univ., India
Pravin Wakte (Hon'ble Pro-vice Chancellor)	Dr. B A M Univ., India
Sadhana Pande (Registrar)	Dr. B A M Univ., India
Suresh Chandra Mehrotra	Dr. B A M Univ., India
Karbhari Kale	Dr. B A M Univ., India

Honorary Chairs

P. Nagabhushan	IIIT, Allahabad, India
P. S. Hiremath	KLE Technological Univ., India
B. V. Dhandra	Symbiosis International Univ., India

General Chairs

Jean-Marc Ogier	La Rochelle Université, France
D. S. Guru (Conference Steering Committee)	Univ. of Mysore, India
Sameer Antani	National Library of Medicine, USA

Conference Chairs

Bharti Gawali	Dr. B A M Univ., India
K.C. Santosh	Univ. of South Dakota, USA

Organizing Secretary

Pravin Yannawar	Dr. B A M Univ., India

Area Chairs

Szilárd Vajda	Central Washington Univ., USA
Mickaël Coustaty	La Rochelle Université, France
Nibaran Das (Conference Steering Committee)	Jadavpur Univ., India
Nilanjan Dey	Techno International New Town, India

Publicity Chairs

Hubert Cecotti	California State Univ., Fresno, USA
Alba García Seco de Herrera	Univ. of Essex, UK
Alireza Alaei	Southern Cross Univ., Australia
Sabine Barrat	Univ. de Tours., France
Do Thanh Ha	VNU Univ. of Science, Vietnam
B. Uyyanonvara	Thammasat Univ., Thailand
Sk. Md. Obaidullah	Univ. de Évora, Portugal
V. Bevilacqua (Conference Steering Committee)	Polytechnic Univ. of Bari, Italy
R. S. Mente	Solapur Univ., India
Partha Pratim Roy	Indian Inst. of Technology (IIT) Roorkee, India
Manjunath T. N.	BMSIT, India

Finance Chairs

Ramesh Manza	Dr. B A M Univ., India
Ashok Gaikwad	Institute of Management Studies and Information Technology, India

Advisory Committee

Daniel P. Lopresti	Lehigh Univ., USA
Rangachar Kasturi	Univ. of South Florida, USA
Sargur N. Srihari	Univ. at Buffalo, USA
K. R. Rao	Univ. of Texas at Arlington, USA
Ishwar K. Sethi	Oakland Univ., USA
G. K. Ravikumar	CVS Health/Wipro, Texas, USA
Jose Flores	Univ. of South Dakota, USA
Rajkumar Buyya	Univ. of Melbourne, Australia
Arcot Sowmya	UNSW Sydney, Australia
Antanas Verikas	Halmstad Univ., Sweden
B. B. Chaudhuri	Indian Statistical Institute, India
Umapada Pal	ISI, India

Contents – Part I

Data Science and Machine Learning

Document Understanding and Recognition

Contents – Part II

Signal Processing and Pattern Recognition

Computer Vision and Applications

Detection of Road Sign Using Edge Detection Method

Prabal Deep Das$^{(\boxtimes)}$ and Bhavesh D. Shah$^{(\boxtimes)}$

Vidyalankar School of Information Technology, Wadala, Mumbai, India
{prabal.das,bhavesh.shah}@vsit.edu.in

Abstract. Automobile industries have developed many features for providing safety to the vehicles. Among these, a feature known as road sign detection system is under the research topic in Automobile safety. Thus, this paper has proposed a feature which will be present in a vehicle and will help the driver to detect the road sign through image processing. It includes the algorithm regarding the detection of a road sign by using three stage detection method which are color, shape and sign respectively. The method used has been applied to a set 100 images in which the results have also been discussed and it was found that around 98% cases the proposed system is found to be effective. It has also considered the various exceptions which occurred during the implementation.

Keywords: Road sign · Pre-processing · HSI model · Grayscale · Morphological operation · Sobel filter

1 Introduction

Road Signs are the groups of unique symbols which are placed on the either sides of the roads. These signs help to provide the information regarding the recent threats or the condition of the roads which helps in to reduce the number of accidents. They are divided into two types; some road signs are known as Compulsory road sign which are represented in Circular board and another group is known as Prohibitory road signs which are represented in Triangular Board. In India, there are 67 Road signs of which 40 are Compulsory and 27 are mandatory road signs. In India, these road signs are present on a white board with Red boundaries. In Compulsory, there are some road signs which are Prohibitory and are represented in the form of a circle with a cross sign as shown below.

The research for the implementation of the feature had been occurring from the decades and various ideas have been proposed for its deployment. All The road signs are represented by red color at the boundary, so therefore identification of Red color is required as discussed by E. Shobha et al. [2], that the red color can be detected by using HSI color model. As the color gets detected, the shape is to be determined to identify whether the give road sign is Compulsory (Circular) or Mandatory (Triangular). The shape detection can be done by calculating the area covered by the shape to the total cropped area as suggested by Salah et al. The actual road sign detection will take place

© Springer Nature Singapore Pte Ltd. 2021
K. C. Santosh and B. Gawali (Eds.): RTIP2R 2020, CCIS 1380, pp. 3–11, 2021.
https://doi.org/10.1007/978-981-16-0507-9_1

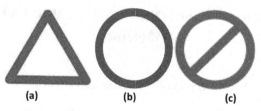

Fig. 1. Road sign boundary shapes (a) Cautionary (b) and (c) Prohibitory

if and only if the previous two detection occurs. The actual road sign detection occurs by considering a focused region of interest as proposed by Huda Noor et al. [1]. But a road sign could be connected or non-connected as shown in the figure below. These unconnected rod signs cannot be detected by using a simple cropping algorithm. Thus, this paper has tried to provide a universal system which will help to detect both connected as well as unconnected road signs.

This paper contains the methodology of the algorithm for the implementation of the proposed system followed by a brief description of the flowchart and the results as well as the observations have been mentioned on the basis of available data sets. The abstract of this paper has been explained with the help of the figures shown below (Fig. 2).

Fig. 2. (a) RGB image (b) B/W image with red color removed (c) Boundary box without using Edge detection (d) Boundary Box after using Edge detection (Color figure online)

The Figure 'a' shows the real image which is a prohibitory sign, indicating not to overtake. In the next figure 'b' binary or black and white image has been obtained from the given raw image. If the boundaries of the image are considered then there will be more than one number of Boundary Boxes as shown in figure 'c'. The above-mentioned problem has occurred because the extracted binary image is not continuous, hence such images are known as Non-connected images. This problem has been overcome by using edge detection method which helps to form a single Boundary box for any type of road sign as shown in figure 'd'. The above problem has been pictorially described by using a signal flow diagram (in Fig. 3) of another example.

2   Proposed Methodology

The proposed method follows a three-way extraction steps which includes: Color Extraction, Shape Extraction and Sign extraction.

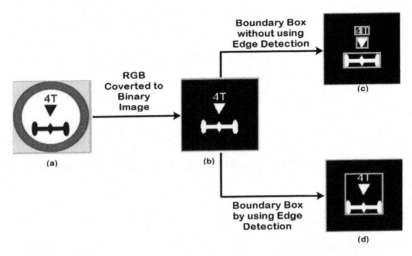

Fig. 3. Signal flow diagram of the proposed system

2.1 Color Extraction

A captured raw image is to be preprocessed for determining the content of red color from a given image. The red color is used exclusively for marking the boundary of the road sign as shown in the Fig. 1. The extraction of red color is performed by using conversion of and RGB (Red Green Blue) model to HSI (Hue Saturation Intensity) model. The figure below has defined the relation between two Color models in the form of Coordinate systems. The HSI model has been realized in the form of Conical structure which has been mapped with rectangular co-ordinate system of RGB color model (Fig. 4).

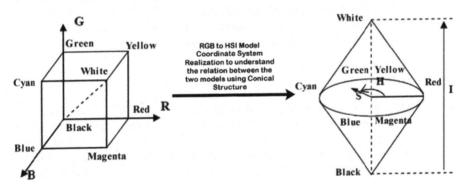

Fig. 4. RGB to HSI coordinate system realization

The conversion of an RGB color model to HSI color model occurs by normalizing the values of every pixel in the corresponding matrices. These normalized values are used in the following mathematical expressions [3].

$$\theta = \begin{cases} \theta & for\ B \leq G \\ 2\pi - \theta\ for\ B > G \end{cases} \tag{1}$$

$$\theta = \cos^{-1}\left\{\frac{0.5[(R-G)+(R-B)]}{[(R+G)^2+(R-B)(G-B)]^{\frac{1}{2}}}\right\} \tag{2}$$

$$Intensity = \frac{R+G+B}{3} \tag{3}$$

$$Saturation = 1 - \frac{3}{(R+G+B)}\{min(R,G,B)\} \tag{4}$$

Where, R, G and B are the values of Red, Green and Blue Matrices of an RGB color image.

2.2 Shape Extraction

This preprocessing method is performed after extracting the Red color from the image to ensure the existence of the road sign based on their shapes. The road signs are differentiated on the basis of their shapes like Triangle, Circle and Pentagon. To recognize these shapes, either pattern recognition or area of interest computation method can be used [3–5]. In this paper area of interest computation [6] is used to simplify the complete process and acquire the results in real time. In this method, the color detected parts are cropped and filtered to form a regular solid structure whose ratio of the number of pixels are determined which is mathematical expressed as:

$$Ratio = \frac{Number\ of\ pixels\ in\ solid\ structure}{Total\ number\ of\ pixels} \tag{5}$$

Where the denominator remains constant due to normalizing every cropped image to 60×60 pixel image. Hence, the total number of pixels will be 360. To use this method, it is mandatory that the cropped image should be a continuous image because the image is needed to be filled by using Morphological operations for developing a solid structure.

2.3 Sign Detection

After detecting the type of road sign by identifying the shape of the boundary, detection of the actual road sign occurs. This is done by using edge detection method among which Sobel filter has been used. To extract the road sign, it is important to redefine the given region of interest because all the road signs are having white background over which the road signs are made by using black color. To extract the non-chromatic colors, following mathematical formula is needed to be applied.

$$Achr = \frac{abs(R-G)+abs(G-B)+abs(B-R)}{3D} \tag{6}$$

In the above equation, the value of D has been taken as 20. The achromatic black color is extracted by comparing the achromatic binary image with the grayscale image of the road sign. The achromatic binary image is formed by using thresholding method, where the threshold for converting an Achromatic image to a binary image is 1. If the value at a particular pixel is greater than 1, then the value will be 0 (Black) otherwise 1 (White). The grayscale image is also converted into the binary image. The binary images of both the images are applied to a logical AND gate system through which the required road sign is produced.

The extracted road sign is to extracted or cropped as shown in the previous figures by using edge detection method. Edge detection method followed by thinning the binary image. The thinned binary image is applied to the following algorithm.

i.   Look after the white pixel in the binary image.
ii. Save the x and y coordinates of the pixel at which White color has been detected.
iii. Find the minimum and maximum values from the saved x and y coordinates.
iv. Determine the difference between the minimum and maximum values of x as well as y.
v.   Crop the given road sign image by using the following parameters determined in step (iii) and (iv):

- minimum values of x and y respectively for providing the starting pixel coordinates.
- Height and Width of the desired image calculated in step (iv).

3   Implementation

The incorporation of three different stages used for development of the proposed system can be understood by using a flowchart as mentioned below. The flowchart has also mentioned the threshold value which has been used for the implementation of system.

The RGB image of the locality is converted to HSI color model for red color detection. For red color determination, hue values are to be considered. If Hue is less than 0.04 or greater than 0.833, then the red color gets detected otherwise not. The detected red color will be cropped if and only if the red colored image width is greater than 26 pixels and the difference between their height and width is less than 10 pixels. The cropped images are processed further to find the ratio of the number of pixels being covered by the detected part to the total number of pixels present in the cropped image, so that the shape (Triangle, Circle) of the road sign can be detected. If the ratio is between 0.5 and 0.6 then the cropped sign is considered as Triangle and if the ratio is between 0.7 and 0.8, then the shape is found to be a Circle (The ratio has also been mentioned and verified by Shobha et al.). After detecting the shape of the road sign, the actual road sign is to be cropped by using edge detection method. Before cropping the image, the rod sign is detected by producing grayscale binary image and achromatic binary image. These binary images are mixed by using logical AND as shown in Fig. 5 (which has been depicted as 'X' in the flowchart).

There are some other preprocessing steps which have been used to provide a more robust system like in the image given below there are some objects which are providing an hindrance in detecting the road sign shape, hence to overcome the problem scanning of the complete image is performed to detect the number of black pixels between two white pixels in the same row and if the number is less than 10 then the black pixels will be converted to white pixel the above-mentioned procedure have been described in Fig. 6. During sign detection, to ensure the detection of a valid road sign the ratio of the pixel of interest is determined or the verification of the end image before crops is a completely blacked out image or not.

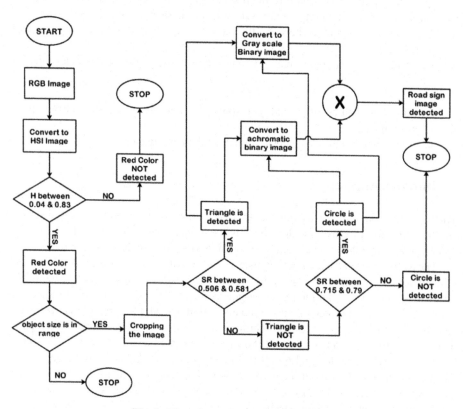

Fig. 5. Flow chart of the proposed system

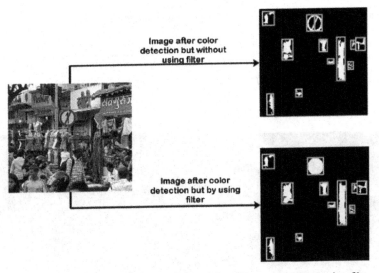

Image after color detection but without using filter

Image after color detection but by using filter

Fig. 6. Comparison of results produced by using filters and without using filters

4 Observations and Results

The image used for testing the system has been taken from mobile. The images were taken in bursts of 20 to 30 images. These images were resized to 640 × 360 for more efficient processing. There were 452 images in which 100 were chosen randomly. Among the 100 images there are 4 images which are having Faded red color (Fig. 7(a)), 14 images contain same background and foreground color (Fig. 8(a)), 4 images are having road sign but are of greater than the prescribed threshold size. There are 15 such images which does not contain road sign (Fig. 7(b)) and 64 images are having road signs with no exceptions (Fig. 8(b)) (Table 1).

Table 1. Observation table

Stages (Number of Images available at the input)	Detected	Not detected	DR (Detection Rate) (%)
Color (64)	64	–	100
Shape (64)	62	2	96.87
Sign (62)	61	1	98.38

Average Sign detected = 61.
Signs not detected = 03.
Detection Rate = 95.31%

Detection rate is determined by using following formula:

$$DR = \frac{Number\ of\ images\ in\ a\ particular\ stage}{total\ number\ of\ images\ available\ at\ the\ input} \qquad (7)$$

$$DR(\%) = DR \times 100$$

Fig. 7. (a) No road sign images (b) Road sign with faded red color (Color figure online)

Fig. 8. (a) Images with same background and foreground color (b) Images with road sign (Color figure online)

5   Conclusion

The proposed system has helped to detect the road sign more accurately as shown in the table above. The system is able to show a higher accurate results if and only if certain conditions are met such as the red color should not fade or become more lighter color because the hue value does not matches the prescribed range used to detect red color, the background and foreground color should not be same because if it happens it will be difficult for the system to detect the shape and if the distance between the camera and the road sign is less or more than the threshold it would not be applied for the shape verification.

References

1. Dean, H.N., Jabir, K.V.T.: Real time detection and recognition of indian traffic signs using Matlab. Int. J. Sci. Eng. Res. 4(5), 684–690 (2013)
2. Shoba, E., Suruliandi, A.: Performance analysis on road sign detection, extraction and recognition techniques. In: 2013 International Conference on Circuits, Power and Computing Technologies (ICCPCT). IEEE (2013)
3. Santosh, K.C., Lamiroy, B., Wendling, L.: Symbol recognition using spatial relations. Pattern Recognit. Lett. 33(3), 331–341 (2012)
4. Santosh, K.C., Lamiroy, B., Wendling, L.: Integrating vocabulary clustering with spatial relations for symbol recognition. Int. J. Doc. Anal. Recognit. 17(1), 61–78 (2014). https://doi.org/10.1007/s10032-013-0205-4
5. Santosh, K.C., Lamiroy, B., Wendling, L.: DTW-radon-based shape descriptor for pattern recognition. Int. J. Pattern Recognit. Artif. Intell. 27(3), 1350008 (2013)
6. Sallah, S.S.Md., Hussin, F.A., Yusoff, M.Z.: Road sign detection and recognition system for real-time embedded applications. In: 2011 International Conference on Electrical, Control and Computer Engineering (INECCE). IEEE (2011)
7. Gonzalez, R.C., Woods, R.E.: Digital image processing [M]. Publishing house of electronics industry 141. 7 (2002)
8. Gonzalez, R.C.: Digital Image Processing Using Matlab-Gonzalez Woods & Eddins. pdf. Education, 609 (2004)
9. https://fourier.eng.hmc.edu/e161/lectures/ColorProcessing/node2.html
10. https://www.indiandrivingschools.com/cautionary-signs.php

Fuzzy Approach to Evaluate Performance of Teaching Staff in Technical Institutions

Vikas J. Magar[1][✉] and Rajivkumar S. Mente[2]

[1] School of Computational Sciences, Solapur University, Solapur, India
magarvjresearch@gmail.com
[2] Department of Computer Applications, Solapur University, Solapur, India
rajivmente@rediffmail.com

Abstract. Higher Education plays a primary role in creating and developing resources within the country and also improves the existence of the people to whom it serves. To construct a highly effective and reliable decision-making system rule-based system has higher significance. Consequently, assessment of teaching faculty helps to characterize well-organized plans to improve teaching quality and learning process. The proposed research paper focuses on Fuzzy based Inference System (FIS) to assess the concert of teaching staff including student feedback reports. Appropriate associative rules and suitable fuzzy inference mechanisms discussed in this research paper. Proposed research work also focuses on the comparative study of classical analysis and fuzzy analysis.

Keywords: Fuzzy logic · Performance appraisal system · Fuzzy Inference System (FIS) · Performance appraisal

1 Introduction

In today's era of competition need to achieve high quality and performance in every sector of human life. Higher Educational sector always plays a significant role in sound quality achievement and to manage highly qualified resources. Teaching faculty is the backbone of the education system. High-quality teaching is essential to improve the academic performance of the student [1]. To enhance high quality in the education system need to appraise teaching faculty from time to time. To assess teacher faculty-student feedback is essential. The proposed article represents a fuzzy rule-based system to evaluate the performance of teaching staff. The conclusion will be encouraging faculty with a meaningful appraisal that improves professional learning and growth. To assess the individual teaching faculty's performance feedback of students is collected. This procedure is planned to achieve confidence for faculty development and to diagnose occasions for supplementary provision wherever essential. Measuring the routine of teaching staff is a very critical task because the quantification of performance dimensions and result may be imprecise and have uncertain. The educational administrators frequently face such issues when annoying to evaluate the performance of faculty like to spend a lot of

© Springer Nature Singapore Pte Ltd. 2021
K. C. Santosh and B. Gawali (Eds.): RTIP2R 2020, CCIS 1380, pp. 12–24, 2021.
https://doi.org/10.1007/978-981-16-0507-9_2

time evaluating each faculty's performance manually [2]. Even if it is time-consuming, sometimes it may lead to errors in calculations. These two problems may lead to increasing human power to appraise performance. The Fuzzy approach can effectively handle imprecise and uncertain data [3]. This approach of evaluation will be useful to the organization for professional judgment in the appraisal of faculties. In the education system, performance evaluation is a procedure of frequently documenting in measurable relations, knowledge, and rule-based criteria for assessment. Estimate is the process of measuring skills, attitude, and beliefs.

Through the student view faculties assessment have several benefits like foreseeing the faculties progress to inform them within time how to change the structure of his/her teaching plan, his/her lacks in teaching quality, suggestions for improvements, etc. faculty can focus and workout to counteractive training or guidance program. Improving the coaching methods and guiding and inspiring students in the direction of active participation in their possess learning is a fundamental role of valuation. Assortment, Certification, education, describing, and cultivating teaching methodology is the primary purpose behind the assessment. Evaluation helps in choosing the right plan. The proposed research article contains both student feedback and self-appraisal of faculty to evaluate performance. The contribution of these two analyzed using a fuzzy approach. A fuzzy approach actively works with linguistic values [4]. Appropriate parameters are necessary to analyze data.

In 1965, Dr. Lofti A. Zadeh Mathematics Professor from U.C.Berkeley introduced Fuzzy Logic, which gives us the language with local syntax and semantics [5]. The Fuzzy reasoning based on fuzzy set theory, where an object's affiliation of a set is regular slightly than just a member or not. Fuzzy logic gives membership value between zero and one by the rule base. Fuzzy logic is useful to convert linguistic experience into scientific information [6]. Fuzzy is a powerful problem-solving technique mostly used for information processing and an embedded system. Fuzzy logic provides a simple approach for concluding the conclusion from unclear, uncertain, or vague information. Fuzzy logic is parallel to human conclusion making with its skill to work from estimated data to find a specific explanation. The implementation of fuzzy logic contains three phases (Fig. 1).

1.1 Phases of the Fuzzy Logic

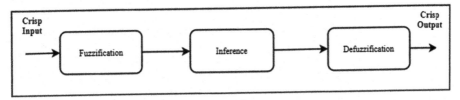

Fig. 1. Phases involved in fuzzy logic

A. Fuzzification: Fuzzification is the first step of inference processing. Fuzzification is the process that converts crisp inputs into fuzzy inputs. Fuzzy inference system processes crisp information with the help of membership function. Fuzzification achieved by using different fuzzy membership functions. Different shapes of membership functions are available like trapezoidal, piecewise, triangular, Gaussian, bell-shaped, etc.

B. Inference: The inference engine determines to fire strength of each rule. Logical product for each standard must be joint earlier than passed on the Defuzzification process for crisp output generation.

C. Defuzzification: Defuzzification means computing a single value to represent the output. This step is followed after the inference. It involves the judgment of value that excellently signifies the information limited to the fuzzy set.

1.2 Different Fuzzy Membership Functions

The representation of different fuzzy membership function is shown in Fig. 2.

a. Triangular MF
b. Trapezoidal MF
c. Gaussian MF
d. Generalized bell MF
e. Sigmoid membership function

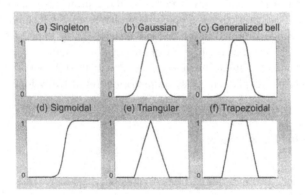

Fig. 2. Different types of fuzzy membership functions

a. Triangular Membership Function

Let a, b, and c represent the x coordinates of the three vertices of $\mu A (x)$ in a fuzzy set A. Where 'a' represents lower boundary, and 'c' represents the upper boundary. Where membership degree is zero, and 'b' represents the center where the membership degree is 1 (Fig. 3) .

$$\mu A(x) = \begin{cases} 0 & \text{if } x \leq a \\ \frac{x-a}{b-a} & \text{if } a \leq x \leq b \\ \frac{c-x}{c-b} & \text{if } b \leq x \leq c \\ 0 & \text{if } x \geq c \end{cases} \tag{1}$$

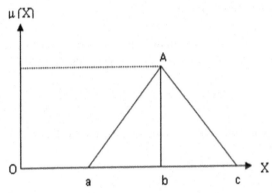

Fig. 3. Triangular membership function

b. Trapezoidal membership function

Let a, b, c, and d stand for the x coordinates of the membership function. Then

$$\text{Trapezoid}(x; a, b, c, d) = 0 \text{ if } x \leq a$$
$$= (x - a)/(b - a) \text{ if } a \leq x \leq b$$
$$= 1 \text{ if } b \leq x \leq c$$
$$= (d - x)/(d - c) \text{ if } c \leq x \leq d$$
$$= 0 \text{ if } d \leq x$$

$$\mu \text{ Trapezoid} = \max\left(min\left(\frac{x - a}{b - a}, 1, \frac{d - x}{d - c}\right), 0\right) \tag{2}$$

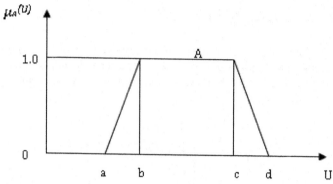

Fig. 4. Trapezoidal membership function

c. Gaussian membership function

The Gaussian membership function frequently represented as Gaussian(x:c,s) where c, s represents the mean and standard deviation, respectively (Fig. 4).

$$\mu_A(x, c, s, m) = \exp\left[-\frac{1}{2}\left|\frac{x-c}{s}\right|^m\right] \tag{3}$$

Here C represents the center, S represents the width, and m represents the Fuzzification factor (Fig. 5).

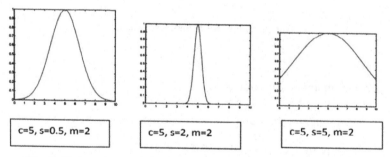

| c=5, s=0.5, m=2 | c=5, s=2, m=2 | c=5, s=5, m=2 |

Fig. 5. Various shapes of Gaussian MFs with different values of s and m.

d. Generalized Bell membership function

A generalized bell membership function has three parameters: a – responsible for its width, c – accountable for its center, and b – accountable for its slopes. Mathematically (Fig. 6),

$$\text{gbellmf}(x\colon a, b, c)\,\frac{1}{1 + \left|\frac{x-c}{b}\right|^{2b}} \tag{4}$$

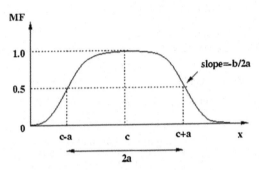

Fig. 6. Generalized bell shaped membership function

e. Sigmoid Membership function

A sigmoidal membership function has two parameters: a responsible for its slope at the crossover point $x = c$. The membership function of the sigmoid function represented as Sigmf (x: a, c) and it is (Fig. 7)

$$\text{Sigmf}(x\colon a, b, c) = \frac{1}{1 + e^{-a(x-c)}} \tag{5}$$

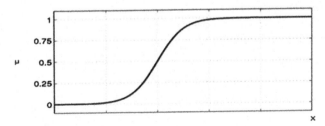

Fig. 7. General structure of sign mode MFs

2 Proposed Method

To evaluate the performance of the teaching staff, the Student side questionnaire is forwarded to the student. The student gives his feedback for the respective faculties. The questionnaire contains different subparts with the appropriate assignment of numerical weight [7, 8]. Some preliminary computations are used to reduce the complexities. Initial computations are an aggregation of weighted data. Here questionnaire distributed among students to fill the feedback. The average of respective input is calculated and further processed for the fuzzy system. To assess the performance of faculties via student feedback, consider the five factors with its 21sub sections having well defined statistical weight. These factors and the associative weights mentioned in Table 1 and Table 2.

Table 1. Fuzzy inference system input parameter and its associated weights

Sr.No	Attribute	Weight
1	Quality of Teaching	350
2	Factors in Learning	50
3	Responsibility and Punctuality	250
4	Assessment of Learning	150
5	Mentoring and counseling	200
Total		1000

A. Algorithm

The algorithm to Evaluate Teaching Staff Performance using Fuzzy Approach:

Step 1: *Collect the sample data from students using a suitable data sampling technique.*
Step 2: *Assign the weight as per given in the above weight table.*
Step 3: *Calculate the average in each section.*
Step 4: *Design the appropriate fuzzy parameters for each section like poor, average, good, very good, and excellent.*
Step 5: *Write rules for inference system.*
Step 6: *Compute the fuzzy output.*

Table 2. Weight assignment to each subsection input

	Attributes	Evaluation parameter				
		1	2	3	4	5
1	**Quality of teaching**					
1.1	Pace of Subject	50	40	30	20	10
1.2	Use good example and illustration	50	40	30	20	10
1.3	Motivation to attend the class	30	24	18	12	6
1.4	Used blackboard efficiently	40	32	24	16	8
1.5	Used audio visual aids	40	32	24	16	8
1.6	Arranging group discussion, seminar etc	40	32	24	16	
1.7	Stimulated my interest in the subject	50	40	30	20	10
1.8	Audibility and clarity of speech	50	40	30	20	10
2	**Factors in learning**					
2.1	Lecture Contributed to my learning	25	20	15	10	5
2.2	Defined learning objectives for each period	25	20	15	10	5
3	**Responsibility and punctuality**					
3.1	Punctuality *(Arrival of class &leave class in time)*	50	40	30	20	10
3.2	Checking Assignment, Journal, Test Result, homework in time	60	48	36	24	12
3.3	Motivate to Students for extra activities	70	56	42	28	14
3.4	Work Dedication	30	24	18	12	6
3.5	Conducting Seminars and Organizing Group Discussion	40	32	24	16	8
4	**Assessment of learning**					
4.1	Feedback on Assignment were useful	50	40	30	20	10
4.2	Problem sets helped me in learn	50	40	30	20	10
4.3	Answer papers evaluated fairly	50	40	30	20	10
5	**Mentoring/Counseling**					
5.1	The teacher was approachable outside the Class	50	40	30	20	10
5.2	Teacher is Sympathetic to academic problems	70	56	42	28	14
5.3	The teacher is sympathetic to the personal problem	80	64	48	32	16

B. Development of Fuzzy Inference System

The proposed architecture of the fuzzy system contains fuzzification, rule inference mechanism, and defuzzification. Matlab tools are applied for the implementation of proposed research work. All the parameters required to appraise the teaching staff performance collected into a single account. Fuzzification of the variables means passing a crisp value to each membership function [9]. The proposed fuzzy system accepts all the parameters mentioned in Table 3. The final result concluded by fuzzy input, prescribed membership functions, and the rule base [10]. The proposed rule base developed using the guidance of academic experts.

Table 3. Input parameter with trapezoidal membership function value

Sr. No	Attribute	Poor	Average	Good	Very good	Excellent
1	Quality of Teaching	[0 20 40 70]	[35 80 100 140]	[120 160 180 210]	[200 245 265 280]	[260 300 330 350]
2	Factors in Learning	[0 3 6 10]	[7 13 18 20]	[16 21 26 30]	[25 32 36 40]	[35 41 45 50]
3	Responsibility and Punctuality	[0 15 35 50]	[40 60 80 100]	[180 110 135 150]	[140 160 180 200]	[180 210 230 250]
4	Assessment of Learning	[0 10 20 30]	[25 40 50 60]	[50 65 80 90]	[75 90 105 120]	[110 125 135 150]
5	Mentoring and counseling	[0 10 25 40]	[30 45 60 80]	[70 85 100 120]	[105 125 145 160]	[150 165 180 200]

C. Fuzzification

Fuzzification is a technique used to convert of crisp value into the grade of membership for linguistic terms. The membership function is responsible for associating a class to each linguistic term.

1. Fuzzy Model with Input and Output Membership

The proposed Fuzzy Inference System is designed using the Mamdani Fuzzy Model. Five evaluation parameters Quality of Teaching, Factors in learning, Responsibility, and Punctuality, Assessment of Learning, Mentoring, and counseling are applied here (Fig. 8).

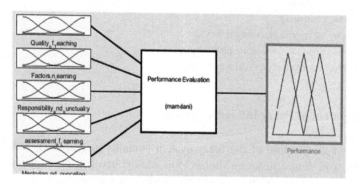

Fig. 8. Fuzzy model to evaluate performance

2. Membership Function

Proposed research work implemented using trapezoidal membership functions. Fuzzification converts crisp values into the grade of membership [11, 12]. A membership function editor is used to describe the properties of the membership function. The membership function is overlapped to achieve a better result. Figure 9 shows the Fuzzification of input parameter 'Quality of Teaching' with an associated weighted value.

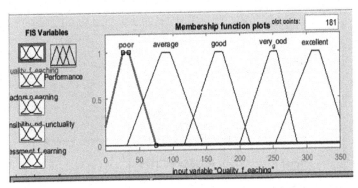

Fig. 9. Membership functions for input 'Quality of Teaching.'

The output of these fuzzy system belongs to performance appraise based on the input parameters. The output generated by this fuzzy system belongs to poor, average, good, very good, and excellent. To create the output, trapezoidal membership function are used. Fig represents defuzzification of output. The output range of this membership function is 0 to 100 (Fig. 10).

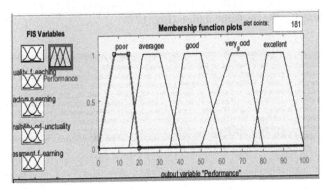

Fig. 10. Membership functions for output variable 'Performance'

D. Fuzzy Rule Base

A fuzzy rule base defines the relationship among the fuzzy input parameter and its associative output parameters [3]. Mostly Fuzzy rule base generated with the guidance of experts of the respective field. The fuzzy rule base is the combination of if-then rules. The fuzzy rule base is used to demonstrate dependency between two and more of the corresponding inputs [13]. The activities of the system depend on the rule base [14]. Rule editor enables the user to define and edit the rules. In this proposed research work, five input parameters with five linguistic terms are used. If 'n' inputs with' linguistic terms for each input, then total rules are m^n (Fig. 11).

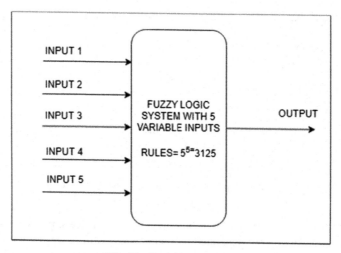

Fig. 11. Basic fuzzy model

The proposed Fuzzy Inference System has five inputs and five linguistic variables. FIS generates 3125 rules with the appropriate combination. Here 91 sample rules are generated to describe the implementation (Fig. 12).

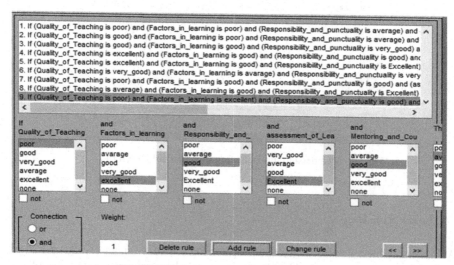

Fig. 12. Rule base for 'Fuzzy Inference System'

3 Experimental Result

Proposed Fuzzy Inference System analyzes the sample data by applying the specified rule base to appraise the teaching staff performance. Rule viewer is a read-only tool available in Matlab which completely displays the Fuzzy Inference System. Table 4 gives the classical and fuzzy analysis of teaching staff.

Table 4. Output values with fuzzy and classical output.

Sr. No	Quality of Teaching (0 to 350)	Factors in Learning (0 to 50)	Responsibility & Punctuality (0 to 250)	Assessment & Learning (0 to 150)	Mentoring & Counseling (0 to 200)	Performance (Fuzzy Output) (0 to 100)	Performance (Classical Output)
1	175.00	25.00	176.00	75.00	56.00	46.90	50.70
2	312.00	25.00	169.00	46.50	174.00	66.40	72.60
3	254.00	25.00	111.00	120.00	131.00	66.10	64.10
4	30.30	25.00	250.00	97.90	54.50	50.00	45.77
5	35.50	6.58	68.10	40.90	93.30	26.90	24.45
6	32.90	45.30	30.80	101.00	18.70	26.90	22.87
7	80.30	34.40	174.00	6.16	18.70	26.90	32.40
8	309.00	44.90	221.00	73.30	137.00	86.90	78.52
9	85.50	25.00	230.00	99.10	17.20	46.90	45.68
10	22.40	25.00	125.00	39.70	17.20	26.90	22.93
11	183.00	33.60	120.00	133.00	57.50	47.00	52.71
12	75.00	33.60	27.10	133.00	57.50	27.00	32.62
13	243.00	14.10	27.10	100.00	162.00	47.00	54.62
14	314.00	43.00	169.00	100.00	175.00	86.90	80.10
15	314.00	3.95	60.60	68.80	99.30	46.90	59.35
16	269.90	40.80	203.40	119.20	146.90	72.20	78.02
17	294.00	39.33	219.06	136.00	174.67	87.00	86.30
18	293.40	45.00	224.30	124.30	162.00	87.00	84.90
19	294.50	44.67	200.00	131.00	168.90	87.10	85.10
20	301.00	40.76	215.00	130.00	158.60	87.10	84.60
21	260.00	35.00	188.00	101.00	142.25	69.66	72.70
22	271.10	42.27	208.50	118.20	164.20	80.43	80.40
23	284.40	41.67	201.80	121.70	158.80	85.94	80.83
24	271.00	40.70	187.00	111.00	160.00	78.68	76.97
25	262.25	38.12	205.50	121.87	149.37	70.87	77.71

4   Conclusion

Proposed research work presents the strategy and development of a soft computing model to evaluate teaching staff performance using fuzzy logic. In this paper trapezoidal function is used. The classical approach is used to calculate the average. Here reading numbers 1, 9, and 15 have classical analysis value 50.7, 45.68, and 59.35 respectively with corresponding fuzzy value 46.9. The reason behind this is reading 1, 9, and 15 belongs to the same category. Value 45.68 and value 59.35 belongs to the same class because of the rule base. The conclusion here is that fuzzy value belongs on the rule base, In the above case even if any Single category found excellent result will not be sure towards the excellence and vice versa. The same happened with other reading also. Here it concludes the fuzzy system decides based on the rule base and its associated membership function.

References

1. Jyothi, G., Parvathi, C., Srinivas, P., Althaf, S.: Fuzzy expert model for evaluation of faculty performance in technical educational institutions. Int. J. Eng. Res. Appl. 4(5), 41–50 (2014)
2. Kamath, R.S.: Design and development of soft computing model for teaching staff performance evaluation. Int. J. Eng. Sci. Res. Technol. IJESRT 3(4), 3088–3094 (2014)
3. Shruti, S.J., Mudholkar, R.R.: Performance evaluation by fuzzy inference technique. Int. J. Soft Comput. Eng. [IJSCE] 3(2), 158–164 (2013)
4. Saneifard, R., Saneifard, R.: A general approach to linguistic approximation and its application in frame of fuzzy logic deduction. Int. J. Ind. Math. 7(3), 261–267 (2015)
5. Zadeh, L.A.: Fuzzy sets. Inf. Control 8(3), 338–353 (1965)
6. Bordogna, G., Pasi, G.: A fuzzy linguistic approach generalizing boolean information retrieval: A model and its evaluation. J. Am. Soc. Inf. Sci. 44(2), 70–82 (1993)
7. Yadav, R.S., Ahmed, P., Soni, A.K., Pal, S.: Academic performance evaluation using soft computing techniques. Curr. Sci. 106(11), 1505 (2014)
8. Vikas, J.M., Arjun, P.G.: Use of questionnaire as knowledge acquisition tool for expert system to evaluating teaching staff performance in technical. Int. J. Innov. Adv. Comput. Sci. 7(3), 475–481 (2018)
9. Bai, S.-M., Chen, S.-M.: Evaluating students' learning achievement using fuzzy membership functions and fuzzy rules. Exp. Syst. Appl. 34(1), 399–410 (2008)
10. Pavani, S., Gangadhar, P., Gulhare, K.K.: Evaluation of teacher's performance using fuzzy logic techniques. Int. J. Comput. Trends Technol. 3(2), 200–205 (2012)
11. Nolan, J.R.: A prototype application of fuzzy logic and expert systems in education assessment. In: IAAI-98 Proceedings, vol. 1134 (1998)
12. Bhosale, G.A., Kamath, R.S.: Fuzzy inference system for teaching staff performance appraisal. Int. J. Comput. Inf. Technol. 2(3), 381–385 (2013)
13. Rasmani, K.A., Shen, Q.: Data-driven fuzzy rule generation and its application for student academic performance evaluation. Appl. Intell. 25(3), 305–319 (2006)
14. Mankad, K., Sajja, P.S., Akerkar, R.: Evolving rules using genetic fuzzy approach: an educational case study. Int. J. Soft Comput. 2(1), 35–46 (2011)

Detection and Learning of Color Objects Using Kernelized Support Correlation Filter

Kishor S. Jeve[1][(✉)] and Ashok T. Gaikwad[2][(✉)]

[1] College of Computer Science and Information Technology, Latur, Maharashtra, India
kishoryog@gmail.com
[2] Vivekanand College, Aurangabad, Maharashtra, India
drashokgaikwad@gmail.com

Abstract. Moving Object detection and tracking are important for many computer vision applications. The support vector machines (SVMs) are used to reduce the cost of computation and to increase the efficiency of computation. Kernelized correlation filters are used for efficient object tracking. In this method, the patches of translated images are used through dense sampling to form the circulant matrix. Support correlation filtering is an approach which is composed using combination features of the support vector machine and circulant matrix. We use a discrete Fourier transform to pose the tracking problem. We further use kernel function with support correlation filters to improve the performance of the object tracking algorithm. Kernelized support correlation filter is a good alternative to improve the accuracy and speed of the object tracking process.

Keywords: Support vector machine · Circulant matrix · Kernelized SVM

1 Introduction

The aim of the tracking of an object is to locate an object in the sequence of images or videos. The detection and tracking of the color object is difficult due to occlusion, deformation, scale variation, low resolution, background clutters, motion blurs as well as fast-motion [1, 2, 4]. Apart from its difficulty, it has great real-time significance in surveillance, robotics, traffic monitoring, and so on [4].

Many different robust algorithms are being used for object tracking. Object tracking algorithms are mainly categorized into generative and discriminative [10]. The Generative algorithm consists of an algorithm based on templates, Methods based on subspace analysis, Methods based on sparse representation. An algorithm based on templates includes a wavelet-based mixture model, incremental principal component analysis, and so on. Generative Methods based on subspace analysis consist of the probabilistic Markov model, an incremental covariance model, etc. Generative Methods based on sparse representation consist of real-time compressive sensing tracking and sparse matrix representation [11].

The Discriminative algorithm consists of methods that rely on an online feature selection, online updating classifiers, and online metric learning. The feature selection

© Springer Nature Singapore Pte Ltd. 2021
K. C. Santosh and B. Gawali (Eds.): RTIP2R 2020, CCIS 1380, pp. 25–32, 2021.
https://doi.org/10.1007/978-981-16-0507-9_3

method includes feature space analysis, linear discriminant analysis, and texture features analysis, and so on. The method which is based on updating classifiers in online mode consists of a methodonline-Ada-Boost-based classifier, online multiple instance learning, nearest-neighbor classification, naive Bayesian classifiers, attentional visual tracking (AVT) algorithm, etc. Methods based on online metric learning includes Euclidean metric based learning. It also includes learning based on Kullback–Leibler divergence metric and learning based on the Bhattacharyya coefficient, and so on.

Support vector machines are one of the discriminative methods used for object detection and tracking [3, 5, 7]. The SVM method uses sampling and budgeting methods. The set of samples is generated using a sampler. The budgeting is used for online-learning. Another method that is popularly used for object tracking is correlation filters and it is based on a circular property of matrices [14]. A circular Structure Tracker with the Kernel (CSTK) is a method used for dense sampling. An improved KSCF algorithm is based on the CSTK algorithm which is used to increase accuracy and speed by dense sampling.

2 Support Correlation Filtering

The correlation filters use a circulant matrix and Fourier transform and are accurate and efficient to locate an object [9]. The cyclic nature of the row elements is characteristic of the circulant matrix. First, consider, the circulant data matrix Y of the digital image y. The circulant data matrix Y is formed using a translated version of y. The row of the circulant data matrix Y represents the features of a target object. As the name suggests, a circulant matrix Y includes the possible cyclic translation of the target image [9, 12, 13]. The tracking of an object is formulated as determining a row. The eigenvectors of Y are the base vector F of the DFT [12]:

$$Y = FDiag\left(\hat{y}\right)F^H \tag{1}$$

Where $\hat{y}$ is the Fourier transform of image y, and F^H is the Conjugate transpose of F. Eigen decomposition of circulant data matrix Y is shown in Eq. 1.

The goal is to classify y_i and learn w and b, where w is the support correlation filter and b is an error [12].

$$x_i = \Gamma\left(w^T y_i + b\right) \tag{2}$$

As discussed above, the circulant data matrix Y is formed by using a translated version of y and every sample in Y are classified by using,

$$x = \Gamma\left(\mathcal{F}^{-1}\left(\hat{y}^* \circ \hat{w}\right) + b\right) \tag{3}$$

Where $\mathcal{F}^{-1}$ is the Inverse of Discrete Fourier Transform, $\hat{y}^*$ is the complex conjugate of $\hat{y}$. The operator $\circ$ is the multiplication operator.

The complexity of classification of y_i using the Eq. (2) is O(n^4), and the complexity of classification of samples of Y using the Eq. (3) is O($n^2 \log n$).

Consider the training set of a circulant matrix $Y = [y_1; y_2; \ldots; y_{n^2}]$ and the corresponding class labels $X = [x_1; x_2; \ldots; x_{n^2}]$. The squared hinge loss of the Support Vector Machine can be determined as:

$$\min_{w,b,\xi} ||w||^2 + C\sum_i \xi_i^2$$

$$x_i\left(W^T y_i + b\right) \geq 1 - \xi_i \tag{4}$$

Where $\xi = [\xi_1, \ldots \xi_2, \ldots \xi_{n^2}]$ is the slack variables in the form of vector. The hinge-loss function is preferably used in most computer vision applications besides LSVM (least-squares SVM). It helps to perform robustly and also punished if an error occurs.

Similar to the Eq. (3), it is possible to form the SVM model equivalently as,

$$\min_{w,b,\xi} ||w||^2 + C||\xi||_2^2$$

$$x \circ \left(\mathcal{F}^{-1}\left(\hat{y}^* \circ \hat{w} + b_1\right)\right) \geq 1 - \xi \tag{5}$$

Where Y is circulant and 1 represents a vector of 1's.

2.1 Class Labels

Consider p* is the center of y*. Similarly p_i is the position of y_i, where y_i is the translated image and y* is the target object. In the object identification process, the ratio of overlapping of the translated image y_i is used to measure the similarity between target object y* and translated an image y_i. Here, the overlap ratio is used to guide the labeling of the y_i. Samples are considered positive if samples are above the predefined upper threshold. If the samples are below the predefined threshold then they are considered as negative. Both optimal thresholds for KSCF are predefined and they are determined empirically.

The class label can be defined as follows,

$$m(P_i, P^*) = \gamma \exp(-\propto ||P_i - P^*||^\beta) \tag{6}$$

The above Eq. (6) plays an important role in defining the class labels. Where γ is a normalization constant, $\propto$ is the scale parameter and β is the shape parameters. Based on Eq. (6), we divide the samples into a labeled subset Ω^l and an unlabelled one Ω^u,

$$i \in \begin{cases} \Omega^u, & \text{if } \theta_l < m(P_i, P^*) < \theta_u, \\ \Omega^l, & \text{Otherwise,} \end{cases} \tag{7}$$

Where Ω^l is the lower threshold and Ω^u is the upper threshold. The class labels for the labeled samples are defined as:

$$X_i \in \begin{cases} 1, & \text{if } m(P_i, P^*) \geq \theta_u, \\ -1, & \text{if } m(P_i, P^*) \leq \theta_l, \end{cases} \tag{8}$$

The sample classified in Ω^u is the unlabelled sample, and it's a class label $X_i \in \{1, -1\}$ is determined in the learning stage.

2.2 Similarities or Dissimilarities with Existing CF-Based Trackers

The existing Correlation Filter based trackers use the RLS model [6, 12] with the continuous confidence map m. It uses to minimize the mean squared error between the actual outcome and predefined confidence map.

This is given by,

$$\min_{w} \lambda \|w\|^2 + \left\| Y^T w - m \right\|_2^2 \tag{9}$$

which has the generally accepted solution,

$$\hat{w} = \frac{\hat{Y}^* \circ \hat{m}}{\hat{Y}^* \circ \hat{Y} + \lambda} \tag{10}$$

The accomplishment of CF-based trackers should be accounted more to the dense sampling. The well-known non-CF based trackers are dependent on Support Vector Machines [5, 7]. To improve the performance of object tracking, a combination of dense sampling and SVM is beneficial.

Unlike the RLS-based and CF-based trackers, the proposed approach uses the squared hinge loss function. Thus, the output of Support Correlation Filtering can be greater for positive samples, and low for negative samples. To reduce the label ambiguity problem, we can use semi-supervised learning. The importance of label ambiguity and SVM is demonstrated in object detection [8]. The proposed method uses dense sampling to copes with classification and labels ambiguity problems.

2.3 Kernelized SCF

Consider the proposed Kernelized SCF model, where given the kernel function $K(y, y') = \langle \psi(y), \psi(y') \rangle$. The proposed KSCF model can be used to understand the nonlinear decision function:

$$f(y) = W^T \psi(y) + b = \sum_i \alpha_i \, K(y, \, y') + b \tag{11}$$

where $\alpha = [\alpha_1, \alpha_2, \ldots \ldots, \alpha_{n^2}]$ denote coefficient vector and $\Psi(y)$ stands for the nonlinear feature mapping. Nonlinear feature mapping is clearly determined by the kernel function $K(y, \, y')$. The kernel matrix with $K_{ij} = K(y_i, y_j)$ is denoted by K which is circulant [9]. The first row of the circulant matrix K is denoted using k^{yy}. Therefore, K α can be efficiently computed via Discrete Fourier Transform:

$$K \, \alpha = \mathcal{F}^{-1}\left(\hat{k}^{yy} \circ \hat{\alpha} \right) \tag{12}$$

where K α is the matrix-vector multiplication.

And we have

$$\|w\|^2 = \alpha^T \, K \, \alpha = \alpha^T \, \mathcal{F}^{-1}\left(\hat{k}^{yy} \circ \hat{\alpha} \right) \tag{13}$$

Based on Eq. 12 and Eq. 13, the proposed KSCF model is devised as

$$\min_{\alpha,b,e,x_i(i\in\Omega^u)} \alpha^T \mathcal{F}^{-1}\left(\hat{k}^{yy} \circ \hat{\alpha}\right) + C \, \|y \circ (\mathcal{F}^{-1}\left(\hat{k}^{yy} \circ \hat{\alpha}\right) + b1) - 1 - e\|_2^2 \quad (14)$$

Where e is greater than or equal to 0. We use an optimization algorithm to solve e, $\{\alpha, b\}$ and $y_i(i\in\Omega^u)$. The solution of the subproblems with e and $y_i(i\in\Omega^u)$ are similar to the SCF model. Now, we can reformulate $\{\alpha, b\}$ by fixing e as the following,

$$\min_{\alpha,b} \alpha^T K \alpha + C\|K\alpha + b1 - q\|_2^2 \quad (15)$$

Where $q = y + y \circ e$ Consider the circulant property of K, we define the K_c as:

$$K_C = K - \bar{k}11^T \quad (16)$$

Where K_c is the centered kernel matrix and $\bar{k}$ is the mean of k^{yy}. The first row of the centered circulant matrix K_C is denoted by k_c^{yy}.

2.4 Optimization Algorithm

Considering unlabeled samples, we can modify the model in (5) and propose alternating optimization. The modified model in (5) can be devised as,

$$\min_{w,b,e,x_i(i\in\Omega^u)} \|w\|^2 + C\|x \circ (\mathcal{F}^{-1}\left(\hat{y}^* \circ \hat{w}\right) + b1) - 1 - e\|_2^2 \quad (17)$$

This formulation provides closed-form solution of e, $\{\alpha, b\}$ and $y_i(i\in\Omega^u)$ when other variables are given. Let $e_0 = x \circ F^{-1}\left(\hat{y}^* \circ \hat{w}\right) + b1) - 1$, by putting the value of e_0 in Eq. (17), we get,

$$\min_e \|e - e_0\|^2 \quad (18)$$

Where $e_0 \geq 0$.
The closed form solution of e subprolems is dvised by,

$$e = \max\{e_0, 0\} \quad (19)$$

The following algorithm shows the training of the proposed algorithm which receives input as Training Image, and center position p* and generate output as: $(\hat{w}, b)$.

Algorithm 1 Support Correlation Filter Training

Input: Training Image, center position p*

Output:$(\hat{w}, b)$

1: Initialize Correlation filter, bias, upper threshold, lower threshold,

2: For all $i \in \Omega^l, X_i = \begin{cases} 1, & \text{if } m(P_i, P^*) \geq \Theta_u, \\ -1, & \text{if } m(P_i, P^*) \leq \Theta_l, \end{cases}$

3: While not converged do

4: $s = x_t \circ \mathcal{F}^{-1}(\hat{y}_t^* \circ \hat{w}_{k-1} + b_1) - 1$

5: Update e_k using $e_k = \max(0, s)$,

6: Update q_k using $q_k = x_t + x_t^\circ d_k$

7: Update b_k using $b_k = \text{mean}(q_k)$,

8: Update p_k using $p_k = q_k - b_k 1$,

9: $Y_c = Y_t - \bar{y}_t 1$,

10: $\hat{w}_k = \frac{\hat{Y}_c^* \circ P_k}{\hat{Y}_c^* \circ \hat{Y}_c + 1C^{-1}}$

11: For all $i \in \Omega^u, X_i = \begin{cases} 1, & \text{if } w^T Y_t(i) + b \geq 0 \\ -1, & \text{if } w^T Y_t(i) + b < 0, \end{cases}$

12: $k \leftarrow k+1$

13: end while

---

3 Experimental Result

To evaluate and assess the performance of the KSCF method, many experiments are performed on the dataset of 10 different image sequences. These image sequences are annotated with 8 different attributes such as Scale Variation (SV), Blur Motion (BM), Fast Motion (FM), Occlusion (OC), In-Plane Rotation (IR), Deformation (DF), Out-of-Plane Rotation (OPR) and Background Clutters (BC). For the uniformity and fair comparison, the bounding box is provided for the target object and then we evaluate the performance of the KSCF method. We evaluate the performance of the proposed method using precision plots and success plots. This evaluation is based on bounding box overlap metrics and error in position according to the ground truth object location. The precision plot displays the percentage of accurately tracked frames for the range of distance threshold. The distance precision (DP) threshold for the precision plot is 20 pixels. The tracker is more accurate if it gives a higher precision value at a low threshold. It also computes frames per second (FPS).

3.1 Experiments on Image Sequences

We implement KSCF on skaters, running race, moving cars, etc. image sequences. The skater's image sequence is annotated with SV, FM, IR, OPR, and DF attributes. Running race image sequence is annotated with attributes such as IR, DF, OC, and OPR. Moving car sequence is annotated with SV, FM, and BM. The following figures illustrate the precision plot of skaters, running race, and moving car image sequence (Figs. 1, 2 and 3).

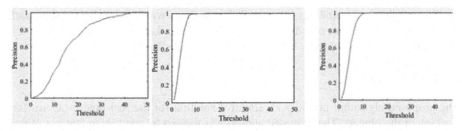

Fig. 1. Precision plot of skaters, running race and moving car image sequences with feature_type = 'HOG_CN_Color' and kernel_type = 'gaussian';

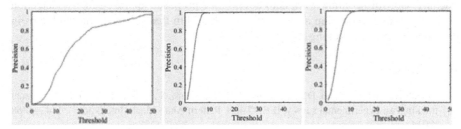

Fig. 2. Precision plot of skaters, running race and moving car image sequences with feature_type = 'HOG_CN_Color' and kernel_type = 'polynomial';

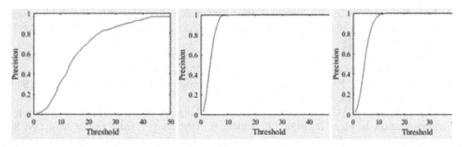

Fig. 3. Precision plot of skaters, running race and moving car image sequences with feature_type = 'HOG_CN_Color' and kernel_type = 'linear';

Table 1. Findings of KSCF with Linear, Polynomial and Gaussian kernels

Kernels	Linear	Polynomial	Gaussian
Mean DP (%)	90.43	90.26	90.56
Mean FPS (s)	76.28	60.94	48.51

Table 1 shows the findings of the KSCF algorithm with Linear, Polynomial, and Gaussian kernels. The proposed algorithm with Gaussian kernel gives better results for Mean DP (90.56%) and Linear kernel gives better results for Mean FPS.

4 Conclusion

The proposed algorithm provides an effective solution for the real-time problems for tracking of the objects. The proposed approach is formed by combining features of the support vector machine and a circulant matrix. We use an optimization algorithm based on DFT to learn Support correlation filters. The kernelized SCF algorithm performs efficiently on object tracking problem. It also works effectively to increase the speed of tracking. Our forthcoming work is to develop the proposed approach for the detection of an object and to develop a more efficient algorithm that solves all the problems in object detection and tracking.

References

1. Smeulders, A.W.M., Chu, D.M., Cucchiara, R., Calderara, S., Dehghan, A., Shah, M.: Visual tracking: an experimental survey. IEEE Trans. Pattern Anal. Mach. Intell. **36**(7), 1442–1468 (2014)
2. Wu, Y., Lim, J., Yang, M.-H.: Online object tracking: a benchmark. In: IEEE Conference on Computer Vision and Pattern Recognition, pp. 2411–2418 (2013)
3. Avidan, S.: Support vector tracking. IEEE Trans. Pattern Anal. Mach. Intell. **26**(8), 1064–1072 (2004)
4. Jeve, K.S., Gaikwad, A.T., Yannawar, P.L.: Automatic color object detection and learning using continuously adaptive mean shift with color, scale, and direction. Int. J. Comput. Appl. **165**(11), 1–3 (2017)
5. Hare, S., Saffari, A., Torr, P.H.: Struck: structured output tracking with kernels. In: IEEE International Conference on Computer Vision, pp. 263–270 (2011)
6. Rifkin, R., Yeo, G., Poggio, T.: Regularized least-squares classification. NATO Sci. Ser. Sub Ser. III Comput. Syst. Sci. **190**, 131–154 (2003)
7. Zhang, J., Ma, S., Sclaroff, S.: Meem: robust tracking via multiple experts using entropy minimization. In: Fleet, D., Pajdla, T., Schiele, B., Tuytelaars, T. (eds.) ECCV 2014. LNCS, vol. 8694, pp. 188–203. Springer, Cham (2014). https://doi.org/10.1007/978-3-319-10599-4_13
8. Girshick, R., Donahue, J., Darrell, T., Malik, J.: Rich feature hierarchies for accurate object detection and semantic segmentation. In: IEEE Conference on Computer Vision and Pattern Recognition, pp. 580–587 (2014)
9. Henriques, J.F., Caseiro, R., Martins, P., Batista, J.: High-speed tracking with kernelized correlation filters. IEEE Trans. Pattern Anal. Mach. Intell. **37**(3), 583–596 (2015)
10. Supreeth, H.S.G., Patil, C.M.: An adaptive SVM technique for object tracking. Int. J. Pure Appl. Math. **118**(7), 131–135 (2018)
11. Bao, C., Wu, Y., Ling, H., Ji, H.: Real time robust L1 tracker using accelerated proximal gradient approach. In: IEEE Conference on Computer Vision and Pattern Recognition, Providence, RI, pp. 1830–1837 (2012)
12. Zuo, W., Xiaohe, W., Lin, L., Zhang, L., Yang, M.-H.: Learning support correlation filters for visual tracking. IEEE Trans. Pattern Anal. Mach. Intell. **41**(5), 1158–1172 (2019)
13. Gray, R.M.: Toeplitz and Circulant Matrices: A Review. Found. Trends® Commun. Inf. Theory, **2**(3), 155–239 (2006). http://dx.doi.org/10.1561/0100000006
14. Boddeti, V.N., Kumar, B.V.: Maximum margin vector correlation filter. arXiv preprint arXiv: 1404.6031 (2014)

Recent Advances in IoT Based Smart Object Detection and Its Authentication by BlockChain Approaches

Ahmed A. A. Shareef[✉] and Pravin L. Yannawar[✉]

Vision and Intelligence System Lab, Department of Computer Science and IT,
Dr. Babasaheb Ambedkar Marathwada University, Aurangabad, MH, India
shareef.kin@gmail.com, pravinyannawar@gmail.com

Abstract. With the rapid improvement of the modern digital world and IoT-based systems, the accurate detection of objects moving in a dynamic scene has become an important and critical task. The object presented in videos and images is detected and recognized using various techniques, its information is extracted, transferred through the internet and displayed on the main monitoring system. The recognized object can be anything we repeatedly observe in our daily life such as human, animal, car, bicycle, etc. To detect such objects in a video or an image, the system needs to do a complex task using hardware and software components in order to complete the function as expected. This paper offers a review of the different techniques that have been used to detect an object, categorize it, localize it, extract its features, and many more, in images and videos. The comments are drawn from the studied literature that is related to IoT based object detection. Some perspectives solutions for object reorganization and tracking are also presented. This paper may significantly help researchers in this domain to start with essential knowledge for developing their own efficient schemes.

Keywords: IoT-based system · Computer vision · Video surveillance · Object detection & Recognition

1 Introduction

Object detection, tracking, and recognition recently have been amongst the most interesting topics for research in computer vision and its applications, including video surveillance, image processing, and object detection [1]. Since the computer vision has become one of the research domains that have been involved in various applications, it is very important to have efficient systems to detect, track and recognize the objects in videos and images. Even though there are many efficient systems and algorithms for detecting and recognizing objects in videos and images, however, still we need real improvements comparing with the current technological revolution [2–4]. IoT-based video-surveillance system identifies, in real-time, moving objects and scene changes of particular locations that

© Springer Nature Singapore Pte Ltd. 2021
K. C. Santosh and B. Gawali (Eds.): RTIP2R 2020, CCIS 1380, pp. 33–43, 2021.
https://doi.org/10.1007/978-981-16-0507-9_4

need continuous monitoring and immediate decision-making for higher security and protection. Such systems should determine if the changes are temporary or permanent and apply a particular strategy based on the type of targeted objects and the level of action required [5]. As IoT-based nodes used in object detection system are constrained (i.e., have limited bandwidth and batteries), and data transmission is power consuming, it is important that efficient detection schemes are highly encouraged from researchers with taking into account a robust securing of data transferred between the camera node and output system used by the authorized users as shown in Fig. 1 [6].

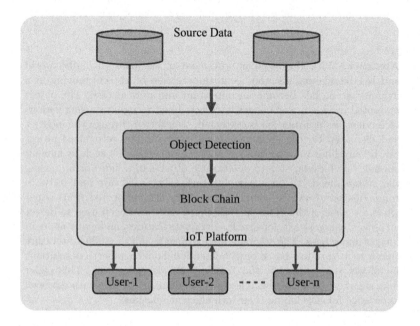

Fig. 1. Object detection and tracking based on IoT framework

The Internet of Things (IoT) is a worldwide network that connects a huge number of heterogeneous devices and objects including humans. Each device/object in IoT is given a unique address, so they can interconnect with each other easily [7,8]. The development of IoT makes such heterogeneous devices able to communicate and interact for data gathering and exchange. This interoperability between these various devices is a main feature of IoT-based systems to remotely work together and cooperate for achieving complex and distributed tasks. Furthermore, the IoT is a group of devices that initial, process, and transfer a critical and privacy-sensitive data that need a higher level of security, safety, and protection, and hence are appealing targets for cyber-attacks [9].

A blockchain is a series of blocks, which are related with each other using crypto graphy. Each block has a crypto graphic hash of the previous one, and transaction data. Purposely, a blockchain is reluctant to update data. It is a distributed ledger that can make transactions between two ends efficiency and in a securable mode [10]. The blockchain was introduced in 2008 by Nakamoto, it is such as bitcoin, which is a public ledger that provides a verification, it tends to store and update data distributive [11]. The Blockchain is basically a distributed structure that does not rely on central authority anymore.

The IoTChain (ITC) is optimized as a system software that uses the idea of a blockchain, allowing data to be stored and exploited in a exploited manner and providing security with a number of IoT nodes in the network. Technology will lead to the wisdom of participating in sharing the Internet of Things (IoT) devices, energy-efficient environment can be used as support for the development of artificial intelligence while rewarding users for providing this support [12,13].

2   Literature Review on IoT Based Object Detection

In [14], Zhang, Lei and Yang have proposed a simple effective and efficient tracking algorithm based on features extracted. The authors have used multi scale filter bank and multi scale image features. The results have shown that their proposed algorithm performs well in terms of accuracy and speed.

Zhang, Wang, Chan, Wei and Ho [15], have proposed a framework for achieving object detection and tracking in non-overlapping multiple camera networks. The study introduced has used novel filter with Simplified Gaussian Mixture. The scheme of has achieved highest recognition compared with other traditional methods.

In [16], A review study on image Processing approaches for Object Tracking in Video Surveillance has been implemented by Ojha and Sakhare. The authors have focused on important and useful tracking methods. They provided brief techniques like region based, active contour based, and so on. Further, they have compared color models. The result of their study has shown great results over many objects in different weather conditions.

A new approach for fast motion detection has been developed by Chia, Wang and Sheu [17], which is able to recognize tracking objects without ambient noise. The authors have used depth edge detection and depth clustering for recognize object. The proposed technique speed was 36.14 faster compare with other techniques.

Mishra and Saroha [18], have proposed background subtraction, statistical and temporal frame difference to determine the various methods in moving object detection and tracking. The scheme provided for object detection, and video tracking has shown successful performance.

In [19], Ren et al. have used feature extractor, region feature and object classifier methods to demonstrate the object classification. The authors claimed that they achieved excellent object detection accuracy by using effective faster R-CNN and ResNet.

Rozantsev, Lepetit and Fua [20], have used sliding window method to detect flying object such as Unnamed Aerial Vehicles (UAVs). The introduced method has shown a better performance for pedestrian detection effectively.

In [21], a new algorithm for monitoring a wireless robot for surveillance is developed by Bokade and Ratnaparkhe. They have used an application work in android platform. The experiment has showed that the getting of a good quality video is efficiently achieved and the clarity reaches to 15 FPS.

Patil, Ambatkar and Kakde [22], have introduced a safekeeping alert device spending little handling power by IoT. The authors have used frame differencing, comparing frames and images methods to make the system working well.

In [23], Jain and Rajankar (2017) have surveyed SIFT, SURF and ORB to combine the object detection methods with IoT concept. The system worked completely for real time detection and recognition.

A novel data augmentation technique have proposed in [24] by Wang et al. The study is to track and recognize objects from existing automated image datasets. The authors provided a deep learning approach to efficiency detect eminent regions in videos. The results have shown that their methods generate high quality results.

Schwarz et al. [25], have developed an intelligent deep learning algorithm that combined object detection and semantic segments. The experimental results have shown that such approach can be applied to real world manipulation functions.

Imran and Sathish [26], have provided a new method to assure the security and surveillance system to the home through internet. Their system has controlled the door of home successfully.

In [27], a Node MCU ESP module has been used by Singh and Nandgaonkar to implement mini robot. The proposed method in the system aimed to produce live stream video, audio, and image transfer.

Lande and Mulajkar [28], have proposed a new approach to recognize moving objects based on foreground detection or background subtraction. The system has given good results in detecting human body. The Table 1 below provides summary of IoT based object detection literature review.

3   Literature Review on BlockChain Based Security and Privacy

Dorri and Kanhere [29], have delved deeper and outlined the different components and tasks of the smart home tier. The authors have discussed the diverse procedures and transactions related to it. The results of this study demonstrate the overheads incurred by its method is low and manage for low IoT devices. The authors planned to investigate the applications of their framework to other IoT domains.

Alphand, Amoretti and Claeysy [30] have proposed IoTChain, a scheme that combines OSCAR and the ACE authentication framework. It provide an Exchange to exchange solution to prevent unauthorized access to IoT resources. The authors have introduced several applications on top iotchain to assess its durability and performance.

Qu, Tao, Zhang, Hong and Yuan [31] have estimated a structure with layers, intersect and self-organizing blockchain structures, that is organized by

Table 1. A summery of IoT based object detection review

Authors & Reference	Objective	Database	Technical methods	Results
Kaihua Zhang et al. [14]	To propose a simple effective and efficient tracking algorithm based on feature extracted	Collect and download datasets from Internet	Multiscale filter bank, Multiscale image features, pare measurement matrix and compressed vectors	The results validates the effectiveness of the scale invariant features and Coarse to the all search strategy
Shuai Zhang et al. [15]	To propose a technique for achieving these tasks in a non-interfacing multiple camera network	Captured multiple videos as dataset	Weight colour histogram, Improved mean shift, BKF-SGM and super pixel represen-tation, SP-EMD	The result displays that their techniques has the best rate comparing with previous
S. Ojha & S Sakhare [16]	To focus on important and useful tracking methods	Record more than 10,000 faces by their own cameras	Background subtraction, foreground extraction and compare colour models in connecting frames	Their study has shown great results with many objects in good weather condition
Chi-Chia et al. & S Sakhare [17]	To make a new algorithm that recognizes object without ambient noise	–	Frame differencing and depth edge detection	The experiment results have proved that the proposed method is faster and has more accuracy
P. K. Mishara & G. P. Saroha [18]	Determine the various methods in static and moving object detection	Using captured images and videos	Background subtraction, statistical method and temporal frame differencing	The research phases for object detection and video tracking is done successful
Shaoqing Ren et al. [19]	To design deep neural network model for object recognition	PASCAL VOC dataset	Feature extractor, indicate region and object classifier	The results of this study have achieved excellent object detection accuracy

(continued)

Table 1. (*continued*)

Authors & Reference	Objective	Database	Technical methods	Results
Artem Rozantsev et al. [20]	To propose approach for detecting flying objects such as Unnamed Aerial Vehicles (UAVs)	UAV dataset, Aircraft dataset	Sliding window, motion compensation and object detector	The resulting algorithm works very well for pedestrian detection and outperforms most of the single-frame methods
A. U. Bokade & V. R. Ratnaparkhe [21]	To propose a method for controlling a remote robot for monitoring	acquires mjpeg dataset and sends it on HTTP session	–	The experimental result has shewed that the getting of a good accuracy and speed 15 FPS
Neha Patil et al. [22]	To define a safekeeping alert device spending little handling power by IoT	Snapshots, videos captured by web camera	Frame differencing Comparing frames and images	The monitoring system working well
S. K. Jain & S. O. Rajankar [23]	To combine the object recognition technique with IoT concept	Pre-existing database	SIFT, SURF and ORB	The system worked perfectly in real-time
Wengguan Wang et al. [24]	Proposed a deep learning model to completely detect salient video regions	DAVIS FBMS	State of the art	Displayed that they have gotten a very good results and high quality regions
Max Schwarz et al. [25]	To develop a deep learning algorithm that combined object detection and semantic segmentation	ImageNet, Visual Genome dataset	Conv features, region feature and SVM or softmax	The experiment result has held such approaches to do real time object detection

(*continued*)

Table 1. (*continued*)

Authors & Reference	Objective	Database	Technical methods	Results
S. A. I. Quadri & P. Sathish et al. [26]	To provide monitoring system for mart home security	Collecting data through sensors and actuators then send it to the mobile phone or a personal computer through a wireless	–	The authors have developed a system to control all component of smart home
D. Singh & A. Nandgaonkar et al. [27]	To implement new technique for mini robot	Database of user names and passwords	NodeMCU ESP module	This technique is able to detect objects in live video as well as images
R. Lande & R. M. Mulajkar et al. [28]	To give a new method to recognize objects based on foreground extraction or background subtraction	Collect their own data and label it	Frame separation, Background subtraction and Noise removal	The method applied is able to detect objects successfully

Blockchain technology. The authors decided to make solutions for some problems like how to control the height of the tree and for large scale IoT environment.

Miraz and Ali [32] have investigated the research question "To what tide can BlockChain be used to improve public security of the Internet of Things?" and how the two technologies work, the authors of this paper differentiated some challenges associated with such application of the BlockChain. They hence to bring up potential solutions for Blockchain based IoT security systems.

Ferrag, Derdour and Mukherjee [33] have presented a overall review of the existing blockchain records for the internet of things networks. The authors have provided a survey of the application domains for blockchain technologies with IoT. They have met many challenging research areas, such as Flexibility against common attacks is a dynamic and adaptive security framework.

Kumar and Mallick [34] have highlighted the possibilities of applications for IoT with blockchain technologies. They have given basic ideas to identify the need of blockchain for IoT. They have discussed the studies related to the potential implication in various fields with appropriate demonstrative models.

Jesus, Chicarino, Albuquerque and Rocha [35] have presented a new technology. That has provided security and privacy in IoT, the provided access control between devices in smart home.

4 Literature Review on BlockChain Based Video Processing

Lazaroiu and Roscia [36] have used new technologies as blockchain and IoT to design a smart city. The authors have connected smart home devices and sensors through secure and reliable network. They did it through IoT and Blockchain technology. They made a new improve in life through their research.

Liu, Shang, Shi and Wang [37] have proposed a method based on blockchain to enclose the security of video surveillance, which is called video-chain. It is basically a blockchain method, but there are some difference from digital currency such as Bitcoin. The authors took a campus video surveillance application scenario as an example. The authors used a blockchain and traditional data storage method. They design two parts of the blockchain system. Safety and proficiency analysis demonstrate that VideoChain is practically suitable.

Nikouei, Xu, Nagothu and Chen [38] have implemented a novel method that make blockchain scheme to protect the data through encrypt and secure channel between all nodes. It is also reduces the attacks on edge and fog devices. The experimental results showed that the proposed method is a feasible solution for the event-oriented applications.

Nagothu, Xu, Nikouei and Chen [39] have introduced a novel secure smart surveillance system based on blockchain technology with micro services architecture. The blockchain technology synchronize securely the video analysis database and provides juggle directory of data tampering in securely network environment.

Gallo, Pongnumkul and Nguyen [40] have introduced blocksee, it is a blockchain based video surveillance system that provides validation to camera settings and makes it ready to authorized users in case of events.

5 Conclusion

The technological revolution is exponentially growing up all around the world, which leads to a higher volume of critical communication and data exchange including text, audio, pictures, videos, and a hybrid of them. Security, protection, and real-time interaction have become challenges on the way of developing robust systems and applications. Object detection and tracking have been active research topic in the field of computer vision. This paper has presented a progress review of popular IoT-based object detection secured by blockchain system, recognition and tracking methods developed up to present. It discusses the main concept of each method and presents the strategies used for secure IoT using the blockchain ecosystem. Potential future work is planned to develop a novel solution for a higher level of robustness.

References

1. Khan, A., Janwe, J.N.: Review on moving object detection in video surveillance. IJARCCE **6**(4), 664–670 (2017)

2. Abdul-Qawy, A.S.H., Srinivasulu, T.: SEES: a scalable and energy-efficient scheme for green IoT-based heterogeneous wireless nodes. J. Ambient Intell. Humaniz. Comput. **10**(4), 1571–1596 (2018). https://doi.org/10.1007/s12652-018-0758-7

3. Santosh, K., Lamiroy, B., Wendling, L.: DTW for matching Radon features: a pattern recognition and retrieval method. In: Blanc-Talon, J., Kleihorst, R., Philips, W., Popescu, D., Scheunders, P. (eds.) ACIVS 2011. LNCS, vol. 6915, pp. 249–260. Springer, Heidelberg (2011). https://doi.org/10.1007/978-3-642-23687-7_23

4. Santosh, K., Lamiroy, B., Wendling, L.: DTW-Radon-based shape descriptor for pattern recognition. Int. J. Pattern Recogn. Artif. Intell. **27**(03), 1350008 (2013)

5. Santosh, K.C., Hangarge, M., Bevilacqua, V., Negi, A. (eds.): RTIP2R 2016. CCIS, vol. 709. Springer, Singapore (2017). https://doi.org/10.1007/978-981-10-4859-3

6. Santosh, K.C., Hegadi, R.S. (eds.): RTIP2R 2018. CCIS, vol. 1036. Springer, Singapore (2019). https://doi.org/10.1007/978-981-13-9184-2

7. Atzori, L., Iera, A., Morabito, G.: The Internet of Things, a survey. Comput. Netw. **54**(15), 2787–2805 (2010)

8. Abdul-Qawy, A.S., Pramod, P.J., Magesh, E., Srinivasulu, T.: The Internet of Things (IoT): an overview. Int. J. Eng. Res. Appl. (IJERA) **5**(12), 71–82 (2015)

9. Sicari, S., Rizzardi, A., Grieco, L.A., Coen-Porisini, A.: Security, privacy and trust in Internet of Things: the road ahead. Comput. Netw. **76**, 146–164 (2015)

10. Rosic, A.: What is blockchain technology? A step-by-step guide for beginners. J. Chem. Inf. Model. (2013)

11. Nakamoto, S.: Bitcoin: A peer-to-peer electronic cash system. Bitcoin **4** (2008). https://bitcoin.org/bitcoin.pdf

12. Zhuopeng, X.: IoT chain mainnet launch (2018). https://medium.com/iot-chain/the-iot-chain-mainnet-launch-stage-observation-7248880d2f59

13. Abdul-Qawy, A.S.H., Srinivasulu, T.: Greening trends in energy-efficiency of IoT-based heterogeneous wireless nodes. In: International Conference on Electrical, Electronics, Computers, Communication, Mechanical and Computing (EECCMC), pp. 1–10, January 2018

14. Zhang, K., Zhang, L., Yang, M.H.: Fast compressive tracking. IEEE Trans. Pattern Anal. Mach. Intell. **36**(10), 2002–2015 (2014)

15. Zhang, S., Wang, C., Chan, S.C., Wei, X.G.: New object detection, tracking and recognition approaches for video surveillance over camera network. IEEE Sens. J. **15**(5), 2679–2691 (2014)

16. Ojha, S., Sakhare, S.: Image processing techniques for object tracking in video surveillance- a survey. In: International Conference on Pervasive Computing (ICPC), pp. 1–6. IEEE (2015)

17. Sun, C., Wang, Y., Sheu, M.: Fast motion object detection algorithm using complementary depth image on an RGB-D camera. IEEE Sens. J. **17**(17), 5728–5734 (2017)

18. Mishra, P., Saroha, G.P.: A study on video surveillance system for object detection and tracking. In: 3rd International Conference on Computing for Sustainable Global Development, pp. 221–226. IEEE (2016)

19. Ren, S., He, K., Girshick, R., Zhang, X., Sun, J.: Object detection networks on convolutional feature maps. IEEE Trans. Pattern Anal. Mach. Intell. **39**(7), 1476–1781 (2016)

20. Rozantsev, A., Lepetit, V., Fua, P.: Detecting flying objects using a single moving camera. IEEE Trans. Pattern Anal. Mach. Intell. **39**(5), 879–892 (2016)

21. Bokade, A.U., Ratnaparkhe, V.R., Pi, A.R.: Video surveillance robot control using smartphone and Raspberry Pi. In: International Conference on Communication and Signal Processing (ICCSP), pp. 2094–2097. IEEE (2016)

22. Patil, N., Ambatkar, S., Kakde, S.: IoT based smart surveillance security system using Raspberry Pi. In: International Conference on Communication and Signal Processing (ICCSP), pp. 344–348. IEEE (2017)
23. Jain, K., Rajankar, S.: Real-time object detection and recognition using Internet of Things paradigm. Int. J. Image Graph. Signal Process. **9**(1), 18 (2017)
24. Wang, W., Shen, J., Member, S., Shao, L.: Video salient object detection via fully convolutional networks. IEEE Trans. Image Process. **27**(1), 38–49 (2017)
25. Schwarz, M., Milan, A., Periyasamy, A.S., Behnke, S.: RGB-D object detection and semantic segmentation for autonomous manipulation in clutter. Int. J. Robot. Res. **37**(4–5), 437–451 (2018)
26. Quadri, S.A.I., Sathish, P.: IoT based home automation and surveillance system. In: International Conference on Intelligent Computing and Control Systems (ICICCS), pp. 861–866. IEEE (2017)
27. Singh, D., Nandgaonkar, A.: IOT-based Wi-Fi surveillance robot with real-time audio and video streaming. In: Iyer, B., Nalbalwar, S.L., Pathak, N.P. (eds.) Computing, Communication and Signal Processing. AISC, vol. 810, pp. 639–647. Springer, Singapore (2019). https://doi.org/10.1007/978-981-13-1513-8_65
28. Lande, R., Mulajkar, R.M.: Moving object detection using foreground detection for video surveillance system. Int. Res. J. Eng. Technol. (IRJET) **17**(6), 517–519 (2018)
29. Dorri, A., Kanhere, S., Jurdak, R., Gauravaram, P.: Blockchain for IoT security and privacy: the case study of a smart home. In: International Conference on Pervasive Computing and Communications Workshops (PerCom Workshops), pp. 618–623. IEEE (2017)
30. Alphand, O., et al.: IoTChain: a blockchain security architecture for the Internet of Things. In: IEEE Wireless Communications and Networking Conference (WCNC), pp. 1–6 (2018)
31. Qu, C., Tao, M., Zhang, J., Hong, X., Yuan, R.: Blockchain based credibility verification method for IoT entities. Secur. Commun. Netw. **2018** (2018)
32. Miraz, M.H., Ali, M.: Blockchain enabled enhanced IoT ecosystem security. In: Miraz, M.H., Excell, P., Ware, A., Soomro, S., Ali, M. (eds.) iCETiC 2018. LNICST, vol. 200, pp. 38–46. Springer, Cham (2018). https://doi.org/10.1007/978-3-319-95450-9_3
33. Ferrag, M.A., Derdour, M., Mukherjee, M., Derhab, A.: Blockchain technologies for the Internet of Things: research issues and challenges. IEEE Internet Things J. **6**(2), 2188–2204 (2018)
34. Manoj, N., Kumar, P.: Blockchain technology for security issues and challenges in IoT. Procedia Comput. Sci. **132**(1), 1815–1823 (2018)
35. Jesus, E.F., Chicarino, V.R.L., Albuquerque, C.V.N.D., Rocha, A.A.D.A.: A survey of how to use blockchain to secure Internet of Things and the stalker attack. Secur. Commun. Netw. **2018**(9675050), 1–27 (2018)
36. Lazaroiu, C., Roscia, M.: Smart district through IoT and blockchain. In: International Conference on Renewable Energy Research and Applications (ICRERA), pp. 454–461. IEEE (2017)
37. Liu, M., Shang, J., Liu, P., Shi, Y., Wang, M.: VideoChain: trusted video surveillance based on blockchain for campus. In: Sun, X., Pan, Z., Bertino, E. (eds.) ICCCS 2018. LNCS, vol. 11066, pp. 48–58. Springer, Cham (2018). https://doi.org/10.1007/978-3-030-00015-8_5
38. Nikouei, S.Y., Xu, R., Nagothu, D., Chen, Y., Aved, A., Blasch, E.: Real-time index authentication for event-oriented surveillance video query using blockchain. In: IEEE International Smart Cities Conference (ISC2), pp. 1–8. IEEE (2018)

39. Nagothu, D., Xu, R., Nikouei, S.Y., Chen, Y.: A microservice-enabled architecture for smart surveillance using blockchain technology. In: IEEE International Smart Cities Conference (ISC2), pp. 1–6. IEEE (2018)
40. Gallo, P., Pongnumkul, S., Nguyen, U.Q.: BlockSee: blockchain for IoT video surveillance in smart cities. In: IEEE International Conference on Environment and Electrical Engineering and 2018 IEEE Industrial and Commercial Power Systems Europe (EEEIC I and CPS Europe), pp. 1–6. IEEE (2018)

MINU-EXTRACTNET: Automatic Latent Fingerprint Feature Extraction System Using Deep Convolutional Neural Network

Uttam U. Deshpande[1][(⊠)] and V. S. Malemath[2]

[1] Department of Electronics and Communication Engineering, KLS Gogte Institute of Technology, Belagavi, Karnataka, India
uttamudeshpande@gmail.com
[2] Department of Computer Science and Engineering, KLE Dr. M. S. Sheshgiri College of Engineering and Techology, Belagavi, Karnataka, India
veeru_sm@yahoo.com

Abstract. The performance of any fingerprint identification system depends on the accuracy of the feature extraction stage. Many latent fingerprint matching methods failed to produce good results because of the presence of background noise. To improve the performance, we propose a simple Deep Convolutional Neural Network (DCNN) model called "Minu-ExtractNet". Firstly, latent fingerprint pre-processing is implemented using a Convolutional Neural Network (CNN) model called "Pre-ProcessNet". This model enhances the quality of the latent and produces the orientation information along with different segmentation masks. Secondly, pre-processed information is then used to extract the minutiae feature points using another CNN model called "ExtractNet". This feature extractor model performs the image quality assessment to determine the threshold value to filter out spurious minutiae points. A dynamic thresholding algorithm is developed to achieve this goal. Experiments are carried out on both plain (FVC2004) and latent (NIST SD27) public fingerprint datasets. The results show significant improvement in precision, recall and Fl score values under different settings in comparison with the state-of-the-art CNN methods.

Keywords: Deep Convolution Neural Network (DCNN) · Minu-ExtractNet · Pre-ProcessNet · ExtractNet · Dynamic thresholding algorithm · FVC2004 · NIST SD27

1 Introduction

Biometric is a term referred to as certain features of human characteristics that distinguish one person from another. Biometric authentication refers to the usage of different biometric features which could be physical or behavioral characteristics [1]. Examples of these biometric identifiers are facial patterns, voice or typing cadence, DNA matching, iris matching, fingerprint recognition, palm print recognition, etc. This method has been a reliable source for the identification of an individual because of its uniqueness

© Springer Nature Singapore Pte Ltd. 2021
K. C. Santosh and B. Gawali (Eds.): RTIP2R 2020, CCIS 1380, pp. 44–56, 2021.
https://doi.org/10.1007/978-981-16-0507-9_5

property. Out of all available biometric techniques, fingerprint recognition is considered as the most reliable, most robust, and less expensive [1] means of individual identification. Nowadays, Fingerprint Recognition is most widely used in industries because of its ease of using it.

Here are a few of the advantages of Fingerprint Recognition:

- No two fingerprints have same ridge characteristics.
- Fingerprint does not get affected by diseases.
- Consumes less storage space compared to other biometric methods.
- Matching is extremely quick. Hence saves time.
- Easy to use.
- Low maintenance cost.
- User doesn't have to make conscious effort to get their fingerprint scanned which makes it user friendly.

Manual fingerprint recognition consumes more time and is prone to introduce errors. Hence, automatic fingerprint recognition is being developed from the past several decades [8]. The success of a good automatic latent fingerprint recognition system depends on how accurately it determines and extracts the fingerprint features from the query fingerprint compared to the ground truth fingerprint of the database. The conventional automatic fingerprint recognition system involves pre-processing and minutiae extraction steps before matching. In Pre-processing, ridge extraction and thinning are carried out before extracting minutiae [10, 14]. Published results revealed that the system produced good minutiae extraction when tested on normal fingerprint images. But the minutiae extraction accuracy got reduced when the system was tested on low-quality fingerprint images.

Neural Network-based systems are being widely developed in fingerprint applications and have produced good results. Yoon et al [2] proposed a method using Gabor filtering to determine the presence of noise and provide a level of confidence for extracted minutiae. This method gave better results compared to earlier algorithms, but the results suffered due to the presence of background noise in the image. Jiang et al. [3] presented two networks: JudgeNet: to classify minutiae patches, and LocateNet: to locate minutiae location. Although this approach uses neural networks, it doesn't provide minutiae orientation information, and also it utilizes more time due to the sliding window method employed for extracting minutiae.

Tang et al. [4] used the object detection method to identify minutiae patches. The performance of the model suffers because of the hard thresholding influences to delete the minutiae patches. He later proposed "FingerNet" that uses fixed weights and maps enhancement, orientation, segmentation, and extraction information to a neural network. Published results showed improvement in the precision and recall values. But the hard thresholding affected the performance of the model.

Dinh-Luan Nguyen et al. [5] proposed an automatic minutiae-extractor based model on Deep-Neural Networks (DNN), called "MinutiaeNet". To achieve fast matching, this model utilizes a compact feature representation. MinutiaeNet contains 1st network called "CoarseNet". This network estimates the minutiae score-map, and orientation based on fingerprint domain-knowledge (enhanced image, orientation field, and segmentation map). 2nd network, called "FineNet", filters the minutiae locations based on minutiae score-map.

Darlow et al. [6] proposed a neural network model called "MENet". Here each pixel of the input fingerprint is fed to this model to determine whether it corresponds to a minutia or not. It uses the sliding window method. The model has independent modules for minutiae location and orientation estimates. Hence the model is slow and time consuming.

To summarize, the approaches used in the work carried out so far suffer from hard threshold problems eliminating true minutiae points during post-processing. In the published state-of-art work carried out so far, most of the methods use the plain network to classify candidate region patch. In our proposed work we combine the fingerprint domain-knowledge and deep networks to investigate if there is any improvement in the extraction result. The contributions to the proposed work are as follows:

- A Robust image enhancement model to suppress the background noise and enhance the quality of the image using Gabor filters.
- An Automatic Minutiae Extraction and classifier model using a convolutional neural network to locate minutiae points using dynamic thresholding to improve precision, recall, and F1 scores of minutiae patches.

2   Related Work on Fingerprint Matching

Our feature extraction framework Minu-ExtractNet has two modules,

1. **Pre-ProcessNet:** A residual learning-based CNN model. It is a Robust image enhancement model that takes input as a fingerprint image and enhances the image for further operation. This model also generates orientation estimates and segmentation masks as output.
2. **ExtractNet:** It's a CNN based minutiae extractor model that takes the output of the robust image enhancement model as input and extracts feature points from the fingerprint image. Feature points could be ridge ending, bifurcation, core points, etc. The model gives output feature points as X and Y coordinates, the orientation angle θ, and the confidence score of each feature point.

2.1   Pre-ProcessNet

To improve the minutiae extraction accuracy, the proposed model uses the additional fingerprint domain knowledge [17] information i.e. orientation map, and automatically extracted segmentation map from the input fingerprint image. This is a learning-based segmentation method shares some features like gradient coherence, local mean, and variance along with orientation estimation. For minutiae patch classification a multi-layer model is used to predict the probability of appearance each input pixel in a region, and to output a segmentation score map with the size of H/8 * H/8. Hence the entire multi-scale feature maps with the orientation estimation. The primary objective of the Pre-ProcessNet is to enhance the quality of the fingerprint image by suppressing the background noise. This step is used to increase the number of extracted fingerprint features and help in improving the fingerprint minutiae prediction. Figure 1 shows the detailed architecture of the Pre-ProcessNet network. This CNN model takes fingerprint as input and generates orientation field estimates and segmentation masks. Input fingerprint is passed through the Gabor filter enhancement model, this along with the orientation field is used to enhance the fingerprint image. The enhanced image is masked with a segmentation mask to remove background noise. This image obtained is enhanced and is suitable to be an input for feature extraction.

Orientation and Segmentation Feature: Proposed model use a deep residual-based learning method with an increased number of pooling layers to decrease the region patch. The number of convolution layers used here is less and simple compared to the CoarseNet [5] architecture. This arrangement helps in reducing the pre-processing time without compromising on the quality of the enhancement results. This Neural network flows to multiple layers. We get the output after 2nd, 3rd, 4th pooling layers and it feeds to a combined network at different rates to obtain multi-scale segmentation.

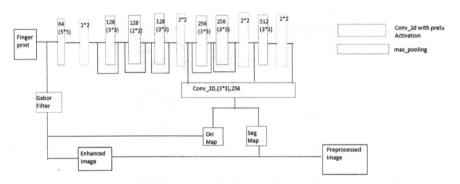

Fig. 1. Pre-ProcessNet: Proposed robust image enhancement model.

This results in output with no loss of information. With four pooling layers, the output at level 3, 4 will perform course evaluation and level 2 performs a fine evaluation of input fingerprint.

Segmentation Map: Segmentation Map and orientation map [11] share the same neural network. A multi-level approach [17] as discussed above will help in obtaining the probability maps for each level. These maps will be in the corresponding region of an input image. For instance, if there exist features at the level 'k', then to get finer details the probability map will be processed at 'k/2' levels. If the feature points are found at level 'k' then it will keep the image in that region. While in the absence of fingerprint features it masks the output because there exists noise. Hence, the segmentation map performs a masking operation and removes all the regions with noise.

Orientation Map: To obtain the full minutiae information, results are fused [11] with orientation results obtained from Pre-ProcessNet to produce ridge orientation estimate of the input image. The orientation estimate and segmentation mask are tested on different database images from FVC2002, FVC2004, and NIST SD27 is as shown in Fig. 2.

Gabor Enhanced Image: Gabor enhancement map is formed by taking an average of Gabor filtered image and orientation map to obtain ridge flow estimation. To suppress the unwanted background noise, the segmentation map is applied to the obtained enhancement map. This pre-processed image is fed to ExtractNet for further operation.

Training Data for Pre-ProcessNet: Due to the lack of ground truth dataset, we generate weak labels from the approach used by Nguyen et.al. [5]. Pre-ProcessNet uses minutiae location and orientation generated from this method. These weak labels are used for training segmentation and orientation modules.

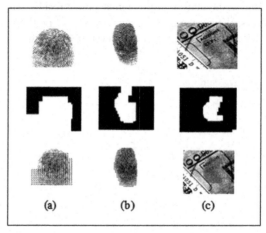

(a)   (b)   (c)

Fig. 2. Original image, Orientation and Segmentation results obtained by Pre ProcessNet for (a) FVC2002 (b) FVC2004 (c) NIST SD27 databases.

2.2 ExtractNet

Minutiae Extractor model "ExtractNet" is a multi-layered convolutional neural network. The model takes the enhanced fingerprint image generated from the Pre-ProcessNet model as the input and outputs the minutiae feature points like ridge ending, and bifurcation, etc. The minutiae feature points will be in terms of minutiae location with x-y Cartesian co-ordinates, ridge orientation, and confidence level. The architecture of ExtractNet is shown in Fig. 3.

The input image is passed through the convolutional layer with a filter size of 9*9. Each filter in the convolution layer recognizes special objects (points) in the image. The filter slides with a sliding window across the image with the image patch getting

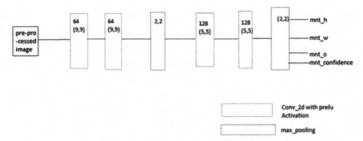

Fig. 3. ExtractNet: Proposed minutiae extractor model.

higher value if the particular feature point is present in the patch. The values of the filter are based on weights and bias of the network architecture which is obtained during the training phase. The weights and biases are determined by the activation function. Here, we perform the sum of products of inputs(X) with their corresponding Weights (W) to activate function f(x). The obtained output is fed as an input to the next layer. Our model utilizes ReLu (Rectified-Linear Unit) as an activation function. This activation function is supported by Keras. This is shown in Fig. 4.

ReLu: It is the most used activation function to determine the output of the Neural Network and the output will be in the form of yes or no decision. It maps the resulting values between 0 to 1 or 1 to −1. It has properties like non-linear, simpler mathematical operation as shown in Eq. 1.

$$A = max(O, x) \tag{1}$$

To get the precise minutiae location, each level of Pre-ProcessNet is fused to get the minutiae score-map. The size of the score map has to be of size (ht/16*wt/16), where 'ht' and 'wt' are the respective 'height' and 'width' of the image. The minutiae points obtained from ExtractNet is shown in Fig. 5.

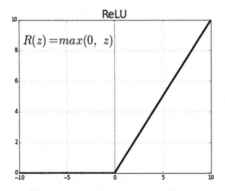

Fig. 4. Activation function - ReLu.

Dynamic Threshold Filtration Algorithm: The confidence level of minutiae points as predicted by ExtractNet directly depends upon the quality of the image. ExtractNet extracts both true and spurious points that have to be filtered before passing it to further operation. The presence of a significant number of spurious points or lost true minutiae points affects the accuracy of the future matching process. Hence, an efficient filtering process has to be implemented. If a static thresholding mechanism is applied then true minutiae points will be filtered out. This is because the degraded image will detect a true minutia point with a lower confidence level. Hence to overcome these drawbacks we propose a dynamic thresholding algorithm. The algorithm uses the Gaussian distribution function (y) and is given in Eq. (2).

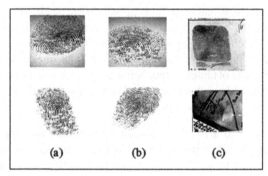

(a)   (b)   (c)

Fig. 5. Minutiae points extracted using ExtractNet for (a) FVC2002 (b) FVC2004 (c) Latent NIST SD27 databases.

The Dynamic Threshold (DT) is given by DT = 2*σ. Our Extractor model performs image quality assessment to determine the threshold to be set to filter out spurious minutiae points. This value is set up by the model itself and it is based on the quality of input image. i.e. If the value of DT < 0.5 then the algorithm set DT = 0.5.

$$y = \frac{1}{\sigma\sqrt{2\pi}} e^{-\frac{(x-\mu)^2}{2\sigma^2}} \tag{2}$$

Where,
μ = Mean,
σ = Standard Deviation.
X = Confidence level.
Π = 3.1428.
e = 2.71828.

Algorithm 1 Dynamic Thresholding Filtration

Input ← Minutiae extracted image(img) from the database (db) using ExtractNet
Output ← Filtered Image (fimg)
for each **img** ∈ {fingerprint image img in db } **do**
    σ ← Calculate Standard Deviation (SD).
    $Dynamic\ Threshold(DT)$ ← $2 * \sigma$
    if $DT > 0.5$ **then**
        DT ← 0.5
    end if
end for

Losses: Due to improper fingerprint placement over fingerprint sensor and dry/wet fingerprint surface the noise or distortion could get introduced. Which can affect the performance of the ExtractNet. To overcome this problem, we use Centre Loss [9] over Softmax loss. The advantage of using Centre loss is that it tries to bring features of the same class more and more close. Consider Total Loss (TL), Centre Loss (CL), Softmax Loss (SL), and Orientation Loss (OL). For training, the TL is calculated as,

$$TL = aCL + (1 - \alpha)SL + \beta OL \tag{3}$$

where 'α' is the balance factor between Centre (intra-class) and Softmax (inter-class). 'β' is the factor used to determine the precision of minutiae orientation. We set the values of $\alpha = 0.5$, and $\beta = 2$. We then set the batch size of 100 and initialize the variables randomly as N (0, 0.01) by using a Gaussian distribution function. The learning rate is set as 0.01 at the beginning and later is reduced as much as ten times after completing 50K iterations. Max epoch is set at 200K with a weight decay of 0.9.

3 Results

The Minu-ExtractNet model is tested on FVC2004 [7], and latent fingerprint database NIST SD27 [18] in different settings. We use two-parameter setting thresholds, they are Distance (D) and Orientation (O). Score maps are determined from correct and incorrect minutiae extractions from test images with a trained image. Experiments are set up and implemented on TensorFlow. The performance is observed by executing on Google Colab which uses Nvidia GTX GeForce graphic processor.

3.1 Datasets

To overcome the lack of ground truth dataset, the minutiae extractor model Minu-ExtractNet uses minutiae-location and minutiae-orientation provided by datasets generated by Nguyen et al. [5]. Similarly, we have trained for the FVC2004 fingerprint database using the FVCViewer tool to get ground truth minutiae points for the FVC database. Separate models are generated for the different databases to prevent the overfitting of the model. We used a total of 80 images from FVC2004 and 258 images from NIST SD27.

Feature Extraction Evaluation: To test the robustness of our model, we use different evaluation procedure for different function in the end to end framework. Feature extraction has a significant effect on the accuracy of the automatic fingerprint matching system. The feature extracted should be accurate enough to sustain the entire working of the model. For evaluating the robustness of the Minu-ExtractNet model, results are compared with approaches published in [5]. Two datasets i.e. FVC 2004 and NIST SD27 with different criteria for distance and orientation thresholds are used. Consider (lpr, lg) and (opr, og) to be coordinates of minutia location and orientation of the ground-truth minutia. The minutia value predicted is considered to be true if the following conditions are satisfied,

$$\left\{ \begin{array}{l} ||lpr - lg|| \le D \\ ||opr - og|| \le O \end{array} \right\} \tag{4}$$

Here, 'D' represents the pixel threshold, and 'O' represents the threshold in degrees. For our experiment, we set the distance (D) between actually detected and the ground-truth minutiae in the range of 8 to 16 pixels. We set Orientation (O) in the range of 10 to 30 degrees. The threshold value was maintained below or equal to 0.5. These values are chosen to compare the obtained results with the results published earlier. This can be seen in the table below.

Table 1, 2, and 3 shows the comparisons of precision and recall obtained under different approaches with different settings. Precision and recall are very important evaluation metrics used in minutiae feature extraction. Precision refers to the percentage of relevant results. Whereas, recall refers to the total percentage of relevant results that are correctly classified by an algorithm. There is another metric called F-1 score is used. It is a Harmonic-Mean (H.M) of precision and recall values.

Table 1. Comparison of minutiae extraction (Precision, Recall, and F1-Score) values obtained by different methods using FVC 2004 and NIST SD 27 Databases with setting-1 ($D = 8, O = 10$).

Dataset	Methods	Precision	Recall	F1-Score
FVC 2004	MINDTCT [12]	30.8%	64.3%	0.416
	VeriFinger [13]	39.8%	69.2%	0.505
	FingerNet [17]	68.7%	62.1%	0.643
	MinutiaeNet [5]	79%	80.1%	0.795
	Proposed method	82.41%	84.7%	0.836
NIST SD27	MINDTCT [12]	8.3%	14.7%	0.106
	VeriFinger [13]	3.6%	40.1%	0.066
	FingerNet [17]	53.2%	49.5%	0.513
	MinutiaeNet [5]	69.2%	67.7%	0.684
	Proposed method	73.33%	78.57%	0.758

"Precision" is defined as the number of True Positives (TP) divided by the number of TP plus the number of False Positives (FP). Here TP is the cases where the model correctly labels positive class and FP are the cases where the model incorrectly labels as a positive and negative class. Precision expresses the proportion of the data points our model says were relevant. "Recall" expresses the ability to find all relevant instances in a dataset.

$$Precision = TP/TP + FP \qquad (5)$$

Table 2. Comparison of minutiae extraction (Precision, Recall, and F1-Score) values obtained by different methods using FVC 2004 and NIST SD 27 Databases with setting-2 (D = 12, 0 = 20).

Dataset	Methods	Precision	Recall	F1-Score
FVC 2004	MINDTCT [12]	37.7%	72.1%	0.495
	VeriFinger [13]	45.6%	77.5%	0.574
	FingerNet [17]	72.9%	70.4%	0.716
	MinutiaeNet [5]	83.6%	83.9%	0.837
	Proposed method	85.2%	87.6%	0.864
NIST SD27	MINDTCT [12]	10.0%	16.4%	0.124
	VeriFinger [13]	5.3%	47.9%	0.095
	FingerNet [17]	58%	58.1%	0.580
	MinutiaeNet [5]	70.5%	72.3%	0.714
	Proposed method	78.2%	88.1%	0.831

Table 1, 2, and 3 contains the state-of-art work carried out by different researchers. "MINDTCT" is open source biometric image software developed by NIST. While "VeriFinger" is a commercial SDK software developed for minutiae extraction and matching. From Table 3., it can be observed that our proposed model outperforms the state-of-the-art techniques with different parameters i.e. 'D = 16' and '0 = 30' (thresholds) for both FVC 2004 and NIST SD27 databases. The precision-recall curves for FVC 2004 and NIST SD27 database by different state-of-art work are shown in Fig. 6. The obtained results are found similar to the ground truth minutiae of FVC 2004 and NIST SD27 databases. The proposed work can work well with partial fingerprint images and images with noisy backgrounds. Although the model performs well, in some cases the model fails to detect the true minutiae or identifies the spurious minutiae. This is because of discontinuous ridges, presence of minutia near fingerprint edge point. The performance of the model can be improved for latent fingerprints of poor-quality images.

Table 3. Comparison of minutiae extraction (Precision, Recall, and F1-Score) values obtained by different methods using FVC 2004 and NIST SD 27 Databases with setting-3 (D = 16, 0 = 30).

Dataset	Methods	Precision	Recall	F1-Score
FVC 2004	MINDTCT [12]	42.1%	79.8%	0.551
	VeriFinger [13]	51.8%	81.9%	0.635
	Gao et.al. [15]	48.8%	82.7%	0.614
	FingerNet [17]	76%	80.0%	0.779
	MinutiaeNet [5]	85.9%	84.8%	0.853
	Proposed method	87.5%	93.33%	0.903
NIST SD27	MINDTCT [12]	11.2%	18.9%	0.141
	VeriFinger [13]	7.6%	58.35%	0.134
	Gao et.al. [15]	23.5%	8.7%	0.127
	Sankaran et. al. [16]	26.4%	63.1%	0.372
	Tang et.al. [4]	53.0%	53.4%	0.532
	FingerNet [17]	63%	63.2%	0.631
	MinutiaeNet [5]	71.2%	75.7%	0.734
	Proposed method	86.67%	92.85%	0.896

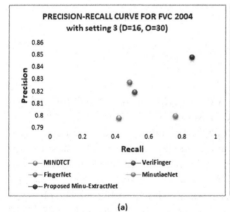 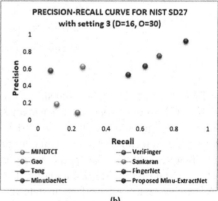

(a)   (b)

Fig. 6. Precision-Recall curves for a) For FVC 2004 b) NIST SD27 datasets based on published data in Table 3.

4   Conclusion and Future Scope

We have presented a framework "Minu-ExtractNet" for fingerprint minutiae extraction. This model combines the fingerprint domain-knowledge, deep network to suppress background noise and in turn improves the extraction results. We implemented the following two separate independent neural networks each with specific functionality.

– **PreProcessingNet:** It is a CNN model, that automatically removes the noise present in the image, enhances the quality of the image, and suppresses the background noise.
– **ExtractNet:** It is a CNN model, that automatically extracts the minutiae without hard thresholding. It provides information about minutiae orientation, location, and confidence level based on the quality of the image.

A Dynamic threshold filtering is proposed to filter out spurious minutiae points based on the confidence level produced by ExtractNet. Experimental results reveal that the proposed model performs well especially in terms of precision, recall, and Fl-scores under different settings of Distance (D) and Orientation (O) over published state-of-the-artwork done by various researchers using FVC 2004 and NIST SD27 datasets. The proposed model can be further improved by,

• Testing the results on a large database and observing the network behavior over application involving large fingerprint images.
• Improving extraction time by development in the neural network model as per the future developments in hardware and software in the Deep Neural Network stream.
• Developing and integrating a Matching Model to develop an end-to-end system that recognizes the fingerprint identity present in the database or not in less time.

References

1. Biometrics. http://biometrics.pbworks.com/w/page/14811357/FrontPage
2. Yoon,S., Feng, J., Jain, A.K.: Latent fingerprint enhancement via robust orientation field estimation. In: Proceedings of IEEE IJCB, pp. 1–8 (2011)
3. Jiang, L., Zhao, T., Bai, C., Yong, A., Wu, M.: A direct fingerprint minutiae extraction approach based on convolutional neural networks. In: Proceedings of IEEE IJCNN, pp. 571–578 (2016)
4. Tang, Y., Gao, F., Feng, J.: Latent fingerprint minutia extraction Using fully convolutional network. In: Proceedings of IEEE IJCB (2017)
5. Nguyen, Dinh-Luan., Cao, K., Jain, A.: Robust Minutiae Extractor: Integrating Deep Networks and Fingerprint Domain Knowledge. Michigan State University, East Lansing (2016)
6. Darlow, L., Rosman, B.: Fingerprint minutiae extraction using deep learning. In: Proceedings of IEEE IJCB (2017)
7. FVC2004. https://bias.csr.unibo.it/FVC2004/
8. Jain, A.K., Nandakumar, K., Ross, A.: 50 years of biometric research- accomplishments, challenges, and opportunities. Pattern Recogn. Lett **79**, 80–105 (2016)

9. Wen, Y., Zhang, K., Li, Z., Qiao, Y.: A discriminative feature learning approach for deep face recognition. In: Leibe, B., Matas, J., Sebe, N., Welling, M. (eds.) ECCV 2016. LNCS, vol. 9911, pp. 499–515. Springer, Cham (2016). https://doi.org/10.1007/978-3-319-46478-7_31

10. Jain, A., Hong, L., Bolle, R.: On-line fingerprint verification. IEEE Trans. PAMI **19**(4), 302–314 (1997)

11. Yang, X., Feng, J., Zhou, J.: Localized dictionaries-based orientation field estimation for latent fingerprints. IEEE Trans. PAMI **36**(5), 955–969 (2014)

12. Watson, C.I., et al.: User's guide to NIST biometric image software (NBIS). NIST Interagency/Internal Report 7392 (2007)

13. Verifying. Neuro-technology (2010)

14. Feng, J.: Combining minutiae descriptors for fingerprint matching. Pattern Recogn. **41**(1), 342–352 (2008)

15. Gao, X., Chen, X., Cao, J., Deng, Z., Liu, C., Feng, J.: A novel method of fingerprint minutiae extraction based on Gabor phase. In: Proceedings of 17th IEEE ICIP, pp. 3077–3080 (2010)

16. A. Sankaran, P. Pandey, M. Vatsa, and R. Singh: On latent fingerprint minutiae extraction using stacked denoising sparse autoencoders. In Proc. IEEE IJCB, pp.1–7, (2014).

17. Tang, Y., Gao, F., Feng, J., Liu, Y.: Fingernet- a unified deep network for fingerprint minutiae extraction. In: Proceedings of IEEE IJCB (2017)

18. Garris, M.D., McCabe, R.M.: NIST special database 27 - Fingerprint minutiae from latent and matching tenprint images. NIST Technical Report NISTIR 6534 (2000)

Texture Based Material Classification Using Gabor Filter

Shubhangi S. Sapkale$^{(\boxtimes)}$ and Manoj P. Patil

School of Computer Sciences, Kaviyatri Bahinabai Chaudhari,
North Maharashtra University, Jalgaon, India
sssapkalenmu@gmail.com, mpp145@gmail.com

Abstract. The image can be classified using various feature extraction techniques. Problem defined material class using properties of texture. The novel approach of this paper is to extract features of an image using the Gabor filter. Authors defined the method which combines Color, Luminance and Texture features. Texture features extracted by calculating the phase and magnitude of the Gabor Filtered image. The classification is carried out using KNN classifier with four different distance measures. Compare the statistics of the result under different distances types used in experiments.

Keywords: Texture · Feature extraction · GLCM · Gabor filter · Euclidean distance · Manhattan distance · Chebyshev distance · Minkowski distance · K-nearest neighbors classifier

1 Introduction

Human categorized an image by analyzing its optical features like color, shape, texture. This paper approach is to find a robust descriptor and suitable technique to classify an image. The texture is the main features described in this paper. Texture found on the surface of an object. The surface can fine, coarse, grained, smooth, etc. Different kinds of surface patterns give important class information. GLCM and Gabor filter techniques extracted texture feature. These techniques extract the texture feature of grayscale images. Author tries to improve these techniques by combining it with color and luminance feature extraction technique. In this experiment ten texture classes of FMD dataset used. Figure 1 indicates a few FMD images of texture samples [15].

T his paper collocated following segments: Section 2 inspect the associated work. Feature and feature extraction methods deliver in Sect. 3 and Sect. 4. Section 5 and Sect. 6 contains K-Nearest Neighbors Classifier using different distance measures and Result and discussions. Conclusions were in segment Sect. 7.

© Springer Nature Singapore Pte Ltd. 2021
K. C. Santosh and B. Gawali (Eds.): RTIP2R 2020, CCIS 1380, pp. 57–68, 2021.
https://doi.org/10.1007/978-981-16-0507-9_6

Fig. 1. FMD images of texture samples [15].

2   Literature Review

This segment includes a literature review on the classification of material.

Hiremath et al. [1] presented a method using the color, texture and shape features and achieve a better retrieval performance. The image divided into a non-intersecting block of the same area. Moment of color and texture as Local descriptor estimates using Gabor filter. Color, texture, shape features used to produce an efficient characteristic for image retrieval.

D S Guru et al. [16] proposed automated classification of flowers using K-Nearest Neighbors Classifier. Author used a different size of the database and 750 flower images for the experiment. The author noted that texture features give an accuracy of classification compared with other available literature results.

Christoph Palm et al. [17] noticed the color feature shows to enhance intensity and intensity independent-pattern of texture features. Gabor features Concerns phase energy which complements amplitude energy and showing similar capabilities.

Kunal Hossaina et al. [18] proposed texture recognition system based on the GLCM with the color feature. The proposed system tested on 105 images from Web sites. The wood, leaves, rock these three classes used for the experiment.

Li-Yu Hu et. al. [19] presented KNN classifier with different distance measures. The author concludes that there is no exact distance function for all the datasets.Author determines Euclidean and Minkowsky distance functions classification accuracy almost same. It was observed K-NN performance not affected.

3   Features

3.1   Color Feature

The human vision system is very receptive to understand color information than gray level, so the color is the first candidate used for feature extraction [2]. Color has been a great feature to identify material from many years. Color features of each pixel of an image obtained three component RGB (red, green, blue). RGB component used in visual recognition of an image [15]. The color image with its RGB matrices shows in Fig. 2 [15].

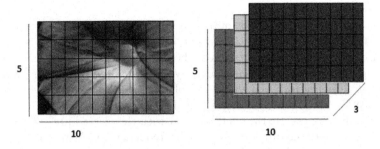

Fig. 2. RGB matrix of color image [15].

3.2   Luminance Feature

Luminance is the illumination of the color. Brightness is one of the most significant pixel characteristics. It is a part of various image-editing algorithms such as contrast or highlight [4]. Wyszecki and Stiles [5] define Brightness as an attribute of a visual awareness according to which visual object has more or less intensity or the area in which visual object appears to emit more or less light. Brightness range varies from bright to dim (Fig. 3).

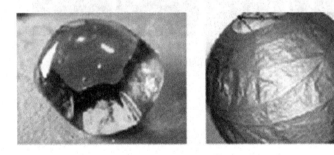

Fig. 3. Images with different luminance spectrum [15].

3.3   Texture Feature

3.3.1   GLCM Feature

GLCM is a texture analysis method used for the classification of an image. GLCM is a second-order statistical method that estimates image features [5]. Different intensities of the recurrence pattern of local pixels hold by Images [6]. The gray-scale image is used to compute the GLCM [5]. GLCM calculates how a pixel point and its neighboring pixel point occurs in image frequently [8]. GLCM method extracted statistical features as Energy, Contrast, Correlation, Entropy, Homogeneity, and IDM in the paper [15].

3.3.2   Gabor Feature

Gabor filter used for the analysis of texture. Parameter of the Gabor filter plays an important role in deciding the output image. [10] Gabor Filter selects the phase, size, frequency, the orientation of the resulting image as a parameter [11]. Each image pixel features are measured by the parameter of Gabor filters like selected size, orientation, frequency, and phase. [20] A phase difference is used for the election of relevant filter size [12]. Features of each pixel are extracted by changing brightness, texture and position with the elected area of the Filter. Gabor Filter adopts the direction and bright frequency bandwidth as well as the center frequency and obtains the best resolution in the frequency domain and spatial domain.

When Gabor is applied, the highest response gets at edges and the point where the texture changes of the image. The following images show a Glass image and its transformation after the filter is applied (Fig. 4).

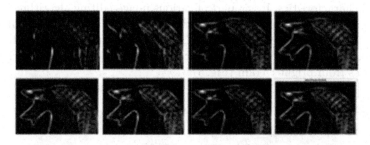

Fig. 4. Test image and its transformation after Gabor filter

4   Features Extraction

4.1   Color Feature Extraction

Every color obtained from three basic colors: Green, Red and Blue [7], In this experiment, histogram-based features are calculated from basic color components for each color channel. The image class retrieved using these statistical values. Folliage material images can give Green, Red and Blue values that show in the figure [15] (Fig. 5).

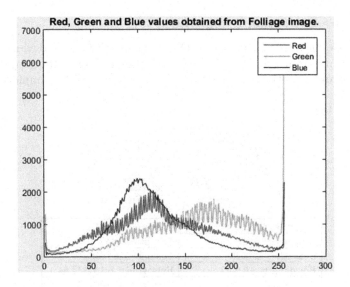

Fig. 5. Green, Red and Blue values of Folliage image [15]. (Color figure online)

4.2   Luminance Feature Extraction

Luminance gives illuminance information of an image without color [7]. Increasing or decreasing Luminance values makes colors lighter or darker, respectively [3]. Luminance, which is defined by [15],

$$Y_{Luminance} \leftarrow 0.3R + 0.59G + 0.11B\,(15) \tag{1}$$

The glass image luminance is larger than the Plastic and Metal images luminance shows in Fig. 6.

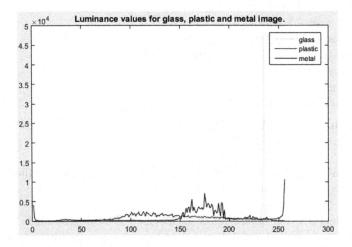

Fig. 6. Luminance values of wood, glass, and stone images [15].

4.3   Feature Extraction Using GLCM

Gray Level Co-Occurrence Matrix (GLCM) is a statistical method which extracts texture feature from images. The author represents six important features, Energy, Entropy, Contrast, Homogeneity, Correlation, IDM in implementation [15] (Fig. 7).

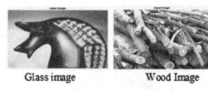

Glass image   Wood Image

Energy = 0.0523	Energy = 0.0097
Entropy = 7.3887	Entropy = 9.5152
Contrast = 72.0929	Contrast = 526.1666
Homogeneity = 0.0027	Homogeneity = 1.1214e-04
Correlation = 3.7658e-04	Correlation = 2.8004e-04
IDM = 45.738	IDM = 7.856

Fig. 7. GLCM feature of Glass and wood image

4.4   Feature Extraction Using Gabor

2-D Gabor filter used to extract features and texture analysis. The 2-D Gabor function is defined as [9]

$$G(X, Y; \lambda, \theta, \psi, \sigma, \gamma) = exp(-\frac{X'^2 + \gamma^2 Y'^2}{2\sigma^2})cos(2\Pi\frac{X'}{\lambda} + \psi) \qquad (2)$$

where,
$X' = X cos\theta + Y sin\theta$ [9]
$Y' = -X cos\theta + Y sin\theta$ [9]
$\lambda \rightarrow$ sinusoidal factor wavelength [9]
$\theta \rightarrow$ Rotation angle of a Gabor function [9]
$\psi \rightarrow$ phase offset [9]
$\sigma \rightarrow$ sigma [9]
$\gamma \rightarrow$ spatial aspect ratio [9]

Wavelength(λ): Gabor filter cosine factor is called the wavelength. Wavelength values designated in pixels [13]

Orientation(θ): Rotation angle of a Gabor function. Its value specified between 0 and 360 degrees are considered Valid values [13].

Phase Offset(ψ): The phase offset ψ specified is in degrees. The phase offset specified in degrees 0 and 180 correlate to center-symmetric 'center-on' and 'center-off' functions and −90 and 90 correlate to anti-symmetric functions [13].

Sigma(σ): The value of σ depends on the bandwidth b. The default value of bandwidth is 1, means σ and λ are connected as follows: $\sigma = 0.56\lambda$. The bandwidth is inversely proportional to σ [13].

Aspect Ratio(γ): Aspect ratio stipulates Gabor function ellipticity support. The circular support, γ value is 1. The support is parallel, γ value is less than 1. γ default value is 0.5 [13] (Figs. 8 and 9).

The images obtain the highest response on edges and where the texture change on Gabor applied. The following images show a test image and Gabor filter applied transformed image.

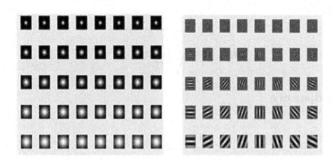

Fig. 8. Magnitudes of Gabor filters and Real parts of Gabor filters

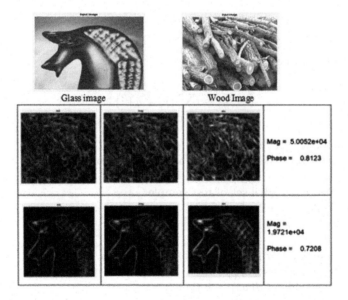

Fig. 9. A test image and Gabor filter applied transformed image.

5   K-Nearest Neighbors Classifier

K-Nearest Neighbors Classifier scrutinized neighbors and used four different distance measures to compute the distance between neighbors [1]. All distance measure combine with KNN and try to find which distance measure rectifies the class of the image accurately.

Distance Measures: Distance Measure can be computed by summarizes two objects difference using distance function $Dist(x; y)$ where x and y are objects composed of N features such that $x = x_1, \ldots, x_N, y = y_1, \ldots, y_N$ [14].

Euclidean distance

$$d(x, y) = \sqrt{\sum_{i=0}^{N} x_i^2 - y_i^2} \tag{3}$$

Manhattan distance

$$d(x, y) = \sum_{i=0}^{N} |x_i - y_i| \tag{4}$$

Chebyshev distance

$$d(x, y) = max_i(|x_i - y_i|) \tag{5}$$

Minkowski distance

$$d(x, y) = (\sum_{i=0}^{N} |x_i - y_i|^P)^{\frac{1}{P}} \tag{6}$$

Procedure: Find label for class.
Input: k, total closest Nearest_Neighbors; *Stest*, set of test sample; *Strain*, set of training sample
Output: *Label*, class label set of test sample
1. Read DataFile (Training_DataSet)
2. Red DataFile (Testing_DataSet)
3. *Label*= {}
4. For each *dist* in *Stest* and each *train* in *Strain* do
5. Nearest_Neighbors(*dist*)= {}
6. If (Nearest_Neighbors(*dist*)) < k then
7. Nearest_Neighbors(*dist*)=Distance(*dist*,*train*) ∪Nearest_Neighbors(*dist*)
8. End if
9. If Nearest_Neighbors(*dist*))= k then
10. Break

11. *Label*=Test_Class (Nearest_Neighbors(*dist*)) ∪ *Label*
12. End For [15]
Notes :
Nearest_Neighbors(*dist*) return k nearest neighbors of *dist*
Distance(*dist*, *train*) return the nearest elements of *train* in *dist*
Test_Class (*Sclass*) return the class label of *Sclass* [14]

6 Result and Discussions

Experiments accomplished using Flickr Material Database (FMD) contains ten different texture classes. The experiments performed on 1000 images of FMD dataset. Each class contains 100 images for learning and testing 50 images used. Three feature vectors (i.e. red, blue, green) and one luminance feature extract from the color and luminance feature extraction techniques. Six features extracted from the GLCM feature extraction technique and Gabor filter extract sixteen features. Author compare two extraction techniques GLCM and Gabor filter combined with Color and Luminance features. In all the experiments author used KNN classifier and changed only the distance measures between the Feature vectors. The result of experiments is composed in Table. In this table explains how different distance measures affect recognition accuracy (Figs. 10, 11 and Table 1).

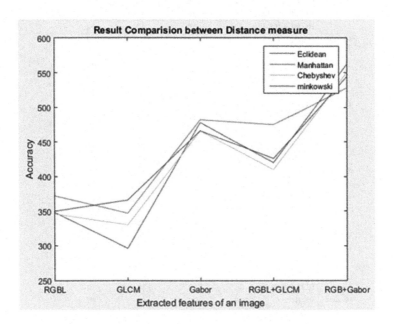

Fig. 10. Result comparision between distance measure

Table 1. Category wise classification accuracy of FMD dataset according to distance measure.

Class	Feature	Distance			
		Euclidean	Manhattan	Chebyshev	Minkowski
Fabric	RGBL	40	42	46	42
	GLCM	26	28	28	32
	Gabor	88	88	88	86
	RGBL+ GLCM	44	44	48	32
	RGBL+ Gabor	90	90	90	90
Foliage	RGBL	82	82	76	72
	GLCM	52	52	46	76
	Gabor	80	78	80	80
	RGBL+ GLCM	82	84	80	76
	RGBL+ Gabor	88	88	88	88
Glass	RGBL	68	68	68	64
	GLCM	24	24	24	22
	Gabor	56	56	58	58
	RGBL+ GLCM	68	68	68	64
	RGBL+ Gabor	70	68	68	66
Leather	RGBL	22	32	32	32
	GLCM	40	34	34	34
	Gabor	46	50	46	48
	RGBL+ GLCM	42	49	50	42
	RGBL+ Gabor	48	48	54	50
Metal	RGBL	32	30	28	28
	GLCM	28	44	40	42
	Gabor	42	42	38	46
	RGBL+ GLCM	30	46	42	44
	RGBL+ Gabor	52	48	40	52
Paper	RGBL	24	28	22	22
	GLCM	22	26	24	24
	Gabor	34	54	32	34
	RGBL+ GLCM	30	30	28	30
	RGBL+ Gabor	40	46	38	40
Plastic	RGBL	16	16	14	16
	GLCM	20	18	18	20
	Gabor	44	40	48	44
	RGBL+ GLCM	20	24	24	20
	RGBL+ Gabor	48	48	48	42
Stone	RGBL	20	30	18	30
	GLCM	18	50	44	44
	Gabor	16	18	22	16
	RGBL+ GLCM	20	52	46	46
	RGBL+ Gabor	32	20	40	36
Water	RGBL	24	24	24	24
	GLCM	16	26	26	26
	Gabor	32	30	30	32
	RGBL+ GLCM	26	28	28	26
	RGBL+ Gabor	34	32	34	32
Wood	RGBL	20	20	18	20
	GLCM	50	46	46	46
	Gabor	40	26	24	22
	RGBL+ GLCM	58	50	46	46
	RGBL+ Gabor	60	40	50	48

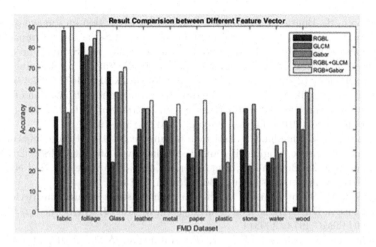

Fig. 11. Result comparision between different feature vector

7 Conclusions

texture properties provide useful information for material classification [15]. In this experiment, GLCM and Gabor filters used for texture classification, Gabor filter combined with color and luminance features gives higher accuracy than GLCM implementations. Gabor filter can efficiently isolate images having regions altering in one of the following properties: Spatial frequency, the density of elements, orientation, phase and energy. The higher number of differences gives better separation. In this experiment GLCM feature vector work more efficiently with Minkowski distance measure to give better accuracy. The author compared four distance measure with KNN classifier. Each distance measures plays different role for each class of FMD dataset. Euclidean distance shows better accuracy on Foliage, Glass, Metal, Plastic classes. Chebyshev distance measure gives better accuracy result on Fabric, leather, water, wood classes whereas paper and stone class result gets good using Manhattan distance measure.

References

1. Hiremath, P.S., Pujari, J.: Content based image retrieval using color, texture and shape features. In: 15th International Conference on Advanced Computing and Communications (ADCOM 2007), Guwahati, Assam, pp. 780–784 (2007). https://doi.org/10.1109/ADCOM.2007.21
2. Wu, J.K., Kankanhalli, M.S., Lim, J.K., Hong, D.: Perspectives On Content-Based Multimedia Systems, pp. 49–67. Kluwer Academic Publishers, New York/Boston/Dordrecht/London/Moscow (2002)
3. Tsai, C.-M., Lee, H.-J.: Binarization of color document images via luminance and saturation color features. IEEE Trans. Image Process. **11**(4), 434–451 (2002)

4. Bezryadin, S., Bourov, P., Ilinih, D.: Single color extraction and image query. In: Brightness Calculation in Digital Image Processing, International Symposium on Technologies for Digital Photo Fulfillment, 1st International Symposium on Technologies for Digital Photo Fulfillment, pp. 10–15(6). Society for Imaging Science and Technology (2007). https://doi.org/10.2352/ISSN.2169-4672.2007.1.0.10

5. Chadha, A., Mallik, S., Johar, R.: Comparative study and optimization of feature-extraction techniques for content based image retrival. Int. J. Comput. Appl **52**(20), 0978887 (2012). https://doi.org/10.5120/8320-1959

6. Srinivasan, G.N., Shobha, G.: Statistical texture analysis. In: Proceedings of World Academy of Science, Engineering and Technology, vol. 36 (2008). ISSN 2070–3740

7. Lewandowski, Z., Beyenal, H.: Fundamentals of Biofilm Research, 2nd edn. CRC Press, Taylor and Francis Group, Boca Raton (2013)

8. Haralik, R.M., Shanmugam, K.: Its'hak dinstein dinstein: texture features for image classification. IEEE Trans. Syst. Man Cybern. **3**, 610–621 (1973). https://doi.org/10.1109/TSMC.1973.4309314

9. Premalatha, K., Anantha Kumar, T., Natarajan, A.M.: A dorsal hand vein recognition-based on local gabor phase quantization with whitening transformation. In: 2009 Fifth International Conference on Natural Computation (2009). https://doi.org/10.14429/dsj.64.4659

10. Tou, J.Y., Tay, Y.H., Lau, P.Y.: TA comparative study for texture classification techniques on wood species recognition problem. In: Fifth International Conference on Natural Computation, ICNC 2009, Tianjian, China, 14–16 August 2009, vol. 6 (2009). https://doi.org/10.1109/ICNC.2009.594

11. Krishan, A.: Evaluation of gabor filter parameters for image enhancement and segmentation. Int. J. Adv. Res. Comput. Eng. Technol. (IJARCET) **1**(7) (2012)

12. Khan, J.F., Adhami, R.R., Bhuiyan, S.M.A.: Color image segmentation utilizing a customized Gabor filter. In: IEEE SoutheastCon 2008 (2008). https://doi.org/10.1109/SECON.2008.4494353

13. Petkov, N., Wieling, M.B.: Gabor filter for image processing and computer vision. University of Groningen, Department of Computing Science, Intelligent Systems (2004)

14. Collins, J., Okada, K.: Improvement and comparison of weighted k nearest neighbors classifiers for model selection. J. Softw. Engi **10**(1), 109–118 (2016). https://doi.org/10.3923/jse.2016.109.118

15. Sapkale, S.S., Patil, M.P.: Material classification using color and texture features. In: Santosh, K.C., Hegadi, R.S. (eds.) RTIP2R 2018. CCIS, vol. 1035, pp. 49–59. Springer, Singapore (2019). https://doi.org/10.1007/978-981-13-9181-1_5

16. Guru, D.S., Sharath, Y.H., Manjunath, S.: Texture features and KNN in classification of flower images. In: IJCA Special Issue on "Recent Trends in Image Processing and Pattern Recognition" RTIPPR (2010)

17. Palm, C., Lehmann, T.M.: Classification of color textures by Gabor filtering. Mach. Graph. Vis. **11**(2/3), 195–219 (2002)

18. Hossaina, K., Parekhb, R.: Extending GLCM to include color information for texture recognition. In: AIP Conference Proceedings, vol. 1298, p. 583 (2010). https://doi.org/10.1063/1.3516370

19. Hu, L.-Y., Huang, M.-W., Ke, S.-W., Tsai, C.-F.: The distance function effect on k-nearest neighbor classification for medical datasets. SpringerPlus **5**(1), 1–9 (2016). Article number: 1304

20. Fogel, I., Sagi, D.: Gabor filters as texture discriminator. Biol. Cybern. **61**, 103–113 (1989). https://doi.org/10.1007/BF00204594

Optimization of Face Retrieval and Real Time Face Recognition Systems Using Heuristic Indexing

Dattatray D. Sawat[1]([✉]), K. C. Santosh[2], and Ravindra S. Hegadi[3]

[1] Department of Computer Science, Solapur University,
Solapur 413255, Maharastra, India
sawat.datta@gmail.com

[2] Department of Computer Science, University of South Dakota,
414 Clark st, Vermilion, SD 57069, USA
santosh.kc@usd.edu

[3] Department of Computer Science, Central University of Karnataka,
Kadaganchi, Kalaburagi 585367, India
rshegadi@gmail.com

Abstract. Retrieving fast and accurate information is the key factor in real time biometric systems. The indexed data provides fast access to the pool of closest matching patterns in the database or the input given to the real-time systems. This paper aims to demonstrate the impact of heuristic indexing in realtime face recognition and on face retrieval systems using face skin color and complexion. This paper also presents the comparison of face recognition techniques with and without heuristic indexing and their impact on realtime performance. Proposed method works on both the indexed and non-indexed database. The survey shows that indexing not only improves retrieval speed but also rejects the wrong samples to be inspected, speeding up the overall system. We have proposed a novel heuristic indexing algorithm which locates key pixels on a face, calculates Skin Complexion Value (SCV) and their tolerance range, reduces search space and finally performs classification. The proposed approach yields significant improvement in terms of speed and reduction in False Acceptance Ratio (FAR).

Keywords: Real time face recognition · Heuristic indexing · Face indexing · Skin complexion and optimization · Query Skin Complexion Values (QSCV)

1 Introduction

Biometrics is one of the fields where time constrained processing is required in order to justify the system. There are some inherent applications which require matching of templates to be done in real time such as realtime face recognition. Face retrieval system is also one of the problems where matching of query

© Springer Nature Singapore Pte Ltd. 2021
K. C. Santosh and B. Gawali (Eds.): RTIP2R 2020, CCIS 1380, pp. 69–81, 2021.
https://doi.org/10.1007/978-981-16-0507-9_7

and database contents is required [24]. Although face retrieval systems do not have any hard time constraints, however, the timely retrieval is always desired. There are several factors such as the size of the database and complexity of the recognition algorithm, which affect the performance of the biometric system in terms of speed and False Acceptance Ratio (FAR). These factors present above challenges to realtime processing and information retrieval systems in various biometric applications including fingerprint recognition, iris recognition, and palm print recognition.

The performance of realtime system depends upon how accurate the system is along with its speed and false acceptance as well as false rejection ratio. The following paragraph discusses the factors which reduce the performance of realtime and offline biometrics systems.

1.1 Size of Search Space

In offline biometrics systems, the templates to be matched are stored in the database. When the query is submitted to verify it against the templates in a database, these systems have to perform the following actions:

1) They have to search the entire database to retrieve templates.
2) They have to match each sample with the query sample. i.e. 1:N matching takes place.

Huge search space and 1:N matching (N is the size of the database) affects the performance not only in terms of speed but also increases false acceptance rate because of submission of undesired samples.

1.2 Complexity of Recognition Algorithm

The FAR increases due to the processing of unnecessary samples. Following equation shows the verification complexity V_c for the population size of N in terms of iterations:

$$V_c = Q_n \times N \tag{1}$$

where Q_n is a number of queries. For $Q_n = 1$, the verification complexity is almost of the $O(N)$. The FAR could increase with population size hence it is possible to reduce both verification complexity V_c and FAR along with population size N as follows:

$$V_c = Q_n \times (P_r \times N) \tag{2}$$

where P_r is population reduction factor. For $Pr = 0.7$, the verification complexity reduces by 30%, according to Eq. 2.

1.3 Face Recognition Systems

The face recognition systems retrieve the query face from the database or from realtime video frames. In order to recognize the face, it has to be detected in the first place. The detected face is then processed using face recognition algorithms. While retrieving query face the system has to process the entire database or all the detected faces from the realtime situation. Such systems suffer from processing overhead of face images, which are not expected to be there in the search space for given query image. In particular such overhead is not feasible for realtime systems because of the imposed time limit.

The solution is to reduce search space which not only will limit the number of face images to be processed but also reduces the false acceptance ratio.

Our contribution includes novel heuristic indexing algorithm which locates key pixels, calculates Skin Complexion Value (SCV) and their tolerance range, performs reduction of search space by comparison of the SCV of database image to the Query Skin Complexion Value (QSCV) and tolerance range and finally does classification.

2   Literature Survey

Apart from face recognition there are several applications where features are used for optimal retrieval of images such as Content-Based Image Retrieval (CBIR). In the following paragraph we discuss these works and in the subsequent paragraph, we discuss indexing for face recognition systems.

CBIR systems fetch images based on query description, the retrieval system has to search the images having the desired characteristics. Several researches used the descriptors for optimal retrieval of images. Ceccarell et al. [3] used a multi scale textual gradient as a cue to retrieve the images. They defined a unified model having shape and texture with the multi scale analysis using morphological filters. Their algorithm worked efficiently with large image datasets. Chatzichristofis [4] proposed descriptors which has color and texture features extracted using the fuzzy approach. Further, they have introduced Auto Relevance Feedback (ARF) which improvised retrieval score significantly. Young et al. [25] used improvised versions of SIFT and Gaussian Mixture Model (GMM) which helped the algorithm to optimize the storage space for descriptors subsequently increasing matching speed. K-Means clustering algorithm was used to initialize the GMM to improve the convergence.

An image representation using Bag of Words model and incremental learning the was used for image retrieval by Nguyen et al. [14]. The algorithm worked without having prior knowledge about the database. Vu et al. [23] proposed a hybrid algorithm in which the Principal Component Analysis(PCA) of the face images was performed and the triangular algorithm was used to normalize the face in order to improve the performance along with preprocessing including illumination reduction, background removal and color space transformation. Mirhosseini et al. [12] proposed a Binary Imperialist Competitive Algorithm (BICA) algorithm which algorithm allows to explore a more significant number of possible solutions. Authors used proper transfer function and optimal parameter setting to enhance the performance. Zhou et al. [26] proposed extraction of two types of histograms and effective fusion of them, the histograms of from color and local directional pattern (LDP) were used along with feature normalization and a new similarity metric for the comparison of images.

A new rotation and scale-invariant line-based color-aware descriptor RSILC has been proposed by Candemir et al. [2]. This descriptor is useful for object recognition particularly objects which are line rich, such as faces. The descriptor combines local information such as intensity, color and gradient as well as global key point information having lines, circles and their spatial arrangement [6]. The descriptor is robust, but it needs classification to be used as an index, it might increase time complexity while searching the images. In the field of biometrics, the focus always remained on enhancing recognition techniques. A recent survey shows some state of art face recognition methods [15, 18, 19, 21], but the use of indexing is less explored. The following paragraph presents the survey of some of the existing techniques.

There are two types of scenarios where indexing can be used to reduce search space. In the first scenario, some researchers used face database partitioning to reduce search space. The calculation of features for indexing is a key part of these studies. Lin et al. proposed a method [9] to calculate indexes of faces in the database using eigenfaces [22]. Each of the face images in the database will be processed for computation of eigenfaces and they were ranked according to the closest of eigenface value to the eigenface value of query face image. A condensed database will be formed using selected faces from original dataset and it will be used for face recognition. Mohanty et al. [13] developed a technique for linear subspace approximation of faces. A linear rigid and non-rigid transformation of face images was performed. For the transformation of nonlinear or affine subspace the distance between training face images, which was calculated by face recognition algorithm, has taken into consideration, Similarly for the transformation of rigid subspace Principal Component Analysis was used.

Kaushik et al. [7] proposed indexing of face database using Speeded Up Robust Features (SURF). They used SURF features for hashing of the database. They proposed preprocessing of images using mean centering, principal components and rotation along with normalization so that they will be invariant to translation, rotation and scaling.

Dewagan et al. [5] proposed a method for face indexing using SURF features. They created a two-level indexed space. Indexed space was further divided into cells and the SURF descriptor was stored into those cells using a hash function. They used a data structure called kd-tree to store SURF descriptors within the cells created earlier in indexed spaces. By applying a hash function on query key points, the kd-tree based nearest neighboring search is performed.

A permutation-based indexing method was proposed by [10] in which they calculated permutation for images and based on permutation value the images were stored optimally in order to accelerate the search process.

Each of the methods discussed above takes too much CPU time to calculate features. Either calculation of eigenfaces or linear transformation with PCA or SURF [1] must be done on each of the database images; hence it is an overhead if recognition time is considered. Also in the second scenario, where the images are indexed at the time of processing instead of database partitioning, one such example is realtime face identification. In real time system the search space changes with each new video frame, hence it is necessary to perform the indexing on every new search space. In such cases, the computational overhead by indexing methods which are discussed above cannot justify their effectiveness for face recognition within certain time limits.

Hence there is a need of an effective indexing technique which will perform indexing with consideration of time limits for realtime as well as for offline databases.

3   Proposed Approach

The human face is uniquely identifiable by the features present on it. All the methods discussed above create indexes using feature descriptors used by the accompanied face recognition method. Methods discussed in literature create feature descriptor either by using derived formulas or by learning techniques. These methods require a large amount of processing time. Whereas the proposed method employs skin complexion as an index. As compared to other methods the proposed method extracts skin complexion value of query image in very less time. The average time required to calculate skin complexion by the proposed method for each image in the ORL database is 0.2944 ms. Skin Complexion Values (SCV) of faces in the database is compared with lower and upper Query Skin Complexion Values (QSCV). The iterative algorithm is implemented which calculates complexion value for the face. If SCR value is not in acceptable range, then algorithm skips current face and proceeds to next face. Figure 1 shows the architecture used in the proposed methodology.

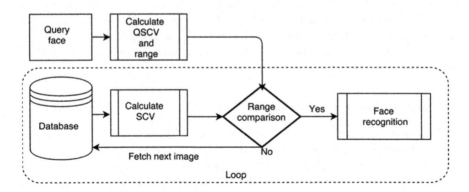

Fig. 1. Architecture of proposed methodology

The SCV (Skin Complexion Value) is calculated to avoid searching in the avoidable search space in the biometric database. The aim of this study is to apply this indexing to search for a person in real-time videos where there is a negligible chance of variation in the original skin complexion of that person (or Person of Interest). It is difficult to change the skin complexion value during real-time video due to time constraints. Using this assumptions a heuristic can be formed that a skin complexion value can act as indexing to the real time videos which contains the face images without alteration. The proposed methodology is discussed in paragraphs below.

3.1 Preprocessing

The submitted query may vary because of its color map or its color scheme; hence the query image has to be preprocessed according to database images. The query image is divided into color query and gray level query accordingly.

The gray level intensities or color pixel values will define the skin complexion of the face being searched. It is possible that the images in the database to be processed or realtime image frames can have different color maps than the query image. In such a situation, the query image can be converted to an identical color map of database images or realtime feed. For this experiment we have converted all the query color images to RGB color map since the images in the database has the same color map, by doing so, the algorithm will proceed reliably.

3.2 Localization of Key–Pixels

The system assumes that the input to the system is query face already detected by the algorithm used in the existing system. To improve the accuracy of the proposed algorithm the face is pre-processed for key pixel localization. In this method, a center of the image is calculated, and the rectangular strip (as shown in Fig. 1) is extracted from the image by using center position, 5 rows onwards of the center and 3/5th columns of total columns in the face image. The position of the rectangular strip having key pixels can be adjusted in the proposed method for better representation of face complexion based on the face area included by the face detector. Only skin pixels are selected for further processing using RGB skin pixel threshold range defined in [8].

3.3 Skin Color and Skin Complexion

The proposed method uses skin complexion as a heuristic to avoid inspection of the undesired face. If the query face is a grayscale image, then the skin complexion value (SCV) is calculated by taking an average of key pixel intensities from a strip located at the center of the face image. The proposed method first calculates skin complexion by taking average pixel intensities of pixels or color channels in case of color images from a rectangular strip extracted from the center of the facial image. Further, the average is calculated for all the training images representing the class. Only skin pixels in the strip are selected to represent skin complexion of the face. Figure 2 shows the rectangular strip containing skin pixels on the face.

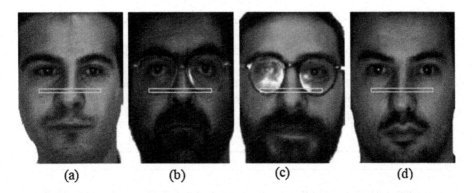

(a)　　　　　　(b)　　　　　(c)　　　　　　(d)

Fig. 2. Strip representing skin pixels on the face images from AR Face Database

If the query image is in color form then the average of the individual color channel is taken as skin complexion. To avoid the illumination effect on the SCV the gamma correction with $gamma = 1.4$ is applied to both training images and the testing images. The extreme gamma values make pixels darker or lighter. The localization and selection procedure of pixels is similar for both color and grayscale images as discussed in Sect. 3.2.

3.4 Tolerance Range

An average intensity of query face calculated in earlier stage may not truly represent skin complexion of the face. In some cases, the face to be searched might have different illumination conditions or there may be intended changes in face complexion due to image processing software and hardware. This difference in face complexions lessens the real time search space for the face. To avoid the non-desired rejection of faces to be inspected the proposed method uses skin complexion (Sc) range that can be searched for. Lower $Sc(L)$ and upper $Sc(H)$ limit of skin complexion can be defined by using tolerance operator T as follows

$$Sc(L) = QSCV - T \tag{3}$$

$$Sc(H) = QSCV + T \tag{4}$$

If the skin complexion (SCV) of the face to be inspected is outside the range $Sc(L)$ and $Sc(H)$ defined by tolerance operator T then the face is skipped and the algorithm can proceed with next face image. The proposed methodology assumes that the face detection is already performed and input to this algorithm is a detected face as per ground truth. To select skin pixels within rectangular strip we have used modified version of RGB skin pixel range defined in [8]. The mean intensity for each channel in color images is calculated using following equations:

$$avgR = mean(R(R > 95\&G > 40\&B > 20\&R > G\&R > B\&abs(R - G) > 15)) \tag{5}$$

$$avgG = mean(G(R > 95\&G > 40\&B > 20\&R > G\&R > B\&abs(R-G) > 15))$$
$$(6)$$
$$avgB = mean(B(R > 95\&G > 40\&B > 20\&R > G\&R > B\&abs(R-G) > 15))$$
$$(7)$$

Where R, G and B are the individual channels of the color image and $avgR$, $avgG$ and $avgB$ are means of the respective channels. Following algorithm states the entire methodology:

Algorithm 1

---

1) Start
2) Locate and select the skin pixels from the rectangular strip on query face which will be used to represent complexion of skin
3) Calculate and store QSCV as well as tolerance range Sc(L) and Sc(H) for query face using Eq.3, 4, 5, 6 and 7
4) Train a model using the existing Face recognition method
5) Search face database and check Skin Complexion Value (SCV) with tolerance range Sc(L) and Sc(H) of QSCV, if it is within range then go to step 6, otherwise, repeat step 5.
6) Perform face recognition on database image and store the results.
7) Calculate processing time and False Acceptance Ratio.
8) Stop

---

4   Database Used

In this experiment, we tested the proposed method on "The Database of Faces" formerly named as ORL database of faces by Olivetti Research Laboratory. The database contains 4000 images of 40 subjects, each having 10 images. In this database, images are 92×112 in size, 256 grey levels. The database has images with variation in expression and different light conditions.

For the color images, we have used cropped AR face database [11]. It contains a total of 2600 images form 100 subjects. The database has 50 male and 50 female subjects each of which has 26 images. The images in the database are correctly cropped which makes this database usable for the further procedure.

5   Face Recognition

The accuracies of facial recognition systems have been improved a lot especially using Deep Neural Networks (DNN) [16]. Both the hand designed and learned representation using DNNs are used to classify the face images. Most of the face recognition systems search database image by image and perform classification. We have coupled one of the most reliable face recognition with heuristic indexing. The system uses gabor filter [20] to extract features from the query face image.

The extracted features are then used to train Support Vector Machine classifier (SVM) with Cubic kernel. The parameter setting of SVM classifier is similar to the classifier used in [17] The Experiment is then carried out with indexing using Algorithm 1 and the search time along with False Acceptance Ratio is recorded. The same experiment is performed without using the proposed indexing to calculate search time and False Acceptance Ratio.

In order to search database same Gabor filters are used to extract features from database images one by one and checked for similarity against query face. The proposed method yields result shown in Tables 1, 2, 3 and 4 without affecting recognition accuracy because the proposed indexing only rejects the undesired images without interfering with face recognition technique.

6   Evolution Metrics

Execution time: The aim of this work is to reduce search time while looking for a query in the database and especially in real time video search. The search time is calculated as the time required for searching the entire database for multiple occurrences of the query. The unit of measure is seconds.

False Acceptance ratio (FAR): It is calculated as a number of impostors among a number of false samples submitted. To calculate the False Acceptance Ratio following formula is used.

$$False Acceptance Ratio = \frac{Number of impostors}{Number of False samples} \tag{8}$$

Similarly, we evaluated the algorithm on AR face database having color images. 5 random query images are searched in the database. Table 3 and 4 show the search time and FAR respectively.

6.1   Comparative Results

The literature reveals that indexing CBIR techniques are mostly used for image retrievals rather than face retrieval. The following table shows the comparison with few methods which performed indexing on face dataset.

The aim of this study was to highlight the effect of indexing on search speed and space reduction. The methods shown in the table have focused on hit ratio. Additionally, we have provided the average processing time required for calculating index on each image. Comparatively these methods take a large amount of time to process each image for indexing which is not desirable in real-time (Table 5).

Table 1. ORL Database search time using $T = 20$.

Face recognition method	Database	Random face query number	Time required to search database (in seconds)		Speed up in %
			Without index	With proposed index	
Gabor features	ORL database	Query 1	47.9716	32.0871	33.11%
		Query 13	47.4716	30.8244	35.07%
		Query 19	47.6578	32.4553	31.90%
		Query 25	46.1692	29.6136	35.86%
		Query 38	48.0318	33.7222	29.79%

Table 2. False acceptance ratio using $T = 20$ for the ORL database for 390 impostors for each class

Face recognition method	Database	Random face query number	False acceptance ratio	
			Without index	With proposed index
Gabor features	ORL database	Query 1	0.0128%	0.0076%
		Query 13	0.0128%	0.0102%
		Query 19	0%	0%
		Query 25	0%	0%
		Query 38	0.0025%	0%

Table 3. AR face database search time using $T = 20$

Face recognition method	Database	Random face query number	Time required to search database (in seconds)		Speed up in %
			Without index	With proposed index	
Gabor features	AR face database	Query 7	822.7558	405.3000	49.26%
		Query 19	820.3312	411.0768	50.10%
		Query 26	821.5315	395.3561	48.12%
		Query 28	822.0400	366.3418	44.56%
		Query 48	823.1705	383.7222	46.62%

Table 4. False acceptance ratio using $T = 20$ for the AR face database for 1276 impostors for each class

Face recognition method	Database	Random face query number	False acceptance ratio	
			Without index	With proposed index
Gabor features	AR face database	Query 7	0.3924%	0.3924%
		Query 19	0.8634%	0.4709%
		Query 26	0.5494%	0.1569%
		Query 28	1.4913%	0.7064%
		Query 48	0.7849%	0.3139%

Table 5. Comparative results

Method	Dataset	Improvement	Retrival time/image	System details
Geometric hashing [7]	FRGC 206	18.61% penetration ratio	–	–
SURF [5]	FRGC	12.5% penetration ratio	–	–
Eigenfaces [9]	ORL (523 images)	25% condensed space	1 s	2.4 GHz
Proposed (SCV)	ORL (4000 images)	35% speed up	0.2944 ms	2.6 GHz

7 Platform Used

This experiment is carried out using MATLAB 2016b on the Windows10 operating system. The Laptop with an i7 processor and 2.6 GHz clock speed, 8 GB RAM was used for the implementation and execution. While calculating search time all other user applications were terminated except MATLAB.

8 Conclusion

Using a heuristic The proposed approach works in real time and non-indexed database using any of the existing face detection and recognition techniques. It reduces the processing time required to search an image in non-indexed databases by reducing search space significantly which resulted in 30–35% reduction of search time for the gray scale dataset and up to 50.10 % in case of a color dataset. Along with the reduction of search space, the False Acceptance Ratio is also reduced when the proposed heuristic indexing method is used with the face recognition algorithm. By varying the value of the tolerance operator T, an additional reduction in search time as well as FAR can be achieved. This approach can be used on the database which is already indexed by other methods for further reduction of search space. In future attempts, simple statistical measures can be used to improve the skin complexion value (SCV). The descriptor such as RSILC can be integrated along with the proposed indexing method for further enhancement.

Acknowledgments. Authors thank the Ministry of Electronics and Information Technology (MeitY), New Delhi for granting Visvesvaraya Ph.D. fellowship through file no. PhD-MLA\4(34)\2014-15 Dated: 10/04/2015.

References

1. Bay, H., Tuytelaars, T., Van Gool, L.: SURF: speeded up robust features. In: Leonardis, A., Bischof, H., Pinz, A. (eds.) ECCV 2006. LNCS, vol. 3951, pp. 404–417. Springer, Heidelberg (2006). https://doi.org/10.1007/11744023_32

2. Candemir, S., Borovikov, E., Santosh, K., Antani, S., Thoma, G.: RSILC: rotation-and scale-invariant, line-based color-aware descriptor. Image Vis. Comput. **42**, 1–12 (2015)

3. Ceccarelli, M., Musacchia, F., Petrosino, A.: Content-based image retrieval by a fuzzy scale-space approach. Int. J. Pattern Recognit. Artif Intell. **20**(06), 849–867 (2006)

4. Chatzichristofis, S.A., Zagoris, K., Boutalis, Y.S., Papamarkos, N.: Accurate image retrieval based on compact composite descriptors and relevance feedback information. Int. J. Pattern Recognit. Artif Intell. **24**(02), 207–244 (2010)

5. Dewangan, J., Dey, S., Samanta, D.: Face images database indexing for person identification problem. Int. J. Biometrics Bioinform. **7**(2), 93–122 (2013)

6. Fawwad Hussain, Md., Wang, H., Santosh, K.C.: Gray level face recognition using spatial features. In: Santosh, K.C., Hegadi, R.S. (eds.) RTIP2R 2018. CCIS, vol. 1035, pp. 216–229. Springer, Singapore (2019). https://doi.org/10.1007/978-981-13-9181-1_20

7. Kaushik, V.D., Gupta, A.K., Jayaraman, U., Gupta, P.: Modified geometric hashing for face database indexing. In: Huang, D.-S., Gan, Y., Gupta, P., Gromiha, M.M. (eds.) ICIC 2011. LNCS (LNAI), vol. 6839, pp. 608–613. Springer, Heidelberg (2012). https://doi.org/10.1007/978-3-642-25944-9_79

8. Kolkur, S., Kalbande, D., Shimpi, P., Bapat, C., Jatakia, J.: Human skin detection using RGB, HSV and YCbCr color models. arXiv preprint arXiv:1708.02694 (2017)

9. Lin, K.H., Lam, K.M., Xie, X., Siu, W.C.: An efficient human face indexing scheme using eigenfaces. In: Proceedings of the 2003 International Conference on Neural Networks and Signal Processing, vol. 2, pp. 920–923. IEEE (2003)

10. von Lücken, C., Jarmila, L., Brítez, G.: Face recognition through a novel indexing method based on permutations. In: Computing Conference (CLEI), 2015 Latin American, pp. 1–10. IEEE (2015)

11. Martínez, A.M., Kak, A.C.: PCA versus LDA. IEEE Trans. Pattern Anal. Mach. Intell. **2**, 228–233 (2001)

12. Mirhosseini, M., Nezamabadi-pour, H.: BICA: a binary imperialist competitive algorithm and its application in CBIR systems. Int. J. Mach. Learn. Cybern. **9**(12), 2043–2057 (2018)

13. Mohanty, P., Sarkar, S., Kasturi, R., Phillips, P.J.: Subspace approximation of face recognition algorithms: an empirical study. IEEE Trans. Inf. Forensics Secur. **3**(4), 734–748 (2008)

14. Nguyen, N.V., Boucher, A., Ogier, J.M.: Keyword visual representation for image retrieval and image annotation. Int. J. Pattern Recogn. Artif. Intell. **29**(06), 1–37 (2015)

15. Parkhi, O.M., Vedaldi, A., Zisserman, A., et al.: Deep face recognition. In: BMVC, vol. 1, no. 6 (2015)

16. Srinivasa Perumal, R., Santosh, K.C., Chandra Mouli, P.V.S.S.R.: Learning deep feature representation for face spoofing. In: Santosh, K.C., Hegadi, R.S. (eds.) RTIP2R 2018. CCIS, vol. 1035, pp. 178–185. Springer, Singapore (2019). https://doi.org/10.1007/978-981-13-9181-1_16

17. Sawat, D.D., Hegadi, R.S.: Unconstrained face detection: a deep learning and machine learning combined approach. CSI Trans. ICT **5**(2), 195–199 (2017)

18. Schroff, F., Kalenichenko, D., Philbin, J.: FaceNet: a unified embedding for face recognition and clustering. In: Proceedings of the IEEE Conference on Computer Vision and Pattern Recognition, pp. 815–823 (2015)

19. Sengupta, S., Chen, J.C., Castillo, C., Patel, V.M., Chellappa, R., Jacobs, D.W.: Frontal to profile face verification in the wild. In: 2016 IEEE Winter Conference on Applications of Computer Vision (WACV), pp. 1–9. IEEE (2016)
20. Štruc, V., Pavešić, N.: Gabor-based kernel partial-least-squares discrimination features for face recognition. Informatica **20**(1), 115–138 (2009)
21. Tran, L., Yin, X., Liu, X.: Disentangled representation learning GAN for pose-invariant face recognition. In: CVPR, vol. 3, p. 7 (2017)
22. Turk, M., Pentland, A.: Eigenfaces for recognition. J. Cogn. Neurosci. **3**(1), 71–86 (1991)
23. Vu, L., Alsadoon, A., Prasad, P., Rahma, A.: Improving accuracy in face recognition proposal to create a hybrid photo indexing algorithm, consisting of principal component analysis and a triangular algorithm (PCAaTA). Int. J. Pattern Recognit. Artif Intell. **31**(01), 1756001 (2017)
24. Wang, H., et al.: An empirical study: ELM in face matching. In: Santosh, K.C., Hegadi, R.S. (eds.) RTIP2R 2018. CCIS, vol. 1035, pp. 277–287. Springer, Singapore (2019). https://doi.org/10.1007/978-981-13-9181-1_25
25. Yong, H., Qingjun, W.: Research and improvement of content based image retrieval framework. Int. J. Pattern Recognit. Artif. Intell. **32**(12), 1850043 (2018)
26. Zhou, J., Liu, X., Xu, T., Gan, J., Liu, W.: A new fusion approach for content based image retrieval with color histogram and local directional pattern. Int. J. Mach. Learn. Cybern. **9**(4), 677–689 (2016). https://doi.org/10.1007/s13042-016-0597-9

Estimation of Human Age and Gender Based on LBP Features Using Two Level Decision by SVM

S. P. Raghavendra[1(✉)], M. J. Adarsh[1], Shoieb Ahamed[2], and J. Shree Hari[3]

[1] Department of College of Engineering, JNN College of Engineering, Shimoga, Karnataka, India
raghusp.bdvt@gmail.com, adimj24@gmail.com
[2] Department of Computer Science, GFGC, Sorab(T), Shimoga, Karnataka, India
shoiabahmed@gmail.com
[3] Siemens Technology and Services India Pvt Ltd., Bangalore, Karnataka, India
sriharijshimoga@gmail.com

Abstract. Automated face and age recognition is becoming an important technology due to the huge amount of biometric transactions will be carried and processed daily by Authorization agencies. Now a days Estimation of human age is a very significant characteristic in terms of identity authentication. In order to assess one's individual age, selection of features from the human face is significant and vital with the perspective of experimental accuracy. Some of the Real world Age estimation applications are Biometrics, Security management, 3D face construction and cosmetology. Statistical and regression based are the traditional and earlier techniques commonly used age estimation technique which works on results of interrelationship and correlation among the different values of age for face images. The current work is an enhancement of existing techniques used previously for feature extraction using Local binary patterns with regional features of 2D Wavelet transformation image and age estimation can be accomplished by using SVM Classifier.

Keywords: 2D Wavelet · Local binary patterns · Support vector machine · Shape features · FG-NET

1 Introduction

Face identification is the procedure of ascertaining one or more person images or videos by inspect and equating patterns. Calculations and estimation for age commonly take out facial highlights and features which assess to a knowledgebase to locate the best match. Face acknowledgment is a very important in biometric, security measures, perception frameworks and in addition picture and video ordering frameworks. Face acknowledgment and age estimation with gender classification uses computer vision in order to segregate data from facial pictures or machine learning methods which demonstrates the presence

© Springer Nature Singapore Pte Ltd. 2021
K. C. Santosh and B. Gawali (Eds.): RTIP2R 2020, CCIS 1380, pp. 82–94, 2021.
https://doi.org/10.1007/978-981-16-0507-9_8

of countenances. Machine learning frameworks can be applied to the geometrically invariant robust features to perform and request as a test face image using coordinated supervised learning methods of insight, for instance Support vector machines (SVM) and decision trees, KNN Classifiers and Convolutional Neural networks with deep learning. Face affirmation structure with age estimation takes the bundle of business, military, security and investigates applications. The proposed methodology focuses on weight encoding configuration in setting the most coherent age estimation with gender classification mechanism by means of which another face sorting out methodology, called the 'Adaptable Matching Framework'.

2 Related Work

Many authors have proposed different state of the art methods in estimation of human age based on human face features some of them are, Andreas Lanitis [1] design classifiers that accept the model based representation of unseen images and produce an estimate of the age of a person in the corresponding face image. Chin-Teng-Lin [2] proposed a mechanism for estimation of age automatically by means of Computer vision which uses global face features by adopting mixture of Orthogonal locality preserving projections and Gabor Wavelets. Dat Tien Nguyen [3] presents research, that effects of gender and facial expression on age estimation using support vector regression (SVR) method are investigated, age estimation using a single level local binary pattern (LBP) and a multilevel LBP (MLBP) are compared. Divyarajsinh N. Parmar [4] describes concepts of face recognition methods & its applications which can provide the readers a better understanding about face recognition methods & applications.

D. Ravichandran [5] show how to represent 1D, 2D and 3D Discrete Wavelet Transform (DWT) mathematically. Haibin Liao [6] presented a technique in image processing by utilizing deep learning approach in order to fetch strong face features and deploys model for factor analysis by means of age estimation purpose and convolutional neural networks and adopts factor analysis model in terms of age estimation function based and sequential study of rank based age estimation learning methods is used and then a divide and rule face age estimator is proposed. Manir Ahmed [7] proposes an eye localization method that can locate the eye centers more precisely in facial images captured under the above mentioned complexities, this method consists of three stages: eye candidate detection, eye candidate verification, and post processing. In eye candidate detection, the possible eye candidates are extracted using two new features namely Semi Circular Edge. M. Kafai [8] proposed RFG based face recognition algorithm is robust to the changes in pose and it is also alignment free. The RFG recognition is used in conjunction with DCT locality sensitive hashing for efficient retrieval to ensure scalability.

Pratibha Sukhija [9] proposed a Genetic Algorithm (GA) based approach for face recognition. The algorithm recognizes an unknown image by comparing it with the known training images stored in the database and gives information regarding the person recognized using PCA and LDA. Rajeev Ranjan [12] propose a novel face detector, Deep Pyramid Single Shot Face Detector (DPSSD), which is fast and capable of detecting faces with large scale variations (especially tiny faces). Raphael Angulu [13] proposes a technique for the analysis of recent research carried in the field of aging and estimation of age and focuses on significant algorithms, models used and related them each other.

R. R. Atallah [14] provides a survey of face recognition, including the age estimation which was discussed. Moreover, the research outlines several challenges faced in face recognition area that had been explored. Raghavendra S P [11] proposed a novel technique for recognition of hand written signature using feed forward neural network and Euclidean distance as metric. Shwetank Arya [15] presents a detailed and time to time review of the literature on Face Recognition in Infrared Spectrum. Vishnu Prasad Verma [16] focuses on conducting a survey on face age estimation techniques for both classification and regression based.

V. S. Manjula [17] proposed approach which is very useful and helpful in very huge real time application. Thus, the Face Detection, Identification and Tracking mechanism which is proposed to detect the faces in videos in the real time application by using the PRDIT (Proposed Rectangular Detection Identification and tracking) algorithm. Utkarsh Trehan [18] has designed and implemented a smart security system for areas where access is limited to people whose faces are available in the database. Xin Geng [19] proposes the AGES (Aging pattern Subspace) method for automatic age estimation. The basic idea is to model the aging pattern, which is defined as a sequence of personal aging face images by learning a representative subspace.

The Proposed research work focuses on devising a novel methodology for automatic age estimation system using 2D wavelet transformation with LBP features. The methodology has been divided into four main phases: (i) face Detection using viola jones algorithm (ii) 2D wavelet analysis; (iii)SVM classification for gender; and (iv) SVM classification for age.

3   Proposed Methodology

The proposed methodology has been divided into two major phases Training and Testing. In case of training an FG-NET aging database of sample images had been considered around 500 sample images of different categories of people with varying age. These images are trained using SVM classifier and the repository of knowledgebase is stored and will be used for testing in the future. In case of testing, the query face image will be preprocessed and face regions are segmented using Viola-Jones algorithm upon which two kinds of geometrically invariant features are extracted viz, (i) 2D Wavelet LBP Features (ii) Shape based features. These features are extracted based on facial expression and combined in order to compose a feature vector, which are compared with the knowledgebase for attaining two level decisions for estimation of age and gender of the query image. The proposed methodology can be depicted using the following block diagram:

Sample experimental results of the proposed system is illustrated as below (Figs. 1, 2 and 3).

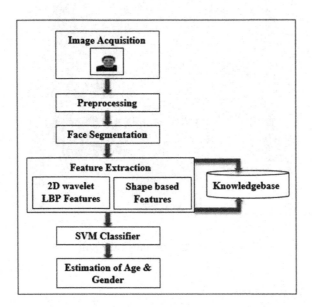

Fig. 1. The block diagram of age & gender estimation.

Fig. 2. Sample experimental results.

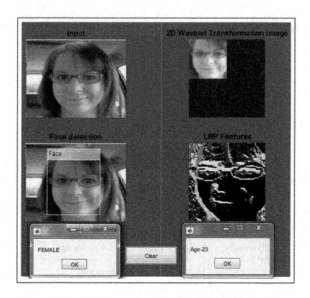

Fig. 3. Sample experimental results.

3.1   Image Acquisition

Consider the input image $f(x, y)$ acquired from a FG-NET database of around 1002 images by considering the gender factor as the combination of male and female subjects along with different variations and combinations with age parameter which demonstrates supervised classification in the later stage and used for training and creation of knowledgebase.

3.2   Preprocessing

Normalize the Query image $f(x, y)$ to standard size which is further used for feature extraction later on.

3.3   Segmentation

Face region is detected and segmented from a given Query image by means of Viola-Jones algorithm. This algorithm is extensively utilized for the identification of objects. It takes more time for this algorithm in order to be get trained, however detection process is fast using Haar basis feature filters.

The integral image generated using Viola-Jones algorithm can be depicted by the following set models:

$$II(y, x) = \sum_{p=0}^{y} \sum_{q=0}^{x} Y(p, q) \tag{1}$$

In the given query image, the Haar features can be evaluated by making summation of 4 number values, as an illustration consider the image area of A B C

D in the following diagram, the integral summation value can be evaluated by using the following formulae (Fig. 4),

$$II(y_A, x_A) - II(y_B, x_B) - II(y_C, x_C) + II(y_D, x_D) \tag{2}$$

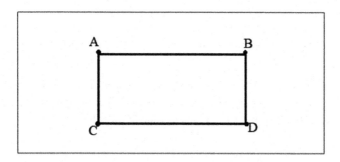

Fig. 4. Image area integration using integral image.

Identification of region of interest happens inside detection window, for which specific range of minimum and maximum bounds will be fixed with a window as a filter mask and this detection process will scan across the query image for possible detection of face region.

Face regions are detected inside mask detection window with different window size will be selected with minimum and maximum values dimension and for each dimension sliding step value will considered. This window will be scanned across the whole image for possible face detection. The cascaded face recognition filter contains multiple classifiers (N filters) and in turn focuses towards a rectangular subclass of the detection window and verifies the region under consideration is face or not and if the detected region is face then the next classifier is employed and the process continues if all the classifiers results in a positive decision then the corresponding region will be declared as a face region else the detection window shifts to next immediate region in the query image.

Every single classifier is comprised of Haar features which is the subjective summation of 2-D assembly of minor quadrilateral sections enclosed to one another. The weights may procure assessment of ±1. Figure 5 depicts instances of Haar features comparative to the encircling the detection frame or window. Black sections contains positive weight and white regions contains a negative weight (Fig. 5).

The result of the classifier is given by:

$$C_m = \begin{cases} 1, & \sum_{i=0}^{l_m-1} F_{m,i} > \theta_m \\ 0, & Otherwise \end{cases} \tag{3}$$

$$F_{m,i} = \begin{cases} \alpha_{m,i}, & if(f_{m,i} > t_{m,i}) \\ \beta_{m,i}, & Otherwise \end{cases} \tag{4}$$

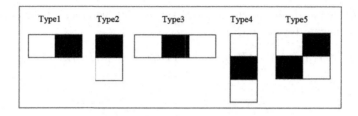

Fig. 5. Detection window with rectangular features.

in the above equation $f_{m,i}$ is considered as the weighted sum of the 2-D integrals which stays as threshold value with respect to i^{th} feature extractor. θ_m is nothing but evaluation threshold for the mth classifier (Fig. 6 and 7).

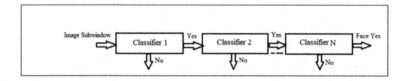

Fig. 6. Detection of object using Viola-Jones mask filter.

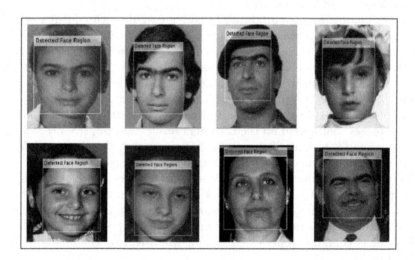

Fig. 7. Face detection using Viola-Jones Algorithm.

4   Feature Extraction

In the proposed methodology two kinds robust geometrically invariant features are extracted viz- 2D wavelet-based LBP features and region-based shape features. The segmented face image will be further divided into 4 quadrants using

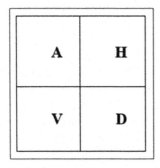 

Fig. 8. (a) AHVD 2D Wavelet Feature decomposition (b) Query image wavelet decomposition.

2D Wavelet transformation. The scaled and translated basis elements of the 2D wavelet transform are given by (Fig. 8):

$$LA = \phi^A(x, y) = \phi(x).\phi(y) \tag{5}$$

$$LH = \psi^H(x, y) = \psi(x).\phi(y) \tag{6}$$

$$LV = \psi^V(x, y) = \phi(x).\psi(y) \tag{7}$$

$$LD = \psi^D(x, y) = \psi(x).\phi(y) \tag{8}$$

where the super scripts A, H, V, and D denotes to the decomposition direction of the wavelet features. Two-dimensional wavelets are utilized as a part of image manipulation. The multi resolution representation of scaling and wavelet functions for the 2-D face image is given below:

$$\phi_{j,m,n}(x, y) = 2^{\frac{j}{2}}\phi(2^j.(x - m), 2^j.(y - n)) \tag{9}$$

$$\psi^i_{j,m,n}(x, y) = 2^{\frac{j}{2}}\psi^i(2^j.(x - m), 2^j.(y - n)) \tag{10}$$

where i = A, H, V, D
Scaling function of the 2D wavelet transformation is:

$$W_\phi(j_0, m, n) = \frac{1}{\sqrt{MN}} \sum_{x=0}^{M-1} \sum_{y=0}^{N-1} f(x, y).\phi_{j_0}, m, n(x, y) \tag{11}$$

Once the wavelet transformation is applied, all the corresponding bands will be chosen in order to fetch the Local binary patterns and shape features from the face image is as given below: $LBP_{P,R}$ operator by meaning is robust and invariant feature values in contradiction of any monotonic transformation of the gray scale feature values.By Providing the order of the gray values which remains the similar, the outcome of the $LBP_{P,R}$ operator will remains constant.

$$LBP_{P,R} = \sum_{p=0}^{p-1} s(g_p - g_c)2^p[W_\phi(j_0, m, n)] \tag{12}$$

where

$$s(x) = \begin{cases} 1, & x \geq 0 \\ 0, & x < 0 \end{cases} \tag{13}$$

The regional shape features which are geometrically invariant in nature will be extracted using the region properties of the face region viz Eccentricity, Perimeter, Orientation and solidity. The perimeter [length] is going to evaluated as the amount of pixels around the object under consideration. Provided that (x1 ..., xn) is a border list of an object, the perimeter is estimated by:

$$Per = \sum_{i=1}^{N-1} d_i = \sum_{i=1}^{N-1} |x_i - x_{i+1}| \tag{14}$$

The distance d_i matches to 1 for 4-connected components and higher than 1 for 8-connected components where as the term Eccentricity is nothing but the proportion of the measure of the short (minor) axis to the measure of the long (major) axis of an object:

$$Eccr = \frac{Axis\ length_{short}}{Axis\ length_{long}} \tag{15}$$

For a given object the measures of density in it can be considered as the solidity which can be estimated as the proportion of the area of an object with respect to its area of its convex hull:

$$Sol = \frac{Area}{Convex\ Area} \tag{16}$$

The overall direction of the shape can be extracted using angle of rotation of the given shape descriptors (θ). Local shape descriptors are combined to form a shape feature vectors as given below:

$$Shape\_feat = \sum_{i=1}^{x} \sum_{j=1}^{y} f(x, y)[Per * Ecc * Sol * \theta] \tag{17}$$

5   Age Estimation

With the 2D Wavelet global features obtained using LBP and the local shape features obtained using regional shape properties, a final feature vector is constructed by concatenating the two normalized features using the following model:

$$f_i^{norm} = \sum_{i=1}^{x} \sum_{j=1}^{y} W_\phi(j_0, m, n) + Shape\_feat \tag{18}$$

The Combined and normalized feature vectors are stored in a repository in the form of a knowledgebase during training phase itself and for query face image also same sets of features are extracted and the feature vectors thus obtained will fed to the Support vector machine classifier along with the knowledgebase. In the proposed methodology the SVM classifier is used to predict two level decisions one for identifying gender and the next one is to estimate the age factor.

For gender classification the hypothesis function h as:

$$h(x_i) = \begin{cases} +1, & if(w.x + b) \geq 0 \\ -1, & if(w.x + b) < 0 \end{cases} \tag{19}$$

Where $(w.x+b)$ is derived from two-dimensional vectors. But in fact, it also works for any number of dimensions and is the equation of the hyperplane. The point above or on the hyperplane will be classified as class $+1$ as Male gender, and the point below the hyperplane will be classified as class -1 for female gender. For age estimation the SVM classifier is trained with all combinations of different aged faces from a predefined knowledgebase by using the following hypothesis, for all the training example points as face feature vectors in a knowledgebase, the point which is closest to the hyperplane as $\beta = |w.x + b|$.

The Learning function is given by

$$z_i = \sum_{i=1}^{n} f_i^{norm} + \beta \tag{20}$$

Where f_i^{norm} indicates normalized feature vector and β indicates training database. Among different classes of face the query face age will be estimated by using the value of y with highest value of index to be considered as the approximated age value of the query face image by applying the Eq. (21)

$$y_i = max \int_{i=1}^{n} (y, i) \tag{21}$$

where n: Defines numerous supervised dataset of face images (in our case $n = 1002$) Once the face has been identified for the given query face image, age can be estimated by using above equation.

6   Experimental Results

The database used in the proposed methodology is the FG–NET Aging Database. FG-NET is one of the most popular publicly obtainable database comprising of around 1002 high resolution color and grey–scale face images with huge disparities in pose, expression, illumination and lighting (Fig. 9).

Fig. 9. Sample images of the same object at different ages.

There are nearby over all 82 subjects (multiple faces) vary between age from 0 to 69 years. The proposed methodology uses the criterion mean absolute error (MAE) to assess the performance of respective age assessment. The MAE signifies the mean of the absolute errors among the actual age and assessed age. The mathematical function is defined as:

$$MAE = \sum_{k=1}^{N} |\hat{l}_k - l_k| \tag{22}$$

where $\hat{l}_k$ declared as the age of the query image k under consideration and l_k is the age assessed age and N is the overall number of test images under consideration.

The following table shows the experimental results of the proposed methodology in which the evaluated MAE value is compared with the state-of-the-art methods by means of FG-NET age database. The proposed wavelet-LBP method has the MAE of 5.70 which is considerably lesser compared to other existing methods (Table 1).

Table 1. Comparative analysis.

Method	MAE
Chin-Teng Lin_SVM [2]	5.71
Chin-Teng Lin_KNN [2]	8.43
Andreas Lanitis_MLP [1]	6.98
Xin Geng_WAS [17]	8.08
Xin Geng_AGES [17]	6.77
Proposed methodology	**5.70**

The Success rate is illustrated by using the below graph which shows the cumulative aggregate score of the various methodologies with MAE's among which the proposed methodology is g comparative to the state of the art methods, the method of Chin-Teng Lin_SVM is closer to our method 2Dwavelet_LBP method and the results obtained are satisfactory over different methodologies discussed (Fig. 10).

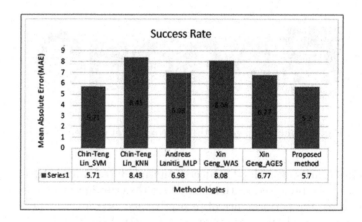

Fig. 10. Bar chart of MAE's of various methodologies.

7   Conclusion

A new and novel methodology for automatic age estimation of face images has been proposed in this paper. A 2D wavelet transformation with LBP features is presented for age estimation to accomplish fully automatic aging feature extraction. SVM's have substantial capability as classifier of thin training data and can provide accurate simplification proficiency.

Face detection is accomplished by using viola jones face recognition algorithm, and face image is decomposed into 4 quadrants as AHVD using 2D wavelet transformation, the face image with A(all) from AHVD features are considered for extracting both LBP and shape based regional features which are fed to SVM classifier with knowledgebase for two level decisions making for estimation of age and gender, the proposed methodology gives success rate in terms of lower MAE value of around 5.7 and success rate of 94.3% which better and comparative with the state of the art methods.

References

1. Lanitis, A., Draganova, C., Christodoulou, C.: Comparing different classifiers for automatic age estimation, IEEE Trans. Syst. Man Cybern. Part B Cybern. **34**(1), 621–628 (2004)
2. Lin, C.-T., Li, D.-L., Lai, J.-H., Han, M.-F., Chang, J.-Y.: Automatic age estimation system for face images. Int. J. Adv. Robot. Syst. 216 (2012). https://doi.org/10.5772/52862
3. Nguyen, D.T., Cho, S.R., Shin, K.Y., Bang, J.W., Park, K.R.: Comparative study of human age estimation with or without pre classification of gender and facial expression. Sci. World J. 905269, 15 p. (2014). https://doi.org/10.1155/2014/905269
4. Parmar, D.N., Mehta, B.B.: Face recognition methods & applications. Int. J. Comput. Technol. Appl. (IJCTA) **4**(1), 84–86 (2013). ISSN 2229-6093
5. Ravichandran, D., Nimmatoori, R., Gulam Ahamad, M.: Mathematical representations of 1D, 2D and 3D wavelet transform for image coding. Int. J. Adv. Comput. Theory Engineering (IJACTE) **5**(3) (2016). ISSN (Print): 2319-2526
6. Liao, H., Yan, Y., Dai, W., Fan, P.: Age estimation of face images based on CNN and divide-and-rule strategy. Math. Probl. Eng. **2018**, Article ID 1712686, 8 p. (2018). https://doi.org/10.1155/2018/1712686
7. Ahmed, M., Laskar, R.H.: Eye center localization in a facial image based on geometric shapes of iris and eyelid under natural variability. Image Vis. Comput. **88**, 52–66 (2019). https://doi.org/10.1016/j.imavis.2019.05.002 0262-8856/Elsevier
8. Kafai, M., An, L., Bhanu, B.: Reference face graph for face recognition. IEEE Trans. Inf. Forensics Secur. **9**(12), 2132–2143 (2014). https://doi.org/10.1109/TIFS.2014.2359548
9. Sukhija, P., Behal, S., Singh, P.: Face recognition system using genetic algorithm. In: International Conference on Computational Modeling and Security (CMS 2016), Published by Elsevier B.V. an open access article under the CC BY-NC-ND license (2016). http://creativecommons.org/licenses/by-nc-nd/4.0/. 1877-0509

10. Raghavendra, S.P., Danti, A.: A novel recognition if Indian bank cheque names using binary pattern and feed forward neural network. IOSR J. Comput. Eng. (IOSR-JCE) **20**(3), Ver I, 44–59 (2018). UGC Approved Journal (Jr. No. 5019). e-ISSN: 2278-0661, p-ISSN: 2278-8727

11. Raghavendra, S.P., Danti, A.: Recognition of signature using neural network and Euclidean distance for bank cheque automation. In: Santosh, K., Hegadi, R. (eds.) Recent Trends in Image Processing and Pattern RecognitionInternational Conference on Recent Trends in image Processing (RTIP2R) 2018 Solapur, Communication in Computer and Information Science (CCIS), vol. 1037, pp. 228–243. Springer, Singapore (2019). https://doi.org/10.1007/978-981-13-9187-2_21

12. Ranjan, R., et al.: A fast and accurate system for face detection, identification, and verification. J. Latex Class Files **14**(8) (2015)

13. Angulu, R., Tapamo, J.R., Adewumi, A.O.: Age estimation via face images: a survey. EURASIP J. Image Video Process. **2018**, 42 (2018). https://doi.org/10.1186/s13640-018-0278-6

14. Atallah, R.R., Kamsin, A., Ismail, M.A., Abdelrahman, S.A., Zerdoumi, S.: Face recognition and age estimation implications of changes in facial features: a critical review study. IEEE Access **6**, 28290–28304 (2018). https://doi.org/10.1109/ACCESS.2018.2836924

15. Arya, S., Pratap, N., Bhatia, K.: Future of face recognition: a review. Procedia Comput. Sci. **58**(2015), 578–585 (2015). In: Second International Symposium on Computer Vision and the Internet (VisionNet 2015). Elsevier

16. Verma, V.P., Verma, D.: A survey on facial age estimation techniques. IJSE Int. J. Comput. Sci. Eng. **6**(8) (2018). E-ISSN: 2347-2693. Open Access Survey Paper

17. Manjula, V.S., Baboo, S.S.: Face detection identification and tracking by PRDIT algorithm using image database for crime investigation. Int. J. Comput. Appl. (0975-8887) **38**(10) (2012)

18. Trehan, U., Awasthi, A.K., Gupta, S., Singh, P.: Security authentication system using facial recognition. J. Netw. Commun. Emerg. Technol. (JNCET) **8**(4) (2018). http://www.jncet.org

19. Geng, X., Zhou, Z.H., Zhang, Y., Li, G., Dai, H.: Learning from facial aging patterns for automatic age estimation. In: MM 2006, Santa Barbara, California, USA, 23–27 October, Copyright 2006 ACM (2006). 1-59593-447-2/06/0010 ...$5.00

20. Yadav, D., Singh, R., Vatsa, M., Noore, A.: Recognizing age separated face images: humans and machines. PLoS ONE **9**(12), e112234 (2014). https://doi.org/10.1371/journal.pone.0112234

Assistive Technologies for Visually Impaired Persons Using Image Processing Techniques – A Survey

Suraj R. Pardeshi[1(✉)], Vikul J. Pawar[2], Kailas D. Kharat[3], and Sachin Chavan[4]

[1] Department of M.C.A, Govt. Engg. College, Aurangabad, Maharashtra, India
surajrp@geca.ac.in
[2] Department of Computer Science and Engineering, University College of Engineering,
Osmania University, Hyderabad, Telangana, India
vikul.pawar@geca.ac.in
[3] Department of CSE, Govt. Engg. College, Aurangabad, Maharashtra, India
kailashdkharat@gmail.com
[4] Department of CS and IT, Dr. B.A.M. U., Aurangabad, Maharashtra, India
sach.chavan@gmail.com

Abstract. Acquiring information of objects or obstacles ahead and accordingly deciding navigation direction is one of the major problems that visually impaired persons face in their day to day life. However there had been a lot of efforts taken for research towards helping the blinds, yet there is no any concrete, globally accepted and used solution available till date. Vision assistive devices are transferable electronic equipment that can also be hold in hands or easily wear by the users to help them sense the obstacles ahead. This paper tries to identify the currently available assistive technologies for visually impaired persons which use advanced image processing techniques. There is an increasing interest in using those techniques for the use of development of cost effective, easily wearable, hassle free, comfortable to operate and user approachable assistive technique for visually damaged population all over the world. These techniques if combined with some other technical components such as sensors, ultrasonic pulse-echo, infrared light transceivers, GPS systems, acoustic feedback techniques, vibration pads etc. can bring forth a very feature enriched assistive system that can overcome many of the lacunas of previously proposed solutions.

Keywords: Visually impaired · Obstacle detection · Assistive devices · Image processing · Sensors · Ultrasonic pulse-echo · Infrared light transceivers · GPS systems · Acoustic feedback · Vibration pads

1 Introduction

As derived from—World Health Organization report and fact sheet updated on October 2017 on visual impairment, the estimated number of people living with vision impairment is about 253 million; 36 million are completely vision impaired while 217 million populations is having restrained to extreme vision impairment.

© Springer Nature Singapore Pte Ltd. 2021
K. C. Santosh and B. Gawali (Eds.): RTIP2R 2020, CCIS 1380, pp. 95–110, 2021.
https://doi.org/10.1007/978-981-16-0507-9_9

Vision is being the most important and vital modality of human life, its loss affects almost all of the daily activities hampering the persons' quality of life, social standard of living, relationships and professional environment also. Assistive Technology (also referred to as AT) normally refers to equipment intended for persons having certain disability or deficiency (or aged folks). It is a combination of multiple advanced technical innovations from a variety of disciplines. The assistive technology for visually impaired encompasses technologies, systems, equipments, processes, interfaces (hardware/software), components or environments that assists them to sense the presence of objects or obstacles (moving or stationary) ahead and accordingly take decision for navigation. Vision AT assists local navigation for visually impaired by identifying the obstacle ahead, conveying the obstacle description and information to the user through auditory or tactile senses and providing navigation help. During the most past recent ten years there has been a substantial increase in research enthusiasm for this area and huge advancements have occurred as novel (scaled down) easy to wear electronic travel helps (ETAs), smart walking sticks, (easy to wear) structure factors, PDA based gadgets and applications, material presentations and interfaces, cortical and retinal inserts (bionic eyes), and so on. This paper shows knowledge into the present status and flow condition of AT innovation for the outwardly impeded and visually impaired individuals, with an accentuation on what can be gained from the most recent twenty years of distributed research and what the potential patterns are. This work is an overview of the cutting edge in exploration in the area dependent on data examination of a database of logical exploration distributions. The distributions are pertinent to assistive innovation for the outwardly impeded and dazzle people crosswise over different fields of innovation, medication and related sub-disciplines.

The electronic navigation devices can be roughly categorized as (Fig. 1):

a)   **Vision Replacement Devices**
b)   **Vision Enhancement Devices**
c)   **Vision Substitution Devices**

Category (a) **Vision Replacement** includes showing the data straightforwardly to the visual cortex of the individual mind or by means of the optic nerve. We won't manage this class since they deal into logical, mechanical and therapeutic issues whose review is past the motivation behind this study. Category (b) **Vision Enhancement**, includes getting key in from a camera, process the data, and show the yield on a visual display. In its least complex structure it might be a small scale head-mounted camera with the yield on a head-mounted visual presentation (as utilized in a computer generated simulation frameworks). Category (c) **Vision substitution** is like vision enhancement, however with the yield being non-visual, ordinarily tangible or sound-related or a blend of the both and in a view of the fact that the faculties of touch and audio have a good deal of lower data limit than visualization, it is fundamental to treat the data to a stage that can be taken care of by the client. The class that we wish to focus here is the "**Vision Substitution**".

Vision Substitution subdivisions are shown in Fig. 2. We are for the most part inspired by ETAs and all the more, explicitly in hurdle recognition arrangements, not accentuating in GPS highlights.

For Simple understanding categories of Electronic Navigation Devices can be represented graphically as follows (see Fig. 1):

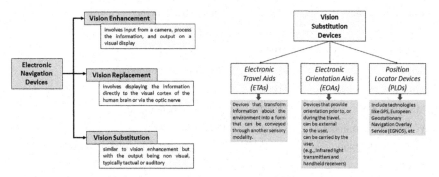

Fig. 1. Electronic navigation devices   **Fig. 2.** Vision substitution devices

Electronic Travel Aids (ETAs) can be broadly distributed as (see Fig. 3):

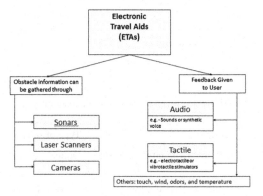

Fig. 3. Electronic Travel Aids

2   Existing ETA Products

2.1   Ultrasonic Sensor or Sonar Based systems

Use acoustic waves in the frequency range beyond human hearing ability (typically from 20 kHz up to several gigahertz), and detect the signals bounced back by the obstacles which are then translated into either audio or tactile feedback forms to the blind people. Table below summarizes few such devices (Table 1):

Table 1. Ultrasonic sensor or sonar based systems

Name of device	Year	Comments (if any)
1. Ultrasonic Cone	1972	Fails in bad whether
2. Polarone	1980	Very Costly
3. Walkmate	1993	Beam may vary
4. Sensory 6	1994	Head Position important
5. Russell Pathsounder	1996	–
6. Miniguide US	2004	$545, still being used
7. Wheelchair Pathfinder	2011	Expensive
8. LaserCane-N-2000	2000	Expensive ($2650), still being used
9. GuideCane	1998	–
10. BAT-K Sonar Torch Cane	2003	–
11. Trisensor	1990	–
12. Ultracane	Still used	Available Commercially online with price $635

2.2 Infrared Sensors based Systems

See Table 2.

Table 2. Infrared sensors based systems

Sr. No	Name of device/system	Type of sensor used
1	FAV & GPS (Fusion of Artificial Vision and GPS)	Optical Sensor
2	Banknote Rec (Banknote Recognition)	ivCAM Sensor
3	CAS Blip	3D CMOS Sensor
4	Low Cost Nav (A low cost outdoor assistive navigation system)	3 Axial Accelerometer Sensors
5	CG System (Cognitive Guidance System)	Kinect Sensor
6	Sili Eyes (Silicon Eyes)	24-bit Color Sensor
7	PF Belt (Path Force Feedback Belt)	IR Sensor
8	Eye Ring	Atmel 8-bit Microcontroller
9	Finger Reader	Atmel 8-bit Microcontroller
10	Navigation Assistance Using RGB-D Sensor	RGB-D Sensor
11	Ultrasonic Assistive Headset for Visually Impaired People	4 DYP-ME007 Sensors
12	SUGAR system	Ultra Wide Band (UWB) Sensors

3 Literature Review

An extensive literature review of almost 37 national / international research articles from Scopus and Web-of-Science journals and conference proceedings has been performed to understand the current status of assistive technologies for vision impairment. The review process tries to discover the timely technological evolution and advancements that affected the maturity of AT devices at various levels from early 90s to 2019.

Early work (1944–1951) on guidance aids for blind used Sonic and Ultrasonic waves with light beams and short electro-magnetic waves. The sonic systems were reported to be unreliable in a high wind condition [1]. The Vector Field Histogram (VHF) method demonstrates an hurdle dodging scheme for mobile robots that uses experimental mobile robot CARMEL permits nonstop and quick movement of the portable robot ceaselessly for deterrents. VFH technique particularly fit to the convenience of incorrect sensor information, for example, that delivered by ultrasonic sensors, just as sensor combination [2]. The GuideCane, under development at the University of Michigan's Mobile Robotics Lab, encompasses ten Ultrasonic sensors which detects obstacles and steers the cane with a noticeable physical force in the direction avoiding the obstacle [3].

Jack M. Loomis proposed a navigation system, that claims that specialized sound will be more effective in conveying obstacle information than synthesized speech [4].Leslie Kay used a high resolution octave band air sonar for spatial sensing of object imaging. The system is coupled to the auditory system for neural processing and spatial imaging [5].

Young Jip Kim had proposed an acoustic direction arrangement for the visually impaired using ultrasonic-to-audio signal conversion. The system consists of multiple wide beam angle ultrasonic sensors to discover objects over a wider range and converts it to binaural acoustic information using appropriate method [6].

In [12] RFID is used in a glove to permit the user to explore the data, the obtained knowledge is sent to a Personal Digital Assistant vis Bluetooth which then is conveyed through audio. But for this the obstacles are labeled with RFID tags in a controlled in-house environment. Experiment was carried out with containers of paper plastic and glass. [24] - As we know we need feature extraction methods to detect objects which area of interest from whole image is detected and represented for further processing. Using Scale Invariant Feature transform (SITF) objects are identified from image and compared with the database stored references. Objects are identified by feature matching. Identified objects names are conveyed to user by auditory feedback.

Another approach use two cameras, used to take images from two different sides connected to blind person's specs. It also consists of a stick and sensor based obstacle detection system. Infrared sensors are used. The system is designed specially to protect the area near the head and provides buzzer and vibration feedbacks [25].

One research work cited here is using image processing and ANN algorithms to identify and match scanned objects with objects already stored in database. Feedback is given to user regarding recognized objects using text to speech synthesizers [26]. A cost effective scene perception system is proposed for visually impaired using an android system integrated with USB camera and USB laser attached to the chest of the subject. The system is capable of identifying objects along with their distances from the user with a voice feedback. The object detection and classification exploits multi-model fusion based faster RCNN using motion, sharpening and blurring filters for efficient feature representation [33].

Alberto Rodriguez and others in their paper in the journal "Sensors-1012" utilizes signal sounds with various frequencies and reiterations to notify the blind person about the existence of objects. An intense disparity map is calculated from the pictures of a stereo camera conveyed by the blind person which can recognize potential impediment in 3D in indoor and outdoor scenarios [13]. One more framework incorporates a camera, an implanted PC and a haptic gadget to give response when an obstruction is distinguished. It utilizes practices from computer vision and motion planning to distinguish walk-capable space, plan bit by bit a protected movement direction in the space perceive and find particular kinds of objects. A belt with installed vibration motors that gives vibration response to indicate hurdles to its user, is utilized. Utilizing depth data from a camera, the framework recognizes walk-capable free space [31].

"The Blind Guider" application is an ongoing application for identifying impediments, for example, staircases, potholes, passerby intersections and moving vehicle recognition and getting present position by GPS and providing instructions to move out here and there utilizing the cell phone camera with voice guidelines. The framework utilizes Haar-Cascade, BLOB and SURF calculations [32]. One anticipate includes helping the incognizant in regards to perceive traffic sign example just as hindrances around and to cross the street without relying upon others, likewise targets actualizing GPS module to guide the client to close by ordained spots. The framework comprises of a glass with camera and sensors, an equipment and a sound framework. It utilizes the MATLAB programming to recognize hindrances around just as traffic sign example [27].

One assistive system for blind people uses the matrix of electrode and a mobile Kinect. It is made up of 2 main modules: 1) Acquiring surroundings knowledge and evaluating it and illustration of this information. Undeniably, not every user can completely become accustomed to this type of apparatus and the freedom of movement however is subject to their natural feeling and inclination. Not all visually impaired are completely sightless and they can adhere to the guidance by light signal [38].

Android based object recognition into voice input software eliminates the need of isolated devoted gadgets for obstacle identification and movement recognition. This undertaking proposes a principal component analysis algorithm (PCA) to identify the obstacle. To help ongoing examining of articles, a key frame extraction algorithm is built up that consequently recovers top notch outlines from constant camera video stream of cell phones. The series roughly catch 3 frames for each second. The obstacle is identified and changed over into text, BY text-to-speech application it is changed over into the voice yield [18].

One out-door navigation system uses a programmed insight framework, in view of computer vision algorithms and profound convolutional neural network. The framework can deal with impediments, abrupt camera/object position changes, pivot or different complex changes. The yield of this framework is changed into a lot of acoustic indications transmitted to the blind person through bone directing earphones [30]. One framework utilizes infrared sensor which is utilized to examine a previously identified region around visually impaired by transmitting reflecting waves. The reflected sign got from the hindrance obstacles are utilized as key-ins to PIC microcontroller. The microcontroller is then used to decide the direction and space of the obstacles around the visually impaired. The system includes a wearable equipment consists of head hat and mini hand stick [14].

One system utilizes three types of devices including IR sensor, sonar sensor and camera. The system is implemented using raspberry pi. A microcontroller processes the reflected signals from all devices in order to classify front obstacle. Python is used to program the hardware and OpenCv is used to setup and run the object detection model with python [35]. One proposed system identifies various public transport means and helps VI(Visually Impaired) to get onboard. It uses an integrated system of a mobile phone connected wirelessly via Bluetooth to Arduino controlled array of uniquely placed ultrasonic sensors complemented with vibro motor for haptic feedback. The system detects obstacles in all four directions. It employ image-based recognition based on the visual information obtained from a mobile phone camera to detect vehicles like bus, car, truck, two-wheelers, auto-rickshaw (three-wheeler) as well as objects [36].

One framework utilizes the ultrasonic sensors, microcontroller, Raspberry pi, Headphone, and Power supply. Ultrasonic sensor is utilized to check a previously identified territory around visually impaired by emanating reflecting waves. The reflected sign got from the obstacles are utilized as key-ins to Arduino microcontroller, Which at that point complete the issued directions and after that convey the status of a given machine or gadget back to the headphones utilizing Raspberry pi speech synthesizer [15].

David A. Ross & Bruce B. Blasch, in their research article in international conference on Assistive Technology at Arlington, Virginia, USA, claimed three wearable orientation interfaces – a sonic guide, speech output and a shoulder tapping system to increase usability and flexibility for VI users. Amongst which the shoulder tapping system of (3X3 tapping interface grid) proved to be of better yield in all aspects [7]. One article in January 2001 by M. Loomis and others summarize all the current as well as past ETAs and categorize them according to navigation and obstacle detection [8]. Radio Frequency identification (RFID) tags are used successfully in robot-assisted indoor navigation for blinds [9].

An Elsevier conference paper in 2004 by J.L. Fernandez and others uses Beam method (BM) & Curvature Velocity method (CVM) for obstacle avoidance for mobile robots in cluttered and unknown or partially unknown environments [10]. One more project demonstrates an android based app that can be downloaded in to smart phones having camera, voice processing unit and internet access. Object detection is achieved by using Tensor Flow Models GitHub fountain which contains a huge number of pretrained models aimed at numerous machine learning jobs, and one of the outstanding method is using object detection API which will be used for identifying objects in a video or image, voice interaction is achieved by using Google voice API and android Talkback engine [34].

A conference proceedings on Human Factors in Computing Systems, Glasgow, Scotland UK in 2019 explain a project **"BBeep"** which uses preemptive sound warnings to free pathway by notifying the visually impaired person and nearby walkers, predicting threat of their future clash [37]. Zraqou Jamal and two others proposes a system containing two cameras mounted on visually impaired user's glasses, GPS free service and ultra-sonic sensors are engaged to deliver the essential information concerning the encompassing surroundings. The two cameras produce the depth information by generating a disparity map of the scene [29].

Varun Raj S P, Annie R Das propose a low cost outdoor navigation system called "Pathfinder", uses audible feedback for navigation, portable camera, GPS, external memory and a microcontroller module to generate sound based on direction of navigation [20]. Hyochang Ahn, Sang-Burm Rhee in their research paper proposed a low multifaceted nature and powerful object acknowledgment and following framework utilizing propelled highlight coordinating for continuous condition. Their algorithm identifies obstacles utilizing invariant highlights and diminishes measurement of feature descriptor to manage the issues [21].

El-hariri and others in a conference paper in Elsevier, presents an indoor obstacle identification framework dependent on the histogram of oriented gradient and Machine Learning (ML) algorithms, for example, Support Vector Machines (SVMs), Random Forests (RF) and Linear Discriminant Analysis (LDA) algorithms, for categorizing various indoor items to improve nature of older individuals' life. It consists of segmentation, feature extraction, and classification [23].

4   General Discussion About Assistive Technologies

From the literature review performed above, various techniques & algorithms, tools, hardware-software interfaces proposed by the various researchers gives a glimpse of the step by step development that has occurred in the field of assistive technology right from its inception till date. The literature considered for review encompasses all the reputed (Conferences and Journals) articles from early 90s till 2019.

The feature list that needs to be taken care of while designing of any assistive technology can be summarized from the above literature as follows [16]:

1. *Real Time:* The system must process fast such that the information given to the user will be useful. E.g. A system that takes 20 s to detect and inform user about an object at 12 feet from user is not real time.
2. *Wearable:* The device must be capable of being easily worn by the user as an ordinary accessory keeping his head, hands, legs, voice, ears and other body parts/functions free for natural movements.
3. *Handy:* The device must be light weight, small in size so that to be able to carry easily anywhere.
4. *Consistent:* The system gives accurate results in normal as well as abnormal situations.
5. *Cheap:* The System must be of low cost so that all users can afford it globally.
6. *User Friendly:* The system must be easy to learn, adopt and operate easily by the user.
7. *Simple:* It should incorporate easy hardware and software components that are simple to design, build and integrate.
8. *Robust:* The system must work in adverse conditions and survive from failures.

9. *Wireless:* The system should have a wireless connectivity to tis computer or processor unit.
10. *Performance:* The system performance should be optimal in all aspects viz. Operating speed, processing time and result accuracy.
11. *Novelty:* The system must be an innovative idea of scientific technological invention.
12. *Availability:* The system must be easily available globally to all audiences as a completely furnished product.
13. *Future Scope:* In this continuous changing era of science and technology, the system must be easily adoptable to surrounding changes in its domain.

The feature enlisted above not only echoes user's view point but also designer's outlook. An ideal assistive system for VI will offer all these features and functionalities. One significant conclusion can be mentioned here that there is no such system currently exists incorporating the above feature set in one.

5 Shortcomings Observed in Current Assistive Devices

Currently available assistive devices for blinds can be separated in to two categories [11]. Firstly, the devices that gives warning of objects and obstacles ahead of the forward path of the user. These devices gives very little information regarding the overall characteristics of the obstacle like its position, size, distance from user and its dimensions etc. with respect to object identification. The feedback is given to user by using vibrations, sound warnings or buzzers. The problem with such devices is they are not able to warn user about depth information such as potholes, aerial hindrances such as floating or hanging objects etc.

Secondly, the devices may be of more precision and accuracy (e.g. laser based), but may provide simplistic feedback like binary signals or may use complex sonar techniques that accepts ultrasonic signals bounced back by the obstacles and convert those signals into synthetic. But these converted signals are not humanly. These devices negotiate over the natural sound hints necessary for blind persons.

Many current products have complex human-machine interfaces because of which none of them is globally accepted and widely used in spite of providing mobility as well as safety.

Deficiencies observed may be listed down as [17, 20, 27]:

1) Complicated and time consuming operations, processes or algorithms: Many devices use sonars or laser beams to scan the environment, to sense the information, understand and interpret it, take a decision and provide feedback to user about navigation. This may affect the normal walking speed of the user.
2) Some devices provide acoustic feedback which may affect the blind person's natural hearing ability. These continuous artificial sounds may degrade in born hearing sense. The reason being the designers and engineers of such devices are from technological background having little or no care of medical and health care issues. Most of these devices are observed to be adopting robotic vision.

3) Sensors are having limited range, hence detect nearest objects. While dealing with moving objects such as vehicles passing nearby that may not be useful enough.
4) RFID also requires tags, hence indoor use is possible but for outdoor environment it is not possible to use, as larger area needs to be tagged.
5) These devices are quite disturbing, interrupting the overall environment with scanning and feedback mechanisms.
6) They still need to be carry as backpacks, are bulky and hence portability is not achieved 100%.

6   Proposed System: Use of Image Processing in Assistive Technology Devices

On the basis of the information gathered from literature review, it is observed that the assistive devices developed and under development had undergone through sweeping technological evolution with respect to hardware and software aspects. The main hurdle in design of these devices is object recognition. An adequate amount of efforts invested in image acquisition, image enhancement, restoration, processing can result in more proper perception of the environmental scene captured from ahead of the bind person.

Further image segmentation, representation and description leads to object recognition. Object identification must be coupled with depth identification (potholes, downstairs etc.) and aerial object identification (e.g. hanging objects, top edge of entrances etc.). Once objects are identified from the captured scene, priorities to those objects may be assigned considering their distances from the user to identify which objects are closer and which are farther from the blind person. According to distances identified navigation information (acoustic, vibrations etc.) must be conveyed to the blind person.

The requirements for such system would be high definition cameras to capture images and a fast working algorithm that would perform the entire image processing operations in least possible time and convey feedback for navigation as quick as possible. The time factor is a major concern here so as to allow the user to navigate or walk with normal speed. The hardware components such as processors and voice system also play a crucial role in obtaining optimum performance in least possible time.

A major part of this research area is object detection [19]. Object detection is nowadays used in many consumer electronics such as in smart phones, face detection, security products, automated driving technologies etc. but still we are very far from human level perfection and ease [28]. One more challenge while designing of such system is achieving Human – Machine interaction. As the blinds are lacking vision sense, they are more dependent and sensitive towards hearing and touch senses. Emphasis must be given to designing a hassle-free, hands free, ear free, portable, wearable and simple device as if a fashion accessory. Google's Android and Apple's iOS—both gives a huge assortment of assistive applications by utilizing the inherent sensors of the cell phones, and connecting this tangible data with the capability of overseeing huge datasets, notwithstanding cloud assets and publicly supported commitments progressively. An ongoing H2020 venture was propelled to build up a navigational gadget running on a cell phone, fusing profundity touchy cameras, spatial sound, haptics and advancement of preparing techniques [22].

By the virtue of this survey conducted we can arrange the near future trends and disciplines in assistive technology for visually impaired or blinds in graphical manner as follows (see Fig. 4, 5 and 6):

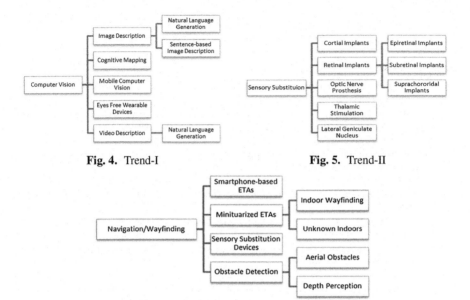

Fig. 4. Trend-I   **Fig. 5.** Trend-II

Fig. 6. Trend-III

Some of the leading journals with publishers, where quality research articles on assistive technologies for vision disability people or people with blindness are published, are given here [28]:

1) ACM SIGACCESS Accessibility and Computing (ACM)
2) ACM Transactions on accessible Computing (ACM)
3) Procedia Computer Science (Elsevier)
4) International Journal of Human Computer Studies (Elsevier)
5) Interacting with Computers (Elsevier)
6) ACM Transactions on Applied Perception (ACM)
7) Journal of Visual Impairments and Blinders (AFB Press)
8) Assistive Technology (Taylor and Francis)
9) Personal and Ubiquitous Computing (Springer)
10) Neuroscience and Biobehavioral Reviews (Elsevier)
11) ACM Transactions on Computer-Human Interactions (ACM)
12) International Congress Series (Elsevier)

7   Listing of Some Recent Research and Development Projects in Assistive Technology

See Table 3.

Table 3. Assistive technology projects

Sr. No	Project title	Organisation	Link
1	A 3D printing solution to solve parents' pain with orthotics services	Project Andiamo	https://andiamo.io/contact-us/
2	AAL-VUK: Active and Assisted Living – Visionless supporting Framework	Erlang Solutions	www.erlang-solutions.com/contact.html
3	AAL-WELL: ambient assistive living technologies for wellness, engagement, and long life	University of Sheffield	www.catch.org.uk/contact-us
4	accessibility-enabled Health (aHealth)	Dolphin Computer Access	www.yourdolphin.com/contact
5	Accessible routes from crowdsourced cloud services	University College London	https://www.disabilityinnovation.com/projects/arccs
6	Acoustic signal processing and scene analysis for socially assistive robots	Imperial College London	www.imperial.ac.uk/people/c.evers
7	ADAM: anthropomorphic design for advanced manufacture	University of Nottingham	www.nottingham.ac.uk/engineering/people/ian.ashcroft
8	Adaptive assistive rehabilitative technology: beyond the clinic	University of Warwick	www.aartbc.org/index.php/contact
9	Additive manufacture value chain to deliver bespoke orthotics within 48 h with greatly improved health economics	University of Salford; FDM Digital Solutions	www.salford.ac.uk/health-sciences/health-academics/rhs067
10	AeroPlus pressure ulcer care recliner device for plus sized users	Medstrom	www.medstrom.com/contact-us
11	ATTILA trial: assistive technology and telecare to maintain independent living at home for people with dementia	South London & Maudsley NHS Foundation Trust	robert.j.howard@kcl.ac.uk
12	Balance Right in Multiple Sclerosis (BRiMS): A guided self-management programme to reduce falls and improve quality of life, balance and mobility in people with Multiple Sclerosis	Plymouth Hospitals NHS Trust	www.plymouth.ac.uk/research/balance-right-in-multiple-sclerosis
13	ColourSpecs: a wearable colour identification system for people with impaired colour vision	University of Dundee	www.computing.dundee.ac.uk/about/staff/15
14	Dementia and imagination: connecting communities and developing well-being through socially engaged visual arts practice	Bangor University	https://gtr.rcuk.ac.uk/projects?ref=AH%2FK00333X%2F1

(continued)

Table 3. (*continued*)

Sr. No	Project title	Organisation	Link
15	F.R.A.M.E. (facial remote activity monitoring eyewear) An inconspicuous, non-invasive, mobile sensor device for real-time control of assistive technologies through facial expression	Nottingham Trent University	www.ntu.ac.uk/staff-profiles/archit ecture-design-builtenvironment/phi lip-breedon
16	GetAMoveOn: transforming health through enabling mobility	University College London Interaction Centre	https://uclic.ucl.ac.uk/research/hea lth-and-well-being/gamo
17	GyroGlove: tremor-reducing device for Parkinson's disease	GyroGear	https://gyrogear.co/contact
18	Home Service -voice-enabled assistive technology	University of Sheffield	www.catch.org.uk/contact-us/
19	The MARQUE project: Managing Agitation and Raising QUality of Life. A project to improve quality of life in people with moderate or severe dementia	University College London	www.ucl.ac.uk/psychiatry/marque/ about-the-project
20	Mobility and Quality of Life: Improving methods of economic evaluation of assistive technology for adults and children with impaired mobility	Bangor University	https://cheme.bangor.ac.uk/Nathan BrayBiography.php

8 Conclusion

The survey can be summarized as the existing assistive technology devices have restricted number of features and functions, lesser scientific or technological significance, and are costly. From the survey conducted, guidelines for the next research and design of a prototype to be built for vision impaired can be identified. The problem is not that a system with all the features mentioned here can be productized or not, but a novel idea that conceives a AT that lasts in time and can be adopted globally is still awaited. The rapid increase and advancements in mobile technologies, novel inventions in image processing and computer vision, shrinking size of electronic devices and pioneering medical advancements will surely drive this area of research further towards more successful assistive devices.

References

1. Kay, L.: An ultrasonic sensing probe as a mobility aid for the blind. Ultrasonics, 2(2) (1964). https://doi.org/10.1016/0041-624X(64)90382-8. https://www.sciencedirect.com/jou rnal/ultrasonics/vol/2/issue/2.
2. Koren, J., Borenstein, Y.: The vector field histogram-fast obstacle avoidance for mobile robots. IEEE Trans. Robot. Autom. 7(3) (1991).https://doi.org/10.1109/70.88137. https://ieeexplore. ieee.org/document/88137/citations#citations.
3. Borenstein, J., Ulrich, I.: The guidecane-a computerized travel aid for the active guidance of blind pedestrians. Paper presented at the IEEE International Conference on Robotics and Automation, Albuquerque, NM, USA, 25 April 1997 (1997)

4. Loomis, J.M., Golledge, R.G., Klatzky, R.L.: Navigation system for the blind: auditory display modes and guidance. Presence **7**(2), 193–203 (1998). https://doi.org/10.1162/105474 698565677. https://ieeexplore.ieee.org/document/6788010

5. Kay, L.: Auditory perception of objects by blind persons using bioacoustic high resolution air sonar. J. Acoust. Soc. Am. **107**, 3266–3275 (2000). https://doi.org/10.1121/1.429399

6. Kim, Y.J., Kim, C.-H., Kim, B.K.: Design of an auditory guidance system for the blind with signal transformation from stereo ultrasonic to binaural audio. Artif. Life Robot. **4**(4) (2000). https://doi.org/10.1007/BF02481178

7. Ross, D.A., Blasch, B.B.: Wearable interfaces for orientation and wayfinding. Paper presented at the Fourth International ACM Conference on Assistive Technologies, Arlington, Virginia, USA, 13–15 November 2000

8. Loomis, J.M., Golledge, R.G., Klatzky, R.: Gps-Based Navigation Systems for the Visually Impaired. Fundam. Wearab. Comput. Augment. Reality **429**, 46 (2001)

9. Kulyukin, V., Gharpure, C., Nicholson, J., Pavithran, S.: RFID in robot-assisted indoor navigation for the visually impaired. In: IEEE/RSJ International Conference on Intelligent Robots and Systems, Sendai, Japan, 28 September–2 October 2004

10. Fernández, J.L., Sanz, R., Benayas, J.A., Diéguez, A.R.: Improving collision avoidance for mobile robots in partially known environments: the beam curvature method. Robot. Auton. Syst. 46, 205–219 (2004). https://doi.org/10.1016/j.robot.2004.02.004. www.elsevier.com/locate/robot

11. Calder, D.J.: Assistive technology interfaces for the blind. In: 3rd IEEE International Conference on Digital Ecosystems and Technologies, Istanbul, France. IEEE, 1–3 June 2009 (2009)

12. Dionisi, A., Sardini, E., Serpelloni, M.: Wearable object detection system for the blind. Paper presented at the IEEE Instrumentation and Measurement Technology Conference (2012)

13. Rodríguez, A., Yebes, J.J., Alcantarilla, P.F., Bergasa, L.M., Almazán, J., Cela, A.: Assisting the Visually Impaired: Obstacle Detection and Warning System by Acoustic Feedback. Sens.—Open Access J. **12**(2), 17476–17496 (2012). https://doi.org/10.3390/s121217476. www.mdpi.com/journal/sensors

14. Al-Fahoum, A., Al-Hmoud, H., Al-Fraihat, A.: A smart infrared microcontroller-based blind guidance system. Active Passive Electron. Compon. **2013**, 1–7 (2013). https://doi.org/10.1155/2013/726480

15. Sharma, P., Shimi, S.L., Chatterji, S.: Design of microcontroller based virtual eye for the blind. Int. J. Sci. Res. Eng. Technol. (IJSRET), **3**(8), 1137–1142 (2014). https://doi.org/10.17148/IJIREEICE.2015.3306. www.ijsret.org

16. Dakopoulos, D., Bourbakis, N.G.: Wearable obstacle avoidance electronic travel aids for blind: a survey. IEEE Trans. Syst. Man Cybern. Part C (Appl. Rev.) **40**(1), 25–35 (2014). https://doi.org/10.1109/TSMCC.2009.2021255.

17. Gurubaran, G.K., Ramalingam, M.: A survey of voice aided electronic stick for visually impaired people. Int. J. Innov. Res. Adv. Eng. (IJIRAE) **1**(8) (2014). www.ijirae.com

18. Prakash, J., Harish, P., Deepika, K.: Android based object recognition into voice input to aid visually impaired. Int. J. Adv. Technol. Eng. Sci. **3**(1) (2015). www.ijates.com

19. Verschae, R., Ruiz-del-Solar, J.: Object detection: current and future directions. Front. Robot. AI **2**, 29 (2015). https://doi.org/10.3389/frobt.2015.00029. https://www.frontiersin.org/article/10.3389/frobt.2015.00029

20. Varun Raj, S.P., Das, A.R.: A low cost outdoor assistive navigation system for blind people. Int. J. Innov. Res. Comput. Commun. Eng. **3**(6), 5767–5774 (2015). https://doi.org/10.15680/ijircce.2015.0306149. IJIRCCE. https://www.ijircce.com/upload/2015/june/149_43_A%20LOW.pdf

21. Ahn, H., Rhee, S.-B.: Research of object recognition and tracking based on feature matching. In: Park, J., Stojmenovic, I., Jeong, H., Yi, G. (eds.) Computer Science and its Applications, vol. 330, pp. 1071–1076. Springer, Heidelberg (2015). https://doi.org/10.1007/978-3-662-45402-2_152

22. Csapó, Á., Wersényi, G., Nagy, H., Stockman, T.: A survey of assistive technologies and applications for blind users on mobile platforms: a review and foundation for research. J. Multimod. User Interfaces **9**(4), 275–286 (2015). https://doi.org/10.1007/s12193-015-0182-7

23. El-hariri, E., El-Bendary, N., Hassanien, A.E., Snasel, V.: An assistive object recognition system for enhancing seniors quality of life. Paper presented at the International Conference on Communication, Management and Information Technology, ICCMIT 2015 (2015)

24. Mohane, V., Gode, C.: Object recognition for blind people using portable camera. In: World Conference on Futuristic Trends in Research and Innovation for Social Welfare (WCFTR 2016), Coimbatore, India, 29 Feb–1 March 2016. IEEE (2016)

25. Udgirkar, S., Sarokar, S., Gore, S., Kakuste, D., Chaskar, S.: Object detection system for blind people. J. Paper Int. J. Innov. Res. Comput. Commun. Eng. **4**(9) (2016). https://doi.org/10.15680/IJIRCCE.2016.0409040

26. Parkhi, S., Lokhande, S.S., Thombare, N.D.: Vocal vision android application for visually impaired person. Int. J. Sci. Eng. Technol. Res. (IJSETR) **5**(6) (2016). www.ijsetr.org

27. Mohanapriya, R., Nirmala, U., Pearlin Priscilla, C.: Smart vision for the blind people. Int. J. Adv. Res. Electron. Commun. Eng. (IJARECE) **5**(7) (2016)

28. Bhowmick, A., Hazarika, S.M.: An insight into assistive technology for the visually impaired and blind people: state-of-the-art and future trends. J. Multimod. User Interfaces **11**(2), 149–172 (2016). https://doi.org/10.1007/s12193-016-0235-6

29. Zraqou, J.S., Alkhadour, W.M., Siam, M.Z.: Real-time objects recognition approach for assisting blind people. Int. J. Curr. Eng. Technol. **7**(1), (2017). NPRESSCO. https://inpressco.com/category/ijcet

30. Mocanu, B., Tapu, R., Zaharia, T.: Seeing without sight — an automatic cognition system dedicated to blind and visually impaired people. In: IEEE International Conference on Computer Vision Workshops (ICCVW), pp. 1452–1459 (2017). https://ieeexplore.ieee.org/document/8265382

31. Wang, H.-C., Katzschmann, R.K., Teng, S., Araki, B., Giarré, L., Rus, D.: Enabling independent navigation for visually impaired people through a wearable vision-based feedback system. Paper presented at the IEEE International Conference on Robotics and Automation (ICRA), Singapore, 29 May–3 June 2017 (2017)

32. Yashas, M., Maalik, K.S., Ashfaq, M.Z.M., De Silva, K.P.S.H., Ragulan, S.: Blind guider: an it solution for visually impaired people. Int. J. Sci. Res. Publ. **7**(11), 700–703 (2017). https://www.ijsrp.org/research-paper-1117.php?rp=P716990

33. Kaur, B., Bhattacharya, J.: Scene perception system for visually impaired based on object detection and classification using multimodal deep convolutional neural network. J. Electr. Imaging **28**(01), 1–16 (2019). https://doi.org/10.1117/1.JEI.28.1.013031

34. Usha, B.A., Sangeetha, K.N., Vikram, C.M.: Blinds personal assistant application for android. Int. J. Res. Appl. Sci. Eng. Technol. (IJRASET) **7**(1), 138–144 (2019)

35. Koharwal, S., Awwad, S.B., Vyakaranam, A.: Navigation system for blind - third eye. Int. J. Innov. Technol. Explor. Eng. (TM) **8**(5) (2019). IJITEE. https://www.ijitee.org/download/volume-8-issue-5/

36. Ponnada, S., Yarramalle, S.: Object identification to assist visually challenged. Int. J. Eng. Adv. Technol. (IJEAT) **8**(4) (2019): D6619048419/19. Blue Eyes Intelligence Engineering Sciences Publication. https://www.ijeat.org/download/volume-8-issue-4/

37. Kayukawa, S., et al.: Bbeep: a sonic collision avoidance system for blind travellers and nearby pedestrians. Paper presented at the CHI 2019 Proceedings of the 2019 CHI Conference on Human Factors in Computing Systems, Glasgow, Scotland, UK, 04–09 May (2019)
38. Hoang, V.-N., Nguyen, T.-H., Le, T.-L., Tran, T.-H., Vuong, T.-P., Vuillerme, N.: Obstacle detection and warning system for visually impaired people based on electrode matrix and mobile kinect. Vietnam J. Comput. Sci. 4(2), 71–83 (2016). https://doi.org/10.1007/s40595-016-0075-z

Script Identification of Movie Titles from Posters

Mridul Ghosh[1]([✉]), Himadri Mukherjee[2], Sayan Saha Roy[3],
Sk Md Obaidullah[4], K. C. Santosh[5], and Kaushik Roy[2]

[1] Department of Computer Science, Shyampur Siddheswari Mahavidyalaya,
Howrah, India
mridulxyz@gmail.com
[2] Department of Computer Science, West Bengal State University, Kolkata, India
himadrim027@gmail.com, kaushik.mrg@gmail.com
[3] Department of Radio Physics and Electronics, Calcutta University, Kolkata, India
sayansaharoy97@gmail.com
[4] Department of Computer Science, and Engineering, Aliah University,
Kolkata, India
sk.obaidullah@gmail.com
[5] Department of Computer Science, University of South Dakota,
Vermillion, SD, USA
santosh.kc@usd.edu

Abstract. In this work, a new problem of script identification in movie posters has been addressed. Movie posters contain an amalgamation of different types of objects like images of actors, sceneries, different graphic symbols, several texts having disparate fonts, colors, textures, etc. Such a complex set of components makes it a challenging task in the automatic identification of the script of the movie titles for further processing. Before identifying the script of the titles, localization of the texts is very much necessary. Using transfer learning and non-maximum suppression the text localization has been performed followed textural feature-based script identification among Bangla, Devanagari, and Roman. We experimented with these poster images from Tollywood, Bollywood, and Hollywood and obtained the highest accuracy of 90.65%.

Keywords: Transfer learning · Script identification · Textural features

1 Introduction

Optical character recognition [1] has a fundamental reliance on script identification system particularly when the processed data is multi-lingual or multi-scripted. Due to the randomly enhancing volume of multimedia data, particularly recorded by mobile terminals, the recognition of text content in natural scenes has emerged as a crucial necessity in the domains of pattern recognition,

K. C. Santosh—Senior Member in IEEE.

© Springer Nature Singapore Pte Ltd. 2021
K. C. Santosh and B. Gawali (Eds.): RTIP2R 2020, CCIS 1380, pp. 111–124, 2021.
https://doi.org/10.1007/978-981-16-0507-9_10

computer vision, and multimedia. Diverging from earlier efforts developed for document images [2,3] and videos, the present research concentrates on recognizing the script/language types of texts in natural images, at the word, text line, or character level [4–7]. Text in natural scenes is accompanied by rich and developed semantics with complex graphic styles [8]. Automatic text recognition in scene images involves three main parts:

- Automatic text localization
- Script identification
- Text recognition using OCR engine.

Automatic text localization in scene images has been studied extensively [9,10] but, due to diverseness in text, background complexity, low resolution, etc., the solution is yet to be concluded. If the localization and script identification is perfect the text recognition is trivial since script depended OCR engines are available. Today we are very much concerned about automatic text localization and script identification from scene images. Different document images have been discussed in the literature for text localization, script identification, or text recognition [11,12]. But, text extraction from movie poster images has not been reflected in the state of art so far. Movie poster images contain artistic writing, images of artists in the movie, different graphic symbols and scenarios, different texts like a movie title, production house, director, short explanation of the title, sponsors, etc. So, the total contents in poster images are very complex as it is an amalgamation of many components to attract people to watch. Here is the challenge lies in extracting not only the text regions but also to take out only the movie title. Movie in three different languages namely, Bengali, Hindi, English have been considered in this present work since a large mass of people in India watches these three types of the movie which are produced in Tollywood, Bollywood and Holywood industry or other words, due to huge popularity of these three types movie, it is justified to work on script identification for non-native spoken or written persons.

Movie titles reflect the subject of the movie but, it is not always possible for non-native speaking/written person to know the movie title from posters in theatre which lead to non-interest in that movie, motivates us to work in this topic. Also, since a large mass of people uses Bengali, Hindi, and English in their daily communication and education medium, encourages us to work on these scripts.

The following are the contributions in this work:

- Using the transfer learning-based approach and non-maximum suppression method the texts in the posters are extracted.
- By tuning the parameters of the bounding boxes the titles are extracted.
- Using textural features the script identification has been done considering machine learning classifiers.

In Fig. 1 the flowchart of our proposed method has been depicted.

The organization of the rest of this paper is as follows: In Sect. 2 literature study on the subject of different types of text localization and script identification has been presented. Dataset collection has been discussed in Sect. 3. In Sect. 4, the proposed method has been discussed. Section 5 describes the experiment followed by conclusion in Sect. 6.

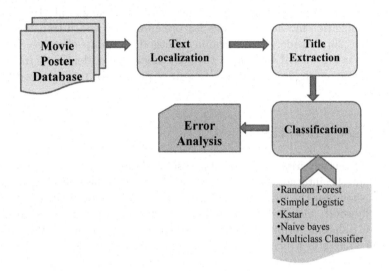

Fig. 1. Flowchart of our proposed method.

2   Literature Study

In [13] Shi et al. discussed a deep learning-based framework for script identification in natural images and videos. Deep feature maps were obtained from the pre-trained CNN model and discriminative clustering on extracted features along with mid-level illustration was amalgamated. Texture based feature extraction methods was discussed in [14] and also MAP adaptation was considered for making a global script model having prior knowledge of different script classes. Shi et al. in another paper [15] proposed a novel method for scene text detection by graph model through MSERs technique. Using MSERs method the text and non-text regions were labeled and from geometrical features and using cost function on the min-cut/max-flow algorithm the potential text blocks were identified and using ICDAR 2011 dataset the robustness of this method was tested. Bhunia et al. in [16] proposed a CNN-LSTM framework for scene text images and video scripts identification. They converted images into patches and fed it to CNN-LSTM network and local and global features were extracted from the intermediate layers and the last layer of the network respectively followed by fusion technique. Latin based languages were identified by word wise from degraded documents as discussed in [17,18]. Obaidullah et al. [11] presented a page-level handwritten Indian document image dataset and distinguished those Indic scripts using different directional strokes and structural features. Ghosh et al. [6] discussed the identification of artistic texts in images at the character level, considering real and synthetic image data. They proposed an isotropic dilation algorithm to join broken components of characters. Features were extracted using geometrical as well as texture-based features. Before script identification text localization is an important aspect in the system. Huang et al. [19] proposed the text localization method by stroke feature and stroke width transform. Neumann et al. [20] considered the pruning method to group effective character regions and using MSER technique the text blocks were identified. In another work, Neumann et al. [21] proposed a two-stage process for text localization and recognition.

3   Dataset Collection

To carry out our experiment, we created a small dataset by collecting the poster images from the internet since there is no standard dataset available on this topic. To showcase the diversity and make this work more challenging, Tollywood, Bollywood, and Hollywood movie posters were considered where we can have three different scripts of Bangla, Devanagari, and Roman. We collected 695 poster images in which the movie titles in 149 images are printed in Bangla scripts, in 145 images titles are in Devanagari and in 401 instances where titles are printed in Roman.

4   Proposed Method

The proposed method can be categorized into two phases: first phase concerns about text localization and movie title extraction while in the second phase, feature extraction and classification have been discussed for script identification.

4.1   Text Localization

In the first phase of our work, the automatic text localization method was in concern i.e., extraction of only the text portions in the movie posters. This process was accomplished with the help of transfer learning [22] based approach. Before that, the images were normalized with the size of [300, 300] for removing the size disparity. In transfer learning a related pre-trained model which was trained by a large dataset was considered and by tuning the parameters of the neural network, our model was developed. In this work, the pre-trained model named, frozen-east-text -detection was taken in deep neural network (DNN) [23] framework and this network was tuned by setting the parameter value scale factor and confidence level. The scale factor was used in normalizing the values of R, G, B plates of the images, and the confidence level to help in-text localization by adjusting its value. In this work, we experimentally set the scale factor as 1, 1.8, and 2.5, and the confidence level was taken 0.4. Blobs/rectangles were created from this network. Blob detection signifies the finding of points or regions where there is a considerable dissimilarity in colors, contrasts, brightness compared to the adjacent regions. Blobs are having related pixel values enclosing some portion of an image. After blobs extraction the correct blobs are selected in two phases i.e., probability calculation and coordinate extraction. By probability value of each blob the score of the blobs were calculated and using coordinates extraction of the correct bounding boxes are extracted. Those blobs were considered in this process whose probability is higher and lower scored blobs are ignored.

In the real world, texts in the posters may not always be horizontally placed but it may get oriented. Considering this situation, we need to find out the coordinates of the rectangle which makes an angle θ with the x-axis. Let the initial coordinates of the rectangle or offset value is (A, B). The following are the equations to find out the other required coordinate (C, D) of the rectangle.

$$C = A + Br * cos\theta + He * sin\theta \tag{1}$$

$$D = B - Br * sin\theta + He * cos\theta \tag{2}$$

Here, He and Br represents the length of the two sides of the rectangle. This procedure is shown in Fig. 2.

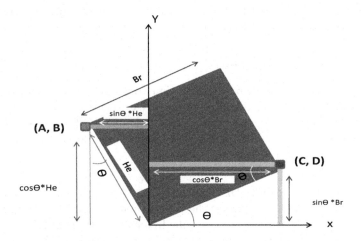

Fig. 2. Coordinate extraction for bounding box when the text line is oriented.

After the bounding boxes were determined, genuine boundary boxes were detected from the best scoring boxes and suppressing the remaining low scoring boxes compared to the best one using non-maximum suppression [24], and thus localized texts were obtained.

4.2 Movie Title Extraction

In a movie poster, many text blocks are there for representing movie information like a movie title, names of the production house, producer, director, actors, sponsors, etc. To extract only the movie title boxes amid different text boxes, we assumed that the movie titles were written in large fonts compared to other texts in the poster and if the title consisted of in dissimilar sized fonts that will also be close to the large fonts. Considering this assumption in the account, we found out the boundary box with a large area, height, and width compared to the rest boxes and also found out the boxes which follow the rule as mentioned below.

if $(l \geq float(L/2)$ && $w \geq float(W/2)$ && $ar \geq A/1.2)$
$S = BoundingBox(B_{l,w,ar})$

where, L, W, and A denote the length, width, and area of the biggest bounding box, and l, w, ar represents the same parameters of the other bounding boxes which were small compared to the large bounding box.

In Fig. 4 sample movie poster images of Tollywood, Bollywood, and Hollywood movies from our dataset are shown. We created images having zero intensity value and of the same size as the original normalized images and copied the bounding boxes into these black images which are shown in Fig. 5 as localized text images. In Fig. 5 it is observed that all the texts in the poster images and the fonts of the movie titles are larger compared to the rest. This clue helps us in detecting and extracting the titles. In Fig. 6 the extracted movie titles as discussed in process Sect. 4.2 are shown.

4.3   Feature Consideration

After text localization feature consideration could be a major job during this work. Features should be robust enough to categorize the scripts into corresponding classes and at an equivalent point, it should be effortlessly computable. During this paper, three differing kinds of texture-based feature extraction techniques were considered to spot the scripts.

Discrete Gabor Wavelet: Discrete Gabor wavelet [7, 25] capable of extracting low-level features and eliminating the time-frequency duality of Fourier transform, capable of extract energy at specific frequency and direction. The discrete Gabor wavelet transform of an image $I_m(k, l)$ of dimension $M \times N$ can be written as

$$\gamma_{pq}(k, l) = \sum_m \sum_n I_m(x - m, y - n)\psi^*_{pq}(m, n) \tag{3}$$

Where m, n are the filter mask sizes and p, q denotes scale and orientations respectively. ψ^* is the complex conjugate of mother wavelet ψ. For 5 scales and 8 orientations the real part of Gabor wavelet is shown in Fig. 3.

Gray Level Co-occurrence Matrix (GLCM): The spatial dependencies in the gray level image can be found out by using GLCM [7, 26]. GLCM is generally calculated using the pixel number and orientations of the pixels. GLCM

Fig. 3. The real part of Gabor wavelet having 5 scales and 8 orientations.

calculates how often a pixel with gray-level value occurs either horizontally $(0°)$, vertically $(90°)$, or diagonally $(-45°, -135°)$ to adjacent pixels and the average value of each distance of the resultant orientations makes the resulting value.

Zernike Moment: Moments measure the distributions of pixels around the center of gravity of an entire image. The reason for using Zernike moment [27] is that it has rotation-invariant features and capable of preserving image information with the least amount of information redundancy. Considering the gray level value of individual pixels $g(i, j)$, in generalized form Zernike moment of order p with repetition r of over an image can be represented as

$$Z_{pr} = \frac{p+1}{\pi} \sum_i \sum_j [A_{p,r}]^* g(i, j), i^2 + j^2 \leq 1 \qquad (4)$$

where, $A_{p,r}$ represents Zernike polynomials.

It is not possible to consider all features extracted from these three extractors because of the feature dimension issue. From Gabor wavelet for 5 scales and 8 orientations, we were having 2560 numbers of features. All these features will not be required in our work because many features were redundant and consequently could make classification complexity high. To reduce the complexity of classification, we exploited a very popular feature reduction technique PCA [28] and retained our Gabor wavelet feature dimension to 50. From GLCM and Zernike moment, 22 features and 20 moments were extracted respectively. Thus our total feature dimension became 92 × 695.

4.4   Classification

To test the efficiency of our method, we used different well-known machine learning classifiers namely, Random Forest [29], Naive Bayes [30], Multiclass Classifier

Fig. 4. Movie poster images from our dataset (source: Internet)

[31], Simple Logistics [32], Kstar [33]. In testing, a k-fold cross-validation approach was used where one set was treated as a testing set and rest as the training
set and next time another set was picked up as testing and rest as the training
set and this process was repeated n times.

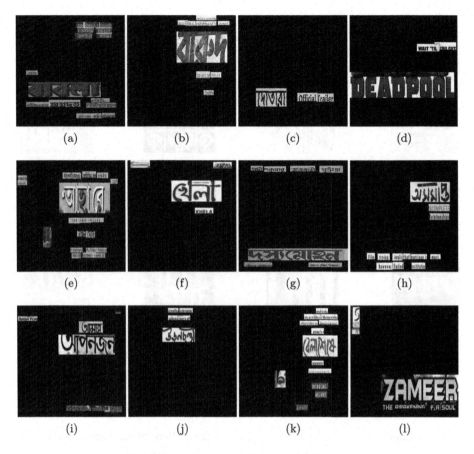

Fig. 5. Localized texts from poster images

5 Experiment

5.1 Result and Discussion

During experimentation, 5 fold cross-validation was considered for all 5 classifiers. From Table 1 it is observed that using Random forest, the accuracy obtained is highest compared to the other classifiers. The parameters used in Table 1 was discussed in [6]. Since the random forest produced the best result, we further explored the accuracy by changing the number of folds from 5 to 25 having 5 fold cross-validation interval which is shown in Table 2.

In Table 2 it is seen that at 25 fold, the accuracy of the random forest becomes 89.64% which is best among other folds. Keeping this fold, we experimented with random forest by changing the number of iterations which is reflected in Table 3. At 2500 iteration we got the best accuracy value of random forest of 90.65%. The confusion matrix for 25 fold cross-validation and 2500 iteration of random forest is shown in Table 4.

Fig. 6. Extracted movie titles from localized texts.

Table 1. Classifier performance with different parameters.

Classifier	Accuracy	Kappa Statistic	Root Mean Square Error
Naive Bayes	71.94	0.5551	0.4067
Kstar	79.42	0.5994	0.3659
Multiclass Classifier	80.43	0.6584	0.3157
Simple Logistic	88.77	0.8032	0.2332
Random Forest	89.21	0.8056	0.2727

Table 2. Cross validation fold vs. Accuracy of random forest classifier.

Folds	Accuracy (%)
5	89.21
10	87.76
15	89.21
20	89.06
25	89.64

Table 3. Iteration vs. Accuracy for random forest in 25 fold cross validation

Iteration	Accuracy (%)
200	90.21
500	90.22
800	89.93
1000	90.07
1500	89.92
2000	90.53
2500	90.65

5.2   Error Analysis

From Table 1 it can be observed that using Bayes classifier the classification error rate of 28.06% is higher among all five classifiers followed by Kstar of 20.58%, Multiclass classifier of 19.57%, Simple logistic of 11.23% and Random forest having 10.79%. Using a 25 fold cross-validation random forest gives the lowest error rate of 10.36% and after 2500 iteration with the same fold, the error rate drops to 9.35%. The confusion matrix of the random forest using 25 fold cross-validation and 2500 iteration is shown in Table 4. It is observed that for Bangla script 10 and 22 number of scripts was misclassified to Devanagari and Roman. Using Devanagari script 9 and 19 number of scripts were misclassified to Bangla while Roman 2 and 3 scripts were wrongly classified to Bangla and Devanagari. The possible reasons for misclassification are that there are similarities in geometrical shapes in a few characters in Bangla, Devanagari, and Roman scripts and the issue of quality of data. Since the data were collected from the internet, it was supposed that there was no specific high configuration camera was used for capturing data: results low illumination issues. Also, after movie title extraction (shown in Fig. 6), it is observed that there were dissimilar, complex, graphics in the background that makes it difficult in script identification.

Table 4. Confusion Matrix of Random forest classifier at 25 fold cross validation and 2500 iteration.

	Bangla	Devanagari	Roman
Bangla	117	10	22
Devanagari	9	117	19
Roman	2	3	396

6   Conclusion

In this paper, a novel problem of movie title extraction from movie posters of Tollywood, Bollywood, Hollywood movies, and script identification of titles was discussed. Using transfer learning and non-maximum suppression the bounding boxes for texts were identified. By experimentation, amid many bounding boxes, the movie title boxes were extracted. The textual features were considered for script identification and by using machine learning classifiers the accuracies of our proposed method were obtained. The low quality of data was one of the reasons for high error rate also since the background removal method was not adopted, different background textures were also responsible for the error in this work. Though the assumption was taken that the movie titles were having larger fonts, this may not hold for all images. In a few posters, the reverse stuff also experienced. In the future, we will consider these issues and also experiment with deep learning-based classification techniques for gaining a commendable accuracy rate. Also, we will consider other Indic scripts like Marathi, Gurumukhi, Telegu, Tamil, etc. for text localization context.

References

1. Peng, X., Cao, H., Setlur, S., Govindaraju, V., Natarajan, P.: Multilingual OCR research and applications: an overview. In: Proceedings of the 4th International Workshop on Multilingual OCR, p. 1. ACM (2013)
2. Obaidullah, S.M., Santosh, K.C., Halder, C., Das, N., Roy, K.: Word-level thirteen official Indic languages database for script identification in multi-script documents. In: Santosh, K.C., Hangarge, M., Bevilacqua, V., Negi, A. (eds.) RTIP2R 2016. CCIS, vol. 709, pp. 16–27. Springer, Singapore (2017). https://doi.org/10.1007/978-981-10-4859-3_2
3. Roy, K.: Document image analysis for a major Indic script Bangla - advancement and scope. In: Santosh, K.C., Hangarge, M., Bevilacqua, V., Negi, A. (eds.) RTIP2R 2016. CCIS, vol. 709, pp. 125–134. Springer, Singapore (2017). https://doi.org/10.1007/978-981-10-4859-3_12
4. Pati, P.B., Ramakrishnan, A.G.: Word level multi-script identification. Pattern Recogn. Lett. **29**(9), 1218–1229 (2008)
5. Shi, B., Yao, C., Zhang, C., Guo, X., Huang, F., Bai, X.: Automatic script identification in the wild. In: 2015 13th International Conference on Document Analysis and Recognition (ICDAR), pp. 531–535. IEEE (2015)
6. Ghosh, M., Obaidullah, S.M., Santosh, K.C., Das, N., Roy, K.: Artistic multicharacter script identification using iterative isotropic dilation algorithm. In: Santosh, K.C., Hegadi, R.S. (eds.) RTIP2R 2018. CCIS, vol. 1037, pp. 49–62. Springer, Singapore (2019). https://doi.org/10.1007/978-981-13-9187-3_5
7. Ghosh, M., Mukherjee, H., Obaidullah, S.M., Santosh, K.C., Das, N., Roy, K.: Artistic multi-script identification at character level with extreme learning machine. Procedia Comput. Sci. **167**, 496–505 (2020)
8. Santosh, K.C.: Complex and composite graphical symbol recognition and retrieval: a quick review. In: Santosh, K.C., Hangarge, M., Bevilacqua, V., Negi, A. (eds.) RTIP2R 2016. CCIS, vol. 709, pp. 3–15. Springer, Singapore (2017). https://doi.org/10.1007/978-981-10-4859-3_1

9. Yi, C., Tian, Y.: Assistive text reading from complex background for blind persons. In: Iwamura, M., Shafait, F. (eds.) CBDAR 2011. LNCS, vol. 7139, pp. 15–28. Springer, Heidelberg (2012). https://doi.org/10.1007/978-3-642-29364-1_2

10. Yan, C., et al.: A fast Uyghur text detector for complex background images. IEEE Trans. Multimed. **20**(12), 3389–3398 (2018)

11. Obaidullah, S.M., Halder, C., Santosh, K.C., Das, N., Roy, K.: PHDIndic_11: page-level handwritten document image dataset of 11 official Indic scripts for script identification. Multimed. Tools Appl. **77**(2), 1643–1678 (2018)

12. Pal, U., Sharma, N., Wakabayashi, T., Kimura, F.: Off-line handwritten character recognition of Devnagari script. In: Ninth International Conference on Document Analysis and Recognition (ICDAR 2007), vol. 1, pp. 496–500. IEEE (2007)

13. Shi, B., Bai, X., Yao, C.: Script identification in the wild via discriminative convolutional neural network. Pattern Recogn. **52**, 448–458 (2016)

14. Busch, A., Boles, W.W., Sridharan, S.: Texture for script identification. IEEE Trans. Pattern Anal. Mach. Intell. **27**(11), 1720–1732 (2005)

15. Shi, C., Wang, C., Xiao, B., Zhang, Y., Gao, S.: Scene text detection using graph model built upon maximally stable extremal regions. Pattern Recogn. Lett. **34**(2), 107–116 (2013)

16. Bhunia, A.K., Konwer, A., Bhunia, A.K., Bhowmick, A., Roy, P.P., Pal, U.: Script identification in natural scene image and video frames using an attention based Convolutional-LSTM network. Pattern Recogn. **85**, 172–184 (2019)

17. Shijian, L., Tan, C.L.: Script and language identification in noisy and degraded document images. IEEE Trans. Pattern Anal. Mach. Intell. **30**(1), 14–24 (2007)

18. Lu, S., Tan, C.L., Huang, W.: Language identification in degraded and distorted document images. In: Bunke, H., Spitz, A.L. (eds.) DAS 2006. LNCS, vol. 3872, pp. 232–242. Springer, Heidelberg (2006). https://doi.org/10.1007/11669487_21

19. Huang, W., Lin, Z., Yang, J., Wang, J.: Text localization in natural images using stroke feature transform and text covariance descriptors. In: Proceedings of the IEEE International Conference on Computer Vision, pp. 1241–1248 (2013)

20. Neumann, L., Matas, J.: Text localization in real-world images using efficiently pruned exhaustive search. In: 2011 International Conference on Document Analysis and Recognition, pp. 687–691. IEEE (2011)

21. Neumann, L., Matas, J.: Real-time scene text localization and recognition. In: 2012 IEEE Conference on Computer Vision and Pattern Recognition, pp. 3538–3545. IEEE (2012)

22. Krizhevsky, A., Sutskever, I., Hinton, G.E.: ImageNet classification with deep convolutional neural networks. In: Advances in Neural Information Processing Systems, pp. 1097–1105 (2012)

23. Hinton, G., et al.: Deep neural networks for acoustic modelling in speech recognition. IEEE Signal Process. Mag. **29** (2012)

24. He, W., Zhang, X.Y., Yin, F., Liu, C.L.: Deep direct regression for multi-oriented scene text detection. In: Proceedings of the IEEE International Conference on Computer Vision, pp. 745–753 (2017)

25. Zhang, D., Wong, A., Indrawan, M., Lu, G.: Content-based image retrieval using Gabor texture features. IEEE Trans. PAMI **13** (2000)

26. Soh, L.K., Tsatsoulis, C.: Texture analysis of SAR sea ice imagery using gray level co-occurrence matrices. IEEE Trans. Geosci. Remote Sens. **37**(2), 780–795 (1999)

27. Khotanzad, A., Hong, Y.H.: Invariant image recognition by Zernike moments. IEEE Trans. Pattern Anal. Mach. Intell. **12**(5), 489–497 (1990)

28. Jolliffe, I.T.: Principal components in regression analysis. In: Jolliffe, I.T. (ed.) Principal Component Analysis. SSS, pp. 167–198. Springer, Heidelberg (2002). https://doi.org/10.1007/0-387-22440-8_8

29. Rodriguez-Galiano, V.F., Ghimire, B., Rogan, J., Chica-Olmo, M., Rigol-Sanchez, J.P.: An assessment of the effectiveness of a random forest classifier for land-cover classification. ISPRS J. Photogram. Remote Sens. **67**, 93–104 (2012)

30. Rish, I.: An empirical study of the Naive Bayes classifier. In: IJCAI 2001 Workshop on Empirical Methods in Artificial Intelligence, vol. 3, no. 22, pp. 41–46 (2001)

31. Li, T., Zhang, C., Ogihara, M.: A comparative study of feature selection and multiclass classification methods for tissue classification based on gene expression. Bioinformatics **20**(15), 2429–2437 (2004)

32. Gardezi, S.J.S., Faye, I., Eltoukhy, M.M.: Analysis of mammogram images based on texture features of curvelet Sub-bands. In: Fifth International Conference on Graphic and Image Processing (ICGIP 2013), vol. 9069, p. 906924. International Society for Optics and Photonics (2014)

33. Thepade, S.D., Kalbhor, M.M.: Image cataloging using Bayes, Function, Lazy, Rule, Tree classifier families with row mean of Fourier transformed image content. In: 2015 International Conference on Information Processing (ICIP), pp. 680–684. IEEE (2015)

Ensemble of Nested Dichotomies for Author Identification System Using Similarity-Based Textual Features

Ankita Dhar[1(✉)], Himadri Mukherjee[1], Sk. Md. Obaidullah[2],
and Kaushik Roy[1]

[1] Department of Computer Science, West Bengal State University, Kolkata, India
`ankita.ankie@gmail.com, kaushik.mrg@gmail.com`
[2] Department of Computer Science and Engineering, Aliah University, Kolkata, India
`sk.obaidullah@gmail.com`

Abstract. Author identification appears to be one of the blooming research areas in the domain of Natural Language Processing (NLP) which helps in identifying the particular author of a respective piece of text. Every author has a unique style of writing based on the linguistic and stylistic study that helps in identifying one author from another. This paper aims to present an author identification technique that uses similarity-based textual features to train the ensemble of nested dichotomies learning model for identification of different authors depending on their writing patterns. Experiments were performed over 12,000 passages (approx.) with 32,37,80,594 tokens from 50 authors obtained from Bangla literature and the highest accuracy of 96.67% was obtained.

Keywords: Author identification · Similarity-based · Textual features · Ensemble of nested dichotomies

1 Introduction

The author identification problem has grabbed the attention of various researchers. It is generally believed that the authors have a definite style of writing [1] which is noticeable in their piece of art in the form of words and grammar. Author identification has various real-world applications such as cybersecurity, intelligence, law agreement detection, plagiarism detection, and identification of ghost author. One of the most common features used by the researchers for identifying authors is n-gram based feature [2] among which encouraging outcomes have been obtained with the application of bigrams in linguistic forms [3]. The author identification problem is widely been studied in English [4,5]; however very few algorithms have been proposed for a less-resourced language such as Bengali.

Anisuzzaman and Salam [2] proposed a hybrid method by merging n-gram and Naïve Bayes and obtained better accuracy of 95% compared to the individual application of Naïve Bayes. Pandian et al. [6] used text-based features to

© Springer Nature Singapore Pte Ltd. 2021
K. C. Santosh and B. Gawali (Eds.): RTIP2R 2020, CCIS 1380, pp. 125–133, 2021.
https://doi.org/10.1007/978-981-16-0507-9_11

train the J48 algorithm for the identification of authors of poems. Chakraborty and Choudhury [7] implemented 3 graph-based techniques and for each technique, they have clustered the graphs and the weighted graph was generated using a simple graph traversal algorithm. The experiment was performed on the documents from 6 authors and obtained an accuracy of 94.98%. Rakshit et al. [8] experimented with semantic along with stylistic features for identification of poems from 4 categories using SVM and obtained an accuracy of 92.3%.

Digamberrao and Prasad [9] also worked with lexical and stylistic features for identifying 5 authors from 15 philosophical Marathi documents and achieved 80% accuracy using SMO with J48 classifier. Otoom et al. [10] extracted 12 features and using traditional classifiers tested their experiments on 456 texts written by 7 authors and obtained an accuracy of 82%. Rexha et al. [11] experimented with two approaches for determining the authors based on the content matching. Their first study provides the conclusion about the content and stylometric features and their other study shows how the methods and features were evaluated and the decisions were made. Abbasi and Chen [12] worked on a multi-lingual (Arabic and English) approach that generates language-specific characters for identifying authors of online messages.

In the rest of the paper: Sect. 2 illustrates the proposed methodology followed by the experimental results in Sect. 3 and Sect. 4 finally concludes the paper showing some future works in this field.

2 Proposed Methodology

In this study similarity-based textual features were proposed in order to train the ensemble of nested dichotomies learning models for identifying the author of a given piece of text. The idea behind using the proposed approach is to get the similarity of distribution of tokens occurred in different pieces of art written by various authors together with the degree of similarity as well. The working of the proposed method is diagrammatically presented in Fig. 1.

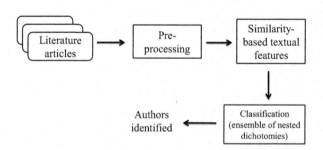

Fig. 1. The workflow of the proposed approach.

2.1 Data

The literature survey shows the unavailability of author identification datasets in Bangla and thus a dataset need to be developed for the experiment consists of around 12,000 passages written by 50 authors from different generations. The present work faces challenges while procuring the articles from various authors in Bengali literature which, being the 6th most spoken languages in the world lacks an adequate amount of resources [13]. The authors are, to name a few, Rabindranath Tagore, Kazi Nazrul Islam, Michael Madhusudan Dutt, Sarat Chandra Chattopadhyay, Bibhutibhushan Bandyopadhyay, Bankim Chandra Chattopadhyay, Jibananda Das, Humayun Ahmed, Samaresh Basu, Shirshendu Mukhopadhyay, Samares Mazumdar, Vivekananda, Sunil Gangopadhyay, Sukumar Ray, Ashapoorna Devi, Suchitra Bhattacharya, Sukanta Bhattacharya, Joy Goswami, Jasimuddin, Tarasankar Bandyopadhyay, Narayan Gangopadhyay, Atul Sur, Buddhadeb Guha, Anisul Hoque, Sharadindu Bandyopadhyay and others whose articles have been procured from www.ebanglalibrary.com. The dataset includes articles covering novels, essays, poems, short and big stories from several authors of different ages having similarities in their writing patterns as well as with lexical stocks.

2.2 Pre-processing

The texts were split into individual 'tokens' using space delimiter before carrying out further experiments and the process is said to be 'tokenization'. The total token count results to be 32,37,80,594. Each extracted token in the set is not informative and essential to be in the feature set for further identification task. These tokens are referred to be as 'stopword' and were removed from the set to get error-free outcomes. The list of stopwords varies according to a specific task, and thus, in this experiment, the list was followed as given in [14]. The total token count after stopword removal task results to be 26, 76, 32, 425.

2.3 Feature

In the present study proposed similarity-based textual features have been proposed that involve different metrics such as word similarity $Word_{sim}$-similarity of tokens between an article and the article in question; article similarity $Article_{sim}$-similarity of an article in question with the number of articles in the total dataset; author similarity $Author_{sim}$-similarity of an article in question with the number of associated authors in total category list; similarity of an article sim-similarity of an article in question in the entire list; average similarity Avg_{sim}-similarity of all the article in a total dataset; and deviation of similarity Dev_{sim}-deviation of the similarity of an article in question with the average similarity. In this study, the similarity-based approach not only estimate the similarity between two given articles but also measure the degree of similarity as well.

Let D_p represent one article and D_q represents the article in question. The similarity metrics can be computed as follows.

$D_p = t_1, t_2, t_3, ..., t_u, D_q = t_1, t_2, t_3, ..., t_v.$

$$Word_{sim}(D_q) = \frac{Ovr(D_q, D_p)}{Tw_{D_q}}. \tag{1}$$

$$Ovr(D_q, D_p) = t_i | t_i \in (D_q, D_p). \tag{2}$$

$$Article_{sim}(D_q) = \frac{Ovr1(D_q, T_{doc})}{T_{doc}}. \tag{3}$$

$$Ovr1(D_q, T_{doc}) = n_{doc} | n_{doc} \in (D_q, T_{doc}). \tag{4}$$

$$Author_{sim}(D_q) = \frac{Ovr2(D_q, c_{cat})}{c_{cat}}. \tag{5}$$

$$Ovr2(D_q, c_{cat}) = n_{D_q} \in (D_q, c_{cat}). \tag{6}$$

$$sim(D_q) = 1/(e^W ord_{sim}(D_q) + Article_{sim}(D_q) + Author_{sim}(D_q)). \tag{7}$$

$$Avg_{sim} = \frac{\sum_1^{T_{doc}} sim)}{T_{doc}}. \tag{8}$$

$$Dev_{sim}(D_q) = sim(D_q) - Avg_{sim}. \tag{9}$$

2.4   Ensemble of Nested Dichotomies

Nested dichotomies can be represented as a standard statistical model where binary trees recursively segregate the multi-class classification problem into a set of dichotomies. Each set of dichotomies forms an ensemble classifier based on the inference of a certain tree depends on the information of a category. This model uses both C4.5 and logistic regression algorithms and performs better compared to the direct application of C4.5 and logistic regression as classifiers [15].

Let us observe Fig. 2, which illustrates 2 different sets of nested dichotomies for the six-domain task. It can be observed that two different trees often lead to two different paths and the classification outcomes will be influenced depending on the tree being chosen. Based on the successful predicting nature of ensemble learning, it is effective to work with all possible nested dichotomies for a given task and measure the average probability. However, this becomes impracticable as the count of possible sets of nested dichotomies for a d-domain task is (2d 3)!! as illustrated in Table 1 that shows set of ND and subset of ND for 10 domain problem [15, 16] and thus considering the subset becomes essential.

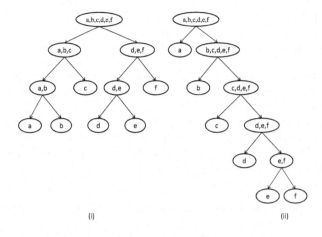

Fig. 2. Two different set of nested dichotomies for six-domain task.

Based on the tree in Fig. 2 likelihood of domain 6 for a sample s can be determined by

case(i): $l(dom = f|s) = l(dom \in \{d, e, f\}|s) * l(dom \in \{f\}|s, dom \in \{d, e, f\})$.

case(ii): $l(dom = f|s) = l(dom \in \{b, c, d, e, f\}|s) * l(dom \in \{c, d, e, f\}|s, dom \in \{b, c, d, e, f\}) * l(dom \in \{d, e, f\}|s, dom \in \{c, d, e, f\}) * l(dom \in \{e, f\}|s, dom \in \{d, e, f\}) * l(dom \in \{f\}|s, dom \in \{e, f\})$.

Table 1. Number of all possible trees.

Domain	Set of ND	Subset of ND
2	1	1
3	3	3
4	15	3
5	105	30
6	945	90
7	10,395	315
8	135,135	315
9	2,027,025	11,340
10	34,459,425	113,400

3   Experiments

3.1   Our Results

In the present work, the experiment was performed on the dataset consists of around 12,000 passages with 26,76,32,425 tokens after pre-processing. The ensemble of nested dichotomies has been used as a classifier with default parameters: cross-validation folds being 5, batch size as 100, and the number of iterations to be 10 and obtained an accuracy of 95.67%. A further experiment was carried out with different types of nested dichotomies (ND) having the same parameter values and the result is given in Table 2.

Table 2. Results for different types of nested dichotomies (ND).

Types of ND	Accuracy (%)
ND	**95.67**
Class balanced ND	92.58
Data near balanced ND	92.92
Random pair ND	94.50
Further centroid ND	80.25

Since the maximum accuracy was obtained for simple nested dichotomies; therefore, a further experiment was performed using ND with different values of iterations keeping the same batch size and cross-validation folds. The obtained result is given in Table 3.

Table 3. Accuracy obtained for different number of iterations.

Iterations	5	10	15	20	25	30
Accuracy (%)	94.33	95.67	95.75	95.58	**96.17**	95.46

The maximum accuracy was obtained for the number of iterations being 25, thus keeping the iteration value fixed; the further experiment was performed for different cross-validation folds. The result is illustrated in Table 4 which shows that the highest accuracy of 96.67% is achieved for 15 fold cross-validation.

Table 4. Accuracy obtained for different cross-validation folds.

Folds	5	10	15	20	25
Accuracy (%)	96.17	96.25	**96.67**	96.25	96.25

3.2   Comparison with Other Classifiers

The experimental result was also compared with other standard classification algorithms using 15 fold cross-validation with the help of WEKA [17] to test the performance of the proposed system whose results are displayed in Table 5. From the table, it can be observed that the ensemble of nested dichotomies performed better compared to all and also it outperformed the application of the C4.5 and logistic regression algorithm when applied as an individual learning model (as mentioned in Sect. 2.4).

Table 5. Comparison with other classifiers.

Classifiers	Accuracy (%)
Ensemble of ND	**96.67**
C4.5	78.75
Logistic regression	86.28
Rule-based	86.25
Naive Bayes	49.92
Random forest	78.33

3.3   Comparison with Existing Works

The proposed system has been compared with some of the existing algorithms in Bangla. Rakshit et al. [8] worked with semantic and stylistic features and identified authors with 92.30% using SVM. Islam et al. [18] performed statistical analysis of different features (frequently occurred terms, term length, sentence length, WH words, Number, and others) and obtained 85% accuracy using neural network for author identification. The obtained accuracies are presented in Table 6 where it can be seen that the performance of the proposed model is better compare to all existing algorithms. Also, our dataset used in the present study is quite large in comparison to the mentioned works.

Table 6. Comparison with existing works.

Reference	Accuracy (%)
Rakshit et al. [8]	92.30
Islam et al. [18]	85.00
Present study	**96.67**

4   Conclusion

This study presents an author identification system using similarity-based textual features to train the ensemble of nested dichotomies learning models for the identification of several authors depending on their writing patterns. Experiments were performed over 12,000 passages (approx.) with 26, 76, 32, 425 after stopword removal from 50 authors obtained from Bangla literature and the highest accuracy of 96.67% was obtained. The proposed methodology outperformed other existing models in Bengali.

In the future, experiments can be done using stylistic features as well. To the best of our knowledge, these experiments seem to be the first substantiated work in Bengali, more importantly to the number of authors as well as articles. Also, there is a plan to explore other various real-world scenarios such as sentiments analysis, named entity recognition, and others.

Acknowledgement. One of the authors thanks DST for support in the form of an INSPIRE fellowship. Also, we thank Dr. Amitabha Biswas, Assistant Professor of Bengali department, WBSU, Ankita Shaw, and Shilpa Roy, students of Comp. Sc. Dept, WBSU for their help while developing the dataset used in the experiment.

References

1. Stamatatos, E.: A survey of modern authorship attribution methods. J. Am. Soc. Inform. Sci. Technol. **60**(3), 538–556 (2009)
2. Anisuzzaman, D.M., Salam, A.: Authorship attribution for Bengali language using the fusion of N-gram and Naïve Bayes algorithms. Int. J. Inf. Technol. Comput. Sci. **10**, 11–21 (2018)
3. Das, S., Mitra, P.: Author identification in Bengali literary works. In: Kuznetsov, S.O., Mandal, D.P., Kundu, M.K., Pal, S.K. (eds.) PReMI 2011. LNCS, vol. 6744, pp. 220–226. Springer, Heidelberg (2011). https://doi.org/10.1007/978-3-642-21786-9_37
4. Madigan, D., Genkin, A., Lewis, D.D., Argamon, S., Fradkin, D., Ye, L.: Author identification on the large scale. In: Proceedings of the Meeting of the Classification Society of North America, vol. 13 (2005)
5. Alharthi, H., Inkpen, D., Szpakowicz, S.: Authorship identification for literary book recommendations. In: Proceedings of the 27th International Conference on Computational Linguistics, pp. 390–400 (2018)
6. Pandian, A., Manikandan, K., Ramalingam, V., Bhowmick, P., Vaishnavi, S.: Author identification of Bengali poems. Int. J. Eng. Technol. **7**, 17–21 (2018)
7. Chakraborty, T., Choudhury, P.: Authorship identification in Bengali language: a graph based approach. In: 2016 IEEE/ACM International Conference on Advances in Social Networks Analysis and Mining (ASONAM), pp. 443–446. IEEE (2016)
8. Rakshit, G., Ghosh, A., Bhattacharyya, P., Haffari, G.: Automated analysis of Bangla poetry for classification and poet identification. In: Proceedings of the 12th International Conference on Natural Language Processing, pp. 247–253 (2015)
9. Digamberrao, K.S., Prasad, R.S.: Author identification using sequential minimal optimization with rule-based decision tree on Indian literature in Marathi. Procedia Comput. Sci. **132**, 1086–1101 (2018)

10. Otoom, A.F., Abdullah, E.E., Jaafer, S., Hamdallh, A., Amer, D.: Towards author identification of Arabic text articles. In: 2014 5th International Conference on Information and Communication Systems (ICICS), pp. 1–4. IEEE (2014)
11. Rexha, A., Kröll, M., Ziak, H., Kern, R.: Authorship identification of documents with high content similarity. Scientometrics **115**(1), 223–237 (2018)
12. Abbasi, A., Chen, H.: Applying authorship analysis to extremist-group web forum messages. IEEE Intell. Syst. **20**(5), 67–75 (2005)
13. Ethnologue. https://www.ethnologue.com/language/ben, 2019
14. Stopword. https://www.isical.ac.in/~fire/data/stopwords_list_ben.txt
15. Frank, E., Kramer, S.: Ensembles of nested dichotomies for multi-class problems. In: Proceedings of the Twenty-First International Conference on Machine Learning, p. 39. ACM (2004)
16. Dong, L., Frank, E., Kramer, S.: Ensembles of balanced nested dichotomies for multi-class problems. In: Jorge, A.M., Torgo, L., Brazdil, P., Camacho, R., Gama, J. (eds.) PKDD 2005. LNCS (LNAI), vol. 3721, pp. 84–95. Springer, Heidelberg (2005). https://doi.org/10.1007/11564126_13
17. Hall, M., Frank, E., Holmes, G., Pfahringer, B., Reutemann, P., Witten, I.H.: The WEKA data mining software: an update. ACM SIGKDD Explor. Newsl. **11**(1), 10–18 (2009)
18. Islam, M.A., Kabir, M.M., Islam, M.S., Tasnim, A.: Authorship attribution on Bengali literature using stylometric features and neural network. In: 2018 4th International Conference on Electrical Engineering and Information & Communication Technology, pp. 360–363. IEEE, September 2018

Feature Combination of Pauli and H/A/Alpha Decomposition for Improved Oil Spill Detection Using SAR

Kinjal Prajapati[1]([✉]), Payal Prajapati[1], Ratheesh Ramakrishnan[2],
Alka Mahajan[1], and Madhuri Bhavsar[1]

[1] Institute of Technology, Nirma University, Ahmedabad, Gujarat, India
kinjal1292@gmail.com,payalprajapati2808@gmail.com,
alkamahajan@gmail.com,madhuri.bhavsar@nirmauni.ac.in
[2] Space Application Centre-ISRO, Ahmedabad, Gujarat, India

Abstract. Oil spill detection techniques using various decomposition algorithms have been studied by researchers and are still evolving. In this paper, two oil spill detection approaches based on Polarimetric decomposition are studied and a combination of useful features is used for efficient oil spill detection and differentiation. The first approach is based on coherent decomposition algorithm i.e. Pauli Decomposition and the second is based on the incoherent decomposition algorithm i.e. $H/A/\alpha$ decomposition. The $H/A/\alpha$ decomposition detects the different types of weathered oil spill but fails to discriminate the oil spill from look alike. Pauli decomposition detects and discriminates oil spill from the look-alike but fails to discriminate the type of oil spill. An improved technique is proposed to detect and characterize the type of weathered oil using the combination of the features of $H/A/\alpha$ and Pauli decomposition. The proposed approach is implemented and validated using the L band UAVSAR data acquired from the Deepwater Horizon Oil spill at Gulf of Mexico in June 2010. The accuracy analysis of the proposed approach using the SVM classification shows that the proposed combination not only detects the oil spill patches but also distinguishes the type of weathered oil with higher accuracy as compared to individual approaches.

Keywords: Oil spill detection · Ocean · UAVSAR · Deepwater horizon · Feature combination · $H/A/\alpha$ decomposition · Pauli decomposition · Weathered oil · SAR · SVM

1 Introduction

The marine pollution due to oil spills is a major issue as it pollutes the ocean, leaving an adverse effect on the marine ecosystem. Oil spill detection on the ocean surface and discrimination from look alikes has been of research interest since decades especially with remote sensing owing to the wide coverage

© Springer Nature Singapore Pte Ltd. 2021
K. C. Santosh and B. Gawali (Eds.): RTIP2R 2020, CCIS 1380, pp. 134–147, 2021.
https://doi.org/10.1007/978-981-16-0507-9_12

area of satellites. SAR has proved its potential for detecting oil spill on the ocean surface as it provides a high spatial resolution image in all weather conditions. In addition to oil spill detection, it is equally important to distinguish the oil spill from its lookalikes like low wind speed area, biogenic slicks, rain cells, internal ocean waves, ocean currents, shadows near a coastal region, ship wakes, upwelling zones, freshwater runoff etc. [19]. Also, after the oil spill on the ocean surface, the oil spreads in different directions due to wave currents or wind direction and over a period of time, this oil undergoes weathering effects like evaporation, emulsification, submerged oil sinking, dispersion, sedimentation, dissolution, oil-mineral aggregation, photolysis etc. changing its physical and chemical properties [1,11,16]. Hence, a technique for oil spill detection & discriminating different types of weathered oil is required so that proper containment and cleaning process is carried out accordingly.

A number of coherent and incoherent decomposition techniques like Pauli, $H/A/\alpha$, Freeman-Durden [2,7] have been developed and are still evolving for oil spill detection on the ocean surface using SAR. Discrimination of oil spill and look alikes is carried out with the support of ancillary data like sea surface temperature, wind current, ocean color etc. [14]. As ocean surface targets are distributed targets, incoherent decomposition algorithms like $H/A/\alpha$ are best suited for ocean target detection. $H/A/\alpha$ decomposition proposed by Cloude and Pottier [4,5] has proved to be an effective potential decomposition technique in detecting and discriminating the types of oil spill (thick surface oil, thin surface oil, oil-water emulsion) using SAR polarimetric data [3,13,18]. $H/A/\alpha$ eigenvector decomposition analyzes the scattering properties of the oil slick relative to surrounding water. The eigenvalue based parameters Entropy (H), Anisotropy (A) and Alpha (α) signify the properties of surface oil based on their polarimetric scattering behaviour enabling the detection and discrimination of the type of oil spill from the surface water. Other than $H/A/\alpha$ decomposition, the coherent decomposition algorithm, Pauli decomposition, basically developed for detection of land features, also detects oil spill on the ocean surface in the form of dark patches. Apart from the decomposition algorithms, a number of other features like the degree of polarization, pedestal height, conformity coefficient, Ellipticity, etc are also analysed for oil spill detection [12] and combination of these features is also studied for efficient oil spill detection using SAR [15].

In this paper, the features of Pauli and $H/A/\alpha$ decomposition algorithm are combined to use the strength of both the algorithms leading to efficient and improved oil spill detection. The full polarimetric L band UAVSAR dataset used is described in Sect. 2. The strengths and limitations of the Pauli and $H/A/\alpha$ Decomposition algorithms for oil spill detection are presented in Sect. 3 and 4. The features which contribute more in identifying and characterizing the type of weathered oil are combined to propose an improved technique for detection and characterization of weathered oil. The extracted features are classified using the SVM classification.

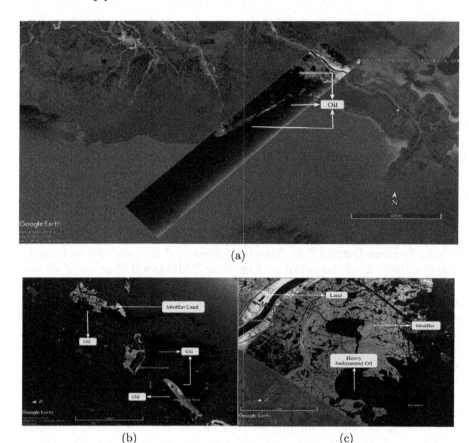

Fig. 1. (a) UAVSAR L band Full polarimetric image of Barataria Bay (BB), Lousiana and the barrier islands at the entrance to BB; BB is in the upper part of the image – Lamrsh_04201 (23 June 2010 23:05 UTC). Patches considered in study: (b) Weathered oil on the GOM side of the barrier islands labeled as Oil water Emulsion & oil on the immediate bay side of the barrier islands that has partially mixed with sediment labeled as Near Coast Oil; (c) Oil heavily mixed with sediment and other surfactants that have moved into the interior bay labeled as Heavy Sedimented Oil. (Color figure online)

2   Dataset and Tools

Fully polarimetric L band UAVSAR data acquired during the Deepwater Horizon oil spill accident at the region of Gulf of Mexico in 2010 is used for analysis and validation of the algorithms. The UAVSAR platform developed at NASA, Jet Propulsion Lab is a Gulfstream-3 aircraft instrumented with a L-band polarimetric SAR that operates 80 MHz bandwidth from 1.2175 to 1.2975 GHz. [17]. The UAVSAR images a 22-km-wide ground swath at 22° to 65° incidence angles with the image resolution of 7 m. The combination of the UAVSAR full polarization capability with an extremely low noise floor makes it an excellent instrument for polarimetric SAR studies. The UAVSAR data image used in study is LAmrsh_04201_10054_003_100623_L090_CX_01 (collection time 23:05:17 UTC on 23rd June, 2010) acquired during the flight over the Grand Isle island region of Gulf of mexico. The Deepwater Horizon (DWH) oil spill was one of the largest accidental oil spills in the U.S. petroleum industry history which started on April, 2010 and ended on July, 2010, with the total oil leak of $7,00,000\,m^3$ [6]. The image acquired near the coastal region of Barataria Bay as shown in Fig. 1a is used as it depicts the Deep water horizon oil transported at the coastal region contaminating the ocean water and coast with different stages of weathered oil. A few patches, shown in Figs. 1b and 1c, containing different types of weathered oil were taken from this UAVSAR image to ascertain the detection and discrimination efficiency of the proposed algorithm.

The Barataria bay coastal region had experienced extensive shoreline oil spill impact transported from the DWH oil spill. Figure 1 shows the image acquired near the coastal region of Barataria Bay where the transported oil from the oil rig explosion region (black in image), labeled as oil slicks in Fig. 1a, is collected at the coastal region due to ocean currents and wind effect. During the period of transportation the oil had undergone weathering effects like evaporation and emulsification resulting into change in its physical and chemical properties. Once the oil reached the coast, it would have mixed with the sediments and other surfactants changing the physical properties of the oil. For better understanding the image was cropped in two patches - Figs. 1b and 1c, consisting of oil spill with varying stages of weathering effect. The presence of the oil spill and the weathering effect at the deep water horizon and gulf coast region, has been reported in a number of research papers, where the researchers have analyzed the image acquired near the deep water horizon oil rig consisting of fresh released oil [9–11,13] thereby confirming the presence of oil in the respective image. The dark features in Fig. 1b show the oil floating on the ocean surface near the coastal region marked in green & yellow while the dark features on the left of the image consist of the weathered oil partially mixed with sediment. In patch Fig. 1c, the land on the top left of image has bright features while the dark features at the bottom are heavily weathered and sedimented oil. The weathering effect is caused due to transportation over a period of time and low bathymetry causes the oil to be mixed with coastal sediments. The changes in physical and chemical properties of the oil spill near the coastal area due to weathering and sedimentation is observed in this image which helps in validation of the proposed approach.

3 Proposed Methodology

Figure 2 shows the flow diagram of the methodology adopted in this paper for oil spill detection using SAR image. The full polarimetric L band UAVSAR data acquired near Barataria Bay region of Gulf of Mexico is used as input data as it includes various stages of weathered oil. The input data set is first pre-processed

to remove noise followed by the polarimetric decomposition for physical interpretation of the target object and classification. Lee filter is used to reduce the
effect of speckle noise on the input data. Further, the Hermitian Coherency (T3)
matrix is generated using Stokes parameters obtained from the radar backscatter
image. In the first phase, the standard polarimetric decomposition algorithms,
Pauli and H/A/Alpha decomposition are applied on the T3 matrix in order
to study their efficiency in oil spill detection and discrimination of types of oil
spill. Features which perform better in detection of desired targets are then
identified and the selected features are combined as RGB components resulting into a feature combination image. This feature combination of H/A/Alpha
and Pauli decomposition comprises of the features that contribute in efficient
detection and discrimination of the types of weathered oil from the ocean water
and coastal land. The proposed approach is finally evaluated and analyzed using
the SVM (Support Vector Machine) classification algorithm. SVM classify data
with different class labels by determining a set of support vectors that outline a
hyperplane in the feature space [8]. Since various features are studied for multi-
polarimetric SAR data, SVM is found to be trustworthy classification approach
for multi class classification for SAR data especially for coastal application by
researchers [8, 20].

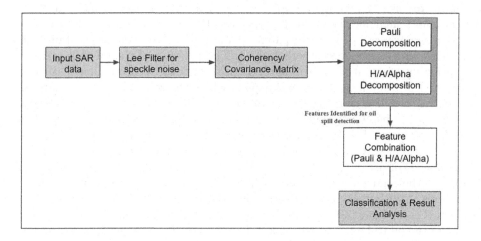

Fig. 2. Flow diagram of proposed methodology

The results and analysis of the individual decomposition techniques and those
of the proposed feature combinations are presented in the following sections.

4   Pauli Decomposition

Pauli Decomposition is majorly used for land classification but it is also identified
as an efficient algorithm for oil spill detection. For fully polarimetric SAR data,

the backscattering properties of the object are described using the backscattering matrix as

$$S = \begin{bmatrix} S_{HH} & S_{HV} \\ S_{VH} & S_{VV} \end{bmatrix} \tag{1}$$

where S_{XY} is the scattering component with x as transmit polarization and y as receive polarization. The Pauli decomposition is the combination of scattering components as shown in Eq. (2) where each component signifies the dominant behaviour of Surface, Double-bounce and Volume scattering over the target object respectively.

$$P = 1/\sqrt{2} \begin{bmatrix} |S_{HH} + S_{VV}| \\ |S_{HH} - S_{VV}| \\ 2|S_{HV}| \end{bmatrix} \tag{2}$$

The surface scattering is dominant over the ocean surface hence the first Pauli component (P1) has higher dominance for ocean surface as compared to other components. In the presence of oil spill, the backscattering intensity is reduced due to dampening of ocean waves resulting into dark signature at the oil covered area. Figure 3a shows the identified oil spill, land and mudflats in the selected patch of image. The dark signature near the coastal region in the Pauli decomposed image is oil. The thickness of the oil near the coastal region is high and hence the backscatter will be lower resulting into more darker signature compared to ocean water. The land and mudflats are identified with yellow and green signature due to the partial dominance of surface and double bounce scattering due to the presence of vegetation. It is also observed from the result in Fig. 3a, that Pauli decomposition can detect oil spill as dark features but cannot discriminate the types of weathered oil.

The analysis of each component of Pauli decomposition is done using the histogram of each component of Pauli decomposition and Figs. 3b–3b show the histogram of first, second and third Pauli components (P1, P2 & P3) respectively. Due to weathering the thickness of the sedimented oil is high hence the backscattering behaviour of sedimented oil is different from the surface scattering observed for oil water emulsion. However, the Pauli decomposition is unable to bring out this differentiation. As observed from the histograms there is a minor variation in the ranges but it is not possible to distinguish clearly between oil water emulsion and heavy sedimented oil. It is thus concluded that Pauli decomposition can detect oil spills and land features efficiently but fails in distinguishing the type of oil spill.

5   H/A/Alpha Decomposition

The eigenvalue/eigenvector based, H/A/α decomposition algorithm is widely used for detecting ocean surface targets especially oil spill detection. Here the three non-negative real eigenvalues and eigenvectors are calculated using the Hermitian Coherency matrix for each pixel of the image. The eigenvector analysis provides a basic invariant description of the scatterer and a decomposition into the types of scattering mechanisms. The rotation invariant H/A/α parameters

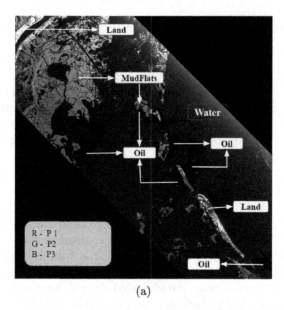

(a)

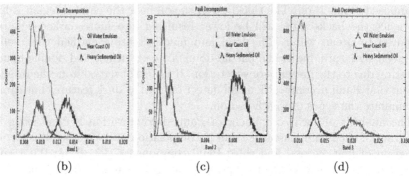

(b)   (c)   (d)

Fig. 3. (a) Pauli decomposition result & Histogram of H/A/Alpha parameters for different type of weathered oil and land. (b) Histogram of First Pauli Component (c) Histogram of Second Pauli Component (d) Histogram of Third Pauli Component (Color figure online)

(Entropy, Anisotropy(A) and Scattering angle(α)) are calculated based on the eigenvalues as shown in Eq. (3), (4) and (5) respectively [5].

$$H = -\sum_{i=1}^{3} P_i log_3 P_i \quad with \quad P_i = \lambda_i / (\lambda_1 + \lambda_2 + \lambda_3) \quad (3)$$

The randomness of the backscattered radiations can be evaluated using pseudo probability of the eigenvalues P_i as shown in Eq. (3) defined as entropy. At moderate wind speed, the clean water will have single dominant backscattering mechanism(surface scattering) hence the entropy will be low (near to 0) while in the presence of surface oil, the backscattering will be the mixture of multiple scatter of comparable strength hence the entropy will be comparatively high.

The amount of multiple backscattering behaviour of the target object is evaluated using anisotropy (A). As shown in Eq. (4), anisotropy is calculated as the ratio of difference and sum of second and third eigenvalues.

$$A = \frac{\lambda_2 - \lambda_3}{\lambda_2 + \lambda_3} \tag{4}$$

Anisotropy mostly helps in distinguishing the features of the target object when the entropy of the target is too low or medium (as low entropy indicates single dominant scattering with low value of second and third eigenvalues). In case of oil spill detection on the ocean surface, surface scattering is the most dominating scattering behaviour, hence the probability of multiple backscattering behaviour is less.

The third parameter, Alpha is the mean scattering angle that identifies the type of dominant scattering of the target object.

$$\bar{\alpha} = \sum_{i=1}^{3} p_i \alpha_i \tag{5}$$

For the oil spill surface, alpha is expected to be below $45°$ as surface scattering is dominant here while in case of objects like ships or oil rig, alpha is expected to be greater than $45°$ owing to dominance of double bounce scattering.

The Fig. 4 shows the H/A/α decomposition result for the full polarimetric L band UAVSAR image acquired near the coastal region of Barataria Bay region. Here the H/A/α decomposition is plotted as entropy (H) as red, anisotropy(A) as green and scattering angle (α) as blue. Using visual interpretation, the oil spill (green and pink) are distinguished from the clean water (blue). The bright green areas in Fig. 4, right-center of image have less entropy and alpha values while intermediate range of anisotropy indicating minor impact of multiple backscattering which corresponds to the oil water emulsion; the light pink and white indicate the intermediate range of entropy, anisotropy and alpha indicating equivalent eigenvalues corresponding to partly multiple scattering behaviour which corresponds to the near coast oil partially mixed with sediment and coastal region; the pink indicates the heavily sedimented oil (upper left) with high range of entropy and alpha. Similar range of entropy and alpha is observed for the land region resulting into pink signature. Hence, the type of weathered oil are clearly distinguished using H/A/α decomposition but due to similar scattering behaviour, some land area in the island and heavily sedimented oil has similar signature leading to false alarm. The Fig. 4b shows the histogram of entropy for different type of weathered oil observed in the full polarimetric L band UAVSAR image of Barataria Bay coastal region. The oil on the ocean surface dampens the ocean waves resulting into reduced random backscattering i.e for oil water emulsion (i.e. <0.4) as shown in entropy histogram in Fig. 4b. Due to constant accumulation of weathered oil near the coastal area, the thickness of the oil is comparatively more and when it gets mixed with the coastal sediments due to

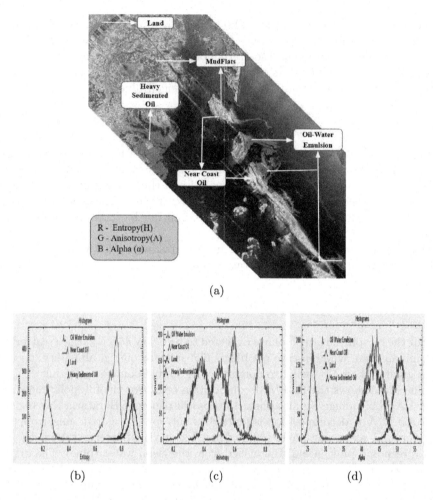

Fig. 4. H/A/Alpha decomposition result & Histogram of H/A/Alpha parameters for different type of weathered oil and land. (b) Histogram of Entropy (c) Histogram of Anisotropy (d) Histogram of Mean Scattering Angle Alpha (Color figure online)

low bathymetry the randomness of backscattering is comparatively more. Thus, the entropy of the near coast oil (light pink and white) and heavy sedimented oil (pink) in Fig. 4 is high (>0.6). Owing to random scattering due to sedimented oil, the entropy of the heavy sedimented oil seems to be equivalent to that of the land near the top left corner. Thus though entropy plays a major role in distinguishing the type of weathered oil spills on the ocean surface it fails to distinguish heavy sedimented oil from land. From the histogram for anisotropy in Fig. 4c, the range is low for heavy sedimented oil, intermediate for oil water emulsion and high for near coast oil while the land has range in between heavy sedimented oil and oil water emulsion. The Fig. 4d shows the histogram of scattering angle(α) for different types of weathered oil observed in the full polarimetric L band UAVSAR image of Barataria Bay coastal region. The value ranges from 25° to 35° signifying the dominant behaviour of surface scattering for the oil water emulsion and variation in the surface scattering for the near coast oil and heavy sedimented oil as it ranges from 35° to 55°. Hence a subsequent increase in value of is observed with the increasing weathering effect on the oil. Also the range of α for land is in the same range (35° to 55°) as near coast oil due to partial dominance of surface scattering for land region.

6   Proposed Feature Combination Technique

It is clear from the results of H/A/α decomposition as shown in Fig. 4, that the types of oil spill are clearly discriminated using this technique but the signature of the land and the heavy sedimented oil are almost similar. It was also observed from the histogram in Figs. 4b and 4d, that the entropy and scattering angle value increases with the increasing weathering effect on the oil resulting into clear discrimination of type of weathered oil. However, the values of entropy and alpha for land is getting mixed with highly sedimented oil. The histogram of anisotropy, Fig. 4c, shows that it plays a limited role in discrimination of different stages of oil spills. Hence after analysing each feature of H/A/α- Entropy(H), Anisotropy(A) and mean scattering angle(α) - it was found that entropy and the scattering angle alpha have more potential to detect and discriminate between the different stages of oil spill however they fails to differentiating it from land. In the case of Pauli decomposition technique, the second (P2) and third (P3) Pauli components signify the dominant behaviour of double bounce and volume scattering over the target object. Thus P2 and P3 majorly contribute in distinguishing the land features from the ocean water and oil spills. It was also observed in the histogram in Fig. 3 that P2and P3 can differentiate among different stages of oil to some extent as compared to the first component.

Hence, in this paper two combinations of H/A/α and Pauli Decomposition features are proposed for the efficient detection and discrimination of types of weathered oil spill from that of man-made targets i.e. land/buildings. The first combination generates an image by combining the Entropy/H(red), second Pauli component/P2 (green) and Scattering angle/α (blue). In this H/P2/α combination, H and α contribute more towards the oil spill discrimination and the pauli component P1 helps in enhancing the land features resulting into unambiguous differentiation among land and types of weathered oil. Similarly the second combination, H/P2/P3, comprises image generated by keeping Entropy(red), second pauli component (green) and third pauli component/P3 (blue) where P2 and P3 focus on land features and highlighting the oil spill on the ocean surface while the entropy makes differentiation among the types of weathered oil possible.

7   Result Analysis

The combined strength of Pauli and H/A/α decomposition algorithm for efficient detection and discrimination of oil spill by means of both the feature combina-

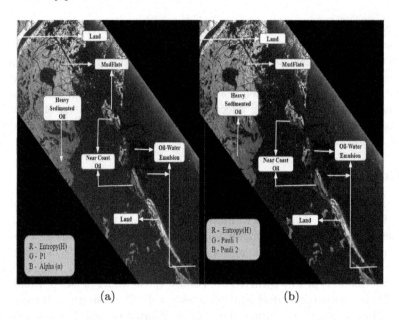

Fig. 5. Feature Combination Results: (a) Feature Combination 1 - Two feature of H/A/Alpha and one component of Pauli decomposition - H/P1/Alpha (b) Feature Combination 2 - One feature of H/A/Alpha and two component of Pauli decomposition - H/P1/P2

tions - (H/P1/α) & (H/P1/P2) - is shown in Fig. 5. As it is seen from Fig. 5, the weathered oil is clearly differentiable from ocean water, oil-water emulsion and land/mudflat areas using both the combinations, which is not possible with either pauli or H/A/α decomposition algorithm considered alone. Comparison of pauli and H/A/α alone with the combinations is shown in Fig. 6. The H/A/α decomposed image in Fig. 6a and 6b discriminates the oil water emulsion and near coast oil but the land signature is similar to near coast oil. Similarly in case of Pauli decomposed image in Fig. 6c and 6d the land and oil are clearly discriminated but the type of weathered oil has same signature throughout the image. The proposed feature combination results shown in Fig. 6e not only discriminates the type of weathered oil but also has unique signature for the land region hence overcomes the limitation of H/A/Alpha and Pauli decomposition. It is also observed that the minute properties of the land region like building or mudflats are also identified in the top left corner of Fig. 6e and 6g. Hence along with the discrimination of different stage of weathered oil, the land features are also enhanced using the feature combination approach. Further the results are analysed using the SVM classification. It is observed that the oil spill and type of weathered oil are classified with the precision of 90% by existing individual algorithms while the proposed approach classifies the weathered oil and discriminates the lookalikes by 92% (for first feature combination) and 96% (for second feature combination) accuracy (Table 1).

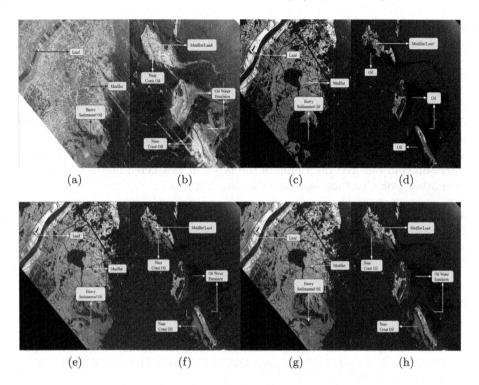

(a)   (b)   (c)   (d)

(e)   (f)   (g)   (h)

Fig. 6. Patch Comparison: (a) & (b) H/A/Alpha Decomposition patch (c) & (d) Pauli Decomposition patch (e) & (f) Feature Combination 1 patch (g) & (h) Feature Combination 2 patch

Table 1. Comparison of standard decomposition algorithm with the proposed decomposition algorithm

Decomposition Algorithm	Oil Spill	Oil Water Emulsion	Near Coast Oil	Heavy Sedimented Oil	Land/Mudflats
Pauli	Yes	No	No	No	Yes
H/A/Alpha	Yes	Yes	Yes	Yes	No
Combination 1	Yes	Yes	Yes	Yes	Yes
Combination 2	Yes	Yes	Yes	Yes	Yes

8   Conclusion

A technique combining features of coherent and incoherent polarimetric decomposition algorithms i.e Pauli & H/A/α, is proposed for efficient detection and discrimination of oil spill using L band full polarimetric UAVSAR data. It was observed from the results that the Pauli decomposition can detect oil spill but cannot discriminate type of oil while H/A/α decomposition can discriminate type of oil spill but its signature gets mixed with land signature. Hence independent features of Pauli and H/A/α are first studied and analyzed to identify the best suitable feature combination for oil spill characterization. The proposed feature combination is observed to have better results as compared to individual decomposition algorithm, in terms of distinguishing various stages of weathered oil and differentiating them from the land, mudflat, ocean water and oil-water emulsion. It is also observed that the land features are more enhanced using the feature combination. The classification accuracy assessment is carried out using SVM classification which shows that the proposed feature combination (1) H/P2/α identities and discriminates weathered oil spills with 92% accuracy while the feature combination (2) H/P2/P3 does the same with 96% accuracy. Hence, with some variation both the proposed feature combinations not only effectively detect oil spill but also discriminate the types of weathered oil, distinguish oil from other look alikes and enhance the land features.

Acknowledgement. The research work was carried out as a part of the NISAR L & S band project entitled "SAR Polarimetry for Detecting Ocean Surface Target" funded by Indian Space Research Organisation (ISRO) at Institute of Technology, Nirma University, Ahmedabad.

References

1. Alpers, W., Holt, B., Zeng, K.: Oil spill detection by imaging radars: challenges and pitfalls. In: International Geoscience and Remote Sensing Symposium (IGARSS), vol. 2017-July, pp. 1522–1525 (2017). https://doi.org/10.1109/IGARSS.2017.8127258
2. An, W., Cui, Y., Yang, J., Member, S.: Three-Component Model-Based Decomposition for Polarimetric SAR Data (March) (2014). https://doi.org/10.1109/TGRS.2010.2041242
3. Angelliaume, S., et al.: SAR imagery for detecting sea surface slicks: performance assessment of polarization-dependent parameters. IEEE Trans. Geosci. Remote Sens. **56**(8), 4237–4257 (2018). https://doi.org/10.1109/TGRS.2018.2803216
4. Cloude, S.R., Pottier, E., Boerner, W.: Unsupervised image classification using the entropy/alpha/anisotropy method in radar polarimetry. In: NASA-JPL, AIRSAR-02 Workshop, vol. 44, no. 1334, pp. 04–06 (2002). http://airsar.jpl.nasa.gov/documents/workshop2002/papers/T2.pdf
5. Cloude, S.R., Pottier, E.: A review of target decomposition theorems in radar polarimetry. IEEE Trans. Geosci. Remote Sens. **34**(2), 498–518 (1996)
6. Crone, T.J., Tolstoy, M.: Magnitude of the 2010 Gulf, p. 2010 (2010)
7. Freeman, A., Member, S., Durden, S.L.: A three-component scattering model for polarimetric SAR data. IEEE Trans. Geosci. Remote Sens. **36**(3), 963–973 (1998)
8. Gou, S., Li, X., Yang, X.: Coastal zone classification with fully polarimetric SAR imagery. IEEE Geosci. Remote Sens. Lett. **13**(11), 1616–1620 (2016)
9. Jones, C.E., Holt, B.: Experimental L-band airborne SAR for oil spill response at sea and in coastal waters. Sensors (Switzerland) **18**(2) (2018). https://doi.org/10.3390/s18020641
10. Jones, C.E., Minchew, B., Holt, B., Hensley, S.: Studies of the DeepWater Horizon oil spill with the UAVSAR radar. In: Monitoring and Modeling the Deepwater Horizon Oil Spill: A Record Breaking Enterprise (June), pp. 33–50 (2013). https://doi.org/10.1029/2011GM001113

11. Leifer, I., Clark, R., Jones, C., Holt, B., Svejkovsky, J., Swayze, G.: Satellite and airborne oil spill remote sensing: state of the art and application to the BP DeepWater Horizon oil spill. In: Proceedings of the 34th AMOP Technical Seminar on Environmental Contamination and Response, pp. 270–295 (2011). http://www.scopus.com/inward/record.url?eid=2-s2.0-80955165034&partnerID=40&md5=00dbb34cffd9e2b2f5492e7f5cb3c52a
12. Migliaccio, M., Gambardella, A., Tranfaglia, M.: SAR polarimetry to observe oil spills. IEEE Trans. Geosci. Remote Sens. **45**(2), 506–511 (2007). https://doi.org/10.1109/TGRS.2006.888097
13. Minchew, B., Jones, C.E., Holt, B.: Polarimetric analysis of backscatter from the DeepWater Horizon oil spill using l-band synthetic aperture radar. IEEE Trans. Geosci. Remote Sens. **50**(10 PART1), 3812–3830 (2012). https://doi.org/10.1109/TGRS.2012.2185804
14. Müllenhoff, O., Bulgarelli, B., Ferraro, G., Perkovic, M., Topouzelis, K., Sammarini, V.: Geospatial modelling of metocean and environmental ancillary data for the oil spill probability assessment in SAR images. In: Remote Sensing for Environmental Monitoring, GIS Applications, and Geology VIII, vol. 7110 (October), p. 71100R (2008). https://doi.org/10.1117/12.799717
15. Singha, S., Ressel, R., Velotto, D., Lehner, S.: A combination of traditional and polarimetric features for oil spill detection using TerraSAR-X. IEEE J. Sel. Top. Appl. Earth Obs. Remote Sens. **9**(11), 4979–4990 (2016). https://doi.org/10.1109/JSTARS.2016.2559946
16. Skrunes, S., Brekke, C., Eltoft, T.: Characterization of marine surface slicks by Radarsat-2 multipolarization features. IEEE Trans. Geosci. Remote Sens. **52**(9), 5302–5319 (2014). https://doi.org/10.1109/TGRS.2013.2287916
17. Wheeler, K., Hensley, S., Lou, Y., Miller, T., Hoffman, J.: An L-band SAR for repeat pass deformation measurements on a UAV platform. In: Proceedings of the 2004 IEEE Radar Conference (IEEE Cat. No. 04CH37509), pp. 317–322. IEEE (2004)
18. Zhang, B., Perrie, W., Li, X., Pichel, W.G.: Mapping sea surface oil slicks using RADARSAT-2 quad-polarization SAR image. Geophys. Res. Lett. **38**(10) (2011). https://doi.org/10.1029/2011gl047013
19. Zhang, Y., Li, Y., Lin, H.: Oil-spill pollution remote sensing by synthetic aperture radar. Adv. Geosci. Remote Sens. (2014). https://doi.org/10.5772/57477
20. Zou, T., Yang, W., Dai, D., Sun, H.: Polarimetric SAR image classification using multifeatures combination and extremely randomized clustering forests. EURASIP J. Adv. Signal Process. **2010**, 4 (2010)

A Fast and Efficient Convolutional Neural Network for Fruit Recognition and Classification

Himanshu Naidu[1(✉)], S. Rajkumar[1(✉)] iD, K. C. Santosh[2(✉)] iD,
and P. V. S. S. R. Chandra Mouli[3(✉)] iD

[1] VIT University, Vellore, Tamil Nadu, India
himanshunaidu12161997@gmail.com, rajkumars@vit.ac.in
[2] University of South Dakota, Vermillion, USA
santosh.kc@usd.edu
[3] Central University of Tamil Nadu, Thiruvarur, India
chandramouli@cutn.ac.in

Abstract. Image recognition and classification using Convolutional Neural Networks (CNN) are the two popular applications of computer vision. The advances in deep learning-based models make it possible to recognize complex images. This paper presents an efficient CNN based method that performs fruit recognition and classification. The data-set used is Fruits-360, which consists of simple and complex fruit images. A series of experiments are conducted to improve the accuracy of the classification method. Experimental results and analysis show that the results are exemplary and exhibit better performance over other methods.

Keywords: Convolutional Neural Network (CNN) · Fruits-360 · Classification · Rectified linear unit (RELU) · Adam optimizer

1 Introduction

In recent years, increasing advancements in fields of machine learning, deep learning, and computer vision have noticed tremendous success in a wide variety of applications [7]. The medical and food industries have benefited from the image processing capabilities of deep learning. CNN has especially shown excellent accuracy in applications like image classification, retrieval, etc. Modern CNNs have shown to outperform even humans in different visual applications like the ImageNet challenges [2]. This concept is being used in several applications like visual recognition, which includes video recognition and classification [5], face recognition [12], handwritten digit recognition [11], fruit recognition [9] etc. each of which has seen CNNs achieve human level accuracy.

CNN [13] has a similar architecture and concept as the general Artificial Neural Network (ANN). It consists of an input layer, two or more hidden layers, and an output layer. The hidden layers, each of which contains several neurons, have the responsibility of learning and analyzing different features of the images.

© Springer Nature Singapore Pte Ltd. 2021
K. C. Santosh and B. Gawali (Eds.): RTIP2R 2020, CCIS 1380, pp. 148–157, 2021.
https://doi.org/10.1007/978-981-16-0507-9_13

The neurons in the hidden layer are responsible for learning the low-level and high-level image features.

The usage of CNN's gives high accuracy but has a problem of taking too much training time due to more number of hidden layers required for training. In this paper, we show that a CNN that is relatively thin, compared to existing successful models, gives an acceptable accuracy with less time compared to other existing models like AlexNet [7], DCNN [8], Fruit Classifier [10].

2   Existing Work

A lot of work on fruit recognition and classification has already taken place. In this section, we briefly discuss in brief the existing literature.

2.1   Image Classification

In this section, two prevalent algorithms used for classification namely Decision trees and Support vector machines are briefed. These algorithms do not fall under the umbrella of deep learning but have been used effectively for image recognition and classification [4].

Decision Tree is an algorithm predominantly used for classification if the given data is given with labels. A rooted tree is formed from which a set of rules are generated as conjunction of disjunctions. Each rule is a unique path from the root node to the leaf node.

Support Vector Machines (SVM) is also a classification approach that separates the data into possible classes by partitioning over hyper plane. SVM gives promising results for the classification problem using support vectors that are separated by marginal distance.

2.2   Deep Learning

Deep Learning is the current locale of research which has been proved in solving complex machine learning problems. Convolutional Neural Networks (CNNs) are extensively used for image classification and object detection [7].

The disadvantage of deep learning is the amount of training time the classifier requires. Reducing the training time is the prime motivation for us to propose a thin and efficient CNN for fruit classification. The method proposed has been compared with other CNN models that are known for their high accuracy.

2.3   Fruit Classification

Several factors can make fruit recognition a challenging task. Some of these factors include flaws in image quality like uneven brightness, obstruction, and also the fact that many fruits have a similar shape, color, and texture.

Extensive research has taken place in recent years to handle the challenge. Hung et al. [3] have proposed a Sparse Autoencoder (SAE) to learn features for segmentation.

There are also various deep learning approaches also used for fruit detection and classification. Sa et al. [9] proposed a region-based CNN model is trained using RGB and NIR images (Near Infrared). Their research achieved remarkable success in deep learning-based image classification. Adnan Qayyum et al. [8] shows a model based on the successful AlexNet to train on a medical image data set and then use for content-based image classification (CBIR) applications.

3   Proposed Method

The overall architecture proposed is represented in Fig. 1.

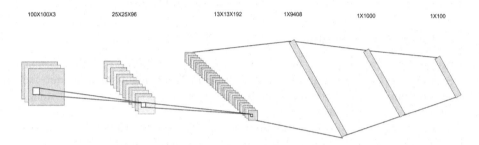

100X100X3   25X25X96   13X13X192   1X9408   1X1000   1X100

Fig. 1. CNN Architecture of the proposed system

The network consists of an input layer, a pair of Convolutional and max pool layers. Two fully connected layers follow the convolutional part. The architecture is shown in Fig. 1.

An Image of size $100 \times 100 \times 3$ is the input to the CNN architecture. A Convolutional layer with 96 filters have been connected to the input layer. The stride for the first layer is taken as 4.

The second convolutional layer contains 192 filters, each of which has a size of $3 \times 3 \times 96$. The stride for this layer is 1 across all dimensions.

Both the convolutional layers use the ReLU activation function. The ReLU function improves the performance at the end of the convolutional layers. ReLU seems to provide the best overall performance enhancement compare to other activation functions [1]. ReLU function is given in Eq. (1).

$$R(z) = max\{0, z\} \tag{1}$$

where z is the input to the function.

Both the convolutional layers are followed by max-pooling layers. The max pooling layer is used to reduce the dimensionality of the input that would be passed to the next layer. The filter size of both the max-pooling layers is 2×2, with a stride of 2×2. The max-pooling layer visits each 2×2 region of the input, and selects only the pixel with the largest value as the output for that region, and then moves on to the next region either in the horizontal or vertical region.

Every neural network is susceptible to over-fitting at some stage of training. Over-fitting refers to a high testing error that results when a network is too closely fit a limited set of training points. This leads to a very low training error, which is misleading because the network will not be able to perform well for points it has not seen during training. In order to avoid this, some regularization measures need to be carried out. In this network, dropout is used for the task.

Dropout is a regularization technique that, as the name suggests, drops out a fixed number of random neurons of the network during training. By dropping out a neuron, the neuron is temporarily eliminated from the network, along with its incoming and outgoing connections. At each training step, a different set of neurons are dropped out. This has a number of advantages. It makes sure that the neurons that are not left out, train on the data set themselves, and thus do not start depending on their neighboring neurons for the correct output. This helps in preventing over-fitting. The dropout used in this layer has a dropping probability of 0.25, which means that 25% of the neurons would be dropped at each step.

The dropout is then followed by a flattening layer that converts the 2-Dimensional output of the max-pooling layer into a 1-Dimensional feature vector. This is used in order to connect to the fully-connected layers that follow after.

The flattening layer has been connected to a fully-connected layer, which consists of 1000 neurons, uses the ReLU activation function, and is also followed by a dropout, with the dropping probability being 0.5.

Finally, the first fully connected layer is connected to the second fully connected layer which contains the output 100 neurons.

The softmax classifier activation is used for the class prediction. It is a logistic regression that normalizes the input value to follow a probability distribution. The softmax function is defined in Eq. (2).

$$S(z_i) = \frac{e^{z_i}}{\sum_{k=1}^{100} e^{z_k}} \tag{2}$$

Finally, the optimizer and the loss function are required for the neural network. The optimizer plays an important role to improve the performance in each step. For our neural network, we have used the Adaptive Movement Estimation (Adam) optimizer because of its efficient optimization technique [6]. The Adam optimizer has various advantages such as computational efficiency, low memory requirements, and efficient adaptability. Equations (3) and (4) show the general implementation of Adam optimization.

$$n_t = b_1 \times n_{t-1} + (1 - b_1) \times g_t \tag{3}$$

$$s_t = b_2 \times s_{t-1} + (1 - b_2) \times g_t^2 \tag{4}$$

where n_t and s_t are the first and second moments, g_t is the gradient, b_1 and b_2 are hyper parameters.

The learning rate used for the network is 0.0001. The low learning rate ensures that the gradient keeps drifting slowly towards the desired output and does not overshoot into a higher error region. In order to assess the model performance, a loss function is needed. Since the output is measured by probabilities, it has been decided that the cross-entropy function would be the best choice. The cross-entropy is defined in Eq. (5).

$$L_i = -\sum_y y_{i,j} \times log(p_{i,j}) \tag{5}$$

where p is the predicted class and y is the actual class.

4   Experimental Results

In this paper, we have used a free and open source software library called TensorFlow. This Python library is used for various machine learning applications. All the simulations for this word were carried out on Dell Inspiron 7572 with Windows 10, in-built with Intel Core i7 - 8550U CPU with 8 GB RAM, and equipped with the NVIDIA GeForce MX150.

4.1   Dataset

The dataset used is the Fruits-360, which is available publicly on Github and Kaggle [9]. The images were taken by placing the fruits in the shaft of a low speed motor and recording a short film of 20 s. Behind the fruits, a white sheet of paper is placed as background for better extraction of the fruits from the background. A dedicated algorithm was developed for the extraction process.

The training and testing sets for the data set are already segregated, which makes the task easier. The total number of images available in the training set and test set are 56, 781 and 19, 053 respectively. Each image has the dimensions of 100 × 100 pixels.

Of the 103 fruits classes in the data set, 100 were used. Three classes, namely, Mangostan, Pear Kaiser, and Tomato Maroon, were ignored. Some sample images of the classes used are shown in Table 1.

5   Performance Comparison

In this classification, we have implemented a deep convolutional neural network, with the aim to create a model that efficiently captures the required features for the classification, and at the same time, does not take as long as the existing models for either training or testing.

For comparison, we have used three existing convolutional neural networks, the traditional AlexNet [8], a DCNN created by Adnan et al. [10], and an existing fruits classifier that was also developed on the Fruits-360 data set by Shadman et al. [12]. The model that we have created is comparatively thinner and takes lesser

Table 1. Fruits-360 Data set Sample Images.

Apple Braeburn	Apple Golden 1	Apple Red 1	Avocado
Banana Ladyfinger	Cactus Fruit	Clementine	Grape White
Hazelnut	Lemon	Pear	Tomato Cherry

time to train and run. To give an idea, the configuration of each neural network used for the experiment is also given along with their respective performances in Table 2. It indicates that our network on an average, performs significantly better than the other three networks. Also, our network takes much lesser time for the training and testing tasks, thus having an edge on efficiency.

5.1   Training Performance

Since, each of the 100 classes contain at least 522 images in their training set, we have selected 522 images per class, thus giving us 52, 200 images for training. Batches of 200 images were used for every epoch, which averaged out to 2 images per class. Thus, the neural network could train over the entire data set in 261 epochs. It was decided that each network would train over the data set seven times, thus every network was trained in 1827 epochs.

Figure 2 shows the training trends of the four neural networks, showing how the performance of all the networks improve over the epochs. We have plotted the training result for every 10 epochs.

The DCNN line in the graph refers to the model of Adnan et al. [8], while the fruits line refers to the new fruits classifier model [10]. As the legend indicates, the cyan-colored plot line named as new, is our model. As the graph suggests, the four neural networks do not display very different results, in terms of performance improvement in every epoch, with every network eventually giving a training accuracy of 0.97 0.99. This would be seen as a positive result as our neural network is much thinner than the rest.

Table 2. Comparative analysis of the proposed model with other models

Model	Color	Configuration			Average testing accuracy (%)	Total testing time (in secs)
Proposed Model	Cyan	Convolutional	5 × 5	96	97.54	97.54
		Max-Pool	2 × 2	1		
		Convolutional	3 × 3	192		
		Max-Pool	2 × 2	1		
		Fully Connected	– –	1000		
DCNN Adnan et al.	Green	Convolutional	11 × 11	64	94.81	578.63
		Max-Pool	3 × 3	1		
		Convolutional	5 × 5	192		
		Max-Pool	3 × 3	1		
		Convolutional	5 × 5	384		
		Convolutional	3 × 3	256		
		Convolutional	3 × 3	256		
		Fully Connected	– –	4096		
		Fully Connected	==	4096		
		Fully Connected	– –	4096		
Fruits Shadman et al.	Cyan	Convolutional	3 × 3	64	96.48	76.80
		Max-Pool	2 × 2	1		
		Convolutional	3 × 3	64		
		Max-Pool	2 × 2	1		
		Fully Connected	– –	500		
Alex Net	Blue	Convolutional	11 × 11	96	96.40	513.94
		Max-Pool	3 × 3	1		
		Convolutional	5 × 5	256		
		Max-Pool	3 × 3	1		
		Convolutional	5 × 5	384		
		Convolutional	3 × 3	384		
		Convolutional	3 × 3	256		
		Fully Connected	– –	4096		
		Fully Connected	==	4096		
		Fully Connected	– –	4096		

5.2 Testing Performance

For testing purposes, each of the 100 classes have at least around 140 images in the test set. Thus, 140 images are taken for every class, totaling to 14, 000 images for testing, and batches are created, each of which contain 200 images. Thus, the testing is carried out over 70 steps for each neural network to cover the entire testing set.

As the graph of Fig. 3 suggests, the four neural networks give around the same average testing accuracy for the first 50 batches. However, in the last 20 batches, we see that our model gives much better testing results. A possible reason for this difference between our model and the deeper networks could be over-fitting on the training data.

Our network runs over the 70 batches in just over 39 s, compared to 500–600 s required by AlexNet and the other DCNN. This significant efficiency improvement combined with better testing accuracy makes our network a much better alternative.

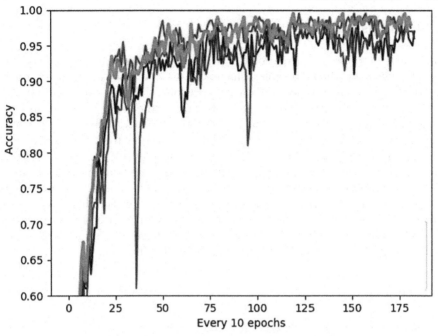

Fig. 2. Comparison of training results

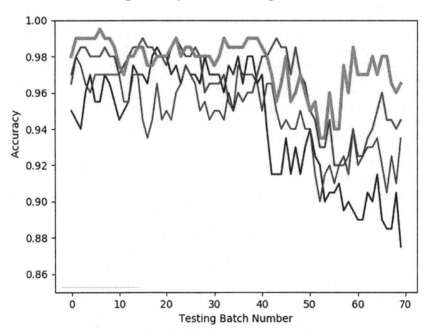

Fig. 3. Comparison of testing results

6 Conclusion

This paper proposes a convolutional neural network that is capable of classifying different images based on color, shape, texture and other features. The main aim of this research is to develop a neural network, that contains lesser number of connections than other existing models, and at the same time captures the required features for the classification task more efficiently, thus aiming at better accuracy and quicker process execution. The proposed neural network gives significantly better classification results, and also executes the process much faster compared to its counterparts. The resultant network gives an average accuracy of 97.54%, at least 1% better than the other networks, and also takes under 40 s to run over 14,000 images, which is at least twice as quicker than its counterparts, thus achieving the objectives with success. Our intention is to take this research further and apply this model for other image processing applications such as content-based image retrieval and video classification.

References

1. Agarap, A.F.: Deep learning using rectified linear units (RELU). arXiv preprint arXiv:1803.08375 (2018)
2. Girshick, R., Donahue, J., Darrell, T., Malik, J.: Rich feature hierarchies for accurate object detection and semantic segmentation. In: Proceedings of the IEEE Conference on Computer Vision and Pattern Recognition, pp. 580–587 (2014)
3. Hung, C., Nieto, J., Taylor, Z., Underwood, J., Sukkarieh, S.: Orchard fruit segmentation using multi-spectral feature learning. In: 2013 IEEE/RSJ International Conference on Intelligent Robots and Systems, pp. 5314–5320. IEEE (2013)
4. Kamavisdar, P., Saluja, S., Agrawal, S.: A survey on image classification approaches and techniques. Int. J. Adv. Res. Comput. Commun. Eng. 2(1), 1005–1009 (2013)
5. Karpathy, A., Toderici, G., Shetty, S., Leung, T., Sukthankar, R., Fei-Fei, L.: Large-scale video classification with convolutional neural networks. In: Proceedings of the IEEE Conference on Computer Vision and Pattern Recognition, pp. 1725–1732 (2014)
6. Kingma, D.P., Ba, J.: Adam: a method for stochastic optimization. arXiv preprint arXiv:1412.6980 (2014)
7. Krizhevsky, A., Sutskever, I., Hinton, G.E.: ImageNet classification with deep convolutional neural networks. In: Advances in Neural Information Processing Systems, pp. 1097–1105 (2012)
8. Qayyum, A., Anwar, S.M., Awais, M., Majid, M.: Medical image retrieval using deep convolutional neural network. Neurocomputing 266, 8–20 (2017)
9. Sa, I., Ge, Z., Dayoub, F., Upcroft, B., Perez, T., McCool, C.: Deepfruits: a fruit detection system using deep neural networks. Sensors 16(8), 1222 (2016)
10. Sakib, S., Ashrafi, Z., Siddique, M., Bakr, A.: Implementation of fruits recognition classifier using convolutional neural network algorithm for observation of accuracies for various hidden layers. arXiv preprint arXiv:1904.00783 (2019)
11. Siddique, F., Sakib, S., Siddique, M.A.B.: Handwritten digit recognition using convolutional neural network in python with tensorflow and observe the variation of accuracies for various hidden layers (2019)

12. Sun, Y., Chen, Y., Wang, X., Tang, X.: Deep learning face representation by joint identification-verification. In: Advances in Neural Information Processing Systems, pp. 1988–1996 (2014)
13. Xu, L., Ren, J.S., Liu, C., Jia, J.: Deep convolutional neural network for image deconvolution. In: Advances in Neural Information Processing Systems, pp. 1790–1798 (2014)

Copy-Move Image Forgery Detection Using Discrete Wavelet Transform

Vivek Mahale[1]([✉]), Pravin Yannawar[2], and Ashok Gaikwad[1]

[1] Institute of Management Studies and Information Technology, Aurangabad 431001, Maharashtra, India
mahalevh@gmail.com, drashokgaikwad@gmail.com
[2] Vison and Intelligent System Lab, Department of CS and IT, Dr. Babasaheb Ambedkar Marathwada University, Aurangabad, Maharashtra, India

Abstract. To expressing visual information Digital images play a significant role. On social media this information in form of digital image is continually increasing. Now a day easily digital images are misrepresented by peoples because availability of software using for image processing. In this paper we represent novel approaches which identify Copy-Move forgery in image using DWT. First we read image and convert this image into grayscale image. Then apply wavelet transform. Extract overlapped high contrast blocks of the coarsest level. Then lexicographically sorting and calculate phase correlation between rows. Extract blocks from reference and match region. Then draw the duplicate region. For evaluation of our system we calculate TPR, FPR, Accuracy and AUC. Our system accuracy $\simeq$ 94.58%.

Keywords: Copy-move · DWT · FAR · FRR

1 Introduction

Digital images play a very special role in expressing visual information. Since images are potent radices of communication because they are of impressive meaning and human visual system gains pictorial information faster than text and other kinds of information. Digital images have wide significant use in all orbits, like police investigation process, evidence in court, medical diagnosis, magazines, fashion and photo human bugs that state in our email [1]. Now a day people can record, store and share a large number of digital images and data because of easy and cost-effective devices that enables the acquisition of visual data at the same time increase of popularity of digital media and image editing software such as sophisticated photo editing tools has growing widespread for venomous purpose [2] that's why digital image has decreased or lost its pureness. An image can be transfiguring with various aim [3]. If, an image was transfigured for improve the quality and carry same information of original but clearer and better useful so that type of editing is called Innocent. If transfigure image carry some added, hidden information then that type of editing is called Malicious. Innocent image editing can be done by enhancement. Enhancement of image can be done by Histogram equalization,

© Springer Nature Singapore Pte Ltd. 2021
K. C. Santosh and B. Gawali (Eds.): RTIP2R 2020, CCIS 1380, pp. 158–168, 2021.
https://doi.org/10.1007/978-981-16-0507-9_14

color modification, contrast adjustment, filtering tools. Malicious image editing can be done by geometric modification and content modification. Geometric modification deals with rotation, zooming, cropping, resizing etc. Content modification deals with Copy-Paste, Copy-Move, Splicing, etc. In image analysis, transfigure or manipulated image has different questions such as [4].

Is image true or original? Or digitally alter.

1) If image is original, then what is genuine details of it.
2) If the image is digitally raised, then what is manipulated, and how ?
3) If image is computer generated, how was it produced?

In order to address questions method were broadly classified under three classes such as,

- **Observation**
  By close observation of image, some time with the help of shadows, secular heights, reflection, scale, color tone image inconsistency can be directly identified.
- **Basic Image Enhancement**
  With the different algorithms such as, re-coloring, scaling blurring, sharpening.
- **Advance Image Analysis**
  This involves LBP, DWT, PCA, Light direction or gradient and HOG Copy-Move image inconsistency is evil and normally used by a large population of users for various purposes; it may be for authorized or unauthorized.

Active [5–7] and passive or blind [8, 9] are two types method for image forgery detection. Prior information of image is need in active forgery detection method. Where as in case of passive forgery detection method, there is no need for prior information. Figure 1 shows methods involved image forgery detection and its types.

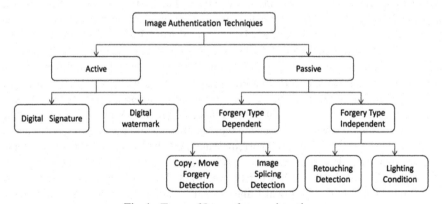

Fig. 1. Types of Image forgery detection.

Active Method
In an active method, adding image details like name, date i.e. calling water marking and digital signature [10] to mark the inconsistency of digital image like implant (embedding) the signature or coding in the image and watermark is a mark or message which hide in a picture to protect image copyright at the time of image acquisition [11].

Passive Method
Passive method is capable without prior information of image passive method was not needed to add additional information to detect image inconsistency. This is an assumption base technique because if tempered image does not have any visual passive this method has again two types i.e. forgery type dependent and forgery type in dependent. Forgery type dependent method are designed only for copy-move and splicing while forgery type independent base on artifact traces left and during process of re- sampling to lighting inconsistencies [12].

2   Related Work

In past so many work reported on image inconsistency detection. Passive copy move image detection by Ghulam et al. [13] used DWT method. They proposed that input image disintegrate LL1 and HH1, then segmented both in overlapping blocks and calculate Euclidean distance. Sort distance array in ascending order of both LL1 and HH1. Then match Euclidean distance values of LL1 and HH1 using threshold and take decision image is forge or genuine. In an image forgery detection by Saurabh A. et al. [14] used co-occurrence based texture operator in frequency domain. They work on CASIA, Columbia and DSO-1 dataset. They apply robust texture based on co-occurrences of LBP pair in SWT domain and for classification they were used SVM binary classifier. In paper copy – move forgery detection by Mohamad F.H. et al. [15] using DWT and SIFT feature. They first convert color image into grayscale image. Then apply DWT and segment image into 4 sub-band i.e. LL, HH, LH and HL. Then apply SIFL on LL properties. Extract key features and match repeating feature and mark it as a forge. Image Inconsistency Detection by Mahale V.H. et al. [16] use Histogram Oriented Gradient methods. They were using COMOFOD dataset. They divide dataset in train and test and perform acquisition, preprocessing, feature extraction, matching and decision. In acquisition they read image from dataset. In preprocessing the convert it into grayscale and apply Gaussian filter. In feature extract divide that gray image into 2x2 blocks and apply Histogram Oriented Gradient on each blocks. In matching process they calculate Euclidian distance and then take decision that the image is forge or original. They apply this method on 100 (50 forge and 50 original) and 200 (100 forge and 100 original) and calculate FAR and FRR. They conclude FAR = 0.63 and FRR = 0.37 when dataset is 100. FAR = 0.77 and FRR = 0.22 when dataset is 200. Image inconsistency detection by Vivek Mahale et.al [17]. Use Local Binary Pattern. They propose algorithm automatic forgery detection. In this algorithm first read image and then convert into gray scale. Divide this grayscale image into overlapping blocks. And apply LBP feature on each block. This feature array short by lexicographical sorting algorithm and then match similar blocks and dark that part of image which is forge. Then analyses result with calculating True Positive and False Positive Rate. In this paper calculate TPR and FPR for 2 × 2, 4 × 4, 8 × 8 and 16 × 16 blocks. Finally conclude that good results are coming on 2 × 2 block size. Image inconsistency detection by Vivek Mahale et.al [18] use Discrete CosineTransform (DCT). In their algorithm first preprocessing second feature extraction by DCT and then matching process. After matching process they find exact forge region and mark it. They Evaluate their system by calculating TPR, FPR and AUC of 0.3372, 0.5278 and 0.949 respectively.

3 Proposed Methodology

3.1 Preprocessing

In preprocessing we convert color image into grayscale image with following formula:

$$I = 0.299R + 0.587G + 0.114B \tag{1}$$

Here R means red, G means green, B means blue. After image convert into gray segment it into fix size overlapping blocks.

Here we initialize the parameters i.e. Block Size, No. of wavelet levels, Contrast threshold, Padding, Padding for second Phase; for each side, No of pre and post blocks to be compared and Phase correlation threshold.

3.2 Feature Extraction

Outputed pre processing of gray image is the inpute of feature extraction process. Apply Discrete Wavelet Transform (DWT) up to the specified level "L" to the gray image. The basic idea of using DWT is to reduce the size of the image at each level, e.g., a square image of size 2j × 2j pixels at level "L" is reduced to size 2j/2 × 2j/2 pixels at level L + 1. At each level, the image is decomposed into four sub images. The sub images are labeled LL, LH, HL and HH. Meanwhile LL corresponds to the coarse level coefficients or the approximation image. The matching is performed on the LL image at level 'L' referred to by LL_L.

Low Contrast Elimination: Calculate the contrast for each block in "A", then ignore blocks where contrast is the least, i.e. the contrast is less than the specified threshold (Fig. 2).

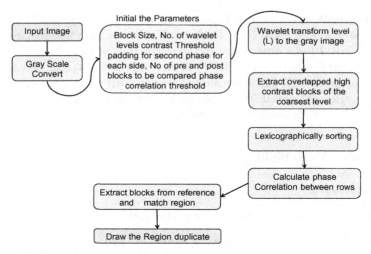

Fig. 2. The propose of study of detect image inconsistency using DWT

Algorithm 1: Automatic Forgery detection using DWT

Input: Image for determination of inconsistencies check

Output: Either Original or Forge image if Forge, dark forge area by Red color

Begin:

Step 1:Read Image

Step 2: Convert Color Image in to Gray scale image

Step 3: Initial the parameter Block Size, No. of wavelet levels, Contrast threshold, Padding, Padding for second Phase; for each side, No of pre and post blocks to be compared, Phase correlation threshold

Step 4: Apply Wavelet (Daubechies db1) transform up to specified level "L" to the gray image.

Step 5: Extract overlapped high contrast blocks of the coarsest level.

Step 6: Lexicographically sorting

Step 7: Find Phase correlation between rows.

Step 8: Extract blocks from reference and match region

Step 9: Take decision using threshold value that image is original or forge

Step 10: Draw the forge part.

End.

3.3 Matching Process

In the case of DWT, for each LL_{L-I} level in the image pyramid, where $I = 3,...L - 1$. There are two cases which was detection of the references and matching the block while the second was comparison and matching the block.

A. Case 1: Detection of Reference and Match Blocks

- Lexicographically Sorting: In this step lexicographic sorting is carried out on the rows of matrix "A". This type of sorting is applied on the rows of the matrix.
- Phase correlation: Calculate the phase correlation for the block corresponding to the current row "i" with the blocks corresponding to "p" rows above and below the current row. If the calculated maximum phase correlation value exceeds a preset threshold value "t", then store the top left coordinates of the corresponding reference block and the matching block from "B" matrix in a new row of a new matrix. The resulting candidate block is progressed to the next phase "Comparison of Reference and Match blocks"

B. Case 2: Comparison of Reference and Match Blocks

- Forming the regions: The candidate blocks, resulting from the previous phase, is considered as a region in "LL_{L-1}" level in the image pyramid. For each row in the matrix B that stored the coordinate of candidate block (reference and match blocks), the "reference" and "matching" regions are formed by padding "m" pixels on all the sides of the "b × b" for each of them (note that b is doubled in each iteration).
- Regions comparisons: For each "b × b" overlapped block in the reference region:
  - Find corresponding match in "matching region" based on Phase correlation but search process has to be opted for a selected part of the matching region.
  - If the computed maximum phase correlation value exceeds a preset threshold value, then the top left coordinates of the corresponding reference block and the matching block are stored in a new row of a new matrix.
- Iterative Comparisons: The previous steps is repeated and iterative region is compared directly on "LL_{L-i}" image, where i = 3, 4, 5..., L−1.
- Finally, Block detection: To identify the segments that have been copied and moved, the regions are directly compared on an original image through doubled blocks detection. The blocks are plotted as copied and pasted regions on the given input image.

Algorithm 2: describes the matching process of forgery detection methods step by step.

Algorithm 2: *Matching*

1:   **Input :** feature vector
2:   **Output:** distance matrix, Threshold values, detection part and marked
3:   **Begin :**
4:   **For** each LL$_{L-I}$ level in the image pyramid, where $i = 3,...L-1$. **do**
5:   **For** each row of the matrix **do**
6:     *A.* Form a reference region by padding "*m*" pixels on all the sides of the $b{\times}b$ reference block.
      B. Form a matching region by padding "m" pixels on all the sides of the $b{\times}b$matching block.
      C. Get all overlapped block in reference region by extracting the resulting pixel values byrows into a row of matrix "refReg", and store the topleft co-ordinates "indRef".
      D. Get all overlapped block in matching region by extracting the resulting pixel values byrows into a row of matrix "matchReg", and store the top-left co-ordinates "indMatch".
      E. Merge two matrices "refReg" and "matchReg" in "*A*", by labeling each block Of them with unique value in order to indicate the reference block and matching one in the merge.
      F. Sort matrix "*A*" lexicographically.
      G. Compare the current row with block corresponding to "*p*" rows below the current row. If the computed maximum phase correlation value exceeds a preset threshold value "*t*", then store the top left coordinates of the corresponding reference block and the matching block from the "index" matrix in a new row of a matrix.
7:   **End**
8. **End**
9. Plot the blocks as copied and pasted regions on the given input image.

---

4   Evaluation

The evaluation system based on True Positive Rate (TPR) and False Positive Rate (FPR) with the help of threshold value, which was generated from distance matrix from training and testing set. For evolution we have read 100 images out of it 50 original and 50 forge. Then extract feature and save it as template. Then load this template file and divide it train and test set. After that calculate Euclidian Distance (ED) with the help of Eq. 2.

$$d_{st} = \sqrt{\sum_{j=1}^{n}|x_i - y_i|^2} \qquad (2)$$

Then configuring the threshold (TH) and comparing Euclidian Distance with threshold values,

If, ED $\leq$ TH then count it as genuine.
Else, Count it as imposter.

With the help of genuine and imposter we calculate TPR and FPR respectively. Then plot ROC curve of FPR Vs TPR. Then from ROC curve we calculate AUC.

Parameter for Evaluation [18, 19]:

1.

$$TPR = \frac{TP}{TP + FN} \tag{3}$$

2.

$$FPR = \frac{FP}{TN + FP} \tag{4}$$

3.

$$\text{Accuracy} = \frac{(TP + TN)}{(TN + TP + FN + FP)} \tag{5}$$

4.

$$\text{AUC} = \frac{1}{2}\left(\frac{TP}{TN + FN} + \frac{TN}{TN + FP}\right) \tag{6}$$

5 Result and Discussion

The propose method is evaluated on COMOFOD dataset [20]. We download this dataset from Video Communication Laboratory (VLC), University of Zagrab, Croatia, and department of wireless communication. Image size is 512×512. We use laptop Intel Core i3, with 4 GB RAM and Hardware interface with MATLAB 2013, necessary toolbox.

The Fig. 3 shows some of the samples taken from COMOFOD database into cases original and forge.

(a) Original Image

(b) Forge Image

Fig. 3. Sample image taken from COMOFOD dataset (a) Original (b) Forge

In preprocessing initial the parameter i.e. Block Size = 8, number of wavelet levels L = 3, Contrast threshold = .440214, padding = 6, Padding for second Phase; for each side P = 4, No of pre and post blocks to be compared Phase correlation threshold Tr = 0.45. Then apply wavelet transform (Daubechies db1) up to specified level "L" and then extract overlapping blocks. After overlapping blocks lexicography sort is apply. Then measure correlation between blocks of training and testing. Then finally we found copy move forge part of image then colour that forge part. Following Fig. 4 shows examples of forge image and to detect forge part.

Fig. 4. Forge image with exact forge area detect and color that forge area (Color figure online)

Evaluation of our system, involves 100 images and applied algorithm and store feature in the template. Then calculate evaluation matrix True Positive Rate (TPR) and False Positive Rate (FPR) with the help of threshold values (Table 1).

Table 1. Shows evaluation result of our system extracting DWT features.

Dataset size	FPR	TPR	AUC
100	0.3192	0.5303	0.9686

The Fig. 5 shows the ROC curve of the system by FPR, TPR and area under curve.

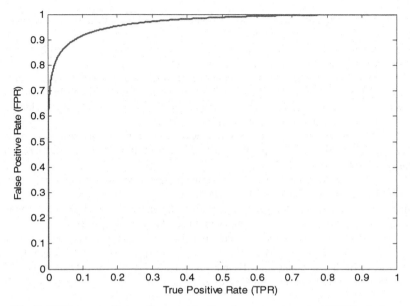

Fig. 5. ROC curve of image forgery detection the system by using DWT technique.

6 Conclusion

The paper present a significant method of copy-move forgery detection method based on DWT technique. The method was evaluated on COMOFOD dataset. On this dataset we apply DWT for feature extraction and then with calculating correlation we got exact forge part of an image. We calculated efficiency of the system using True positive Rate (TPR), False Positive Rate (FPR), Accuracy and Area under an ROC Curve (AUC). The evaluation from the proposed work shows TPR is 0.5303, FPR is 0.3192, accuracy $\simeq$ 94.58% and AUC is 0.9686.

References

1. Lee, J.-C., Chang, C.-P., Chen, W.-K.: Detection of copy–move image forgery using histogram of orientated gradients. Inf. Sci. **321**, 250–262 (2015)
2. Farid, H.: Image forgery detection. IEEE Signal Process. Mag. **26**(2), 16–25 (2009)
3. Piva, A.: An overview on image forensics. ISRN Signal Processing 2013 (2013)
4. Krawetz, N.: A Pictures Worth Digital Image Analysis and Forensics. Black Hat Briefings, pp. 1–31 (2007)
5. Cheddad, A., Condell, J., Curran, K., McKevitt, P.: Digital image steganography: survey and analysis of current methods. Signal Process. **90**(3), 727–752 (2010)

6. Rey, C., Dugelay, J.-L.: A survey of watermarking algorithms for image authentication. EURASIP J. Adv. Signal Process. **2002**, 218932 (2002). https://doi.org/10.1155/S11108657 02204047

7. Yeung, M.M.: Digital watermarking: marking the valuable while probing the invisible. Commun. ACM **41**(7), 31–35 (1998)

8. Lee, J.-C., Chang, C.-P., Chen, W.-K.: Detection of copy–move image forgery using histogram of orientated gradients. Inf. Sci. **321**, 250–262 (2015)

9. Mahdian, B., Saic, S.: Blind authentication using periodic properties of interpolation. IEEE Trans. Inf. Forensics Secur. **3**(3), 529–538 (2008). https://doi.org/10.1109/TIFS.2004.924603

10. Thajeel, S.A., Bin Sulong, G.: State of the art of copy-move forgery detection techniques: a review. Int. J. Comput. Sci. Issues **10**(6), 174183 (2013)

11. Vaidya, S.P., Mouli, P.V.S.S.R.C., Santosh, K.C.: Imperceptible watermark for a game-theoretic watermarking system. Int. J. Mach. Learn. Cybern. **10**(6), 1323–1339 (2018). https://doi.org/10.1007/s13042-018-0813-x

12. Mushtaq, S., Mir, A.: Digital image forgeries and passive image authentication techniques: a survey. Int. J. Adv. Sci. Technol. **73**, 15–32 (2014)

13. Muhammad, G., Hussain, M., Bebis, G.: Passive copy move image forgery detection using undecimated dyadic wavelet transform. Digit. Invest. **9**(1), 49–57 (2012)

14. Agarwal, S., Chand, S.: Image forgery detection using co-occurrence-based texture operator in frequency domain. In: Sa, P.K., Sahoo, M.N., Murugappan, M., Wu, Y., Majhi, B. (eds.) Progress in Intelligent Computing Techniques: Theory, Practice, and Applications. AISC, vol. 518, pp. 117–122. Springer, Singapore (2018). https://doi.org/10.1007/978-981-10-3373-5_10

15. Hashmi, M.F., Hambarde, A.R., Keskar, A.G.: Copy move forgery detection using DWT and SIFT features. In: 2013 13th International Conference on Intelligent Systems Design and Applications (ISDA), pp. 188–193. IEEE (2013)

16. Mahale, V., Yannawar, P., Gaikwad, A.T.: Image inconsistency detection using histogram of orientated gradient (HOG). In: 2017 1st International Conference on Intelligent Systems and Information Management (ICISIM), pp. 22–25. IEEE (2017)

17. Mahale, V.H., Ali, M.M., Yannawar, P.L., Gaikwad, A.T.: Image inconsistency detection using local binary pattern (LBP). Procedia Comput. Sci. **115**, 501–508 (2017)

18. Sokolova, M., Lapalme, G.: A systematic analysis of performance measures for classification tasks. Information Process. Manag. **45**(4), 427–437 (2009)

19. Gornale, S.S., Babaleshwar, A.K., Yannawar, P.L.: Content based video retrieval for indian traffic signage's (2019)

20. CoMoFoD database. https://www.vcl.fer.hr/comofod

A Comprehensive Survey of Different Phases for Involuntary System for Face Emotion Recognition

Dipti Pandit[1,2(✉)] and Sangeeta Jadhav[3]

[1] Vishwakarma Institute of Information Technology, Pune, India
dppandit@gmail.com
[2] D Y Patil College of Engineering, Pune, India
[3] Army Institute of Technology, Pune, India
hodit@aitpune.edu.in

Abstract. Involuntary recognition of basic and non-basic emotions has started great curiosity in research area. Developing a fully automated computational model for face emotion analysis is quite difficult a human face is complex, multi-dimensional and has different meaningful visual messages to pass. A big research augmented in Human Computer Interaction over decades but still many queries are still clueless as in what should be the important signs and expressions to be evaluated for meaning encoding of messages. In this paper fundamental components, as face image acquisition, registration, pre-processing or dimensionality reduction, feature extraction and learning, classifiers, recognition, datasets and new designs for involuntary expression identification is been reviewed in detail. The paper also enlightens some core problems like illumination variations, registration faults, occlusions due to head movements or glasses, age and any disorders.

Keywords: Face emotion recognition · Registration · Dimension reduction · Feature representation · Classifiers · Datasets · Challenges

1 Introduction

Face is a very imperative biometric feature of human being. Face emotions can be understood mainly by two ways, verbal i.e. audible form or nonverbal i.e. facial expression, action body postures and gesture form of communication. Research shows that maximum communication can be through facial expression then verbal [1]. Facial expressions or emotions are sensed, interpreted and analyzed in different disciplines like biology, neuro science, advertisement, website testing, sociology, security, computer science, psychology and many more. Psychological science always needs help to develop tools and models for understanding the mental health and promoting well-being [2–9]. Cognitive Science provides the guide lines to encode the facial representation. According to the research, the facial expressions or emotions are marked according to the time duration i.e. macro expressions (typically last for 3/4th to 2 s) or micro expressions (typically

© Springer Nature Singapore Pte Ltd. 2021
K. C. Santosh and B. Gawali (Eds.): RTIP2R 2020, CCIS 1380, pp. 169–182, 2021.
https://doi.org/10.1007/978-981-16-0507-9_15

last for 1/25th to 1/3rd seconds) and their representation approaches are focused on three types: Holistic Matching, Feature based or structural based and Hybrid methods.

The main challenges in involuntary expression or emotion recognition may appear due to non-accurate computation, spontaneous affective behavior, lighting variation because of head movements, registration techniques cause registration faults, accessories or camera movements may cause occlusions, subject independent expressions cause for identity errors and wrinkles caused due to aging may miss or give false expressions [61] (Fig. 1).

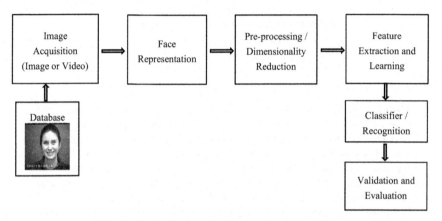

Fig. 1. Block diagram for face emotion recognition

This paper is break down in sections of fundamental components like Sect. 2, face acquisition and registration, Sect. 3, pre-processing and dimensionality reduction, Sect. 4, datasets, Sect. 5, feature extraction and learning, Sect. 6, recognition or classifiers. The paper will also discuss the different validation and evaluation methods in Sect. 7, used for measuring the accuracy of different algorithms. Challenges in expression recognition as well as dealing with them in each module is discussed in detail.

2 Face Acquisition and Registration

Face acquisition and its registration is the fundamental set for expression recognition. Facial behaviors are usually recorded using good resolution cameras and the participants are informed accordingly to posed and non-posed emotions. Ekman and his colleagues developed a basic emotion recognition model where they claimed about some emotions are hard wired in human brains [13]. Viola-Jones method [46] and Subspace Constrained Mean-shifts [49] can be used for face detection and tracking. Viola-Jones method for object and face detection is the well-known method used for face detection and uses the Harr technique [62]. Registration technique can be categorized as landmarking and generic depending on the technique applied on the region of interest.

In landmark based registration, detecting face and to locate the distance between the eye to eye or eye-nose-mouth is performed for detecting facial landmarks. Computing more points enhances the advantages as the registration becomes more inflexible/less sensitive to errors and also cope-up with the head-pose variations. Flexible registration like Active Appearance Models (AAM) works on portion-wise affine transformations around each landmark [19, 20]. More then 60–70 points are used in computation for Active Appearance Models (AAM) [20, 22], Free-Form Deformation (FFD), enables local registration and can suppress registration errors [18]. Generic registration techniques are normally more exact when subject is known in prior and is used as template. Techniques such as Lucas-Kanade or Robust FFT are one of these approaches used in sequence registration and inflexible registration. Generic techniques such as SIFT (Scale Invariant Feature Transform) flow can be used for flexible registration [49, 64]. SIFT flow for facial sequence registration uses a technique called Avatar image registration technique. Convolution of 3D morphable face models (3DMM) shape and texture is used for robust face recognition [56] (Fig. 2).

Primary landmarks		Secondary landmarks	
Number	Definition	Number	Definition
16	Left eyebrow outer corner	1	Left temple
19	Left eyebrow inner corner	8	Chin tip
22	Right eyebrow inner corner	2-7, 9-14	Cheek contours
25	Right eyebrow inner corner	15	Right temple
28	Left eye outer corner	16-19	Left eyebrow contours
30	Left eye inner corner	22-25	Right eyebrow corners
32	Right eye inner corner	29, 33	Upper eyelid centres
34	Right eye outer corner	31, 35	Lower eyelid centres
41	Nose tip	36, 37	Nose saddles
46	Left mouth corner	40, 42	Nose peak (Nostrils)
52	Right mouth corner	38-40, 42-45	Nose contours
63, 64	Eye centres	47-57, 53-62	Mouth contours

Fig. 2. Red dot denote utmost fiduciary and green dots are the secondary points. (Fig. ref [22]) (Color figure online)

3   Pre-processing and Dimension Reduction Techniques

Pre-processing is an operation performed with image for grey scaling or scaling down the image, or enhancement of some image features by suppressing the unwanted distortions as well as for correction required due to any artifacts and occlusions. Many times, image pre-processing is equivalent to mathematical normalization in many feature selection methods. Dimensionality reduction is usually plotting of data to a beneath dimensional space which is closely correlated like clustering the data but the goals can differ and can be used for eliminating illumination variation, registration errors and identity bias [21, 23]. Depending on the feature selection different pre-processing methods are used; as in color SIFT algorithm [23] will require different pre-processing technique then that of a local binary feature which uses grey scale data. For improving illumination effect, Laplacian of Gaussian or histogram equalization, global normalization [16]; Eigen Phases and Nuclear Norm based Matrix Regression (NMR) models for partial face registration [25, 26] are used as pre-processing techniques. In 1981, for image alignment in computer vision, a widely used Lucas-Kanade algorithm was proposed.

Fourier spectrum of the LBP histogram used to provide rotational invariance [19]. Non-linear optimization and Supervised Decent Method (SDM) methods are used to solve the problems due to camera calibration, image alignment, structure from motion and many more [27]. Sparse-representation for visual tracking considers holistic representation for reconstruction error and may fail with similar objects and occlusions therefore structural local sparse modelling is used [28, 29, 54]. 3D facial model restored from 2D images also provide enhancement of robustness like motions, head rotations and partial occlusions [57]. To improve the Multiview face detection patch scaling is done before Deep Convolution Neural Network on FDDB data set [30].

Pooling techniques is normally applied on many small regions across the image for dimensionality reduction can be applied to spatial as well as spatio-time-based [11]. Some of the different pooling techniques are histogram, binning features overload, sampling the min or max value, calculating the average or sum of feature across the neighborhood. By normalizing the output of pooling, its sensitivity to illumination can be solved [33]. Methods like FEDIP is also used for dimension truncate through feature abstraction [32]. Selection of feature is for filtering irrelevant or redundant features from datasets which is also used as dimension reduction. Different feature selection techniques are selecting and weighting certain spatial regions manually [31], generic techniques like data driven feature selection and boosting are designed for prediction [36].

4 Datasets

Using few hardware synchronized cameras with good resolution, facial behavior can be recorded. Participants are instructed to pose a series of basic emotions or even the small video is displayed to capture the instant emotions. The Facial Action Coding System (FACS) [59] helps in computing facial movement in terms of component actions and it consists of facial action units (AU) which has four time-based segments: neutral, apex, onset and offset; which are well analyzed in psychology [14–16]. The sentiments are categorized as basic emotions like happy, surprised, sad, anger, disgust, fear and non-basic emotions such as power, expectation, valence, contempt, relief, pain and many more.

Most broadly used posed type datasets like the Ekman, CK and MMI datasets include elementary emotions and facial action units (AU) remarks. The complete CK dataset with its intensity annotations for 14 AU is provided frame-by-frame in Enhanced CK dataset. Spontaneous recording and original subjects, with remarks and labels for non-basic emotions, contempt, are included in CK + dataset [14]. MMI-Facial Expression database comprises recording of the time-based pattern of a facial expression (neutral, apex, onset and offset) including the basic emotions with a single FACS Action Unit (AU) [13]. Natural sentimental behavior is added in MMI with non-posed numerous emotion recognition situation like action units, dimensional emotion and pain detection. SEMAINE [16] is a non-posed dataset, with 3 basic and 10 non-basic emotion video datasets. The dataset collected from professional actors called GEMEP [7], includes 6 basic emotions and 15 non-basic emotions. Japanese Female Facial Expression (JAFFE) has 7 expressions out of which 6 are basic and 1 neutral, posed by Japanese females [35]. The Facial Expression Recognition (FERA) contest determined AU detection with separate sentiments cataloguing for 4 basic sentiments and 1 non-basic sentiment [14, 16]. The Audio/Visual Emotion Challenges (AVEC) [17] gauged dimensional affect models and highlights the limitations which dealing with impulsive affective behavior (Table 1).

Table 1. Outline of available Datasets

	Dataset	BE	NBE	Action units	Variations	No. of subjects	Images	Videos	Image sizes
Posed	CK	6+N		Yes		97		486	640 × 490
	MMI	6+N		Yes		75	484	2420	
	GEMEP$	6+N	15	Yes		10		7000	
	FERET	N				1199	14126		384 × 256
	ORL	2*				40	400		92 × 112
	AR	6+N	6			130	3000		
	CMU-PIE	6+N		Yes	Illumination	337	750000		
	Film Ground hog day	6+N		Yes	Pose, illumination and partial occlusion		300		
	IMM Face					40	240		640 × 480
Posed and Non-Posed	CK+	6+N	1	Yes		123		593#	10 to 60 frames
	MMI	6+N	1	Yes		75	484	2420#	
	JAFFE	6+N				10	213		576 × 768
Non-Posed	SEMAINE	3	10	Yes		150		959	780 × 580
	HUMAINE		2			4		23	
	RU-FACS	3				100		100	

*Eyes open and closed, smiling and nonsmiling
#Spontaneous behavior recording.
$Audio data available.

5   Feature Extraction and Learning

Feature Abstraction is a set of technique that allows a system to remove unwanted variances from a dataset and helps to inevitably learn the representations which is required for feature detection or classification. The downstream classifiers or regression estimators can perform better [32] and can be adaptive or non-adaptive because of feature extraction and learning. The most popular adaptive transform is Principal Component Analysis [28, 29] and Discrete Cosine Transform is the non-adaptive transformation. LDA (Linear Discriminant Analysis) is a supervised alternative to PCA [31] where labelled information is used to learn to differentiate between differently labelled representation and it also can handle more than 2 classes [34].

Facial extraction and learning can be classified according to the type of data encoded as: appearance or shape [12]. Shape type learning are less common then the appearance-based image but are used for point learning or in landmarking techniques. Appearance based image learning is of low-level and high-level information encrypting. Different techniques used for facial learning are spatial [10] i.e. encrypt image sequences frame after frame and spatio-time-based [11] where a small region of frames is to be considered and neural network. Spatio-time-based considers series of borders within a time-based space as a solitary object and embodies expression more competently by enabling modelling time-based properties. It can categorize the expressions that look alike in space and enable the combination of area facts from psychology point of view which relates muscular movement with posed and spontaneous expressions (Table 2).

Table 2. List of appearance based learning techniques

Appearance based	
Spatial	Spatio-time-based
Low level histogram	LBP-TOP
LBP	LQP-TOP
LPQ	LGBP-TOP
Gabor	3D HoG
Data driven-BoW	HOOF
HoG	CLBP-TOP
NMF	Multi Kernel Learning
Sparse coding	MDMO
	Dynamic Harr
	Time-based BoW

5.1 Appearance Based Learning

Low level histogram [10] extracts local features and then encodes them in changed image, later, collects these features into unvarying regions. It is computationally simple, allows real time operation, robust to registration error and illumination variation but suffers from identity bias. LBP (Local Binary Pattern), [34, 35] defines local texture variation along with circular region learning. LBP along with feed-forward neural network is also used for facial expression detection [37]. To blur the insensitive texture classification LPQ (Local Phase Quantization) descriptor was used with local Fourier transform [38]. HOG method (Histogram of Gradients), removes limited attributes by using gradient operators and encodes the output in relation of scale and position [19, 37, 39]. Convolution of Gabor filters of diverse balances and alignments with input image is done to achieve the Gabor representation.[39]. The Gabor filter encodes componential information like features or contrast [39, 40]. This type of learning is sturdy to registration faults and to small translations and rotations of the image as well as due to convolution computation becomes costly. Bag-of-words learning, in sentiment recognition labels limited regions by mining limited attributes, by measuring the scale invariant feature transform from fixed points and computing the similar features. This type of learning overcomes various problems like illumination variation and small registration faults (Table 3).

Table 3. List of shape based learning techniques

Shape based	
Spatial	Spatio-time-based
Facial points	Geometric Feature
	Space Time Interest Points

NMF (Non-negative Matrix Factorization) may also be called as clustering method which are not unique and are designed for various semantic interpretations which creates no of basis images from where the features are pulled out from the coefficients of the base image. Illumination and registration faults are subject to data used for training purpose [41]. Maximum coefficients of the new image are zero with Sparse code approach [42]. Most popular approach in spatial as well as in spatio-time-based learning is the feature extracting from three orthogonal planes (TOP). LBP extended to LBP-TOP [43] to be used for emotion and AU recognition, whereas, for AU and time-based segment recognition LQP-TOP is used [44]. Dealing with real time processing can be attained depending on the dimensions of the spatial and time-based window operators by LBP-TOP and LPQ-TOP even if they are complex in computation. Both are robust with variations in illuminations but sensitive to registration errors and identity bias. The previous results of LGBP with TOP extensions of other feature selection methods are then combined to form three orthogonal planes of LGBP [45]. Many more methods can be seen used in micro-expression recognition, like 3DHOG, HOOF, Complete Local Binary Pattern CLBP, extended CLBP as CLBP-TOP as well as Multi kernel learning and Main Directional Mean Optical Flow MDMO [47]. Wrapping strategy upsurges the accuracy of detection in optical flow [24]. Encoding the time-based differences in the input sequence with its binary values by applying a threshold to each frame is achieved in Dynamic Haar feature approach [46]. Depending on features selected and time-based sequential window size, Dynamic Harr learning can be done [62]. Time-based Bag-of-words learning are specific to AU detection and represents arbitrary subset where each frame from subset is denoted by means of SIFT learning and compressed with PCA to get framewise vector. This type is sensitive to registration errors, identity bias, illumination variation and head pose variations.

5.2 Shape Based Learning

Geometric features learning describes face shape and movement from the fiducial points. It compares the current frame with the neutral face with respect to length and angle of lines. The computation for this type of learning is simple but sensitive to registration error and the depends on accurate point learning. Space Time Interest Points is also one of the methods built on spatio-time-based features used for computation on videos for body movements [11].

5.3 Neural Networks

Low-level learning is robust to light variations and registration errors whereas issues like identity bias and creating features which are interpretable can be solved by using high-level learning. Hybrid feature learning approach which bridges the low-level and high-level together is also called as deep learning. Deep learning is an architype that acquires useful data from multi-layered graded learning. There are mainly two layers, where in the first layer, different filter and the input is convolved and second layer that totals the convolved output using pooling. The higher-level layers in deep learning normally are designed for various purpose such as tacking aging and partial occlusion. Here the filtering and pooling improves the registration process against illumination and registration error. Dimension reduction of an image is must in any system using deep learning. The size and number of convolution filters is overhead or a bottleneck of the learning process.

Convolution with smooth filters, represents time-based variation in textural variation with features by convolving with filters. Different filters are used depending on the application such as Gabor filter, Independent Component (IC) filters, IIR and Laplacian filter. As Gabor and IC filters assume time-based registration through-out the successive images in a sequence, they are more sensitive to registration faults and more over they have a lot of computation as they involve three-dimensional convolution with many filters. The filtering methods which filter each pixel with its local spatial neighborhood are usually very efficient; like anisotropic diffusion, bilateral filter. Regularization can be used for the same smoothing purpose. Drop out is one of the methods for regularization [58]. Most optimization-based approaches are time consuming and so new approaches train a deep neural network using the smoothened images generated by existing different smoothing algorithms.

6 Recognition

The quality of data used for training as well as the method or algorithm used for machine learning decides the performance of the recognition. For classification many of the times Gabor wavelet coefficients and linear discriminant analysis (LDA) are used. Most expression recognition systems use a generic model such as SVM. Several models addressed issues like modelling of time-based variation of expressions, using domain knowledge, expression dimensions and personalizing existing models. Typically for time-based variation of facial expression models like HMM [48], to enhance prediction are combined with SVM or Boosting. Personalization for motion recognition can be modelled by reweighting the training samples with respect to data input using discriminative classifiers such as SVM [50, 51, 56, 60]. Recognition of real time tracking of mouth shapes is done by author Oliver et al. using HMM with maximum likelihood. Support Vector Clustering (SVC) algorithm as unsupervised learning method is stimulated by support vector machines [52]. Expression like valence and arousal are intercorrelated and can be recognized by extended RVM and CRF (Conditional Random Fields) [53]. Sparse Representation base Classification (SRC) can be used when the face is partly corrupted or occluded [54]. Arithmetical models such as Relevance Vector Machine and Dynamic Bayesian Network are inspired to learn time-based dependencies in supervised as well as unsupervised manner. Face movement is limited by face muscular limitation. Some face movements actions are completely isolated where as others cannot be displayed simultaneously. The AU recognition system improves these needs through arithmetical models as Deep Belief Networks (DBN) or Restricted Boltzmann Machines (RBM) [40]. Spotting time-based segmentation of facial expression is also done using the strain impact on the skin due to muscle movement over the region with duration. In [62], for strain magnitudes in micro expressions, use of global threshold for macro and local threshold for time-based duration is done.

Deep learning algorithm is considered as a break-through in the field of recognition. It can automatically extract useful features from raw data unusual as for the feature extractor techniques like HOG, SIFT, LBF which require manual efforts for extraction. Deep learning networks are trained using database to set the weights of the trained network and then used on testing set of data base. Deep learning using neural networks for learning approaches consist of layers like convolution layers, drop-out layer, max pooling layers, activation function as well as fully connected layers. Alex Net [55], VGG-CNN [55, 56], ResNet [56] and Random Forest algorithm [57] are some of the type of methods for deep learning. Hui chen et al. [57] have used random forest algorithm which concurrently integrates regression for face tracking as well as constant emotion estimation. In [58], Random Forest algorithm consists of many classification and regression trees and can deal with great amount number of training samples without overfitting. An activation function is used for convolution layers like ReLU (Rectifier Linear Unit) for preventing gradient vanishing problem [16, 58]. For regularizing of the network drop out method is used. The filter sizes may vary for convolution layer as well as for pooling. The network models use the multi-nominal logistic regression also known as SoftMax activation function for classification [58]. SoftMax classification is widely replaced by SVM for classification. In [55], for static face emotion recognition, transfer learning approach is used for small dataset in wild. Combination of Alex Net and VGG-CNN with supervised training showed up better performance.

7   Validation and Evaluation

Mostly the emotion recognition systems are authenticated on posed type of datasets, differing completely from realistic dataset in terms of illumination, head position variation, and spontaneous expressions. The non-posed type of datasets also exists and include categorial basic and non-basic sentiments, AU and pain recognition. Even micro expressions dataset for spontaneous expression are available but not in naturalistic data form. Typical validation decorum is to compared with the autonomous cross validation for evaluating a system. Some of the mostly adopted versions are: 7-fold-cross validation [40, 63]; leave-one-subject-out cross validation [60], allowing use of the most data for individual data-independent validation; for balanced binary classification task [60], ROC curve is designed; F1 Score for harmonic mean precision and recall for imbalanced data [60]. Highlighting the abilities of an algorithm and to analyze the method towards generalization is done using Cross-database validation where the dataset for training and testing are different [51]. The evaluation of emotion recognition algorithms has been done using ROC metrics, average recognition rate, root mean square error and mean absolute error. Confusion/error matrix is also used for describing the performance of a classifier [55]. The best accuracy in confusion matrix is one and worst is zero.

8   Conclusion

Expressions are signals used to convey a message whereas emotions are referred to the message through expressions. Humans can detect and recognize emotions without fail which is studied to be used in computerization implementation. Due to its applications face expression recognition still remains very challenging for researchers. This paper presented complete review of the face emotion\expression recognition system addressing all possible techniques with steps starting from face acquisition, datasets, feature extraction and representation learning, recognition / classifier and validation methods. Representation approaches which can be categories as holistic matching, structural based and hybrid methods. There are many challenges like non accurate computation and registration errors like illumination variation, spontaneous emotional behavior, head movements and many more. Face acquisition or registration can be done by methods like Viola Jones and Subspace Constrained Mean Shift. Generic registrations are more accurate with prior known subject. Methods like Viola-Jones for detection and AAM for flexible registration works well on portion wise affine transformations. Techniques like Lucas Kanada or Robust FFT, SIFT, 3DMM are few of the techniques used for robust recognition. Pre-processing works on artifacts, like illumination variation registration error and removing unwanted distortion. Eigen phases, NMR, SIFT are few of the techniques mostly used. Pooling technique, Random projection and manifolds are computationally less expensive in dimensional reduction. In deep learning holistic feature learning with convolution of filters according to its application is applied. SRC, RVM, RBM are some dominating classifiers, while in deep learning, fully connected layers with trained algorithms work compatibly well. ReLu activation function normally seems to be used for preventing gradient vanishing problem. Dealing with natural expression and prediction of emotions still remains a good challenge. The research objective is to facilitate and connect the psychophysics, neuroscience and the computer vision communities.

References

1. Mehrabian, A.: Communication without words. Psychol. Today. **2**, 53–56 (1968)
2. Altamura, M., et al.: Facial emotion recognition in bipolar disorder and healthy aging. J. Nerv. Mental Disease **204**(3), 188–193 (2016). https://doi.org/10.1097/NMD.0000000000000453
3. Schulze, L., Domes, G., Köppen, D., Herpertz, S.C.: Enhanced detection of emotional facial expressions in borderline personality disorder. Psychopathology **46**, 217–224 (2013)
4. Harms, M.B., Martin, A., Wallace, G.L.: Facial emotion recognition in autism spectrum disorders: a review of behavioural and neuroimaging studies. Neuropsychol. Rev. **20**, 290–322 (2010). https://doi.org/10.1007/s11065-010-9138-6
5. Kohler, C.G., et al.: Facial emotion recognition in schizophrenia: intensity effects and error pattern. Am. J. Psychiatry **160**(10), 1768–1774 (2003)
6. Ricciardi, L., et al.: Facial emotion recognition and expression in Parkinson's disease: an emotional mirror mechanism. PLOS ONE **12**, e0169110 (2017)
7. Adolphs, R.: Perception and emotion: how we recognize facial expressions. Assoc. Psychol. Sci. **15**(5), 222–226 (2006)
8. O'Leary-Barrett, M., et al.: Personality, attentional biases towards emotional faces and symptoms of mental disorders in an adolescent sample. PLOS ONE: Pers. Atten. Biases Predictors Psychopathol. **10**, e0128271 (2015)
9. Addington, D., Addington, J., Schissel, B.: A depression rating scale for schizophrenics. Schizophrenia Res. **3**(4), 247–251 (1990)
10. Caponetti, L., Castellano, G.: Low-level image processing. In: Caponetti, L. (ed.) Fuzzy Logic for Image Processing, pp. 15–37. Springer, Heidelberg (2017). https://doi.org/10.1007/978-3-319-44130-6_2
11. Huang, H., Shen, L., Zhang, R., Makedon, F., Pearlman, J.: A spatio-temporal modeling method for shape representation. In: Third International Symposium on 3D Data Processing, Visualization, and Transmission (3DPVT 2006), pp.1034–1040. IEEE, Chapel Hill (2006)
12. Georghiades, A.S., Belhumeur, P.N., Kriegman, D.J.: From few to many: illumination cone models for face recognition under variable lighting and pose. IEEE Trans. Pattern Anal. Mach. Intell. **23**(6), 643–660 (2001)
13. Ekman, P., Friesen, W.: Facial Action Coding System: A technique for the Measurement of Facial Movement. Consulting Psychologists Press, Palo Alto (1978)
14. Ding, X., Chu, W.-S., De la Torre, F., Cohn, J.F., Wang, Q.: Facial action unit event detection by cascade of tasks. In: 2013 IEEE International Conference on Computer Vision (ICCV), pp. 2400–2407 (2013)
15. Eleftheriadis, S., Rudovic, O., Pantic, M.: Joint facial action unit detection and feature fusion: a multi-conditional learning approach. IEEE Trans. Image Process. **25**(12), 5727–5742 (2016)
16. Gudi, A., Tasli, H.E., Den Uyl, T.M., Maroulis, A.: Deep learning based FACS action unit occurrence and intensity estimation. In: 11th IEEE International Conference and Workshops on Automatic Face and Gesture Recognition (FG), Ljubljana, pp. 1–5 (2015)
17. Cruz, A.C., Bhanu, B., Thakoor, N.S.: Vision and attention theory based sampling for continuous facial emotion recognition. IEEE Trans. Affect. Comput. **5**(4), 418–431 (2014)
18. Koelstra, S., Pantic, M., Patras, I.: A dynamic texture-based approach to recognition of facial actions and their temporal models. IEEE Trans. Pattern Anal. Mach. Intell. **32**(11), 1940–1954 (2010)
19. Chew, S.W., et al.: In the pursuit of effective affective computing: the relationship between features and registration. IEEE Trans. Syst. Man Cybern. Part B Cybern. **42**(4), 1006–1016 (2012)
20. Edwards, G.J., Cootes, T.F., Taylor, C.J.: Active appearance models. IEEE Trans. Pattern Anal. Mach. Intell. **23**(6), 681–685 (2001)

21. Harsanyi, J.C., Chang, C.I.: Hyperspectral image classification and dimensionality reduction: an orthogonal subspace projection approach. IEEE Trans. Geosci. Remote Sens. **32**(4), 779–785 (1994)
22. Çeliktutan, O., Ulukaya, S., Sankur, B.: A comparative study of face landmarking techniques. EURASIP J. Image Video Process. **2013**(1), 1–27 (2013). https://doi.org/10.1186/1687-5281-2013-13
23. Burges, C.J.C.: Geometric methods for feature extraction and dimensional reduction: a guided tour. In: Rokach, L., Maimon, O. (eds.) Data Mining and Knowledge Discovery Handbook: A Complete Guide for Practitioners and Researchers. Kulwer Academic Publishers (2004)
24. Brox, T., Bruhn, A., Papenberg, N., Weickert, J.: High accuracy optical flow estimation based on a theory for warping. In: Pajdla, T., Matas, J. (eds.) ECCV 2004. LNCS, vol. 3024, pp. 25–36. Springer, Heidelberg (2004). https://doi.org/10.1007/978-3-540-24673-2_3
25. Savvides, M., Kumar, B.V.K.V., Khosla, P.K.: Eigenphases vs eigenfaces. In: 17th International Conference on Pattern Recognition, Cambridge (2004)
26. Yang, J., Luo, L., Qian, J., Tai, Y., Zhang, F., Xu, Y.: Nuclear norm based matrix regression with applications to face recognition with occlusion and illumination changes. IEEE Trans. Pattern Anal. Mach. Intell. **39**(1), 156–171 (2017)
27. Xiong, X., De la Torre, F.: Supervised descent method and its applications to face alignment. In: IEEE Conference on Computer Vision and Pattern Recognition, pp. 532–539 (2013)
28. Jia, X., Lu, H., Yang, M.H.: Visual tracking via adaptive structural local sparse appearance model. In: IEEE Conference on Computer Vision and Pattern Recognition, USA (2012)
29. Wagner, A., Wright, J., Ganesh, A., Zhou, Z., Mobahi, H., Ma, Y.: Towards a practical face recognition system: robust alignment and illumination by sparse representation. IEEE Trans. Pattern Anal. Mach. Intell. **34**(2), 372–386 (2012)
30. Zhang, C., Zhang, Z.: Improving multiview face detection with muti-task deep convolutional neural networks. In: IEEE Winter Conference on Applications of Computer Vision, USA (2014)
31. Loog, M., Duin, R.P.W., Haeb-Umbach, R.: Multiclass linear dimension reduction by weighted pairwise fisher criteria. IEEE Trans. Pattern Anal. Mach. Intell. **23**(7), 762–766 (2001)
32. Tariq, A., Karim, A.: Fast supervised feature extraction by term discrimination information pooling. In: 20th ACM International Conference on Information and Knowledge Management, CIKM 2011, Scotland, pp. 2233–2236 (2011)
33. Zhang, P., Peng, J., Domeniconi, C.: Kernel pooled local subspaces for classification. IEEE Trans. Syst. Man Cybern. Part B: Cybern. **35**(3), 489–502 (2005)
34. Ahonen, T., Hadid, A., Pietikainen, M.: Face description with local binary patterns: application to face recognition. IEEE Trans. Pattern Anal. Mach. Intell. **28**(12), 2037–2041 (2006)
35. Shan, C., Gong, S., McOwan, P.W.: Facial expression recognition based on local binary patterns: a comprehensive study. Image Vision Comput. **27**(6), 803–816 (2009)
36. Friedman, J., Hastie, T., Tibshirani, R.: Additive logistic regression: a statistical view of boosting. Ann. Stat. **28**(2), 337–407 (2000)
37. Gritti, T., Shan, C., Jeanne, V., Braspenning, R.: Local features based facial expression recognition with face registration errors. In: 8th IEEE International Conference on Automation Face and Gesture Recognition (2008)
38. Jiang, B., Valstar, M., Martinez, B., Pantic, M.: A dynamic appearance descriptor approach to facial actions temporal modelling. J. LATEX Class Files **6**(1), 1–14 (2011)
39. Cruz, A., Bhanu, B., Thakoor, N.S.: Facial emotion recognition with anisotropic inhibited gabor energy histograms. In: IEEE International Conference on Image Processing (2013)
40. Zhao, X., Shi, X., Zhang, S.: Facial expression recognition via deep learning. J. IETE Tech. Rev. **32**(5), 347–355 (2015)

41. Zafeiriou, L., Nikitidis, S., Zafeiriou, S., Pantic, M.: Slow features nonnegative matrix factorization for temporal data decomposition. In: IEEE International Conference on Image Processing (2014)
42. Zhang, M., Sawchuk, A.A.: Human daily activity recognition with sparse representation using wearable sensors. IEEE J. Biomed. Health Inform. **17**(3), 553–560 (2013)
43. Zhao, G., Pietikainen, M.: Dynamic texture recognition using local binary patterns with an application to facial expressions. IEEE Trans. Pattern Anal. Mach. Intell. **29**, 915–928 (2007)
44. Ojansivu, V., Heikkilä, J.: Blur insensitive texture classification using local phase quantization. In: Elmoataz, A., Lezoray, O., Nouboud, F., Mammass, D. (eds.) ICISP 2008. LNCS, vol. 5099, pp. 236–243. Springer, Heidelberg (2008). https://doi.org/10.1007/978-3-540-69905-7_27
45. Almaev, T.R., Valstar, M.F.: Local gabor binary patterns from three orthogonal planes for automatic facial expression recognition. In: IEEE: Humaine Association Conference on Affective Computing and Intelligent Interaction (2013)
46. Viola, P., Jones, M.J.: Robust Real-Time Face Detection. International Journal of Computer Vision **57**(2), 137–154 (2004). https://doi.org/10.1023/B:VISI.0000013087.49260.fb
47. Liu, Y.J., Zhang, J.K., Yan, W.J., Wang, S.J., Zhao, G., Fu, X.: A main directional mean optical flow feature for spontaneous micro-expression recognition. IEEE Trans. Affect. Comput. **7**(4), 299–310 (2016)
48. Chen, J.-L., Kundu, A.: Rotation and gray scale transform invariant texture identification using wavelet decomposition and hidden Markov model. IEEE Trans. Pattern Anal. Mach. Intell. **16**(2), 208–214 (1994)
49. Berretti, S., Amor, B., Daoudi, M., del Bimbo, A.: 3D facial expression recognition using SIFT descriptors of automatically detected keypoints. Vis. Comput. **27**(11), 1021–1036 (2011). https://doi.org/10.1007/s00371-011-0611-x
50. Brahnam, S., Chuang, C.F., Shih, F.Y., Slack, M.R.: Machine recognition and representation of neonatal facial displays of acute pain. Artif. Intell. Med. **36**(3), 211–222 (2006)
51. Zhang, X., Mahoor, M.H., Mavadati, S.M.: Facial expression recognition using lp-norm MKL multiclass-SVM. Mach. Vis. Appl. **26**(4), 467–483 (2015)
52. Lee, J., Lee, D.: An improved cluster labelling method for support vector clustering. IEEE Trans. Pattern Anal. Mach. Intell. **27**(3), 461–464 (2005)
53. Baltrušaitis, T., Banda, N., Robinson, P.: Dimensional affect recognition using continuous conditional random fields. In: 10th IEEE International Conference and Workshops on Automatic Face and Gesture Recognition, Shanghai (2013)
54. Cotter, S.F.: Sparse representation for accurate classification of corrupted and occluded facial expressions. In: IEEE International Conference on Acoustics, Speech and Signal Processing (2010)
55. Ng, H.W., Nguyen, V.D., Vonikakis, V., Winkler, S.: Deep learning for emotion recognition on small datasets using transfer learning. In: ACM on International Conference on Multimodal Interaction, ICMI 2015, Washington, pp. 443–449 (2015)
56. Tuan Tran, A., Hassner, T., Masi, I., Medioni, G.: Regressing robust and discriminative 3D morphable models with a very deep neural network. In: IEEE Conference on Computer Vision and Pattern Recognition, pp. 5163–5172 (2017)
57. Chen, H., Li, J., Zhang, F., Li, Y., Wang, H.L.: 3D model-based continuous emotion recognition. In: IEEE Conference on Computer Vision and Pattern Recognition, pp. 1836–1845 (2015)
58. Lee, I., Jung, H., Ahn, C.H., Seo, J., Kim, J., Kwon, O.: Real-time personalized facial expression recognition system based on deep learning. In: IEEE International Conference on Consumer Electronics (2016)
59. Bartlett, M.S., Hager, J.C., Ekman, P., Sejnowski, T.J.: Measuring facial expressions by computer image analysis. Psychophysiology **36**(2), 253–263 (1999)

60. Chu, W.S., De la Torre, F., Cohn, J.F.: Selective transfer machine for personalized facial expression analysis. IEEE Trans. Pattern Anal. Mach. Intell. **39**(3), 529–545 (2017)
61. Lou, Z., Alnajar, F., Alvarez, J.M., Hu, N., Gevers, T.: Expression-invariant age estimation using structured learning. IEEE Trans. Pattern Anal. Mach. Intell. **40**(2), 365–375 (2018)
62. Shreve, M., Godavarthy, S., Goldgof, D., Sarkar, S.: Macro- and micro-expression spotting in long videos using spatio-temporal strain. In: IEEE Conference on Face and Gesture (2011)
63. Davison, A.K., Lansley, C., Costen, N., Tan, K., Yap, M.H.: SAMM: a spontaneous micro-facial movement dataset. IEEE Trans. Affect. Comput. **9**(1), 116–129 (2018)
64. Verma, M.K., Dwivedi, R., Mallick, A.K., Jangam, E.: Dimensionality reduction technique on SIFT feature vectore for content based image retrival. In: Santosh, K., Hegadi, R. (eds.) Recent Trends in Image Processing and Pattern Recognition, vol. 1035. Springer, Singapore (2018). https://doi.org/10.1007/978-981-13-9181-1_34

Classification of Vehicle Type on Indian Road Scene Based on Deep Learning

K. L. Arunkumar[1(✉)], Ajit Danti[2], H. T. Manjunatha[1], and D. Rohith[3]

[1] Department of MCA, Jawaharlal Nehru National College of Engineering, Shimoga, Karnataka, India
{arunkumarkl,manjudeepa}@jnnce.ac.in

[2] Computer Science and Engineering, CHRIST (Deemed to be University), Bengaluru, Karnataka, India
ajit.danti@christuniversity.in

[3] NMIT, Banglore, Karnataka, India
rohitdanti98@gmail.com

Abstract. In Recent days an intelligent traffic system [ITS] is implemented on indian traffic sytem. Different applications are widely used to improvies the performance of the system. To improve the intelligence of the system deep learning can used to classify the vehicles into three different classes. The combination of Faster RCNN classifier and RPN can used to detect the objects and classify those objects into different classes. Analysis of the experimental results shows the improved accuracy and efficiency in classifying the vehicles on indian roads into different categories.

Keywords: Intelligent traffic system (ITS) · Deep learning · Faster R-CNN · Region Proposal Network (RPN)

1 Introduction

In most of the developing countries traffic survillence plays a very important role. Nowadays an intelligent traffic system has been introduced for traffic survillence. In ITS detection and recognition of vehicles and traffic sign boards [9,10] plays a vital role. So an efficient algorithm implementation is very necessary to achieve the high accuracy rate and improved efficiency in the system. In this work our aim is referred to vehicle detection, which usually consists of different subtasks such as vehicle type detection, pedestrian detection, and bus detection. We have proposed a method for classification vehicle based on geometrical invariant features under complex background images [1] and to estimate the vehicle distance [2,13]. In recent days vehicle detection are achieved using different techniques in advanced computer vision technology like different deep neural network techniques [3–6]. Many traditional feature extraction methods are used to detected vehicles, now deep learning techniques are giving better results with more efficiency when compared with traditional methods. The deep learning technology is very widely used for segmentation, detection and recognition of different

© Springer Nature Singapore Pte Ltd. 2021
K. C. Santosh and B. Gawali (Eds.): RTIP2R 2020, CCIS 1380, pp. 183–192, 2021.
https://doi.org/10.1007/978-981-16-0507-9_16

objects in the image and videos [8]. In earlier decades vehicle classifications are developed using the traditional computer vision techniques such HOG or SVM classifiers. For natural scene images these classifiers are failed to give the better results. Results obtained using deep learning using faster-RCNN have higher accuracy rate and which are much applicable for natural scene images, hence getting more popular in recent research work [14]. So deep learning techniques are implemented here to construct more intelligent traffic system [11,12].

In this work deep neural network is implemented with advanced faster R-CNN for detection of vehicle with more efficiency. A multi layered convolution neural network is used to detect and classify the vehicles more accurately.

2   Related Work

2.1   Related Work on Vehicle Classifications

Various types of techniques are proposed for vehicle detection and classification by many researchers in past few years [7,19]. Shaoyong Yu et al. [15], has proposed a model using deep learning for fine grained vehicle classification. This models consists of two parts vehicle detection model and fine grained vehicle classification model. CNN model is used to extract the features and to detect the vehicle in first part. Then bayesian network is used in second part for fine grained vehicle classification. Linkai Chen et al. [8], has presented an effective and efficient framework for recognition of vehicle and to classify into different classes using deep neural network. Feature fusion technique is proposed to detect and classify the vehicles belongs to of different size and dimension. An unsupervised model was constructed by Hai Wang et al. [5], this model was built on the basis of hypothesis distribution on multiple feature subspaces.

2.2   Background of Convolution Neural Network

Different algorithms like R-CNN, Fast-CNN and Faster-CNN are developed under convolution neural network in order to detection and recognition of objects and drawing the bounding box around the detected objects. In the R-CNN technique specific regions are selected based on the selective search and extracting those region features and verifying those features with object features. If features are matched then a bounding box will be drawn around the detected object in that particular region. Drawback of R-CNN is, it get very slow in process due to multiple steps are involved in it.

Fast R-CNN is the advanced version of R-CNN, in this technique complete input image is given to the convolution neural network this generates the regions of interest where objects can be detected. Here the manual selection of regions is reduced. Hence this technique seems to be fast when compared with R-CNN.

Faster R-CNN technique provide the improvisation for the Fast R-CNN and R-CNN by implementing the Region Proposal Network instead of selective to find out the region of interest to extract the features. Faster R-CNN generate the results much faster when compared with both R-CNN and Fast R-CNN. Hence Faster R-CNN technique is used in this work to detect and classify the vehicles on traffic roads.

3   Methodology

In this paper Faster R-CNN method is implemented for progressive vehicle detection approach. Region Proposal Network is used to generate the region of interest. Which extracts the features of the region and matches those features with proposed object features.

Proposed Methodology

Step 1: An image is captured and give as an input for convolution neural network which generates feature map. Which is the result obtained after extracting the features from the input image. The resultant image is used for the next step.

Step 2: For those feature maps extracted in the previous step region proposal network is applied. Region proposal network is applied in order to reduce the computational requirements. Then objectness score is returned for those features maps for the object proposal.

Step 3: A ROI pooling layer is applied those proposals extracted in the step 2 inorder to resize all the proposals into the equal sizes and shapes which are fully connected layers. This is a type of pooling layer which converts all the non-uniform sizes and generates a small feature maps. This mainly helps in speedup the training and testing time of the system.

Step 4: In the last step a completely connected layer is constructed, the proposals of the step 3 process are given as input to this connected layer which has a softmax layer for the processing. On the top of this connected layers a linear regression layer is designed. The role of this layer is to classify the vehicles in different classes and clear boundary box to draw around the detected vehicles.

Working Principle. Vehicle detection and recognition begins with, the preprocessing an input image and then pass it through the CNN [16,17]. Feature maps are generated for the input image, these feature maps are then pass as an input for the Faster R-CNN. Region proposal network uses these features maps and apply the sliding window over all these feature maps, this is applied on every individual window. As a result Region proposal network generates n different fixed boundary boxes of various shapes and sizes as shown in the figure. These fixed boundary boxes are called as Anchor Boxes. Based on the objects found in the image, anchor boxes are placed on the entire image with different shape and sizes. Multitasking loss function is applied on every image at time of training. Multitasking loss function formula is as shown in Eq. 1 (Fig. 1).

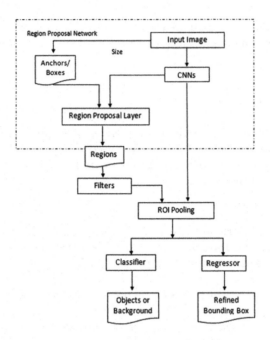

Fig. 1. Showing proposed methodology.

$$L(\{P_i\}, \{t_i\}) = \frac{1}{N_{cls}} \Sigma_i L_{cls}(P_i, P_i^*) + \lambda \frac{1}{N_{reg}} \Sigma L_{reg}(t_i, t_i^*) \qquad (1)$$

Where total number of anchors are indicated using i, probability of anchor having object is represented as P_i. Positive anchors are indicated using $P_i^* = 1$ and negative anchors are having the value as $P_i^* = 0$. t_i is representing the predicted bounding box having 4 coordinates. P_i^* is a label representing positive anchors. The two normalization parameters are N_{cls} and N_{reg}. Balancing parameter is indicated by λ and is assigned with value 10.

Regression-loss of the bounding box is described using below equation.

$$L_{reg}(t_i, t_i^*) = smooth_{L_1}(t_i - t_i^*) \qquad (2)$$

Where robust regression loss function is represented by $smooth_{L_1}$. Below formula describes regression loss.

$$smooth_{L_1}(x) = \begin{cases} 0.5x^2 & |x| < 1 \\ |x| - 0.5 & |x| > 1 \end{cases} \qquad (3)$$

Further these anchor boxes and region proposal network are used to predict two things

One: In the entire input image the probability of detecting the objects irrespective of to which class it belongs to.

Two: Placing the anchor boxes on objects where it fits more accurately using the bounding box regressor.

Now ROI pooling layer is used where these anchor boxes of different sizes and shape which are not classified into any classes are passed as input. This ROI pooling layer consider each proposals and crop each proposals in such way that every proposals contains an object. Then extract the fixed size feature maps of the every bounding box objects.

For the classification of these feature maps a fully connected layer is used which consists of both softmax and linear regression layer. For this fully connected layer feature maps obtained in the ROI pooling layer are given as inputs. Then classification of obejcts is done based on feature matching obtained from ROI pooling layer [17] (Fig. 2).

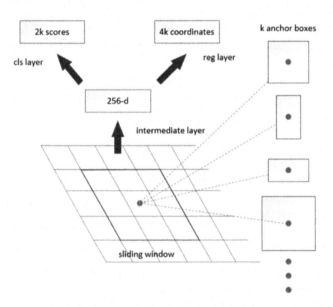

Fig. 2. Region proposal network architecture.

3.1   Foreground and Background Classification

In classification of vehicles into different classes the basic thing we need to consider here is identifying the foreground and background of the image [15]. To solve this problem first we need to have the training data set [18]. After processing and ground-truth boxes of the training dataset anchors are obtained. by labeling these anchors majority of the problem get solved. The logic behind this is if anchors are having the higher convergence value with ground-truth boxes are considered to be as foreground and anchors with lower convergence value with ground-truth boxes are considered as background. Like this every anchors will have labels.

In the next level features of the objects within this anchors are extracted for further processing. Consider an image with size of 600 × 800 which is shrinked repeatedly until image reduces upto 39 × 51 which is nearly 16 times reduction in this case. This is considered as feature maps which are obtained when CNN is applied on the image. Each feature maps have approximately 9 anchors in each positions and for every anchors have two labels foreground and background. Like this, training of the dataset is completed by obtaining features and labels as outcome of the process.

3.2   Regressor

Regressor is the process of refining anchor boxes obtained the previous step. In regressor anchors labelled as background are not considered for regression because they dont have the ground-truth boxes. The feature maps are having depth of 32. Here we use smooth-L1 loss on the position (x,y) of top-left of the box, heights and widths of the logarithm is retained with the same values as in Fast R-CNN.

$$L_{loc}(t^u, v) = \Sigma_{i \in \{x,y,w,h\}} smooth_{L1}(t_i^u - v_i) \tag{4}$$

in which

$$smooth_{L1}(x) = \begin{cases} 0.5x^2 & if |x| < 1 \\ |x| - 0.5 \} & otherwise \end{cases} \tag{5}$$

4   Experiment and Results

4.1   Dataset

The exemplary Faster RCNN accomplishes high precision for classifying and testing more than 2000 traffic images. In this paper we tried to solve the problem of classification of vehicles on indian traffic into different classes using India Driving Dataset (IID) from IIIT Hydrerabad as standard dataset. The training images consists of different objects like car, bus, truck, person, etc. Here classification of these objects into three classes as person car and Bus. In this paper sample dataset of the vehicles is produced as follows: Images: 4024/JPG, Labels: 4024/XML, Bounding Boxes: Car 4012/ Rectangles, Bus 642/Rectangles, Persons: 1432/Rectangles. With this results different types of vehicle data sets are collected.

Table 1. Information of Total Dataset, Trained Data and Test Data.

Class	Total dataset	Trained set	Test set	Accuracy
Car	4024	3014	1010	94%
Bus	642	533	109	96%
Person	1432	1044	388	93%

4.2 Experimental Results

In this work training sample images are given from IDD standard dataset as original input image. In the picture consists of different types of vehicles and other objects. These input images are processed and trained according to the requirements. Further with this trained images different kinds of vehicles are identified and classified into different classes such as car, bus and person. The experiment is conducted with different number of samples as mentioned in the Table 1. In Fig. 3 three different types of objects are detected recognized in different sample sizes. Result analysis clearly depicts that the accuracy rate of vehicle classification will be increased by moderatley increasing the number of samples. As sample number increases the depth of the network have more number of convolution layers as a result more number of features are extracted. If more number of features are extracted then accuracy rate will also increase.

Fig. 3. Sample results

4.3 Result Analysis

In this proposed work, experiments are conducted with different algorithms of the CNN families like R-CNN, Fast R-CNN and Faster R-CNN with the same dataset. The comparitive results are as shown in the below table. To analyse the performance of the proposed method, an image which consists of different vehicles like car, bus and persons are given as input and get the results. same set input images are also experimented with different algorithms like R-CNN, Fast R-CNN and obtain the results. By analysing the results of all the algorithms with respective to time complexity the proposed algorithm performance is much better when comapred with other algorithms. Comparatively the proposed method is providing the amazing results. Brief comparison is given the Table 2.

Table 2. Comparision of Faster R-CNN performance with other algorithms

Algorithm	Features	PT/ Image	Limitations
CNN	Multiple regions are created for input image and classify those regions into different classes	–	A lot of computation time is needed to predict each region to achieve high accuracy rate in prediction
R-CNN	Selective search method is used to create the regions. Approximately 2000 regions are extracted from each region	40–50 s	Since large number of regions at created high computation time is required
Fast R-CNN	Features are extracted by using the combination of both CNN and R-CNN method	2 s	Since using the selective method for feature extraction which is a time consuming method
Faster R-CNN	Region Proposal Network method is used instead of selective search for region creation which made the method very faster	0.2 s	Dependency on the previous method makes algorithm a time consuming and it has to work with different systems one after the other

5   Conclusion

In this paper Faster R-CNN model is implemented to detect the vehicles in the complex background captured on Indian traffic roads and classify the vehicles in the image into three different classes like car, bus and person. In this work all vehicles in images are not detected, hence 100% accuracay is not obtained. We found that the vehicle detection and classification into different classes can achieved higher accuracy using faster R-CNN compared to the other deep learning algorithms. Also this experimental results shows comparatively better results when compared with other traditional methods in detecting and classifying the vehicles. In the future work the results of this vehicle classification are best suitable for detecting the make and model of the vehicle with highest accuracy rate using more number of features.

References

1. Arunkumar, K.L., Danti, A., Manjunatha, H.T.: Classification of vehicle make based on geometric features and appearance-based attributes under complex background. In: Santosh, K.C., Hegadi, R.S. (eds.) RTIP2R 2018. CCIS, vol. 1035, pp. 41–48. Springer, Singapore (2019). https://doi.org/10.1007/978-981-13-9181-1_4
2. Arunkumar, K.L., Danti, A., Manjunatha, H.T.: Estimation of vehicle distance based on feature points using monocular vision. In: IEEE Proceedings of the International Conference on Data Science and Communication (IconDSC), March 2019. https://doi.org/10.1109/IconDSC.2019.8816996
3. Dong, Z., Wu, Y., Pei, M., et al.: Vehicle type classification using a semisupervised convolutional neural network. In: IEEE Trans. Intell. Transp. Syst. **16**, 2247–2256 (2015)
4. Fang, J., Zhou, Y., Yu, Y., Du, S.: Fine-grained vehicle model recognition using a coarse-to-ne convolutional neural network architecture. IEEE Trans. Intell. Transp. Syst. **18**(7), 1782–1792 (2017)
5. Wang, H., Yu, Y., Cai, Y., Chen, L.: A vehicle recognition algorithm based on deep transfer learning with a multiple feature subspace distribution. Sensors **18**, 4109 (2018). https://doi.org/10.3390/s18124109. www.mdpi.com/journal/sensors
6. Suhao, I., Lin, J., Li, G., Bai, T., Wang, H., Pang, Y.: Vehicle type detection based on deep learning in traffic scene. In: 8th International Congress of Information and Communication Technology (ICICT-2018). Elsevier (2018). https://doi.org/10.1016/j.procs.2018.04.281
7. Arunkumar, K.L., Danti, A.: A novel approach for vehicle recognition based on the tail lights geometrical features in the night vision. Int. J. Comput. Eng. Appl. **XII** (2018). ISSN 2321-3169
8. Chen, L., Ye, F., Ruan, Y., Fan, H., Chen, Q.: An algorithm for highway vehicle detection based on convolutional neural network. EURASIP J. Image Video Process. **2018**(1), 1–7 (2018). https://doi.org/10.1186/s13640-018-0350-2
9. Manjunatha, H.T., Danti, A.: Indian traffic sign board recognition using normalized correlation. Int. J. Comput. Eng. Appl. **XII** (2018). ISSN 2321-3169
10. Manjunatha, H.T., Danti, A., ArunKumar, K.L.: A novel approach for detection and recognition of traffic signs for automatic driver assistance system under cluttered background. In: Santosh, K.C., Hegadi, R.S. (eds.) RTIP2R 2018. CCIS, vol. 1035, pp. 407–419. Springer, Singapore (2019). https://doi.org/10.1007/978-981-13-9181-1_36
11. Druzhkov, P., Kustikova, V.: A survey of deep learning methods and software tools for image classification and object detection. Pattern Recogn. Image Anal. **26**(1), 9 (2016)
12. Felzenszwalb, P.F., Girshick, R.B., McAllester, D., Ramanan, D.: Object detection with discriminatively trained part-based models. IEEE Trans. Pattern Anal. Mach. Intell. (TPAMI), **32**(9), 1627–1645 (2010)
13. Psyllos, A., Anagnostopoulos, C.N., Kayafas, E.: M-SIFT: a new method for vehicle logo recognition In: 2012 IEEE International Conference on Vehicular Electronics and Safety (ICVES), 24–27 July 2012, pp. 261–266 (2017)
14. Ren, S., He, K., Girshick, R., Sun, J.: Faster R-CNN: towards real-time object detection with region proposal networks. IEEE Trans. Pattern Anal. Mach. Intell. **39**(6), 1137–1149 (2017)
15. Yu, S., Wu, Y., Li, W., Song, Z., Zeng, W.: A model for ne-grained vehicle classification based on deep learning. Neurocomputing **257**, 97–103 (2017). https://doi.org/10.1016/j.neucom.2016.09.116:0925-2312

16. Zhang, F., Xu, X, Qiao, Y.: Deep classification of vehicle makers and models: the effectiveness of pre-training and data enhancement. In: 2015 IEEE International Conference on Robotics and Biomimetics (ROBIO), pp. 231–236 (2015)
17. Zeiler, M.D., Fergus, R.: Visualizing and understanding convolutional networks. In: Fleet, D., Pajdla, T., Schiele, B., Tuytelaars, T. (eds.) ECCV 2014. LNCS, vol. 8689, pp. 818–833. Springer, Cham (2014). https://doi.org/10.1007/978-3-319-10590-1_53
18. Zhao, Z., Zheng, P., Xu, S., Wu, X.: Object detection with deep learning: a review. IEEE Trans. Neural Netw. Learn. Syst. (2018). https://doi.org/10.1109/TNNLS.2018.2876865
19. Sun, Z., Bebis, G., Miller, R.: On-road vehicle detection using optical sensors: a review. In: The International IEEE Conference on Intelligent Transportation Systems Proceedings, pp. 585–590 (2004)

Indian Road Lanes Detection Based on Regression and clustering using Video Processing Techniques

H. T. Manjunatha[1](✉), Ajit Danti[2], K. L. ArunKumar[1], and D. Rohith[3]

[1] Department of MCA, Jawaharlal Nehru National College of Engineering,
Shimoga, Karnataka, India
{manjudeepa,arunkumarkl}@jnnce.ac.in
[2] Computer Science and Engineering, CHRIST (Deemed to be University),
Bengalore, Karnataka, India
ajit.danti@christuniversity.in
[3] NMIT, Banglore, Karnataka, India
rohitdanti98@gmail.com

Abstract. Detecting the road lanes from moving vehicle is a difficult and challenging task because of road lane markings with poor quality, occlusion created by traffic and poor road constructions. If the driver is not maintaining the road lanes properly, the proposed system detects the road lanes and gives the alarm to the driver so that driver can take the corrective actions there by we can avoid the accidents. The paper mainly focusses on detection of road lanes from sequence of image taken from the video from moving vehicle. The Methodology mainly consisting of lane segments merging and fitting using clustering and weighted regression techniques to fit the curve in the place of group of lane segments and curve fitting separately.

Keywords: Lane segments · Regression · Clustering

1 Introduction

India has second largest road network in the word. According to the World Health organization statistics around 3800 people will die every day because of rash driving, driver laziness and often changing road lanes that leads accidents. The applications of computer vision give more impact on various domains like medical, transportations retail etc. For example, automatic road sign, obstacles, potholes and road lanes detection systems. In order to avoid accidents, cost and road are the two important aspects. The bad condition of the road that adversely affects the quality of the vehicle fuel consumptions thus the road users. The detection and recognition of road lanes is one of the important significances in the context of highway maintenance. According to the survey conducted by the Automobile Association the one of the major reasons for road accidents is

© Springer Nature Singapore Pte Ltd. 2021
K. C. Santosh and B. Gawali (Eds.): RTIP2R 2020, CCIS 1380, pp. 193–206, 2021.
https://doi.org/10.1007/978-981-16-0507-9_17

frequently changing the road lanes. The main intension of lane detection is finding and track the boundaries of lane in road images so that vehicle can maintain the host lane boundaries. The proposed work facing several challenges like lighting conditions, dense traffic, faded road lanes occlusion by vehicles tree shadows and many more. We have proposed the Advanced Driver Assistance Systems (ADS) for detecting the road lanes then sends the alarm to the driver when the driver abruptly changing the road lanes. The advantages road lane detection system is to identify and predicts the instant lane changing locations that will be displayed on the integrated board present in the highly advanced automobiles. These driver assistance systems avoid the collision with other vehicles. Intelligent transportation systems (ITS) such as lane detection and tracking (LDT), lane departure warning (LDW) and lane marking recognition (LMR) systems are called for by industry [12, 14]. The one best method to detect the road lanes is Model driven method that provides better results in lane detection application, only the loophole is it needs more computation. Feature driven methods faces many problems like blur, noise and irreverent features [11]. In the proposed approach adopted feature-based method for detecting the lanes from video frames. The Fig. 1 shows the block diagram of abstract methodology for lane detection and recognition system.

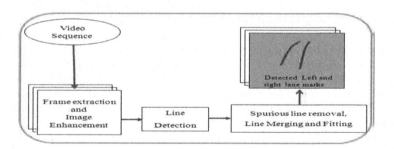

Fig. 1. Block diagram of detection and recognition of lanes.

The brief description of methodology (Fig. 1) contains the following steps (i) Sequence of frames has been extracted from the source video and processing near image and farther image separately. (ii) To enhance the input image by removing the paper salt noise by using median filters that leads efficient edge detection (iii) The lane detection algorithms identifies the disconnected road lanes. There are two types of lane marks the one is line like lane segments and curve like lane segments. The proposed line detection method detects the segments of small lines in the lane curve those are not continuous in the slope and space and further process these line segments separately and merge them as a continuous lanes. (iv) Removing the unwanted (spurious) lines and lines are merged, grouped based on their slope and closeness of the relative pixels. Spurious lines are removed based on the hypothesis that road lanes are parallelly to each other and they meet at vanishing point. (v) Finally detect the left and right road lanes.

2   Related Work

There are several method have been developed for lane detection problem but in our proposed work related to feature based methodology (e.g., edge, colour, gradient). Most of the literature focussed only the clustering based detection technique but in our methodology concentrated on clustering as well as regression technique for detecting the road lanes using video processing approaches. L N P Boggavarapu, R S et al. proposed the multi-colour lane marking detection technique for Indian scenario. The proposed method uses HSV colour segmentation for recognizing white and yellow road lines and concentrated only still images with accuracy is only 80% but in our approach, we have achieved 92% accuracy for detection of road lanes using video processing [8,13,21]. The pre-processing is one the key aspect for reducing computational time. Navarro, J. Deniel et al. developed the system for detecting and classifying the road lanes using colour and edge-based segmentation technique. The methodology uses perwitt and sobel filter for enhancing the road edges, Haugh transformation technique is used for detecting road line segment [2,3,15]. H.-Y. Cheng et al. described the environmental classification and hierarchical lane detection method for handling both structured and unstructured roads and used mean shift segmentation for divide the road scene into regions [6]. The different methods have been proposed in the literature to handle edges, pixel intensities, colours and textures and other features. ZuWhan Kim et al. used a unique method for lane detection which contains probabilistic line segment grouping and lane hypotheses generation [20]. It is observed that only few researches used weighted regression technique for detection of road lanes. A. Broggi et al. uses several morphological features such as Gaussian filters and median filters for smoothing, periwitt canny edge detectors are used for extracting the road edge segment [5]. Lucia Vanesa Araya et al. proposed a system which detects the road lanes by using Haugh Transformation technique for extracting the road line. The methodology is not focussed for images under cluttered background. The methodology contains yellow and white mask for segmenting yellow and white lines [9]. Yinghua He et al. uses road area extraction module contains road boundary determination, road surface colour computation, road area extraction. The proposed methodology highlighting that projection relationship is very essential for road curvature determination and used SVM for classification [19]. Mingfa Li et al. describes the various feature extraction methods for lane detection. The proposed methodology uses KNN classifier for classifying the road lane images [10]. Shriyash Chougule et al. uses CNN as a regression network for detecting and classifying reliable multi lane in Indian roads. The author uses Enet and FCN for generating the segment mask but author focused only edge-based feature extraction method not colour based [17]. Rudra N. Hota et al. proposed a lane detection system which uses hierarchical structural for grouping the line segments and contains weighted regression for fitting the line segments with accuracy of 89%, but author not focussed the colour-based extraction technique [16]. Hang yuan et al. has proposed the lane detection based on normal map. The proposed method uses depth map for classifying right and left road lanes. al has discussed a review of lane detection system which uses methodologies like canny edge detection, bilateral filter and Haugh Transformation technique for detecting the road lanes but not used any classifiers for classifying the different types of road images [7]. Ajit danti et al. uses Haugh Transformation technique for identifying the road line, colour thresholding is implemented for detecting the road lane images and road lane image is recognized by using KNN classifiers [1, 4]. Krzysztof Slot et al. proposed the lane detection system that eliminates the high curvature edges. The methodology uses HSV colour space for further processing [7, 18].

3 Methodology

Methodology contains the following phases (i) Video Acquisition (ii) preprocessing (iii) Line segment detection (iv) Line segment clustering technique (v) Line fitting and regression (vi) Classification of yellow and white colour lanes (vii) Experimental result. In the first phase of proposed methodology describes preprocessing methodology like segmenting small line like structure using Canny edge and Sobel gradient operator. The Haugh transformation is applied for identifying the line like segment there after line segment grouping is done by clustering. Clustering can be done in two stages (i) slopes of the line segment (ii) again clustering on Y intercept. In second phase methodology uses weighted regression for line fitting after line grouping and merging. The flow chart of proposed methodology is as shown in the Fig. 2.

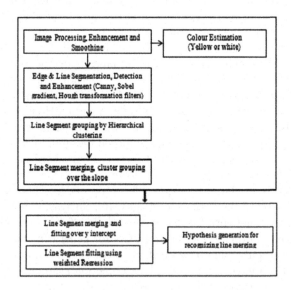

Fig. 2. Flow chart of proposed methodology.

3.1 Video Acquisition

Video acquisition is process of extracting road lane images from the sample video as a series of continuous frames by interval of 20 ms. Those images fed for further processing as a jpeg image

3.2 Preprocessing

Main intension to use pre-processing is to remove noise and enhance the image. Pre-processing is inevitable for preliminary stage of image processing. The pre-processing stage mainly contains image smoothing, edge detection and line segmentation detection. The Firstly sequence of RGB image frames are converted into grey scale for minimizing the processing time. The multistage algorithms called Sobel gradient operator and Canny edge detector is used for extracting small line like segments form the input image. The functionality of these two algorithms is to find the Sharpe changes in luminosity that defines the sharp edges. The presence of noise usually hinders the extraction of road lane edges. In this regard filters are very essential in order to remove the noise because noise leads false edge detection. The 4*4 Gaussian filter and winner filter is applied one after the other for accurate edge detection. The smoothened image is again fed into the Roberts, or Prewitt operator along x axes and y axes for determining whether the edges are diagonal, horizontal or vertical.

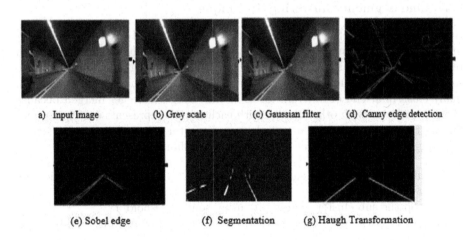

a) Input Image   (b) Grey scale   (c) Gaussian filter   (d) Canny edge detection

(e) Sobel edge   (f) Segmentation   (g) Haugh Transformation

Fig. 3. Flow chart of proposed methodology.

The Fig. 3 shows the different pre-processing stages such as Fig. 3(a), (b) shows input image and grey scale image and Fig. 3(c), (d) shows the Gaussian filter and canny edge detector. The Fig. 3(e) and (f) and (g) shows the Sobel edge detection, Segmentation and Haugh transformation detected image.

3.3   Lane Segment Detection

In the proposed methodology the Haugh transformation technique is used for locating and identifying the line segments. The probabilistic Hugh transformation method is used for detecting the lanes by using some randomly selected edge points. The quality of Hough transform depends on quality of input image. Haugh transformation uses the parameter rho (ρ) and theta (θ) for detecting the lines by putting the similar edge points to these parameters shown the Eq. 1

$$r = x * \cos\theta + y * \sin\theta \tag{1}$$

where (ρ) and theta (θ) are the distance and angle between the from the line to the origin. The Fig. 3(b) shows line detection by Haugh transform. The algorithm for probabilistic Hough transformation technique is as follows

Step 1: If an empty input image list, then terminate.
Step 2: If the pixel is selected randomly from the input image update the accumulator.
Step 3: Remove pixel from each input image.
Step 4: Find the longest pixel segments in the accumulator. If the line segment is exceeding minimum length and put that into the output list.
Step 5: Go to step 1.

3.4   Line Segment Clustering Technique

In proposed methodology uses Agglomerative Hierarchical clustering for merging different line segments after detecting the lines by Haugh transformation technique. The Fig. 4 shows the representation of clustering technique with nine samples. The technique uses bottom up approach because the method starts with many clusters at end of different levels of clustering all are get merged because of their closeness with other cluster with each sample represents one cluster and finding the closeness between two cluster play vital role for cluster formation. The Agglomerative Hierarchical clustering algorithm is shown below

Input: Take Set of input samples Y = a1, a2, a3, . . ., an of n is the indicators of set of line segments.
T- Stop the sub cluster merging by using some threshold T.
Output: Size of the Clusters with of each inter class distance greater than T.
Step 1: Processes starts with n number clusters each one act as independent cluster.
Step 2: Determine the similar pair of clustering by finding the distance between two clusters. Similar pair of clusters are merged into a one single cluster if the similarity value is less than the given threshold T then fed the single cluster for further processing.
Step 3: Decrease the n (number of clusters) by 1.

Step 4: Again repeat step 1, 2 and 3 until there is no two clusters less than the threshold value T.

Step 5: Got o step 1.

The finding the similarities between the cluster by determining average distance between one cluster to all other member of the clusters as shown in the Eq. 2

$$d(C_i, C_j) = mean_{(x_1, x_2) \in (c_1 * c_2)} d(x_1, x_2) \tag{2}$$

Where d (Ci, Cj) represents the distance between two clusters.

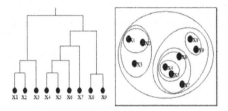

Fig. 4. Agglomerative clustering representation diagram

The Firstly we need to find the slope and Y intercepts for each segmented lane then clustering will be applied on them there after stop the merging of clusters to extract the lane groups by using different threshold values. The reason for using slope is to extract the parallel lane segments which will have a similar angles with respect to x axis and Y intercepts are used to exclude and discard all the line segments which are outside or too far away from the group but they may be parallel to each other. The Y intercept and slope representation are shown in the Fig. 5. The result after the clustering method is the set of all road lane segments which similar Y intercepts and slopes.

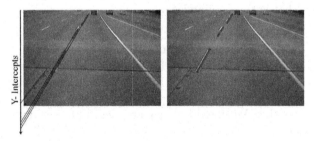

Fig. 5. Clustering based on Y intercept.

3.5   Lane Fitting and Regression

Regression is one of the important statistical tools for fit the line or curve on segmented data points there by reduce the distance between the data points. In real case line segments are disconnected not in continuous. In order to combine all the disconnected lane segments as a one continuous line, methodology uses weighted regression technique to fit all the line segments as one continuous line. Weighted regression is the best technique for fitting the lane segments.

3.5.1   Line Fitting by Least Square Regression

Least square regression line reduces the distance between pixel values (data points) to the regression line as small as possible the processes is called as least square. The main intension to use this technique in the proposed work is to connect all lane segments as one continuous line. Least square regression computes the equation that will give the best fit for curve or line for set of datapoints. The Fig. 6 shows the distance between the data points and regression line.

$$E(a, b) = \sum_{n=1}^{N} (y_n - (ax_n + b))^2 \qquad (3)$$

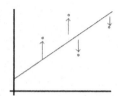

Fig. 6. Graph representing distance between data points and regression line.

The data points (x1, y1), . . ., (xn, yn), Error associated with the equation y = ax + b shown in the Eq. 3. Where E (a,b) represents the error between the two points a and b. The error estimation can be computed sum and square of all data points that is to be minimized.

3.5.2   Weighted Regression Technique

In a weighted regression line fitting technique gives a less weight for less precise measurement and give more weight to the more precise measurement. If any lane segments which are away from cluster group and it is not prominent for detecting the road lanes then Weighted least square method fit the data points to the prominent degree of importance. This method increases the efficiency of parameter estimation. The least square parameter and weight factor can calculate using Eq. 4.

$$\beta = (X^* T \omega X^*)^{-} 1 (X^* T \omega Y) \qquad (4)$$

$$\begin{bmatrix} w1 & 0 & 0 & 0 \\ 0 & w2 & 0 & 0 \\ 0 & 0 & w3 & 0 \\ 0 & 0 & 0 & w_n \end{bmatrix}$$

Where wi are weighted factors representing in a diagonal matrix. In lane mark detection phase the regression-based line fitting uses the points from each lane segments. The points are weighted based on line weighing method that is presented in the next subsection. The fitting of lane segment after detection is as shown in the Fig. 7(e).

3.5.3 Line Segment Weight Factor Determination

Each of the lane segments are weighted by using weight factor because to minimise the impact of spurious lane segments which are not similar to the line present in the cluster and too far away from the group. The weight factor is determined by finding the distance between the line segments in the same set is determined by Eq. 5 is as follows

$$w_i = \sum_{j=1}^{n} exp^{-d(x_i, x_j)} \tag{5}$$

Where wi are the weighted factor for line segments starts from 1 to n and d(xi yj) is the distance between the line two-lane segments xi and xj. The Fig. 7(c) shows the clustering method to representing the merging or grouping the lines from different set. The proposed method determines the slope and Y intercept for segmented line which are used for agglomerative hierarchical clustering by fixing the threshold in slope and Y intercept as shown in the image of Fig. 7(d).

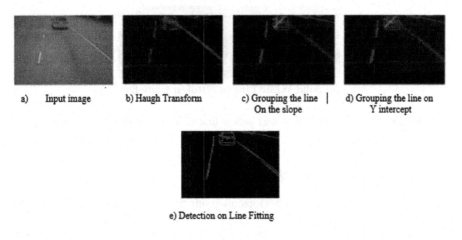

a)   Input image   b) Haugh Transform   c) Grouping the line | d) Grouping the line on
                                                    On the slope   Y intercept

e) Detection on Line Fitting

Fig. 7. Different stages of detection process.

3.6 Detection of White and Yellow Lines

There is different marking of road lanes are broken white lines, solid white lines, single solid yellow lines and double solid yellow lines. Broken white line means you can change the road lanes and allowed to overtake. Solid white line means you are not supposed to overtake. Solid yellow lines are used in the low visibility areas, it indicates you are not allowed to overtake. Double solid yellow lines indicate dangerous road, it does not allow anybody crossing over into the lane. yellow and white lines are not strictly visible on the road hence the proposed methodology distinguishing the white and yellow lines because of tree shadows, occluded by other vehicle and rough texture of the road. The RGB values of yellow and white pixels are of range (255, 255, 0) and (255, 255, 255). The value of channel B clearly distinguishes between yellow and white colours. If the pixel value of Blue(B) channel is less than the mean value of Red and Green then that will consider as a yellow pixel value otherwise if the pixel value of B is much greater than average of G and R pixel value then that will be considered as White pixel. The Fig. 8(a) and (b) shows the detection of solid yellow line and broken yellow line and Fig. 8(c) and (d) shows the detection of solid and broken white lines.

(a) Solid yellow line (b) Broken yellow line

(c) Solid White Line (d) Broken white line

Fig. 8. Detection of White and yellow line segments (Color figure online)

3.7 Result and Observations

In this section we compare the performance our proposed method with the other line regression for fitting and line grouping in clustering method and also describe the performance or efficiency of detecting left and right lane marks. In our proposed work we have tested 500 image frames and 300 for testing image frames form the captured video and image frame of size 250*352. The performance analysis has been done based on number of proper detection rate. The rate of detection depends on area between annotation and detection lane mark. The detection goodness rate is computed using the below Eq. 6

$$DR = Numberofcorrectlydetectedlanes \div Totalnumberoflanesinvideo \quad (6)$$

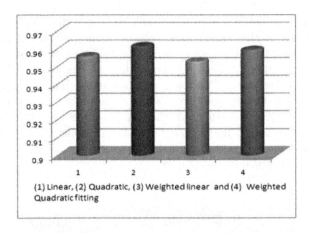

(1) Linear, (2) Quadratic, (3) Weighted linear and (4) Weighted Quadratic fitting

Fig. 9. Different approaches of detection rate.

The Fig. 9 shows that Quadratic regression gives the best performance than the linear regression for both weighted regression and clustering. The processing time for weighted linear and weighted quadratic is less compare to linear and quadratic regression. Weighted linear and weighted quadratic takes an average of 30 frames per second to process as shown in the Table 1.

Table 1. Processing time comparison of different regression method.

SI. NO	Regression method	Average frames per second (fps) processed
1	Linear	25.39
2	Quadratic	26.50
3	Weighted Linear	30.47
4	Weighted Quadratic	30.20

The proposed methodology is compared with different authors methodology is shown in the Table 2.

Table 2. Comparative analysis

Methods	No of images per frame	Detection technique	Efficiency (%)
[6]	100	HMaxima	60
[7]	200	CNN	92.21
[9]	150	Normalized cross correlation method	90
Our Method	110	Regression and Clustering	95

The randomly selected frames along with some key challenges, the detection results are shown in the Fig. 11. The column 2 shows the input frames. The lane detection results of clustering, regression followed by weighted regression are shown in the column 3 and 4. Consider the frame number 24 both methods are correct and doing good. The frame number 48 there is disconnected line in the right-hand side but weighted regression representing the proper road lane segment. The road lane is occluded by the vehicle and its curved in nature. There is small and disconnected line segments as shown in the frame number 302 in these two cases our proposed methodology works better. The sample database of road lanes is as shown in the Fig. 10.

Fig. 10. Sample database for road lanes.

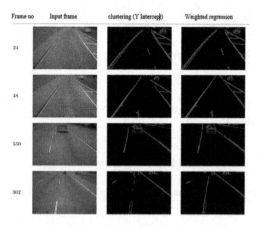

Fig. 11. Detection result of some random frames with frame number.

3.8   Conclusion and Future Work

In this paper we have developed robust system that detects road lanes using clustering regression-based technique. The Proposed methodology focuses both edge and colour-based segmentation (yellow and white) for locating road lanes in an Indian scenario. The main contribution of this paper is to extract the road lines by using hierarchical clustering for grouping and merging of road lane segments and weighted regression for fitting the datapoints on line segments. The proposed method achieves an accuracy of 90%. In future planned to detect and classify using hybrid classifier with different feature extraction technique under cluttered background with high accuracy.

References

1. Danti, A., Kulkarni, J.Y., Hiremath, P.S.: Processing approach to detect lanes, pot holes and recognize road signs in Indian roads. Int. J. Model. Optim. **2**(6), 658–662 (2012)
2. Arunkumar, K.L., Danti, A., Manjunatha, H.T.: Classification of vehicle make based on geometric features and appearance-based attributes under complex background. In: Santosh, K.C., Hegadi, R.S. (eds.) RTIP2R 2018. CCIS, vol. 1035, pp. 41–48. Springer, Singapore (2019). https://doi.org/10.1007/978-981-13-9181-1_4
3. Arunkumar, K.L., Danti, A., Manjunatha, H.T.: Estimation of vehicle distance based on feature points using monocular vision. In: IEEE Proceedings of the International Conference on Data Science and Communication (IconDSC), March 2019. https://doi.org/10.1109/IconDSC,8816996
4. Hechri, A., Mtibaa, A.: Lanes and road signs recognition for driver assistance system. IJCSI Int. J. Comput. Sci. Issues **8**(6), 1 (2011)
5. Bertozzi, M., Broggi, A.: GOLD: a parallel real-time stereo vision system for generic obstacle and lane detection. IEEE Trans. Image Process. **7**(1), 62–81 (1998)
6. Cheng, H.Y., Yu, C.C., Tseng, C.C., Fan, K.C., Hwang, J.N., Jeng, B.S.: Environment classification and hierarchical lane detection for structured and unstructured roads. IET Comput. Vis.-ISSN 1751–9632
7. Ślot, K., Strzelecki, M., Krawczyńska, A., Polańczyk, M.: Road lane detection with elimination of high-curvature edges. In: Bolc, L., Kulikowski, J.L., Wojciechowski, K. (eds.) ICCVG 2008. LNCS, vol. 5337, pp. 33–42. Springer, Heidelberg (2009). https://doi.org/10.1007/978-3-642-02345-3_4
8. Boggavarapu, L.N.P., Vaddi, R.S., Anne, K.R., Vankayalapati, H.D., Munagala, J.K.: A robust multi color lane marking detection approach for Indian scenario (IJACSA). Int. J. Adv. Comput. Sci. Appl. **2**(5), (2011)
9. Araya, L.V., Espada, N., Tosini, M., Leiva, L.: Simple detection and classification of road lanes based on image processing. Int. J. Inf. Technol. Comput. Sci. (IJITCS) **10**(8), 38–45 (2018). https://doi.org/10.5815/ijitcs.2018.08.06
10. Li, M., Li, Y., Jiang, M.: Lane detection based on connection of various feature extraction methods. Hindawi Advances in Multimedia, vol. 2018, Article ID 8320207, 13 p. (2018). https://doi.org/10.1155/2018/8320207
11. Shafique, M., Fahim, M., Pydipogu, P.: Robust lane detection and object tracking. Masters Thesis Electrical Engineering Signal Processing
12. Aly, M.: Real time detection of lane markers in urban streets. In: IEEE Intelligent Vehicles Symposium, pp. 7–12 (2008)

13. Manjunatha, H.T., Danti, Ajit, ArunKumar, K.L.: A novel approach for detection and recognition of traffic signs for automatic driver assistance system under cluttered background. In: Santosh, K.C., Hegadi, R.S. (eds.) RTIP2R 2018. CCIS, vol. 1035, pp. 407–419. Springer, Singapore (2019). https://doi.org/10.1007/978-981-13-9181-1_36

14. Manjunatha, H.T., Danti, A., Arun Kumar, K.L.: Detection and classification of potholes of indian roads using wavelet based energy field. In: IEEE Proceedings of the International Conference on Data Science and Communication (IconDSC) (2019). https://doi.org/10.1109/IconDSC.2019.8816996

15. Navarro, J., Deniel, J., Yousfi, E., Jallais, C., Bueno, M., Fort, A.: Influence of lane departure warnings onset and reliability on car drivers' behaviors. Appl. Ergon. **59**, 123–131 (2017)

16. Hota, R.N., Syed, S., Bandyopadhyay, S., Radhakrishna, P.: A simple and efficient lane detection using clustering and weighted regression. SET Labs, Infosys Technologies Ltd, Hyderabad, India

17. Chougule, S., Ismail, A., Soni, A., Kozonek, N., Narayan, V., Schulze, M.: An efficient encoder-decoder CNN architecture for reliable multilane detection in real time. In: IEEE Intelligent Vehicles Symposium (IV) Changshu, Suzhou, China, pp. 26–30 (2018)

18. Saito, Y., Itoh, M., Inagaki, T.: Driver assistance system with a dual control scheme: effectiveness of identifying driver drowsiness and preventing lane departure accidents. IEEE Trans. Human-Mach. Syst. **46**(5), 660–671 (2019)

19. He, Y., Wang, H., Zhang, B.: Color-based road detection in urban traffic scenes. IEEE Trans. Intell. Transp. Syst. **5**(4), 309–318 (2017)

20. Almazan, E.J., Tal, R., Qian, Y., Elder, J.H.: MCMLSD: a dynamic programming approach to line segment detection. IEEE digital Explorer (2018)

21. Franke, U., Gavrila, D., Gorzig, S., Lindner, F., Puetzold, F., Wohler, C.: Autonomous driving goes downtown. Intell. Syst. Appl. **13**(6), 40–48 (2018)

Detection of Emotion Intensity Using Face Recognition

Alhasan Ali Alharbi$^{(\boxtimes)}$, Mukta Dhopeshwarkar$^{(\boxtimes)}$, and Shubhashree Savant$^{(\boxtimes)}$

Department of CS and IT, Dr. Babasaheb Ambedkar Marathwada University, Aurangabad, Maharashtra, India
hss.harbi1@gmail.com, drmuktanaik@gmail.com, shubhashree.savant@gmail.com

Abstract. The area of face recognition can help to understand the emotional states of user, along with the intensity of those emotions at that particular time, emotion is detected by using feature extraction and process the data to detect the intensity of the emotion.The objective of this paper is to recognaize the intensity of emotions and find out its percentage, for which, a real live video is preperded, Accordingly to the individaul expression in the live video, the emotions are catgorsized in to angry, disgust, scared, happy, sad, surprised, and neutral, emotion intensity is also calculated in real time.

Keywords: Emotion · Facial expression · Intensity · CNN · Facedetection · Python · mini-xception

1 Introduction

The ICT technology has brought enormous changes and rapid development. But the ability to understand human emotion is still a complex area that has to be developed. For this to happen, the emotional state of a user has to be recognize accurately.

Face recognition is one of the areas where emotion is detected through this paper, a method proposed is a new for calculation of emotion intensity through face recognition [1]. Emotion depends on the circumstances of the human; it is complex and changeable over time. Many studies have been used to detect emotions, some of them worked on facial expressions, text, social media, behavior and so on.

The intensity of the emotions can be identified and calculated by using facial expressions and comparing those faces in the dataset with the live video.

This method will be the suitable way to calculate emotional intensity through face recognition. This paper, addressesthis calculation and recognition of faces by using the fer2013 dataset, and find out the emotionsfrom human faces which are captured through live videos.

_mini_XCEPTION.102–0.66.hdf5 model is used for analysis and classification of emotions. For image processing Convolutional Neural Network (CNN) is used, and recognition is used in Artificial Neural Networks to process the pixels. CNN is a

© Springer Nature Singapore Pte Ltd. 2021
K. C. Santosh and B. Gawali (Eds.): RTIP2R 2020, CCIS 1380, pp. 207–213, 2021.
https://doi.org/10.1007/978-981-16-0507-9_18

very popular image-processing model used in Artificial Intelligence and deep learning technologies [2].

Also Keras library built the CNN and processes the image as a pixel, which takes the image and divide the image to pixels or squares.

In addition, the file Haarcascade_frontalface_default.xml is used as classifier to detect the objects from the sources. And openCv for detection of the faces which also detects the features as well.

Facial recognition and intensity are very important and many research and project works are going on, algorithms where intensity from informal and short text messages to identify emotional intensity [3].

To identify the degree of emotion in a sentence,the emotional intensity from a short text like positive and negative words belonging to the same emotion category can be helped.

Therefore, these algorithmsare used to solve the problem of intensity identification using sentences in social media and try to get the emotion according to that.

Another approach used to identify emotions from micro-expressions, the research work on the eyes and faces have been done, based on the color intensity estimation and the Viola –Jones algorithm two algorithms are used [3].

The results of these algorithms for images of the people with the different skin colors are useful to perform the preliminary processing in the pipeline of the micro-expression recognition. These algorithms based on the color intensity estimation as well as suitable for color images are also easier and faster for the small images. The algorithm applied by Viola – Jones to grayscale images is faster for a clear higher resolution images [4].

2   Related Work

Much research work was done on the facial recognition intensity and most of them tried to identify the facial emotions through the text, social media [1, 2, 5, 6]. These researchers used neural network method, an integral projection method has been proposed for face detectionto support the performance of the system. With the noise and illumination this method is very sensitive. Varying background images are not appropriate to use. The system achieves a recognition rate of 86.85%. 140 images have been trained and successfully recognized, whereas the 45 images were not trained and successfully recognized [7]. Some researchers proposed the Regional Covariance Matrix (RCM) based method representation of facial images,and developed a new discriminant analysis theory, aiming to reduce the dimensionality of the facial feature vectors while preserving the most discriminative information, Under the Gaussian Mixture Model (GMM) an estimated multiclass Bayes error derived by minimizing. Further to solve the optimal discriminant vectors an efficient algorithm proposed discriminant analysis method [9].

Another approach made was investigation of the possibility of automated emotion representation, recognition and prediction. Moreover, existing work has been presented, possibilities and existing methods to analyse emotion in video, text, image, physiological signals and sound and. Finally,outlines the existing projects, and presented the available platform, which deals with multimodal emotion analysis [8].

3   Proposed Design

This work is divided into some stages like capturing the real time video, detecting the face using the openCV model, emotions recognition based on the Fer2013 dataset and the mini-Xception model classification and evaluation by using CNN model which gives the percentage of the emotional intensity.The different stages of methodology are as follows (Fig. 1):

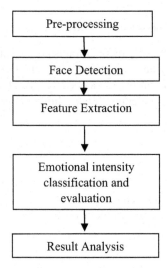

Fig. 1. Methodology

3.1   Pre-processing

The Fer2013 dataset is loaded, read and converted it to pixels. Each row in the Fer2013.csv dataset converted to image with dimension 48 * 48 and emotion is labeled using load_fer2013 function.

After this pre-process input function is used to scale images between -1 to 1. This range is calcultedby dividing by 255, subtracting by 0.5 and multiplying by 2, i.e. $[-1, 1]$ which is better for CNN model and computer vision.

3.2   Face Detection

Open Source Computer Vision (openCV) library is used in face detection to read, detect the faces and its features like eyes, lips in real-time video which is a collection of frames and each frame is an image i.e. collection of pixels.

3.3   Feature Extraction

After face detection features are extracted like eyes, teeth, eyebrows and the widening of eyes, lips. Then face detection propagation and visualization is done by using mini-Xception model and then feed them to the CNN model.

CNN is used for extraction of the features from the image. It has a standard architecture fully connected layer. The functions that are used for feature extractions are softmax, BatchNorm and Conv2D for image normalization.

3.4   Emotional Intensity Classification and Evaluation

The last step of emotional intensity recognition is classification and evaluation process which is done by comparing the learned features of the last convolution and complete the pipeline with the input of real-time video, CNN filters the image and recognizes the features like teeth, eyebrows, widening of eyes, lips and each feature fixed in the same class.

3.5   Result Analysis

After the evaluation and classification, the output is given in the windows one is video captured and face detected and emotion the other one is a canvas that shows the percentageof the emotion intensity simultaneously.

4   Dataset

Dataset that have been used is fer2013, it is open-source dataset, which is the standard datashared for a Kaggle database website [8].

This dataset contains 35.887 grayscale images of faces each with 48 × 48 pixel. In the dataset faces have been automatically registered, so that the face is more or less centred and occupies into the same amount of space in each image.

Each faceisclassifiedin data based on the emotions seven categories of facial expression shown namely 0 is Angry, 1 is Disgust, 2 is Fear, 3 is Happy, 4 is Sad, 5 is Surprise, 6 is Neutral. It has also published in International Conference on Machine Learning (ICML) 6 years ago, which is used to recognize the emotions.

Emotion labels in the dataset are as follows (Table 1):

Table 1. Fer2013 database

No	No. of images	Emotion type
0	4593	Angry
1	547	Disgust
2	5121	Fear
3	8989	Happy
4	6077	Sad
5	4002	Surprise
6	6198	Neutral

5 Implementation

The implementation has been done by using Python language where 3 files are used named:

- load_and_process which has uploaded the Fer2013 dataset and converted it to images.
- real_time_video this file captures the images from the live video and detect the face using openCV and extracts the features and classify them and get the results.
- train_emotion_classifier, this file uses for training purpose.

Models like CNN model, _mini_XCEPTION.102–0.66 model and haarcascade_frontalface_default classifier are used. They are used for detection and classification for emotion and emotional intensity regcognition. The Fig. 2 shows the flow of the work.

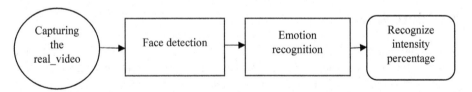

Fig. 2. General steps of the work

6 Results

The emotional intensity is calculated succesfully for seven emotions of human and give the percentage of the intensity in real time depending on the Fer2013 dataset and the models that are mentioned previously.

These are the samples of the emotions after the processing and classification, which gives the live video and the real emotions. Also the percentage of the emotional intensity is calculated. For example the Fig. 3 for natural emotional intensity is 90% as well as happy emotional intensity in Fig. 4 its percentage is 97%. The intensity differs from person to person.

Fig. 3. Sample natural emtion and intensity   **Fig. 4.** Sample happy emtion and intensity

7 Conclusion

In today's scenario, imparting knowledge about emotional states of a person is necessary; use of this system is not only the application of this work. It can also be used in the clinical field for assessing the emotion states of a patient who is enabled to convey it. Extending this to prediction of future emotional states along with its intensity will improve accuracy and will have a wider range of application. This emotional recognition coupled with intensity calculation will make the sphere of affective computing progress to its next level of advancement.

This paper has tried to calculate the intensity by taking real time video of a person and has given a new idea for calculation of emotion intensity.

8 Future Scope

New models can be developed through this aspect especially in the medical field for the patients of ICU who cannot convey their states. Their feeling can be calculated, by their facial expressions intensity by following this model.

Acknowledgment. We are thankful to Kaggle for providing the data required for this paper. We are also thankful to Dept. of CS and IT, Dr. Babasaheb Ambedkar Marathwada University, Aurangabad for this opportunity to share our paper .

References

1. M.F., Wang, H., Santosh, K.C.: Gray level face recognition using spatial features. In: Santosh, K.C., Hegadi, R.S. (eds.) RTIP2R. CCIS, vol. 1035, pp. 216–229. Springer, Singapore (2019). https://doi.org/10.1007/978-981-13-9181-1_20

2. Srinivasa, R., Santosh, K.C., Chandra , P.V.S.S.R.: Learning deep feature representation for face spoofing. In: Santosh, K.C., Hegadi, R.S. (eds.) RTIP2R. CCIS, vol. 1035, pp. 178–185. Springer, Singapore (2019). https://doi.org/10.1007/978-981-13-9181-1_16

3. Mashal, S.X., Asnani, K.: Emotion Intensity Detection for Social Media Data. 978–1–5090–4890–8/17/$31.00 ©2017 IEEE

4. Sergeeva, A.D., Savin, A.V., Sablina, V.A.: Emotion Recognition from Micro-Expressions: Search for the Face and Eyes. 978–1–7281–1740–9/19/$31.00 ©2019 IEEE

5. Candemir, S., Borovikov, E., Santosh, K.C., Antani, S.K., Thoma, G.R.: RSILC: rotation- and scale-invariant, line-based color-aware descriptor. Image Vis. Comput. **42**, 1–2 (2015)

6. Wang, H., et al.: An empirical study: ELM in face matching. In: Santosh, K.C., Hegadi, R.S. (eds.) RTIP2R. CCIS, vol. 1035, pp. 277–287. Springer, Singapore (2019). https://doi.org/10.1007/978-981-13-9181-1_25

7. Kushwah, K., Sharma, V., Singh, U.: Neural Network Method Through Facial Expression Recognition, PROF. Vikrant Sharma, 978–1–5090–5686–6/17/$31.00 ©2017 IEEE

8. Kaggle. https://www.kaggle.com/deadskull7/fer2013/downloads/fer2013.zip/1. Accessed 09 Sept 2019

9. Github. https://github.com/omar178/Emotion-recognition#p1. Accessed 09 Sept 2019

10. Pythonprogramming.   https://pythonprogramming.net/convolutional-neural-network-cnn-machine-learning-tutorial/. Accessed 10 Sept 2019

11. Zheng, W., Tang, H., Lin, Z., Huang, T.S.: Emotion recognition from arbitrary view facial images. In: Daniilidis, K., Maragos, P., Paragios, N. (eds.) ECCV. LNCS, vol. 6316, pp. 490–503. Springer, Heidelberg (2010). https://doi.org/10.1007/978-3-642-15567-3_36

12. Marechal, C., Mikołajewski, D., Tyburek, K., Prokopowicz, P., Bougueroua, L., Ancourt, C., Węgrzyn-Wolska, K.: Survey on AI-based multimodal methods for emotion detection. In: Kołodziej, J., González-Vélez, H. (eds.) High-Performance Modelling and Simulation for Big Data Applications. LNCS, vol. 11400, pp. 307–324. Springer, Cham (2019). https://doi.org/10.1007/978-3-030-16272-6_11

13. Mehta, D., Siddiqui, M.F.H., Javaid, A.Y.: Recognition of emotion Intensities using machine learning algorithms: a comparative study. Sensors **19**, 1897 (2019). https://doi.org/10.3390/s19081897

14. Martinez, A., Du, S.: A model of the perception of facial expressions of emotion by humans: research overview and perspectives. J. Mach. Learn. Res. **13**, 1589–1608 (2012)

15. Pandey, R.K., Karmakar, S., Ramakrishnan, A.G., Saha, N.: Improving Facial Emotion Recognition Systems Using Gradient and Laplacian Images

Double Authentication System Based on Face Identification and Lipreading

Priyanka P. Kapkar[✉] and S. D. Bharkad

Government College of Engineering, Aurangabad, Maharashtra, India
priyankakapkar123@gmail.com, sangita.bharkad@gmail.com

Abstract. With the amercing new technologies more advanced security systems are developed. Security system means difficult to be attacked by any intruder, complicated design, expensive and requires additional software and hardware resources. Biometric system comes over all the simple security system. Since the biological data is used for the security purpose and its cheap, simple design and much easy to handle. But now-a-days these systems are also hacked and more advanced, secured system is to be developed. So to overcome all these problems new biometric technique of lipreading is brought into implementation as authenticating system. In this paper, double biometric authentication system is developed. This system is based on face identification as "ID" and then after identification lipreading is used as "Password". In the process of face identification the KAZE features are used which gave 90.1923% of accuracy using the KNN classifier. After the correctly identification of face, lipreading process starts. In the lipreading part, hybrid based technique feature are extracted. By making use of multi-class SVM, this gave 80% accuracy for lipreading in MATLAB 2018a software. This developed system can be used in various areas like banking, highly secured areas and also for the locker systems.

Keywords: Face identification · Lipreading · Feature extraction · Classifiers

1 Introduction

Amercing each of new technologies in our day-to-day life bring us to more advance and security to access a system. Highly secured system means more difficult to hacked, very complex to design, costly and require additional software and hardware resources. When new authenticating system is developed, it's essential to take into account its efficiency, cost of it, simplicity and social acceptance. Now a day's, rather than using a password, authenticating a unique identity by using biological information in secured system is mostly used. Mainly used biometric systems are fingerprint, iris scans, face recognition [1–4], voice recognition, signature recognition, and retinal scan, DNA, Hand geometry and many more. Biometric is a methodologically studying of analysis of biological data used for the purpose of person's identification or person's authentication. "Biometric" was originally the Greek word, where "Bio" means 'life' and "metrics" means 'measurements'. Biometric system provides all the requirements and quite reliability.

© Springer Nature Singapore Pte Ltd. 2021
K. C. Santosh and B. Gawali (Eds.): RTIP2R 2020, CCIS 1380, pp. 214–224, 2021.
https://doi.org/10.1007/978-981-16-0507-9_19

Still biometric systems are more efficient and safe, but it has some disadvantages inspit of it. Also while designing a biometric system we have to take into consideration its advantages and disadvantages.

Now a days various new biometric system are used liked face recognition. It is most cheapest technology available, but still system can also be easily hacked by applying mask of individual on other one. So was not such effective one. The next one is the voice recognition one, similar to face recognition cheap in technology and requires less time to execute. But has low efficiency and if individual is not well then change in little voice causes difficulties during identification. This system can also be easily hacked by only storing the voice of individual, which operate a system in absence of that authenticating individual. Retinal scan one of the promising technique for biometric but very costly. Also more exposure of eyes to the system causes harm to eyes. Iris recognition is more amercing new technique in biometric system with more accuracy rate. But the drawback is that it's more expensive and requires more memory to store data and takes more time to generate output. By applying contact lenses on individual person's it can easily be hacked and identified. Fingerprint recognition is the cheapest one and more accuracy one biometric system. Much wildly used, now a day's in cell phones e-cards and many more. But still has drawback that the fingerprints are left on the system by individual during authentication which will give error for other individual to authenticate and left fingerprint also can be used for the hacking purpose.

Biometric technique which overall comes with all these drawbacks is the lipreading technique. Yiu-ming Cheung full professor of the department of the Computer Science by a Hong Kong Baptist University, has proposed lipreading and spoken passwords. Every individual on this planet has different ways of lip movements and even the twins cannot mimicries it, had been proved in [14]. So it's a kind of unique biometric feature which can be used for authentication.

Recently, much of work had been done on lipreading and it's applications. By making use of the most advanced tool's in image processing, signal processing and machine learning tool. Researchers taking now much interest in improving lipreading processes, which will work automatically. Basically lipreading work was done on lip detection on 2D image. In this paper, lipreading is implemented using short video based database.

Each frame of videos is processed and used for feature extracting process. This lipreading process is used as the "password" for the authentication purpose. This lipreading will be implemented only when the face identification is done.

Rest of paper is organised as follows: Sect. 2 gives the literature survey of lipreading Sect. 3. Has developed system with its processes used Sect. 3. Has the face identification algorithm used Sect. 3. Has lipreading process used for system development Sect. 4 summarizes the different systems results for lipreading. Conclusion and future scope for the work are been presented in Sect. 5.

2 Literature Survey

The processes for lipreading is divided into following parts; which are database, pre-processing, feature extracting techniques and classifiers. For evaluating classifier, the important part which play's a very vital role is the database been used. Various database are been used for various systems which are implemented. M2VTS is the database which contains audio as well as video based signals in it. Zero to nine digit's are been pronounced in French which has 185 recording of 37 individuals in [9, 20]. PKU—AV database is used by [23] and [20] had used XM2VTS database which are having AV-letter based database. Oulu-VS database, that consists of 20 individuals utterance of 10 phrase of each five times is used in [23].

Various pre-processing techniques are implemented. Alizedeh et al. [9] had used SMQT (successive mean quantization transform) based technique for localization of lower facial part. Chen et al. [10] had made to automatically locate lips with the use of Haar transform and is also used to separate luminance from chrominance of the mouth's region. Rathee et al. [22] has studied many pre-processing techniques which are based on colour luminance, transforms and thresholding of gray scale values.

For feature extracting the techniques used, which are mainly classifieds as first one based on geometric feature of lips. Here the ratio of mouth's height to width is been use as feature [9, 20]. Sharma et al. [15] had used bivariated Distribution of filtered of image taken after extracting the region of interest (ROI). Thabet et al. [25] has made use of height and the width of lips which are concatenated are used as feature. Mathulaprangsan et al. [20] has made use of area of mouth as feature. The second one is the appearance features extracting technique which uses the area of tongue see, teeth's as feature using pixel based data for feature extracting [16] and binarisation of image of the lips as feature in [4]. Lenung et al. [7] had used opened mouth area which consisted of tongue and the teeth's which are used as the feature. ASM (active shape model) was been used for contour based detection of lip [8]. In the texture based technique for feature extracting. By applying morphological process, mouths centre is used while movements of lips are taking place in it [11]. Liu et al. [19] had extracted feature by making use of discrete Cosine transform, discrete Wavelet transform and principal Component analysis. In the most advanced technique developed for feature extracting from other techniques is the hybrid technique. Talea et al. [13] used the red exclusion algorithm, for having transform of ROI of mouth which had recognised mouth's centre from vertical position. Ahmad [18] has made use of combination of geometric feature and discrete wavelet transform and taken its mutual probability as feature. Aleksic et al. [6] has used jumping snake model that founded features of lips contour.

After the feature extracting classification is done of it. Different classifiers used are SVM (support vector machine) [8] which is mainly used. GMM (Gaussian Mixture Model) which has more approximation that HMM (Hidden Markov Model) [17] is used. Multi-dimensional-convolutional neural network was used for classification in [26]. So many classifiers where used for the classification with different features but the supervised were more appropriate one.

3 Proposed System

Since there are various security system developed, but having here doubly authenticating system is developed. The block diagram of proposed system is shown below;

Figure 1 shows Proposed system block diagram. In this diagram, the first part is used for face identification which works as "ID" to the system and after face identification

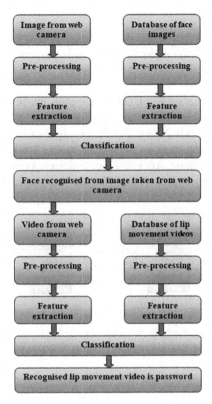

Fig. 1. Proposed system block diagram

is done correctly then only lipreading as password comes. After the verification of both the systems then only the secured system opens.

Here the database for the face recognition and lipreading is taken differently. Image database is used for face recognition and short video database is used for lipreading. Pre-processing used in both parts is the histogram equalisation. For face recognition KAZE detector features are used. In the lipreading part lips height to width ratio is used as feature. Classifiers are used for the classification of face based database and similarly for lipreading. But after the face is recognised only, then the lipreading part will take place.

3.1 Face identification

Face identification is the first part of the developed system which consists of following parts:

- Face based database
- Pre-processing
- Feature extraction
- Classification

Face Based Database

For face identification part face image database is required. Since this proposed system is for security purpose so the individuals who are going to handle specific secured system their database is only required. So here the database created is of 104 people's having 15 images of each.

For classification of the system it takes real time image for testing and database for training. The database created has some pre-processing done on it while storing the data from software MATLAB 2018a. Before storing data of specific individual in its subfolder the pre-processing steps are, first the snapshot is taken then converted colour image to gray scale image done. After that face is detected using Viola-Jones algorithm and then resizing the face image to 150 × 150 and then stored it (Fig. 2).

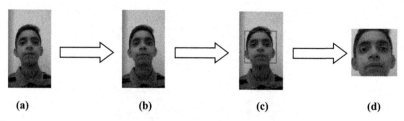

| (a) | (b) | (c) | (d) |

Fig. 2. Processes for creating database. (a) snapshot, (b) converted colour to gray scale image, (c) face detected using Viola-Jones Algorithm (d) cropped and resized

Pre-processing

After the database is created still it requires some pre-processing before actual feature extraction takes place. Since images in database are not in correct contrast with its gray levels. So histogram equalization is technique to process an image for adjusting the contrast of image, by changing the intensities distribution of the histogram [27]. The formula for histogram equalization is;

$$h = \left| \frac{C_1 - C_0}{(m \times n) - C_0} \times (l - 1) \right|$$

where C_0 is the minimum non-zero values of the Cumulative distribution function. mxn is the pixels in the image and l is the no. of grey level used in image. C_1 is the cumulative distribution function of that point which had to be found.

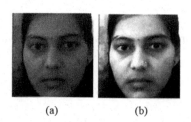

| (a) | (b) |

Fig. 3. (a) Before histogram equalization and (b) After histogram equalization

Histogram equalization is mainly used because of its simple to use than other techniques and also only the contrast needed to set.

Feature Extraction
After pre-processing feature extraction takes place. For feature extraction, the KAZE-featuresare used. Other feature extraction techniques like SURF and SIFT didn't gave accuracy as compare to KAZE feature while identifying in the process of classification. Where KAZE means 'wind' in Japanese words. KAZE feature used is the combination of non-linear space scale, through non-linear diffusion filter. KAZE Detector based, on the normalised scale, determinant of Hessian matrix.

Hessian matrix can be expressed as follow,

$$H(a, \sigma) = \begin{bmatrix} L_{aa}(a, \sigma) & L_{ab}(a, \sigma) \\ L_{ba}(a, \sigma) & L_{bb}(a, \sigma) \end{bmatrix}$$

Where, $L_{aa}(a, \sigma)$; convolution of the Second Order Gaussian derivative of image atpoint 'a'. Similarly, $L_{ab}(a, \sigma)$ and $L_{bb}(a, \sigma)$ are same.

For non linear space scale Hessian matrix is taken and then for standard non linear diffusion filter taken as,

$$\frac{\partial l}{\partial t} = div(c(a, y, t).\nabla L)$$

Where, c; conductivity of the function, div; divergence, l; luminance, ∇; gradient of operator.

KAZE feature is unchanged even if rotated, or scaled. These features have distinctiveness with varying scales (Fig. 4).

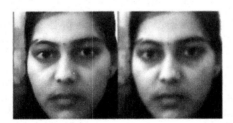

Fig. 4. Show the KAZE feature on left and Gaussian one on right

Classifiers
There are various classifiers available for classification. But here the supervised KNN (K-Nearest Neighbor) and multi-class SVM (Support vector machine) is been used. KNN uses the Euclidian distance for the classification of features. Multi class SVM used one to one comparing while using classifier.

Simple and more efficient classifier to be used is SVM classifier. SVM classifier classifies according to binary classification of database which is selected. According to linear classification of classifier, SVM classifier works. Assume a linear separatable problem:

$$[(a_i, b_i)]_{i=1}^k \quad \text{and} \quad b_i = [-1, +1]$$

Where a_i is a k dimensional vector and b_i are labels to the vectors taken. Classifier concept separates two classes is called hyperplane.

$$We^T a + n = 0$$

Where 'a' is input-variable, 'We' is weight of the vector and 'n' is bias. Optimal hyperplane parameters 'We' and 'n' are found to maximize of the Geometric margin $2/\|W_e\|$;

$$b_i \left(We^T a + n \right) \geq +1$$

KNN classifier checks the nearest neighbor points by taking minimum distance between the nearest neighbor points. Here the for minimum distance Euclidian distance is taken.

3.2 Lipreading

After identification of face only lipreading part will take place. It has got similar steps as that for the face identification part as;

- Video database
- Pre-processing
- Feature extraction
- Classification

Video Database

As lip movements are taken as the database for lipreading. So the lip movements are stored in video format, hence short video database is used. The database consisted of short video of 18 people used for identification of lipreading. Each video is of 28 frames per second.

Pre-processing

In the pre-processing part of lipreading, the video is first converted to fames. Means the images can be used for further processing. Images which are taken on which face detection is done, then the colour image is converted to gray scale and resized to 150 × 150. After the resize of image histogram equalization is applied on it for contrast equalization. Because its more simplex to implement and showed more accuracy while classifying the video frames.

Feature Extraction

For the feature extraction part here the first mouth is detected using Viola-Jones algorithm and then the ratio of lips height to width is stored as feature for classification purpose.

Viola-Jones algorithm is more robust while identifying the facial parts. The ratio of lips height to width in each video for every person is different. Since each video consisted of 28 frames per second so the sequence of ratio of lips height to width is different for every person in the video database.

The lip detection is been done by the use of Viola-Jones Algorithm. So the steps in Viola-Jones algorithm are.

1. Haar feature
2. Integral of image
3. Adaboost
4. Cascading

Haar features are similar to edge detection but only specified kernels are used for the feature extracting purpose. 24 × 24 window is used as base for evaluating features from the image. More the 160,000 features are extracted.

So the reduce the number of features integral image is done. In this feature gray scale values which are coming under the black box are summed then subtracted from the summed white box gray scale values.

Integral image for image can be taken as;

$$\Delta = \text{black} - \text{white} = \frac{1}{n} \sum_{\text{black}}^{n} I(x) - \frac{1}{n} \sum_{\text{White}}^{n} I(x)$$

Where, Δ; is the integral of image, n; number of pixels, I; is the image taken, x; is the pixel intensity values.

Using this, the feature values are reduced. But for still reducing Adaboost classifier is used. In Adaboost, the Haar kernel which is applied is relevant or irrelevant is identified and features are reduced. Adaboost does the combining of weak classifier means the features to form a strong classifier.

After Adaboost, cascading classifier is applied. Where in cascading process first the first kernel is applied, checks if the facial part is detected the it goes further for whole image to be scanned or if it does not match with the kernel then the next image is taken. This way the time is reduced and more appropriate facial parts are detected.

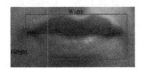

Fig. 5. Figure shows mouth detected with lips height and width

By using this process of Viola-Jones, mouth is detected. The detected mouths, lips height to width ratio is stored as .mat file in MATLAB for classification purpose as shown in Fig. 5.

Classification

Similar to face identification the classifier used here are the multi-class SVM and KNN. For calculating the accuracy of the classifier, testing video upon the total number of videos are taken while calculating.

4 Results

Various feature are taken into account while extraction like SURF, SIFT, BRISK and many more. This has showed low accuracy after the classification. Zahra Saleem et al. [27] had also studied different feature extraction techniques and also came to conclusion that KAZE was much better among the different feature extracting techniques and detector. So KAZE feature has specifications like distinctiveness' when scaled, the is no effect of rotation of image and scaling of it. By using KNN as classifier for classification 90.1923% accuracy which was much better than using the multiclass SVM with 60.0385% accuracy for the face recognition.

While in lipreading hybrid based technique is used for feature extracting purpose. So here in the hybrid based technique various combinations of methods are used for extracting the features. So here first mouth is detected and then the ratio of lips height to width is taken.

Lee et al. [24] had used Long Short Term Memory for the neural network based classifier and got 68.4% accuracy with feature as Eigen values for lipreading. Thabet et al. [25] has shown the use of different classifiers for lipreading and had done the comparative study with it. They used various classifiers, but with SVM they got 59.4% of accuracy using the only geometric features. Lesani et al. [21] had also implemented the same biometric system for mobile phones but with image database. They had taken contour corner points as features. Got 70% accuracy for lipreading.

But by making use of the short videos database in the proposed system, I had got 80% accuracy with multiclass SVM classifier and 40% with KNN classifier. So, multiclass SVM classifier is having more accuracy then the KNN classifier. By making use of one to one comparing of the videos during the classification process in multiclass SVM.

Table.1. Comparative study of various paper with proposed system

	Lee et al. [24]	Thabet et al. [25]	Lesani et al. [21]	Proposed system
Feature	Eigen values	Geometric	Contour corner points	Hybrid features
Accuracy	68.4%	59.4%	70%	80%

5 Conclusion and Future Scope

This paper has developed a more secured system which can be used in banking systems, in locker system, in highly secured areas. Since by making use of KAZE feature as for identification in real time proved more robust then the other feature extracting techniques like SURF and SIFT, because by rotating the image also it showed correct identification for real time system. Since we are using only visual part of the video, so we can use this system in very crowed or noisy area also. Here the system is making use of hybride feature extracting technique so that while authenticating the password as lipreading showed more robustness. Since here the system uses the authentication twice so more hard to be attacked by intruder. The individual who has enrolled this ID can change its password also at any time.

By making use of unsupervised classifier from machine learning than supervised one the system authentication can be increased. This system is implemented in MATLAB 2018a, so it's not a open source and has many disadvantages also. So we can make use of open source software's like python, java or SQL for implementation of system. This system the lipreading is using alphabet as password, we can make use of some special lip movements instead making use of words or alphabets. Since they are special for every individual and cannot be mimicked and recalled by any other individual. Also by making use more high resolution camera the more clear features can be extracted and more accuracy can be gained.

References

1. Srinivasa Perumal, R., Santosh, K.C., Chandra Mouli, P.V.S.S.R.: Learning deep feature representation for face spoofing. In: Santosh, K.C., Hegadi, R.S. (eds.) RTIP2R 2018. CCIS, vol. 1035, pp. 178–185. Springer, Singapore (2019). https://doi.org/10.1007/978-981-13-9181-1_16
2. Fawwad Hussain, M., Wang, H., Santosh, K.C.: Gray level face recognition using spatial features. In: Santosh, K.C., Hegadi, R.S. (eds.) RTIP2R 2018. CCIS, vol. 1035, pp. 216–229. Springer, Singapore (2019). https://doi.org/10.1007/978-981-13-9181-1_20
3. Wang, H., Hussain, M.F., Mukherjee, H., Obaidullah, S.M., Hegadi, R.S., Roy, K., Santosh, K.C.: An empirical study: ELM in face matching. In: Santosh, K.C., Hegadi, R.S. (eds.) RTIP2R 2018. CCIS, vol. 1035, pp. 277–287. Springer, Singapore (2019). https://doi.org/10.1007/978-981-13-9181-1_25
4. Candemir, S., Borovikov, E., Santosh, K.C., Antani, S.K., Thoma, G.R.: RSILC: rotation- and scale-invariant, line-based color-aware descriptor. Image Vis. Comput. 42, 1–12 (2015)
5. Gomez, E., Travieso, C.M., Briceno, J.C., Ferrer, M.A.: Biometric identification system by Lip shape. In: Proceedings. 36th Annual 2002 International Carnahan Conference on Security Technology, pp. 39–42 (2002)
6. Aleksic, P.S., Katsaggelos, A.K.: Audio-visual biometrics. Proc. IEEE 94(11), 2025–2044 (2006)
7. Leung, S.H., et al.: Automatic lipreading with limited training data. In: 18th International Conference on Pattern recognition (ICPR 2006), pp. 881–884 (2006)
8. Wang, S.L., Liew, A.W., Lau, W.H., Leung, S.H.: An automatic lipreading system for spoken digits with limited training data. IEEE Trans. Circuits Syst. Video Technol. 18(12), 1760–1765 (2008)
9. Alizadeh, S., Boostani, R., Asadpour, V.: Lip feature extraction and reduction for HMM-based visual speech recognition systems. In: 2008 9th International Conference on Signal Processing, pp. 561–564 (2008)

10. Chen, J., Tiddeman, B., Zhao, G.: Real-time lip contour extraction and tracking using an improved active contour model. In: Bebis, G., Boyle, R., Parvin, B., Koracin, D., Remagnino, P., Porikli, F., Peters, J., Klosowski, J., Arns, L., Chun, Y.K., Rhyne, T.-M., Monroe, L. (eds.) ISVC 2008. LNCS, vol. 5359, pp. 236–245. Springer, Heidelberg (2008). https://doi.org/10.1007/978-3-540-89646-3_23

11. Wang, M.: Lip feature selection based on BPSO and SVM. In: IEEE 2011 10th International Conference on Electronic Measurement & Instruments, pp. 56–59 (2011)

12. Travieso, C.M., Zhang, J., Miller, P., Alonso, J.B., Ferrer, M.A.: Bimodal biometric verification based on face and lips. Neurocomputing **74**(14–15), 2407–2410 (2011)

13. Talea, H., Yaghmaie, K.: Automatic combined lip segmentation in color images. In: IEEE 3rd International Conference on Communication Software and Networks, pp. 109–112 (2011)

14. Marouf, H., Faez, K.: Zernike moment based feature extraction for facial recognition off identical twins. Int. J. Comput. Sci. Eng. Inf. Technol. **3**(6), 1–8 (2013)

15. Sahu, V., Sharma, M.: Result based analysis of various lip tracking systems. In: International Conference on Green High Performance Computing (ICGHPC), pp. 1–7 (2013)

16. Liu, H., Fan, T., Wu, P.: Audio-visual keyword spotting based on adaptive decision fusion under noisy conditions for human-robot interaction. In: IEEE International Conference on Robotics and Automation (ICRA), pp. 6644–6651 (2014)

17. Sangve, S., Mule, N.: Lip recognition for authentication and security. IOSR J. Comput. Eng. (IOSR-JCE), **16**(3), 18–23 (2014)

18. Hassanat, A.: Visual passwords using automatic lip reading. Int. J. Sci.: Basic Appl. Res. (IJSBAR), **13**, 218–231 (2014)

19. Liu, X., Cheung, Y.: An exemplar-based hidden Markov model with discriminative visual features for lipreading. In: Tenth International Conference on Computational Intelligence and Security, pp. 90–93 (2014)

20. Mathulaprangsan, S., Wang, C., Kusum, A.Z., Tai, T., Wang, J.: A survey of visual lip reading and lip-password verification. In: International Conference on Orange Technologies (ICOT), pp. 22–25 (2015)

21. Lesani, F.S., Ghazvini, F.F., Dianat, R.: Mobile phone security using automatic lip reading. In: 9th International Conference on e-Commerce in Developing Countries: With Focus on e-Business (ECDC), pp. 1–5 (2015)

22. Rathee, N., Ganotra, D.: Analysis of human lip features: a review. Int. J. Appl. Systemic Stud. **6**(2), 137–184 (2015)

23. Wu, P., Liu, H., Li, X., Fan, T., Zhang, X.: A novel lip descriptor for audio-visual keyword spotting based on adaptive decision fusion. IEEE Trans. Multimedia **18**(3), 326–338 (2016)

24. Lee, D., Myung, K.: Read my lips, login to the virtual world. In: IEEE International Conference on Consumer Electronics (ICCE), pp. 434–435 (2017)

25. Thabet, Z., Nabih, A., Azmi, K., Samy, Y., Khoriba, G., Elshehaly, M.: Lipreading using a comparative machine learning approach. In: First International Workshop on Deep and Representation Learning (IWDRL), pp. 19–25 (2018)

26. Ding, R., Pang, C., Liu, H.: Audio-visual keyword spotting based on multidimensional convolutional neural network. In: 25th IEEE International Conference on Image Processing (ICIP), pp. 4138–4142 (2018)

27. Tareen, S.A.K., Saleem, Z.: A comparative anaylsis of SIFT, SURF, KAZE, AKAZE, ORB, and BRISK. In: 2018 International Conference on Computing, Mathematics and Engineering Technology-iCoMET 2018, Sukkur, pp. 1–10 (2018)

28. Ruikar, D.D., Santosh, K.C., Hegadi, R.S.: Contrast stretching-based unwanted artifacts removal from CT images. In: Santosh, K.C., Hegadi, R.S. (eds.) RTIP2R 2018. CCIS, vol. 1036, pp. 3–14. Springer, Singapore (2019). https://doi.org/10.1007/978-981-13-9184-2_1

Safety Gear Check at Industries and Laboratories Using Convolutional Neural Network Based on Deep Learning

R. Sandhya[1]([✉]), J. Shree Hari[2], and S. N. Jagadeesha[3]

[1] Department of Computer Application, JNN College of Engineering,
Shimoga, Karnataka, India
mysoresandhya@gmail.com
[2] Siemens Technology and Services India Pvt Ltd., Bangalore, Karnataka, India
sriharijshimoga@gmail.com
[3] Department of Computer Science and Engineering,
PES Institute of Technology and Management, Shimoga, Karnataka, India
jagadeesha2012@gmail.com

Abstract. There are plethora of industries and laboratories around the world, they have a necessity to maintain their safety standards especially with respect to safety gear (safety wearable's such as apron or high visibility jackets). Indeed, and this is a difficult task to monitor if the subject (person) is wearing appropriate safety apparatus or not in hazardous environments. A methodology is proposed herein to identify whether the subject is wearing appropriate safety gear or not. Using the dataset available, a neural network is trained to suit this need.

Keywords: Safety gear check · Tensor Flow · Inception-v3 · Convolutional networks

1 Introduction

Safety is a crucial part of industrial environments. Accidents or mishaps often occur especially in these kinds of environments, often injuring the subject. These mishaps must be avoided at all cost as each and every life is precious. Laboratory coats are used to avoid contact with dirt and the small chemical particles or spills in doing laboratory scale work. The laboratory coat can be worn as a protection for primary clothing and as well as exposure to the wearer. Present days are difficult for the security persons to identify the persons entering the laboratory or industry, whether the employees are wearing the safety gears or not and it takes more time to check each person, Security guards should be hired in order to check. In this paper, a method is proposed to classify the subject is wearing safety wearable or not.

Convolutional neural network (ConvNets or CNNs) is one of the main techniques for image recognition and image classifications.

© Springer Nature Singapore Pte Ltd. 2021
K. C. Santosh and B. Gawali (Eds.): RTIP2R 2020, CCIS 1380, pp. 225–236, 2021.
https://doi.org/10.1007/978-981-16-0507-9_20

CNNs are widely used for object detections, recognition of faces etc.,. In recent years, deep learning, is regarded as a convolutional neural network (CNN, or ConvNet) which is a class of deep neural networks and is applied in analyzing images. Convolutional Neural network (CNN) based image processing provides a feasible solution in classification. Using the large available dataset, a neural network is trained. Multiple features of safety gears are taken during the training process by the neural network. Using the trained network, subject can be classified as pass or fail(wearing or not).

S. M. Sofiqul Islam, et al. [1] proposed a methodology to identify the garment design based on AlexNet and VGGNet and some feature extraction method. On two different garment datasets for training and testing, they applied two well known deep Convolutional Neural Network (CNN) models Alex Net and VGG_S. Finally, with the existing models, the accuracy of proposed system was compared. Marianna Bedeli, et al. [2] proposed a model to identify persons based on the image information resulting from their apparel. To train the computer, deep learning was used to categorize images based on contents of the apparel and reveal garment classification by using a large dataset. However proposed models carry out comparatively weak garment classification on a dataset that have trendy logos and well known trade name images. Alexander Schindler, et al. [16] gave center of attention on an observed study of applying deep Convolutional Neural Networks (CNN) to the chore of fashion and apparel image classification for e-commerce applications. On two small and large scale dataset, three different tasks, person detection, product and gender classification of models were reported. Huizhong Chen, et al. [12] proposed an automated system in identifying attributes of the clothes on human body and introduced a novel application in analyzing style of the dress, by finding semantic attributes of the clothes. Brian Lao and Karthik Jagadeesh [15] gave a proposal in identifying clothing item in a image and used several tasks in classifying the cloth type, cloth attributes.

Saitoh and Kaneko [3] proposed a method to recognize flowers, where two images are needed, one of the flowers and other of the leaf. This method requires the user to place a black cloth behind the flower or leaf to recognize it. This is not feasible and is inconvenient for the user to use this method in real time scenario. In this method, noise is reduced using K-Means algorithm by applying a small blur on the input image. Xiaoling Xia and Cui Xu [4] proposed a model based on the Inception-V3 model of TensorFlow platform and transfer Learning technology to classify the flowers. The Inception-V3 model of TenserFlow platform is well suited to train Convolutional Neural Network for large dataset of leaves.

2   Convolutional Neural Networks

Deep learning is a family of machine learning methods rooted in artificial neural networks. Deep Learning can be supervised, semi supervised or unsupervised. Deep neural networks, deep belief networks, recurrent neural networks and convolutional neural network architectures have been applied in the several fields of computer applications [17].

CNN [11] is applied in deep learning, artificial neural networks that have been useful productively for exploring the visual layers. These networks resemble the connection pattern of the neurons of an animal visual cortex. CNN contains an input layer and an output layer with many hidden layers in the middle. Middle layers contain convolutional layers, pooling layers and fully connected (FC) layers. The connection of neurons in the middle layers is used for training purpose. The input image is taken as a 3-dimensional volume where RGB values of the image is arranged in the form of a cube. Filters of various sizes are applied for each layer to get a convoluted next layer. Number of filters applied depends upon the resolution of an image. Figure 1 shows various layers of convolutional neural networks and their connections.

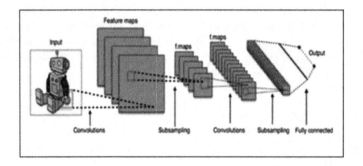

Fig. 1. CNN architecture.

The output is taken from fully connected layer through activation function. Each neuron consists of two units: summing function and a nonlinear element. Summing function gives the sum of the product of each pixel value and its associated filter weights as shown in Fig. 2.

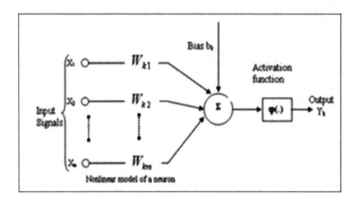

Fig. 2. Nonlinear model of a neuron.

Nonlinear element uses activation function to give the output. Sigmoid and ReLu are the two common activation functions used in CNNs. ReLu can be applied to the hidden layers and used for the regression type problems. This paper proposes the use of sigmoid function to classify the wearable to their classes. Sigmoid function ϕ is defined as:

$$\phi_{sigmoid}(z) = \frac{1}{1+e^{-z}} \tag{1}$$

where the input z is

$$z = w_0 x_0 + w_1 x_1 ..... w_m x_m = w^T X \tag{2}$$

Where w is the weight vector, where $w = [w_0, w_1, w_2 ...... w_m]$ and X is the feature vector of training sample where $X = [x_0, x_1, x_2 ...... x_m]$ and w_0 is the bias unit.

The output from the sigmoid function is compared with the previously trained network for accuracy. The obtained weight difference is used to back-track and weight co-efficients are applied to minimize the error signal produced by each neuron of the network [19].

3   Architecture

Many architectures and algorithms have been proposed to implement convolutional neural network.

3.1   KNN Algorithm

It is a decision rule of finding K-nearest neighbors [5,7]. It is a well recognized, high routine pattern recognition technique used for feed back neural networks.

1. Find, parameter K = number of nearest neighbors.
2. Compute the length between all the training samples and query instance.
3. Arrange the length in ascending order and find nearest neighbors based on the Kth minimum length.

It is a clustering algorithm which uses previous use cases to predict new use cases [9]. But its sequential implementation is inherently slow.

3.2   Alex NetModel

Alex NetModel is a CNN developed with CUDA (Compute Unified Device Architecture) is an API using GPU support to run [8]. The architecture of the model is shown in Fig. 3. In this model only one filter is used for layer to get convolved next layer. The layers become denser after applying filter to each layer. Finally, all the features will get convolved in fully connected layer. The FC layer output is compared with new case to find similarity.

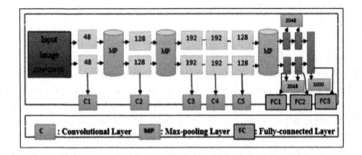

Fig. 3. Full architecture of AlexNet model.

3.3 Inception-V3 Model

Inception-v3Model [4] is a model developed by Google which is one of the pre trained model, developed on the TensorFlow [6]. TensorFlow is a open source software library, meant for dataflow and programming across a variety of jobs. Tensor flow consists of math library and used in machine learning applications [18]. It is difficult to train all the layers of this network, but TensorFlow provides tutorials to keep final layer of inception's for new grouping and learning [6].

The main advantage of this model compared to other conventional models is that, it uses many filters for a single layer to get more features convolved for the final layer. In this architecture 3×3, 5×5 filters and 1×1 filters are used as shown in Fig. 4, which helps number of computations and storage space on the device.

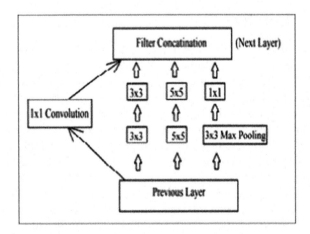

Fig. 4. Layers of Inception-v3 model.

3.4 Data Set

The images have been collected from various sources, like Google images, e-commerce web sites. Primarily, only upper part of the body was considered. Over a thousand images of each type were taken, namely, Laboratory Coats, High Visibility Jackets and Regular Dresses for training purposes. Around two hundred images of each type were also used for validation purposes. Figure 5(a), (b) and (c) shown represents the typical type of images taken for training and validation purposes. Images taken are of high quality and are rich in details, so that right set of features are considered for increasing accuracy. All the images considered are color images.

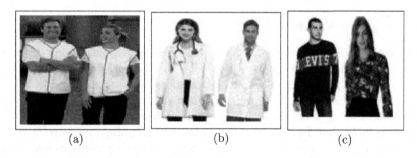

(a)   (b)   (c)

Fig. 5. (a) Visibility jackets (b) Lab gown (c) Regular dress Sample Images taken for training and validation

4 Proposed System

Test images are fed to CNN shown in Fig. 1., which was previously trained on taken dataset using Inception-v3 [4,13] architecture to identify if it's a PASS/FAIL. CNN consists of multiple layers, each layer consist of multiple neurons, which are interconnected with the neurons of neighboring layers through weights. The last layer is a fully connected layer through which the output (number of Pass/Fail) is obtained. First, the input is given to the neural network to be trained for the various images. After training, each image is split into features like edges, structures and collection of various shapes [11,13]. Then features of each image are fed into CNN.

The basic steps of the proposed model are shown in Fig. 6. Input image is treated as a 3-dimensional volume consisting of RGB colors. Filters are used to apply for the input image to extract the various features which are present in the image such as color density, structure and pattern of worn clothes [13,14]. A filter is just a matrix consisting of some values. These initial values are given at random in the beginning. Later various filters are convolved on the input image. Convolution or applying the filter means performing dot product of input image pixel values and filter values of the matrix. These filters are applied to various parts of the image to get more features and these values are summed up to get denser image for the next layer. Pooling is done through the application of either max ( ), sum ( ) or average ( ) after convolution. Finally features extracted in this way look like magnified pieces of original image. These features are fed into a fully connected neural network and probabilities for each image (based on network trained on dataset) are calculated after each feed forward pass through the network. The network is trained, which means that the parameters(weights) and filter matrices are optimized through back propagation (minimization of mis classification error). Feed forward is essential to recognize the image, once the image is fed in to trained network. The accuracy of predicting the new image in the network is through back propagation by correcting the error values in each neuron [10,19,20].

After presenting several examples of images, the network gets used to small details; middle sized features resemble whole image, if they come up very often. Each layer of the deep network reinforces some features and passes on to the next. Thereby, the fine details or pattern in the worn cloths are extracted and used to predict the test images as pass/fail. This increases the accuracy in predicting the test images.

Using multiple features from multiple filters improve the performance of the network. After performing the 1×1 convolution, the inception block job is do the cross-channel correlations, and avoiding the spatial dimensions. Then cross-spatial and cross-channel correlations using the 3×3 and 5×5 filters are followed [19]. For the network to be trained, a large collection data set is required for each

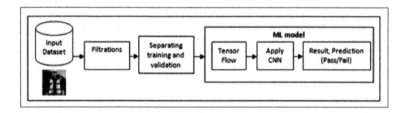

Fig. 6. Basic steps of proposed model.

type, consisting of 1000 images each. Larger the data, better the classification. The input image is then fed to network and compared with previously trained network. The difference obtained from comparison is used for backtracking and correcting the weight co-efficient of each neuron. Finally output is obtained.

5   Experimental Results

This section describes the implementation of the proposed method and obtained results are presented. First, standard dataset was separated into two categories, training dataset and validation dataset. Then, the training dataset is prepro-cessed and used to train the machine to build a correct model. Classification is accomplished using sigmoid function [Eq. (1)], as the sigmoid function can be applied to get binary output pass/fail.

Performance of the proposed model is evaluated using the accuracy and loss values. The learning curve plots of the proposed model are constructed. The model accuracy is calculated on training data set and the validation dataset. The validation accuracy gives a measure of accuracy of the model in classifying images and is expressed as a number. The loss value is a measure of error and should be within a certain range and expressed as a number. Loss value implies how well/poorly, the model behaves, after each iteration. Loss value close to zero implies, the error has been minimized after several iterations. The interpretation is done on, whether the output obtained is close to the actual output and hence the training of the model was successful [2].

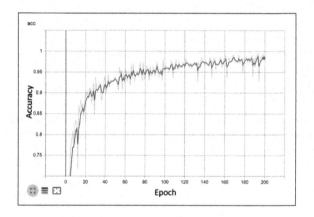

Fig. 7. Model accuracy on training dataset.

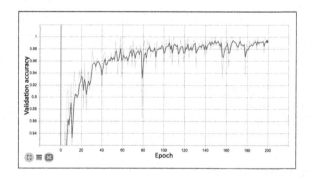

Fig. 8. Model accuracy on validation dataset.

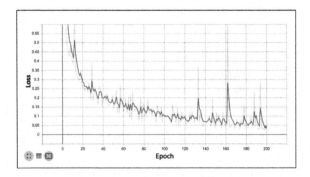

Fig. 9. Model loss on training dataset.

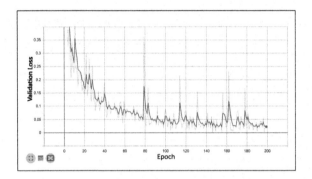

Fig. 10. Model loss on validation dataset.

Table 1. Accuracy percentage.

Index	Success rate
Accuracy of training dataset	90%–96%
Accuracy of validation dataset	92%–94%
Loss of training dataset	6%–16%
Loss of validation dataset	3%–20%

The results of the proposed method shown in the learning curve plots Figs. 7, 8, 9 and 10. Figure 7, depicts the machine is learning progressively from the training dataset and the Fig. 8 shows how well the model is converging as the validation dataset increases. Fig. 9 depicts the training loss decrease and shows how well model is minimizing the errors. Figure 10 shows how the validation loss is decreases as the epoch increases which implies that the parameter of the model are being optimized and Validation loss stabilizes at 3%. Accuracy percentage was calculated from the result obtained and is shown in the Table 1, which implies that, the machine learnt very well, which identifies the person is wearing the safety gear or not.

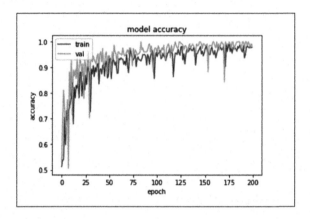

Fig. 11. Accuracy comparison between trained and validated dataset.

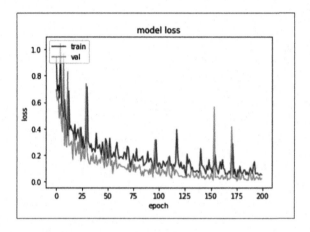

Fig. 12. Loss comparison between trained and validated dataset.

Figure 11 shows that as epoch increases, the accuracy also increases and there is a minimal gap between the training accuracy and validation accuracy. Figure 12 depicts as epoch increases, the loss decreases and shows that there is no much gap in training loss and validation loss, that implies a good fit model. Training loss and validation loss are decreasing parallelly as epoch increases and both comes to a point of stability which shows how well the process is progressing. This identifies the person is wearing safety gear or not.

6   Conclusion

The proposed technique is used to classify, whether the person in the image is in right safety gear or not and is based on Convolutional neural networks. It is based on the Inception-v3 [4] model of Tensor Flow pattern to train a Pass/Fail model on dataset. The input images are fed into neural network and compared with features obtained from previously trained dataset to classify. The accuracy and loss values have been used as the metrics and the results are promising. Further studies are required and the proposed method to be compared with other alternate techniques proposed in the literature.

References

1. Islam, S.M.S., Dey, E.K., Tawhid, M.N.A., Hossain, B.M.M.: A CNN based app-roach for garments texture design classification. Adv. Technol. Innov. **2**(4), 119–125 (2017)
2. Bedeli, M., Geradts, Z., van Eijk, E.: Clothing identification via deep learning: forensic applications. Forensic Sci. Res. **3**(3), 219–229 (2018)
3. Saitoh, T., Kaneko, T.: Automatic recognition of wild Flowers. In: Proceedings of the 15th International Conference on Pattern Recognition, vol. 2, pp. 507–510 (2000)
4. Xia, X., Xu, C.: Inception-v3 for flower classification. In: 2017 2nd International Conference on Image, Vision and Computing. 978-1-5090-6238-6
5. Chen, Y.Q., Damper, R.I., Nixon, M.S.: On neural network implementations of k-nearest neighbor pattern classifiers. IEEE Trans. Circ. Syst.-I: Fundam. Theory Appl. **44**(7) (1997)
6. Abadi, M., Agarwal, A., et al.: TensorFlow: Large-Scale Machine Learning on Het-erogeneous Distributed Systems. CoRR abs/1603.04467.2016
7. Na, S., Liu, X., Guan, Y.: Research on K-means clustering algorithm: an improved K-means clustering algorithm. In: 2010 3rd International Symposium on Intelligent Information Technology and Security Informatics (IIITSI). 978-1-4244-6743-3
8. Sun, J., Cai, X., Sun, F., Zhang, J.: Scene image classification method based on alex-net model. In: 2016 3rd International Conference Informative and Cybernetics for Computational Social Systems (ICCSS). https://doi.org/10.1109/ICCSS.2016.7856482
9. Qi, J., Yu, Y., Wang, L., Liu, J.: K*-means: an effective and efficient k-means clus-tering. In: 2016 IEEE International Conference Big Data and Cloud Computing (BDCloud), Social Computing and Networking (SocialCom), Sustainable Com-puting and Communications (SustainCom). https://doi.org/10.1109/BDCloud-SocialCom-SustainCom.2016.46
10. Raghavendra, S.P., Danti, A.: Recognition of signature using neural network and euclidean distance for bank cheque automation. In: Santosh, K.C., Hegadi, R.S. (eds.) RTIP2R 2018. CCIS, vol. 1037, pp. 228–243. Springer, Singapore (2019). https://doi.org/10.1007/978-981-13-9187-3_21
11. Liu, M., Shi, J., Li, C., Zhu, J., Liu, S.: Towards better analysis of deep convolu-tional neural networks. IEEE Trans. Vis. Comput. Graph. **23**(1) (2017). https://doi.org/10.1109/TVCG.2016.2598831
12. Chen, H., Gallagher, A., Girod, B.: Describing clothing by semantic attributes. In: Fitzgibbon, A., Lazebnik, S., Perona, P., Sato, Y., Schmid, C. (eds.) ECCV 2012. LNCS, vol. 7574, pp. 609–623. Springer, Heidelberg (2012). https://doi.org/10.1007/978-3-642-33712-3_44
13. Bankar, J., Gavai, N.R.: Convolutional neural network based inception v3 model for animal classification. IJARCCE **7**(5) (2018). https://doi.org/10.17148/IJARCCE.2018.7529

14. Farhadi, A., Endres, I., Hoiem, D., Forsyth, D.: Describing objects by their attributes. In: 2009 IEEE Conference on Computer Vision and Pattern Recognition. https://doi.org/10.1109/CVPR.2009.5206772
15. Lao, B., Jagadeesh, K.: Convolution neural network for fashion classification and object detection, 26 June 2016. http://cs231n.stanford.edu/reportsBLAO_KJAG_CS231N_FinalPaperFashionClassification.pdf
16. Schindler, A., Lady, T., Karner, S., Hecker, M.: Fashion and Apparel Classification using Convolutional Neural Networks. Published in Forum media technology (2017)
17. Deep learning in neural networks. https://en.wikipedia.org/wiki/Deep_learning
18. Tensorflow. https://en.wikipedia.org/wiki/TensorFlowcite_noteYoutubeClip5
19. Padmashree, S., Shree Hari, J., Sujan, Y.M., Vasuki, B.R.: Leaf classification and disease detection using convolution neural network. In: ICIVBS 2018 Conference (2018)
20. Raghavendra, S.P., Danti, A.: A novel recognition of indian bank cheque names using binary pattern and feed forward neural network. IOSR J. Comput. Eng. (IOSR-JCE) **20**(3), 44–59 (2018). e-ISSN 2278–0661, p-ISSN 2278–8727. UGC Approved Journal(Jr. No. 5019)

Analysis of Changing Trends in Textual Data Representation

Ksh. Nareshkumar Singh[1], A. Dorendro[1(✉)], H. Mamata Devi[1(✉)],
and Anjana Kakoti Mahanta[2(✉)]

[1] Department of Computer Science, Manipur University, Imphal, India
`nareshksh2711@gmail.com`, `ah.dorendro@gmail.com`,
`mamata_dh@rediffmail.com`
[2] Department of Computer Science, Gauhati University, Guwahati, India
`anjana@gauhati.ac.in`

Abstract. The most efficient way to convey human knowledge is through natural language text. In order to manage the exponential growth of digital data, it is high time to build a robust text information system. The system performs various techniques such as classification, clustering, summarization, etc. to organize the huge unstructured text data into well-defined forms. Text representation is the fundamental task in text mining and text retrieval. Just like a backbone gives structure to human body, text representation lays the foundation step for various other downstream tasks of Natural Language Processing (NLP), text mining and text retrieval. This paper concentrates on the analysis of various text representation models and also discusses major changing trends in textual data representation. This paper could be beneficial to those who wish to study and work on text data in NLP domain. The challenges and drawbacks of the existing text representation models are also discussed in this paper.

Keywords: NLP · Text representation · Machine learning · Word embedding

1 Introduction

Text data is the most abundant resource for information among other resources in the Internet as well as within the Intranets. Huge amounts of textual data are available and ever-growing exponentially day by day. A conceptual framework of text information system for solving challenging problems like searching, analysing, and organizing large amount of collected electronic text is shown in Fig. 1. Many scholars and scientists have been researching in the fields of text retrieval and text mining to tackle these problems. A large deal of machine learning algorithms has been developed so that systems can automatically perform clustering of documents with similar content or classify the documents into predefined categories. One of the most challenging tasks in today's machine learning is the numeric representation of text documents. There are various representation models to represent the text data into numeric form so that machine learning algorithms can work on it.

© Springer Nature Singapore Pte Ltd. 2021
K. C. Santosh and B. Gawali (Eds.): RTIP2R 2020, CCIS 1380, pp. 237–251, 2021.
https://doi.org/10.1007/978-981-16-0507-9_21

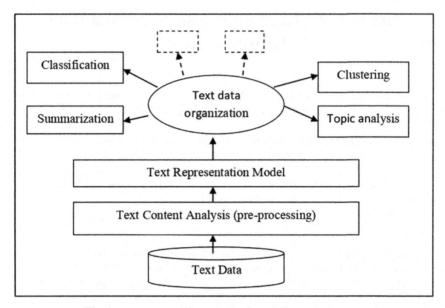

Fig. 1. A conceptual framework of text information system

Since the raw text data cannot be used directly with machine learning algorithms, it needs to be first converted into numeric form like vector of numbers. Such representation forms the backbone of many other tasks like web search, spam filtering, document retrieval, topic modelling etc. [20, 32].

As a computerized approach of analysing the text, a field called "Natural Language Processing (or NLP)" comes striving forward first. There have been great changes in NLP landscape from last 2 years. NLP develops various tools and techniques so that computers can understand and manipulate the natural language text or speech. Text representation is the prerequisite step for many of the NLP tasks, information retrieval and text mining methods specially document classification or clustering. The quality of clustering or classification results not only depends on its ML algorithms used but also on the way text is represented in the algorithms.

Earlier, document representation was mainly based on word level. In recent years, researchers have been working on word representations commonly known as embedding, which is aware of the contextual meaning in the sentence. They have been working hard to extend word level to achieve phrase-level representation, sentence-level representation, and paragraph or document level representation [27, 28].

The remainder of this paper are arranged according to the following: the various existing text representation models are discussed in Sect. 2 along with their pros and cons. In Sect. 3, we make a comparison among the representation models. Conclusion is mentioned in Sect. 4.

2 Growth of Text Data

From the last two decades, text data has been growing really fast. For instance, the number of emails sent in the year 2003 was 610 billion representing 11,000 TB [35]. The number of emails sent in 2010 was 107 trillion which was counted in 2012 [36]. Even during this short period, a large amount of text data is generated. It grows exponentially and continues to grow so. The estimated growth rate of text data is 2.5 Exabytes (10^{18} bytes), that is 2.5 million TB (Terabytes), a day. It is expected to grow up to 40 Zettabyte (10^{21} bytes) that is 40 billion TB by 2020 according to recent estimates [37]. The digital world is expected to expand by a factor of 300 during 2005–2020, from 130 Exabytes to 40 trillion gigabytes which is equivalent to 5200 gigabytes of data for every human on Earth [23]. NLP's current technology still has not achieved a level that machine can accurately understand the natural language text. This is one of the challenges which we are facing even today. Many scientists and academics have used a broad variety of various statistical and heuristic approaches to find suitable text representation so that the machine can precisely understand. Another challenging task is how to organize such explosive growth of text data with minimum human effort in a short lesser period.

2.1 Word Level Representation

Bag-of-Words (BoW). It was first found in the linguistic context of Zellig Harris's 1954 article on "Distributional Structure" [1]. It is one of the traditional methods to represent the text data. This method is simply collection of all the words in the document; it neglects the relationship between words, words order and words sense in the document. Various term weighting approaches can be applied on BoW [2, 3]: i) *binary weighting (also called Boolean Weightage)* consider whether the term is present (1) or absent (0) ii) *term frequency (tf)* simply counts the number of term occurrences in the document iii) *Tfidf* weighs the occurrence of a word in the document (tf) with a factor called inverse document frequency (idf) which measure its importance in the whole corpus i.e. gives more importance to rare words. Classification or clustering results are varied due to different term weighting schemes. This representation works well for small dataset like BBC corpus (consist of 2225 documents) but suffers from sparse representation in case of large dataset due to the larger size of vocabulary.

Pros:

i) it is widely used for its less complexity, efficiency and sometimes extraordinary accuracy.

Cons:

i) the word order is ignored, so sentence with the same vocabulary but different meaning can have same representation. For example, a sentence 'Tom can run faster than Harry' and another sentence, 'Harry can run faster than Tom' can have identical representation due to the ignorance of words order in the sentences.
ii) sparsity and semantic problems which are most prevalent in the textual document and cannot be solved by this model.

n-gram Representation. It is one of the most widely used methods in NLP. In the year 1913, Markov first suggested fundamental concepts of the n-gram to predict whether an upcoming letter would be a vowel or consonant in Pushkin's Eugene Onegin. In 1948, Shannon started to apply its computation on English word sequence. This is the probabilistic language model, which assigns probability to word sequences. Markov assumed that probability of a word relies entirely on the previous word. Using this assumption, it can predict next word given the previous one. Basically, n-gram representation is a sequence of n words just like moving a window of n boxes on the document body. It is so-named because it characterizes a sequence of n words. In case of bigram model where n = 2, it predicts the existence of a word given its preceding word. Experiment of bigram count for the words in the Berkeley Restaurant Project Corpus was conducted. Similarly, trigram model (where n = 3) predicts the next word provided its previous two words. In general terms, the representation of n-gram predicts the occurrence of a word based on the occurrence of its n-1 preceding words [4].

Pros:

i) it can store some spatial information within the words. So it can make next word predictions. ii) it can also assist in fixing spelling mistakes. As an example, the terms "drink cofee" should be changed to "drink coffee" since the term "coffee" has a strong probability of occurring after the term "drink" and also a high possibility of letters corresponding between "coffee" and "cofee".

Cons:

i) n-gram model suffers from data sparsity and the issue of high dimensionality.

Bag-of-words and n-gram representations are unsatisfactory as they don't consider any natural language relationship between words that don't occur together. The following two representation models are used to alleviate this problem: a) *Ontology based text representation:* Ontology is one of the important pillars to manipulate the text data semantically. Extracting conceptual features from text data using ontology have also revealed that ontology improves the performance of text mining [5]. For instance, the words "honest" and "sincere" are treated as unrelated but they are semantically correlated. To solve this problem, lexical database like WordNet [6] can be used to find the semantic relationship between every pair of words in the corpus vocabulary. According to WordNet, the words like 'beautiful', 'attractive', 'pretty', 'lovely' and 'stunning' are semantically related to each other. After considering the semantic relationship between each pairs, the original terms in vector space is updated b) *Dependency graph:* The document dependency graph G is referred to as G = (V,E), while V = $\{v_1, v_2, \ldots v_n\}$ is the collection of vertices where each vertices v_i represents the word (w_i) that can be used as the document's meta-descriptions, and E = $\{e_1, e_2, \ldots e_n\}$ is the collection of edges where each edge e_i implies a certain association between words in the document [7, 8]. Each edge can be drawn without crossing over the words. Parsing phase is also required to construct dependency graph. The output from dependency graph is considered as tree that explains how sentence connects the words to each other. This graph can be further extended with some constraints to improve the quality of document clustering

[9, 10]. Dependency graph reduces the sparsity and semantic problem which are faced by traditional methods.

2.2 Rise of Word Embedding

In the year 2013, the era of word embedding techniques emerged. Popularity of word embedding is increasing since then. It has the capability of capturing a word context in a document, word relationships, semantic and syntactic similarities, etc. Basically, word embedding may be divided into two groups- static and dynamic. In static word embedding, same word will have same representation regardless of the context where it occurs. In dynamic word embedding, same word can have various representations depending on their context. The most commonly used static word embedding models are word2vec and GloVe. Both models are unsupervised methods that are focused on the distributional hypothesis to produce word vectors. Later on, in the years around 2016–2018, two more notable models of word embedding came into picture: FastText (static) and ELMo (dynamic).

Word2vec. Word2vec is one of the most popular methods for learning word embedding with a shallow neural network. In the year 2013, at Google, a researcher team led by Tomas Mikolov developed perhaps the first word embedding pattern called word2vec [11]. Word2vec works on a wide range of text and creates a vector space with unique words in the corpus. Each word is represented by a unique vector in the vector space. For words that have common context and similar meaning in the corpus, their vectors are positioned closed to each another in vector space. For example, "Bank", "money" and "accounts" are used in similar situation, with similar surrounding words like "dollar", "loan" or "credit". These words are represented by a similar vector representation under the assumption of word2vec. The model trained word vector on a part of the Google News dataset (100B tokens).

Word2vec can use either of the two approaches - i) Skip Gram: this approach takes the word as input, and the output is the context words that surround the word input. The number of words in left or right context for the input word is defined by the hyper-parameter window size or ii) Continuous Bag of Words (CBoW): the input consists of several words which are merged through vector addition to predict the word which is most likely to appear in it [22, 33]. Conferring to the Mikolov, Skip Gram operates best on small dataset and is found to represent the rare words well whereas CBOW is faster and has better representation for more frequent words.

This learns word embedding can preserve the semantic and syntactic relationships between words. For instance, the analogy "Doctor is related to Patient as Lawyer is related to Client" can perform simple algebraic operations in the vector space. Say vector ("*Lawyer*") − vector ("*Doctor*") + vector ("*Patient*") yields a result which is closed to the vector representation of word "*Client*". Thus, it can indicate the preservation of semantic relations (such as Doctor-Patient) as well as syntactic relations (e.g. present tense - past tense) between the words [12]. The parameters that can be sensitive on the results of word2vec training are: corpus size, training algorithm, sub-sampling, dimensionality and context window.

Pros:

i)   it gives useful word representation and also works well for large size corpus.

Cons:

i)   word sense is not considered separately. For example the word "cell" could have different sense of meaning related to "prison" or "phone" or "biological cell", etc. but gives same vector representation for all the cases.
ii) word2vec is insensitive to word order.
iii) it never calculates the statistical information regarding word co- occurrences i.e. the sub-linear relationship are not clearly defined [24].

GloVe (Global Vectors). GloVe is a new model with log-bilinear regression that incorporates the benefits of two approaches – global matrix factorization and local context window. Global matrix factorization is the process of using matrix factorization methods to reduce large term frequency matrices. Local context window methods are CBOW and Skip-Gram. GloVe model demonstrates that online scanning approach used by word2vec is suboptimal as it never calculates the statistical information regarding word co-occurrences. For word representation of all unsupervised methods, the primary source of information comes from the statistical information of occurrences of word in a corpus. GloVe uses the global statistical information contained in the document. The model trained word vector on Wikipedia, Gigaword and Common Crawl (840B tokens) and experimented on the CoNLL-2003 dataset [13, 21].

Pros:

i)   it takes less training time than word2vec and some benchmark shows that it does better semantic tasks compared to word2vec.

Cons:

i)   GloVe doesn't consider the subword-level information. Thus, during training the words which are not seen i.e. out-of-vocabulary (OOV) words GloVe is not able to deal with them.
ii) Nor does GloVe catch polysemy, phrases definition and expression of multi-word.

FastText. In the year 2016, an extension of word2vec called FastText was created by Tomas Mikolov's team who suggested word2vec framework in 2013 [14].The main improvement of FastText in comparison with word2vec model is the addition of character n-grams where n could lie in the range of 1 to total length of word. For example, the word 'funny' is composed of [fun, funn, funny], [funny, unny, nny] etc. It is different from gensim word vectors. Unlike word2vec, FastText doesn't consider every single word as the smallest unit vector, instead it can break down the word using character n-gram. Using FastText, already trained word vectors are available for 157 different languages, trained on dataset which is composed of a mixture of Wikipedia and Crawl [25].

FastText's key benefit over word2vec and gloVe is that it can offer vector representation for terms that did not exist in the training data [26]. For example, suppose the word 'annemedobeatificbeautifully' did not occur in the vocabulary. Word2Vec and GloVe both fail to give vector representation of this word because it is not present in the vocabulary. In the case of FastText, this word can be broken down in chunks using character n-grams. Vectors for those chunks are used to create the final vector for the word. In this example, the final vector may be closed to vectors of the words like 'beatific' and 'beautifully'. Thus, it gives the vector representation for all the words and more helpful for rare words.

Cons:

i) Like word2vec, FastText is not able to capture the multi-sense embedding.

Embeddings from Language Models (ELMo). ELMo, a state-of-the-art revolutionary in word embedding was developed by Mattew et al. [15] at Allen Institute for Artificial Intelligence in early June of 2018. ELMo is a deep contextualized word representation. To create contextual word embedding it uses a bi-directional LSTM (Long Short-Term Memory) which is skilled on a large text corpus (1B Word Benchmark). Some of the special features of ELMo over the other word embeddings are:

a. every word is allotted a vector that is a feature of the whole input sentence containing that word. Therefore, the same word can have different word vector representation due to different contexts. A couple of sentences can be considered as an example: i) I read the book yesterday. ii) You can read the book now. Here, the word 'read' both have the same vector in case of traditional word embedding but in ELMo, 'read' would have different word vector. Let us see one more example, "The doctor carried his *cell* phone to prison *cell* to extract blood *cell* from the inmate's pancreatic cells." In the models like word2vec word embedding, the word "*cell*" would have same vector representation regardless of its context but ELMo can generate the context dependent representation i.e. the word "*cell*" has different representation based on the context. This type of representation is much better for downstream tasks like named entity recognition etc.
b. on the same word distinct layers of language model encodes the distinct kind of information. For example, lower level layers of a bidirectional Language Short Term Memory (biLSTM) is used to encode the part-of-speech tagging while word-sense disambiguation is well encoded in higher-levels. So, in ELMo, several activations layers of the bidirectional Language Models (biLMs) are concatenated.
c. Word2vec and GloVe don't consider the word order in their training while ELMo takes into account word order.

Pros:

i) this word embedding can handle the polysemy wherein a word could have multiple meaning or sense

Cons:

i) it takes more time on training because vector assigned to each word depends the entire corpus sentences wherein they belong.

2.3   Rise of Sentence/Paragraph/Document Embedding

Presently, many competing approaches are there to learn sentence embedding. Some of these embedding types are:

Doc2vec (or Paragraph Vector). A year later, word2vec was introduced, doc2vec was developed as an extension concept of word2vec and was presented by Le and Mikilov [16]. Doc2vec name comes from Gensim library where it was implemented. It is the simple extension of learning embedding from words to word sequences where granularity of word sequences can be sentence, paragraph or document. Like word2vec, there are also two approaches within doc2vec: dbow which means *distributed bag of words* and dmpv meaning *distributed memory model of paragraph vector*. The dbow functions similarly to skip-gram, except that input is document vector to predict words in the output. In the document the order of words is ignored thus it is named as distributed bag of words. Dmvp and cbow's way of working is same, the only difference in the way of giving input, in dmpv concatenation of paragraph vector with word vectors works as input for prediction of next word in a text window. Doc2vec computes the feature vector for every document in the corpus. The vectors generated from Doc2vec are used to measure similarity between documents/paragraphs/sentences. Doc2vec is a very simple technique, easy to use, performs particularly well over longer documents and gives good results. The benefit of doc2vec diminishes for shorter documents. The performance gap between word2vec and doc2vec is large for longer documents, but for shorter documents the gap is small. Like word2vec, the hyper-parameters that can be affected on the results of doc2vec training are: corpus size, training algorithm, sub-sampling (most important hyper-parameter), dimensionality and context window size. Standford Sentiment Treebank dataset (consists of 11855 sentences) and IMDB dataset (consists of 100,000 movie reviews) were used while conducting the experiment of this model [17, 30].

Pros:

i)   it can solve the words semantics problem.
ii) it takes word order into account.
iii) Doc2Vec are of significantly lower dimension and less prone to overfitting when used.
iv) it can operate well for tasks with inadequate labelling of data.

Cons:

i)   the vector quality of Doc2Vec is highly dependent on the quality of word vector.

Skip-Thoughts Vectors. It is an unsupervised learning of sentence embedding based on encoder-decoder. It rather predicts the surrounding sentences (S_{i-1}, S_{i+1}) of a given sentence (S_i), instead of predicting the surrounding words of a given word as in case of skip-gram model for word embedding. An encoder is used to map sentence to a vector and the surrounding sentences are generated by a decoder. The encoder-decoder pair can be a CNN (Convolutional Neural Network)-RNN (Recurrent Neural Network) [31] or RNN-RNN [18] or LSTM-LSTM (Long Short Term Memory). For training this model, a large collection of novels, namely BookCorpus dataset is used. Many variations of skip-thought vectors are yet to be explored, including- deep encoders and decoders, larger context windows, encoding and decoding paragraph etc. More exploration in this space will result in higher quality representation [18].

Pros:

i)   it allows expansion of the vocabulary size. So, OOV (out of vocabulary) words can be managed by studying a linear mapping between their RNN word embedding space and a wider word embedding like word2vec. After training, any word that appears in the word2vec can be mapped into RNN word embedding space for encoding sentences.
ii) sentences having common semantic and syntactic nature will have similar vector representation.
iii) skip-thought vectors not only consider the word order but also consider the sentence order.

Cons:

i)   skip-thought vector requires the sentences to be ordered in a semantically meaningful way. So, this method is difficult to use for domain like social media text since there may have incomplete sentences, using slang words in communication between friends, using neologism (e.g. use "gr8" instead of "great", "u" instead of "you") etc.
ii) it is slow to train on large amount of data.

Quick-Thoughts Vectors. It is simply a reformulation of the task of Skip-thoughts vectors. It predicts the target sentence which has nearest meaning to the given sentence as a classification task. Instead of using decoder, a classifier is used which selects the target sentence from a group of candidate sentences. Fig. 2 shows the working of Quick-thoughts for sentence classification. For example, the sentence "Oily fish is rich in omega-3 fatty acid" is the given sentence in the classifier. The classifier will select the next sentence from within the candidate sentences collection. As an output, the classifier gives the third sentence which is more related to the given sentence. The model trained on the BookCorpus and UMBC dataset.

Pros:

i)   its training speed is fast as compared to skip-thought vectors so it can exploit the massive amount of dataset in lesser time.

Cons:

i)   parameter sharing between encoder and classifier is a significant concern when the model is trained on small corpus.

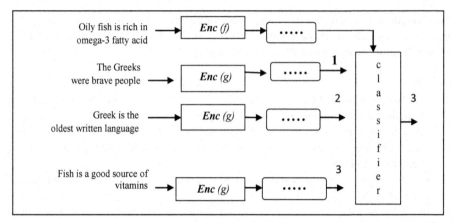

Fig. 2. Quick-thoughts process for classification task to choose the target sentence from set of candidate sentences [19].

3   Comparison between Different Representation Models

Here, we make a comparison among different representation models. The following tables show the comparison between them.

3.1   BoW vs N-gram

BoW	N-gram
1. It is the simplest n-gram representation with n = 1	1. n-gram can be bigram (n = 2), trigram (n = 3), four-grams (n = 4) and so on
2. The problems faced on this model are: multi-word expression ("Vitamin A" has its own meaning but when it is broken down into pieces. Each pieces "Vitamin" and "A" have their own meaning), synonym words are treated as different features (e.g. "surprising" and "amazing" are treated differently), polysemy words (e.g. the word "bank" has many possible meanings but it is treated as one single feature), lack of generalization for the similar terms (e.g. "apple" and "banana" are the hyponyms of "fruit")	2. The problems of multi-word expression and polysemy are minimized in the n-gram model by varying the value of n. Bag-of-bigram representation is much more powerful than BoW representation and gives better results in the task like document classification [29]

3.2 GloVe vs Word2vec

GloVe	Word2vec
1. It uses the global statistical information contained in the document 2. It is global in the sense that it goes through the corpus and counts the co-occurrence frequencies of the words 3. It is better to work in tabulated training data. It can reduce the data size, easier to work and extend. But it doesn't maintain the information order so when we try to add more data, it needs to do the fitting all over again	1. It never calculates any global statistics 2. It iteratively runs through the corpus, sees a couple of words at a time and learns and tries to predict from that. In this sense, word2vec is completely local 3. It takes longer time to train data but it captures the information order

3.3 ELMo vs FastText

ELMo	FastText
1. Input is character-based rather than words. So, it can handle the out of vocabulary (OOV) words 2. It can generate different vector representations for a word that captures the context of a word i.e. it is context dependent 3. It belongs to dynamic word embedding category	1. Like ELMo, it can learn sub-words. Hence, it can handle the OOV problem 2. FastText is context independent 3. FastText includes to static word embedding

3.4 BoW vs Word Embedding (Word2vec or GloVe) Models

BoW	Word2vec or GloVe
1. BoW gives one number value (may be word occurrence count, tfidf, etc.) for each word 2. Challenges of BoW representation models: dimensionality, sparsity, evolving non-standard vocabulary, etc. [34] 3. In some situations, BoW is preferred over word embedding: a) to build the baseline model b) if the dataset is small and context is domain specific	1. Word2vec and GloVe produce one vector for each word 2. Word embedding is the successful way to solve the text related problems like the semantic and syntactic relationships between words, dimensionality, etc. 3. Word embedding have better performance than BoW in many NLP tasks

3.5 Comparison Among the Approaches: Traditional Approaches, Word Embedding, and Document Embedding

Traditional approaches	Word embedding	Document embedding (or paragraph or sentence embedding)
1. These approaches convert the documents into their numerical form of vectors in an n-dimensional space where n indicates the number of unique terms in the vocabulary 2. Features are based on word-level representation and fixed in length 3. These models train efficiently by ignoring the word order, so the training process is fast 4. Ignoring words order, have sparsity and semantic problems	1. These approaches represent each word in the form of numerical vectors 2. Features are based on word(or subword) vector representation. Several factors such as size and nature of training data, size of vectors etc. affects the quality of the word vectors 3. It takes longer time to train data 4. It can handle the problems of polysemy, OOV, etc.	1. Simple extension of learning embedding from words to word sequences where sentences or paragraphs are treated as atomic units rather than as a compositional function of its words 2. Different lengths of text features can be there like sentences, paragraphs or documents 3. It is slow to train on large amount of data as it considers the words order as well as sentences order 4. Solve the problems occurs due to the ignorance of words order, semantic and dimensionality problems

The following Fig. 3 shows the area covered by the different text representation models based on their uses. Traditional representation (BoW + N-gram) models occupy the largest area followed by word embedding which is currently active in use. Most commonly used Vector Space Model (VSM) for text representation in Information Retrieval (IR) is BoW model.

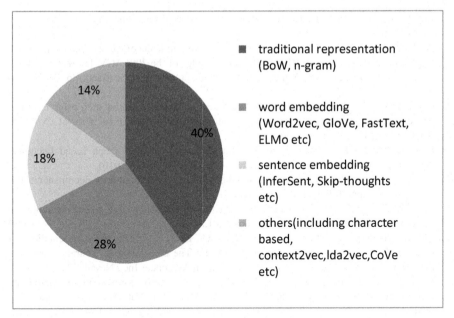

Fig. 3. Approximately area covered by different representation models.

4   Conclusion

Now we have discussed various text representation models. It is observed that the accuracy of clustering or classification results not only depends on applied ML algorithms but also on the way text is represented in the algorithms. As most of the representation models are language specific, there is no specific formula to select suitable representation model. Generally, traditional methods are still used for Corpora other than English. We could prefer to use word embedding methods for large English text corpus as they greatly reduce dimensionality space without compromising accuracy. Other than nature of corpora, we should also consider easiness, efficiency and time complexity etc. while selecting the representation model. Finally, we could conclude that any single model cannot be given global advantage over the others.

References

1. Harris, Z.: Distributional structure. Word **10**, 146–162 (1954)
2. Manning, C.D., Schutze, H.: Foundations of Statistical Natural Language Processing. MIT press, Cambridge (2002)
3. Manning, C.D., Raghavan, P., Schutze, H.: Introduction to Information Retrieval. Cambridge University Press, Cambridge, England (2008)
4. Jurafsky, D., Martin, J.H.: Speech and language processing: an introduction to natural language processing. In: Computational Linguistics and Speech Recognition. 1st edn. Prentice Hall PTR, Upper Saddle River (2000)
5. Hotho, A., Maedche, A., Staab, S.: Ontology-based text document clustering. KI J. **16**, 48–54 (2002)

6. Jing, L., Zhou, L., Ng, M.K., Huang, J.Z.: Ontology-based distance measure for text clustering (2006)
7. Wang, Y., Ni, X., Sun, J.T., Tong, Y., Chen, Z.: Representing document as dependency graph for document clustering. In: CIKM 2011 Proceedings of the 20th ACM International Conference on Information and Knowledge Management, Glasgow, Scotland, pp. 2177–2180 (2011)
8. Chow, T.W., Zhang, H., Rahman, M.K.M.: A new document representation using term frequency and vectorized graph connectionists with application to document retrieval. Exp. Syst. Appl. **36**(10), 12023–12035 (2009)
9. Rafi, M., Amin, F., Shaikh, M.S.: Document clustering using graph based document representation with constraints. Pak. J. Eng. Appl. Sci. **18**, 56–68 (2016)
10. Abdulsahib, A.K., Kamaruddin, S.S.: Graph based text representation for document clustering. J. Theor. Appl. Inf. Technol. **76**(1) (2015)
11. Mikolov, T., Chen, K., Corrado, G., Dean, J.: Efficient estimation of word representations in vector space. CoRR J. (2013). Volume: abs-1301.3781
12. Mikolov, T., Sutskever, I., Chen, K., Corrado, G., Dean, J.: distributed representations of words and phrased and their compositionality. In: The proceeding of Neural Information Processing Systems (NIPS), pp. 3111–3119, Curran Associates Inc., Nevada (2013)
13. Pennington, J., Socher, R., Manning, C.D.: Glove: global vectors for word representation. In: Proceedings of the 2014 Conference on Empirical Methods in Natural Language Processing (EMNLP), pp. 1532–1543. Association for Computational Linguistics, Doha (2014)
14. Joulin, A., Grave, E., Bojanowski, P., Mikolov, T.: Bag of tricks for efficient text classification. In: Proceedings of the 15th Conference of the European Chapter of the Association for Computational Linguistics: Volume 2, Short Papers, pp. 427–431, Association for Computational Linguistics, Valencia (2017)
15. Peters, M.E., et al.: Deep contextualized word representations. In: Proceedings of the 2018 Conference of the North American Chapter of the Association for Computational Linguistics: Human Language Technologies, Volume 1 (Long Papers), pp. 2227–2237. New Association for Computational Linguistics, Orleans (2018)
16. Le, Q., Mikolov, T.: Distributed representations of sentences and documents. In: Proceedings of the 31st International Conference on Machine Learning, JMLR: W&CP, Beijing, China, vol. 32, pp. 1188–1196 (2014)
17. Lau, J.H., Baldwin, T.: An empirical evaluation of doc2vec with practical insights into document embedding generation. In: Proceedings of the 1st Workshop on Representation Learning for NLP, pp. 78–86. Association for Computational Linguistics, Berlin (2016)
18. Kiros, R., et al.: Skip-thought vectors. In: the proceeding of Neural Information Processing Systems (NIPS), pp. 3294–3302. Curran Associates Inc., Montreal (2015)
19. Logeswaran, L., Lee, H.: An efficient framework for learning sentence representations. In: International Conference on Learning Representations (2018)
20. Zhai, C., Massung, S.: Text Data Management and Analysis – A Practical Introduction to Information Retrieval and Text Mining. Association for Computing Machinery and Morgan & Claypool Publishers (2016)
21. Huang, E.H., Socher, R., Manning, C.D., Ng, A.Y.: Improving word representations via global context and multiple word prototypes. In: Proceedings of the 50th Annual Meeting of the Association for Computational Linguistics, Jeju, Republic of Korea, pp. 873–882 (2012)
22. Levy, O., Goldberg, Y.: Dependency-based word embeddings. In: Proceedings of the 52th Annual Meeting of the Association for Computational Linguistics, pp. 302–308. Association for Computational Linguistics, Baltimore (2014)
23. Gantz, J., Reinsel, D.: The Digital Universe in 2020: Big Data, Bigger Digital Shadows, and Biggest Growth in the Fast East, IDC Report (2012)

24. Ling, W., Dyer, C., Black, A.W., Trancoso, I.: Two/too simple adaptations of Word2Vec for syntax problems. In: Proceedings of the 2015 Conference of the North American Chapter of the Association for Computational Linguistics: Human Language Technologies, pp. 1299–1304. Association for Computational Linguistics, Denver, (2015)
25. Grave, E., Bojanowski, P., Gupta, P., Joulin, A., Mikolov, T.: Learning word vectors for 157 languages. In: Proceedings of the International Conference on Language Resources and Evaluation (2018)
26. Bojanowski, P., Grave, E., Joulin, A., Mikolov, T.: Enriching Word Vectors with Subword Information. arXiv:1607.04606v2 [cs.CL] 19 June (2017)
27. Mitchell, J., Lapata, M.: Composition in distributional models of semantics. Cognit. Sci. **34**(8), 1388–1429 (2010)
28. Zanzotto, F.M., Korkontzelos, I., Fallucchi, F., Manandhar, S.: Estimating linear models for compositional distributional semantics. In: COLING (2010)
29. Yoav, G.: Neural Network Methods in Natural Language Processing (Synthesis Lectures on Human Language Technologies). Morgan & Claypool Publishers (2017)
30. Dai, A.M., Olah, C., Le, Q.V.: Document Embedding with Paragraph Vectors. arXiv:1507. 07998v1 [cs.CL] 29 July (2015)
31. Gan, Z., Pu, Y., Henao, R., Li, C., He, X., Carin, L.: Unsupervised learning of sentence representations using convolutional neural networks. arXiv preprint arXiv:1611.07897 (2016)
32. Perone, C.S., Silveira, R., Paula, T.S.: Evaluation of sentence embeddings in downstream and linguistic probing tasks. arXiv:1806.06259v1 [cs.CL] 16 June (2018)
33. Rong, X.: word2vec Parameter Learning Explained. arXiv:1411.2738v4 [cs.CL] 5 June (2016)
34. Giannakopoulos, G., Mavridi, P., Paliouras, G., Papadakis, G., Tserpes, K.: Representation models for text classification: a comparative analysis over three Web document types. In: Proceedings of the 2nd International Conference on Web Intelligence, Mining and Semantics, Craiova, Romania, vol. 13 (2012)
35. Lyman, P., et al.: How much information? https://www2.sims.berkeley.edu/research/projects/how-much-info-2003.
36. Roe, C.: The growth of unstructured data: what to do with all those zettabytes? https://www.dataversity.net/the-growth-of-unstructured-data-what-are-we-going-to-do-with-all-those-zettabytes/
37. Applied Text Mining in Python, University of Michigan. https://www.coursera.org/lecture/python-text-mining/handling-text-in-python-MeheH

Detection of Falsary Happening on Social Media Using Image Processing: Feature Extraction and Matching

Kshipra Ashok Tatkare[1,2](✉) and Manoj Devare[2]

[1] Ramrao Adik Institute of Technology, Nerul, Navi Mumbai, India
kshipra.tatkare@rait.ac.in
[2] Amity University, Panvel, Mumbai, India
mhdevare@mum.amity.edu

Abstract. In last decade and half, especially generation Z (Gen Z) has witnessed a drastic change in their communication pattern due to paradigm shift in digital media. Social media is the largest medium to connect any part of the world via internet is considered to be the trend changer. Increasing use of mobile internet and easy availability of mobile compatible softwares have changed the way of expression on social media in both apt and inept manner. Forged images known as memes are, nowadays, trending on social media like Facebook, Instagram, Twitter, Whatsapp and what not. These memes on social media are used to appreciate or to troll on particular cause to someone or group of people. The plethora of memes usage leads to image processing where feature extraction and feature matching can be done. Matching of features that are invariant to transformation includes geometric invariance and photometric invariance. This paper presents the comparative analysis of images (memes) matching algorithms of feature, which will definitely helpful for future researchers to identify the best matching technique to be fit in desired area. Authors have also included the implemented results of various traditional matching techniques invariant to translation, rotation, scaling, brightness and exposure.

Keywords: Feature extraction · Feature matching · Falsary detection

1 Introduction

In past few years, image forging plays significant role in Newspapers, Banners, Magazines, social media etc. Social media is the biggest hub of tampered images rather these images have become discussions on any type of incidences. These tampered images have given a sweet name as 'Memes'. To detect tamper in these memes, feature extraction is an important step. Image features can be extracted from an image using various feature extraction algorithms. For Dimensional reduction, various feature extraction techniques are used. If input to the system is of huge size then to compute this, it is better to reduce the input data into smaller scale in the form of feature vectors for future computations. There are various feature extraction algorithms, discussed in literature. The

© Springer Nature Singapore Pte Ltd. 2021
K. C. Santosh and B. Gawali (Eds.): RTIP2R 2020, CCIS 1380, pp. 252–260, 2021.
https://doi.org/10.1007/978-981-16-0507-9_22

most discussed algorithms for feature extraction in literature are SIFT, SURF, Zernike Moments, Hue Moments, Principle Component Analysis (PCA) etc. After feature extraction, feature matching plays a vital role in object recognition, duplicated region detection, tracking of motions, pattern recognition etc. Feature matching is process where feature vectors are matched with other feature vectors. In this process high similarity feature vectors are found as a matched feature vectors. The extracted feature vectors are matched using various techniques like Euclidean distance, Lexicographic sorting, kd-tree algorithm, Best-Bin-First search, Brute force matching etc. Significantly the feature matching techniques are used in various applications like Pattern recognition, Surveillance system, Digital evidence matching, Digital Forensics investigations, Intelligence system, Medical imaging, Journalism etc. Image feature matching is dependent on various factors like contrast between distinctiveness of the found feature, differences between orientations, texture, etc. The example of this type of Meme is shown in Fig. 1:

Fig. 1. Example of Meme

One Day International Cricket world cup 2019, had witnessed the undecidable final match, where England had been declared winner on the basis of number of 4's and 6's hit due to match tied on both occasions that are 50 overs and Super Over. This incidence was responsible for flood of Memes on social media as shown above. People on social media wanted to express that England won the final against England.

The original image before World Cup Final had been published on "India Today" News portal. Figure 2 was the original image.

Pakistan cricket team once again lost a world cup ODI match against India, which had resulted into hug frustration in Pakistan cricket team supporters. It had caused an old image into a hilarious meme. The upper original image in Fig. 3 shows the demand of Pakistanis about 'Azadi'. The meme of Azadi image is smartly tampered in demand for Virat Kohli as he was in his golden era of cricketing career.

Thus, in this paper researchers intended to carry out comparative analysis of various image matching algorithms for various feature extracted to identify the falsary changes in images used to trend them on social media as memes.

Fig. 2. Original image for meme [1]

Fig. 3. Example of meme [2]

This paper comprises with Image Feature extraction algorithm, matching algorithm for features, results of some matching algorithms and ended with conclusion.

2   Related Work

As discussed earlier, an image feature extraction is very basic component in the processing of modern image applications. Extraction of Features from an image and matching is not a new or upcoming technique in image processing. It is carried out since 1980's for the application of stereo matching with a corner detector by Moravec [3]. Some feature extraction algorithms are listed below:

2.1 Scale Invariant Feature Transform (SIFT)

In the SIFT algorithm, the SIFT feature vectors are calculated from the digital image, which are then matched with each other. Drawback of this method is the high dimensionality of the SIFT descriptors [4]. SIFT algorithm consists of following steps: Construct Scale Space, get Difference of Gaussians, find DoG Extrema, Filter, allocate Key Points directions, construct Key Point Descriptors, and Go Play with Features [5]. There is scope for improvement in the existing techniques [6].

2.2 Speed Up Robust Feature (SURF)

In SURF, detection of key point uses basic Hessian-matrix approximation. The key point descriptors are created by using Haar wavelet responses in the neighborhood of the specified key point. For the matching in pattern recognition the Nearest Neighbor approach is used.

2.3 Zernike Moments

There are different types of moments in the literature; these moments are better-quality among all in their information content, inconsiderateness to noise in an image and facilitating the adroitness of faithful image representation in literature. As the scales of these moments are mathematically invariant to rotation, the accuracy of matching region invariant to rotation is at higher side. This method, is not giving required results, if scaling prior to thrashing or other tampering which is relevant to affine transform [7].

2.4 Hue Moments

These seven moments are formed by group of random focused moment expressions. The output is a bundle of moments which are rotation invariant. These are used for pattern identification for position, rotation and scale invarient [8].

Using these feature extraction techniques, image feature can be extracted. After extracting features, the next step is to match the feature with other features of that image. There are some common feature matching techniques in literature:

Lexicographic Sorting
This is Block-based type of feature extraction, where, initially an image splits into intersected or non-intersected blocks. Feature vector is evaluated for each block. Lexicographic sorting is the first choice for the most of the authors for matching of feature vectors [9].

Euclidean Distance
Typically, it is utilized for corresponding measures. This type of distance is computed

based on the number of matching key-points. The generalized formula to compute this is as follows:

$$d(a, b) = \sqrt{(bx - ax)^2 + (by - ay)^2} \qquad (1)$$

Brute Force Matcher

It is straightforward technique for matching of feature in an image processing. In first step, it grabs the descriptor of a feature and then it is mapped with other features in the next step using distance computation. Then it returns the nearest one at the end [10].

Best-Bin-First Search

This method is based on an algorithm which is kd-tree, to acquire estimated nearby neighbors. This method is usually used for key-point based approach [9].

These are some matching techniques, which can be used for image feature matching. As per discussed in literature, there are some advantages and disadvantages of exiting systems depend on various factors. Thus as per necessity, researcher can use matching technique.

3 Experimental Results

The experimental results of various techniques with MICC F220 database (having 220 images) are discussed below:

3.1 Matching Algorithm for MSER Features

The MSER (Maximally Stable Extremal Regions) algorithm extracts co-variant portion of an image [11]. This method is defined by function of intensity and outer border, because of which this method gives key characteristics of region. The result of MSER feature matching is shown in Fig. 4.

Fig. 4. Matching algorithm for MSER features

3.2 Matching Algorithm for SURF Features

SURF is highly efficient algorithm as per the time complexity point of view. This algorithm detects the features based on local minimum and maximum value [12]. The result of feature extraction with SURF and feature matching with Euclidean distance is shown in Fig. 5.

Fig. 5. Matching algorithm for SURF features

3.3 Matching Algorithm for SIFT Features

SIFT is highly recommended feature extraction algorithm, as this is invariant to rotation. In literature almost all authors used Best-Bin-First algorithm for matching SIFT features. The result of this technique is shown in Fig. 6.

Fig. 6. Matching algorithm for SIFT features

3.4   Matching Algorithm with Harris Detector

Harris corner detector is commonly used algorithm in computer vision to extract image features of corner. The result of this is shown in Fig. 7.

Fig. 7. Matching algorithm with Harris Detector

3.5   Brute Force Matching

This type of matching uses trial and error concept for matching of feature vectors. The result of Brute force matching is shown in Fig. 8.

Fig. 8. Brute-Force matching result

These are some experimental result of matching techniques for various traditional feature extraction algorithms.

4   Comparative Analysis

Table 1 shows comparative analysis of some of the above mentioned techniques with Recall, Precision, F1-score and Accuracy as parameters for comparison.

Table 1. Comparative analysis

Techniques	Recall	Precision	F1-Score
SIFT	79.17	88.37	90.53
SURF	89.58	91.49	90.53
Harris Detector	76.44	84.78	80.39

The comparative analysis graph of SIFT, SURF and Harris Detector is shown in Fig. 9.

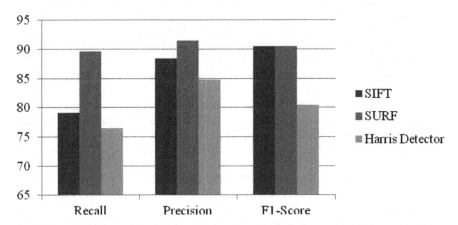

Fig. 9. Comparative analysis graph of SIFT, SURF and Harris Detector

5   Conclusion

Above experimental results show, the detection of falsary in memes on social media. It concludes that the feature extraction of memes with feature matching of different variety can identify the tamper in an image with Recall, Precision and F1-Score as analytical parameters. Figure 8 shows that SURF give better results than other techniques. If a researcher wants to develop a system for pattern recognition, to stop destructive involvement of memes in society pertaining to social cause, the concentration on corner key-points in an image is important, then the researcher should use matching algorithm with Harris corner detector. Thus using this paper researchers will comprehend, the desired combination of type of system applications, feature extraction with feature matching algorithms.

References

1. Ramesh, A.: World Cup 2019 final: England, New Zealand seek history and bragging rights. India Today, 14 July 2019. https://www.indiatoday.in/sports/cricket-world-cup-2019/story/world-cup-2019-final-england-new-zealand-seek-history-and-bragging-rights-1568583-2019-07-14

2. Vidya: India-Pakistan match, India Today, 18 June 2019. https://www.indiatoday.in/fact-check/story/fact-check-an-old-meme-resurfaces-with-a-new-twist-on-india-pak-match-155 1386-2019-06-18

3. Babri, U.M., Tanvir, M., Khurshid, K.: Feature based correspondence: a comparative study on image matching algorithms. (IJACSA) Int. J. Adv. Comput. Sci. Appl. 7(3), 206–210 (2016)

4. Amtullah, S., Koul, A.: Passive image forensic method to detect copy move forgery in digital images. IOSR J. Comput. Eng. (IOSR-JCE) 16(2), 96–104 (2014)

5. Ryu, S.-J., Lee, M.-J., Lee, H.-K.: Detection of copy-rotate-move forgery using zernike moments. In: Böhme, R., Fong, P.W.L., Safavi-Naini, R. (eds.) IH 2010. LNCS, vol. 6387, pp. 51–65. Springer, Heidelberg (2010). https://doi.org/10.1007/978-3-642-16435-4_5

6. Singh, V.K., Tripathi, R.C.: Fast and efficient region duplication detection in digital images using sub-blocking method. Int. J. Adv. Sci. Technol. 35, 93–102 (2011)

7. Yan, C.-P., Pun, C.-M.: Multi-scale difference map fusion for tamper localization using binary ranking hashing. IEEE Trans. Inf. Forensics Secur. 12(9) (2017)

8. Guo, Y., Cao, X., Zhang, W., Wang, R.: Fake colorized image detection. IEEE Trans. Inf. Forensics Secur. 13(8) (2018)

9. Christlein, V., Riess, C., Jordan, J., Riess, C., Angelopoulou, E.: An evaluation of popular copy-move forgery detection approaches. Proc. IEEE Trans. Inf. Forensics Secur. 1–26 (2012)

10. OpenCV by doxygen - 1.8.12, Role of reference elements is under the Feature Detection and Description with Feature Matching (2018). https://docs.opencv.org/3.4.3/dc/dc3/tutorial_py_matcher.html

11. Śluzek, A.: Improving performances of MSER features in matching and retrieval tasks. In: Hua, G., Jégou, H. (eds.) ECCV 2016. LNCS, vol. 9915, pp. 759–770. Springer, Cham (2016). https://doi.org/10.1007/978-3-319-49409-8_63

12. Lyu, D., Xia, H., Wang, C.: Research on the effect of image size on real-time performance of robot vision positioning. EURASIP J. Image Video Process. 2018(1), 1–11 (2018). https://doi.org/10.1186/s13640-018-0328-0

Development of Multi Faces Recognition System Using HOG Features and Neural Network Classifier in Real Time Environment

Narayan Kulkarni$^{(\boxtimes)}$ and H. S. Fadewar

School of Computational Sciences, Swami Ramanand Teeth Marathwada University, Nanded 431606, India
kulkarninarayan@rediffmail.com

Abstract. The face recognition field is not limited to personal identification and verification, recently it is highly applicable in a real-time application, security, and authentication purpose. It becomes an interested, challenging, and growing topic for a researcher in the area of Computer Vision In this paper, the researcher proposed GUI based development system for multiple faces recognition in video images using a Histogram of Oriented Gradient (HOG) and Neural Network classifier. This system can also be implemented for multi-face recognition and identification for class attendance purposes. In experimental work, the HOG algorithm and NN technique are incorporated. In this recognition system, the SEAS-FR-DB video database consists of HD multi faces of 5 subjects and each subject consists of 300 frames. The result shows correct recognition and a higher recognition rate near about 100% in a real-time environment with much lower computational time.

Keywords: Multi faces recognition · HOG · Neural network

1 Introduction

Face detection and recognition play a crucial part in the task of a face-based authentication system [1, 3, 11]. There are several techniques and methods are used by researchers like Principal Component Analysis (PCA) is statistical-based techniques for dimensionality reduction. Eigen face approach which is well famous and accepted in pattern recognition and categorization many types of research applied successfully in face recognition techniques [4]. Local Binary Pattern (LBP) it is used for the texture of the digital image description, the texture operator which marks the pixels of the computerized picture by thresholding the area of every pixel and rewarded as the consequence of a double number. The LBP code in images is composed into a histogram. The categorization is done on the basis of histogram similarities. [6], Linear Discriminant Analysis (LDA) for the classification purpose LDA is better to perform than PCA. The basic idea of LDA is to find linear transformation; feature cluster is separable after transformation.

HOG (Histogram of Oriented Gradient): HOG is one type of features used to detect objects in human computer interaction, and digital image processing. A feature descriptor

© Springer Nature Singapore Pte Ltd. 2021
K. C. Santosh and B. Gawali (Eds.): RTIP2R 2020, CCIS 1380, pp. 261–269, 2021.
https://doi.org/10.1007/978-981-16-0507-9_23

is an agent of a picture or a or an image patch that rearranges the image by separating the valuable data and throwing undesirable data. This procedure counts occurrences of gradient orientation in localized portions of a picture detection window or region of interest descriptor among the all and commonly used for object recognition. HOG descriptor decomposed images into tiny squared cells computes the histogram of oriented gradients in each region. It is the distribution of measurements in the image region and needful for the identification of texture objects with different shapes [8].

Basic Structure of HOG Feature Extraction: During the HOG feature extraction, the face picture is first part into a few little cells. Furthermore, for every cell register a histogram of inclination bearings or edge directions for the pixels inside the cell. The HOG highlight extraction process appeared in the following diagram.

The HOG feature extraction consist following steps:

Step 1: Gradient calculation: To find a HOG descriptor, first, we need to compute the X and Y gradients, then we can determine the histogram of gradients calculated by the following formula (Fig. 1).

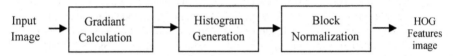

Fig. 1. Block diagram of HOG Feature extraction

For X gradient:

$$f(x + 1, y) - f(x - 1, y) \tag{1}$$

For Y gradient:

$$f(x, y + 1) - f(x, y - 1) \tag{2}$$

Gradient Magnitude:

$$M(x, y) = \left(gx^2 + gy^2\right)^{1/2} \tag{3}$$

Gradient Orientation:

$$\theta(x, y) = \tan^{-1}(gy/gx) \tag{4}$$

Step 2: Histogram Generation: The second step of calculation is making the cell histograms. Every pixel inside the cell makes a weighted choice for a direction put together histogram channel based with respect to the qualities found in the gradient calculation.

Step 3: Block Normalization: for removal of noise a normalization can be done after calculating histogram vectors (Fig. 2).

Neural Network Classification: Neural network is type of classification model, is a specific set of algorithm frequently used in machine learning which solved complex problem [23]. NN is a good programming approaches that broken down big program to many small piece of program. NN structure consist of layer 1, called input layer, hidden layer is a layer 2, and finally layer 3 is an output layer shown in following Fig. 3.

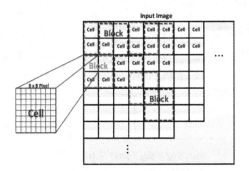

Fig. 2. Cell and Block for HOG

Input Layer: Represents external input or data input.

Hidden Layer: It is layer of NN, but which is not the part of neither Input nor Output. Neural Network can have many hidden layers.

Output Layer: That represent the target field or result on input data.

Each layer is connected through strength called weights, Input data are presented to the input layer, and values are transmitted from each neuron to every neuron in the next layer. Finally, a result is delivered from the output layer.

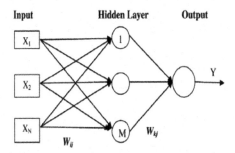

Fig. 3. Three layer NN classification model

2 Proposed Face Recognition System

Figure 4 shows block diagram of proposed system. The experimental setup contains a real time video data of 5 person is an input picture. It is implemented in MATLAB 16 through GUI based system, consists mainly two phases Trained phase and Test phase. In the trained phase frontal face features for single person in different positions are trained using HOG algorithm. The test phase consist of following steps.

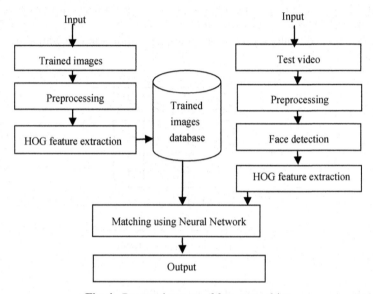

Fig. 4. Proposed system of face recognition

Face detection the system automatically done multiple face detection using vision. CascadeObjectDetector function.

- Feature extraction using HOG algorithm.
- Matching the trained and Test images using Neural Network classification (Figs. 5, 6, 7, 8 and 9).

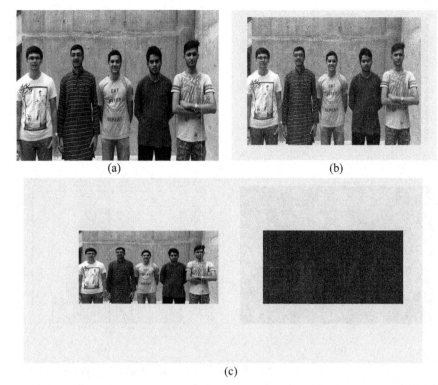

(a)   (b)

(c)

Fig. 5. (a) Test video (b) HOG feature over original image (c) Original image and HOG feature.

3 Experimental Result and Analysis

The experimental result shows that input video contains5 person with varying position after applying HOG descriptor and Neural Network classifier it gives all match face as shown in Fig. 10 the output.

Table 1 shows related work done by various researchers using Histogram Oriented Gradients algorithm, it is also indicated in table rate of recognition and database used for their experiments.

Face recognition rate for above database using HOG feature extraction and neural network classification with time taken for feature extraction, classification, and time required for recognition as shown in Table 2.

Data-Sets: SEAS-FR (School of engineering and applied Science-Face Video Database). It consist full HD -1080p multi subject off line and real time video inputs. Database consist video of 5 subjects, each subject consist of 300 frame, total frames are 5*300 = 1500 frames, duration of video is 10 s with frame rate 30 fps.

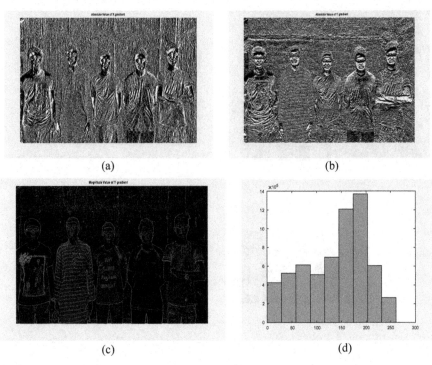

Fig. 6. (a) X-gradient Image (b) Y-gradient Image (c) Magnitude image of Y gradient (d) 9 bin histogram

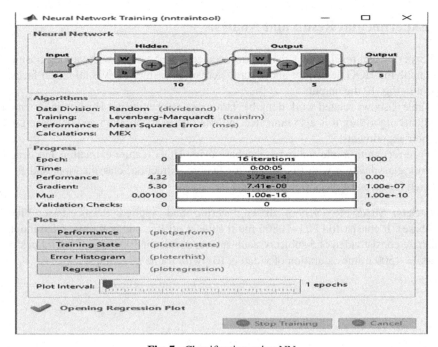

Fig. 7. Classification using NN

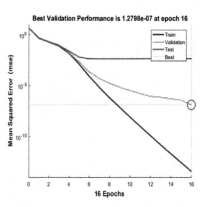

Fig. 8. NN Classification performance plot   **Fig. 9.** ROC curve

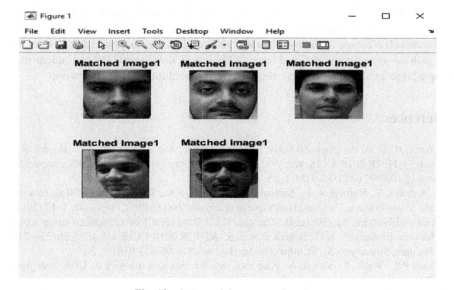

Fig. 10. Output of the proposed system

Table 1. Classification of HOG techniques

Sr. no	Title of paper	Author name	Data set used	Rate of recognition
1	Face recognition using HOG-EBGM [18]	Alberto Albiol	Yale, CVL	98.2
2	Face Recognition using Histogram of Oriented Gradients [17]	Sourabh Hanamsheth	Yale	85.0

Table 2. Recognition rate

Subjects	Total frames	Time taken for feature extraction	Time taken for classification	Time taken for recognition	Face recognition rate
S - 1	300	38.74	9.40	2.80	100%
S - 2	300				
S - 3	300				
S - 4	300				
S - 5	300				

4   Conclusion

In this proposed system we have implemented HOG feature extraction and neural network as a classifier using multi faces video. Our experiment shows. HOG descriptors feature which is robust to change in rotary motion, illumination, and higher recognition rate with minimum computational time. In the future, the system may be implemented using a large dataset and deep learning such as a convolutional neural network.

References

1. Wang, H., et al.: An empirical study: ELM in face matching. In: Santosh, K.C., Hegadi, R.S. (eds.) RTIP2R 2018. CCIS, vol. 1035, pp. 277–287. Springer, Singapore (2019). https://doi.org/10.1007/978-981-13-9181-1_25
2. Candemir, S., Borovikov, E., Santosh, K.C., Antani, S.K., Thoma, G.R.: RSILC: rotation- and scale-invariant, line-based color-aware descriptor. Image Vis. Comput. **42**, 1–12 (2015)
3. Fawwad Hussain, M., Wang, H., Santosh, K.C.: Gray level face recognition using spatial features. In: Santosh, K.C., Hegadi, R.S. (eds.) RTIP2R 2018. CCIS, vol. 1035, pp. 216–229. Springer, Singapore (2019). https://doi.org/10.1007/978-981-13-9181-1_20
4. Suri, P.K., Walla, E., Verma, A.: Face recognition techniques using PCA, LDA, histogram, Eigen faces
5. Xiao, D., Lin, J.: Face recognition using a new feature selection method. In: Proceeding of the 27th Chinese Control Conference, 6–18 July 2008
6. Kulkarni, O.S., Deokar, S.M., Choudhari, A.K.: Real time face recognition using LBP features. In: Third International Conference on Computing, Communication, Control and Automation (2017)
7. Subban, R., Soundararajan, S.: Human face recognition using facial feature detection techniques. In: International Conference on Green Computing and Internet of Things (2015)
8. Shu, C., Ding, X.: Histogram of the Oriented Gradient for Face Recognition. Tsinghua Science and Technology, April 2011
9. Li, Y., Su, G.: Simplified histogram of oriented gradient feature extraction algorithm for the hardware implementation. In: International Conference on Computers, Communications and Systems (2015)
10. Awais, M., Iqbal, M.J.: Real-time surveillance through face recognition using HOG and feedforward neural networks, 10 September 2019

11. Ade-Ibijola, A., Aruleba, K.: Automatic attendance capturing using histogram of oriented gradients on facial images. In: IIMC International Information Management Corporation (2018)
12. Mary Prasanna, D., Ganapathy Reddy, Ch.: Development of real time face recognition system using OpenCV. Int. Res. J. Eng. Technol. **4**, 791 (2017)
13. Ronanki, S., Gundu, S.: Face detection and identification using SVM. Int. J. Adv. Res. Sci. Eng. (2017)
14. Kim, S., Cho, K.: Fast calculation of histogram of oriented gradient feature by removing redundancy in overlapping block. J. Inf. Sci. Eng. **30**, 1719–1731 (2014)
15. Surasak, T., Takahiro, I.: Histogram of oriented gradients for human detection in video. In: 5th International Conference on Business and Industrial Research (2018)
16. Zhang, S., Wang, X.: Human detection and object tracking based on histograms of oriented gradients. In: Ninth International Conference on Natural Computation (2013)
17. Bardeh, N.G., Palhang, M.: New approach for human detection in images using histograms of oriented gradients (2013)
18. Kulandai Josephine Julina, J., Sree Sharmila, T.: Facial recognition using histogram of gradients and support vector machines. In: IEEE International Conference on Computer, Communication, and Signal Processing (2017)
19. Ho, H.-H., Nguyen, N.-S.: Accurate and low complex cell histogram generation by bypass the gradient of pixel computation. In: 4th NAFOSTED Conference on Information and Computer Science (2017)
20. Hanamsheth, S., Rane, M.: Face recognition using histogram of oriented gradients. Int. J. Adv. Res. Comput. Sci. Manag. Stud. (2018)
21. Albiol, A., Monzo, D.: Face recognition using HOG-EBGM. Pattern Recogn. Lett. **29**, 1537–1543 (2008)
22. Zhang, X., Gonnot, T.: Real-time face detection and recognition in complex background. J. Signal Inf. Process. **8**, 99–112 (2017)
23. Hegadi, R., Navale, D., Pawar, T., Ruikar, D.: Osteoarthritis detection and classification from knee X-ray images based on artificial neural network. In: Santosh, K.C., Hegadi, R.S. (eds.) RTIP2R 2018. CCIS, vol. 1036, pp. 97–105. Springer, Singapore (2019). https://doi.org/10.1007/978-981-13-9184-2_8

Extraction of Key Frame from Random Videos Based On Discrete Cosine Transformation

Shivanand S. Gornale[1], Ashvini K. Babaleshwar[1(✉)], and Pravin L. Yannawar[2]

[1] Department of Computer Science, Rani Channamma University, Belagavi, Karnataka, India
shivanand_gornale@yahoo.com, ashw.babaleshwar@gmail.com
[2] Vision and Intelligent System Lab, Department of Computer Science and IT, Dr. Babasaheb Ambedkar Marathwada University, Aurangabad, Maharashtra, India
pravinyannawar@gmail.com

Abstract. Video Analysis has rooted tremendously in many applications with the development of new technologies. Video Analysis plays vital role in many real time event applications where the small content from video gives a full story of the whole video. In such case the analysis of video becomes important to study the data contents present in the videos rather than its attributes. Key frame extraction is a method used for video indexing and in video retrieval applications. The proposed work presents the extraction of key frames from a given video using Discrete Cosine Transform (DCT). The expirmenatal result obtained show competative outcomes with 82.75% completeness of video with 32×32 pixel coeffecent as compared to 64×64 and 128×128 coefficients of frames by good time and space complexity compared to results reported in literature.

Keywords: Video · Shot · Frames · Key frames

1 Introduction

A video contains a huge set of information both objective as well as subjective. The contents of videos like text, image, visual objects, different textures and audio are in great demand of study and analysis for the storage and reusing of the information [8]. The demand of such multimedia applications is rapidly increasing in day-to-day life because of the rapid capturing devices and technologies. Applications based on multimedia data are getting attention by research community, therefore among the key elements for the success of these applications are the method of storing and effective management of voluminous data, whereas it also becomes important to provide user-friendly access to the stored data were considered on priority. In the video analysis the first processes is to do a video composition analysis which consists the process of segmenting the smallest unit of video called frames. Whereas a key frame is the frame that superlative content of a shot or a sub shot. Key frames are used as the records of the video information for video indexing and retrieval. Hence the key frame extraction plays a vital role in Content Based video retrieval systems (CBVRS) [6], in this paper we are presenting an algorithm, to select the best key frames from a given video that can be used in the process of video summarization and retrieval [1].

© Springer Nature Singapore Pte Ltd. 2021
K. C. Santosh and B. Gawali (Eds.): RTIP2R 2020, CCIS 1380, pp. 270–278, 2021.
https://doi.org/10.1007/978-981-16-0507-9_24

The organisation of work is given in Sect. 2 that presents the related work; Sect. 3 rivals the Methodology, Sect. 4 gives the result analysis and Sect. 5 gives the conclusion of the work.

2 Related Work

Liu et al. [1] have presented a novel for key-frame-extraction approach, which was combination of motion-based temporal segmentation and color-based shot detection. They assumed key frame as turning point of motion acceleration and deceleration of each motion pattern. In this approach, the number of key frames and the location of the key frames in a given videos are determined automatically by the perceived motion patterns of the video. This approach there were no threshold and accordingly performance was fast, since motion information in MPEG video directly utilized in the motion analysis. The algorithm measures visual content complexity of a shot by action events and determines the number of key frames to abstract a video by action events give a very good percentage of result up to 77% to 86% for different videos.

Huang et al. [2] have proposed a method for integrated key frame extraction for video. authors have made use of OpenCV to select key frames based on shot boundary and Visual content frames. For similarity, comparison of histogram, Chi-Square method was applied. Experiments show that algorithm requires a less time and space complexity.

Liu et al. [3] have also proposed an algorithm for key frame extraction based on MPEG video stream. An improved histogram matching method is proposed for segmentation and key frames where extracted by different technique like shod activity, macro-block, and based on motion analysis. In their method, they classify frames as I-frames, P-frames, B-frames and use features for each sub-lens. The average performance of their algorithm was 99.48% with average fidelity of 0.76%, and thus extracted good and accurate key frames.

Zhao et al. [4] proposed key frame extraction and shot retrieval approach. The system gives a new metric to measure the distance between query image and a shot based on the concept of Nearest Feature Line (NFL). Feature trajectory of a video was used as key frames and the lines that pass through the points represent the shot in a video. The experiments were conducted on color histogram as features. The results obtained for + NFL method gives batter performance as compared to NN, WL methods.

Nasreen et al. [5] presented a key frame extraction using Edge Change Ratio for shot segmentation. The extracted key frame represents the video as a whole. Their proposed method starts with pre-processing for frames by converting color frame to gray scale frame and then to edge frame, the sober method was provided for detection of edges from gray scale image vector. Then edge change ration method was applied on frame vector, later by using adaptive threshold value the candidate frames were selected. The method found effective for key frame extraction with high efficiency and robustness.

Qu et al. [6] have presented key frame extraction methods based on histogram method and pixel based method respectively. For segmentation of videos into shots Histogram intersection, non-uniform portioning and weighting are calculated and then by using this shot result, an improved clustering algorithm is applied for video shot segmentation. The tentative outcome demonstrates that the algorithm gives an improvement in recall and precision of shot detection to certain degree. In addition extracted key frame with the entropy method represent the contents of video shots better.

Thepade et al. [8] have presented the key frame extraction method based of DCT fractional coefficient. The experimentation have carried on five different videos like clock, mice, cookie, super, snow, with 25 % are found as better coefficient with more than 80% of completeness in an average for all five set of videos. Authors conclude that the technique of key frame extraction proposed have achieved higher performance resulting in saving of space and time.

Selvaganesan et al. [7] have proposed a work for key frame extraction for face recognition using clustering approach. Methods like SURF, k-means clustering are used in the experimentation. The system was tested on Honda/UCSD database 1. The experimental results obtained good number of key frames to recognize the face in a given video dataset.

Kelm et al. [9] used a motion feature based approach for extraction of key frames. The frames were evaluated using Mean opinion score by obtaining 3.62 score as compared to IBM Multimedia Analysis and Retrieval System (IMARS). The experimentation was carried on different YOUTUBE videos.

Padmakala et al. [10] has proposed a video retrieval system based on optimal key frame feature, color and texture features. The key frames were selected by generating correlation coefficient between first and second frames based on DCT method and, further different descriptor like LBP are used for retrieval of videos. The experiments were carried on 50 videos of different classes with 150 to 250 frames.

Rathod et al. [11] presents a key frame extraction and shot boundary detection method based on histogram difference of consecutive frames and thresholding method. The system was tested on 40 videos, as a result the system have obtained good results.

Shi et al. [12] proposed a video key frame extraction based on color difference between consecutive frames and further with the structural characteristic difference between adjacent frames of alternative sequence. The optimization is included for the effectiveness of video copyright protection process.

Ghatak et al. [13] have proposed a key frame extraction from news videos based on 3 descriptors called color histogram, Edge Direction Histogram, and wavelet statistics. The approach has obtained good number of key frames that are sufficient to represent a whole video.

Aote et al. [15] have presented a work on video annotation based on two level of key frame extraction method. The system assumes first frame as key frame in level one and further in level two the fuzzy-c means clustering technique is used to select the prominent key frames. Methods like Color Histogram Difference and Edge change Ratio are used in video annotation process. The results obtained are found competitive.

Qi et al. [16] have proposed key frame extraction system based on CNN based for face recognition in a video. The system use make use of one person and multi person videos using Chokepoint dataset and private video dataset. The results obtained are found to reduce the data volume by 90 % improving face recognition process. Authors conclude that the GPU accelerated key frame extraction reach higher than real time process speed.

3   Methodology

The objective of the proposed system is to extract key frames from a given video based on Discrete Cohesion Transformation (DCT) of consecutive still images. In Fig. 1 which represents the system architecture.

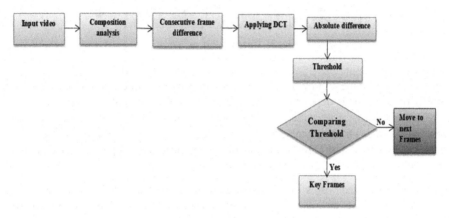

Fig. 1. System architecture

Algorithm:
Input: Video stream.
Output: Key Frames.
Step1: Read input video.
Step 2: Read Consecutive Frame.
Step 3: Apply DCT2 Command on the Frames.
Step 4: Extract these frames R, G, and B which has energy information concentrates it in a few Coefficients.
Step 5: Find Absolute difference of consecutive frames between i and i+1.
Step 7: calculate threshold using mean and standard deviation.
Step 8: If Absolute difference is greater than threshold than select it as a Key frame, Store the Frames else Not Key frame discard and move to next.
Step 9: List the Key Frames in Output Folder.

Database: The experimentation was carried on different class videos like Entertainment, Sports, and Cartoon is taken into consideration to meet the system objective. Each of these videos is of different size like 118 kb to 2 MB with different frame size for each of the sample videos.

Composition Analysis: In content based video analysis the first phase is to breaking down of video into its smallest sub units. The hierarchy of video clips, scenes, shots and frames are arranged in a descending manner is basically known as composition analysis, as shown in the following Fig. 2.

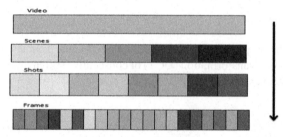

Fig. 2. Composition analysis

Candidate Key Frame: A key frame is a superlative image content of a video shot. The number of key frames depends on the video type and its content. Key frames can be used as the records of the video information for manipulations, such as indexing and browsing of videos from a database. The proposed system extracts the key frames based on the DCT method and Thresholding technique on different samples of video datasets taken from YOUTUBE Commercial website [14].

Discrete Cosine Transforms (DCT): In digital image processing the Discrete Cosine Transform represents an image as a sum of sinusoids of varying magnitudes and frequencies. In this work we make use of two dimensional DCT, as it provides significant information with few coefficients of DCT. The two dimensional DCT is given in the Eq. 1 as follows [10].

$$F[k, l] = \alpha(k)\alpha(l) \sum_{m=0}^{N-1}\sum_{n=0}^{N-1} f(m, n) \cos\left[\frac{(2m+1)\pi K}{2N}\right] \cos\left[\frac{(2n+1)\pi l}{2N}\right] \quad (1)$$

Where $\alpha(k) = \left\{\sqrt{\frac{1}{N}}\right.$ if k = 0 and $\alpha(k) = \left\{\sqrt{\frac{2}{N}}\right.$ if k $\neq$ 0, similarly for $\alpha(l)$
The threshold (Th) is defined in the following Eq. 2.

$$Th = \mu + \sigma \quad (2)$$

Where μ is mean of absolute difference and σ is standard deviation of absolute difference. Once the threshold is obtained, key frames are determined by comparing the difference of frames against threshold.

4   Expirimental and Result Analysis

The system is implemented on the MATLAB 2018a, computer vision tools are employed here. The proposed model accepts the input video in the format ".mp4" and the size of the video ranges from 811 KB to 1.46 MB. The datasets consists of different videos taken from the YouTube like Entertainment, Sports, and Cartoon. The results of different samples are listed below in sample 1, sample 2, and sample 3.

Sample 1: Entertainment Video

Fig. 3. Video shot of sample Entertainment of size 1.46 MB with total number of frames 738

key_32_1.jpg   key_64_1.jpg   key_128_3.jpg

Fig. 4. Extracted key frames for entertainment of coefficient fame size 32 × 32, 64 × 64, 128 × 128.

The Fig. 3, Fig. 5, Fig. 7, and Fig. 9 shows the different video types used in the experiment for extraction of key frames. Whereas the Fig. 4, Fig. 6, Fig. 8 and Fig. 10 shows the screen shot of extracted key frames for different DCT coefficient as 32 × 32, 64 × 64, 128 × 128 respectively as follows.

Sample 2: Sports Video

Fig. 5. Video shot of sample Sports of size 811 KB with total number of frames 811

key_32_83.jpg   key_64_78.jpg   key_128_82.jpg

Fig. 6. Extracted key frames for sports of coefficient fame size 32 × 32, 64 × 64, 128 × 128

Sample 3: Cartoon Video

Fig. 7. Video shot of sample cartoon of size 1.42 MB with total number of frames 854

key_32_1.jpg   key_64_409.jpg   key_128_159.jpg

Fig. 8. Extracted key frames for cartoon of coefficient fame size 32 × 32, 64 × 64, 128 × 128

Sample 4: News Video

Fig. 9. Video shot of sample news video of size 256 KB with total number of frames 854

key_32_19.jpg   key_64_19.jpg   key_128_42.jpg

Fig. 10. Extracted key frames for news video of coefficient fame size 32 × 32, 64 × 64, 128 × 128

The system is implemented on four different categories of random videos each of three samples are presented in Table 1. The frames are normalized and observed to find the key frame. These key frames are expected to evaluate the completeness of the system proposed. The completeness can be computed [8] using the following Eq. 3.

$$Completeness = \frac{number\ of\ key\ frames}{total\ number\ of\ frames} \tag{3}$$

The system involves three different coefficients of frames of size 32 × 32, 64 × 64, 128 × 128 to measure a performance of completeness as presented in the following Table 1.

Table 1. The performance of key frame extraction completeness on different video samples.

Video	Samples	Completeness %		
Proposed coefficients of frame		32 × 32	64 × 64	128 × 128
Entertainment	Sample 1	89.83	97.69	99.08
	Sample 2	91.04	45.52	37.28
	Sample 3	81.33	62.11	69.22
Sports	Sample 1	78.29	66.30	70.20
	Sample 2	80.53	71.06	85.33
	Sample 3	81.88	73.07	81.87
Cartoon	Sample 1	73.78	50.11	74.55
	Sample 2	57.76	48.11	77.41
	Sample 3	88.52	60.30	77.28
News	Sample 1	87.23	90.12	98.43
	Sample 2	89.51	95.16	99.19
	Sample 3	93.33	86.66	99.16
Average completeness		**82.75**	**70.51**	**80.75**

The expected number of key frames of 12 random videos is used to calculate the completeness. For different coefficient frame size of 32 × 32, 64 × 64, 128 × 128 are presented in the above Table 1. The 32 × 32 DCT coefficients the average completeness is 82.75%, whereas for 64 × 64 achieved 70.51%, and for 128 × 128 have obtained 80.75%.

5   Conclusion

This work presents the key frame extraction process based on the DCT technique for random videos of four different types with different samples. The algorithm presented has given higher completeness performance with 32 × 32 coefficient by obtaining 82.75% of average completeness than compared to 64 × 64 and 128 × 128 frame size. The system can be one of the good methods for video summarization and retrieval efficiency by saving space and time.

References

1. Liu, T., Zhang, H.-J., Qi, F.: A novel video key-frame-extraction algorithm based on perceived motion energy model. IEEE trans. Circ. Syst. video technol. **13**, 1006–1013 (2003)
2. Huang, M., Xia, L., Zhang, J., Dong, H.: An integrated scheme for video key frame extraction. In: 2nd International Symposium on Computer, Communication, Control and Automation. Atlantis Press (2013)
3. Liu, G., Zhao, J.: Key frame extraction from MPEG video stream. In: Proceedings of the Second Symposium International Computer Science and Computational Technology(ISCSCT 2009) Huangshan, P. R. China, pp.7–11 (2009)
4. Zhao, L., Qi, W., Li, S.Z., Yang, S.-Q., Zhang, H.J.: Key-frame extraction and shot retrieval using nearest feature line (NFL). In: Multimedia 2000 Proceedings of the 2000 ACM Workshops on Multimedia, USA, pp. 217–220 (2000)
5. Nasreen, A., Shobha, G.: Key frame extraction using edge change ratio for shot segmentation. Int. J. Adv. Res. Comput. Commun. Eng. **2**, 4421–4423 (2013)
6. Zhong, Q., Lin, L., Gao, T., Wang, Y.: An improved keyframe extraction method based on HSV colour space. J. Softw. **8**, 1751–1758 (2013)
7. Selvaganesan, J., Natarajan, K.: Unsupervised feature based key-frame extraction towards face recognition. Int. Arab J. Inf. Technol. **13**, 777–783 (2016)
8. Thepade, S.D., Tonge, A.A.: Extraction of key frames using discrete cohesion transform. In: International Conferences on Control, Instrumentation Communication and Computational Technologies ICCICCT, pp.1294–1297. IEEE (2014)
9. Kelm, P., Schmiedeke, S., Sikora, T. : Feature-based video key frame extraction for low quality video sequences. IEEE (2009)
10. Padmakala, S., Mala, A., Shalini, M.: an effective content based video retrieval utilizing texture, color and optimal key frame features. In: International conference on Image Information Processing (ICIIP). IEEE (2011)
11. Rathod, G., Nikam, D.: An algorithm for shot boundary detection and key frame extraction using histogram difference. Int. J. Emerg. Technol. Adv. Eng. **3**, 155–163 (2013)
12. Shi, Y., Yang, H., Gong, M., Liu, X., Xia, Y.: A fast and robust key frame extraction method for video copyright protection. J. Electr. Comput. Eng. **2017**, 1–7 (2017)
13. Ghatak, S., Bhattacharjee, D.: Extraction of key frames from news videos using EDF, MDF, and HI method of new video summarization. Int. J. Eng. Innov. Technol. (IJEIT) **2** (2013)
14. https://www.winxdvd.com/resource/free-download-youtube-videos.htm
15. Shailendra, S.: Aote and archana potnurwar, "an automatic video annotation framework based on two level keyframe extraction mechanism. Mutimed. Tools Appl. **78**, 14465–14484 (2019)
16. Qi, X., Liu, C., Schuckers, S.: Boosting face in video recognition via cnn based ker frame extraction. In: International Conference on Biometrics (ICB). IEEE (2018). https://doi.org/10.1109/ICB2018.2018.00030

Data Science and Machine Learning

Prediction of SO$_2$ Air Pollution Quality Parameter of Kolhapur City Using Time Series Analysis

Aniket Muley$^{(\boxtimes)}$ (iD) and Atish Tangawade (iD)

School of Mathematical Sciences, SRTM University, Nanded, Maharashtra, India
aniket.muley@gmail.com, tangawadeatish@gmail.com

Abstract. This paper deals with the identification of time series predictive model to evaluate the air pollution quality SO$_2$ parameter. In recent years, due to modernization, lots of changes have been done already in the air quality of the environment. A time series model has been developed for SO$_2$ parameter. The performance has been measured through statistical measures. The proposed time series model (2, 0, 1) will be helpful to identify the near future situation of air pollutants may present in the air of Kolhapur city. Further, it will help us to reduce the pollution parameter level and implement some remedies to decrease it.

Keywords: ARIMA · Time series · SO$_2$ · Pollution · Kolhapur · Prediction

1 Introduction

In India, urbanization increasing population gives rise in high level of air pollutants, and particulates in Indian urban centres. It causes acute and chronic effects on health of human being, and is key factor which affects on the health [1, 4, 8, 9, 11, 22]. In the atmosphere, CO slowly oxidizes into carbon dioxide or ozone. Sulphur dioxide (SO$_2$) is an antecedent in the construction of PM and damages forests and global ecology, distressing the human respiratory system. Some researcher has studied the Kolhapur regions noise pollution study [14]. Air pollution study of nearby area Belgaum has been performed [26]. The main purpose is to perform statistical study of SO$_2$ air pollution quality parameter in Kolhapur city. The objectives of the proposed study are: 1) to perform exploratory study of the dataset. 2) To develop optimal time series model for SO$_2$ air pollution data. 3) To test adequacy of the proposed model. 4) To forecast the SO$_2$ of the study area in the next five years.

2 Review of Literature

Researcher performed study for changes of the concentration of air pollutants and sources of air pollutants examined with the help of factor analysis of the Cuic Basin, Romania region [17]. The sources of air pollutants study exhibits due to biomass burning; traffic

© Springer Nature Singapore Pte Ltd. 2021
K. C. Santosh and B. Gawali (Eds.): RTIP2R 2020, CCIS 1380, pp. 281–290, 2021.
https://doi.org/10.1007/978-981-16-0507-9_25

and photochemistry. Along with that, car traffic in cold season and atmospheric stability are also important reasons to the air pollutant sources [27]. The performance of widely used Danish Operational Street Pollution Model (OSPM) under Indian traffic conditions is studied. The comparison between observed and predicted concentration through both statistical and qualitative methods has been performed. Also automobiles are found to be primary source of urban air pollution. The OSPM model perform exceptionally well for the forecasting of parameters whereas NO_2 prediction were poorly predicted were studied various models for forecasting monthly concentration of lead, zinc, iron and RSPM using state space modeling coupled with Kalman filter. Their result shows that SSF model performs better than AR model using least squares model for prediction of concentration of particular month [12]. The health effects of air pollution in large Asian cities data were estimated by using of Japanese compensation system. A comparative study between correlation and relative risk model has been performed. [25] Street Box and Street model used to simulate pollutant concentrations in the street. SPM and SO_2 concentrations were modelled and monitored for a street canyon at Station road, Kolhapur for a period of one week. They observed that, the pollutant concentrations were dependent upon traffic volume, wind direction and wind speeds. New statistical approaches explored, reviewed and summarize the methodological and substantive contributions to time series analysis (TSA) of air pollution. Various TSA methods and aspects were used for analyzing data viz., semi-parametric method, Generalised additive model, multisite time series study, effects of misclassification of exposure, mortality displacement, shape of the concentration–response curve etc. [10, 13, 15, 16, 19, 20, 23, 26, 28–32] used assessment (AirQ) in various cities of Maharashtra. A multivariate vector auto-regression (VAR) model proposed for analyzing the time series of compositional data. PM10 was found in the study area which is to be one of the critical pollutants of API [2, 3, 10, 12, 13, 16, 20, 24].

In the next subsequent sections methodology, result and discussion, and conclusion is discussed in detail.

3   Methodology

3.1   Study Area

Here, secondary dataset of Sulpher dioxide air pollution quality parameter of Kolhapur city has been taken for consideration. The data is collected from the Maharashtra Pollution Control Board website [21]. Kolhapur city consists of three stations which count the air pollution (Fig. 1): Shivaji University campus, Vidyanagar; Ruikar Trust and Mahadwar Road. The available source data record is from the year 2008 to 2018 in the form of frequency two days in a week. Further, we have aggregated the data by aggregation of month and missing values are replaced by its arithmetic mean.

Fig. 1. Location of the study area

3.2 Time Series Model

Time series is a sequence of observations on a variable measured at successive points in time or over consecutive periods of time. It may contain some or all components: trend, cyclic, seasonal and irregular variation [7]. In this study, Time series analysis is performed. Initially, decomposition of additive time series model was completed. Normality was testing for results given by randomly fitted model and best fitted model. Further, divided the whole data into training (70%) and testing (30%) dataset and applied the random model and best fit model on the distributed datasets. Finally, the results were compared to check the efficiency of best model. Autoregressive Integrated Moving Average (ARIMA) Model is applied [5, 6, 18, 22]. ARIMA explains its own past values viz., own lag and forecasted values and errors. If the given no seasonal data does not follows random white noise then, ARIMA is suitable for this situation. It is characterised by p, d and q i.e. p-order of the Auto Regressive model, q-order of Moving Average model and d- required number of differencing for making stationary time series model. If the model shows seasonal variation then it is termed as SARIMA.

The Akaike information criterion (AIC), Bayesian information criterion (BIC) and Ljunge-Box statistics applied to obtain appropriate model. Further, the root mean squared error (RMSE), and mean absolute error (MAE), precision in Eq. (1–3) were used for evaluation of goodness of fit, respectively, during the performance analysis of simulation of training and testing sets [6, 18, 22].

$$RMSE = [n^{-1} \sum\nolimits_{i=1}^{n} (P_i - O_i)^2]^{0.5} \tag{1}$$

$$MAE = \frac{1}{n} \sum\nolimits_{i=1}^{n} \left| P_i - \tilde{O}_i \right| \tag{2}$$

$$MAPE = \frac{1}{n} \sum\nolimits_{i=1}^{n} \left| P_i - \tilde{O}_i \right| \times 100 \tag{3}$$

Where, n is the number of observation, P_i - The predicted values, O_i - The observed data, $\tilde{O}_i$ - The mean values for P_i and O_i, respectively.

The measures viz., AIC, BIC, RMSE, MAE and MAPE were used to check the efficiency of the proposed model with random model. Its efficiency is considered as more with the lower value of the entire above measures.

4   Result and Discussion

In this study, initially, data is split into two parts 70% and 30%. Based on the 70% data time series model is developed. Further, we have analyzed the data through free and open source R software. The library functions: fUnitRoots, lmtest, forecast, FitAR and Metrics were used to prepare R program.

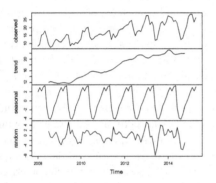
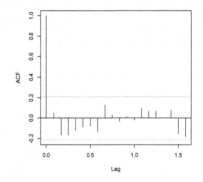

Fig. 2. Decomposition of additive time series

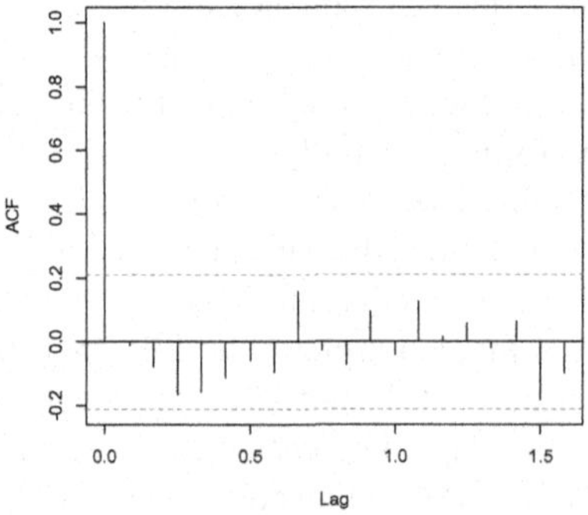

Fig. 3. Fitting residuals for randomly proposed model

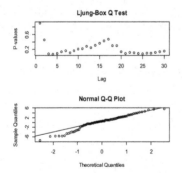

Fig. 4. Normality testing results by proposed random model

Fig. 5. Fitting residuals for best fitted model

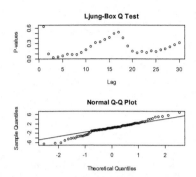

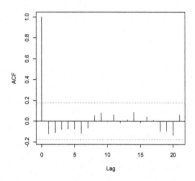

Fig. 6. Normality testing results by best fit model

Fig. 7. Fitting residuals for future prediction of best fitted model

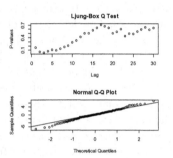

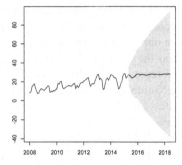

Fig. 8. Normality testing future prediction results by best fit model

Fig. 9. Forecasting future prediction results by random fit model

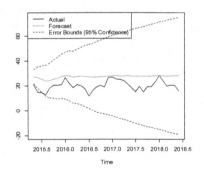

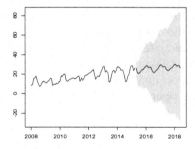

Fig. 10. Prediction area by random model

Fig. 11. Forecasting prediction results by best fit model

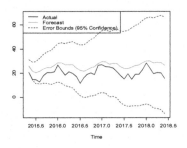

Fig. 12. Prediction area by best model

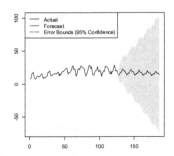

Fig. 13. Forecasting results for future prediction by best fit model

In this study, simulation techniques performed to identify the best ARIMA model. Table 1 represents AIC values. It has been observed that (0, 1, 0) (2, 0, 1) model is found to be more suitable among others. Initially, randomly proposed model (1, 1, 1) (1, 0, 0) has been implemented for the our dataset and it has been tabulated in Table 2. Figure 2 represents the decomposition of the dataset in time series perspective of 2008 to 2018. Figure 3 represents residual plot ACF against the Log values. Figure 4 Ljung Box Q test and Normal qqplot represents the nature of the data. Figure 5 represents the residual for the best fitted model. Figure 4 and Fig. 5 represents Normality plots. Figures 6 and 7 explores autocorrelation function Vs. Lag of the data. Also, the normality of data explains in Fig. 8. The visualization of randomly proposed time series model represents Fig. 9 and 10. Figure 11 and Fig. 12 represents the best fitted model. Also, for future forecasting visualization is represents the overall fluctuation of the data. Table 3 shows comparative significance of the proposed models with Z statistic and with the different level of significance. Table 4 explores the results of the randomly proposed model and generated best fitted model. Table 4 represents the randomly proposed model, optimal generated model obtained through simulating technique. After comparing RMSE, MAE and MAPE values it is observed that ARIMA (2, 0, 1) model is optimal one among all the other ARIMA Models. The next 60 months values of SO_2 air quality parameters are represnted in Fig. 13. Table 5 represents the statistical summary associated to the visualization of predicted results of SO_2 level in the next five years (Fig. 5). The SO_2 has upper limits 50 (unit) defined by MPCB and is observed after prediction results that it will be under control in the next five years.

Table 1. Simulation of ARIMA models

Sr. No.	ARIMA models	AIC
1	(2, 1, 2) (1, 0, 1) [12] with drift	Inf
2	(0, 1, 0) with drift	441.4252
3	(1, 1, 0) (1, 0, 0) [12] with drift	438.0272
4	(0, 1, 1) (0, 0, 1) [12] with drift	438.7657
5	(0, 1, 0)	439.7556
6	(1, 1, 0) with drift	440.464
7	(1, 1, 0) (2, 0, 0) [12] with drift	Inf
8	(1, 1, 0) (1, 0, 1) [12] with drift	Inf
9	(1, 1, 0) (2, 0, 1) [12] with drift	Inf
10	(0, 1, 0) (1, 0, 0) [12] with drift	437.0813
11	(0, 1, 1) (1, 0, 0) [12] with drift	437.5661
12	(1, 1, 1) (1, 0, 0) [12] with drift	439.4553
13	(0, 1, 0) (1, 0, 0) [12]	435.1946
14	(0, 1, 0) (2, 0, 0) [12]	430.7903
15	(0, 1, 0) (2, 0, 1) [12]	430.5291
16	(1, 1, 0) (2, 0, 1) [12]	Inf
17	(0, 1, 1(2, 0, 1) [12]	432.4133
18	(1, 1, 1) (2, 0, 1) [12]	434.2527
19	(0, 1, 0) (2, 0, 1) [12] with drift	432.6647
20	(0, 1, 0) (1, 0, 1) [12]	Inf
21	(0, 1, 0) (2, 0, 2) [12]	431.8331

Table 2. Coefficients of ARIMA models

ARIMA model	sar1	sar2	sma1	$\hat{\sigma}^2$	Log likelihood	AIC	AICc	BIC
Auto model	0.560 s.e. 0.254	0.2508 s.e. 0.1638	−0.4399 s.e. 0.2539	7.273	−211.02	430.04	430.53	439.9
Best model: (0, 1, 0) (2, 0, 1) [12]	0.5605 s.e. 0.2540	0.2506 s.e. 0.1639	−0.4404 s.e. 0.2539	7.022	−211.02	430.04		
Proposed initial model (1, 1, 1) (1, 0, 0) [12]	ar1 −0.2677 s.e. 0.4394	ma1 0.4282 s.e. 0.4083	sar1 0.2480 s.e. 0.1196	$\hat{\sigma}^2$ 8.034	Log likelihood −214.48	AIC 436.97		
Future prediction (0, 1, 0) (2, 0, 1) [12]	sar1 0.6044 s.e. 0.1603	sar2 0.2516 s.e. 0.1152	sma1 −0.4707 s.e. 0.1608	7.245	−304.77	617.54		

Table 3. Z test of coefficients

Models	(p, d, q)	Estimate	Std. Error	z value	Pr(>|z|)
Future prediction: (0, 1, 0) (2, 0, 1) [12]	sar1	0.60435	0.16033	3.7695	0.0001636 ***
	sar2	0.25164	0.11523	2.1839	0.0289689 *
	sma1	−0.47075	0.16084	−2.9268	0.0034245 **
Initial model: (1, 1, 1) (1, 0, 0) [12]	ar1	−0.26774	0.43941	−0.6093	0.54231
	ma1	0.42822	0.40833	1.0487	0.29431
	sar1	0.24804	0.11958	2.0743	0.03805 *
Best model: (0, 1, 0) (2, 0, 1) [12]	sar1	0.56051	0.25403	2.2065	0.02735 *
	sar2	0.25056	0.16390	1.5287	0.12634
	sma1	−0.44040	0.25392	−1.7344	0.08285

Sig.: 0 '***' 0.001 '**' 0.01 '*' 0.05 '.' 0.1 ' ' 1

Table 4. Comparative results

Model	RMSE	MAE	MAPE
Initial proposed model	8.20	7.37	737.42
Best generated model	6.50	6.025	602.56

Table 5. Summary statistics of SO_2 parameter ($\mu g/m^3$)

Results	Average	Min	Max	Standard deviation
Prediction	38.00	24.65	49.81	6.68
Lower	25.91	16.78	33.96	4.56
Upper	55.73	36.09	73.05	9.81

5 Conclusion

In this study, Kolhapur city's SO_2 paramter air pollution quality study has been under-taken. The statistical results explored that, the collected data is normally distributed (Table 4). It is observed that, SO_2, parameter shows the seasonal variation in the study area. Also, the data follows polynomial time series model and its accuracy is checked by performance measures. Further, we have estimated the next five years observations of SO_2 air pollution parameter observed that, SO_2 parameter predicted value ranges 24.65-49.81($\mu g/m^3$), minimum value ranges 16.78–33.96 ($\mu g/m^3$) and maximum value ranges 36.09–73.05 ($\mu g/m^3$). It is found below the permissible limit of MPCB standards. Some of the sources from which SO_2 may increases viz., vehicles, power plants, combustion of fossil fuels, extraction of metals from sulphide ores, paper industry, extraction and distribution of fossil fuel, petroleum refining, combustion of diesel, petrol and natural gas. In future, based on our prediction values of the SO_2 air pollution parameter of the study area we would like suggest: It will be better to increase in the public transport frequency so that, the private transport will get reduce. To develop tree plantation so that, air pollution will get reduce and it helps to reduce the breathing problems occurs due to these parameters. In future, this work can be extended with the interaction of industrial growth, domestic growth, noise pollution and the medicinal aspects viz. health issues of the study area and further it can be compared with the nearby geographical places of the study area to develop more efficient model to reduce air pollution.

Acknowledgment. The authors gratefully acknowledge to Ms. P. S. Waghmode and Ms. A. A. Jadhav for their help in the completion of data collection process.

References

1. Adki, V.S., Jadhav, J.P., Bapat, V.A.: At the cross roads of environmental pollutants and phytoremediation: a promising bio remedial approach. J. Plant Biochem. Biotechnol. **23**(2), 125–140 (2013). https://doi.org/10.1007/s13562-013-0250-6
2. AL-Dhurafi, N.A., Masseran, N., Zamzuri, Z.H.: Compositional time series analysis for air pollution index data. Stochast. Environ. Res. Risk assess. **32**(10), 2903–2911 (2018)
3. Aromolo, R., Moretti, V., Salvati, L.: Exploring time-series of selected air pollution elements in Castelporziano, Rome: the impact on soil and forest ecosystem. Rendiconti Lincei **26**(3), 499–505 (2015). https://doi.org/10.1007/s12210-015-0413-6
4. Chien, L.C., Bangdiwala, S.I.: The implementation of Bayesian structural additive regression models in multi-city time series air pollution and human health studies. Stochast. Environ. Res. Risk Assess. **26**(8), 1041–1051 (2012)
5. Clement, E.P.: Using normalized Bayesian information criterion (BIC) to improve box-Jenkins model building. Am. J. Math. Stat. **4**(5), 214–221 (2014)
6. D'Urso, P., Di Lallo, D., Maharaj, E.A.: Autoregressive model-based fuzzy clustering and its application for detecting information redundancy in air pollution monitoring networks. Soft. Comput. **17**(1), 83–131 (2013)
7. Das, S.: Time Series Analysis. Princeton University Press, Princeton (1994)
8. Dastoorpoor, M., Idani, E., Goudarzi, G., Khanjani, N.: Acute effects of air pollution on spontaneous abortion, premature delivery, and stillbirth in Ahvaz, Iran: a time-series study. Environ. Sci. Pollut. Res. **25**(6), 5447–5458 (2017). https://doi.org/10.1007/s11356-017-0692-9
9. Dionisio, K.L., Chang, H.H., Baxter, L.K.: A simulation study to quantify the impacts of exposure measurement error on air pollution health risk estimates in copollutant time-series models. Environ. Health **15**(1), 114 (2016)
10. Gattu, K.P., et al.: NO_2 sensing studies of bio-green synthesized Au-doped SnO_2. J. Mater. Sci.: Mater. Electron. **28**(17), 13209–13216 (2017)
11. Guo, Y., et al.: Time series analysis of ambient air pollution effects on daily mortality. Environ. Sci. Pollut. Res. **24**(25), 20261–20272 (2017). https://doi.org/10.1007/s11356-017-9502-7
12. Hirota, K., Sakamoto, S., Shibuya, S., Kashima, S.: A methodology of health effects estimation from air pollution in large asian cities. Environments **4**(3), 60 (2017)
13. Holian, M.J.: The effect of social and economic development on air pollution in Indian cities. Environ. Urban. ASIA **5**(1), 1–15 (2014)
14. Hunashal, R.B., Patil, Y.B.: Environmental noise pollution in Kolhapur city, Maharashtra, India. Nat. Environ. Pollut. Technol. **10**(1), 39–44 (2011)

15. Ingle, S.T., Pachpande, B.G., Wagh, N.D., Patel, V.S., Attarde, S.B.: Assessment of daily noise exposure and prevalence of hearing loss in the shopkeepers working near national highway no. 6: a case study of Jalgaon city. Int. J. Sustain. Transp. **3**(1), 54–69 (2009)
16. Kaushik, G., Patil, S., Chel, A.: Air quality status and management in tier II and III Indian cities: a case study of Aurangabad City, Maharashtra. In: Handbook of Environmental Materials Management, pp. 1–22 (2018)
17. Keresztes, R., Rapo, E.: Statistical analysis of air pollution with specific regard to factor analysis in the Ciuc Basin. Romania. Stud. Univ. Babes-Bolyai Chemia **62**(3), 283–292 (2017)
18. Kulkarni, G.E., Muley, A.A., Deshmukh, N.K., Bhalchandra, P.U.: Autoregressive integrated moving average time series model for forecasting air pollution in Nanded city, Maharashtra, India. Model. Earth Syst. Environ. **4**(4), 1435–1444 (2018)
19. Kumar, A., Gupta, I., Brandt, J., Kumar, R., Dikshit, A.K., Patil, R.S.: Air quality mapping using GIS and economic evaluation of health impact for Mumbai city, India. J. Air Waste Manage. Assoc. **66**(5), 470–481 (2016)
20. Maji, K.J., Dikshit, A.K., Deshpande, A.: Human health risk assessment due to air pollution in 10 urban cities in Maharashtra, India. Cogent Environ. Sci. **2**(1), 1193110 (2016)
21. MPCB (2018). http://mpcb.gov.in/envtdata/demopage1.php
22. Odriozola, J.A., Jimenez, J.D., Rubio, J.M., Pérez, I.M., Ortiz, M.P., Rodrigues, P.R.: Air pollution and mortality in Madrid, Spain: a time-series analysis. Int. Arch. Occup. Environ. Health **71**(8), 543–549 (1998)
23. Patil, D., Thanuja, T.C., Melinamath, B.C.: Air pollution monitoring system using wireless sensor network (WSN). In: Balas, V.E., Sharma, N., Chakrabarti, A. (eds.) Data Management, Analytics and Innovation. AISC, vol. 808, pp. 391–400. Springer, Singapore (2019). https://doi.org/10.1007/978-981-13-1402-5_30
24. Ram, S.S., et al.: A review on air pollution monitoring and management using plants with special reference to foliar dust adsorption and physiological stress responses. Crit. Rev. Environ. Sci. Technol. **45**(23), 2489–2522 (2015)
25. Sathe, Y.V.: Air quality modeling in street canyons of Kolhapur City, Maharashtra, India. Univ. J. Environ. Res. Technol. **2**(2), 97–105 (2004)
26. Sathe, A.J., Desai, V.M., Chate, V.R., Hosamani, S.: Air pollution monitoring & control at foundry clusters in belgaum-a case study. Civ. Environ. Res. **7**(5), 63–69 (2015)
27. Sathe, Y., Ayare, A., Kulkarni, G.: Urban air quality modelling and simulation: a case study of Kolhapur (MS), India. Int. J. Civ. Environ. Eng. **2**(1), 6 (2013)
28. Savale, P.A.: Effect of noise pollution on human being: its prevention and control. J. Environ. Res. Dev. **8**(4), 1026–1036 (2014)
29. Shinde, K.A.: Planning for urbanization in religious tourism destinations: insights from Shirdi, India. Plan. Pract. Res. **32**(2), 132–151 (2017)
30. Yadav, J., Kharat, V., Deshpande, A.: Fuzzy description of air quality using fuzzy inference system with degree of match via computing with words: a case study. Air Q. Atmos. Health **7**(3), 325–334 (2014). https://doi.org/10.1007/s11869-014-0239-x
31. Yadav, J., Kharat, V., Deshpande, A.: Fuzzy-GA modeling in air quality assessment. Environ. Monit. Assess. **187**(4), 1–14 (2015). https://doi.org/10.1007/s10661-015-4351-7
32. Yu, B., Huang, C., Liu, Z., Wang, H., Wang, L.: A chaotic analysis on air pollution index change over past 10 years in Lanzhou, northwest China. Stochast. Environ. Res. Risk Assess. **25**(5), 643–653 (2011)

A Big Data Prediction for Weather Forecast Using Hybrid ARIMA-ANN Time Series Model

Rupali D. Patil[(✉)] and Omprakash S. Jadhav

Dr. Babasaheb Ambedkar, Marathwada University Aurangabad, Aurangabad, India
rupali.stat@gmail.com, drjadhav@gmail.com

Abstract. Big data is nothing but as enormous quantity of data set in which necessitate recent tools to construct probable to take out value starting it by capturing and investigation process. Analytics frequently engage revising past historical data to research possible drifts. Weather is the most critical issue in regular human life. The weather prophecy is the appliance of tools to forecast the weather conditions intended for specified place found with the help of historical and current data as appropriate. Weather forecasting flattering more and more fundamental for industry, agriculturists, farmers, calamity administration to identify with the usual phenomenon. Weather situation is the status of environment at a known period in expressions of weather attributes like rainfall, temperature, sunshine, evaporation, humidity, wind and so on to collect the points. Sensors size as well as speed of information in the entire sensor create the data handing out time overriding and multifaceted. This paper aspires to construct investigative Big Data forecasting structure for weather attributes with the help of hybrid time series model.

Keywords: Big data · Data analysis · Weather forecasting · Hybrid time series model

1 Introduction

Climate prediction is necessary study in science and technology toward guess the situation of the environment intended for particular site as well as moment with gathering recording facts points concerning recent status of the ambiance on known locations. The forecast of weather has confirmed to be very significant and valuable for it is for all time connecting toward the conclusion of administration to help care for the enlargement of farming yield, the caution of cyclone, flood etc. Nevertheless, the situations investigation is regularly to joint through huge size of data, which complete it a considerable difficult challenge and excellent applicant for big data tools [5]. Simply, weather forecasting originates to be support on big data analysis. Weather prediction is good appliance for the big data. Weather predicts sector has begun gathering and investigation enormous quantity of facts. They use several sensor record such as maximum temperature, minimum temperature, wind, sunshine, evaporation, relative humidity at AM and PM and rainfall etc to predict the future planning of organization. While the number of sensors rises the data is converted into huge size and the sensors data have high-speed. There is

© Springer Nature Singapore Pte Ltd. 2021
K. C. Santosh and B. Gawali (Eds.): RTIP2R 2020, CCIS 1380, pp. 291–307, 2021.
https://doi.org/10.1007/978-981-16-0507-9_26

requiring of a scalable analytics devices toward development the enormous quantity of data. Since the forename proposes, Big Data mention toward a vast size of data, other than there is no sufficient in the direction of explains the significance of the thought [4]. The framework of big data is immediately upcoming to survival with have unsure birth. The idiom Big Data appear keen on outlook for earliest time during 1998 into a Silicon Graphics (SGI) slide deck by John Mashey through entitle of Big Data and NextWave of InfraStress. The beginning of the Big Data is suitable on the way to information that we be generating massive size of data each data is a gathering of facts situate so bulky and multifaceted that it turn into complicated to procedure by on-hand database organization tools or conventional data handing out purpose [6]. In this article, we planned big data prediction structure of several climate attributes based on hybrid ARIMA-ANN time series model to producing results with help of R open source software.

The Autoregressive integrated moving average (ARIMA) model is an important forecasting tool in time-series analysis or sometimes ARIMA called Box-Jenkins models. The perfect fitted ARIMA model of all weather parameters depend on the minimum assessment of Akaike information criterion (AIC) and Bayesian information criterion (BIC) performance actions. Box and Jenkins (1976) proposed methodology consist four stages: i) Model recognition; ii) Assessment of model factors iii) Investigative examination for recognized model and iv) Forecasting [7].

Main disadvantage for the ARIMA modelling approach is that the chronological sequences under study are produce from linear process and therefore, no nonlinear patterns are able to capture with the ARIMA model. They can be unsuitable if the fundamental mechanism is nonlinear. In detail, actual humanity organisms are frequently nonlinear. Over the past 20 years, artificial neural networks (ANNs) be introduced as well-organized equipment for time series forecasting. ANNs are nonlinear and be capable of estimated every continuous task to any required precision [8].

The ARIMA and ANN techniques contain get achievement during their individual linear or nonlinear province. The estimate of ARIMA models toward difficult nonlinear trouble as well as ANNs model to liner troubles can exist completely improper as well as too create problem within linear and nonlinear correlation structure [1]. The mixture of the ARIMA and ANN form completed the different linear as well as nonlinear pattern in the climate data. The methodology consists of two stages: 1) At initial stage, ARIMA constructed to predict series data set and 2) At next stage, ANN created using the residuals commencing from ARIMA model.

The objectives of present study are

- To construct ARIMA models for the corresponding all weather parameters.
- To construct ANN models for the corresponding all weather parameters.
- To construct hybrid ARIMA-ANN models for the corresponding all weather parameters.
- To compare the forecasting ARIMA, ANN and hybrid models using forecasting measures.
- To take out the prediction of all weather parameters.

2 Review of Literature

Weather forecasting is recently sensitive area. Several researchers, scientist has been done different model and methods.

Khalid Adam et al. [4] studied recently prediction procedure, methods and handling huge size of weather data sets. They presented the big data analysis structure for weather dataset support on map reduce algorithm.

Ning Yand et al. [5] forecasted the barometric pressures using the recorded data from the considerable location and use a novel regression model. In this model fusion the essential aspects of weather data to increase the precision of guess rate.

Mehdi Khashei and Mehdi Bijari [1], latest technique is planned in order to merge the ANNs through ARIMA in charge near rise above restrictions of conventional mixture technologies and give up extra common with more precise hybrid models. Experiential marks by Canadian Lynx point to facilitate the planned methodology be capable of more useful system in sequence to come together linear and nonlinear models mutually than conventional hybrid methodologies.

G. peter Zhang [3], proposed a mixture of time sequence forecasting model. The linear ARIMA and nonlinear ANN model be combine, target to arrest dissimilar appearance of association within time progression records. Combining model techniques construct forecasting presentation as compare to independent models.

In [9], the researcher set up the assignments that want to predict the probability of rainfall with the help of predictive analysis in Hadoop software. Created form imprisons interaction with a lot of feature in the data to allocate achieve or influence outline for upcoming rainfall forecast with using chronological data. The procedure is in capable way for the huge size of data is able to be healthy process in the big data techniques. The major process in support of the study is classifying the humidity data records using Naive Bayes classifier. The organization plan and the design of average, upper limit and precipitation factor of humidity be completed towards get better so as to extra climate in sequence preserve economically forecast with the support of Naive Bayes in Hadoop construction.

3 Data Source

The data set collected from Water and Land Management Institute (WALMI) for Aurangabad division, Maharashtra state. It contains weather information from January 2006 to December 2017 i.e twelve year data set. This data set involve eight weather attributes like maximum temperature, minimum temperature, relative humidity at AM, relative humidity at PM, wind, sunshine, evaporation, rainfall. All data recorded daily but in present study we choose convert monthly data record. We develop the hybrid ARIMA-ANN time series model for individual eight attributes.

4 Research Methodology

In this article there are several time series forecasting models involve like the autoregressive (AR), moving average (MA), and ARIMA are various commonly predictable statistical forecasting representations which forecast view description of a time series on the establishment of several linear roles of historical values and white noise circumstances and also to construct the nonlinear models. Zhang [3] have realistically joint together ARIMA and ANN models in order to significantly raise the prediction precision.

4.1 Hybrid Time Series Model

The ARIMA and ANN models proposed successfully within their individual linear or nonlinear provinces. Practically, ARIMA techniques towards the multifaceted nonlinear trouble may not be possibly satisfactory. Alternatively, linear trouble of data set the ANNs model fails the result. There is so hard to entirely identify features of records set within actual difficulty, hybrid attitude to have mutually linear and nonlinear ability exist to superior approach used for forecasting power expenditure. Adding the two dissimilar forms with altered feature of fundamental patterns can be captured.

It possibly will exist useful to regard as weather time sequence to be collected a linear autocorrelation arrangement and a nonlinear element i.e.

$$y_t = L_t + N_t \tag{1}$$

Where L_t and N_t indicate the linear and nonlinear element correspondingly. Both of these two parameters include being approximate commencing the period sequence data. Foremost ARIMA methods useful for the linear element and their residuals as of the linear form determination enclose just the nonlinear association. Suppose e_t indicate the residuals by period t beginning the linear form, after that:

$$e_t = y_t - \hat{L}_t \tag{2}$$

Where $\hat{L}_t$ is predicted cost from ARIMA model by period t. The investigative verify of the residuals is significant towards decide the sufficiency of the ARIMA techniques. An ARIMA model is not tolerable but convenient at rest linear correlation structures absent inside the residuals. Nevertheless, investigation confirm of the residuals be incapable to identify nonlinear outline in the period sequence data. For this reason, yet if the residuals go by the indicative ensure and the form is a sufficient one, the model can silent not be enough in that nonlinear relationships have not been suitably modelled. Important nonlinear prototype inside the residuals will specify the restriction of the ARIMA. Consequently, the residuals are able to model with help of ANNs to find out nonlinear relationships. Through n enter neurons; the ANN mould used for the residuals will be present:

$$e_t = f(e_{t-1}, e_{t-2}, \ldots, e_{t-n}) + \varepsilon_t \tag{3}$$

Let f be a nonlinear assignment indomitable through the neural system and ε_t is the random inaccuracy. The precise model of acknowledgment is necessary. Designate they guess from above equation, as $\hat{N}_t$ then the dual prediction will be at this point as:

$$\hat{y}_t = \hat{L}_t + \hat{N}_t \tag{4}$$

The processes of the hybrid structure involve the two steps. At prime phase, an ARIMA model be used towards create linear period sequence data set and secondly, a neural network be constructed with the help of residuals commencing the ARIMA mould. Although the ARIMA model unable to build up the nonlinear agreement of the records, the residuals of linear form determination clutch in sequence as look upon the nonlinearity. The grades since the neural system are capable to use as prediction of the error conditions in favour of the ARIMA model. The hybrid method builds up the individual characteristic and power of ARIMA form and ANN mould within influential dissimilar prototype Hence, it is beneficial towards mould linear and nonlinear prototype independently through by disparate form and after that join guess towards acquire healthier the generally modelling along with forecasting appearance [2, 3].

5 Empirical Results

The weather data situate composed from the weather stations comprises the changed statistical features. They have been at length premeditated in the statistical and also in the neural network review. The linear and nonlinear draft contain immediately establishment for this weather data set, yet if more or less nonlinearities have been situate up in this succession. Weather data set engage the maximum temperature, minimum temperature, relative humidity at AM, relative humidity at PM, wind, evaporation, sunshine, rainfall explain the stationarity, seasonality as well as less or more nonlinearity using graphical demonstration (Figs. 1, 2, 3, 4, 5, 6, 7 and 8):

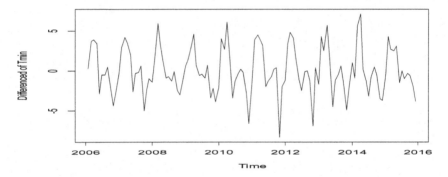

Fig. 1. Time series plot of maximum temperature

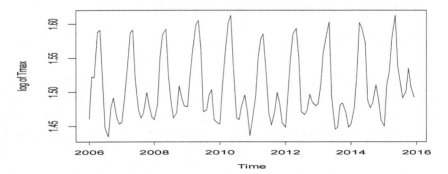

Fig. 2. Time series plot of minimum temperature

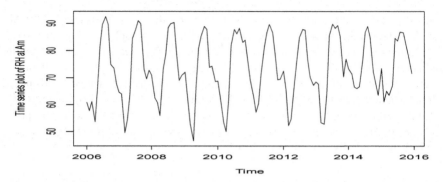

Fig. 3. Time series plot of relative humidity at AM

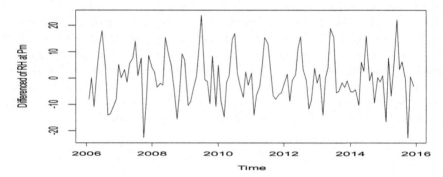

Fig. 4. Time series plot of relative humidity at PM

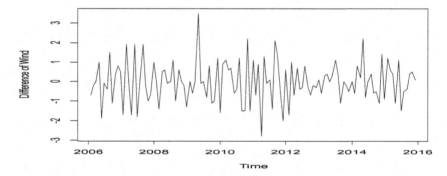

Fig. 5. Time series plot of wind

The climate succession surround the altered the number of constraint interrelated to weather current for each year in WALMI of Aurangabad city. The data points have 144 periods, equivalent to the period 2006–2017. It has to be broadly analysed in the period progression review by a core lying on the nonlinear modelling. The above diagrammatical

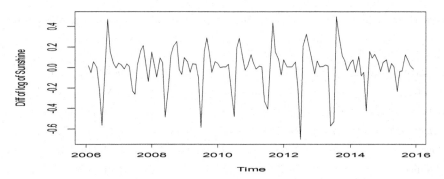

Fig. 6. Time series plot of sunshine

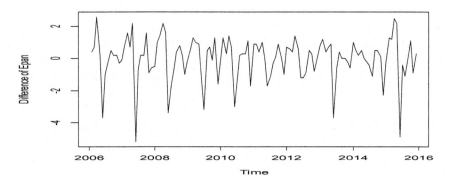

Fig. 7. Time series plot of evaporation

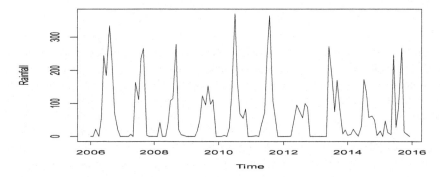

Fig. 8. Time series plot of rainfall

demonstration of several parameters of weather in which the first difference as well as log formats (with the base 10) of the points be use in modelling and forecasting procedure.

After the graphically representation towards locate out the ARIMA and NNAR (neural network autoregressive) model of weather attributes as given below table.

Table 1. Forecasting model comparisons for weather parameter with minimum RMSE measures

Weather Parameters	ARIMA model	ANN model
Max Temp	ARIMA (1, 0, 0) (1, 0, 0) [12]	NNAR (20, 1, 10) [12]
Min Temp	ARIMA (1, 0, 0) (1, 0, 0) [12]	NNAR (1, 1, 2) [12]
Relative humidity at AM	ARIMA (1, 0, 0) (1, 0, 0) [12]	NNAR (13, 1, 7) [12]
Relative humidity at PM	ARIMA (1, 1, 0) (1, 0, 0) [12]	NNAR (2, 1, 2) [12]
Wind	ARIMA (1, 1, 1) (2, 0, 0) [12]	NNAR (16, 1, 8)
Sunshine	ARIMA (2, 0, 4)	NNAR (14, 1, 8) [12]
Evaporation	ARIMA (1, 0, 0) (2, 0, 0)	NNAR (1, 1, 2) [12]
Rainfall	ARIMA (1, 1, 1) (2, 0, 0) [12]	NNAR (18, 1, 8) [12]

The above Table 1 shows the ARIMA and neural network of residual ARIMA model i.e neural network autoregressive model evaluated at minimum value of prediction performance measures like root mean square error. After that table illustrate the combination of both models.

Table 2. Forecasting model comparison for weather parameter with RMSE measures

Models	Tmax	Tmin	Rha	Rhp	Wind	Sunshine	Epan	Rainfall
ARIMA	2.011	1.54	4.83	5.82	0.918	1.843	1.675	18.36
ANN	1.882	1.317	4.71	5.81	0.1517	1.467	1.393	16.76
Hybrid	1.46	1.07	1.67	3.59	0.90	1.17	1.32	11.25

In this paper, the ARIMA, ANN and Hybrid time series model of individual all attribute calculated by help of R programming command and also the neural network autoregressive model built using residual of ARIMA. The root mean squared errors are selected for all attribute models to check the forecasting accuracy measures. The second Table 2 gives the prediction frame result for the weather parameters data set. An autoregressive model of all data set has been set up sufficient moderator by the residual analysis. Results table represent the after use the ANN model be able to get better the prediction accurateness over the ARIMA model of same data set. Now propose to neither the neural net nor the ARIMA mould confine each individual of the prototypes into the facts situate. The outcomes of hybrid model demonstrate so as to with merge two models jointly, in general prediction inaccuracy able to considerably reduced not including wind series where ANN is somewhat improved. The judgment linking the real value and estimate value for four year out of sample is give below graphs (Figs. 9, 10, 11, 12, 13, 14, 15, 16, 17, 18, 19, 20, 21, 22, 23 and 24):

In this paper, result observe the long term forecasting (12 years), together neural set-up and hybrid form be greatly superior into precision as compare the ARIMA mould. For longer period progression, the ANN representation presents equivalent presentation

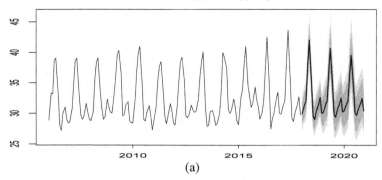

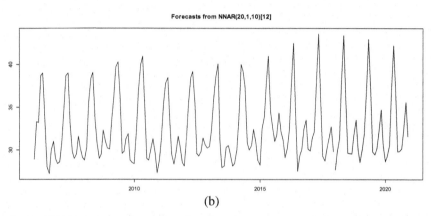

Fig. 9. (a) ARIMA forecasts time series plot of maximum temperature. (b) ANN forecasts time series plot of maximum temperature

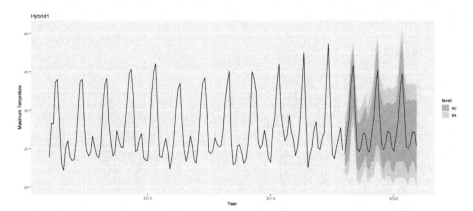

Fig. 10. Hybrid ARIMA-ANN prediction time series plot of maximum temperature

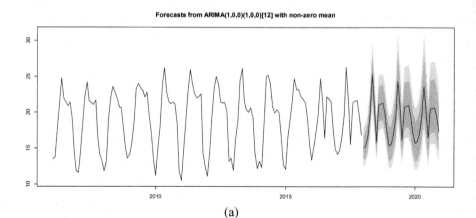

(a)

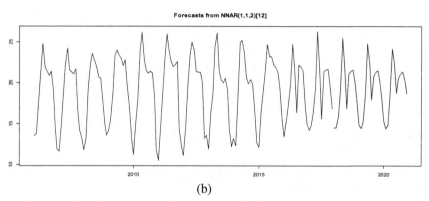

(b)

Fig. 11. (a) ARIMA forecasts time series plot of minimum temperature. (b) ANN forecasts time series plot of minimum temperature

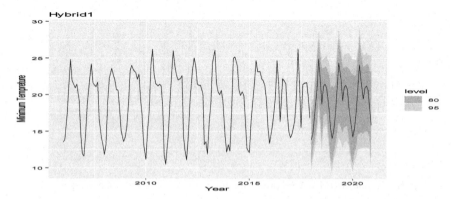

Fig. 12. Hybrid ARIMA-ANN prediction time series plot of minimum temperature

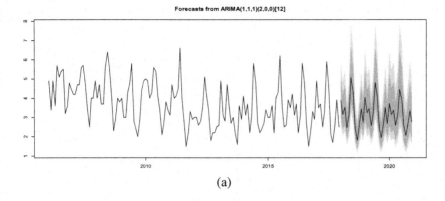

Forecasts from ARIMA(1,1,1)(2,0,0)[12]

(a)

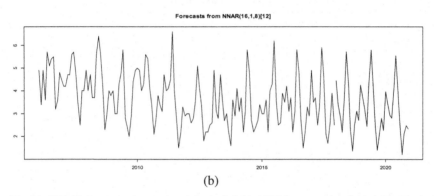

Forecasts from NNAR(16,1,8)[12]

(b)

Fig. 13. (a) ARIMA forecasts time series plot of wind (b) ANN forecasts time series plot of wind

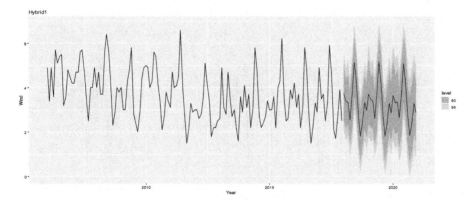

Fig. 14. Hybrid prediction of wind time series plot

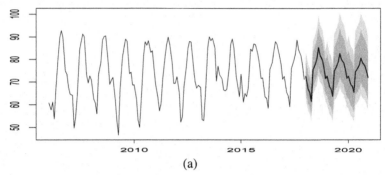

(a)

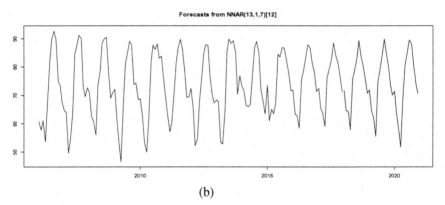

(b)

Fig. 15. (a) ARIMA forecasts time series plot of relative humidity at AM (b) ANN forecasts time series plot of relative humidity at AM

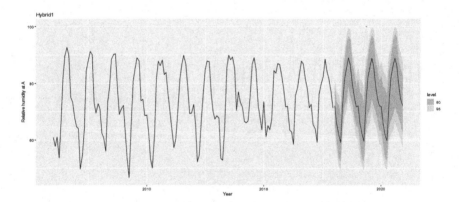

Fig. 16. Hybrid ARIMA-ANN prediction of time series plot of relative humidity at AM

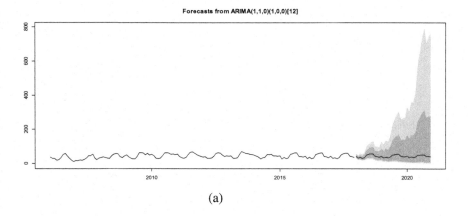

(a)

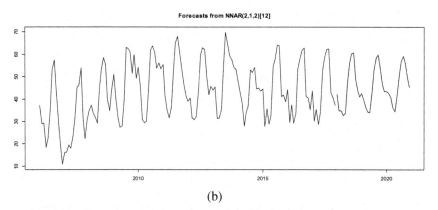

(b)

Fig. 17. (a) ARIMA forecasts time series plot of relative humidity at PM (b) ANN forecasts time series plot of relative humidity at PM

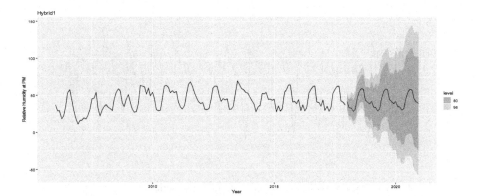

Fig. 18. Hybrid ARIMA-ANN prediction of relative humidity at PM

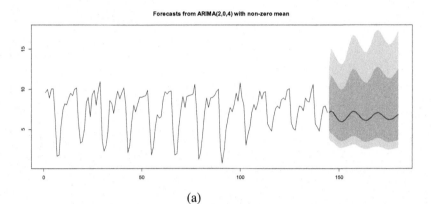

(a)

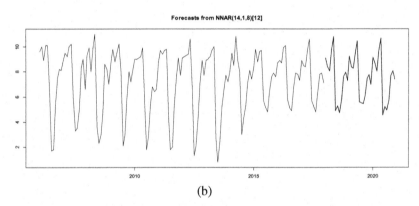

(b)

Fig. 19. (a) ARIMA time series plot of sunshine (b) ANN time series plot of sunshine

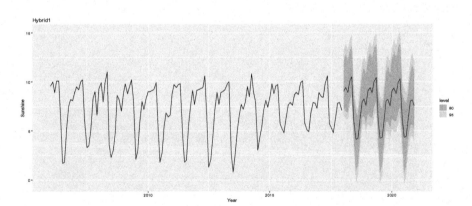

Fig. 20. Hybrid ARIMA-ANN prediction of time series plot of sunshine

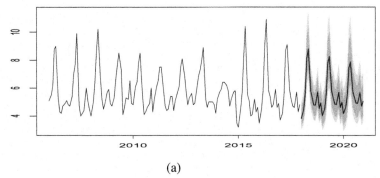

(a)

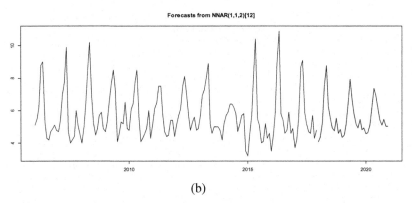

(b)

Fig. 21. (a) ARIMA forecasts time series plot of evaporation (b) ANN forecasts time series plot of evaporation

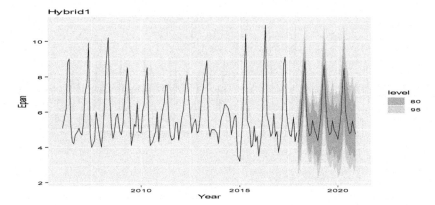

Fig. 22. Hybrid ARIMA-ANN prediction of evaporation

Forecasts from ARIMA(1,1,1)(2,0,0)[12]

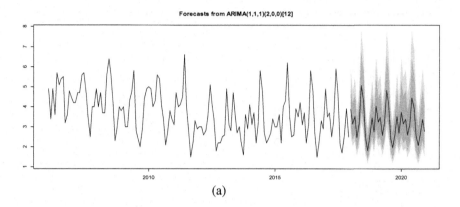

(a)

Forecasts from NNAR(16,1,8)[12]

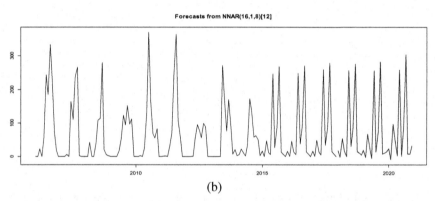

(b)

Fig. 23. (a) ARIMA time series plot of rainfall (b) ANN time series plot of rainfall

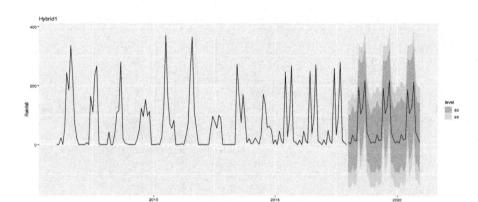

Fig. 24. Hybrid ARIMA-ANN prediction of time series plot of rainfall

towards the ARIMA techniques. The hybrid model performance together ARIMA and ANN model again and again diagonally eight altered weather attributes and by model performance inaccuracy measures even though the development for longer perspective is not extremely inspiring.

6 Conclusion

In study, promulgation big data analysis is used for predicting the weather attributes based on the hybrid ARIMA-ANN time series model to the big data. We proposed to take a combination of time sequence forecasting model. The linear ARIMA model and nonlinear ANN model are used to combine, aim to confine the altered relationship of weather attributes in the moment sequence data. The hybrid model gives better exceptional strong point of ARIMA and ANN within linear and nonlinear modelling. In support of the difficult situation, together linear and nonlinear correlation structures, the mixture methods can be helpful way to get better forecasting presentation. The experimental marks of all weather data sets evidently propose that the hybrid model is capable to do better than every factor model help in segregation.

Acknowledgement. The authors are appreciative to Guide Omprakash S. Jadhav and all staff of Department of Statistics, Dr. Babasaheb Ambedkar Marathwada University Aurangabad for valuable guidance to the work. We also express gratitude to Water and Land Management Institute (WALMI) Aurangabad given that the monthly total twelve year eight parameters data set used in the study.

References

1. Bijari, M., Khashei, M.: A novel hybridization of artificial neural networks and ARIMA models for time series forecasting. Appl. Soft Comput. **11**(2), 2664–2675 (2011)
2. Babu, C.N., Reddy, B.E.: Performance comparison of four new ARIMA-ANN prediction models on internet traffic data. J. Telecommun. Inf. Technol. **1**, 67–75 (2015)
3. Zhang, G.P.: Time series forecasting using a hybrid ARIMA and neural network model. Neurocomputing **50**, 159–175 (2003)
4. Ismail, K.A., Majid, M.A., Zain, J.M., Bakar, N.A.A.: Big data prediction framework for weather Temperature based on MapReduce algorithm. In: 2016 IEEE Conference on Open Systems (ICOS), pp. 13–17 (2016)
5. Yang, N., Westfall, L., Dalvi, P.: A weather prediction model with big data. In: Proceedings of Student-Faculty Research Day, CSIS, pp. 1–7. Pace University (2018)
6. Patil, R.D., Jadhav, O.S.: Some contribution of statistical techniques in big data: a review. Int. J. Recent Innov. Trends Comput. Commun. **4**(4), 293–303 (2016)
7. Patil, R.D., Jadhav, O.S.: Predictive modelling of rainfall data for aurangabad region, by using ARIMA method. Int. J. Eng. Technol. (UAE) **7**(4.10), 1085–1088 (2018)
8. Patil, R.D., Jadhav, O.S.: Predictive modelling of weather parameters by artificial neural network approach. Water Energy Int. **61**(9), 60–63 (2018)
9. Shakila, S., Sunil, N., Pintukumar, Y., Jobin, T.: Weather prediction: a novel approach for measuring and analyzing weather data. In: International Conference on I-SMAC (IoT in Social, Mobile, Analytics and Cloud), pp. 414–417 (2017)

Automatic Detection of Riots Using Deep Learning

Mayur K. Jadhav[✉] and V. A. Chakkarwar

CSE Department, Government College of Engineering, Aurangabad, Aurangabad, India
mj8055x@gmail.com, vrush.a143@gmail.com

Abstract. Riot like situations styles serious consequences on societal and individual security and a simple primary cautioning of any fierce, vehement, vicious, force-full or violent movement could significantly condense these dangers. At present, there are oodles of video surveillance kits applied in civic places, such as bus-stations, highways, airports, Signal-squares, crossings, and railway_stations. This effort focuses on the challenging task of detecting violent situations in video-tapes & aims to propose a fangled way that could automatically distinguish violent behaviors by resources of computer vision methods. For our system, the primary motive is to detect furious activities from either video_streams or pre-recorded video-clips. We take a proportion of videotapes & we train those precise sequences as violent/non-violent situations & once we have a model ready, we deploy for example on intelligent surveillance camera, any action which is close to this precise entity would be classified as violent situation and we can direct an alarm/warning back to the control-room for further necessary steps with highest possible accuracy.

Keywords: Neural networks · Deep learning · Image processing · Riots detection

1 Introduction

1.1 Introduction to the Concept

We stand alive in a digital universe, encircled by electronic devices all over. These devices are designed to assist humans in carrying various tasks easily and efficiently. Surveillance cameras are broadly used and existing all over the world with persistent supervision by humans to check for any anomalies, the main problem ascends with the human part of this, with humanoid supervision we may gain human error along with manipulation possibilities & also the need of a particular experienced human-being in the first place. According to a survey done by British_Security Industry_Authority (BSIA) [2], the total quantity of CCTV cameras in India could be as high as one for every 51 people. With these numbers ever increasing, the human workforce is clearly inadequate to analyze these videos. Even though CCTVs are very useful for analyzing a scene after an event has happened, they are rarely used to detect or predict events. Most of the surveillance videos can be subdivided into 2 categories:

K. C. Santosh and B. Gawali (Eds.): RTIP2R 2020, CCIS 1380, pp. 308–317, 2021.
https://doi.org/10.1007/978-981-16-0507-9_27

A. Involving humans - for e.g. classrooms, footpaths, hallways, shops, road crossings etc.
B. Not involving humans - for e.g. highways, parking lots, industries

In this work, we will solely focus on videos involving humans. Our system proposes the detection of violence in a scene gained from surveillance videotape, as these videos do not comprise any audio tracks the system only can rely on visual features. The idea is to detect crowd-based violence & with crowd arises the issue of too much motion & hence we terminate the use of high-level motion features & analysis & as an alternative, we dive into changes observed in low level features for classification. Short frame-sequences are used to classify the videotapes two ways using a deep learning model. We have used CNN, RNN along with Long Short-Term-storage memory (LSTM) in different combinations and also various other techniques that eventually made our unique system validate its action detection techniques with good efficiency. The videotapes for experiments are obtained from an annotated public database used in a similar project as ours Hassner and Kliper-Gross [29] as well as from other social media resources such as YouTube for local videos.

2 Past Related Work

Violence detection is subtask of action recognition can be frame-based or interest-point based, in situation of motion-based interest-points the tricky problematic state arises when there are too few interest-points or like in the cases of crowds too much motion bag of words approach fails immensely. The frame-based method is efficient but uses a search-based approach which is not practical (Too slow) for real time detection. Liu et al. [2009] Dollar et al. [26] Boiman and Irani [24] proposed an approach that involved categorizing videos as violent by analyzing sudden changes in videos. Hendel et al. [27] defined a probabilistic method to detect sudden changes by using space-time tubes containing an object moving in the scene. This method is known to under-perform with crowd videos. Another approach is to use dynamic features produced by a stochastic process which are stationary in space & time but crowds are not stationary but recently local binary patterns (LBP) have been confirmed to be fairly effective & efficient. Crook et al. [25] Zhao and Pietikainen [30] Hassner, Yossi & Klipper-Gross T. Hassner & Kliper-Gross [29] proposed a unique method for riots detection using their unique feature descriptor called ViF (Violent Flows). They classified surveillance clips as violent/non-violent using ViF-descriptors & Support-Vector-Machines (SVM). In our opinion, their hard-work is by far the best when it comes to making predictions in real time & we strategy to originate motivation, incentive & inspiration from their efforts in our project. Most recently, some deep learning based methods have been discovered in order to recognize actions & activities [18, 24, 29]. Deng et al. projected a deep model [18] to capture distinct actions, pairwise interactions, & group activities. In one more work [18], Deng et al. first estimate the distinct & scene activities which are complementary refined by means of some efficient message_passing algorithm under an outlined framework of a recurrent neural network. In [29], the authors projected a two-staged LSTM model where the first stage captures distinct temporal dynamics trailed by scene activity acknowledgement based on combined discrete information. Furthermore, the current approaches attention on scene activity acknowledgement & overlook the fact that numerous groups with diverse actions are present in the videos. Group level infor- mation can be employed for high-level claims such as irregular activity detection & is significant to understand the scene in its completeness. We shape upon our group detector and detect group-activities as well, sideways with scene activities.

3   The Dataset

Creating a good dataset for group and scene activity is a challenging job, since annota- tions have to be done at various levels. The dataset that is used is an annotated dataset that is a mixture of surveillance data & other in the wild videos acquired from YouTube.

Fig. 1. Non-violent local video dataset screens (Color figure online)

The complete number of videos is about 1230 with half of them annotated as violent & other as non-violent as seen in Fig. 1. The tiniest video is only of approximately 1 s in length & the longest duration length is of 6.52 s with an average duration of 3.6 s vindicating our method to work with a short numeral of frames. The videotapes are fragmented into 5 dissimilar groupings each exhibiting some type of crowd situation whether a sporting or other social gathering with many people with half displaying acts of violence & the other half displaying normal behavior. As our idea is to detect riot like behavior in crowds & perform actions to stop it through surveillance cameras & other forms of monitoring. A rather in-depth motive is to understand crowd behavior from image data analysis. The actual data is in these videos & our neural model is then fed with those images that are the specific frames extracted from those video data with almost a total image count of about 220000 images approximate with 120000 non violent & 100000 violent marked images in separate folders marked as labels before pre-processing comes-in action. The ratio of violent to nonviolent data points is about 6:5 which is least mildly biased towards the violent data. The training: testing split considered is well thought out & is 80:20.

4 Video and Camera

We have also tested the system with live video input from a usb-camera. There are numerous settings which can vary across surveillance video-camera models, the total number of cameras, video resolution, camera motion, the location of recording, proximity to the scene, crowd density & presence of objects like cars to list a few. Before going any further, it's critical to mention all the types of videos we analyzed along with all settings, hence only the settings with best output is considered in this research paper.

5 Approach

5.1 Preprocessing

The initialization part of this approach is to use the video data set as several images. The reason behind it is that the extreme features that are used, are not temporal which that is, the features are a lot suitable for images also the other reason is of data, we begin with a modest number of videos, but converting them to images would let us work with a very rigorous dataset & help the model generalize better. To achieve this OpenCV was used with python scripting & each video was converted into many frames. An advantage that comes along with using images instead of videos is the discrepancy in the length of the videos which if used would have needed normalization that is converting each video to the same length as CNN requires a consistent size of the feature vector. The second step is to select our features from the several images obtained, after contemplating with histogram of orientations which are some spatial features using descriptors like SIFT, but after experimentation we came to the conclusion that using orientation-based features will surely give bad results as the data at hand contain drastic actions which would rattle the descriptors & the number of interest points may be several to very few in number. Thus, we ultimately ended up by way of choosing the extreme intensities of the snap shots as one of our aspects for the neural_network. The sequential subsequent step is to pre_process the information that is extracted for the Convolutional_neural_network being used in addition all down the process. Initially, right here we used a super_vectorized version of almost all photographs are of a unique size (320_x_240) also which used to be humongous massive alongside with our tiny dataset & the community when the training dropped into the difficulties of some memory problems on a computer with infrequently sufficient or fairly precise specifications. Thus, because of it, we made the choice of skewing our information via hand, by way of converting each picture used to a size of (224_x_224). This was firstly accomplished in Matlab & the photos saved for in addition processing. But later on we also carried out on the go with some environment friendly video clipping python programs developed for this purpose, intentionally. Also later the device was upgraded to 32 Gb memory.

5.2   Architecture, Explanation and Workflow

The proposed architecture of the network is displayed in Fig. 2. It has been displayed that the nearby transient elements that ought to be received from the optical_flow are additionally vital in addition to adding the LSTM (which is supposed to extract standard brief features) after the CNN[14]. It has additionally been said that the virtue of optical_flow is due to its appearance invariance as nicely as its accuracy at obstacles and at small displacements[13]. Therefore, in this work, by taking two video_frames as input, the impact of optical_flow must be mimicked. Before finalizing on this architecture, we experimented with including greater FC layers, however more layers resulted in drop of education accuracy. The pre-trained CNN methods the 2 input frames. The first neural community is a Convolutional neural network aimed at extracting high-level photograph facets and lowering input complexity. It makes use of sixteen filters of 2×2 size. The output of these filters was once pressured to be saved the same as the input by means of padding the borders before convolution. Output from this Convolutional_layer was once surpassed through relu_activation & into the max-pooling layer. We use of a pre-trained DarkNet mannequin skilled on the massive visual detection task ImageNet dataset. The two frame outputs of the pre-trained model's backside layer are blended in the very remaining channel and then fed into the extra-additional CNN (labeled in our Fig. 1 by orange color).

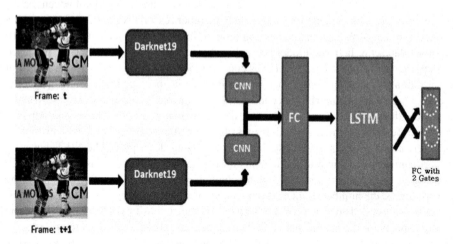

Fig. 2. Proposed architecture

Since the output results from the bottom-back most layers are considered to be the required low-level features, in the end by means of comparing the 2 frames function map, the additional CNN should learn both the local motion features and the look invariant features. The two frame outputs from the pre-trained network's pinnacle layer are additionally concatenated and fed into the other additional CNN to compare the two frames' high-level features.

In order to analyze the customary brief features, the outputs from the two additional CNN are then concatenated and passed to an entirely joined layer and the LSTM cell.

Lastly, the LSTM cell phone outputs are categorized via an utterly joined layer containing two neurons representing the two categories (riots and non-riots), respectively. The blue_colored_layers are pre-trained on the ImageNet dataset and also frozen in the course of its training. On the video-clip dataset, the layers marked via the light-orange color are trained. Due to its exact-accuracy on ImageNet and the stated actual time efficiency, Darknet19 [31] implements the pre-trained model. Since the Darknet19 already includes 19 convolution layers, the extra CNN is applied with the aid of the residual_layers[28] to omit the degradation difficulty.

If we did not use any max-pooling layer, the training accuracy would increase but testing accuracy would go down. We used one batch normalizer between the first pooling layer & the second Convolutional layer. Batch normalizer makes sure that the input weights & bias to the next layer have 0 mean & unit variance. The primary use of batch normalization is to speed up the training process by squashing the range of possible values for weights & bias to a normalized range. This however introduces noise & lowers training accuracy. Normalization can help reduce over fitting. In our case, our training accuracy was already over 99% & we could do with some normalization to reduce over fitting. Testing accuracy with & without batch normalization had a difference of about 2% with the model lacking batch normalization having lower accuracy of the two. Finally, we used a dropout layer with a dropout value of about 0.5. Dropout works by randomly switching a certain proportion of neurons on & the rest off by multiplying by either a 1 or a 0. This process is known to introduce multiplicative noise in the training phase. It's again used to combat over-fitting & helps improve testing accuracy. Leaky Rectified Linear Unit (i.e. Leaky ReLu) standard equations for our LSTM model are as follows:

$$i_t = \sigma\left(w_x^i * I_t + w_h^i * h_{t-1} + b^i\right) \tag{1}$$

$$f_t = \sigma\left(w_x^f * I_t + w_h^f * h_{t-1} + b^f\right) \tag{2}$$

$$\tilde{c}_t = tanh\left(w_x^{\tilde{c}} * I_t + w_h^{\tilde{c}} * h_{t-1} + b^{\tilde{c}}\right) \tag{3}$$

$$c_t = \tilde{c}_t \odot i_t + c_{t-1} \odot f_t \tag{4}$$

$$o_t = \sigma\left(w_x^o * I_t + w_h^o * h_{t-1} + b^o\right) \tag{5}$$

$$h_t = o_t \odot tanh(c_t) \tag{6}$$

In the above equations, '*' represents convolution operation & '$\odot$' represents the Hadamard product. The hidden state ht, the memory cell ct & the gate activations it, ft & ot are all 3D tensors in the case of LSTM.

5.3 Experiment

There are 7 different versions for this model & the gained results for the successful experiments are mentioned here, for our versions 1 & 2 the resulting testing accuracy is very bad hence their confusion matrix is not discussed. For version three, the number of epochs was set to 30 & a drop rate of 0.2 was used with no batch normalization which gave a classification rate of 78% on testing data. The true positives for violence data is far fewer than the non-violence positives, with great accuracy achieved for non-violent testing data.

The next version which is version no. 4 gave us extremely good satisfying results with a super classification rate of 82.75% where the selected number of regular epochs were equal to 100 only with a dropout rate of 0.5 & no batch normalization implemented. The violence data in this case gave extremely good results while the results for non-violence data fell down a bit.

Version 4, 5 and 6 gave satisfactory results for the task at hand but we wanted to experiment with batch normalization, CNN+LSTM, CNN+RNN & thus implemented that for version 7 giving us the best results thus far.

6   Result

At the end-part of this research, some of the most accurate, extremely handy and efficient preferences have been used from the range of preferences handy in each part. The model with fine result was version 5 which gave a classification price of 98.52% which will go around the surrounding neighborhood of values based on the information sequence selected as a random shuffle is carried out to gain a more grounded result. The training accuracy came to about 98.8% which may suggest the model to be over fitting but as the number of data samples are less comparatively over fitting seemed necessary, while using an even larger data set, over fitting will be unnecessary. Here, we can say that for the training portion the model over fits with zero false positives for violent_data & nominal false negatives for some of the non-violent data. The final result can be seen in Fig. 3 as shown in below:

Fig. 3. Output screen of analyzed video

Table 1. Comparison between two proposed models.

Model	Accuracy with violent-flows dataset	Accuracy with our dataset
MoSIFT + KDE+ Sparse coding	89.05+3.26%	91.33%
Three streams + LSTM	93.92%	96.29%
CNN only	92%	94%
Proposed model CNN+LSTM	97+1.33%	98+0.55%

In Table 1, we get to see that CNN model offers less accuracy than CNN + LSTM. CNN solely considers the latest input whilst the proposed model considers the latest input along with the earlier obtained inputs. Because of its internal storage, it could memorize preceding inputs.

RNN also handles sequential information and has a short term storage. However, as we are using LSTM, it has a Long_Short_Term storage. Because of LSTM, training takes less time and also has excessive accuracy. Furthermore it solves the challenge of gradients disappearing.

7 Conclusion and Future Work

Crowd visual analysis is an interesting & newly emerging technical field of computer_vision & with increasing amounts of surveillance cameras set up all over the world, detection of crowd behavior using this type of data is very crucial. The task accomplished here surpasses many research projects in the same domain, but as most of this system is modelled for real-time feedback this result may be not comparable. In conclusion, we can positively say that a high precision riot detection system was implemented using deep learning concepts like Convolutional neural network on video data. The proposed network architecture uses a pre-trained model on ImageNet (Hybrid Darknet19) dataset which also extracts widely wide-spread and local temporal features. CNN is successfully used for frame level feature extraction. The basic idea here is to extend these outputs of the experiment conducted further & achieve a more realistic & better accuracy by tweaking hyper parameters & also by experimenting with our network layer architecture. In terms of future work, there is scope to expand the model to incorporate functionalities with real-time data with implementations of spatial-temporal features to achieve a more functional system. Also, one other thing that can also be usually done is to develop the model into a windows or IOS system for law enforcement departments with real-time machine learning based monitoring of large crowds specifically it would prove very useful for countries with huge populations like India or China. Lastly, future research can be invested in expanding the domain of action detection from crowds & extend it to more diverse actions other than just violence & non-violence detection. In conclusion, we can positively say that a high precision violence & non-violence system was implemented using deep learning concepts like convolutional neural network on video data. We created a machine with an excessive accuracy in detecting furious activities from pre-recorded video-clips as properly as from live input from usb-camera. To discover riots in two real-time frame by frame, we wanted higher processing speed. With similar development & research going about in the area of crowd behavior analysis the system will only get better. In future, we plan to design an online front-end utility where we ought to add video-clips to detect furious activities. Furthermore, we are planning to take our research into subsequent steps via detecting suspicious two tasks in real-time. We will attempt to connect this prototype with CCTV monitoring cameras and a hardware system with alarm so that it ought to discover suspicious projects or crook two tasks. The second the device detects a suspicious or crook project it ought to set off an alarm or alert the safety in-charge or guards.

References

1. Aggarwal, C.C.: A human-computer interactive method for projected clustering. IEEE Trans. Knowl. Data Eng. **16**(4), 448–460 (2004). https://doi.org/10.1109/tkde.2004.1269669. ISSN 1041-4347
2. Barrett, D.: One surveillance camera for every 11 people in Britain, says CCTV survey (2013). http://www.telegraph.co.uk/technology/10172298/Onesurveillance-camera-for-every-11-people-in-Britain-says-CCTV-survey.html
3. Bazzani, L., et al.: Analyzing groups: a social signaling perspective. In: Shan, C., Porikli, F., Xiang, T., Gong, S. (eds.) Video Analytics for Business Intelligence, vol. 409, pp. 271–305. Springer, Heidelberg (2012). https://doi.org/10.1007/978-3-642-28598-1_9
4. Chen, C., Heili, A., Odobez, J.M.: A joint estimation of head and body orientation cues in surveillance video. In: 2011 IEEE International Conference on Computer Vision Workshops (ICCV Workshops), pp. 860–867 (2011). https://doi.org/10.1109/iccvw.2011.6130342
5. Choi, W., Savarese, S.: A unified framework for multi-target tracking and collective activity recognition. In: Fitzgibbon, A., Lazebnik, S., Perona, P., Sato, Y., Schmid, C. (eds.) ECCV 2012. LNCS, vol. 7575, pp. 215–230. Springer, Heidelberg (2012). https://doi.org/10.1007/978-3-642-33765-9_16
6. Choi, W., Savarese, S.: A unified framework for multi-target tracking and collective activity recognition. In: ECCV (2012). http://www-personal.umich.edu/~wgchoi/eccv12/wongun_eccv12.html
7. Choi, W., Shahid, K., Savarese, S.: Learning context for collective activity recognition. In: 2011 IEEE Conference on Computer Vision and Pattern Recognition (CVPR), pp. 3273–3280. IEEE (2011)
8. Choi, W., Shahid, K., Savarese, S.: What are they doing?: collective activity classification using spatio-temporal relationship among people. In: 2009 IEEE 12th International Conference on Computer Vision Workshops (ICCV Workshops), pp. 1282–1289. IEEE (2009)
9. Chollet, F.: Keras (2015). https://github.com/fchollet/keras
10. Cristani, M., et al.: Social interaction discovery by statistical analysis of Formations. In: Proceedings of the British Machine Vision Conference, pp. 23.1–23.12. BMVA Press (2011). ISBN 1-901725-43-X
11. Dalal, N., Triggs, B.: Histograms of oriented gradients for human detection. In: 2005 IEEE Computer Society Conference on Computer Vision and Pattern Recognition (CVPR 2005) (2005)
12. Deng, Z., et al.: Deep structured models for group activity recognition. arXiv preprint arXiv: 1506.04191 (2015)

13. Deng, Z., et al.: Structure inference machines: recurrent neural networks for analyzing relations in group activity recognition. In: Proceedings of the IEEE Conference on Computer Vision and Pattern Recognition, pp. 4772–4781 (2016)
14. Dollár, P.: Piotr's computer vision matlab toolbox (PMT). https://github.com/pdollar/toolbox
15. Dollár, P., et al.: Pedestrian detection: an evaluation of the state of the art. PAMI **34**, 743–761 (2012)
16. Ester, M., et al.: A density-based algorithm for discovering clusters in large spatial databases with noise. In: KDD, vol. 96, no. 34, pp. 226–231 (1996)
17. Ge, W., Collins, R.T., Ruback, R.B.: Vision-based analysis of small groups in pedestrian crowds. IEEE Trans. Pattern Anal. Mach. Intell. **34**(5), 1003–1016 (2012)
18. Hajimirsadeghi, H., et al.: Visual recognition by counting instances: a multiinstance cardinality potential kernel. In: Proceedings of the IEEE Conference on Computer Vision and Pattern Recognition, pp. 2596–2605 (2015)
19. Hall, D., Perona, P.: Fine-grained classification of pedestrians in video: benchmark and state of the art. CoRR abs/1605.06177 (2016)
20. He, K., et al.: Deep residual learning for image recognition. CoRR abs/1512.03385 (2015). http://arxiv.org/abs/1512.03385
21. Hornik, K.: Approximation capabilities of multilayer feedforward networks. In: neural Netw., vol. 4, no. 2, , pp. 251–257 (1991). ISSN 0893-6080. https://doi.org/10.1016/0893-608 0(91)90009-t
22. Hosang, J.H., et al.: Taking a deeper look at pedestrians. CoRR abs/1501.05790 (2015). http://arxiv.org/abs/1501.05790
23. Ibrahim, M.S., et al.: A hierarchical deep temporal model for group activity recognition. In: Proceedings of the IEEE Conference on Computer Vision and Pattern Recognition, pp. 1971–1980 (2016)
24. Boiman, O., Irani, M.: Detecting irregularities in images and in video. In: Tenth IEEE International Conference on Computer Vision (ICCV 2005), vol. 1, pp. 462–469, October 2005. https://doi.org/10.1109/iccv.2005.70
25. Crook, P.A., Kellokumpu, V., Zhao, G., Pietikainen, M.: Human activity recognition using a dynamic texture based method. In: Proceedings of the British Machine Vision Conference, pp. 88.1–88.10. BMVA Press (2008)
26. Dollar, P., Rabaud, V., Cottrell, G., Belongie, S.: Behavior recognition via sparse spatio-temporal features. In: 2005 IEEE International Workshop on Visual Surveillance and Performance Evaluation of Tracking and Surveillance, pp. 65–72, October 2005
27. Hendel, A., Weinshall, D., Peleg, S.: Identifying surprising events in videos using bayesian topic models. In: Kimmel, R., Klette, R., Sugimoto, A. (eds.) ACCV 2010. LNCS, vol. 6494, pp. 448–459. Springer, Heidelberg (2011). https://doi.org/10.1007/978-3-642-19318-7_35
28. Karpathy, A., Toderici, G., Shetty, S., Leung, T., Sukthankar, R., Fei-Fei, L.: Large-scale video classification with Convolutional neural networks. In: Proceedings of the IEEE conference on Computer Vision and Pattern Recognition, pp. 1725–1732 (2014)
29. Itcher, Y., Hassner, T., Kliper-Gross, O.: Violent flows: real-time detection of violent crowd behavior. In: 3rd IEEE International Workshop on Socially Intelligent Surveillance and Monitoring (SISM) at the IEEE Conference on Computer Vision and Pattern Recognition (CVPR), June 2012
30. Zhao, G., Pietikainen, M.: Dynamic texture recognition using local binary patterns with an application to facial expressions. IEEE Trans. Pattern Anal. Mach. Intell. **29**(6), 915–928 (2007). https://doi.org/10.1109/tpami.2007.1110. ISSN 0162-8828
31. Redmon, J., Farhadi, A.: YOLO9000: better, faster, stronger. In: Proceedings of the IEEE Conference on Computer Vision and Pattern Recognition, pp. 7263–7271 (2017)

A New Method for Defining Scale to Estimate the Aspects Oriented Sentiment Polarity of the Tweets

Sudarshan S. Sonawane[1]([✉]) [iD] and Satish R. Kolhe[2] [iD]

[1] Department of Computer Engineering, Shri Gulabrao Deokar College of Engineering,
Jalgaon, India
sudars2000@gmail.com
[2] School of Computer Sciences, Kavayitri Bahinabai Chaudhari North Maharashtra University,
Jalgaon, India
srkolhe2000@gmail.com

Abstract. The positive or negative polarity of an opinion on a product, event, or activity is not strengthen enough if the tweet of opinion exploring about the vivid aspects of the target objective. In this regard, many of the contributions in contemporary research has portrayed for sentiment analysis using supervised learning. However, the content on twitter, which is social media platform to share the opinion on anything, limits the size of each tweet. Hence, the users intend to express negative polarity of the opinion in their tweets. This trend has not consider much in contemporary contributions of sentiment analysis. In this context, the proposal of this manuscript portrayed "A New Method for Defining Scale to Estimate the Aspects Oriented Sentiment Polarity (SEAOSP) of the Tweets". Experimental study evincing the significance of the proposal that scaled by comparing the performance of other contemporary model with the proposed model.

Keywords: Term co-occurrence · Aspects oriented · Sentiment polarity · Fitness evolution · Global polarity deviation

1 Introduction

The significant task in processing of natural language is SA (Sentiment Analysis). It is solving computational processing of subjectivity, opinions, emotions, which collected are summarized and analyzed. Much concentration is attained not only in case of academia yet also in instance of industry, offering real-time feedback by online reviews e.g. like amazon that might take the benefit of opinions of customers on definite services or products. The basic prediction of the task is that, total text is having entire polarity.

Nevertheless, users generally care regarding some definite products features or aspects. An instance of tweet by such concept is "The novel cellular phone series from XYZ brand could be well-fitted with high end version of camera, yet the weight & thickness of the product is not conservative". Here, polarity in the feature of camera could be positive whereas, polarity above weight & thickness could be negative. Therefore, it

© Springer Nature Singapore Pte Ltd. 2021
K. C. Santosh and B. Gawali (Eds.): RTIP2R 2020, CCIS 1380, pp. 318–333, 2021.
https://doi.org/10.1007/978-981-16-0507-9_28

might be ineffective and tiresome for scanning total tweets. Just concentrating on total ratings would not be adequate for the consumer in making decisions; the study of mining divergent tweet factors is in high demand. The work [1–4] proposed ABSA aims to detect polarity that is fine grained towards particular aspect. This paper contribution is to assess the tweet by allotting polarity towards each factor of corresponding tweet that increases accuracy in sentiment polarity detection of specified tweet.

2 Related Work

Huge amount of the literature associated to SA and opinion mining could be identified [5, 6]. Many of the methods are implemented towards twitter. Nevertheless, others were implemented towards the platforms of social-media within the context of micro-blog. Because of this, the methods are technically varied and in link with purpose. The 2 important methods present in SA are unsupervised & supervised. The supervised methods applied classification models such as conditional random fields, KNN, SVM etc. The work [7] stated that SVM were more suitable for the classification of sentiment than generative methods, because of their ability for contributing with the ambiguity. It means dealing with combined feelings. The supervised algorithms were utilized while number of classes and each class representative members are known.

Unsupervised methods are on the basis of linguistic knowledge such as syntactic features and lexicons for inferring polarity [8]. Here, these last methods depict more effective method in context of cross-domain and aimed at multilingual implementations. Algorithms of unsupervised learning could not contribute with the set of training. Unlike, some utilize clustering algorithms to differentiate clusters [9].

As formerly stated, the special instance of implementing SA towards twitter is addressed effectively [10, 11]. By the solutions, which are selected, they focused on the text normalization method [12] and key elements are utilized in the classification method [13]. The others hold benefits of utilizing deep learning methods in this challenge [14].

As per purpose of developed methods, it could be possible for detecting the implementations such as estimation of election results and political sentiment compared to others [15].

The former contribution on the Aspect oriented SA depends mainly on the feature engineering [16, 17] and following methods based on neural network [18–22] has attained maximum accuracy. Contemporarily, the former contribution "Term Co-occurrence Fitness Evolution (TCFE) for sentiment analysis" [23] is exploiting the significance of the terms involved in the given records as n-grams to predict the sentiment polarity, however the method is not considering the aspects as separate entity. The work (TABSA) [24] optimized memory network & implemented it to their method for better capturing of linguistic framework.

3 Methods and Materials

The term aspect denotes the property, event or activity, context which represents a feature or integral part of an individual, product or event that represents the objective of the behavior, state, performance, observation, or feature.

Table 1. Descriptions used for below used formulas

r	Record
T	Corpus
S	Set
vt_s	Vector of tokens
s	Source sentence
VT	Set
a_{vt}	Aspect
l_{vt}	Sentiment lexicon
$plpr$	Positive local polarity ratio
$nlpr$	Negative local polarity ratio
$plpd$	Positive local polarity deviation
$nlpd$	Negative local polarity deviation
$pgpr$	Positive global polarity ratio
$ngpr$	Negative global polarity ratio
$pgpd$	Positive global polarity deviation
$ngpd$	Negative global polarity deviation
nps_l	Local probability scale of the negative polarity
pps_l	Local probability scale of the positive polarity
nps_g	Global probability scale of the negative polarity
pps_g	Global probability scale of the positive polarity
$aps_+(a_i)$	Aspect level probability scale of positive polarity of the aspect a_i
$aps_-(a_i)$	Aspect level probability scale of negative polarity of the aspect a_i

Concerning the Natural Language Processing, the token of words catered as arguments have generally referred as the aspects. The given tweet is an aggregation of set of sentences, and each sentence is the vector of words (tokens). This vector of tokens is the mix of aspect, functionality, appearance or outcome of the respective aspect, and the opinion of the tweet on respective aspect. The proposed model is "A New Method for Defining Scale to Estimate the Aspects Oriented Sentiment Polarity (SEAOSP) of the Tweets". The description of the methods and materials related to the proposal has portrayed in this section.

3.1 Preprocessing

Prune the tweets from the given corpus T of tweets as records that are not having label either positive or negative. Further, the preprocessing phase splits each record $\{r \exists r \in T\}$ (Table 1) in to sentences, and each of these sentences entails the label of the source record as global polarity. The resultant sentences of the corpus T have listed further as a set S. The next phase of the preprocessing splits each sentence $\{s \exists s \in S\}$ listed in set S in to vector of tokens vt_s, such that each token represents a word in the source sentence s. Further, for each vector of tokens vt_s, remove the tokens representing stop words, and stem the "ing", "ed" forms from the leftover tokens. The resultant vector of tokens vt_s of each sentence $\{s \exists s \in S\}$ has accumulated as a set VT, such that each entry of the set VT is a vector of tokens vt_s representing the sentence $\{s \exists s \in S\}$.

3.2 Sentence Level Polarity Estimation (Local Polarity)

This phase discovers the aspect and sentiment lexicon listed in each vector of tokens $\{vt \exists vt \in VT\}$. An aspect a_{vt} is a token that noted as argument under natural language processing rules. A sentiment lexicon l_{vt} is a token of word listed in sentiment lexicon repository, which indicates the opinion under respective aspect. Further, assigns the local polarity to the respective vector of tokens $\{vt \exists vt \in VT\}$ as positive, if the sentiment lexicon l_{vt} is positive, else if the sentiment lexicon l_{vt} negative, then the local polarity of the vector of token vt is negative.

3.3 Aspect Level Local Polarity Ratio

Let the set A represents the list of aspects observed in the given corpus T of records having labels either positive or negative.

Bipartite the vector VT in to two sets VT_+^l, VT_-^l such that the set VT_+^l contains the vector of tokens having the local polarity as positive, and the other set VT_-^l contains the vectors of tokens having the local polarity as negative. Further, find the local polarity of the ratio as follows in (Eq. 1), (Eq. 2).

$$\overset{|A|}{\underset{i=1}{\forall}}\{a_i \exists a_i \in A\} \; Begin \qquad // \text{for each aspect } a_i$$

$$plpr(a_i) = \frac{\displaystyle\sum_{j=1}^{|VT_+^l|}\{1 \exists a_i \in vt_j \wedge vt_j \in VT_+^l\}}{|VT_+^l|} \tag{1}$$

$$// \text{ positive local polarity ratio of the aspect } a_i$$

$$nlpr(a_i) = \frac{\displaystyle\sum_{j=1}^{|VT_-^l|}\{1 \exists a_i \in vt_j \wedge vt_j \in VT_-^l\}}{|VT_-^l|} \tag{2}$$

$$// \text{ negative local polarity ratio of the aspect } a_i$$

End

3.4 Aspect Level Local Polarity Deviation

$$\overset{|A|}{\underset{i=1}{\forall}}\left\{a_i \exists a_i \in A\right\} Begin \qquad // \text{ for each aspect } a_i$$

$$plpd(a_i) = \frac{\sum_{j=1}^{|VT_+^l|}\left\{\sqrt{(plpr(a_i)-1)^2} \exists a_i \in vt_j \wedge vt_j \in VT_+^l\right\}}{|VT_+^l|} \qquad (3)$$

$$// \text{ positive local polarity deviation of the aspect } a_i$$

$$nlpd(a_i) = \frac{\sum_{j=1}^{|VT_-^l|}\left\{\sqrt{(nlpr(a_i)-1)^2} \exists a_i \in vt_j \wedge vt_j \in VT_-^l\right\}}{|VT_-^l|} \qquad (4)$$

$$// \text{ negative local polarity deviation of the aspect } a_i$$

End

3.5 Aspect Level Global Polarity Ratio

Similarly, bipartite the vector VT again in to two sets VT_+^g, VT_-^g such that the set VT_+^g contains the vectors of tokens having positive global polarity, and the other set VT_-^g lists the vectors of tokens having negative global polarity.

Further, find the global polarity of the ratio as follows in (Eq. 5), (Eq. 6):

$$\overset{|A|}{\underset{i=1}{\forall}}\left\{a_i \exists a_i \in A\right\} Begin \qquad // \text{ for each aspect } a_i$$

$$pgpr(a_i) = \frac{\sum_{j=1}^{|VT_+^g|}\left\{1 \exists a_i \in vt_j \wedge vt_j \in VT_+^g\right\}}{|VT_+^g|} \qquad (5)$$

$$// \text{ positive global polarity ratio of the aspect } a_i$$

$$ngpr(a_i) = \frac{\sum_{j=1}^{|VT_-^g|}\left\{1 \exists a_i \in vt_j \wedge vt_j \in VT_-^g\right\}}{|VT_-^g|} \tag{6}$$

// negative global polarity ratio of the aspect a_i

End

3.6   Aspect Level Global Polarity Deviation

$$\overset{|A|}{\underset{i=1}{\forall}}\left\{a_i \exists a_i \in A\right\} \; Begin \qquad \textit{// for each aspect } a_i$$

$$pgpd(a_i) = \frac{\sum_{j=1}^{|VT_+^g|}\left\{\sqrt{\left(pgpr(a_i)-1\right)^2}\exists a_i \in vt_j \wedge vt_j \in VT_+^g\right\}}{|VT_+^g|} \tag{7}$$

// positive global polarity deviation of the aspect a_i

$$ngpd(a_i) = \frac{\sum_{j=1}^{|VT_-^g|}\left\{\sqrt{\left(ngpr(a_i)-1\right)^2}\exists a_i \in vt_j \wedge vt_j \in VT_-^g\right\}}{|VT_-^g|} \tag{8}$$

// negative global polarity deviation of the aspect a_i

End

3.7   Aspect Level Local Probability Scale

The absolute distance of the negative local polarity ratio, and the respective negative local polarity deviation of the aspect a_i has termed as Aspect level Local Probability Scale $nps_l(a_i)$ of the negative local polarity of the aspect a_i. Similarly, the absolute distance of the positive local polarity ratio and the respective positive local polarity deviation has termed as Aspect level Local Probability Scale $pps_l(a_i)$ of the positive local polarity of the aspect a_i is follows in (Eq. 9), (Eq. 10).

$$\bigvee_{i=1}^{|A|} \left\{ a_i \exists a_i \in A \right\} \; Begin \qquad // \textit{for each aspect } a_i$$

$$nps_l(a_i) = \sqrt{\left(nlpr(a_i) - nlpd(a_i)\right)^2} \qquad (9)$$

//local probability scale of the negative polarity

$$pps_l(a_i) = \sqrt{\left(plpr(a_i) - plpd(a_i)\right)^2} \qquad (10)$$

// local probability scale of the positive polarity

End

3.8 Aspect Level Global Probability Scale

The absolute distance of the negative global polarity ratio, and the respective negative global polarity deviation of the aspect a_i has termed as Aspect level global Probability Scale $nps_g(a_i)$ of the negative global polarity of the aspect a_i. Similarly, the absolute distance of the positive global polarity ratio and the respective positive global polarity deviation has termed as Aspect level Global Probability Scale $pps_g(a_i)$ of the positive global polarity of the aspect a_i is follows in (Eq. 11), (Eq. 12).

$$\bigvee_{i=1}^{|A|} \left\{ a_i \exists a_i \in A \right\} \; Begin \; // \textit{for each aspect } a_i$$

$$nps_g(a_i) = \sqrt{\left(ngpr(a_i) - ngpd(a_i)\right)^2} \qquad (11)$$

// global probability scale of the negative polarity

$$pps_g(a_i) = \sqrt{\left(pgpr(a_i) - pgpd(a_i)\right)^2} \qquad (12)$$

// global probability scale of the positive polarity

End

3.9 Aspect Level Positive and Negative Probability Scales

Further, the Probability Scales of the Positive and Negative polarities have derived as follows in (Eq. 13), (Eq. 14):

$$aps_+(a_i) = 1 - \left(pps_l(a_i) * pps_g(a_i)\right) \qquad (13)$$

//Aspect Level Probability Scale $aps_+(a_i)$ of Positive Polarity of the aspect a_i, which has scaled by normalizing the product of local and global probability scales of the positive polarity.

$$aps_-(a_i) = 1 - \left(nps_l(a_i) * nps_g(a_i)\right) \qquad (14)$$

//Aspect Level Probability Scale $aps_-(a_i)$ of Negative Polarity of the aspect a_i, which has scaled by normalizing the product of local and global probability scales of the negative polarity.

3.10 Estimating Sentiment Polarity

For a given record t, perform the preprocessing (as stated in Sect. 3.1) that extracts all aspects exists in the respective record t as a vector A. Further, the positive and negative polarity scores have scaled as follows.

Let the notation $p_+ = 1$ that denotes the positive polarity of the given record t, which is initialized to 1.

$$\overset{|A|}{\underset{i=1}{\forall}}\left\{a_i \exists a_i \in A\right\} \; Begin \; // \, for \, each \, aspect \, a_i$$

     $p_+{}^* = aps_+(a_i)$ // cumulative product of the aspect level probability score of the
                                 positive polarity

     $p_-{}^* = aps_-(a_i)$ // cumulative product of the aspect level probability score of the
                                 negative polarity

     $s_{+ve} = 1 - p_+$
     $s_{-ve} = 1 - p_-$ // normalizing the positive and negative polarity scores of the

               given tweet t

     if $\left(s_{+ve} > s_{-ve}\right)$ // the sentiment polarity of the tweet t is said to be positive

     else if $(s_{+ve} < s_{-ve})$ // the sentiment polarity of the tweet t is said to be negative

        Else, the sentiment polarity of the tweet t is said to be neutral
End

4 Experimental Study

The experimental study carried on benchmark twitter dataset "sentiment140" that portryed by the kaggle [25], which provides benchmark datasets and conducts competitions in machine learning challenges. The dataset sentiment140 has 1600000 records, which labeled as positive, negative, or neutral, among these 26415 records have considered. The performance of the proposed model SEAOSP is scaled by standard metrics [26], which have listed in following description.

- The metric positive predictive value, which denotes often as precision of positive label prediction that estimates as explored in (Eq. 15). The pv_{+ve} is the probability of the true positives against the total records discovered as positives.

$$pv_{+ve} = \frac{t_{+ve}}{t_{+ve} + f_{+ve}} \tag{15}$$

// positive predictive value pv_{+ve} denotes the ratio of true positives t_{+ve} against the sum of true positives t_{+ve} and false positives f_{+ve}.

- The metric negative predictive value, which denotes often as precision of negative label prediction that estimates as explored in (Eq. 16).

$$pv_{-ve} = \frac{t_{-ve}}{t_{-ve} + f_{-ve}} \tag{16}$$

// The negative predictive value pv_{-ve} is the probability of the true negatives t_{-ve} against the total records discovered as negatives $(t_{-ve} + f_{-ve})$, which is the sum of true negatives t_{-ve} and false negatives f_{-ve}.

- The metric True positive rate that often denotes as sensitivity, or recall, which enables to estimate the probability of the truly discovered positives count against the total number of positives given for testing (see Eq. 17).

$$pr_{+ve} = \frac{t_{+ve}}{p} \tag{17}$$

// The true positive rate pr_{+ve} is the probability of the true positives t_{+ve} against the total records of positive label $(p = t_{+ve} + f_{-ve})$ given for testing, which is the sum of true positives t_{+ve} and false negatives f_{-ve}.

- Similarly the metric true negative rate that denotes the probability of the truly detected negative label records against the total number of negative labeled records given for testing (see Eq. 18).

$$nr_{-ve} = \frac{t_{-ve}}{n} \tag{18}$$

// The true negative rate nr_{-ve} is the probability of the true negatives t_{-ve} against the total records of negative label $(n = t_{-ve} + f_{+ve})$ given for testing, which is the sum of true negatives t_{-ve} count and false positives f_{+ve} count.

- The other metric accuracy scales the performance of the label prediction strategy towards the both labels positive and negative (see Eq. 19)

$$accuracy = \frac{t_{+ve} + t_{-ve}}{t_{+ve} + t_{-ve} + f_{+ve} + f_{-ve}} \tag{19}$$

// The accuracy denotes the probability of the sum of the positive labels t_{+ve} and negative labels t_{-ve} truly discovered against the total number of records given for prediction, which is the sum of true positives t_{+ve}, false positives f_{+ve}, true negatives t_{-ve} and false negatives f_{-ve}.

- Harmonic mean is the other considerable metric to estimate the performance advantage of the supervised learning methods adapted for binary classification (number of labels remain two). This metric often denotes as f-measure (see Eq. 20).

$$f - measure = 2 * \frac{(pv_{+ve} * pr_{+ve})}{(pv_{+ve} + pr_{+ve})} \tag{20}$$

// The ratio of the product of precision and recall $(pv_{+ve} * pr_{+ve})$ against the sum of precision and recall $(pv_{+ve} + pr_{+ve})$ has to doubled to estimate the f-measure.

The performance of the proposed model under aforesaid performance metrics has scaled by comparing with the values obtained for corresponding metrics from other contemporary models TCFE [23], TABSA[24]. The statistics of the total records used for training are 12786 (positives), and 13629 (negatives), which are aspect specific those filtered from the millions of records exist in the original dataset. The statics of the records used in testing and count of resultant positive, negatives alongwith true positives, false negatives, true negatives and false positives have visualized in Fig. 1 and Fig. 2.

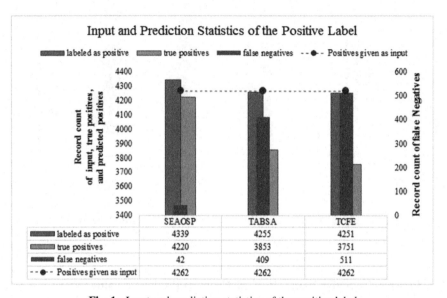

Fig. 1. Input and prediction statistics of the positive label

The Fig. 1 indicating the statistics of the positive label records. The number of records labeled as positve has given as input to the experimental study of the proposal and the other contemporary models (- • -), which are 4262 for all the three methods. The records labeled as positves (▬) by proposed model SEAOSP, and other contemporary models has portrayed, which are 4339, 4255, and 4251 in respective order of the methods SEAOSP, TABSA, and TCFE. The count of true positives (▬) 4220, 3853, and 3751 have observed from the methods SEAOSP, TABSA, and TCFE in respective order. The count of false negatives (▬) listed by proposed model SEAOSP and contemporary methods TABSA and TCFE are 42, 409, and 511 in respective order.

Similarly, the Fig. 2 indicating the statistics of the negative label records. The number of records labeled as negative has given as input to the experimental study of the proposal and the other contemporary models (- • -), which are 4543 for all the three methods. The records labeled as negatives (▬) by proposed model SEAOSP, and other contemporary models has portrayed, which are 4466, 4550, and 4554 in respective order of the methods SEAOSP, TABSA, and TCFE. The count of true negatives (▬) 4424, 4141, and 4043 have observed from the methods SEAOSP, TABSA, and TCFE in respective order.

The count of false positives (▬) listed by proposed model SEAOSP and contemporary methods TABSA and TCFE are 119, 402, and 500 in respective order.

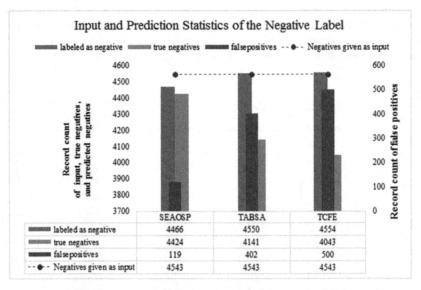

Fig. 2. Input and prediction statistics of the negative label

4.1 Positive Predictive Value (PPV) & Negative Predictive Value (NPV)

The metric PPV denotes the ratio of the true positives against the aggregate of true positives and false positives (see Eq. 15).

Similarly, the metric NPV denotes the ratio of the true negatives against the aggregate of true negatives and false negatives. The statistics observed for these metrics from proposed model SEAOSP, and the other contemporary models TABSA, TCFE are briefed in Fig. 3.

Fig. 3 portraying the statistics of the metrics PPV & NPV, which are scaled from the proposed method SEAOSP and the contemporary methods TABSA & TCFE on given dataset. The ratio of PPV & NPV scaled for proposal SEAOSP, contemporary methods TABSA, and TCFE from the experiments in respective order are 0.9726 (PPV) & 0.9906 (NPV) from SEAOSP, 0.9055 (PPV) & 0.9101 (NPV) from TABSA, and 0.8824 (PPV) & 0.8877 (NPV) from TCFE. The depicted PPV & NPV ratios confirming that the proposed model SEAOSP is having significant advantage that compared to other two contemporary models.

4.2 True Positive Rate (TPR) & True Negative Rate (TNR)

The true positive rate (TPR) indicates the significance of the true positive label prediction, which is the ratio of true positives against the aggregate of the true positives and false

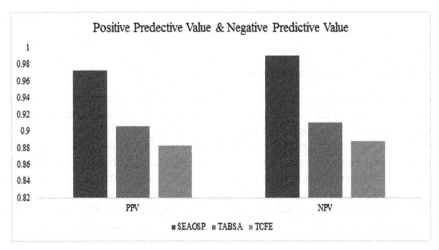

Fig. 3. The statistics observed for the metrics PPV & NPV of the SEAOSP, TABSA, and TCFE

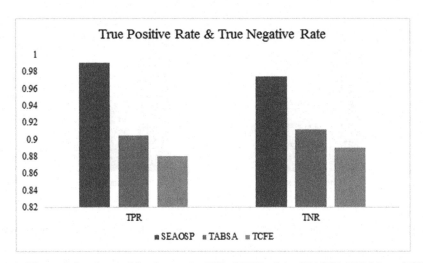

Fig. 4. The statistics observed for the metrics TPR & TNR of the SEAOSP, TABSA, and TCFE

negatives. Similarly, the metric true negative rate (TNR) is the ratio of true negatives against the aggregate of true negatives and false positives, which denotes the significance of negative label prediction. The statistics of the TPR & TNR from the experimental study carried on SEAOSP, and contemporary methods TABSA and TCFE have visualized in Fig. 4.

The values of the metrics TPR & TNR observed for the proposal SEAOSP are 0.99 & 0.9738 in respective order. Similarly, the values of the metrics TPR & TNR observed for the contemporary method TABSA are 0.904 and 0.9115 in respective order. The values of TPR & TNR observed for the contemporary method TCFE are 0.88 and 0.89 in respective order. According to these statistics of the metrics TPR & TNR, the significance and consistence of the proposed model SEAOSP that compared to other contemporary methods is clearly evinced.

4.3   Prediction Accuracy and Harmonic Mean

The metric accuracy is utilized for describing the approximations of measurement towards true-value, which is the ratio of count of true values (the aggregate of the count of true positives and true negatives) against the total count of records given for classification. The other metric harmonic mean denotes the consistency of the values portrayed for the "positive predictive value (precision)" and the "true positive rate (recall or sensitivity)" of the binary classification process, which is double of the ratio of "product of the PPV and TPR" against the "sum of the corresponding PPV and TPR".

The statistics observed for these metrics from proposed model SEAOSP and the other contemporary models TABSA, TCFE are briefed in the following (see Fig. 5).

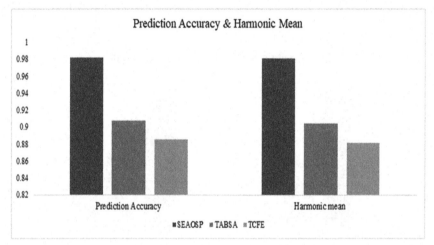

Fig. 5. The statistics observed for the metrics Accuracy & Harmonic Mean of the SEAOSP, TABSA, and TCFE

The ratios of accuracy & harmonic mean observed for proposed model SEAOSP from the experiments are 0.9817 and 0.98122 in respective order of the metrics. Similarly, the values 0.9079, and 0.9047 have observed as accuracy, and harmonic mean of the contemporary model TABSA. The values observed for these accuracy, and harmonic mean from the other contemporary model TCFE are 0.8851, and 0.8812 in respective order.

The computational complexity of the proposed model SEAOSP has observed as linear from the experimental study, which is similar to the other contemporary models. The state of the computational time (process complexity) is not proportionate to the volume of the training corpus. Instead, it is proportionate the volume of the features. However, the features related to the NLP are mostly appear with in context boundaries. Hence, the process complexity of the proposed model has not found as complexed.

5   Conclusion and Future Work

The intent of this contribution is to estimate the sentiment polarity of the given tweet using the sentiment polarity observed for each aspect of the corresponding tweet. Unlike the contemporary methods, the proposal is devising a scale by correlating the aspect level sentiment polarity with tweet level sentiment polarity during training phase. Further, the resultant probability scales of both positive and negative sentiment polarity of each aspect is to predict the sentiment polarity of the given unlabeled tweet. Experimental study evinced the 98% accuracy to identify the sentiment polarity by proposed model SEAOSP that is considerably better than label prediction accuracy of the contemporary models TABSA and TCFE, which is 91% and 89% in respective order. The future research can include this approach to derive the sentiment polarity of a tweet that incurs by multidimensional factors of sentiment representatives such as emoticons, emojis, and many others.

Acknowledgements. The authors are thankful to the UGC, New Delhi for supporting this research work at School of Computer Sciences, KBCNMU, Jalgaon under the SAP DRS-II level.

References

1. Yohan, J., Alice H.: Aspect and sentiment unification model for online review analysis. In: Proceedings of the Fourth ACM International Conference on Web Search and Data Mining, pp. 815–824 (2011). https://doi.org/10.1145/1935826.1935932
2. Pontiki, M., Galanis, D., Pavlopoulos, J., Papageorgiou, H., Androutsopoulos, I., Manandhar, S.: Semeval-2014 task 4: aspect based sentiment analysis. In: Proceedings of the 8th International Workshop on Semantic Evaluation (SemEval 2014), pp.27–35. Association for Computational Linguistics (2014). https://doi.org/10.3115/v1/S14-2004
3. Pontiki, M., Galanis, D., Papageorgiou, H., Manandhar, S., Androutsopoulos, I.: Semeval-2015 task 12: aspect based sentiment analysis. In: Proceedings of the 9th International Workshop on Semantic Evaluation (SemEval 2015), pp. 486–495. Association for Computational Linguistics (2015). https://doi.org/10.18653/v1/S15-2082
4. Pontiki, M., et al.: Semeval-2016 task 5: aspect based sentiment analysis. In: Proceedings of the 10th International Workshop on Semantic Evaluation (SemEval-2016), pp. 19–30. Association for Computational Linguistics (2016). https://doi.org/10.18653/v1/S16-1002
5. Bo, P.: Lee, L: Opinion mining and sentiment analysis. Found. Trends® Inf. Retrieval 2(1–2), 1–135 (2008). https://doi.org/10.1561/1500000011
6. Miguel, A., Martinez, E., Julio, V., Janine, G.: Tass 2015–the evolution of the spanish opinion mining systems. Procesamiento Lenguaje Nat. **56**, 33–40 (2016)
7. Hang, C., Mittal, V., Datar, M.: Comparative experiments on sentiment classification for online product reviews. In: AAAI 2006 proceedings of the 21st national conference on Artificial intelligence, vol. 6, pp. 1265–1270 (2006)
8. Paltoglou, G., Thelwall, M.: Twitter, MySpace, Digg: unsupervised sentiment analysis in social media. ACM Trans. Intell. Syst. Technol. (TIST) **3**(4) (2012). https://doi.org/10.1145/2337542.2337551
9. Li, G., Liu, F.: A clustering-based approach on sentiment analysis. In: 2010 IEEE International Conference on Intelligent Systems and Knowledge Engineering, pp. 331–337 (2010). https://doi.org/10.1109/ISKE.2010.5680859

10. Pak, A., Paroubek, P.: Twitter as a corpus for sentiment analysis and opinion mining. In: Proceedings of the Seventh Conference on International Language Resources and Evaluation (LREC 2010), pp. 1320–1326 (2010)
11. Han, B., Baldwin, T.: Lexical normalisation of short text messages: Makn sens a# Twitter. In: Proceedings of the 49th Annual Meeting of the Association for Computational Linguistics: Human Language Technologies, Association for Computational Linguistics, vol. 1, pp. 368–378 (2011)
12. Ruiz, P., Cuadros, M., Etchegoyhen, T.: Lexical normalization of spanish tweets with pre-processing rules, domain-specific edit distances, and language models. In: Proceedings of the Tweet Normalization Workshop at the Conference of the Spanish Society for Natural Language Processing (SEPLN) (2013)
13. Wang, X., Wei, F., Liu, X., Zhou, M., Zhang, M.: Topic sentiment analysis in twitter: a graph-based hashtag sentiment classification approach. In: Proceedings of the 20th ACM International Conference on Information and Knowledge Management, pp. 1031–1040 (2011). https://doi.org/10.1145/2063576.2063726
14. Santos, C., Gatti, M.: Deep convolutional neural networks for sentiment analysis of short texts. In: Proceedings of COLING 2014, the 25th International Conference on Computational Linguistics: Technical Papers, pp. 69–78 (2014)
15. Bermingham, A., Smeaton. A.: On using Twitter to monitor political sentiment and predict election results. In: Proceedings of the Workshop on Sentiment Analysis Where AI Meets Psychology (SAAIP 2011), pp. 2–10 (2011)
16. Wagner, J., et al.: DCU: aspect-based polarity classification for semeval task 4. In: Proceedings of the 8th International Workshop on Semantic Evaluation (SemEval 2014), pp. 223–229 (2014). https://doi.org/10.3115/v1/S14-2036
17. Kiritchenko, S., Zhu, X., Cherry, C., Mohammad, S.: NRC-Canada-2014: detecting aspects and sentiment in customer reviews. In: Proceedings of the 8th International Workshop on Semantic Evaluation (SemEval 2014), pp. 437–442 (2014). https://doi.org/10.3115/v1/S14-2076
18. Nguyen, T., Shirai, K.: PhraseRNN: phrase recursive neural network for aspect-based sentiment analysis. In: Proceedings of the 2015 Conference on Empirical Methods in Natural Language Processing, pp. 2509–2514 (2015). https://doi.org/10.18653/v1/D15-1298
19. Wang, Y., Huang, M., Zhao, L., Zhu, X.: Attention-based LSTM for aspect-level sentiment classification. In: Proceedings of the 2016 Conference on Empirical Methods in Natural Language Processing, pp. 606–615 (2016). https://doi.org/10.18653/v1/D16-1058
20. Tang, D., Qin, B., Feng, X., Liu, T.: Effective LSTMs for target-dependent sentiment classification. In: Proceedings of COLING 2016, the 26th International Conference on Computational Linguistics: Technical Papers, pp. 3298–3307 (2016)
21. Tang, D., Qin, B., Liu, T.: Aspect level sentiment classification with deep memory network. In: Proceedings of the 2016 Conference on Empirical Methods in Natural Language Processing. pp. 214–224 (2016). https://doi.org/10.18653/v1/D16-1021
22. Wang, B., Liakata, M., Zubiaga A., Procter R.: TDParse: multi-target-specific sentiment recognition on Twitter. In: Proceedings of the 15th Conference of the European Chapter of the Association for Computational Linguistics, vol. 1, pp. 483–493 (2017)
23. Sonawane, S., Kolhe, S.: Feature optimization in sentiment analysis by term co-occurrence fitness evolution (TCFE). Int. J. Inf. Technol. Web Eng. (IJITWE), **14**(3), 16–36 (2019). https://doi.org/10.4018/IJITWE.2019070102
24. Liu, F., Cohn, T., Baldwin, T.: Recurrent entity networks with delayed memory update for targeted aspect-based sentiment analysis. In: Proceedings of NAACL-HLT 2018, pp. 278–283 (2018). https://doi.org/10.18653/v1/N18-2045

25. https://www.kaggle.com/kazanova/sentiment140. Accessed 24 Aug 2019
26. McSherry, F., Najork, M.: Computing information retrieval performance measures efficiently in the presence of tied scores. In: Macdonald, C., Ounis, I., Plachouras, V., Ruthven, I., White, R.W. (eds.) ECIR 2008. LNCS, vol. 4956, pp. 414–421. Springer, Heidelberg (2008). https://doi.org/10.1007/978-3-540-78646-7_38

Protecting Big Data Sets from Unauthorized Users on Cloud

T. N. Manjunath[1,2(✉)], M. R. Shrihari[1,2], R. A. Archana[2,3], and Ravindra S. Hegadi[4]

[1] Department of ISE, BMS Institute of Technology and Management, Bengaluru, India
manju.tn@gmail.com, shrihari.mr@gmail.com
[2] VTU, Belagavi, Karnataka, India
archana.tnm@gmail.com
[3] Sai Vidya Institute of Technology, Bengaluru, India
[4] School of Computational Sciences, Solapur University, Solapur, Maharastra, India
rshehadi@gmail.com

Abstract. The variety of different appearance computing has modified over a segment of instance. It is changed as its commencement from objective to disseminated figure which facilitate one machine-to other machine communications. The novel methods move toward is called as internet based method wherever information to accumulate and different security examine are externalization to public suspicion in compensate per use method. The foundation following this is that present have to be transformed in the corporation in generous assessment to industry data. Ever since the data happen to a quality to institute protect every operation develop into an essential. Through the explosion of intelligence knowledge, satellites and public media present is exponential and exceptional development of data. Such information has acquire the different types such as volume, velocity, variety and value and a appearance by name big data has be present invent to indicate it. In heart, big data is the information which is huge, through dissimilar type of information, the data is incessantly increasing and it adds assessment to the industry which preserves it. By means of big data, inclusive industry intellect can be taken out to make extremely precise planned decision. The difficulty of organization and dispensation big data which is suspicious in Peta bytes is resolve with the appearance of Hadoop wherever huge group of different security methods are preserve and specified on-demand unrestricted access exclusive of resources speculation. Big data is accumulate and development through the facilitate of disseminated encoding structure like Hadoop and which supports the new encoding prototype MapReduce which can switch enormous quantity of information through thousands of product different machines in Hadoop clusters. Though, the data are apprehensive with security of their externalization data. The big data has recognized and declares different safety challenge through reverence to big data protection and protected estimation in disseminated encoding structure. Individuals confront are big data privacy, big data security, communications security and data institute moreover consistency and instantaneous security.

Keywords: Big data · Hadoop · Security · Privacy · Fully homomorphic encryption

© Springer Nature Singapore Pte Ltd. 2021
K. C. Santosh and B. Gawali (Eds.): RTIP2R 2020, CCIS 1380, pp. 334–349, 2021.
https://doi.org/10.1007/978-981-16-0507-9_29

1 Introduction

The appearance of disseminated technology resembling big data disseminated encoding frameworks similar to Hadoop and Map Reduce encoding prototype that can process huge quantity of data, cemented method for a novel computing representation. Since for each of this method to use different potential to farm out storage and dispensation of huge quantity of data identified as big data. Big data is very massive data that is deliberate in peta bytes. Such information cannot be contain in the confined servers. As a result corporations are externalization big data and its mange to public cloud. During this perspective, it is significant to make sure that big data is accumulate and development with comprehensive security [1]. The Cloud Security Alliance recognized four dissimilar challenges through reverence to disseminated encoding structure and big data security. They are associated to protected assessment, solitude of big data, big data protection and reliability. The difficulty of protected estimation demonstrates the significance of perform to the Map and Reduce process properly. Because thousands of service processor is concerned in Hadoop cluster to development big data, therefore present it should be for securing Map Reduce estimation. Since separately this, present is a difficulty of big data confidentiality. Because confidentiality of information is extremely important, present is require for defensive confidentiality of big data. Here in this circumstance, this subject is intended at concentrate on the abovementioned protection difficulty of big data and Map Reduce process. It current novel methodology to covenant with protected estimation in Hadoop cluster, protecting big data confidentiality support on discrepancy confidentiality, protected accumulate and recovery. Dissimilar techniques are planned in this subject to encompass an inclusive clarification that accommodates to the security desires of big data and Map Reduce encoding prototype. Big data is the information so as to be demonstrated by volume, velocity and variety. Such information is voluminous and desires disseminated encoding structure such as Hadoop. Methodological advance in compute industry with big data. Big data is created by satellites, digital sensors, social media and essential applications that demonstrate big data since instant to time. Big data is constructive in application like Microsoft, Yahoo and Google to reveal few. It is also indispensable for big data request to covenant with enormous quantity of information [2].

2 De-identification

Intensity of protection and the level of protection predate the review information compilation. Individuality privacy and information protection methods to enhance the risk: the conventional idea in the secrecy and sensing. Uniqueness is a key device to release the protection of private data that can develop the privacy of data study. However, the delinquent can obtain additional data about peripheral detection sustain huge data, expressive that a huge quantity of data can enhance the possibility of reauthentication. It is as a result not a sufficient amount to defend a extensive variety of data. During assessment of the elasticity, the security of personal data and the protection of information remains complicated. If a convincing privacy protection and conservation of the algorithms are developed a quantity of constraint to classify risks, you preserve revoke the verification to protect privacy and sustain enormous data learning. Present there are three - to security the protection of individual data - technique of detection secret. The subsequent are a small number of essential words of the individual statistics security: detection quality should incorporate data in a clear and express dissimilarity between persons, such as name, identification card, public security number. Normal identifier quality character-izes a set of data. It can preserve to be used by means of additional peripheral data to recognize individuals. Insightful content is classified and individual data. Examples of this consist of disease; salary and extra non-sensitive quality are collective and consis-tent data. This is corresponding class definite in all records by means of the identical identifier [2].

3 Securing Big Data Storage

Security to externalization big data is essential anxieties as data repository servers are delight suspicious as of the user position of inspection. Data are not completely secure to outsource their information. As a result, protected big data in transfer and also in respite subsequent to externalization is mainly essential for the development in handling of public data for externalization data. Conventionally, information is secured by means of cryptographic method. Though, it can be used suspiciously with Hadoop cluster as it deals with huge data. as soon as the data vendor is clever to encrypt and farm out with the intention of will facilitate data vendor to achieve in assurance resting on the protected data storage. The validation after is that Cloud Service Providers are not pleasing concern of encrypting information. Then the data immediately accumulate anything data vendor sends. With the aim of is the major motivation to encompass cryptographic primitives in organize to protection externalization data. In this incident, the investigate accepted elsewhere is accessible within this. As a big data have the excellence known as diversity amazing structured data, unstructured data and semi-structured data, it is essential to machine encryption process and decryption process method carefully [3].

4 Security Issues and Challenges in Big Data

The late information is to be specified additional significance by activity in the exis-tent planet. Once information is particular consequence, each quantity of information is retaining for excellence, exercise and information integration objective. Therefore, massive quantity of information is individual produce in the endeavor. Separately since this a quantity of application that are related through the sensors, endure predict and collective system create massive quantity of data to facilitate has individuality of big data. In big data accumulate and dispensations are most important tribulations as big data reside in reminiscence in petabytes. So the data not to be accumulate and progression in restricted technology. Hadoop cluster is intelligent to supply the necessary storage and work out possessions to resolve the difficulty. Now way days there are several areas that generate massive quantity of data. For occasion insurance, banking and public network-ing is segment to declare a small number of for generating big data. Since corporations are prepared to progression big data to acquire complete industry intellect, they are externalization data to public data and frequently they farm out estimation as well. At this time is the protection difficulty that occur. The data vendors are not positive about externalization while greatly as security of information is disturbed. In addition to this, the vendors encompass security anxiety of their externalization data [4].

The data become very significant to learning organization, government, engineering and healthcare constituent. Consequently, the collect of information desires to be accumulate in public data. Exclusive of data, industry not to produce and administer operation. Data really become a quality to organization in the existent world. The objective of several companies can be attain with the facilitate of information they contain. So as to be the grounds they provide maximum consequence in the direction of information. As a data is focus to data mining, the Industries achieve essential comprehension to formulate fine conversant decision. Security of such information is the current anxiety towards them. The information confirmation within the complete record of human, 90% is collect in the very last few years. Now the present is exceptional increase of data in a variety of segment. The inclination of growing is present in expectations as well. The appearance of Internet of Things is a different rationale that in prospect, all engineering generates additional data. The Sensor networks, public system are producing big data constantly. The majority of the statistics within unstructured data. The additional varieties of big data are existing in the outline of structured data and semi-structured data and the unstructured data is within the appearance of unexciting records that could include multimedia data. The different structured data is accumulate in different relational record wherever the structure of the data is evidently definite. Semi structured data is also seemed similar to unstructured data. Essence in XML library is a model designed for this type of information [5].

The information so as to accumulating in the structure of XML is recognized as semi structured data. While information is in unstructured data, it's not likely to examine it effortlessly with conventional method. To conquer this difficulty disseminated encoding structure like Hadoop move into reality. Since institutes are exasperating to get very constructive development beginning the information, so they are theoretical to method quantity of data that reveal variety and velocity. The novel model to appreciate data, development it, store it and achieve process on it is identified as big data prototype. It is solitary technologies that convey massive modify in the mode corporation covenant through the data. An amount awareness in the existent carry a quantity of subject the length. Through reverence to big data, the concerns are not only connected to diversity of data and quantity of information but also with data protection, data confidentiality and excellence of data. In accumulation to the conventional data issues in security, novel ones within huge extent came into reality through the big data. Since the big data grow to be a authenticity, In present several policy connected to organization and administration to encompass organize in excess of its process and investigation. During this circumstance, attain big data security develop into very imperative. It also turns out to be solitary of obstruction that frequently deliberate behind the velocity of knowledge improvement. While present no security assurance, the necessary altitude of confidence not to be realize by big data. Consequently, it preserve be supposed to big data convey big task. Since the big data protection is disturbed, the big data effective cluster at Cloud Security Alliance recognized a quantity of concern associated to big data protection and they are to be recognized as data confidentiality, data protection infrastructure security and data organization. Since existing in (see Fig. 1), it is apparent so as to the protection of big data is separated interested in four major kinds. They are recognized as data confidentiality correlated security, reliability and deliberate protection, communications security and data organization related security [4].

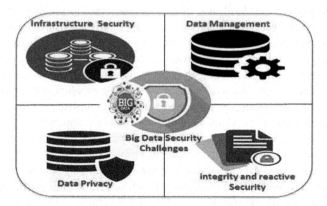

Fig. 1. Big Data security challenges as per cloud security alliance

In this subject, the entire these security characteristic descriptions by CSA are measured. The imparting security in the outline of protected Map Reduce structure within the existence of untrusted design and lower is inspect in addition to a novel structure is planned and realize to concentrate on difficulty and the result [5].

5   Securing Big Data

This segment supply a common explanation to encompass protection to big data as it is externalization to public data. The information is enormous and it desires in the direction of be protected even ahead of it is externalization to private data. Visibly and data vendor has to compose definite protected storage since the information not to be sustain in the neighborhood. In additional terminology, the externalization information not be present in the local machine. This means to enhance the security concern and decrease the wide extend convention of public statistics to accumulate venture data. It is the require for accumulate strongly as externalization to public Hadoop cluster an important inspection is that data externalization to accumulate as it is. The CSP have no commerce through the content. Suchlike the information is sent is accumulate. Though, the big data as soon as it is on transportation or while it is by the respite might be focus to numerous battering. The insider assault or stranger assault can source confusion to institute as their industry determined on the information. Consequently it is essential to encompass protected Hadoop cluster reposition method so as to can be make use of by the data vendor exclusive of should for technical proficiency. Such spontaneous structure can assist data vendor to externalization their information securely and achieves after needed (see Fig. 2) Illustrate the specific structure to facilitate assists in protected reposition and protected data repossession [6].

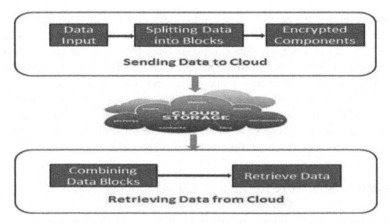

Fig. 2. A structure for secure cloud storage

As shown in (see Fig. 2), it's apparent so as to the data vendor is competent to execute encryption through subsequent plain process. The data are encrypted data and the encrypted information is externalization to social data. The big data is specified as contribution and it is divide into amount of chunk. The amount might be accumulate in dissimilar technology as the CSP supply the essential communications to repossess. Formerly the data is recovered back; all amounts are collective and decrypted data earlier than the conclusion customer perceives the information. It is the plain experiences that make available specific indication of the secure data storage system. In the presented scheme AES encryption is used for the different kinds of data [7].

6 Current Cloud Storage Mechanism

The cloud storage security method is support on the cryptography technique known as AES which was first accessible in 2001 by NIST (National Institute of Standards and Technology). It system is symmetric block cipher that could replace DDES. It supports dissimilar key span like 128, 192 and 256. It is use to encrypt data with elegant method. It go behind a move toward anywhere the data vendor utilize AES for encrypting data and the information is stored in public cloud. The equivalent key is make use of for encryption and decryption. Once data is to be reclaim, the data vendor downloads information records desired from public cloud and carry out decryption development as the data vendor has the key that is make use of for encryption. This phenomenon is as shown below.

Data vendor → Encrypted Data Using AES → Public Cloud

Then the decryption process is as follows. It is very straight forward as the required data is downloaded from cloud and then encrypted with the key available with the data owner.

Public Cloud → Encrypted Data Using AES → Data vendor → Decrypted Data

In the development, the data is separated keen on large quantity and each large quantity is subjected to encryption earlier than transfer it to public cloud. It construct utilize of 128 bit key. Formerly data is separated into block; each mass is individually encrypted and subsequently sent to cloud. The data might be accumulate in different place. On one occasion information is accumulate in public cloud, it cannot be entrance by unauthorized users. Even if the cloud examination supplier acquire it cannot be decrypted and the satisfied is not in once exacting place. The identical is useful to all different kinds of data accumulate in public cloud. The difficulty with this move toward is that it provides equivalent to all different kinds of data [8].

7   Design of Structure for Secure Cloud Storage

These sections provide the information of the planned structure that direct in accumulates and rescue data to the collective cloud through security. For conciseness, the statement user is make use of in the structure. Though, it might submit toward the data vendor or data consumer. The majority of the occasion data vendor and data consumer may be identical. The data vendor produce data, most likely an activity and enormous quantity of data is created, and the information is externalization to collective cloud.

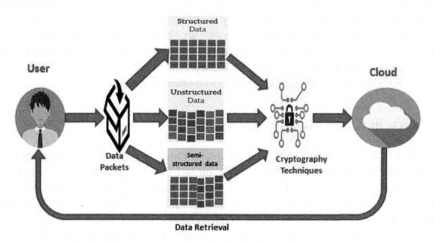

Fig. 3. Planned structure for secure cloud storage and recovery

To achieve in this inspect is to include a sensitive limit intended for end customer so as to make possible him to do process exclusive of the perceptive of existent cryptography or cloud. A representation is creating to focus on the complexity of conference. Usability of the designed organization with the archetype is improved significantly. The execution of the user, exclusive of information on cryptography, is able to use the relevance to carry out their behavior. Consequently the planned structure provide boundary to have communications with collective cloud.

As existing in (see Fig. 3), it is apparent that the planned structure is intelligent to distinguish the big data particular as input. It does indicate to facilitate the information is documented as three groups. There are three clusters survive in big data as a result the planned structure is intelligent to deal through the data quality. They are recognized as structured data, unstructured data and semi structured data. Industry through data quality is the relevant attribute desired as the big data has the attribute known as diversity. The big data approach as of dissimilar resource and in dissimilar system. Consequently it is diversify and classify into the three types abovementioned. The structure is competent to sustain equally storage space and recovery of big data. The explanation is completed through cryptographic relating to facilitate previously be present. Consider as the increase of a individual to be sensitive information and confidential within this environment. In this circumstance discrepancy confidentiality has the competence to celebrate and defend confidentiality of the statistics starting a variety of confidentiality attacks [9].

In classify to attain the abovementioned intention, an algorithm is planned. As stated toward the algorithm on different data sets are measured. It indicates as D and D^1 where D is the innovative data set even as D^1 is consequent by invention modify to the information for confidentiality. Here in this case, observation as a arbitrary algorithm represent as A is competent to convince discrepancy confidentiality intended for the two datasets recognized as contiguous data sets D and D^1 and this is accurate in maintain of the production O of the algorithm A.

$$P_r[A(D) = O] \leq \exp(\epsilon).P_r[A(D') = O]$$ (1)

Amount of confidentiality security is represent as ε.

The intend of an algorithm is to arrangement through big data; it's extremely frequent for the data to have sensitive data. It be capable of be functional to data of several field such as banking, collective networks, healthcare and so on. A lot of anonymization algorithms to facilitate give confidentiality to data might affect data loss. This defeat is appropriate to the conversion of contribution data for as long as privacy to it. As a result, present survive tradeoffs connecting data failure and confidentiality intensity of data. Present in a risk once the recompense is not impartial as it direct to behind convenience of unidentified information and conquer the foremost reason of confidentiality security. The renovation utility planned in illustrates this fact.

$$Fx_i(a) = \frac{\int_{-\infty}^{a} fy(w1 - z)fx(z)dz}{\int_{-\infty}^{\infty} fy(w1 - z)fx(z)dz}$$ (2)

specified n amount of random illustration consciousness and increasing sharing function F_y, the section realizations are expected as $x_1 + y_1$, $x_2 + y_2$ ..., $x_n + y_n$ and F_x. As approximate in Eq. (2), the subsequent sharing is contribute. Correspondingly the assessment of F_X^1 for $x_1 + y_1$, $x_2 + y_2$, ..., $x_n + y_n$ is supply as follow the Equation.

$$Fx_i(a) = \frac{1}{n}\sum_{i=1}^{n} fx_i = \frac{1}{n}\frac{\int_{-\infty}^{a} fy(w1 - z)fx(z)dz}{\int_{-\infty}^{\infty} fy(w1 - z)fx(z)dz}$$ (3)

Solidity occupation f'_x is acquire as pursue by distinguish the F_x.

$$Fx_i(a) = \frac{1}{n}\sum_{i=1}^{n} fx_i = \frac{y(w1 - a)fx(a)}{\int_{-\infty}^{\infty} fy(w1 - z)fx(z)dz}$$ (4)

The contingent progress toward and renovation difficulty to throw an fundamental difficulty that is to supply a quantity of data as well anonymization information foundation leak of sensitive information. This is the motivation such move toward be not measured for the planned clarification. Solitary one constraint connected to privacy is used in Eq. 1 at the same time as two considerations are studied in [9]. As a result (ϵ a), discrepancy Confidentiality is the build that content estimation occupation that believe both D and D^1 as soon as their dissimilarity is a distinct article to facilitate is related with D and not with D^1. It is accurate in support of all amount produced such as $S \subseteq$ Range (F) Eq. (5) is make use of to accomplish this [10].

$$P_r[F(D)\epsilon S] \leq \exp(\epsilon) \times P_r\left[F\left(D^1\right)\epsilon S\right] \tag{5}$$

The consequences of the estimation, it is not likely to state with any possibility to facilitate whether present is convention of any particular input significance for create the preferred invention. This variety of excellence does not provide the facility to discover the incidence or deficiency of several information point, is the most important objective of the planned discrepancy confidentiality create to facilitate is in employment in MapReduce encoding prototype.

8 Proposed Algorithm

```
Selection of data
(type) If (type == 1)
{
Structured data
Data from SQL type data bases
AESEncrypt()
Send to Cloud
}
If (type == 2 or type == 3)

{
Unstructured or semi structured data
Data from HBase or Casandra or MongoDB etc
HomomorphicEncrypt()
}
```

Algorithm 1: Variety of Secure Cloud Data Encryption and Decryption

The planned structures make use of cryptographic method properly to complete secure in sequence storage and recovery as illustrate. As individual volume does not enthusiastic for all, the structure has dissimilar plan to covenant by means of the data protection. Moving towards this, an algorithm is planned. Its name as the same as secure various cloud data.

The encryption algorithm and decryption algorithm covenant by the quality of the big data even as accumulate and recover information from collective cloud. The algorithm is definite in such a method that it create use of suitable cryptographic method in organize to accomplish the preferred protection to big data. AES is useful to structured data even as Homomorphic is make use of for unstructured data. The validation behind this is to facilitate the structured information is accumulate in relational database are encrypted and accumulate. After certainty is prepared they are decrypted and achieve the process. In case of unstructured and semi-structured data, precise explore method on encrypted externalization data are indispensable. Intended for this motivation, such data is encrypted by means of Homomorphic encryption.

As revealed in Algorithm 1, present is preference of the variety of data individual supply for protected externalization. Formerly the information is predictable as a demanding type, equivalent protection is useful. Intended for illustration, the structured data is store in the relational databases. While the association's necessity collect data. The information and Meta information are maintain in the form of associations. Consequently it develops into easier to recognize the variety of encryption so as to can provide particular statistics. The information that is stored in the relational schemas desires dissimilar method. Once the data is accessible in the even records, the planned algorithm preserve recognize and obtain suitable result on the intensity of protection or the variety of cryptography appropriate for the identical system. The algorithms delight three types of big data in to two varieties generally. The foremost type is structured data wherever it's stored in associations within the cloud. The occasion, it does accumulate in Relational Data Storage in Amazon Web Services cloud. It desires dissimilar conduct even as the stage to storage and repossession. The model relevance moreover has definite engines or machine to deal with it. Consequently the foremost class is connected to any type of RDBMS in the globe such as MYSQL, Oracle,, DB2 and SQL Server to declare few [11].

Algorithm AESEncrypt()
{
Infer the arrangement of round keys from the figure key. Introduce the state exhibit with the piece information (plaintext) Add the round key to the beginning state cluster

Perform nine rounds of state control.
Play out the tenth and last round of state control.
Duplicate the last state exhibit out as the scrambled information (ciphertext).

}

Algorithm 2: AES based encryption algorithm

The subsequent type include of collectively unstructured and semi-structured data. This approach of the algorithm is to covenant by means of the unstructured data and semi-structured data in a related method. The foundation following this is to facilitate the unstructured data and semi-structured data. The major comparison is the organizer system. In the cooperation of varieties of data are accumulate in even records. The semi-structured data is essentially not linked by means of relational storage data. Consequently, semi-structured data is distributed as identical as to facilitate unstructured data. An acquire to understood the method the algorithm delight big data through two kinds slightly than the definite three class, at this point are the algorithms associated to cryptography to facilitate are in employment by the planned algorithm.

The Advanced Encryption Standard is solitary of the specialized algorithms to supply cryptographic techniques are necessary. It holds the encryption data and decryption data through elevated velocity and it is working through the model relevance to reveal verification of the model. The algorithm is in fact are make use of in the mode illustrate by the structure shown in (see Fig. 2). The structure consent to data vendor to contain big data divides in to quantity of amount in addition to encrypt earlier than externalization them to collective cloud. In the development, this algorithm in employment. This is particularly competent in provisions of the stage encryption process and decryption process. Formerly it is accepted and the structure does the split of the procedure. During the similar manner, as the planned algorithm discover the information to be of subsequent class i.e., unstructured data or semi-structured data. Consequently, it's to be implicit to the structure summarizes the functional to produce make use of of the protection algorithm requisite. In case of big data, the algorithm in employment intended used for secure infrastructure illustrated [12].

The proposed Algorithm 1 discover information to exist unstructured data or semi-structured data, it formulate an assessment to covenant through the choice is to make use of encryption model so as to be existing in Algorithm 3. As soon as evaluate through the AES algorithm. And this algorithm is further appropriate for the variety of data. Because the data is in even records, the algorithm is able to make available additional encryption process. The variety of encryption process in fact formulates the data recovery also resilient.

Algorithm HomomorphicEncrypt ()

{

Step 1: Select any two prime numbers say p and q.

Step 2: Compute the result of those two prime numbers.

Say N = p * q, where p and q being classified and N is open.

Step 3: Select arbitrary number x and a root g of GF(p),where g and x are smaller than p.

Step 4: Compute y = gx mod p. Utilize this y for encryption.

Step 5: Encryption will be performed in following two stages.

a. Select arbitrary whole number r and apply following homomorphic encryption.

$$E1(M) = (M+r*p) \bmod N.$$

b. Select arbitrary whole number k, and then encryption calculations are:

$$Eg(M) = (a, b) = (gk \bmod p, yk \, E1(M) \bmod p)$$

Step 6: Decrypted calculation

$$Dg() \text{ is } M = b * (hatchet) -1 \pmod p.$$

}

Algorithm 3: Encryption algorithm for unstructured data and semi-structured data

So the motivation behind this is to facilitate the algorithm has confident facility to consent to cloud attendant to encompass potential in the stage subjective process or control on the externalization cloud statistics which is in encrypted variety. In general, such information approach commencing the existent instance cloud database such as Cassandra and MongoDB anywhere unstructured data and semi-structured data is accumulates.

It's not necessary but the information preserve approach since different resource. As soon as the future structure discovers big data, it go behind the different methods as it identify. The structure deal among the quality of the data as illustrate in this segment [13].

9 Experimental Results

Conduct experiment are prepared through a model function to exhibit evidence of the conception. The experiential consequences exposed the convenience of the planned structure. Interpretations are prepared in the expressions of implementation instance for encryption process and decryption, entirely upload instance and largely download instance. The consequences demonstrate the diversity in the projected and presented classification. The different experiments are prepared by means of big data of dissimilar amount such as 10 mega bytes, 50 mega bytes, 100 mega bytes, and 500 mega bytes. The consequences are evaluated through the circumstances of the ability method existing. The conduct experiments are prepared with Amazon AWS anywhere EC2 is make use of as calculate cloud and S3 is used for storage space for cloud [12].

9.1 Assessment Execution and Instant Performance

The implementation time diversity between accessible and planned method is converse in this segment. The consequences are making available used for in cooperation encryption process and decryption process of data in dissimilar amount as mention above.

As illustrate in Table 1, It's apparent to the encryption process time and decryption process time of presented and planned system are offered. The performance time beside big data through dissimilar amount is evidence for investigation.

Table 1. Implementation instance assessment in encryption and decryption execution time

Data size (MB)	Encryption presented	Encryption planned	Decryption presented	Decryption planned
10	0.4057	0.3989	0.3945	0.2921
50	2.2237	2.1956	1.4879	1.3925
100	2.7937	2.5968	2.5472	2.0156
500	13.6537	12.9896	9.6734	9.0132

As revealed in (see Fig. 4), it's apparent that the amount of the big data is revealed in parallel association even as the completion time in succeeding is supply in horizontal affiliation. Presently there are two tendency originate in the consequences.

The foremost development exhibit involvement concerning the amount of information and the success time. The data quantity is control routine instance. Since the data amount is enhanced implementation occurrence is enhanced. The consequent enlargement empirical is associated to the association involving the presented and planned

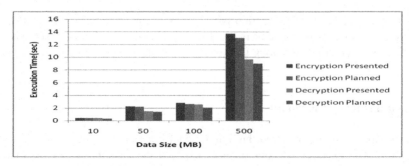

Fig. 4. Execution time comparison in Encryption and decryption

system. Through reverence to encryption process and decryption process, the designed system has enhanced routine than presented organization. The planned method take a smaller amount implementation instance for encryption process and decryption process constantly used for each amount of data measured for research.

9.2 Assessment of Overall Upload Time

The assessment segment provides data concerning the full upload instance of equally presented and proposed method. The overall upload instance refers toward the casing in position in use to encrypt and consignment the data to public cloud. The entire upload instance is considered in subsequent even as the amount of data is deliberate in mega bytes.

Since revealed in Table 2 it is apparent so as to the entire upload moment in seconds to be accessible for equally presented and planned method. The statistics amount is measured to include clarification on the overall upload instance taken.

Table 2. Comparison of data size vs. total upload time

Data size (MB)	Presented method	Planned method
10	0.5862	0.4568
50	2.7162	2.1689
100	4.4762	3.3258
500	17.4262	13.9856

As existing in (see Fig. 5), it is visible to facilitate the instance taken intended for entire upload of data externalization to cloud is supply in upright alliance whereas the straight alliances demonstrate the data volume. While the volume of data is improved, the entire upload instance is also improved.

A different significant inspection is so as to the overall upload point in instance of the planned method is a smaller amount that of the existing method. It discloses the competence of the planned method to upload information to collective cloud with the planned protection method.

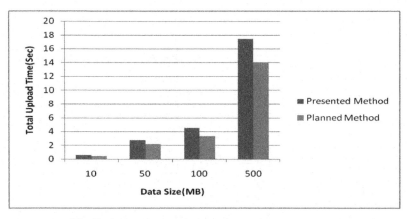

Fig. 5. Execution time for data size vs. total upload time

9.3 Assessment of Total Download Time

This segment supply completion consequences of the model through reverence to interpretation on the entire download instance. The entire download point in time is considered in subsequent and the interpretations are completed with the planned and presented system.

Table 3. Comparison against dissimilar data sizes and total download time

Data size (MB)	Presented method	Planned method
10	0.8058	0.7098
50	2.3237	1.9856
100	3.7937	3.4265
500	13.6537	12.3568

Since the existing in Table 3, it's implicit that here the variation among the instance in use for entire download of information of dissimilar amount. The presented method receive comparatively additional instance while the contrast with to facilitate of the planned method.

As revealed in (see Fig. 6), it's recognize so as to the total download point in time of statistics of different quantity exists in horizontal alliance while the vertical alliance demonstrate the data quantity. In a association between data volume and the entire download point in time.

The difference between planned and presented method. The planned method took a smaller amount instance to download statistics since cloud when evaluate through that of presented method. The presented method is based on AES which is greatly slower than so as to of the planned method. The motivation behind this is that Homomorphic encryption desires fewer composite estimation and it is light mass when evaluate to

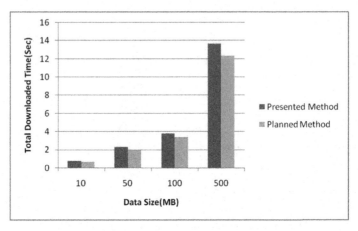

Fig. 6. Data amount vs. entire download time assessment

AES encryption. Consequently, the point in time in use for encryption and decryption is perceptibly less than AES. Intended for uploading and downloading statistics is also enhanced due to the consequence of the planned encryption method. In general point in time in use for upload and download is concentrated moderately.

10 Conclusion

The proposed method for protected cloud storage space. The structure is planned and execute through essential algorithms in organize to encompass two significant process. Protected cloud storage space and protected data recovery. This algorithm planned is identified as Secure Heterogeneous Cloud Data Encryption Process and Decryption Process algorithm. The planned protection architecture acquire the three varieties of data while execute encryption process and decryption process. The three varieties of big data contain structured data, unstructured data and semi-structured data. The algorithms classify the variety of data and supply essential security to the information. The research is prepared with model relevance through interpretation such as encryption time, total upload time and total download time. The consequences discovered that the planned structure is competent of allocate data vendor to achieve process such as encryption process and uploading information to cloud server. Subsequently the data vendor is competent to get requisite statistics and decrypt the process. The planned method is evaluated with a presented method institute in the literature. The consequences demonstrate the presentation enhancement of the planned method over the presented one. The difficulty with the encryption used in this is and that it does not consent to subjective operation on the encrypted and externalization data.

References

1. Philippe Botteri of Accel Partners: Turn big data into big value. White Paper Big Data Analytics, Intel, pp. 1–8 (2013)

2. Ning, Y.X., Li, Y.L.: How we could realize big data value. In: 2nd International Symposium on Instrumentation and Measurement, Sensor Network and Automation (IMSNA), pp. 1–3. IEEE (2013)
3. Gupta, R.: Journey from data mining to web mining to big data. Int. J. Comput. Trends Technol. (IJCTT) **10**(1), 18–20 (2014)
4. Arjun, K., Lee, H., Singh, R.P.: Efficient and secure cloud storage for handling big data, pp. 162–166. IEEE (2013)
5. Lai, J., Deng, R.H., Guan, C., Weng, J.: Attribute-based encryption with verifiable outsourced decryption. IEEE Trans. Inf. Forensics secur. **8**(8), 1–12 (2013)
6. Sharma, P.P., Navdeti, C.P.: Securing big data hadoop: a review of security issues, threats and solution. Int. J. Comput. Sci. Inf. Technol. **5**(2), 1–6 (2014)
7. Rathna, S.S., Karthikeyan, T.: Survey on recent algorithms for privacy preserving data mining. Comput. Sci. **6**(2), 1–6 (2015)
8. Baby, V., Chandra, N.S.: Privacy-preserving distributed a survey data mining techniques. Int. J. Comput. Appl. **143**(10), 1–5 (2016)
9. Aldossary, S., Allen, W.: Data security, privacy, availability and integrity in cloud computing issues and current solutions. Int. J. Adv. Comput. Sci. Appl. **7**(4), 485–498 (2016)
10. Zanoon, N., Al-Haj, A., Khwaldeh, S.M.: Cloud computing and big data is there a relation between the two: a study. Int. J. Appl. Eng. Res. **12**(17), 6970–6982 (2017)
11. Feng, X., Jia, S., Mai, S.: The research on industri al big data information security risks, pp. 19–23 (2018)
12. Stergiou, C., Psannis, K.E., Xifilidis, T., Plageras, A.P., Gupta, B.B.: Security and privacy of big data for social networking services in cloud, pp. 438–443 (2018)
13. Mahmoud, H., Hegazy, A., Khafagy, M.H.: An approach for Big data security based on hadoop distributed file system. In: ITCE 2018. Aswan University, Egypt (2018)
14. Shamsi, J.A., Khojaye, M.A.: Understanding privacy violations in big data systems. IT Prof. **20**(3), 73–81 (2018)
15. Balaga, T.R., Peram, S.R., Paleti, L.: Hadoop techniques for concise investigation of big data in multi-format data sets, pp. 490–495 (2017)
16. Manjunath, T.N., et al.: Data quality assessment model for data migration business enterprise. Int. J. Eng. Technol. (IJET) **5**(1) (2013). ISSN 0975-4024
17. Shrihari, M.R., Archana, R.A., Manjunath, T.N., Hegadi, R.S.: A review on different methods to protect big data sets. (12), 4 (2018)
18. Mehmood, A., Natgunanathan, I., Xiang, Y., Hua, G., Guo, S.: Protection of big data privacy, pp. 2169–3536. IEEE (2016)

Text Categorization: A Lazy Learning-Based Approach

Ankita Dhar[1]([⊠]), Himadri Mukherjee[1], Sk. Md. Obaidullah[2], K. C. Santosh[3], Niladri Sekhar Dash[4], and Kaushik Roy[1]

[1] Department of Computer Science, West Bengal State University, Kolkata, India
ankita.ankie@gmail.com, kaushik.mrg@gmail.com
[2] Department of Computer Science and Engineering, Aliah University, Kolkata, India
sk.obaidullah@gmail.com
[3] Department of Computer Science, The University of South Dakota,
Vermillion, USA
santosh.kc@usd.edu
[4] Linguistic Research Unit, Indian Statistical Institute, Kolkata, India
ns_dash@yahoo.com

Abstract. The instantaneous magnification of digital texts has made text categorization a prime technique for managing and sorting text data. The goal of this study is to present a lazy learning-based text categorization system using text representation features. Experiments were performed on 14,373 texts from nine different categories procured from various online news corpus and magazines. The experimental results show an encouraging outcome of 96.24% accuracy using the K* algorithm. The performance of the system was also tested with other existing approaches and datasets and our system produced a better result.

Keywords: Text categorization · Text representation · Lazy learning · K* algorithm

1 Introduction

The worldwide utilization of the Internet for conveying all kinds of information is amplifying the volume of digital data that is stored and accessed through WWW among various applications. The digital data are mostly in unstructured text form and one of the main sources for search queries and information retrieval tasks. The automatic text categorization systems, that is, assigning the text articles to one or more predefined domains can help the users as well as the information retrieval techniques to fetch the required information. Now, text categorization techniques have various real-world applications such as sentiment analysis, email filtering, topic categorization, and others.

In this paper, a technique has been proposed and evaluated for the development of an automatic text categorization task that aims to categorize 14,373

© Springer Nature Singapore Pte Ltd. 2021
K. C. Santosh and B. Gawali (Eds.): RTIP2R 2020, CCIS 1380, pp. 350–359, 2021.
https://doi.org/10.1007/978-981-16-0507-9_30

Bangla texts from nine domains based on a text representation features using a lazy learning model (K-star algorithms). The system obtained a maximum accuracy of 96.24% using 25 cross-validation folds. The experimental result was also compared with other existing works in Bangla and it can be observed that our system outperformed the existing algorithms in Bangla. The proposed methodology was also tested on the other two standard datasets as well as with other classification algorithms to show the robust nature of the system.

In the rest of the paper, the literature survey is discussed in Sect. 2 followed by the proposed methodology in Sect. 3. In Sect. 4 the results have been discussed and finally Sect. 5 concludes the paper.

2   Literature Survey

The literature study points towards the ample amount of researches for various resourceful languages, however, very few works exist for languages that lack standard databases, resources, and tools such as Indian languages, especially for Bengali. In this section, a few of the recent works performed in various languages have been discussed. For instance, DeySarkar et al. [6] experimented with a clustering-based approach on 13 datasets using Naïve Bayes (NB) algorithm. Guru and Suhil [8] implemented a frequency-based feature along with Support Vector Machine (SVM) and K Nearest Neighbor (KNN) learning models for categorizing 20 Newsgroups articles. Jin et al. [11] experimented with a bag of embeddings models along with stochastic gradient descent (SGD) classifier on 2 standard datasets. Wang et al. [15] tested tf and t-test features on 2 standard datasets and reported quite encouraging outcomes. In the work of Wang and Hong [14], a supervised Hebb rule was used which denotes the tokens and categories as neurons and selects the tokens depending on the criteria that it can be distinctly identified if it stimulates the corresponding categories. Their system was also tested with 7 feature selection schemes on 6 standard databases which shows that their model outperformed all other algorithms.

Al-Salemi et al. [2] experimented with supervised learning algorithms on RTA news dataset. 4 transformation algorithms and 4 adaptation algorithms have been implemented which shows that both RFBoost and Label Powerset along with SVM outperformed other algorithms. Al-Radaideh and Al-Khateeb [1] worked with a rule-based classification model for the development of the Arabic text categorization system. Rakholia and Saini [13] tested the NB algorithm on 280 Gujarati documents from 6 domains and reported an accuracy of 88.96%. Gupta and Gupta [7] tested a hybrid classification approach on 184 Punjabi texts from 7 subcategories of sports domains by fusing NB and Ontological classifiers. ArunaDevi and Saveeth [4] experimented with compound features harvested from Mozhi and CIIL corpus and obtained satisfactory outcomes. Bolaj and Govilkar [5] tested with a dictionary-based approach for classifying Marathi articles along with Modified KNN, ontological, MNB, and SVM learning models. Kabir et al. [12] have applied the SGD classifier and categorizes texts from 9 domains and reported an average accuracy of 93.85%. Islam et al. [10] proposed a model based on tfidf and chi-square methods and obtained an accuracy of 92.57% for the SVM algorithm. Alam and Islam [3] proposed a textual feature-based methodology that categorizes 3,76,226 text articles with a precision of 0.95 using a logistic regression learning model.

3   Proposed Methodology

The paper presents a lazy learning-based text categorization system using some text representation features on 14,373 articles harvested from various online sources. After the collection of articles, pre-processing was performed which includes tokenization and stopword removal followed by the feature extraction schemes discussed in Sect. 3.3 to train K-star algorithm for the classification purpose. The outline of the proposed text categorization technique is shown in Fig. 1.

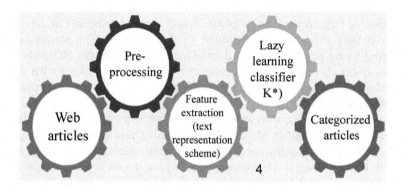

Fig. 1. The workflow of the proposed approach.

3.1   Data

Data is the most major part of any experiment. Since no standard domain-wise datasets are available in Bengali, a dataset was developed consists of 14,373 articles from nine different domains procured from various online news corpus as well as magazines [17–21]. The detailed distribution of the articles for each domain is provided in Table 1.

3.2   Pre-processing

The texts were split into individual 'tokens' using 'space' delimiter before performing further experiments and the process is said to be 'tokenization'. The total token count results to be 57,22,569. Each extracted token in the set is not

Table 1. Document distribution for each domain.

Domain	Distribution
Business (a)	2168
Entertainment (b)	2166
Food and Recipe (c)	1051
Literature (d)	1103
Medical (e)	1047
State affairs (f)	2122
Sports (g)	2134
Science & Technology (h)	1194
Travel (i)	1388
Total	**14,373**

informative and essential enough to be in the feature set for further categorization task. These tokens are referred to be as 'stopword' and were removed from the set to get rid of erroneous results. However, stopwords selection depends on the task being carried out and thus, in the present work, along with the stopwords defined in the list presented in [16], articles and adverbs were treated as stopwords. The total token count after stopword removal task counts to be 44,47,689.

3.3 Feature Extraction

Here, text representation scheme is proposed in order to develop the feature vector. Here, $Article_{Occ}(o_t, doc_s)$ - the occurrence of term in an article and $Dom_{Occ}(doc_s, dom_p)$ - the occurrence of an article in a text domain containing term o_i have been considered as features. Formally, let $O = o_1, o_2, ..., o_i$ represents the set of terms associated with an article, $DOC = doc_1, doc_2, ..., doc_m$ represents the set of articles contains o_i terms, and $DOM = dom_1, dom_2, ..., dom_n$ represents the set of text domains with associated articles.

$$Article_{Occ}(o_t, doc_s) = \frac{AO(o_t, doc_s)}{\sum_{s=1}^{m} AO(o_t, doc_s)}. \tag{1}$$

$$Dom_{Occ}(doc_s, dom_p) = \frac{DO(doc_s, dom_p)}{\sum_{p=1}^{n} DO(doc_s, dom_p)}. \tag{2}$$

The smaller the number of definite text domains where the article occurs with term o_i, the higher the $Article_{Occ}$ and $Dom_{Occ}(doc_s, dom_p)$. The efficiency of these features lies in filtering the terms spread unevenly among various articles;

filtering the articles spread unevenly among various text domains, and eventually evaluates the relevancy of which domains may have the articles associated with given features.

3.4   Classification

K* is a lazy learning-based classifier that learns depending on the instances and aims to enhance its efficiency to deal with missing and actual attributes and simplifying the task. For classification purposes, the similarity is computed between the current and existing instances based on a distance measure and the domain of a close one is assigned to the current instance. The K* algorithm differs from other classifiers in terms of using entropy as the distance measurement function depending on the likelihood of changing an instance into another by selecting randomly among all possible changes. Entropy function is efficient as a distance measure for estimating the distances between the samples. The complexity of changing an instance into another is the distance between the samples obtained in 2 ways: firstly, by defining a definite set of alterations for mapping one sample to another. Secondly, changing one sample to another using code in a definite series of alterations initiating from one and ending at other.

For a given set of unbounded points and pre-defined alterations S, let s denotes the value in S.

$$\bar{s}(i) = s_m(s_{m-1}(...s_1(i)...)) \qquad where, s = s_1..s_m$$

L is a likelihood function on S* satisfying the following characteristics:

$$0 \leq \frac{l(\bar{s}v)}{l(\bar{s})} \leq 1 \tag{3}$$

$$\sum_v l(\bar{s}v) = l(\bar{s}) \tag{4}$$

$$l(\wedge) = 1 \tag{5}$$

As a result satisfying the following:

$$\sum_{s \in l} l(\bar{s}) = 1 \tag{6}$$

The likelihood function l* determines the likelihood of all changes from one sample to another.

$$l*\left(\frac{j}{i}\right) = \sum_{s \in l : s(i) = j} l(s) \tag{7}$$

$$\sum_j l*\left(\frac{j}{i}\right) = 1 \tag{8}$$

$$0 \leq l * \left(\frac{j}{i}\right) \leq 1 \tag{9}$$

The K-star algorithm is determined as follows:

$$K * \left(\frac{j}{i}\right) = -log_2 l * \left(\frac{j}{i}\right) \tag{10}$$

4 Result Analysis

Experimentation was done on the obtained dataset consists of 14,373 Bangla articles from 9 different text domains based on text representation schemes using a lazy learning model (K-star algorithm). The result obtained is given in Table 2.

Table 2. Results using K-star algorithm.

Parameter	Value
Accuracy	96.24%
Kappa statistic	0.9572
Mean absolute error	0.0098
Relative absolute error	5.0233%
TP Rate	0.962
FP Rate	0.006
Precision	0.963
Recall	0.962
F-Measure	0.963

Experimentation was further performed for different cross-validation folds (5, 10, 15, 20, 25, and 30) and the obtained results are provided in Table 3. From the table, it can be observed that the accuracy gets reduced for 30 cross-validation folds. Thus the maximum accuracy obtained for 25 cross-validation folds was considered.

Table 3. Accuracy obtained for different cross-validation folds.

Folds	5	10	15	20	25	30
Accuracy (%)	95.92	96.10	96.14	96.16	**96.24**	96.19

The confusion matrix obtained using 25 cross-validation folds is illustrated in Table 4. The reason behind the number of miscategorization is the higher percentage of similarities of the tokens in the articles of two text categories which made the system unable to identify and categorize articles to the text category it belongs to. The rate of correct and incorrect categorization for all the text domains being considered is given in Table 5 measured using Eq. 11 and Eq. 12.

$$Categorization = \frac{No._-of._-categorized._-articles}{Total._-articles} * 100\% \qquad (11)$$

$$Miscategorization = \frac{No._-of._-miscategorized._-articles}{Total._-articles} * 100\% \qquad (12)$$

Table 4. The confusion matrix for 25 cross-validation folds.

	a	b	c	d	e	f	g	h	i
a	**2047**	4	0	0	1	77	3	36	0
b	2	**2134**	1	0	0	17	11	0	1
c	0	3	**1038**	3	3	0	1	1	2
d	0	8	0	**1079**	1	0	0	0	15
e	9	4	0	0	**995**	30	0	6	3
f	89	12	0	2	7	**1993**	9	3	7
g	10	18	0	0	0	22	**2084**	0	0
h	69	9	0	1	10	5	0	**1098**	2
i	5	2	0	5	0	7	1	3	**1365**

4.1   Comparison with Other Standard Classifiers

The performance of the proposed methodology was also tested with other standard classification algorithms such as Naïve Bayes Multinomial, Random Tree, Decision Table, and SVM using WEKA [9]. The obtained accuracies have been shown in Table 6 from which it can be observed that the lazy learning algorithm (K-star) performed better compared to all other classifiers.

4.2   Comparison with Other Algorithms in Bangla

A comparison of our system's performance was done with other algorithms in Bangla. Since there are no standard datasets available in Bangla, therefore, the framework of each existing methods have been replicated and tested on our obtained dataset consists of 14,373 Bangla text documents. The obtained results for all the algorithms is provided in Table 7 from where it can be observed that our proposed system outperformed the existing algorithms in Bangla.

Table 5. Rate of categorization and miscategorization for all text categories.

Category	Categorization	Miscategorization
Business	94.42%	5.58%
Entertainment	98.52%	1.48%
Food and Recipe	98.76%	1.24%
Literature	97.82%	2.18%
Medical	95.03%	4.97%
State affairs	93.92%	6.08%
Sports	97.66%	2.34%
Science & Technology	91.96%	8.04%
Travel	98.34%	1.66%
Average	**96.27%**	**3.73%**

Table 6. Comparison with other standard classifiers.

Classifiers	Accuracy (%)
K-star	96.24
Naïve Bayes Multinomial	76.96
Random Tree	94.77
Decision Table	71.18
SVM	86.51

4.3 Performance of the System on Other Datasets

The proposed approach was also implemented on two popular and commonly used standard datasets such as Reuters-21578 R8 and 20 Newsgroups to test the performance of the system. The experimental results are given in Table 8 from where it can be observed that our proposed system can work well for Bangla as well as English documents.

Table 7. Comparison with existing algorithms in Bangla.

Reference	Used Feature	Accuracy (%)
Kabir et al. [12]	Tfidf	95.97
Islam et al. [10]	Tfidf & chi-square	95.78
Alam and Islam [3]	Tfidf	95.76
Present work	**Text representation scheme**	**96.24**

Table 8. Performance of proposed approach on other datasets.

Dataset	Size	Accuracy (%)
Reuters-21578 R8	7,674	92.77
20 Newsgroups	18,828	89.52
Our dataset	**14,373**	**96.24**

5 Conclusion

This study presents a lazy learning-based model for categorizing web documents to their respective text domains using text representation schemes. The experiments were tested on 14,373 articles procured from various web news corpora, magazines, and other online sources and obtained a maximum accuracy of 96.24%. The performance of the system was compared with other standard classification algorithms from which it can be noted that the lazy learning-based algorithm (K-star) performed better for categorizing Bangla documents. In the future, the proposed model can be implemented on a larger dataset with text documents from a larger number of text domains. There is a plan to explore other techniques/algorithms such as active learning, deep learning, and clustering-based techniques. In the future, some fusion techniques can also be introduced for text categorization tasks.

Acknowledgement. One of the authors thanks DST for the INSPIRE fellowship.

References

1. Al-Radaideh, Q.A., Al-Khateeb, S.S.: An associative rule-based classifier for Arabic medical text. Int. J. Knowl. Eng. Data Min. **03**, 255–273 (2015)
2. Al-Salemi, B., Ayob, M., Kendall, G., Noah, S.A.M.: Multi-label Arabic text categorization: a benchmark and baseline comparison of multi-label learning algorithms. Inf. Process. Manag. **56**, 212–227 (2019)
3. Alam, M.T., Islam, M.M.: BARD: Bangla article classification using a new comprehensive dataset. In: Proceedings of International Conference on Bangla Speech and Language Processing, pp. 1–5 (2018)
4. ArunaDevi, K., Saveeth, R.: A novel approach on Tamil text classification using C-feature. Int. J. Sci. Res. Dev. **2**, 343–345 (2014)
5. Bolaj, P., Govilkar, S.: Text classification for Marathi documents using supervised learning methods. Int. J. Comput. Appl. **155**, 6–10 (2016)
6. DeySarkar, S., Goswami, S., Agarwal, A., Akhtar, J.: A novel feature selection technique for text classification using Naïve Bayes. Int. Sch. Res. Not. **2014**, 10 (2014)
7. Gupta, N., Gupta, V.: Punjabi text classification using Naive Bayes, centroid and hybrid approach. In: Proceedings of the 3rd Workshop on South and South East Asian Natural Language Processing, pp. 109–122 (2012)

8. Guru, D.S., Suhil, M.: A novel term_class relevance measure for text categorization. In: Proceedings of International Conference on Advanced Computing Technologies and Applications, pp. 13–22 (2015)
9. Hall, M., Frank, E., Holmes, G., Pfahringer, B., Reutemann, P., Witten, I.H.: The WEKA data mining software: an update. SIGKDD Explor. **11**, 10–18 (2009)
10. Islam, Md.S., Jubayer, F.E.Md., Ahmed, S.I.: A support vector machine mixed with TF-IDF algorithm to categorize Bengali document. In: Proceedings of International Conference on Electrical, Computer and Communication Engineering, pp. 191–196 (2017)
11. Jin, P., Zhang, Y., Chen, X., Xia, Y.: Bag-of-embeddings for text classification. In: Proceedings of the 25th International Joint Conference on Artificial Intelligence, pp. 2824–2830 (2016)
12. Kabir, F., Siddique, S., Kotwal, M.R.A., Huda, M.N.: Bangla text document categorization using stochastic gradient descent (SGD) classifier. In: Proceedings of International Conference on Cognitive Computing and Information Processing, pp. 1–4 (2015)
13. Rakholia, R.M., Saini, J.R.: Classification of Gujarati documents using Naïve Bayes classifier. Indian J. Sci. Technol. **05**, 1–9 (2017)
14. Wang, H., Hong, M.: Supervised Hebb rule based feature selection for text classification. Inf. Process. Manag. **56**, 167–191 (2019)
15. Wang, D., Zhang, H., Liu, R., Lv, W.: Feature selection based on term frequency and T-test for text categorization. In: Proceedings of the ACM International Conference on Information and Knowledge Management, pp. 1482–1486 (2012)
16. Stopword. https://www.isical.ac.in/~fire/data/stopwords_list_ben.txt
17. Anandabazar Patrika. https://www.anandabazar.com/
18. Bartaman. http://bartamanpatrika.com/
19. Ebela. https://ebela.in/
20. Ebanglarecipe. https://www.ebanglarecipe.com/
21. Ebanglatravel. https://www.ebanglatravel.com/

Exploring Research Pathways in Record Deduplication and Record Linkage

Vaishali Wangikar[1]([✉]), Sachin Deshmukh[2], and Sunil Bhirud[3]

[1] School of Computer Engineering and Technology, MIT Academy of Engineering, Pune, India
vaishali.wangikar@gmail.com
[2] Department of Computer Science and Information Technology, Dr. Babasaheb Ambedkar
Marathwada University, Aurangabad, India
sndeshmukh@hotmail.com
[3] Department of Computer Engineering and Information Technology, Veermata Jijabai
Technological Institute, Mumbai, India
sgbhirud@vjti.org.in

Abstract. This paper provides a detailed introduction, significance and research progression of record de-duplication (RDD) as well as record linkage (RL) process. The basic study starts with the experimental analysis of various Blocking and Indexing techniques for Record de-duplication process, where Sorted Neighborhood Method (SNM) is found to be the best choice among all the methods. SNM is further improved using Adaptive variants of SNM. The advancements in record de-duplication are further explored and various methods for it are reviewed and implemented. The major two contributions in the unsupervised record de-duplication, FDJ and OATF are implemented and compared where it is observed that OATF which is a completely automated and unsupervised approach performs equally well as compared to unsupervised FDJ approach, where limited automation is achieved.

Keywords: Record linkage · Record de-duplication blocking and indexing ·
Sorted neighborhood method · Unsupervised blocking key formation · Real time
record linkage · Real time record de-duplication · Automated record linkage

1 Introduction

For the correct decision-making process, data need to be collected from several internal as well as external sources. The collection of data, transformation and loading, cleansing of data, detailed analysis and pattern recognition and visualization takes place systematically in a data warehouse framework. As in the data-warehouse repository data are collected from heterogeneous sources having different schema formats and conventions, different data types, different terminologies and also different primary keys. The very first step is to clean the data to assure quality decision making. It is necessary to transform the incoming data into a unified, consistent format for analysis purpose. Proper treatment to the present dirt such as noise, spelling mistakes, missing values, irregular formats,

© Springer Nature Singapore Pte Ltd. 2021
K. C. Santosh and B. Gawali (Eds.): RTIP2R 2020, CCIS 1380, pp. 360–372, 2021.
https://doi.org/10.1007/978-981-16-0507-9_31

redundant values is necessary. Each type of dirt is removed using a unique data cleansing technique [1, 2]. The removal of redundant, duplicate entries from the dataset is an essential task to make correct inferences from the data. The process of removal of duplicate record entries from the data is termed as De-duplication [3, 4]. The duplicate identification and removal take place by two different ways, one with Record De-duplication and other with Record Linkage. In the Record De-duplication process, duplicate record entries are identified and re- moved from the same dataset, while in Record Linkage, two or more datasets having the similar record types are checked to identify whether different records are pointing to the same real-world entity. Record de-duplication and record linkage are having slight difference in processing, in record linkage, duplicates are identified from more than one datasets while in record de-duplication the duplicates from the single datasets are identified. Record linkage is also termed interchangeably as Entity Resolution. The de-duplication and linkage need same techniques to identify duplicates. Thus the technique used for record de-duplication can be used for record linkage; the only difference is in the number of datasets. Both the tasks would have easy if a common unique identifier (unique key) present for the exact matching process, but in practice, as the data is extracted from different heterogeneous sources availability of universal, unique identifier is mostly not possible. Even though the unique identifiers are present in the different data sources, they have different conventions, so the identification of repeated record entries become difficult. So more than one attributes are needed with near similarity to identify duplicates. This paper focuses primarily on the Record De-duplication process [5, 6] though the results and conclusion by this study are equally applicable to the record linkage process.

Applications of Record Linkage and Record De-duplication
In Record linkage, more than one records are linked together to find whether they relate to the identical real-life entity. The entity mentioned here could be some individual, or some family or some business or any identifiable object. Record linking involves linking and merging of more than one datasets into a single file without duplicates. The applications of record linkage or Record de-duplication can be broadly categorized in two different ways. The first application, where two or more databases are combined to produce a single database and removes the repetitive or duplicate entries from it to assure the uniqueness, for example to identify the same patient counted many times for the same disease. The second application, two or more datasets are combined together to assure the more correct search entries (quality data) from different sources, for example, to find the double beneficiary for the same scheme. Many unique entries are reflected in dataset which are not actually unique and refer to the same entity in the dataset, identification of such entries and removing them for improvement in the data quality is the third application of record linkage [7].

The record de-duplication a well as the linkage quality is dependent upon the selection of correct attribute or attributes for matching, and it also depends upon the type of matching, exact matching or approximate matching selection.

2 Literature Survey

This section presents the work done so far in the field of record de-duplication and linkage.

2.1 Deterministic Record De-duplication

Deterministic Record de-duplication [8] is based on the threshold-based similarity match. It is based on the rules of matching similarity so also termed as rule-based de- duplication. While deciding these rules, types of dirt present in the dataset must be considered. The matching rules need a correct selection of attribute or combination of attributes. It also requires the information about the type of data to be matched such as integer, string, date, image or video. The selection of similarity match function, the threshold of acceptance and rejection for similarity match decide the quality of de- duplication.

The deterministic approach is the most straightforward approach of de-duplication. Although to keep the quality of de-duplication, it is necessary to monitor the feasibility of the rules throughout the system, especially when the new data entries are made to the system. If the continuous data entry changes the characteristics of the dataset, then the rebuilding of record de-duplication rules set is required. Thus it may become an expensive and time-consuming task.

2.2 Probabilistic Record Linkage

Several different attributes are taken into consideration to find the distance similarity of the records. Based on the quality of the match, the weights are allocated to these attributes. The probability of match and non-match is calculated by making use of the associated weights. A group records above a certain matching probability threshold are considered as a match and below a threshold are considered as non-match [9].

Probabilistic algorithms allocate similarity/non-similarity weights to the attributes of the dataset by calculating the averages of the two probabilities called as U probability and M probability. U probability can be defined as the probability that an attribute in two non-similar records are found similar. For example, u probability for a 'day' field in Date of Birth attribute is 1/30. The attributes having the non-uniformly distributed values may have different U probabilities, i.e. the attributes with unknown values or missing values. The M probability can be defined as the probability of matching entities in a true duplicate pairs, i.e. for near similar strings, where the distance between the strings is low Jaro-Winkler or Levenshtein distance. This value would be 1.0 in the case of a seamless match. The agreement and dis-agreement weights are calculated based on u and m probability.

2.3 Research Progression in Record De-duplication

The geneticist Howard Newcombe [10] has introduced the concept of record link- age and de-duplication. He used odds ratios of frequencies and the decision rules for describing similar and non-similar record pairs. It is used in many epidemiological applications in health care domain.

$$log2(pL) - log2(pF)$$ (1)

Where, pL is the relative frequency of matches and pF is the relative frequency of non- matches. Further, an approximation is provided to the above odds ratio by the following ratio, as the true matching status is not known.

$$log2(pR) - log2(pR)2$$ (2)

Where, pR is the frequency of a particular string (first name, surname DOB, address, etc.).

Fellegi and Sunter [3] follow Newcombe and a formal mathematical foundations of record linkage is provided through their research. The optimality of the decision rules is demonstrated by the researchers. Further the datasets under considerations are classified the datasets into matches, M and non-matches U. the ratios of these probabilities is given by the Eq. (3).

$$R = P(\gamma\varepsilon\Gamma|M)\ P(\gamma\varepsilon\Gamma|U)$$ (3)

Where, γ is an arbitrary agreement pattern in a comparison space Γ, $\gamma\varepsilon\Gamma$ is a relative frequency of specific attribute. The ratio R is a matching score (or weight).The decision rule is given by:

If R $>$ θ, then mark the pair as a match.

If R $<$ θ, then mark the pair as a non-match.

Where, Θ and θ are the upper and lower cutoff threshold respectively, are determined by a priori error bounds on false matches and false non-matches.

$$If(\theta \leq R \leq \Theta)$$ (4)

Then, the given pairs are treated as a probable match and marked for manual review.

In case of three matching fields and only simple agree/disagree weights are considered, then a conditional independence assumption is shown as

$$P(agree\ first,\ agree\ last,\ agree\ age\ |\ M\ ) =$$
$$P(agree\ first\ |\ M\ )\ P(agree\ last\ |\ M\ )\ P(agree\ age\ |\ M\ )$$ (5)

Similarly,

$$P(agree\ first,\ agree\ last,\ agree\ age\ =\ |\ U) =$$
$$P(agree\ first\ |\ U)\ P(agree\ last\ |\ U)\ P(agree\ age\ |\ U)$$ (6)

Such conditional independence assumption must hold on all combinations of attributes that are used in matching.$P(agree\ first|U)$, $P(agree\ last|U)$, and $P(agree\ age|U)$ are called as Marginal Probabilities while $P(|M)\&P(|U)$ is called the M and U-Probabilities, respectively. A total agreement weight can be defined as the natural logarithm of the ratio R of the probabilities. The logarithms of the ratios of probabilities associated with individual attributes are called the Individual Agreement Weights. The M and U probabilities are also referred to as matching fields. In the conditional independence circumstances, the parameters are calculated through the simple Expectation maximization (EM) algorithm [10]. The EM algorithm which finds the maximum likelihood estimates of parameters is termed a 'Frequentist Approach'. It is mainly used in handling unknown or missing data.

EM is a probabilistic approach which needs availability of the training dataset. EM may not be effective if the dataset has typographical errors and missing values in huge quantity.

On the other hand, for the deterministic approach, there is no need of training dataset, although the intervention of human expert is required to provide appropriate rules for matching pairs. If the deterministic approach is used distance-based algorithms such as Jaro distance, Edit distance, Levenshtein distance algorithms must be chosen with the correct threshold. Availability of domain expert and need of distance-based algorithm with a correct threshold is necessary for the deterministic algorithm. Poor choice of a threshold may lead to poor de-duplication.

Apart from the quality of de-duplication, the process of record de-duplication is further refined for optimization in comparison space. As finding the similarity among the different records is the main task of record de-duplication, the naive approach requires similarity to be measured for all pairs in the entire dataset. The process of matching similarity in a pairwise fashion raises the computational complexity quadratically with the size of the input dataset. Therefore scaling is much more needed for similarity matching especially for large datasets. Also, at many a times, the similarity checking tasks become unnecessary, because many of the record pairs are not similar and just add comparison time unnecessarily.

Blocking methods [11] are introduced to improve the efficiency of similarity match process. Blocking assimilates similar records in a group or blocks using certain criteria. Blocking can be based on pre-specified similarity threshold which groups the similar pairs together based on their similarity distances, for example, Jaro-Winkler distance, Levenshtein distance, Jaccard similarity distance [5] etc. Another way of blocking is to sort the records lexicographically on pre-specified blocking key or token and group them for similarity match. Human intervention is needed for both of these tasks in blocking, one for parameter setting and other for the selection of correct blocking key. A detailed overview of several blocking and indexing techniques is presented by Peter Christen [12]. Sorted Neighbourhood method, Q-gram based indexing, suffix array-based indexing, canopy clustering, string map based indexing are few indexing and blocking techniques discussed by Christen.

The researchers further explored the techniques required to handle de-duplication for web-based systems [13]. An unsupervised online record matching techniques are used to handle web-based De-duplication. Network bottleneck caused during online de-duplication is reduced using the decision tree approach [14]. A progressive sorted neighbourhood method and progressive blocking techniques are used to improve the speed of de-duplication in large datasets [15]. A Map-reduce distributed framework is used for implementing parallel Sorted neighbourhood method for improving speed and scalability of de-duplication, especially for large datasets [16]. A Temporal record linkage approach is used for de-duplication for the records collected over a period of time. For example, in the Customer Care databases, often temporal information is present, such as the time of instance creation or modification. Temporal De-duplication keeps track of changes that happened to a record over the period of time during de-duplication. A regression-based approach is used for temporal De-duplication over the traditional model for temporal datasets [17]. Karapiperis use Bloom filter space and Hamming Locality–Sensitivity hashing for online record linkage. The Bloom filter-based blocking technique improves response time as well as recall which a requirement of online systems [18].

Ma et al. [19] make use of domain type and subtype information of attributes for blocking key formation. A genetic algorithm is used for selecting a correct predicate for de- duplication [20]. A semi-supervised de-duplication is provided using ensemble learning [21]. Unigram based blocking key generation technique is used for automatic blocking key generation by Vogal and Felix Naumann [22]. Fisherman discrimination based blocking scheme is used for unsupervised blocking key generation [23]. A Fisher Dis-Junctive Dynamic Sorted Neighborhood Indexing method is used for unsupervised blocking key formation and extended use of it for real time record de- duplication [24]. Two different semi-supervised approaches are proposed based on recursive feature elimination and rough set approach by Wangikar *et al.* [25, 26]. A fully automated blocking key formation is proposed by Wangikar *et al.* using the relevance feedback mechanism. A real time de-duplication framework is also proposed by the researchers [25].

Thus the record de-duplication research work addresses several issues such as quality of de-duplication, optimization of comparison space, speed and scalability of de-duplication, de-duplication in large datasets, de-duplication in temporal and web-based datasets, Online de-duplication, semi-supervised as well as unsupervised de-, real-time de-duplication. Thus from basic to advanced techniques in de-duplication are discussed by several researchers.

3 Blocking and Indexing Techniques

Peter christen studied and reviewed various blocking and indexing methods. The methods like sorted neighborhood, q gram indexing, canopy clustering, suffix array indexing, string map based indexing are discussed and implemented in this section.

In Sorted Neighborhood Method (SNM), a correct blocking key chosen by the domain expert is used to sort the records and the fixed size widow is used for identifying duplicates within it. Due to sorting and windowing, similar records are grouped together, and comparison space is reduced to the window size, which provides faster de-duplication and reduces complexity [27]. With fixed-sized window, there is always a possibility of missing duplicates, if the size of blocking window is smaller than the number of actual duplicates. On the other hand, there will be unnecessary comparisons if the blocking-window size is larger than the duplicates present. An adaptive approach of SNM uses flexible window size to overcome the issue of fixed window size and provides better efficiency for de-duplication. Adaptive SNM has two approaches Accumulative Adaptive (AA-SNM) and Incrementally Adaptive (IA-SNM) [28]. Felix Naumann *et al.* put forth an alternate adaptive SNM approach which have improved SNM in the flexibility of window size called as Duplicate Count Strategy (DCS) [29].

The Canopy blocking is proposed by McCallum *et al.* [30]. The similarity match algorithm which allows efficient retrieval of all records within pre- defined distance threshold from a randomly selected record. Canopy centres are chosen randomly for forming Blocks which retrieves similar records within a pre-defined threshold.

Q gram based indexing [31] is another approach for blocking as well as indexing where Q grams are the substrings of length q. During similarity checking of two records, the q-grams of both the sets are matched with one another, and the intersecting q-grams are found out. These number of intersecting q-grams are converted into a similarity using coefficient methods.

In suffix array indexing [32] suffixes are used for blocking purpose. TF/ IDF similarity match techniques are used for making clusters of record for de-duplication. String map based indexing uses the distance between the strings to form the group.

A comparison of all blocking and indexing methods with respect to response time is shown in Fig. 1. From the Fig. 1 it can be concluded that SNM outperforms all remaining blocking methods.

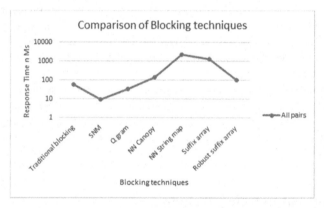

Fig. 1. Response time comparison (log scale) of different blocking and indexing techniques

It has been observed that SNM has gain popularity due to fast response time as compared to other methods. Though SNM has fewer limitations such as unnecessary comparisons when the window size is more than the potential duplicates and missing few duplicates when window size is less than the potential duplicates.

4   Adaptive Variants of SNM

The limitations of SNM are addressed through Adaptive SNM approach. Accumulative Adaptive SNM (AA-SNM), Incrementally Adaptive SNM (IA-SNM), Duplicate count strategy (DCS, DCS++) [28, 29] are all adaptive variants of SNM.

In IA-SNM the boundaries between the two adjacent windows are found out using distance threshold. Window enlargement and retrenchment are performed according to the threshold criteria, and the non-overlapping windows of different sizes are made for comparison [28].

In AA-SNM minimum window size is set initially and the window is enlarged till the records follow the similarity distance threshold criteria. Thus many windows are accumulated to form an enlarged window. The Retrenchment is done to fit only desirable records in the window. Thus a flexible window is created for comparison [28].

For DCS, the blocking-window size is determined on the basis of the already marked duplicates for the window. If more duplicates found, it enlarges the blocking-window to accommodate them. If no duplicates found in neighborhood records, it is assumed that there are no duplicates present and window boundary is decided [29]. DCS++ is a refinement to DCS approach where instead of on adding every duplicate record in the window, the next (w-1) records are added where w is the window size. Transitive closure is calculated to save comparison time [29]. For experimentation two real datasets Cora and Restaurant are used.

A comparative analysis of SNM with all variants of Adaptive SNM is depicted in Fig. 2.

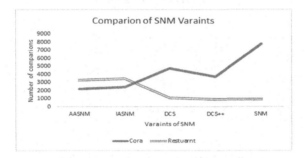

Fig. 2. Comparison of all variants of Sorted neighborhood method

It is observed that all the Adaptive variants of SNM proven better than SNM, especially in terms of the number of matching steps. SNM needs much more comparisons as compared to adaptive methods. It is seen that DCS++ method outperforms in the restaurant while in Cora dataset IA and AA SNM methods perform well.

The evaluation criteria for the de-duplication process is given by the three parameters Pair Completeness (PC), Reduction Ratio (RR) and F-Score.

PC is a measure of true positive coverage, RR is measure how efficiently the blocking schemes the comparison space. High values of RR shows a reduction in comparison space. F score is a harmonic mean of PC and RR values. The Pair completeness, Reduction Ration and F-score comparison of all adaptive SNM approaches for Restaurant dataset are shown in Fig. 3 while Fig. 4 shows it for Cora Dataset.

It is observed that the performance of all adaptive methods is nearly equal for Restaurant dataset. IASNM has shown better performance over the rest of the methods for Cora data. Due to better performance of Adaptive variants of SNM, many researchers prefer ASNM for the advanced research in Record de-duplication.

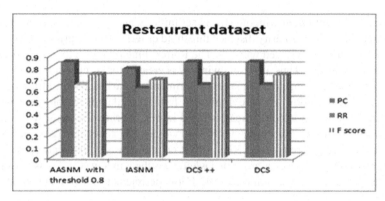

Fig. 3. Comparison of ASNM for restaurant

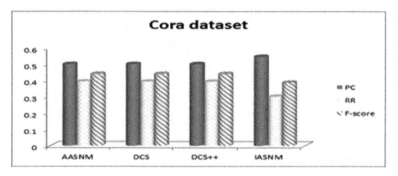

Fig. 4. Comparison of ASNM for CORA

5   Advanced Record De-duplication Techniques

In the current business scenario, maximum businesses are on either on b-based or real times systems. The data is updated and feed to the systems continuously. For making decisions, the fresh real-time data is needed as stale data may hamper decision making. Thus to cater to today's real time systems a scalable, as well as real time de-duplication, is required. Following is the overview of some unsupervised RDD methods which can fulfil the requirements of Real-time environments.

Vogal and Felix Naumann propose an approach of automatic blocking key selection based on unigram indexing [22] which is a step toward automatic de-duplication process. A two-step process is followed for blocking key formation, in the first step, all possible uni-keys are generated, with each of these keys de-duplication is per- formed on the training gold standard dataset. The comparison threshold set for acceptance and rejection of keys. If any of these keys exceeds the number of comparisons, it is discarded else the Blocking key quality is calculated. All the accepted keys are sorted according to the Blocking key quality. This is the first step called as training phase. In the second step, all the shortlisted blocking keys of the training phase are validated against new dataset using de-duplication algorithm. The keys do not follow the specified criteria are discarded while the remaining keys are accepted. Although the algorithm is claimed as unsupervised, it needs a gold standard dataset to validate the similar type of new dataset, thus entire automation of the system is not achieved.

Further, Kejriwal *et al.* [23] explored unsupervised blocking key formation termed as FDJ. The approach is two-step, in the first step, a weakly labelled training set is generated using TF-IDF similarity. From the weakly labelled set, feature vector sets are derived using all pre-specified specific blocking predicates, and a Boolean vector set is made. In the second phase, Fisher discrimination formula is used to find the optimum feature set as a token or blocking key. The fisher based blocking keys performed better than the manual key approach. Though it is claimed as unsupervised but complete automation of the algorithm is not achieved. Human intervention is needed to set specific blocking key predicates.

The research work of Kejriwal is taken forward by Banda Ramdan *et al.* [24]. Ramdan *et al.* use Fisher Discrimination (FD) based record de-duplication termed as FDY-SN approach and used it for Real time Record linkage framework. They use a three-step approach. In the first step, the training dataset is identified. This dataset is used for learning blocking keys. In the second step, TF-IDF similarity match along with special blocking predicates are used to identify the duplicate and non-duplicate groups. In the third step, optimal blocking keys are identified using fisher score, block size and distribution of blocks. A threshold is set to decide the size of the block, the keys which generate block more than the threshold are discarded. Blocks of similar sizes are preferred to avoid the skew.

Thus, the optimal blocking keys made available for real-time record linkage framework. The dynamic similarity aware indexes are used for the real-time framework. Three types of indexes are used Block index (BI), Similarity index (SI), and Record index (RI). Whenever there is any new insertion or modification occurs to the dataset, the attribute values are inserted into RI, based on it, its block is identified, and similarities between the existing and new attributes are calculated and stored in SI. Thus online updations are handled by the real-time framework.

As FD approach which is used by Ramdan as well as Kejriwal needs human intervention for setting specific blocking predicates, also, in FDY-SN approach the optimal size of the blocks is needed to be decided prior by the domain experts. Therefore both these parameter settings make it unsuitable for fully automated real-time environment. While concluding one can say that fully automated blocking keys and fully automated record linkage are remain unattended by both the approaches discussed.

Wangikar *et al.* [25, 26] work on the same line, for unsupervised, automated blocking key formation. A fully automated way of blocking key formation, Optimized Automated Token Formation (OATF) is proposed. It is a two-step approach; in the first step, primary feature set is prepared using distinct and null feature count; in the second step, a recursive feature elimination is used to select the optimal features. The frequent duplicate coverage (FDC) is calculated for each feature, the features having FDC less than the mean FDC are discarded, and the optimal blocking key feature set is made ready. This approach does not need any human intervention for making tokens. However, as it is based on deterministic distance-based de-duplication, the rebuilding of Key formation logic is needed if the data characteristics of the dataset are changed drastically over the period of time.

Wangikar *et al.* use the automated token formation approach further to build Real time De-duplication framework. The Sorted dis-joint indexes (SID) of blocking key values (BKV) are maintained with the repeat count of each index entry. For the new entry of the record, the blocking key value is generated based of blocking key logic, the new BKV is matched with existing BKVs from SID, if the match is found then the repeat count is increased and de-duplication takes place, in case the match is not found in SID then a new entry of BKV is inserted at appropriate place in SID and repeat count is maintained, and de-duplication takes place using DCS++. Thus Automated Record de- duplication is used to build a framework for real-time de-duplication process.

The experimental evaluations of unsupervised tokens formation approaches such as FDJ and OATF with supervised manual tokens for Cora and Restaurant datasets are in shown in Fig. 5 and Fig. 6 respectively.

It is observed that both the unsupervised approaches FDJ by Kejriwal *et al.* and OATF by Wangikar *et al.* outperform supervised manual token. OATF, which is a completely automated approach, perform equally well as that of FDJ approach for Restaurant dataset. OATF shows little low pair completeness for Cora dataset, as the approach is completely automated in comparison with FDJ which is governed by human intervention for setting few parameters of blocking, thus it can be concluded that OATF works equally good and suitable for real time environments where no human intervention is expected.

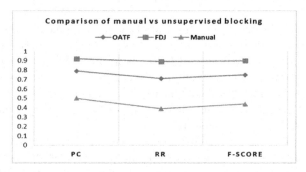

Fig. 5. Comparison of manual and unsupervised, automated blocking for restaurant

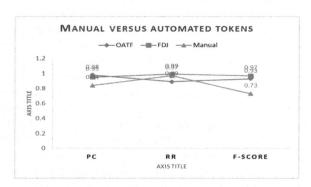

Fig. 6. Comparison of manual and unsupervised automated blocking for cora

6 Conclusions

This paper reviews the entire progress of research in the field of record linkage as well as record de-duplication. The process of identification of duplicates started with the initial concern of identification of correct duplicate and non-duplicate groups from the dataset. The research is further focused on optimizing the task of similarity comparison using blocking and indexing methods. The Comparative analysis of various blocking and indexing methods guided the most suitable and preferred method of blocking, i.e. SNM. The popular blocking method, SNM is further improvised for the scalability, temporal nature of data, web-based data and real time data. The unsupervised and fully automated, real time record de-duplication is explored till date.

The paper presented all pathways of progress in Record linkage and de-duplication systematically and provided an experimental evaluation of many methods wherever needed.

References

1. Li, L.: Data quality and data cleaning in database applications, vol. 242 (2012)
2. Lorenzi, L.: Missing Data Problems in Record Linkage-How to Find Links and Non-. Links, vol. 2001, pp. 1–3 (2013)
3. Fellegi, I.P., Sunter, A.B.: A theory for record linkage. J. Am. Stat. Assoc. **64**(328), 1183–1210 (1969)
4. William, E.: Winkler: Matching and Record Linkage (1983)
5. Elmagarmid, K., Member, S.: Duplicate Record Detection : a Survey (shorter version). IEEE Trans. Knowl. Data Eng. **19**(1), 1–16 (2007)
6. Goiser, K., Christen, P.: Towards automated record linkage. In: Conference on Research and Practice in Information Technology Series, vol. 61, pp. 23–31 (2006)
7. Thomas, W.E.W., Herzog, N., Scheuren, F.J.: Applications of record Linkage Techniques. https://www.soa.org/library/newsletters/the-actuary-magazine/2007/february/link, February 2007
8. Muse, A.G., Mikl, J., Smith, P.F.: Evaluating the quality of anonymous record linkage using deterministic procedures with the New York state aids registry and a hospital discharge file. Stat. Med. **14**, 499–509 (1995)
9. Blakely, T., Salmond, C.: Probabilistic record linkage and a method to calculate the positive predictive value. Int. J. Epidemiol. **31**, 1246–1252 (2002)
10. Newcombe, H.B., Kennedy, J.M., Axford, S.J., James, A.P.: Automatic linkage of vital records. Science PUBMED **130**(1959), 954–959 (1959)
11. Kelley, R.P.: Blocking considerations for record linkage under conditions of uncertainty. In: Proceedings of Social Statistics Section, pp. 602–605 (1984)
12. Christen, P.: A survey of indexing techniques for scalable record linkage and de-duplication. EEE Trans. Knowl. Data Eng. **24**(9), 1–20 (2011)
13. Ravikanth, M., Vasumathi, D.: Record matching over query results from multiple web databases with duplicate detection. J. Adv. Res. Dyn. Control Syst. **10**(4), 2040–2049 (2018)
14. Dey, D., Mookerjee, V.S., Liu, D.: Efficient techniques for online record linkage. IEEE Trans. Knowl. Data Eng. **23**(3), 373–387 (2011)
15. Papenbrock, T., Heise, A., Naumann, F.: Progressive duplicate detection. IEEE Trans. Knowl. Data Eng. **27**(5), 1316–1329 (2015)
16. Kolb, L., Thor, A., Rahm, E.: Parallel Sorted Neighborhood Blocking with MapReduce (2010)

17. Kim, J., Shim, K.: General chairs, preface. Lecture Notes Computer Science (including Subser. Lecture Notes Artificial Intelligence Lecture Notes Bioinformatics), LNAI, vol. 10234, pp. 561–573 (2017)
18. Karapiperis, D.: Summarization algorithms for record linkage. In: Edbt, pp. 73–84 (2018)
19. Ma, Y., Tran, T.: TYPiMatch. In: Proceedings of Sixth ACM International Conference on Web search data Min. - WSDM 2013, p. 325 (2013)
20. De Carvalho, G., Laender, A.H.F., Andre, M., Silva, A.S.: A genetic programming approach to record deduplication. IEEE Trans. Knowl. Data Eng. 24(3), 399–412 (2012)
21. Jurek, A., Hong, J., Chi, Y., Liu, W.: A novel ensemble learning approach to unsupervised record linkage. Inf. Syst. 71, 40–54 (2017)
22. Vogel, T., Naumann, F.: Automatic blocking key selection for duplicate detection based on unigram combinations. In: International Work Quality (2012)
23. Kejriwal, M., Miranker, D.P.: An unsupervised algorithm for learning blocking schemes. In: Proceedings - IEEE International Conference on Data Mining, ICDM, pp. 340–349 (2013)
24. Ramadan, B.: Indexing Techniques for Real-Time Entity Resolution, vol. March (2016)
25. Wangikar, V.C., Deshmukh, S.N., Bhirud, S.G.: An Efficient approach for automated token formation for record de-duplication with special reference to real-time data-warehouse environment. Int. J. Eng. Adv. Technol. 4, 151–159 (2019)
26. Wangikar, V.C., Deshmukh, S.N., Bhirud, S.G.: Rough set based approach for automated token formation in real-time record. J. Adv. Res. Dyn. Control Syst. 11, 380–390 (2019)
27. Hernández, M.A., Stolfo, S.J., Hernandez, M.A.: Real-world data is dirty: data cleansing and the merge/purge problem. Data Min. Knowl. Disc. 2(1), 9–37 (1998)
28. Yan, S., Lee, D., Kan, M.-Y., Giles, L.C.: Adaptive sorted neighbourhood methods for efficient record linkage. In: Proceedings of 2007 Conference Digital Library - JCDL 2007, p. 185 (2007)
29. Draisbach, U., Naumann, F., Szott, S., Wonneberg, O.: Adaptive windows for duplicate detection. In: Proceedings - International Conference on Data Engineering, pp. 1073–1083 (2012)
30. Mccallum, A., Ungar, L.H.: Efficient clustering of high-dimensional data sets with application to reference matching. In: Proceedings of the Sixth ACM SIGKDD International Conference on Knowledge Discovery and Data Mining, pp. 169–178 (2000)
31. Navarro, G.: Indexing text with approximate q –grams. J. Disc. Algorithms 3(2–4), 157–175 (2005)
32. De Vries, T., Ke, H., Chawla, S., Christen, P.: Robust record linkage blocking using suffix arrays and bloom filters, ACM Trans. Knowl. Disc. Data 5(2), 1–27 (2011)

Enhancing Enterprise Business Processes Through AI Based Approach for Entity Extraction – An Overview of an Application

Ankit Dwivedi$^{(\boxtimes)}$, Praveen Vijayan, Rishi Gupta, and Preeti Ramdasi

TCS Data Office, Analytics & Insights, Tata Consultancy Services, Pune, India
{ankit.dwivedi2,praveen.vijayan,rishi.g,preeti.ramdasi}@tcs.com

Abstract. While Industries are growing strong with their digital transformation, advanced analytics are making them stronger through data driven decisions. At the same time traditional automation is getting matured and emerging as cognitive automation. In the era of Industry 4.0, handshake of business process automation, advance analytics and cognitive services have laid down a strong platform for 'Cognitive Bots'. Enterprises can leverage the advent of powerful technologies and approaches, anticipating ultimate goal of the business through more adaptive, self-learning, and contextual applications. This paper explains one of such cognitive bot for finance department where invoices are of utmost importance for the function. The mentioned bot is intended for amount detection and verification; additionally, it can also extract various entities like organization name, location and date which contributes to perform analytics to a great extent. The application reward business in reducing turnaround time and human errors. The accuracy of specially customized trained neural model has achieved state of the art results on the current set of learning data. The proposed framework makes use of Optical Character Recognition and PDFMiner for text extraction from scanned invoices. A Quality Classifier that will reject hand written invoices for any further processing. A spaCy's *Name-Entity-Recognition* predicts the amount, date, organization name and location from extracted unstructured text.

Keywords: Invoice processing · Optical Character Recognition (OCR) · Name Entity Recognition (NER) · Tesseract · spaCy · Convolution Neural Network (CNN) · Image processing

1 Introduction

Invoices in hard copies, as well as soft versions, are referred to everywhere as a proof of financial transactions. The finance department of any organization consumes a lot of time in storing and verifying these documents for further processing [1]. At some organizations, an employee is allowed to claim reimbursement. Whereas there are multiple stakeholders involved for approval of the claims. Also, there is more than one document submitted for the claim along with the claim form. It becomes very critical to verify every document and confirm the relevance of the claim raised and the submitted invoices. At

© Springer Nature Singapore Pte Ltd. 2021
K. C. Santosh and B. Gawali (Eds.): RTIP2R 2020, CCIS 1380, pp. 373–380, 2021.
https://doi.org/10.1007/978-981-16-0507-9_32

the same time tallying the amount consumed as mentioned on invoices and amount that is claimed needs focused attention of the one who is responsible for verifying and passing the claim for further approval. At big organizations like Tata Consultancy Services where more than four lakhs of employees are allowed to claim some or the other type of monetary consumption, there are other transactions with so many vendors, it brings tremendous load on finance department and all its subunits who are stakeholders in the approval process. For the finance staff, it is very stressful job that demands on-time completion of total work, meeting compliance of turnaround time of individual claim and the most implicit demand of correctness. Referring to this, human limitations of work efficiency, scarcity of skilled resources and reduced excitement due to repetitive monotonous nature of work are key risk contributors for incorrect processing at the most important operating unit in any of the organization.

An automated way of processing these claims has become a necessity to address above mentioned issues in manually processing the work. This paper talks about a method proposed to automatically extract intended entity from variety of invoices. The primary target is to identify amount mentioned on the invoice. The experimental results are encouraging and depicts better efficiency and accuracy.

2   Motivation

Researchers are trying to address this area of problem for years. A lot of work has been done on Optical Character Recognition, template matching techniques, handwritten character recognitions and relevant sub areas of the domain. However, success is not satisfactory for developing a generalized solution so as to convert the invention into a product or an application.

There are multiple challenges to address for generalization of the solution as compared to template matching approach. The complexity in problem of recognition increases mainly due to the large variety of invoices. We have studied the variation of invoices; these are mentioned below.

a) Various size or dimension	e) Font size	i) Resolution or clarity
b) Orientation	f) Font color	j) Machine printed
c) Paper color	g) Skewness	k) Handwritten
d) Font types	h) Rotation	l) Language

To overcome these difficulties a framework is designed which is specially customized for invoices and is capable of handling the above stated variations. Following section takes reader to a further technical detail of the said AI based cognitive BOT.

3   High Level Design of Framework

The framework is designed and implemented using Artificial Intelligence at its core. This is a framework of multiple modules intended for independent work. Every module processes the outcome of earlier module and is considered the basis for the next module's outcome. The Reconciliation module finally validates the recognized entity with the information on the claim form. Following diagram in Fig. 1 shows the framework modules and their process workflow. The modules are as below

a) Invoice pre-processing module
b) Image quality classification module
c) Image to text conversion module
d) Entity extraction module
e) Reconciliation module.

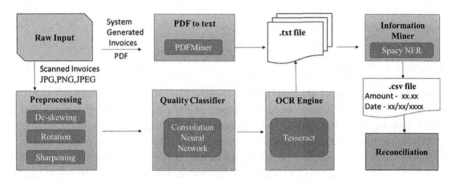

Fig. 1. Architecture of Invoice processing framework

The proposed architecture uses state of the art algorithms in the research domain like, i) a neural network-based quality classifier to identify handwritten invoices. Thus, the proposed system is trained to reject and not invest into processing handwritten invoices. Such invoices are kept for manual verification, ii) Tesseract OCR (Optical Character Recognition) for extracting text from an image, and iii) Neural network based spaCy model to capture invoice entities like amount, date, organization name and location.

With the proposed solution, artificial intelligence is developed in two parts. The first part is for determining the processability of invoices and converting it into textual form. Here unstructured data is collated for accepted invoices for further processing. The second part is for intended information mining from the unstructured digital text. The Reconciliation module produces statistical results of the entire processing. This is an important outcome that helps to derive business intelligence and take strategic decisions.

4   About the Dataset

The data set contains 3000 invoices both handwritten and machine printed. 2500 images are of PNG, JPG and JPEG format and 500 that of PDF format. Such diverse dataset used in this research work includes invoices in different languages like English, Mandarin, and Nihongo. As the initial phase of the work is intended only for amount and date printed on the invoice, the language in which invoices were printed had no role in the analysis.

5 Major Components of the Framework

In this section, components of the proposed invoice processing framework are described in detail. The overall accuracy of the entire framework mainly depends on accuracy of following three components.

1. Quality Classifier
2. Tesseract OCR
3. spaCy information miner

5.1 Quality Classifier

Manually written invoices are improperly processed by OCR and produces shoddy outcomes. Various methods have been implemented for classifying hand written text in images from machine written text. M. Emambakhsh et al. [2] have used pattern matching techniques to classify the images that were hand-written, however, pattern matching techniques does not generalize on a data set having different structure of the invoices. Zagoris et al. [3] used the Bag of Visual Words model (BoVW) to do the same kind of classification and got good accuracy while the local features were extracted using Scale-Invariant Feature Transform (SIFT) [4], and the Speeded-up Robust Features (SURF) [5]. Both the algorithms SIFT and SURF involved licensing and hence it is not considered for this implementation. Therefore, the proposed framework for automatic invoice processing has a quality classifier which uses a 4-layer Convolution Neural Network (CNN) [6] that segregates the handwritten invoices and process only the machine printed invoices. The CNN contains two convolution layers and two dense layers.

The experimental result of training and validation loss with respect to the number of epochs is shown in Table 1 below. While doing the experiment using 2500 invoices, 2000 images were taken for training the model and the remaining 500 for validation. Monitoring the training and validation loss on the balanced dataset for the two classes suggests that the model learns fast and it quickly over fits the training dataset.

Table 1. Experimental results showing training and validation, loss and accuracy at different epochs

Training		Validation		Number of epochs
Loss	Accuracy	Loss	Accuracy	
0.72	0.58	0.68	0.5	1
0.22	0.91	0.37	0.81	25
0.1	0.96	0.26	0.96	50

The Quality Classifier is able to correctly classify hand written invoices from machine printed invoices. Therefore, integration of the quality classifier in the framework segregates hand written invoices so that it can be processed manually.

5.2 Optical Character Recognition (OCR)

Optical character recognition is an instrument that converts scanned documents or images into machine-readable text. This work emphasizes the use of 'Tesseract' OCR engine to extract the text of machine printed scanned invoices. It was developed as a proprietary software by Hewlett Packard Labs. In 2005, it was publicly released by HP as a team with the University of Nevada, Las Vegas. Since 2006 it has been actively developed by Google and many open source contributors [7].

What makes the problem more challenging is the structure of invoices that varies a lot. We could discover invoices of different size or dimensions, direction, paper shading, textual style types, text dimension, textual style shading, skewness, revolution, goals or lucidity. In general, Tesseract is able to serve our purpose. It is observed that the results are impermissible when the input image is blurred, tilted or rotated, or had skewness. Depending on the input, preprocessing [8] methods like deburring, text skew correction [9] are applied to improve the accuracy of the OCR.

The output from Tesseract OCR will be unstructured text extracted from the invoices in digital format. In case, when the invoices are not in English, Tesseract correctly identifies the numerical digits which are needed to detect amount from invoices. Also, one important point to note here is that Tesseract's overall performance may be low, but after image pre-processing and customization for invoices, numerical digits present in the invoices had been quite accurately described by it. Finally, the extracted unstructured text from OCR will be the input to the information miner in the next stage to detect the relevant entities.

5.3 Information Miner

A 'Master-mind' of the proposed framework is Information Miner. This Name Entity Recognition (NER) is to extract entities like amount, date, organization name and location, from the unstructured text from OCR. An open source library for advanced natural language processing, spaCy [10] is used for this purpose. It highlights new neural models for labeling, parsing and element acknowledgment. These models have been specially crafted to give a superior blend of speed and exactness. Model 1, 2 and 3 described below

Table 2. Description of spaCy's models that were used for NER without any further training

Model1: en_core_web_sm	It is the English multi-task CNN trained on OntoNotes [11] It assigns context-specific token vectors, POS tags, dependency parse and named entities
Model2: en_core_web_md	It is English multi-task CNN trained on OntoNotes, with GloVe [12] vectors trained on Common Crawl. It assigns word vectors, context-specific token vectors, POS tags, dependency parse and named entities
Model 3: en_vectors_web_lg	It is a 300-dimensional word vectors trained on Common Crawl with GloVe

are used without any further training on our custom dataset to detect amount from the invoices (Table 2).

The above mentioned models are trained for general named entity recognition, not specifically for detecting relevant entities from invoices. Therefore, to train the model that can detect entities from invoices a corpus of dataset is created in the spaCy's format. The manually created dataset has 2000 entities annotated in the format shown in Fig. 2.

TRAIN_DATA = [("£ 289 is the cost of Indigo ticket on 20/February/2019", {"entities": [(0,5, "MONEY"),(21,27,"ORG"),(38,54,"DATE")]}),

("₹ 7000", {"entities":[(0,6,"MONEY")]}),

("₹ 1001", {"entities":[(0,6,"MONEY")]}),

("₹ 70.05", {"entities":[(0,7,"MONEY")]}),

("₹ 7", {"entities":[(0,3,"MONEY")]})]

Fig. 2. Sample dataset created for training custom NER model using spaCy

The dataset is used to further train four spaCy models specifically for invoices. The list of models trained using transfer learning on the created corpus is described in Table 3.

Table 3. Description of Custom trained spaCy models used for NER

Model4: Custom_trained_sm	This Model 4 is customized using Model 1 by applying transfer learning [13] on the custom dataset
Model5: Custom_trained_none	The learning of Model 5 is done from scratch, and is trained on only custom dataset
Model 6: Custom_trained_md	This Model 6 is customized using Model 2 by applying transfer learning on the custom dataset
Model7: Custom_trained_lg	This Model 7 is trained on our custom training dataset starting with Model 3

In order to test the performance of all the seven models, the independent dataset which contains 500 entities was created. The screenshot of the sample evaluation dataset is given in Fig. 3 below.

Seven different models were evaluated on the evaluation dataset. The precision, recall and f-score of all the models are stated in Table 4. Analysis of the results shows that the performance of the models that were trained using transfer learning was better on the other hand the models that were trained for general NER (i.e. Model 1,2 and 3) does not give satisfactory results on our particular problem. The best performing model, i.e. Custom_trained_lg was trained on large corpus additionally it had been further trained

```
Evaluation_Data= [("$ 500 was the bill amount
paid   at   Uber".[(0.5,  "MONEY"),  (34,  38,
"ORG")]),

("Movie      tickets     cost    ₹    250    on
Tuesday".[(19,24,"MONEY"),(28,35,"DATE")],

("₹ 95 was paid.".[(0,4,"MONEY")]),

("₹ 1899".[(0,6,"MONEY")]),

("₹ 30.50 was the bill amount paid at McDonald's
on   26-Jan-2019".[(0,7,   "MONEY"),   (36,46,
"ORG"),(50,61,"DATE")]),

("$ 350.66 amount paid".[(0,8, "MONEY")]),

("£23.40".[(0,6,"MONEY")])]
```

Fig. 3. Sample dataset created for evaluation of NER models using Spacy

on our custom trained dataset gives best precision, recall and f-score. Further analysis of the results from Table 4 shows that the fifth model, i.e. *Custom_trained_none,* which was trained from scratch only on our training dataset had given very low accuracy.

Table 4. Experimental results showing accuracy per model using test data

Sr. No	Model	Precision	Recall	F-Score
1	en_core_web_sm	56.25	42.85	48.64
2	en_core_web_md	46.66	33.33	38.88
3	en_vectors_web_lg	71.27	58.54	64.44
4	Custom_trained_sm	78.88	66.19	72.05
5	Custom_trained_none	11.76	9.52	10.52
6	Custom_trained_md	71.42	71.42	71.42
7	Custom_trained_lg	73.91	72.55	73.22

The best performing NER model for invoices i.e. Custom_trained_lg was already trained on web data from Common Crawl trained on 840 billion tokens, with around 2.2 million unique tokens, taking care of case sensitivity. Additionally, the model was also customized by training it further with the training dataset. The customization of model has increased the accuracy to a great extent.

6 Conclusion

The proposed framework makes use of open source solutions that uses deep learning algorithms at the backend. The accuracy of the entire framework can further be increased by training Tesseract especially for text involved in invoices. The Quality Classifier has an important role in the current framework, but training Tesseract further for hand-written invoices can make the product more robust as then it can handle more complex hand-written invoices without getting rejected by Quality Classifier. Finally, the accuracy can further be improved by training spaCy neural models on much larger set of custom designed data for invoices.

This innovation can ease down the process of assessing the claims and can result in detection of fraudulent cases. The project is designed and implemented around 'Machine First' approach as one of the pillars for Business 4.0 at our organization. This suggests acceleration, which is achieved through implementation of this bot at the finance department within the branch office. The work produces generalized approach and thus reusable to develop special purpose bots where potential of human resources can be utilized for more skillful work. Its applicability has tremendous scope across health industry, government organizations, insurance companies, where document verification work is carried out at a larger scale. The business benefits are anticipated as effective utilization of resources, quick response to verification tasks, savings in terms of efforts and ultimately cost reduction and enhanced user experience.

References

1. Ming, D., Liu, J., Tian, J.: Research on Chinese financial invoice recognition technology. Pattern Recogn. Lett. **24**(1), 489–497 (2003)
2. Emambakhsh, M., He, Y., Nabney, I.: Handwritten and machine-printed text discrimination using a template matching approach. In: Proceedings of the 12th IAPR International Workshop on Document Analysis Systems DAS, vol. 2016, no. 101779, pp. 399–404 (2016)
3. Emambakhsh, M., He, Y., Nabney, I.: Handwritten and Machine-Printed Text Discrimination Using a Template Matching Approach (2016). https://doi.org/10.1109/DAS.2016.22.
4. Lowe, D.: Distinctive image features from scale-invariant keypoints. Int. J. Comput. Vis. **60**(2), 91–110 (2004). https://doi.org/10.1023/B:VISI.0000029664.99615.94
5. Bay, H., Ess, A., Tuytelaars, T., Van Gool, L.: Speeded-up robust features (SURF). Comput. Vis. Image Underst. **110**(3), 346–359 (2008)
6. Albawi, S., Mohammed, T.A., Al-Zawi, S.: Understanding of a convolutional neural network. In: 2017 International Conference on Engineering and Technology (ICET), Antalya, pp. 1–6 (2017). https://doi.org/10.1109/ICEngTechnol.2017.8308186
7. Vincent, L.: Announcing Tesseract OCR (2006). https://googlecode.blogspot.com/2006/08/announcing-tesseract-ocr.html. Accessed 30 Aug 2006
8. Alginahi, Y.: Preprocessing Techniques in Character Recognition (2010). https://doi.org/10.5772/9776
9. Abdu, A.: Enhanced radon transform skew estimation and correction algorithm for scanned multiple-choice forms, pp. 444–454 (2019). https://doi.org/10.15405/epsbs.2019.05.02.44.
10. Honnibal, M.: Introducing spaCy (2015). https://explosion.ai/blog/introducing-spacy. Accessed 19 Feb 2015
11. Hovy, E., Marcus, M., Palmer, M., Ramshaw, L., Weischedel, R.: OntoNotes: the 90% solution. In: Proceedings of the Human Language Technology Conference of the NAACL, Companion Volume: Short Papers, NAACL-Short 2006, pp. 57–60. Association for Computational Linguistics, Stroudsburg (2006)
12. Pennington, J., Socher, R., Manning, C.D.: Glove: global vectors for word representation. In: EMNLP, pp. 1532–1543 (2014)
13. Tan, C., Sun, F., Kong, T., Zhang, W., Yang, C., Liu, C.: A survey on deep transfer learning. arXiv:1808.01974 (2018)

Web Based GIS Village Information System: A Review

Reena H. Chaudhari[1](✉), Bidoor Noori Ishaq[2], and Bharti W. Gawali[1]

[1] Department of Computer Science and IT, Dr. Babasaheb Ambedkar Marathwada University, Aurangabad 431004, India
reena27reena@gmail.com
[2] Basra Technical Institute, Southern Technical University, Basra, Iraq
bidoornoori@stu.edu.iq

Abstract. This review gives a recapitulation of the Village Information System (VIS). Village information system is a research at the very small scale, which may useful to villagers, government sectors and administrators in planning and making decisions about the development of Village. A village is a legal group of individuals residing in a particular geographical region, characterized by kind consciousness, prevalent lifestyles and numerous extensive social interactions. Village should be at the core in the nation's preparation and growth process. It is acknowledged that the planner scheduling may fail due to insufficient and unavailability of village-related data. VIS helps to provide adequate information. This study reveals VIS growth with numerous tools including different parameters. Remote Sensing (RS) and Geographical Information System (GIS), these are the two robust tools through which VIS can be developed. The advent of Remote Sensing and Geographic Information System as a strong tool for spatial analysis and memory board has effectively alleviated the issue through spatial data computerization. Web-based GIS is a computer network-wide GIS that integrates, disseminates and communicates geographic information on the Web.

Keywords: Remote Sensing · GIS · ArcGIS

1 Introduction

India is a country dominated by the villages. To grow India, villages must first be developed. But villagers do not have adequate understanding about multiple public schemes, funds and taxes, Ration status, Dairy Management, significant village announcement due to the communication gap between villages and central/state government. In order to connect villages with central/state government, city councils and other people, it is possible to introduce Web-based GIS VIS to the village to provide detailed information about the village, which acts as a bridge between them [1]. This bridge enables as a smart village to develop. Smart villages will then promote smart cities that make India smart.

Village Information System (VIS) stores and analyzes vast spatial and non-spatial village information and shows outcomes in tables, charts, graphs and maps. Over the

© Springer Nature Singapore Pte Ltd. 2021
K. C. Santosh and B. Gawali (Eds.): RTIP2R 2020, CCIS 1380, pp. 381–390, 2021.
https://doi.org/10.1007/978-981-16-0507-9_33

years, it has the ability to regularly update data bases, ensuring better accessibility of village data. For more honest alternatives and appropriate planning, VIS is implemented in all areas. VIS is an initiative to develop a village-wise GIS Geo-database, acquiring all household asset information, land holdings, infrastructure, etc. [2]. VIS helps to make the village better. A smart village has detailed information about its villagers, accessible resources, facilities and systems that are relevant. It has knowledge of necessity and moment of that necessity. The Smart Village initiative aims to improve resource efficiency, empower local self-governance, access to guaranteed fundamental facilities and responsive individual and community conduct in order to create a vibrant and happy society [3].

It is more efficient to create the VIS using Remote Sensing (RS) and Geographical Information System (GIS). RS and GIS should be used for the VIS as a multi-faceted tool. The advent of RS and GIS as a strong tool for spatial analysis and storage has effectively alleviated the issue through spatial data computerization. The GIS technology can reduce the cost and time of decision-makers and planners in setting up the information to reach the correct conclusion [5]. Space technology advancement is too helpful to map the Earth's surface using high precision satellite information and can be connected to field attribute information. Cadastral map comprises of each parcel of property having an official number with owners' documents and a person's or group's region. The development of Geo-database is mandatory because it has all information of spatial and non-spatial data regarding village and can be updated frequently or routinely if necessary. Digital database speeds up administrative procedures and facilities to execute development plans at village level [2].

2   Literature Review

Village information system is a way that includes the village's spatial and non-spatial data. VIS is an initiative to become a village-wise Geo-database that collects all information on every household asset, property, infrastructure, etc. [2]. Remote Sensing (RS), Geographic Information System (GIS), Information and Communication Technology (ICT), Global Positioning System (GPS) are some technologies that can be implemented efficiently to generate VIS. For creating VIS application, some front and back end tools can be used like Geo- Referenced Area Management (GRAM++), Arc GIS, .Net, MS Access, Visual Basic, QGIS, PostgreSQL, PostGIS, GeoServer, Web, HTML, JavaScript, Leaflet, MySQL, GIS tools, Adobe Photoshop, ERDAS, Macromedia Dreamweaver, et. A number of charts and maps such as Village Map, Base Map, Cadastral Map, Transport Map, Soil Map, Land Use Land Cover Map, Drainage Network Map, Physiography Map, and Geomorphology are needed for better visualization and evaluation purposes.

In the making of Village Information System, Data can be included as population, gender ratio, birth death marriage records, total geographical area, bank facilities, Land Use Land Cover information, literacy information, Educational center like schools and colleges, hotels, hospitals, post office, religious places like temples, church, Majid, community halls, ATM Machines, Picnic spot, Police Station, Train Facility, Road Infrastructure, Drinking and Utility Water facility, Data of House and Water Tax, Weather and Climate Information, Drainage (sanitation facility), Household Information (house number, location, type, photograph of house, owner and family members, Education, Occupation, Annual Income, Aadhar card, Ration Card, Basic Amenities like Electricity, Water, Telephone, Vehicle.), etc.

According to [2], when creating VIS, GIS is such a platform that makes it simple and provides facilities for the storage of spatial and non-spatial data in one domain, making it simple to access and alter data whenever needed. It is also possible to use the GIS database to compare and recognize modifications that have happened over time [2]. For the assessment of vegetation, they used Quickbird satellite information to analyze land use and land cover and sentinel-2 information. Soil examined by double ring infiltrometer. Cadastral map is developed, along with thematic maps. In [7], GRAM++ GIS software produced VIS. GIS covers geographic data as well as individual's information, locations, including socio-economic data. GIS's real value is its ability to solve problems. GIS can provide responses to better management of resources and environmental security. GIS is a vibrant, dynamic and quickly growing field that generates significant government and private participation. GIS technology has been prepared to embrace latest technical developments such as Internet, World Wide Web, PC and mobile computing. Potential GIS applications include, apart from generating datasets, regular database updates, watershed management, site suitability analysis, planning for optimal use of limited resources, wasteland reclamation, simulation of significant projects impacting big geographic regions to evaluate their effect on the floor before making appropriate choices, and so on [7]. [8] and [9] states that the GIS Village Information System will help improve governance through micro-level decentralization of planning [8]. With the help of GIS technology, the state government can better interpret and assess spatial data by making graphic presentations. The information stores on the database can host the maps which is present on the internet in such a way clients can watch the information query [9].

For keeping, controlling, retrieving and analysis of spatially correlated data, Remote Sensing and GIS serves as a powerful tool [11]. Cost profitable and time worthwhile resource database can be prepared with the potential and capability of Remote Sensing and GIS. Databases which are created by Remote Sensing and GIS techniques build up various aspects of decentralized block level planning through a coordinated approach [10]. WebGIS has many benefits, but the most important is user-convenient and self-standing platform operations. Advantage of GIS is frequently found in elaborate planning of the project receiving a large spatial component, where analysis of the problem is a requirement at the outset of the task. Thematic map generation is possible for one or more than one base maps, example: the generation of a land use map on the footing of a soil composition, vegetation and topography. Such thematic maps are facilitated by the distinctive mixture of certain characteristics. With the different modules within GIS, surface, length, width and distance can be calculated [10]. Basic information assembly is the main step in choosing the correct conclusion in the subject regions' development activities. For Micro-level scheduling, decision makers and planners must rely on geospatial information and attribute data for optimal reading. The researchers in [4] used ArcGIS for VIS. ArcGIS has a advanced model of geographic information to interpret spatial information as spatial information, characteristics and kinds of raster data. ArcGIS supports an accomplishment of the data model for both DBMS and file systems. GIS datasets include file based models, such as shape files, coverages, images and grids triangulated irregular networks (TINs). ArcGIS promotes the rapid accessibility of enormous quantities of images for a wide range of apps and users. ArcGIS offers the substructure that supports various workflows connected with data collection, management, manufacturing, and use of imaging. All spatial data in a GIS is based on a reference frame. The prevalent frame of reference co-ordinate system for most GIS is that of a North-South and East-West conventionally focused plane, Orthogonal Cartesian co-ordinates. This integral operation is called Geo-referencing.. Before it is applied to create thematic maps from satellite data, the same method is also applied to remote sensing information [4]. In [11] they prepared a large-scale base map using RS and GIS methods to integrate primary data collected through a main household level study to achieve the village-level position of basic amenities and social features. Village map, base map, drainage map, transport, map, soil map, land use/cover map, geomorphology, physiography map, all [4, 10–12] produced.

According to [5, 13, 14], the fast growth and combination of spatial techniques such as Geographical Information System (GIS), Global Positioning System (GPS) and Remote Sensing (RS) has created number of tools for supporting spatial decision-making. GPS is a radio navigation and location system based on satellite and land that allows users to determine very precise places on the Earth's surface [13] GPS-based geographic information system routing and scheduling system is used to track the object's position, the front-end platform utilizes embedded equipment, and the background utilizes high-performance servers. The scheme refers primarily to integrated development, GIS, GPS and wireless transmission technology to realize collection, display, query, editing, analysis, path planning, navigation, Points of interest management of the base station information and its surrounding information, So that mobile phone location can be positioned rapidly and react rapidly, saving time and enhancing effectiveness in the workplace [5]. Village Information System is an effort to concentrate on several elements of people's living standards through high-resolution remote sensing information integrated with field surveys with GPS and for generation of databases on various facilities in the village. Using Arc GIS software characteristics, the secondary information could be readily vectorized and integrated [14].

As gone through the [15], GIS and Spatial Data Infrastructure (SDI) (the geodetic control and common base maps) would help to improve the efficiency of village management activities. These techniques have the ability to help with data planning, tracking and exchange between different organizations and village development administration [15].

According to [16–18], Developments in information and communication technology have led to GeoInformatics, which includes frontier technologies such as Remote Sensing, Geographic Information Systems (GIS), Photogrammetry, and Global Positioning System (GPS). GeoInformatics is capable of enriching rural life and bringing revolutionary change [18]. Now a day is efficiently applied to GeoInformatics in different areas such as tourism, health services, utilities, navigation etc. Information facilities are one of the most significant and crucial sectors. It is linked to all in society, i.e. students, parents, scientists, community teachers and representatives of government [16]. The emergence of all-pervading space technology and the speed of ICT (Information Communication and Technology) facilitating information acquisition in near-real-time mode provides the development world with the chance for judicious decision-making at all levels of governance to reduce redundancy and time and optimize the use of scarce resources [17].

3   Village Information System (VIS)

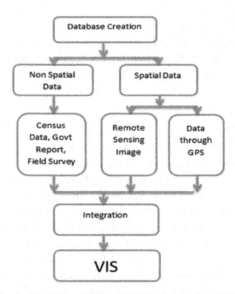

Fig. 1. Creation of Village Information System (VIS)

The Village Information System (VIS) comprises mainly of designing and creating databases of suitable spatial, non-spatial and attribute and Integration of the same to promote the development of different scheduling situations for the planning and management of the facilities. The Overall Methodology is divided into three phases [3] (Fig. 1):

1. Data Collection.
2. Field Work and ground truth data collection.
3. Data Integration and generation of Village Information System.

3.1   Data Can Be Spatial Data, Non-spatial Data, Attribute Data

3.1.1   Spatial Data

Spatial data means the geographic location of Earth's characteristics and borders, such as natural or built characteristics, oceans, and more. Spatial data is generally stored as coordinates and topology and can be mapped as information. Geographic information systems (GIS) often access, manipulate or analyze spatial information. A complex operation involving processes of data capture, verification and structuring is the creation of a GIS spatial database. Raw geographical information, such as toposheets, aerial photographs, satellite imagery and tables, are accessible in many distinct analog and digital types. The toposheet source is of great interest to natural resource scientists and an environmentalist from all these sources. Spatial data may be the Village Boundary Map that contains highways, streets and GPS information collection [3, 5].

3.1.2 Nonspatial Data

Non-spatial data involves home information, data related to water supply, hospitals, education centers, temples, community halls, meteorological data, census data [5]. Non-spatial information is collected by the field survey. It can be natural resources survey and human resources survey and village-level mapping involving local volunteers, officials from Panchayat, etc.

3.1.3 Attribute Data

Attribute data is information attached to spatial characteristics in tabular format. Spatial data is where and attribute data can contain what, where, and why information. Attribute information provide spatial information features. Using automated digitization method, thematic maps are transformed to digital mode. These maps are prepared by distinct symbols or coloring to a certain scale and demonstrate the characteristics of entities. The position of entities on the surface of the Earth is then defined through a coordinated scheme agreed upon. It is compulsory to locate all spatial data in a GIS in relation to a reference frame. For most GIS, the common frame of reference co-ordinate system is that of a plane, Orthogonal Cartesian co-ordinates oriented conventionally North-South and East-West. This entire process is called Geo-referencing (Mark et al., 1994). Before preparing thematic maps from satellite data with the help of remote sensing data, the same method is applied to that remote sensing data [4].

3.2 Consolidation of Spatial and Non-spatial Databases

For the purpose of incorporating spatial and non-spatial databases, the attribute databases were conveniently organized to correspond to the particular areas of planning required, such as education, health, transport, communication, etc. These data sets are linked and integrated into the spatial databases to facilitate the development of the facility planning and management system [4].

3.3 The Spatial Database for the Village Can Be Generated by Satellite Images and Can Be Processed by Following Methods

3.3.1 ICT (Information and Communication Technology)

ICT relates to technologies that provide access to data through telecommunications services. It is comparable to Information Technology (IT), but mainly focuses on communication systems. This involves the Internet, wireless networks, cell phones and other means of communication.

ICT gives facility to collect data on almost real-time mode. Through this judicious decision can make at all levels of governance in the developing world for reduction of redundancy and time and for optimum utilization of the insufficient resources. Crop monitoring system, electronic alarm system, weather forecast system, electronic cold storage system, etc., these are some ICT equipment throught which the Village Information System can be developed [1, 19].

3.3.2 IoT (Internet of Things)

IoT (Internet of Things) is a framework that provides a unique identity for information or data. IoT can tranfer information over a network without needing human-to-human two-way handshaking. It allows the route to connect with anything and anyone ideally using any network topology with a specific service at any time, anywhere. The Internet of Things (IoT) concept is the technology's future prospect. The rationale behind their work is the web, mobile, and information and communications technology merging. It allows different devices to communicate and interact with each other in a scheme to execute their work in a harmonious manner. RFID, 3S, WSN, cloud computing, etc. are the technologies used in IoT [20, 21].

IoT is the communications technology of the future. It is the key to the idea of smart cities and villages. It enables all the objects in a system to behave in a smart way, i.e. they all interact and coordinates with each other for smooth functioning of the system. The objects are connected via a wireless network. The objects or devices will be embedded with intelligent decision making components [9, 10].

3.3.3 Arc GIS

ArcGIS is a geographic mapping and geographic information system. In order to explore information and share location-based ideas, ArcGIS offers contextual tools for mapping and spatial reasoning. ArcGIS generates a deeper knowledge, enabling you to rapidly see where things are going and how data is connected. The technology of the Geographic Information System (GIS) is used for researching, developing, implementing and monitoring the progress of VIS development plans. GIS offers tools for village and city design and mapping. GIS facilitates the development of the VIS decision-making process.

3.3.4 Q-GIS

Quantum-GIS (QGIS) is a geographic information system software that encourages the viewing, editing and evaluation of geospatial data. It is free and open source. It is able to be used on different types of computers or with different software packages. QGIS enables users to assess and modify spatial data as well as to compose and export graphic maps. QGIS promotes both raster data and vector data. In vector data, a description of the world using points, lines and polygons. These information are generated by digitizing the database information. They store data in x and y coordinates. Multiple raster image formats are supported, and georeferenced images can be used by the software. QGIS supports shapefiles, coverages, personal geodatabases, dxf, MapInfo, PostGIS, and other formats. Web services are also endorsed to allow the use of information from external sources, including Web Map Service and Web Feature Service.

3.3.5 Visual Basic

Visual Basic is an event-driven programming language of the third generation that was first published in 1991 by Microsoft. It developed from the BASIC which is version of the previous DOS. BASIC is the abbreviation of Beginners' All-purpose Symbolic Instruction Code. Visual Basic is specially desiged for beginners and it is very user-friendly programming language. With help of Visual Basic GUI window applications can be easily developed.

VB is a front end tool that can be used. You can create application forms with VB. It will be used in the growth of VIS as a front end tool. VB can be used in connection with spatial and non-spatial information [4].

3.3.6 GRAM++

The fullform of GRAM++ is Geo-Referenced Area Management. It is developed at the Centre of Studies in Resources Engineering which is a department of IIT Bombay. It is India's first fully indigenously developed GIS software. This is a extremely competent GIS tool that enables a broad variety of activities such as creating map database, querying and retrieving, analyzing, and viewing. This software has been applied to a broad spectrum of real-life applications such as district and local planning, ideal site choice, urban slum information systems, sustainable agriculture, rural growth indicator creation, etc. [12].

3.4 Creation of Different Maps for VIS

VIS can be very useful and attractive by creating maps like Village Map, Base Map, Cadastral Map, Transport Map, Soil Map, Land Use Land Cover Map, Drainage network Map, Physiography Map, Geomorphology, Thematic Map.

4 Applications of VIS

VIS is customized for facility planning and management. VIS has a number of applications as follows [7],

1) Amenity planning: To construct a new school, college, hospital or any other commercial building, etc., a suitable location can be pinpointed.
2) Monitor the functional status of different village facilities like transformers, hand pumps, schools, hospitals, etc.
3) Keeping track of and assessment of the execution of different programs/schemes for rural development and poverty alleviation (Midday meals scheme for school kids, housing and job assurance schemes, etc.).
4) Road Network Supervision: Provides guidance on particular locations to reach, the planning of new road constructions and the maintenance of road infrastructure.
5) Connectivity of the village to the headquarters of Panchayat: remotely generates a direct bridge between the village and GramPanchayat.

6) Land Holding Analysis: It gives all Land Use Land Cover information like vegetation, urban infrastructure, water, bare soil, wildlife habitat or agriculture etc.
7) House Type Analysis: House type analysis can be done as Soil brick-stone houses, Cement houses out of the soil from stones and bricks, Vita Letters Cement Houses, RCC (Reinforced Cement Concrete) Buildings etc.
8) Income Analysis: It provides an income structure of the village. So it gives financial status of the village.
9) Occupational Analysis: It shows available jobs and profession of the village.
10) Social Strata, and eligibility analysis: It gives social strata of village like farmers. Doctors, teachers, businessman, engineers, police, labors etc.
11) Age Group Analysis for education infrastructure: It gives educational facility information age group wise like primary, secondary and college education.
12) It reduces time: It considerably reduces the time needed to locate hotels nearby, a picnic place, a hospital, an ATM, a police station, a bank in the village.
13) It increases productivity: It increases productivity related to the information associated with particular region such as crop information.
14) It provides a time table for Train and Bus and also shows emergency services.

5 Conclusion

A village information system based on GIS offers comprehensive spatial data for a specific village concerning demographic infrastructure and natural resourceA spatial database can be compiled using remote sensing and geographic data system techniquesThis database is evaluated for the creation of thematic maps in a web GIS platform. These maps will be released on a user-friendly interface over the Internet. Users can browse through interactive maps and obtain comprehensive spatial data information, users can also generate queries to obtain particular data, print maps, and so on. By incorporating spatial and non-spatial data, this information system can support planners in information retrieval; it needs advanced data management systems to manage enormous spatially correlated data.

References

1. Hegade, M.R., Kuber, S.R., Sathe, P.P., Mote, R.R., Bhosale, R.R.: Smart village system. IJSTE - Int. J. Sci. Technol. Eng. 3(04) (2016). ISSN (online) 2349-784X
2. Joshi, R.C., Reza, M.: Building geodatabase on village information system using geospatial technology: an example of Bajoon Village, Central Himalaya, India. IJCRT 6(2) (2018). www.ijcrt.org©. ISSN 2320-2882
3. Shukla, P.Y.: The Indian smart village: foundation for growing India. Int. J. Appl. Res. 2(3), 72–74 (2016)
4. Kavita: Rural level information system using GIS and remote sensing. Int. Res. J. Hum. Resour. Soc. Sci. Impact Factor-3.866 3(10) (2016). ISSN(O) (2349-4085) ISSN(P) (2394-4218)
5. Nagarajan, M., Gupta, C.A.: A GPS and GIS based model for an empirical study of village information system. Int. J. Sci. Eng. Technol. 2(6), 496–504 (2013). (ISSN 2277-1581)

6. Phanindra Kumar, T., Thotapally, R.K., Murthy, D.S.R., Madhava Rao, V.: GeoInformatics based village information system – a case study of Relegoan Siddhi, Ahmednagar District, Maharashtra. IJIR **2**(12) (2016). ISSN 2454-1362. https://www.onlinejournal.in
7. Ghadge, S.N.: Village level Information System of Shahapur Taluka using GRAM++ GIS software. Int. J. Res. Appl. Sci. Eng. Technol. (IJRASET); IC Value: 45.98; SJ Impact Factor: 6.887 **5**(X) (2017). www.ijraset.com. ISSN 2321-9653
8. Saymote, P.A.: Develop a village information system (VIS) application using visual basic (VB) programming. ISSN 2229-6093
9. Ghose, A.: An integrated spatial decision support system (SDSS) for rural development department of Orissa
10. Alajangi, S., Rao Pyla, K., Eadara, A., Prasad, N.S.R.: Web GIS based information system for rural development. Int. J. Sci. Res. (IJSR) Index Copernicus Value (2013): 6.14 I Impact Factor (2015): 6.391. ISSN (Online) 2319-7064
11. Sitender, Kumar, S., Reena: Village information system – a case study of Muklan village, Hisar, Haryana (India). IJRSS **2**(2) (2012). ISSN 2249-2496
12. Asadi, S.S., Vasantha Rao, B.V.T., Raju, M.V., Reddy, A.: Creation of web based mandal level information system using remote sensing & GIS and visual basic programe - a model study. Int. J. Eng. Technol. **3**(6), 361–372 (2011–2012)
13. Sreekanth, P.D., Rao, N.H., Kumar, K.V.: Web based geo-spatial village information system
14. Rai, P.K., Singh, S., Mishra, A.: Village mapping using high resolution remote sensing data and field survey. In: 11th ESRI India User Conference (2010)
15. Adinarayana, J., Raj, F.J., Sharma, V.: Village level information system – a tool for decentralized planning at district level in India. J. Environ. Inform. **4**(2), 56–64 (2004)
16. Yedage, A.S., Baviskar, S.P.: Geospatial analysis for village level social profiling: a case study of Solapur district. Int. J. Recent Sci. Res. **6**(10), 6815–6820 (2015)
17. Phanindra Kumar, T., Thotapally, R.K., Murthy, D.S.R., Madhava Rao, V.: GeoInformatics based village information system – a case study of Relegoan Siddhi, Ahmednagar District, Maharashtra. Imperial J. Interdisc. Res. (IJIR) **2**(12) (2016). https://www.onlinejournal.in. ISSN 2454-1362
18. Singh, H., Krishan, K., Litoria, P.K.: Creation of a village information system of Moga district in Punjab using geoinformatics. In: National Conference on Recent Developments in Computing and its Applications, NCRDCA 2009, 12–13 August 2009 (2009)
19. Santhiyakumari, N., Shenbagapriya, M., Hemalatha, R.: A novel approach in information and communication technology combined with traditional practices for smart villages. In: Humanitarian Technology Conference (R10-HTC), 2016 IEEE Region 10 (2016)
20. Bangera, T., Chauhan, A., Dedhia, H., Godambe, R., Mishra, M.: IOT based smart village. Int. J. Eng. Trends Technol. (IJETT) **32**(6) (2016)
21. Kaur, K.: The idea of Smart villages based on Internet of Things (IoT). Int. Res. J. Eng. Technol. (IRJET) **03**(05) (2016). e-ISSN 2395-0056

Document Understanding
and Recognition

An Approach to Extract the Relation and Location from the Short Stories

Deepali Vaijinath Sawane[(✉)] and C. Namrata Mahender

Department of Computer Science and Information Technology, Dr. Babasaheb Ambedkar
Marathwada University, Aurangabad 431004, MS, India
deepalisawane99@gmail.com, nam.mah@gmail.com

Abstract. Stories are the most wonderful and fascinating thing of childhood.
It creates a whole new world, each character has a different impact and the end
which always states the goodness, helpfulness, courage always empowers and win
on evil things. From childhood we are emotionally bonded with different types
of stories. Stories are Motivational, Funny, Comedy, Puzzled, and Happiest etc.
Each and every story taught us many lessons. Stories are one of the important
medium to share knowledge and express the emotions. It can be classified into
some types described by Christopher Booker such as Overcoming the Monster,
Rags to Riches, The Quest, Voyage and Return, Comedy, Tragedy and Rebirth etc.
Stories are not just a text but a powerful tool, they make us understand the moral
of life, helps to explain difficult or complex event in a simple and understandable
manner. This paper takes into account the stories as the main domain for work and
tries to produce a summary of it in the present work extraction of important aspects
i.e. feature so that a meaningful summary could be generated. The use of POS tag
and NER based relation are used first to extract feature which we decided as Actor,
Relation, Location and Event. For all this main terms a rule based extraction is
written for proper extraction. The extracted terms are used to extract the sentences
and finally sentences are ranked and summary is generated.

Keywords: Relation extraction · Location extraction · Information extraction ·
Events extraction

1 Introduction

Now days large amount of data available on internet due to growth of data, it is difficult to get the relevant content, and it is very tedious approach for human to manually
summarize the text document, the main purpose of the text summarization is to get the
source text into shorter and exact form, and which reduces search time and gives output
in the form of summary and size of it usually less compare to original document. The
applications of text summarization are abstract, movie review, biography etc. there are
two types of text summarization that is abstractive and extractive summarization. The
abstractive text summarization can be done by understanding the important text with
facilitate of linguistic technique. The most important motive of abstractive summarization is to construct the suitable summary that may be able to display information in an

© Springer Nature Singapore Pte Ltd. 2021
K. C. Santosh and B. Gawali (Eds.): RTIP2R 2020, CCIS 1380, pp. 393–406, 2021.
https://doi.org/10.1007/978-981-16-0507-9_34

accurate way that usually wants to a great extent developed language generation process [1]. Extractive summarization is the process to extract essential information from source text document and groups them to generate a summary without changing its abstract [1]. Usually, sentences are systematized in the corresponding order like in the source text document. Therefore in this research we have to extract the features of the text document or stories with the use the of extractive techniques. Feature extraction is the process of extracting relevant text data from a collection of document [2]. Feature extraction is the task of extract the valuable and vital information of relation between original document and structured form [2]. Important and valuable point extraction is a vital part of computational linguistic which performs a vital role in management of database [3]. The general purpose of important data extraction is to identify structured data from unstructured text document [4]. Data Extraction of semantic knowledge is also essential part of Natural Language Processing [5]. Data Extraction inputs are structured database, unstructured database and linguistic tags [6]. The data extraction collects important data or sentences from original text document without changing its meaning as original document. The particular type of information is named entity recognition discovering reference particular kind of relation between entities. The summary is generating through annotated unstructured text database [7]. This technique presents a method for identifying some feature with the help of name entity Recognition [8]. Natural language understanding is critical for bulk information extraction task because the desired information can only be identified by conceptual roles [9]. The proposed methodology is hybrid approach which concatenates the feature of supervised and unsupervised methods are used for extracting the feature such as actor, event, relation and location form the short stories with help of some rules. This method identifies the main characters and sentences relevant to them. Then identified sentences are analyzed for extraction relation and location. The important application is story summarization and analysis of relation and location. The data is extracted by structured data and unstructured data. Structured data are simple, easily available, and easy to access and can be stored in databases. Unstructured data is difficult to organize. Unstructured data does not have identifiable structure [10]. The main purpose of this research is to signify the significant aspects from stories for creating a summary. Three main focuses is on the verb and noun, as verb provides great idea of action and the noun provides the lead actors.

2 Literature Review

See Table 1.

Table 1. Review on text summarization

Author & Year	Method/technique	Description	Lacuna
Sergey Brin (1998) [3]	Knowledge basedmethod	This is the primary category of methods which specially helps in domain- specific work. In the knowledge based method the text are similar and closed set of relations needs to be identified. In this method relations are domain dependent. It is used for document collection get result in less time	Knowledge based method are not simply accessible to another domain
AronCulotta, Andrew McCallum, Jonathan Betz (2006) [14], Nanda Kambhatla (2004) [10]	Supervised method	Supervised methods are automatic extract the relation by using Machine- learning Techniques. This method is domain Specific. This method can easily accessed on another domain	The limitation of this method is development of suitable tagged can take lot of time and effort
Zornitsa Kozareva and Eduard Hovy (2010) [15], Michele Bankoand Oren Etzioni (2008) [7], Eduard Hovyand ZornitsaKozareva, Ellen Riloff (2009) [15]	Weakly-supervised method	Weakly-Supervised Method is also used in bootstrapping to make construction of data easily. This technique is also called "Weakly-Supervised Information Extraction." This method is mostly used for Author identifying of books	The serious problem of this method is Propagation and error to expand named Entity Recognition extracting in Incomplete name
Natalia Konstantinova (2014) [3], Michel Bankoand Oren Etzini (2008) [6]	Self-Supervised method	Self-Supervised Method go further task of information Extraction unsupervised. This method uses set of generic pattern to automatically instantiate relation specific extraction rules	This method repeated all process iteratively. The major problem of this method is that all relation cannot be extracted
Eugene Agichtein, Luis Granno (1999) [1]	Baseline method	This technique is based on frequency of co-occurrence of the organization and the location. It also reports the location that co-occurs in the same line with each organization most often as the headquarters for organization	This method is able to exploit features
Rolf sint, Serbastianschaffert, Stephanie Stroka, and Roland Ferstl [1999] [10]	Dual Iterative Pattern Relation Extraction (DIPRE) method	This method used for extracting relation which makes use of pattern relation duality. This method have two important task ie. Firstly Finding occurrences of books and secondly finding pattern matches	Limitation of this method is both task ie. Finding occurrences of books and finding pattern matches are take place only large database of web document

(continued)

Table 1. (*continued*)

Author & Year	Method/technique	Description	Lacuna
Eugene Agichtein & Luis Gravano (1999) [6]	Snowball method	Snowball presents a novel methodology to Generate patterns and extract tuples from source text documents. Also, Snowball introduces a approach for evaluating the quality of the patterns and the tuples that are produced in each extraction method	There is problem with snowball method, we do not trust, that tend to generate wrong tuples because pattern is not selective, they have low weight
Daniel Santos, NunoMamede, Jorge Baptista (2010) [5]	Kernel methods	This method is used for the extraction of relation among entities. It is based on machine learning	The problem of this method, it depends on another method
David D.Lewis (1990) [18]	Categorization method	Categorization Method is straightforward and in this method proportionality parameter is used	The problem of this method is the highest value on recall and precision are similar
Bhavna Lanjewar (2015) [11]	Feature based mehtod	In this method important sentences are indentified with the help of features such as cue phrases, verb phrases, noun, word frequency, title word andsentences position	This method is calculate summary only in high score sentences

3   Proposed Model

The flow diagram of system is shown in Fig. 1.The system shows taking input as stories and after applying pre- processing step and extracting features it produces summary. Table 2 gives the complete description of the stories.

Table 2. Complete overview of the stories

Sr. no	Story name and nomenclature	Actual length of story	Min. Sentences length in story	Max. Length of sentence in story
1	17 Camels and 3 sons (S1) [16]	16	5	27
2	Cocoon and the butterfly (S2) [16]	23	5	16
3	Gold coins and a selfish man (S3) [16]	4	15	35
4	Health is wealth (S4) [16]	19	5	19
5	Money vs. Family (S5) [16]	19	4	13
6	Powerful prayers (S6) [16]	13	4	19
7	The apple tree and the farmer (S7) [16]	9	7	18
8	The devoted mother (S8) [16]	10	5	16
9	The secret of happiness (S9) [16]	10	5	10
10	The tree and the travelers (S10) [16]	16	8	18

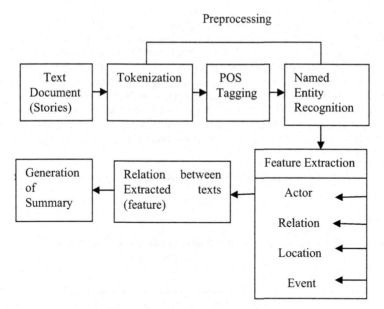

Fig. 1. Proposed system work flow

Each Component is explained below:

3.1 Text Document (Story)

In this process we take text document as ten stories are extracted from the web and text file are referred as s1, s2, s3, s4, s5, s6, s7, s8, s9 and s10. In which all are moral stories. After this formatted text documents are given for further processing.

3.2 Preprocessing

3.2.1 Tokenization

A tokenization process is splitting larger text document into smaller text documents. Tokenization is working as firstly tokenized paragraph into sentences and secondly sentences are tokenized into words of given text document. The text document is divided into tokens therefore they can be used for further analysis. It works by separating words into spaces and punctuation marks.

3.2.2 Sentence Tokenization

In this process the text documents are tokenized into sentences. The example is shown as following Fig. 2.

One day, a man saw a cocoon in flowers garden. ', ' He loved butterflies and had a craze for its wonderful combination of colors.' , ' In fact, he used to spend a lot of time around butterflies.' , ' He knew how a butterfly would struggle to transform from an ugly caterpillar into a beautiful one.' , ' He saw the cocoon with a tiny opening.' , ' It meant that the butterfly was trying to make its way out to enjoy the world.', ' He decided to watch how the butterfly would come out of the cocoon.', ' He was watching the butterfly struggling to break the shell for several hours.' , ' He spent almost more than 10 hours with the cocoon and the butterfly.' , ' The butterfly had been struggling very hard for hours to come out through the tiny opening.'

Fig. 2. Example of sentence tokenization

3.2.3   Word Tokenization

In this process the sentence are tokenized into words. The example is shown as following Fig. 3.

'One', 'day',',' 'a',' man', 'saw', 'a', 'cocoon', 'in', 'flowers', 'garden.', ' He', 'loved', 'butterflies', 'and', 'had', 'a', 'craze', 'for', 'its', 'wonderful', 'combination', 'of', 'colors.' , 'In', 'fact', 'he', 'used', 'to', 'spend', 'a', 'lot', 'of', 'time', 'around', 'butterflies.' , ' He', 'knew', 'how', 'a', 'butterfly', 'would', 'struggle', 'to', 'transform', 'from', 'an', 'ugly', 'caterpillar', 'into', 'a', 'beautiful', 'one.', 'He', 'saw' 'the', 'cocoon', 'with', 'a', 'tiny',' opening.'

Fig. 3. Example of word tokenization

3.2.4   POS Tagging

POS tagging is used for applied text documents, words after tokenization process. POS Tagging is used means labeling words with their appropriate Part-Of-Speech. The POS tagging is explains how words is used in sentences. POS tagging include nouns, verb, adverb, adjectives, pronouns, conjunction and their sub-categories. The example is shown as following Fig. 4.

[('Cocoon', 'NN'), ('and', 'CC'), ('the', 'DT'), ('Butterfly', 'NNP'), ('Many',
'NNP'), ('of', 'IN'), ('us', 'PRP'), ('know', 'VBP'), ('that', 'IN'), ('a', 'DT'), ('beau-
tiful', 'JJ'), ('and', 'CC'), ('colorful', 'JJ'), ('butterfly', 'NN'),
('comes', 'VBZ'), ('from', 'IN'), ('an', 'DT'), ('unappealing', 'JJ'), ('worm', 'NN'),
('!!', '.'), ('Here', 'RB'), ('is' ,'VBZ'), ('the', 'DT'), ('story', 'NN'), ('of', 'IN'), ('a',
'DT'), ('butterfly', 'NN'), ('that', 'WDT'), ('was', 'VBD'), ('never', 'RB'), ('able',
'JJ'), ('to', 'TO'), ('live', 'VB'), ('its', 'PRP$'), ('life', 'NN'), ('as', 'IN'), ('a',
'DT'), ('normal', 'JJ'), ('butterfly', 'NN'), ('.', '.'), ('One', 'CD'), ('day', 'NN'), (',', ','),
('a', 'DT'), ('man', 'NN'), ('saw' ,'VBD'), ('a', 'DT'), ('cocoon', 'NN'), ('in', 'IN'),
('flowers', 'NNS'), ('garden', 'NN'), ('.', '.'), ('He', 'PRP'),
('loved', 'VBD'), ('butterflies', 'NNS'), ('and', 'CC'), ('had', 'VBD'), ('a', 'DT'),
('craze', 'NN'), ('for', 'IN'), ('its', 'PRP$'), ('wonderful', 'JJ'), ('combination',
'NN'), ('of', 'IN'), ('colors', 'NNS'), ('.', '.'), , 'NN'), ('.', '.'), ('He', 'PRP'), ('saw',
'VBD'), ('the', 'DT'), ('cocoon', 'NN'), ('with', 'IN'), ('a', 'DT'), ('tiny', 'JJ'), ('opening'), 'NN'), ('.', '.')

Fig. 4. Example of POS Tagging

3.2.5 Named Entity Recognition

Named Entity Recognition can identify individuals, company, city, places, country and
other entities. Named Entity is the Fundamental step for recognizing the person, relation,
organization and location from the given story. It is used for identifying and extracting
the relation between character pairs and Location of the story. The method identifies the
main characters and gathers the sentences relevant to them. That selected sentences are
analyzed and separated to extract the relation and location. The important application is
story summarization and analysis the main character of stories (Fig. 5).

man NN PERSON
garden NN LOCATION
butterfly NN RELATION
knew NNS EVENT
saw NN EVENT
watch NN EVENT
spent NN EVENT
help NN EVENT

Fig. 5. Example of named entity recognition

4 Experimental Result

In this Process we are extracting some important feature such as actor, event, location
and relation with each other. Actor shows the important entity such as name of person,
animal etc. Event shows the important activity in story and location shows event that

occurs on several particular places, organizations, cities, villages, home, country etc. and relation shows association between two entities. Extracted features are important for summary generation example extracted actor, event as shown in the following tables.

4.1 Actor Extraction

In this process we extract the noun and proper noun consider as actor such as name of person, name of animal etc. as follows in Table 3:

Table 3. Extracted actor

Story name	Extracted actor
S1	Old man, son, camels
S2	Butterfly, man
S3	Daughter, sam, worker
S4	King, people, minister, holy man, doctor
S5	Rama, father, mother, kids, son, daughter
S6	Kim, Ray
S7	Farmer
S8	Mother, duck
S9	Samuel, Timothy, Xander, old women
S10	Travelers

4.2 Relation Extraction

This is the task of extracting the named relationship between entities of the stories. It extracts the important information about the relationship of the interest. It links the relation between one character to another character or organization. For example, ['old man', 'father'], ['Three Kids', 'son'], ['Kim & Ray', 'Friends'] etc. The Extracted relations from stories are as follows in Table 4.

4.3 Location Extraction

This is the task of extraction of location from the stories using named entity recognition. It extracts the place and event of the stories. For example, ['Palace', 'Location'], ['Lake', 'Location']. The following Table 5 shows extracted location of the story.

4.4 Extracted Event

In this process the event present the vital activity in the stories which happening between the actors of the stories. The following Table 6 shows the extracted event of the stories.

Table 4. Extracted relation of the story

Story name	Extracted Relation
S1	Old man, Son, Camel
S2	Butterfly & Cocoon
S3	Friends, Neighbors, Judge, Workers
S4	Generous & Kind hearted king, People, Fatty king, Bulky king, Doctors, Ministers, holy man, kingdom
S5	Kids, sons, Daughter, Mother, Father
S6	Close Companions, Neighbours, Classmates, Colleagues, passengers, beautiful girl, wife
S7	Farmer, little boy, childhood, little animal, neighbourhood, friends
S8	Mother, fox, Little Duckling, Children duckling
S9	Three brothers, Poor women, doorman, servants, wife, beautiful maiden, pretty, wife
S10	Travelers, Hungry man

Table 5. Extracted location of the story

Story name	Extracted location
S1	Deserted village, vicinity of a desert
S2	Flowers garden
S3	Court
S4	Country, Palace, road
S5	Family, home, household, new house, beach house, sea
S6	Close companions, school, at work, sea voyage, strange lands, ship, ocean islands, tree, eastern tip, western tip, sea shore, hometown
S7	Village, forest, apple tree, other plants, home, nests
S8	Lake, Middle of the Lake Cottage, forest, home, house
S10	Huge tree, broad trunk, dry land

4.5 Relation Between Extracted Texts (Feature)

Relationship extraction is the procedure of extracting meaningful relation from a text. Relation is always between two or more entities e.g. PERSON, LOCATION, RELATION and EVENT etc. example of relation between extracted texts is shown in Fig. 6.

In this step summary is generated depends upon the highly ranked sentences consist of maximum number of features are arranged into ascending order and only half of

Table 6. Extracted event of the story

Story name	Extracted event
S1	Lived, shipping, leaving, divided, questioned, stunned, mentioned, bring, brought, remaining, shared, counting, assigned
S2	Unappealing, struggling, remaining, withered, removed, opening, stored, converted, decided
S3	Hesitated, anything, wished, desired, working, identified, decided, shocked, pleaded, examined, questioned, replied, punished
S4	Sleeping, eating, anything, kind hearted, lived, started, something, calling, realized, offered, visited, invited, refused, saying, complimented, requested, treated, walking, asked, regained
S5	Early, eagerly, lives, spent, increasing, passed, shattered, offered, replied, continued, asked, running
S6	Decided, travelled, wrecked, turned, killed, realized, wanted, prayed, requested, decided, felling, referring, heard, requested, offered, enjoying, completing, answering, remembered
S7	Lived, passed, playing, stopped, decided, eating, getting, climbed, chopping, included, entertained, notices, requested, continued, toiling, exclaimed, tested, provided, wanted, realized
S8	Duckling, shouted, sudden, frightened, quickly, devoted, hurried, tired, reached, stopped
S9	Hardworking, continued, hankered, returned, carrying, offered, immediately, approached, expressed, contained, reached, adapted, helping, greeting, attained
S10	Innumerable, located, meeting, walking, cooled, hungry, reached, resting, soothing, crushed, comforted

One day, a man[PERSON] saw[EVENT] a cocoon in flowers[FLOWER] garden [LOCATION]. Man[PERSON] loved butterflies[INSECT] and had a craze[EVENT] for its wonderful combination of colors. In fact, man [PERSON]used[EVENT] to spend[EVENT] a lot of time around butter-flies[INSECT]. Man [PERSON]knew[EVENT] how a butterfly[INSECT] would struggle[EVENT] to transform[EVENT] from an ugly caterpillar into a beautiful one. Man[PERSON] saw[EVENT] the cocoon with a tiny opening[EVENT]. It meant that the butterfly[INSECT] was trying [EVENT] to make[EVENT] its way out to enjoy[EVENT] the world

Fig. 6. Example of Relation between extracted texts

the highly ranked sentences are considered for generation of summary example of it as shown in Fig. 7.

4.6 Generation of Summary

Those sentences are calculating high score in the text document or short stories that sentences included in the summary. In summary compress the text from original document without changing its meaning which is given as source documents. The important words or sentences are extracted using extractive techniques is called the summary or output of the story. In that summary included features are Relation and location of appropriate story.

[1, 3, 'One day a man[PERSON] saw[EVENT] a cocoon in flowers[FLOWER] garden [LOCATION] [LOCATION].']

[3, 1, 'In fact man [PERSON] [PERSON] used[EVENT] to spend[EVENT] a lot of time around butterflies[INSECT].']

[4, 1, 'Man [PERSON] knew [EVENT] how a\n butterfly[INSECT] would struggle[EVENT] to transform[EVENT] from an ugly caterpillar into a beautiful one.']

Fig. 7. Example of summary generation

5 Experimental Result

For this experiment considered 10 stories such as S1, S2, S3, S4, S5, S6, S7, S8, S9, and S10. Features are extracted are by using rule based method and shows the relation between extracted features and only those sentences are part of summary which contains maximum numbers of features such as actor, event, location and relation. Arranged sentences into ascending order of sentence number and only highly ranked sentences are considered as part of summary. Table 7 shows summarized sentences and compression ratio. Selected sentences from 10 stories which reflect the important sentences necessary for the making summary.

S1: Long ago, there lived an old man with his three sons in a deserted village, located in the vicinity of a desert. He had 17 camels, and they were the main. source of his income. He used to rent out camels as a means of shipping in the. desert. One day, he passed away. He had left a will, leaving his assets for his. three sons. After the funeral and the other obligations were over, the three. sons read the will [16].

S3: Kim and Ray were very close companions. They were neighbors, classmates at school, and later, colleagues at work. One day, they decided to go on a sea voyage to explore strange lands. They began their voyage in a cruise ship, and travelled far and wide. However, in the course of their trip, the weather turned very destructive. The ship was wrecked in the middle of the ocean. Most of the passengers were killed, but Kim and Ray could swim to a nearby island [16].

S9: Once upon a time, there were three brothers named Samuel, Timothy and Xander, who lived in a cottage by the woods. They were honest and hardworking. Every day, they would venture into the forest to fell wood. Later, they would sell it in the market where it would fetch a decent price. Thus, their life continued in this manner. However, the brothers were always sad and morose. Even though they lived a good life, they were unhappy. Each one hankered for something or the other and would pine for it [16].

Compression Ratio
Compression Ratio: Compression ratio indicates very short summary, it can bemeasured using following equation.

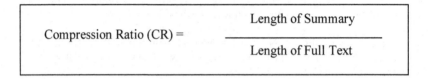

$$\text{Compression Ratio (CR)} = \frac{\text{Length of Summary}}{\text{Length of Full Text}}$$

Table 7. Result of generation of summary

Story name	Length of the story	Summarized sentences	Compression ratio
S1	16	8	8/16 = 50%
S2	23	12	12/23 = 52%
S3	4	2	2/4 = 50%
S4	19	10	10/19 = 52%
S5	19	10	10/19 = 52%
S6	13	7	7/13 = 53%
S7	9	5	5/9 = 55%
S8	10	5	5/10 = 50%
S9	10	5	5/10 = 50%
S10	16	8	8/16 = 50%

6 Conclusion

Stories are essential part of our lives and it performing vital role to identified important features of stories, it classified into seven different types such as Overcoming the Monster, Rags to Riches, The Quest, Voyage and Return, Comedy, Tragedy and Rebirth etc. It is one of the important communication way to develop the growth of human minds. In this paper we use hybrid technology for feature extraction and that method is helpful for extract the feature from stories.Stories allow us to express emotions which are easily understanding therefore summarization necessary. Text summarization is the method to generate exact summary. It is important because its needs, it allows us to get relevant information and more easily. This paper gives more attention on extraction of features such as actor, location, relation, and event. Only those sentences are part of summary which contains highest score, and highest score depends upon the sentences contains of maximum number features and those are arranged into ascending order of that story's sentence number, and the overall compression ratio found to be 50% . In future work we try to work on combining method of abstractive and extractive method for getting improved result and incorporation of these may lead to more prominent summary. In this research paper we generate summary only from single document. In future workmultiple document will use for extracting summary or generate summary from multiple document in single document.

Acknowledgement. Authors would like to acknowledge and thanks to CSRI DST Major Project Sanctioned No. SR/CSRI/71/2015(G), Computational and Psycholinguistic Research Lab for Facility supporting to this work and Department of Computer Science and Information Technology, Dr. Babasaheb Ambedkar Marathwada University, Aurangabad, Maharashtra, India.

References

1. Brin, S.: Extracting patterns and relations from the world wide web. In: Atzeni, P., Mendelzon, A., Mecca, G. (eds.) WebDB 1998. LNCS, vol. 1590, pp. 172–183. Springer, Heidelberg (1999). https://doi.org/10.1007/10704656_11
2. Devisree, V., Raj, P.R.: A hybrid approach to relationship extraction from stories. Proc. Technol. **24**, 1499–1506 (2016)
3. Konstantinova, N.: Review of relation extraction methods: what is new out there? In: Ignatov, D.I., Khachay, M.Y., Panchenko, A., Konstantinova, N., Yavorskiy, R.E. (eds.) AIST 2014. CCIS, vol. 436, pp. 15–28. Springer, Cham (2014). https://doi.org/10.1007/978-3-319-125 80-0_2
4. Leung, C.W.K., Jiang, J., Chai, K.M.A., Chieu, H.L., Teow, L.N.: Unsupervised Information Extraction with Distributional Prior Knowledge, pp. 814–824 (2011)
5. Santos, D., Mamede, N., Baptista, J.: Extraction of family relations between entities. In: Barbosa, L.S., Miguel, P.C. (eds.) INForum 2010 - II Simp'osiode Inform´atica, 9–10, pp. 549–560 (2010)
6. Agichtein, E., Gravano, L.: Snowball : extracting relations from large plain-text collections. In: Proceedings of the fifth ACM conference on Digital libraries, pp. 85–94. ACM (2000)
7. Banko, M., Etzioni, O.: The tradeoffs between open and traditional relation extraction. In: Proceedings of ACL-08 HLT, pp. 28–36 (2008)
8. Riloff, E.: Information extraction as a stepping stone toward story understanding. In: Understanding Language Understanding: Computational Models of Reading, pp. 435–460 (1999)
9. Kazantseva, A.: An approach to summarizing short stories. In: Proceedings of the Eleventh Conference of the European Chapter of the Association for Computational Linguistics: Student Research Workshop, pp. 55–62. Association for Computational Linguistics (2006)
10. Sint, R., Schaffert, S., Stroka, S., Ferstl, R.: Combining unstructured, fully structured and semi- structured information in semantic wikis. In: CEUR Workshop Proceedings, vol. 464, pp. 73–87. Morgan Kaufmann Publishers Inc., San Francisco (2009)

11. Lanjewar, B.: Automatic text summarization with context based keyword extraction. Int. J. Adv. Res. Comput. Sci. Manage. Stud. **3**(5) (2015).
12. Eichler, K., Hemsen, H., Neumann, G.: Unsupervised relation extraction from web documents. In: LREC (2007)
13. Valls-Vargas, J., Zhu, J., Ontañón, S.: Towards automatically extracting story graphs from natural language stories. In: Workshops at the Thirty-First AAAI Conference on Artificial Intelligence (2017)
14. Zhou, D., Xu, H., Dai, X.Y., He, Y.: Unsupervised storyline extraction from news articles. In: Proceedings of the Twenty-Fifth International Joint Conference on Artificial Intelligence (IJCAI), pp. 3014–3020 (2016)
15. Culotta, A., Mccallum, A., Betz, J., Bush, N., Prescott, J.: Integrating Probabilistic Extraction Models and Data Mining to Discover Relations and Patterns in Text (2006)
16. Kozareva, Z., Hovy, E.: Learning arguments and supertypes of semantic relations using recursive patterns. In: Proceedings 48th Annual Meeting Association for Computational Linguistics, pp. 1482–1491 (2010). www.kidsworld.com. Moral stories of the kids world
17. Lewis, D.D.: Feature selection and feature extract ion for text categorization. In: Proceedings MUC-3 (1991).
18. Yogita, K.D., Prof. Prakash, P.R.: Multi-document summarization: approaches and future scope. Int. J. Comput. Technol. Electron. Eng. (IJCTEE), **5**(3) (2015)

Recognition of Partial Handwritten MODI Characters Using Zoning

Sadanand A. Kulkarni$^{(\boxtimes)}$ and Pravin L. Yannawar

Department of Computer Science and Information Technology, Dr. Babasaheb Ambedkar
Marathwada University, Aurangabad, Maharashtra, India
sadanandkulkarni1980@gmail.com, plyannawar.csit@bamu.ac.in

Abstract. Complete pattern of input character image was initial need of any
handwritten optical character recognition (HOCR) system. This research work
proposes a robust technique to deal with the problem of partial, broken or incomplete characters impressed in the document image. On other hand machine interaction for image acquisition. Preprocessing and segmentation, backbone for any
HOCR produces incomplete patterns. Principal interest of this work was to propose Partial Character Recognition (PCR) for MODI script and evaluate efficiency
and performance of proposed system by applying different classifiers. Partial area
of character (PAC) was the percentage of partialness in character image. PAC
was extracted by using various planar geometrical shapes including circle, square,
triangle and rhombus. These shapes were applied to discover patterns, finds area
and length of PAC which helps to estimate incompleteness of the ideal character.
Proposed framework analyzes experimental results using Ensemble bagging with
decision tree, Decision Tree, k-NN, LDA and QDA, Naïve Byase and SVM as
compare to Euclidian distance classifier. Manuscript shows highest 94.92% confidence in recognition rate (CRR) using Zernike moments and 97.68% for Partial
MODI handwritten character using soft computing techniques, ensemble bagging
with integrated approach.

Keywords: MODI script · Zoning · Zernike moments · PAC · PCR

1 Introduction

Lots of things can human do better than machine, ability of recognizing, reading, writing
scripts was one of them. In recent decades machines were tried be to developed and
simulated to compete human communication whether it was oral or written. Human
can accurately recognize handwritten characters if they are or aren't written neatly or
cleanly, but machines find difficult when it was degraded.

Human can handle degradations by using hierarchical information. High context sensitivity in handwritten document makes this task difficult. Simulation of human reading
and recognition ability was an area of intensive research from early days of computer.
Besides to the immense development and ongoing efforts in pattern recognition it was
still far from the final frontier.

K. C. Santosh and B. Gawali (Eds.): RTIP2R 2020, CCIS 1380, pp. 407–430, 2021.
https://doi.org/10.1007/978-981-16-0507-9_35

All efforts were made for targeting universal problem of Optical Character recognition and image processing. Generally, OCR was an act to mimic human ability of recognizing characters or script. Script was identified by its character set, unique representation and state of rules.

India speaks [1], 780 languages and 66 different scripts from which in last 50 years 220 languages was removed from daily transactions and another 150 would vanish in next half century. Among these Devanagari, Bengali, Oriya, Gujarati, Tamil, and Urdu were used frequently for written communication in India also known as Indic script. Ancient Brahmi script was the origin of Indic scripts [2]. Brahmi script was broadly divided in two group, North Indian scripts consists of Devanagari, Oriya, Gurumukhi, Bengali and Gujarati whereas South Indian scripts consists of Telugu, Malayalam, Kannada, and Tamil [3, 4].

Devanagari was widely used to write most Indian languages such as Sanskrit, Konkani, Marathi, Hindi [5, 6]. Sanskrit was an well-known ancient script which is not in use at present for usual transactions but historical handwritten documents presents huge opportunities for extensive research in character recognition and pattern recognition [7–10]. Marathi was an official language of Maharashtra since 19th century also known as Indo-Aryan language. Initially Marathi was prevailing as a descendent of Prakrit and originated from Sanskrit. In the evaluation period from 11th to 19th century Marathi was also known as Balbodh, modified version of Devanagari [11–13] was written in MODI script. About 600 years of time span before 19th century it was used for written communication. In this era handwritten documents of Devanagari (Marathi) was written in 'MODI' script [14–20].

Manuscript gives significance of the script in Sect. 2. Comparative analysis of character representations for Indic scripts Devanagari (Marathi), Sanskrit and MODI was detailed in Sect. 3. Literature review for PCR in Sect. 4. Section 5 illustrates proposed framework for PCR. Section 6 focuses on evaluation of zoning patterns for degradations in Indic scripts. Experimental results in Sect. 7. Concluding remarks were given in Sect. 8 and finally Sect. 9 gives scope for further study.

2 Significance of MODI Script

According to reported work [14–20] ancient MODI script was not in use at present for usual transactions and basically available only in old historical documents with cursive and complex nature of writing. Origin of this script was still ambiguous. Canonically it was began with the objective to speed up writing Devanagari especially Marathi. Initially it was invented by 'Hemadpant' or 'Hemadri' in 12th century. Hemandpant was an administrator in the kingdom of 'Mahadev Yadav' and 'Ramdev Yadav/Ramdevrai' which was the last king of 'Yadav empire' so called Devgiri (1187–1318). In the era of 'Peshwe' (Pune) and 'Chatrapati Shivaji Maharaj' MODI was widely used at all over the Maharashtra. During time span from early 12th century to 17th century many changes were occurred at writing styles of MODI script. In 12th century it was known as 'proto-MODI', 'Adya-Kalin' or 'Yadava-Kalin' then for the period of 13th century it was known as 'Bahamanikalin' and while in 14th to 16th century it was most popular as 'Shivakalin'. Whereas in 17th century it was known as 'Chitnisi'. Moreover during 18th century various 'MODI' styles was began to proliferate and known as 'Peshvekalin', which lasted until 1818. In this period of evolution from 1818 to 1952 MODI script was well known as 'Chitnisi', 'Bilavalkari', 'Mahadevapanti', 'Ranadi' and 'Anglakalin' which was associated with English rule [18].

Reported work [14–20] states that plenty of MODI documents were stored in Tanjavar's Saraswati Mahal, Oriental manuscript section of Chennai's Connemara University, BISM Pune, Rajwade Sanshodhan Mandal Dhule, museums in London, Paris, Spain, and Holland, South Asia, Europe, Denmark and other countries. All of these documents related to political, social and economic history of Maharashtra suffering in some private institutions like palaces, temples, private libraries and are threatened with decay. Even though lot of MODI document source were available in historical documents, due to huge hurdles in process of segmentation in historical documents present technology fails to extract individual characters up to the expected accuracy. This leads to the researchers to mimic such characters by writing with the help of fountain pen to get their glyph.

This was really difficult to handle the original source of characters due to overlapping text lines, touching text lines and characters. On other hand uneven width and height of historically written characters causes serious problems for MODI character extraction due to various concerning properties of historical documents. Initial step was taken by Tamil University to digitize MODI documents. Government of India funds for cataloguing of these records in MODI. Users of computers produced these documents in portable document format or as an image. The technology was immensely developed and various experimental works was going on in the world of pattern recognition to produce promising and highly reliable solutions for different scripts, only digitizing all these documents was not a robust solution. A system must be developed to represent these MODI documents in plain electronic text. Initiatives were taken in reported work [14–19] to deal with the problem of HOCR in MODI script and also to deal with text line segmentation [20]. Strong efforts were going on to develop HOCR for Indian languages especially for 'Devanagari' but negligible efforts were present for 'MODI'. Although MODI was vanished from usual transactions and available only in old historical documents with cursive and complex type of nature, It was originated as well as initially invented as same model of Devanagari (Marathi). Even so writings in MODI script was considerably differs in terms of letterforms, scheme of writing text, rendering behaviors, orthography. Moreover it was completely differ in glyph of the characters as compare to other Indic scripts. Calligraphy and glyph of the characters introduces immense challenging tasks in every stage of the HOCR as compare to other Indic scripts even comparing Devanagari (Marathi).

This leads the problem of MODI character recognition as a superset of problem to other Indian Scripts. Comparison of challenges presented by MODI script from the point of pattern recognition was detailed in Sect. 3. In last few decades OCRs were developed for various foreign or Indic scripts and promising better results according to their experimental data, but still the problem of character and text line segmentation in historical documents as well as in handwritten document was proved to be a major threat in further progress of HOCR in historical documents of MODI script. Due to existence of this savoir problem of segmentation, accuracy of text line, word and character segmentation was in threat. As far as MODI script was concern only reported work [20] was present in literature that deals with text line segmentation from MODI historical documents. Even though technology was growing rapidly, character segmentation from historical MODI documents was still far from the final frontier. Moreover text line segmentation from handwritten document produces heavy degradations that leads to be resulted in partial, missing or incomplete characters. This work was an attempt to deal with partial characters by using different planar geometrical shapes including circle, square, triangle and rhombus. Principal interest of this work was to apply this aforesaid novel zoning approach to discover new patterns in partial area of characters (PAC) as well as apply proposed framework for recognizing ideal character using partial or missing information.

3   Comparative Analysis of Character Representations

Sanskrit was an ancient Indo-Aryan language and vanished from usual transaction but frequently used for ritualism. Sanskrit was liturgical language of Hinduism, Buddhism, and Jainism. Most of ancient poetry, scientific, and technical texts were written in Sanskrit literature [9]. Grammatical and vocabulary base of various Indic languages was originated from Sanskrit and phonetic language which consists of 15 vowels, 33 consonants [21] as shown in Fig. 1.

Vowels

अ, आ, इ, ई, उ, ऊ, ए, ऐ, ओ, औ, ऋ, ॠ, लृ, अं, अः

Consonants

क, ख, ग, घ, ङ, च, छ, ज, झ, ञ, ट, ठ, ड, ढ, ण, त,

थ, द, ध, न, प, फ, ब, भ, म, य, र, ल, व, श, ष, स, ह, ळ.

conjuncts

क्ष, ज्ञ

Fig. 1. Basic characters set (Sanskrit Script)

Sanskrit and Devanagari script was written from left to right. The concept of upper and lower case letters was unavailable. Vowels was independent letters written with variety of diacritical marks ('kana', 'matra', 'velanti' or 'ukar') written at above, below, before or after the consonant. When vowel was written by combining one or more diacritical marks then it was known as modifier and resultant characters was called as conjunction, while relevant consonant were combined to form new shapes [22].

Glyph of this resultant character was known as compound character. All these characters were written with respect to the header called as 'shirorekha'. Different diacritical marks and punctuation marks at 'Shirorekha' increases error rate in segmentation framework for the production of individual characters. Presence of very similar glyphs of character increases complexity in character recognition. At present no standard dataset was present for Devanagari handwritten compound characters [6, 22–24]. In this research basic character set of Devanagari script was considered which consists of 14 vowels and 33 consonants as shown in Fig. 2.

Vowels

अ, आ, इ, ई, उ, ऊ, ऋ, ॠ, लृ, ॡ, ए, ऐ, ओ, औ,
अं, अः, ॲएँ, ऑ.

Consonants

क, ख, ग, घ, ङ, च, छ, ज, झ, ञ, ट, ठ, ड, ढ, ण, त,
थ, द, ध, न, प, फ, ब, भ, म, य, र, ल, व, श, ष, स, ह, ळ.

conjuncts

क्ष, ज्ञ

Fig. 2. Basic characters set (Devanagari-Marathiscript)

MODI was written by 'Boru', 'lekhan' (a pen, created from 'Bambuu', need to lift too often for dipping in the ink.). The MODI script includes 46 distinctive letters, of which 36 are consonants and 10 vowels. As compare to Devanagari and Sanskrit MODI script does not contains long 'i' and long 'u'. Before the commencement of writing in MODI, horizontal line, *'Shirorekha'* was drawn across the page. Characters were written with respect to it. As compare to Devanagari and Sanskrit, intention of writing separate words along with its individual *shirorekha* was absent in MODI script which was used as a major property for word segmentation. No punctuation symbols were used in MODI. There is no such special mark (space) to indicate word or character termination as well as to indicate end of the sentence [14–20]. Such representation of basic character set of MODI Script was shown in Fig. 3.

Fig. 3. Basic characters set (MODI script)

3.1 MODI Script-Superset of the Problem

Unconstrained handwritten character recognition for Indic scripts was becomes an area of extensive research. This HOCR was quite challenging due to the inconsistency in the writing style, similarity in the character shapes, presence of modifiers and other symbolic features of Indic scripts. The complexity of a handwritten character recognition system increases mainly because of various writing styles of different individuals as well as different writing styles of same individual at different environment.

Moreover, similar shaped characters, very minute difference in glyph presenting numerous confusions to the recognition system. As compare to Devanagari and Sanskrit, MODI script was formulated with more number of confusing characters as well as more number of complex glyphs. Actual difference were visible in the behaviors of characters in certain environments, such as calligraphic uniformity of the characters, cursive nature of the script and degraded document. Calligraphic uniformity shows similarity in representations as well as presents huge complexity and confusions for recognizing individual character. Complexity causes serious effect over segmentation process in the paradigm of HOCR. Such Similarity was shown in Fig. 4.

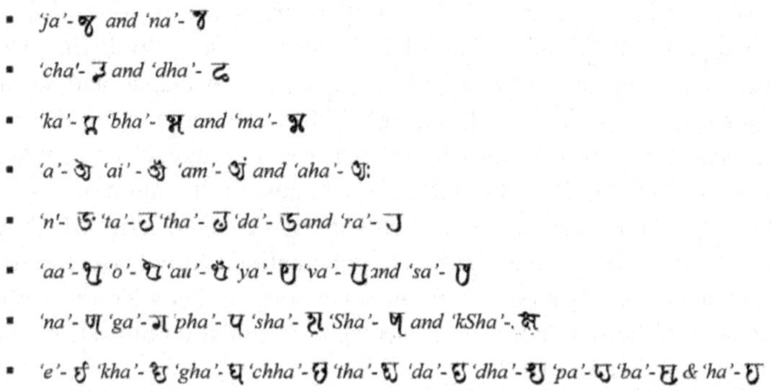

- *'ja'-* ᥨ *and 'na'-* ᥨ
- *'cha'-* ᥨ *and 'dha'-* ᥨ
- *'ka'-* ᥨ *'bha'-* ᥨ *and 'ma'-* ᥨ
- *'a'-* ᥨ *'ai'-* ᥨ *'am'-* ᥨ *and 'aha'-* ᥨ
- *'n'-* ᥨ *'ta'-* ᥨ *'tha'-* ᥨ *'da'-* ᥨ *and 'ra'-* ᥨ
- *'aa'-* ᥨ *'o'-* ᥨ *'au'-* ᥨ *'ya'-* ᥨ *'va'-* ᥨ *and 'sa'-* ᥨ
- *'na'-* ᥨ *'ga'-* ᥨ *pha'-* ᥨ *'sha'-* ᥨ *'Sha'-* ᥨ *and 'kSha'-.* ᥨ
- *'e'-* ᥨ *'kha'-* ᥨ *'gha'-* ᥨ *'chha'-* ᥨ *'tha'-* ᥨ *'da'-* ᥨ *'dha'-* ᥨ *'pa'-* ᥨ *'ba'-* ᥨ *& 'ha'-* ᥨ

Fig. 4. Uniformity in calligraphy of MODI characters

In first case as shown in above, filled area of a tiny circular space at the top of the character distinguishes two character *'ja'* and *'na'*. If degradation occurs exactly at the position of intended area then somehow humans can approach it manually by necked eye, but this was became very critical for the system to differentiate them individually. Similarly, for another four letters *'ka'*, *'bha'*, *'ma'* and *'ksha'* slight curves and tiny filled whole was used as a distinguishable property. When *'cha'* and *'dha'* was rotated then they shows significant similarities. Moreover, as it was illustrated for *'a'*, *'ae'*, *'ai'*, *'am'* and *'aha'* basic structure of representation was unchanged. In this case modifiers were used to distinguish them from other characters. In case of *'n'*, *'ta'*, *'tha'*, *'da'* and *'ra'* similarity has been increased at higher level. While in the writing style of *'aa'*, *'ya'*, *'va'*, *'sa'*, *'e'*, *'kha'*, *'gha'*, *'chha'*, *'tha'*, *'da'*, *'dha'*, *'pa'*, *'ba'* and *'ha'* very minute difference was noticed in the form of curves and glyph. Even though each character present minute difference at carving form but complexity for automated optical hand-written character recognition was immensely increased due to nature of cursive writing, historical calligraphic writing style and real time intentions of writer. Comparison of character representations clearly states that glyph of each character in MODI script was very similar to each other. When similarity in character representation was increased, difficulty in automatic character recognition was increased. This similarity and calligraphic representation produces lots of variations in handwritten MODI characters as compare to any other Devanagari or foreign scripts. Principal interest of the work was to devise an automated system in such way that it should identify any minute difference and similarities to achieve greater recognition rate when the complete character impression was available or not.

Analysis of partialness in digital character image was another decisive feature for partial handwritten characters and partialness in digital character image was highly situational. Partial characters mainly occurs due to degradation, meanwhile in the process of HOCR, by the oldness of the manuscript, timely changes influenced in color of document or impression of ink used at the time of writing and measures used at digitization paradigm. In this proposed work partialness of a character was analyzed using zoning patterns. In recent decades many researchers were attracted towards the problem of PCR.

4 Literature Review for PCR

Partial or broken character recognition was addressed [25] by using multi-level feed forward neural network classifier (MLFNC). Grid level features were used with statistical features to address presence of partialness in the character image. Statistically measured features were used to distinguish Devanagari basic characters.

Two-tier architecture was used [26] with unsupervised and supervised learning for unconstrained handwritten numerals. Different 15 segments were used with different horizontal, vertical and diagonal bars and feature vector was formed by using their respective centroid. This statistical approach was used with self-organizing KNN and LVQ as a classifier to improve classification accuracy. Empirical zoning strategy [27] was used with geometrical shapes for zoning patterns which enhances Latin character recognition in degraded historical documents. Zoning patterns was used with two vertically rectangular zones, two horizontal rectangular zones, two square and three vertically rectangular zones, two square and three horizontal rectangular zones and six equal sized rectangular zones. Whereas feature vector was formed with geometric moments, concavity measurements and shape representation of profile to achieve 78.2% CRR. Projection distance metrics method, zoning and general regression neural network (GRNN) classifier [28] was used to recognize handwritten Kannada numeral. Normalized Input image (50×50) was divided in equal 25 zones. Each zone was represented by a grid of 5 column and 10 rows. Vertical projection was used to construct the feature vector of size 10 features. Total 250 features were extracted with respect to 25 zone. Overall 94 to 98.8% RR was achieved using GRNN classifier.

Fuzzy strokes was proposed [29] for analyzing handwritten Devanagari characters. Average Compressed Direction Codes (ACDC) was used to describe character shape using curves, slanted lines, horizontal and vertical strokes [45–47]. Feature set was formulated by dividing each character into nine zones. Whereas counter for number of strokes, zonal stroke frequency (ZSF) and regional stroke frequency (RSF) was further used for classification. 92.80% CRR was achieved by using Euclidean distance classifier. Handwritten and printed Kannada digits [30] were recognized by using Zone based features. Image was divided into equal 64 zones of size 8×8 pixels. Feature set was represented with pixel density of each zone. 97.32% CRR was achieved in case of handwritten and 98.30% for printed Kannada digits using KNN and SVM.

Zoning [31] was used to create feature set with intersection, shadow feature, chain code histogram and straight line fitting for recognition of off line handwritten Devanagari characters. Intersection features, chain code histogram features and line fitting features were computed for zone while shadow features were computed globally. 92.80% CRR was achieved by using weighted majority voting technique and four Multi-layer Perceptron (MLP). Zone based feature extraction [32] was illustrated for recognition of handwritten Telugu text. 84.80% CRR was achieved by using probabilistic neural networks classifiers.

Multi-scale, multi-oriented character recognition scheme [33, 44] for Bangla & Devanagari basic character recognition was proposed. Each character image was divided in 15 circular zones. Centroid for each zone was used as principal feature. The feature set was extended with spatial distribution of centroid. 99.01% CRR was achieved using 14 circular zones for Bangla and 99.25% CRR for Devanagari characters using PCA based feature selection and SVM. Literature revive states that in every stage of HOCR there exists a possibility of losing character information to produce partial, broken or incomplete character. Zoning was one of the major technique to deal with the problem when system contains partial characters for the recognition. Still there was a room of extensive research for evaluating various zoning patterns. Up till now researchers were considered square, rectangular zoning patterns. This was an attempt to evaluate various zoning patterns and analyze effectiveness for recognizing partial characters using planar geometrical shapes including not only square and rectangle but also with various combinations of circle, triangle and rhombus.

5   Proposed Framework for PCR

Framework for partial character recognition includes similar steps as traditional HOCR. The difference lies in the segmentation process where character image was divided into various PAC using different zoning patterns shown in Fig. 5.

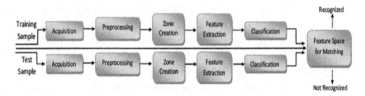

Fig. 5. Proposed framework for PCR.

5.1   Data Acquisition

Character image was captured with the help of scanning device. 100 repetitions of each 46 handwritten characters were taken. Train and test set was constructed with the ratio of 70:30. Further image was divided in 37 zones with six patterns called Partial area of character (PAC). Train set contains 3220 character images with 119140 PAC and 1380 characters images in test set with 51060 PAC. Total 170200 distinct images were used in dataset.

5.2 Pre-processing

Each image from the data set was preprocessed so as to obtain good discriminating features. Preprocessing includes foreground and background separation. Foreground contains information about shape. Morphological 'opening' and 'closing' were performed to strengthen statistical information whereas 'Top Hat' transform were used to extract small elements and details to subtract from original image.

5.3 Extraction PAC

Zone based approach was used to address partialness of a character. Various planner geometrical shapes were used to construct zoning patterns referred as Partial Area of a Character (PAC). PAC not only gives support for character recognition but also help to identify and eliminate degraded PAC from entire character image. Support of PAC shows amount of data and location of degradation. Percentage of Support of PAC was given by using Eq. 1.

$$Support \; of \, PAC = \frac{Available \; PAC \; in \; zone \times 100}{Total \; Area \; of \; the \; Original \; Image} \tag{1}$$

5.4 Feature Extraction

Moment based features were used for feature extraction. In this paper Zernike and Zernike Complex moments were used with zoning to construct feature set.

Zernike Moments. Moments were calculated using a set of complex polynomials which is a form of complete orthogonal set using unit disk as follows:

$$(x^2 + y^2) = 1 \tag{2}$$

$$Z_{mn} = \frac{m+1}{\pi} \iint\limits_{xy} I(x, y)\big[V_{mn}(x, y)\big]dxdy \tag{3}$$

Where m, n represents order of moment and $I(x, y)$ gives gray level of a pixel. The Zernike polynomials $V_{mn}(x, y)$ were expected in polar coordinates as follows:

$$V_{mn}(r, \theta) = R_{mn}(r)e^{-jn\theta} \tag{4}$$

Where, $R_{mn}(r)$ called as orthogonal radial polynomial. Moments Z_{mn} are invariant under rotation and scale.

$$R_{mn}(r) = \sum_{s=0}^{\frac{m-n}{2}} (-1)^s \frac{(m-s)!}{s!\left[\frac{m+|n|}{2} - s\right]!\left[\frac{m-|n|}{2} - s\right]!} r^{m-2s} \tag{5}$$

Zernike Moments [34] derived statistical measures of pixel distribution around center of gravity which allows capturing information just at single boundary point. Global property such as overall image orientation was given by Zernike moments, which was missing in boundary based representation. Zernike moment features [35] was not affected by moderate level noise. These moments were used to recognize various scripts such as Tamil [36], Oriya [34], Isolated Arabic characters [37], Devanagari compound characters [38], and Farsi characters [39].

Zernike Complex Moment. The Zernike polynomials were introduced in 1934 by Fruits Zernike [40]. Zernike Complex moments [41, 42] were constructed by complex polynomials as moment basis set. Complex moments Z_{nm} of order 'n' with repetition 'm' was defined in polar coordinates (r, θ) inside the unit circle:

$$Z_{nm} = \frac{n+1}{\pi} \int_0^1 \int_0^{2\pi} R_{nm}(r)e^{-jm\theta} f(r, \theta) r dr d\theta, \quad o \leq |m| \leq n, \ n - |m| \ is \ even \quad (6)$$

Where $R_{nm}(r)$ is nth order of Zernike radial polynomial was given by:

$$R_{nm}(r) = \sum_{k=0}^{(n-|m|)/2} (-1)^k \frac{(n-k)!}{k![(n-2k+|m|)/2]![(n-2k-|m|)/2]} r^{n-2k} \quad (7)$$

The image reconstructed using set of moments with order M and Zernike Complex moment features (total 66 features) were derived for order n = 10 and repetition m = 2.

$$f(r, \theta) \approx \sum_{n=0}^{M} \sum_{m} Z_{nm} R_{nm}(r) e^{jm\theta} \quad (8)$$

6   Evaluation of Zoning Patterns for Degradations

Proposed Framework follows two major steps, firstly, find nature of incompleteness of PAC in character with zone identification and secondly recognize ideal character using PAC. Various zoning patterns and different 37 zones were used to extract PAC with the help of planner geometrical shapes. Each character image was normalized with size of 60 × 60 pixels as it produces most prominent CRR. Different zones were formed using geometrical shapes like circle, Square, Rectangle, Triangle, Equilateral Triangle and Rhombus. An hypothesis has been stated, justified and proved in experimental outcomes that central pixel values were most considerable and important portion that helps to distinguish every individual character form other in MODI script.

6.1   Circular Zones

Circular zones were extracted with varying radius size from 5 to 30. Considered a circular mask of radius 10, 13, 16, 19, 22 and 25 with support of PAC 8.72%, 14.74%, 22.33%, 31.49%, 40.47% and 54.51% respectively as shown in Fig. 6.

Region of interest (ROI) was an area extracted from character image. Experimental approach considered ROI as zone which then used as individual identical image. In case of circular zones experimental outcome states that use of radius below 10 gives worst CRR as well as from radius 10 it shows improvement in CRR for each considered incremented value of radius. Noticed improvement in CRR causes process to uses image of size 60 × 60, the experimental process uses radius values in the range of 10 to 25 by incrementing 3 pixels at each iteration.

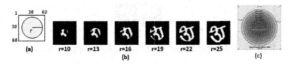

Fig. 6. a. Circular zone b. ROI in character image c. Support of PAC.

6.2 Square and Rectangular Zones

Square zones were derived by segmenting character image in four equal zones (size 30 × 30) and fifth overlapping modified square zone (size 31 × 31 pixels) as shown in Fig. 7. Support of PAC for these four square zones and 5th zone was 25% and 26.69% respectively. Improvement was observed in CRR using such fifth modified overlapping square zone.

Fig. 7. a. Four square zones (30 × 30) b. Fifth square zone (31 × 31) c. ROI. d. Support PAC.

According to the hypothesis square and rectangular zones were formed to analyze core portions in character image which has been justified and proved to be true where fifth overlapping zone of size 31 × 31 shows most promising outcome among all other square zones.

Character image was further divided in nine zones including four square zones (15 × 15), four rectangle zones (30 × 15) and one square zone (30 × 30). Considered support of PAC 6.25% for four square zones, 25% for fifth square zone and 12.5% for four equal sized rectangular zones was considered as shown in Fig. 8.

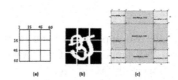

Fig. 8. a. Nine zone b. ROI. c. Support of PAC.

Rectangular zones were extracted by using a rectangular mask. Rectangular ROI is of the size 30 × 60 pixels with 50% Support of PAC as shown in Fig. 9. Vertical and horizontal cut was considered for two rectangular zones.

Fig. 9. a. Rectangular zones b. ROI c. Support of PAC.

6.3 Irregular Hexagonal Zones

Two irregular Hexagonal zones were constructed with the help of hexagonal segment of size 1575 pixels with 43.75% Support of PAC. Size of irregular hexagonal zone was considered accordingly to justify confidence in recognition rate. Hexagonal ROI in character image as shown in Fig. 10.

Fig. 10. a. Irregular hexagonal zones b. ROI c. Support of PAC.

6.4 Triangular Zones

Triangular zones were formed by choosing a triangular segment from character image. Two types of geometric structure of right angle triangle and Isosceles triangle were used for zone formation. Formation of zone was shown in Fig. 11.

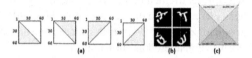

Fig. 11. a. Triangular zones b. ROI c. Support of PAC.

In case of Isosceles triangle two approaches were used. In first case half part of character was considered with 25% support of PAC as shown in Fig. 12, whereas whole image considered with 50% support of PAC in Fig. 13.

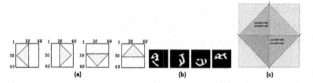

Fig. 12. a. Isosceles triangular zones of size 900, b. ROI in Character, c. Support of PAC.

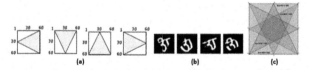

Fig. 13. a. Isosceles triangular zones of size 1800, b. ROI in Character, c. Support of PAC

6.5 Rhombus Zone

Rhombus zone was formed by choosing rhombus mask from character image as shown in Fig. 14. Rhombus zone extracts whole central portion in character image with 50% support of PAC Size considered to justify confidence in recognition rate.

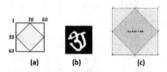

Fig. 14. a. rhombus zone, b. ROI c. 50% Support of PAC.

6.6 Zone Selection

Use of six geometrical structures gives different 37 zones. All zones were sent to feature extraction process. This work assumes that middle portion of each character was important and essential for recognition in case of MODI script. Various zoning combinations were selected for experimentation. Selection criteria of zones were based on the support of PAC at each zone. The principal objective of this research was to achieve maximum CRR with minimum support of PAC. Less support of PAC ultimately represents maximum degradation in character. Moreover middle portion of each character was focused for CRR as degradation occurs at the corner PAC with special attention to MODI script. Pictorial representation was necessarily included for analyzing support of PAC.

7 Experiment and Results

Samples were recognized with derived features from Zernike and Zernike Complex moments using 'Euclidean' distance classifier. Comparative analysis clearly states that

CRR was increased when zone of a PAC was known as shown in Fig. 15. Performance of zone support and CRR for recognizing a zone when zone of PAC is Unknown is shown in Table 1 and when PAC is known is shown in Table 2.

Fig. 15. Comparison for recognizing a zone when zone of PAC is known or unknown.

Table 1. Performance of Zone support and Confidence when zone of PAC is unknown (Search space 37 mean vectors of 119140 PAC images where each vector is a mean feature vector of 3220 images)

Sr. No	Partial Zone	Circular PAC					
		1	2	3	4	5	6
1	Support PAC %	8.72	14.74	22.33	31.49	40.47	54.51
2	CRR in %	64.56	60.07	71.59	60.86	38.11	51.44

		Square PAC-I					Square and rect. PAC-II	
	Partial Zone	7	8	9	10	11	12	13	14
3	Support PAC %	25	25	25	25	26.69	6.25	12.50	**6.25**
4	CRR in %	86.08	73.91	56.37	69.71	68.91	81.81	77.24	**71.30**

		Square and rectangular PAC-II						Rectangular PAC	
	Partial Zone	15	16	17	18	19	20	21	22
5	Support PAC %	12.50	25.00	12.50	6.25	12.50	6.25	50	**50**
6	CRR in %	42.82	38.98	42.31	84.13	30.43	59.56	56.66	**57.31**

		Irr. Hexa. PAC		Right Angle Triangular PAC				Rhombus PAC
	Partial Zone	23	24	25	26	27	28	37
7	Support PAC %	43.75	43.75	50	50	50	50	**50**
8	CRR in %	41.52	42.31	58.47	55.94	77.39	51.30	**18.47**

		Isosceles Triangular PAC-I				Isosceles Triangular PAC-II		
	Partial Zone	29	30	31	32	33	34	35	36
9	Support PAC %	25	25	25	25	50	50	50	**50**
10	**CRR in %**	92.02	73.62	71.95	51.95	49.49	51.81	41.52	51.66

Further performance of features for each zone was evaluated to reduce feature set and find most prominent zones for PCR. Table 3 indicates that when amount support of

Table 2. Performance of Zone support and Confidence when zone of PAC is known.

Sr. No	Partial Zone	Circular PAC					
		1	2	3	4	5	6
1	Search Space	6 mean vectors and 8280 PAC images					
2	Support PAC %	8.72	14.74	22.33	31.49	40.47	54.51
3	CRR in %	64.56	60.07	71.59	60.86	38.11	51.44

Sr. No	Partial Zone	Square PAC-I					Square and rect. PAC-II		
		7	8	9	10	11	12	13	14
4	Search Space	5 mean vectors of 6900 PAC images					9 mean vectors of 12420 PAC images		
5	Support PAC %	25	25	25	25	26.69	6.25	12.50	6.25
6	CRR in %	87.60	80.50	81.59	72.89	68.98	81.81	81.73	71.30

Sr. No	Partial Zone	Square and rectangular PAC-II						Rectangular PAC	
		15	16	17	18	19	20	21	22
7	Search Space	9 mean vectors of 12420 PAC images						2 mean vectors of 2760 PAC images	
8	Support PAC %	12.50	25.00	12.50	6.25	12.50	6.25	50	50
9	CRR in %	50.14	45.86	44.13	84	31.52	59.56	98.98	100

Sr. No	Partial Zone	Irr. Hexa. PAC		Right Angle Triangular PAC				Rhombus PAC
		23	24	37	26	27	28	37
10	Search Space	2 mean vectors of 2760 PAC images		4 mean vectors of 5520 PAC				1 vector 1380 of PAC image
11	Support PAC %	43.75	43.75	50	50	50	50	50
12	CRR in %	86.15	85.72	70	74.78	79.42	69.20	100

Sr. No	Partial Zone	Isosceles Triangular PAC-I				Isosceles Triangular PAC-II			
		29	30	31	32	33	34	35	36
13	Search Space	4 mean vectors of 5520 PAC				4 mean vectors of 5520 PAC			
14	Support PAC %	25	25	25	25	50	50	50	50
15	CRR in %	95.62	93.84	82.39	73.62	93.04	96.66	81.08	73.18

PAC was more, ultimately greater amount of character image was available then CRR was also increased.

Performance of feature set not only illustrates nine most prominent zones but also indicates that for each case Zernike Complex moment has produced better CRR as compare to Zernike moments.

Depending on the performance of features shown in Table 3 experiment was continued. When zone of a PAC was supervised then experiment goes in second part where we have followed two methods with two different approaches.

Table 3. Performance of Features used in recognition for each zone.

Sr No	Zone or Figure	Support PAC in %	Zernike moments			Zernike Complex		
			Hit	Miss	CRR	Hit	Miss	CRR
1	Circle of r = 10 of 6a	8.72	401	979	29.05	681	699	49.34
2	Circle of r = 13 of 6a	14.74	571	809	41.37	884	496	64.05
3	Circle of r = 16 of 6a	22.33	738	642	53.4	1062	318	76.95
4	Circle of r = 19 of 6a	31.49	840	540	60.86	1152	228	83.47
5	Circle of r = 22 of 6a	40.47	958	422	69.42	1211	169	87.75
6	**Circle r = 25 of 6a**	**54.51**	**991**	**389**	**71.81**	**1237**	**143**	89.63
7	1st square of 7a	25.00	847	533	61.37	878	502	63.62
8	2nd Square of 7a	25.00	747	633	54.13	836	544	60.57
9	3rd Square of 7a	25.00	611	769	44.27	732	648	53.04
10	4th Square of 7a	25.00	765	615	55.43	773	607	56.01
11	**5th Square of 7b**	**26.69**	**1047**	**333**	**75.86**	**1099**	**281**	79.63
12	1st Square of 8a	6.25	249	1131	18.04	277	1103	20.07
13	2nd Square of 8a	12.50	729	651	52.82	756	624	54.78
14	3rd Square of 8a	6.25	329	1051	23.84	375	1005	27.17
15	4th Square of 8a	12.50	587	793	42.53	652	728	47.24
16	**5th Square of 8a**	**25.00**	**836**	**544**	**60.57**	**932**	**448**	67.53
17	6th Square of 8a	12.50	447	933	32.39	507	873	36.73
18	7th Square of 8a	6.25	155	1225	11.23	209	1171	15.14
19	**8th Square of 8a**	**12.50**	**559**	**821**	**40.50**	**628**	**752**	45.50
20	9th Square of 8a	6.25	338	1042	24.49	390	990	28.26
21	**Rectangle of 9a**	**50.00**	**966**	**414**	**70.00**	**1204**	**176**	87.24
22	Rectangle of 9a	50.00	922	458	66.81	1168	212	84.63
23	**Irregular hexa. of 10a**	**43.75**	**925**	**455**	**67.02**	**1186**	**194**	85.94
24	Irregular hexa. of 10a	43.75	875	505	63.40	1127	253	81.66
25	Right angle Δ of 11a	50.00	850	530	61.59	1116	264	80.86
26	Right angle Δ of 11b	50.00	805	575	58.33	1058	322	76.66
27	**Right angle Δ of 11c**	**50.00**	**928**	**452**	**67.24**	**1141**	**239**	82.68
28	Right angle Δ of 11d	50.00	769	611	55.72	1032	348	74.78
29	Isosceles Δ of 12a	25.00	728	652	52.75	1000	380	72.46
30	Isosceles Δ of 12b	25.00	720	660	52.17	992	388	71.88
31	**Isosceles Δ of 12c**	**25.00**	**915**	**465**	**66.30**	**1157**	**223**	83.84
32	Isosceles Δ of 12d	25.00	903	477	65.43	1115	265	80.79
33	Isosceles Δ of 13a	50.00	957	423	69.34	1147	233	83.11
34	Isosceles Δ of 13b	50.00	883	497	63.98	1144	236	82.89
35	**Isosceles Δ of 13c**	**50.00**	**982**	**398**	**71.15**	**1188**	**192**	86.08
36	Isosceles Δ of 13d	50.00	877	503	63.55	1164	216	84.34
37	**Rhombus of 14a**	**50.00**	**996**	**384**	**72.17**	**1222**	**158**	88.55

7.1 Distinct and Integrated Approach (Homogeneous Zones)

Nine homogeneous pattern of zoning were considered with six circular zones, five square zones, nine square and rectangular zones, two rectangular zones, two irregular hexagon zones, four right angle triangular zones, four isosceles half size triangular zones, four isosceles triangular zones and one rhombus zone. Rhombus zone was illuminated in case of homogeneous integrated pattern as the group contains only one zone. Performance for distinct approach using homogeneous pattern was shown in Table 4 and integrated approach was shown in Table 5.

Table 4. Performance of homogeneous zones used as distinct vector.

Sr. No	Zone or Figure	Support PAC in %	Zernike moments			Zernike Complex		
			Hit	Miss	CRR	Hit	Miss	CRR
1	Six zones of Fig. 6	54.54	930	450	67.39	1135	245	82.24
2	Five zones of Fig. 7	100.00	1132	248	82.02	1145	235	82.97
3	Nine zones of Fig. 8	100.00	936	444	67.82	1002	378	72.60
4	Two zones of Fig. 9	75.00	961	419	69.63	1187	193	86.01
5	Two zones of Fig. 10	41.66	900	480	65.21	1157	223	83.84
6	Four zones of Fig. 11	100.00	1084	296	78.55	1219	161	88.33
7	Four zones of Fig. 12	50.00	1068	312	77.39	1204	176	87.24
8	Four zones of Fig. 13	100.00	1044	336	75.65	1198	182	86.81

When distinct and integrated approach were considered then train set size was reduced to the particular used zoning pattern as six vectors for circle, five vectors for square, nine vectors for square and rectangle and so on. In case of integrated approach integration of particular zone vectors has been done to represent single vector for each zoning pattern. Zernike complex moment increase CRR as compare to Zernike moments.

Using Zernike moments 88.33% CRR was achieved using four Right angle triangular zones and with Zernike complex 92.39% CRR. These two observations also state importance of Right angle triangular and Isosceles triangular zoning patterns for further improvement in CRR. This study has two parts one that selects a zone and another selects a character depends on available PAC in a zone. Recognition of zone was done by considering two methods, initially when zone of a PAC was known to the process and another when zone of a PAC was unknown.

Table 5. Performance of Features for homogeneous zones used as integrated vector

Sr No	Zone or Figure	Support PAC %	Zernike Moments			Zernike Complex Moments		
			Hit	Miss	CRR	Hit	Miss	CRR
1	Six zones of Fig. 6	54.54	1075	305	77.89	1228	152	88.98
2	Five zones of Fig. 7	100.00	1255	125	90.94	1217	163	88.18
3	Nine zones of Fig. 8	100.00	1246	134	90.28	1237	143	89.63
4	Two zones of Fig. 9	75.00	1108	272	80.28	1239	141	89.78
5	Two zones of Fig. 10	41.66	1103	277	79.92	1223	157	88.62
6	Four zones of Fig. 11	100.00	1211	169	87.75	1275	105	92.39
7	Four zones of Fig. 12	50.00	1255	125	90.94	1274	106	92.31
8	Four zones of Fig. 13	100.00	1149	231	83.26	1242	138	90.00

7.2 Distinct and Integrated Approach (Heterogeneous Zones)

Heterogeneous zoning patters were used by considering various degradation at different parts of the image. In this pattern combination of different zones were applied with different size and shape as well as with different support of PAC when zone of PAC was known.

Sample space used for this pattern was reduced as it depends on zone selection and leads to increase speed and accuracy for CRR. Performance of features for heterogeneous zoning pattern using distinct vector was shown in Table 6 and Table 7 illustrates integrated approach.

These two tables indicates that Zernike complex moment increase CRR as compare to Zernike moments. In case of Zernike moments CRR was increased from 87.46 up to 94.92% and Zernike complex moments increases CRR from 90.43 up to 94.74% when integrated approach was used instead of distinct approach.

Considering support of PAC, size of sample set and time required for recognition Zernike complex moment shows greater prominent results. In case of distinct approach 4 vectors were used for train set and 5520 vectors for test set whereas in case of integrated approach single vectors at train set and 1380 vectors at test set for both Zernike and Zernike complex moments. In case of support of PAC Zernike moment was applied by considering four zones with 62.50% support of PAC and Zernike complex moment with 50.00% PAC.

Table 6. Performance of heterogeneous zones (distinct vector when PAC is known)

Sr. No	Zone or Image	Support PAC in %	Zernike moments			Zernike Complex		
			Hit	Miss	CRR	Hit	Miss	CRR
1	Table 3: 6, 11, 16, 21, 23, 27, 31, 35, 37	94.30	1202	178	87.10	1248	132	90.43
2	Table 4: 4, 6, 7, 8	100	1170	210	84.78	1248	132	90.43
3	Table 4: 3, 4, 6, 7, 8	100	1206	174	87.39	1248	132	90.43
4	Table 4: 6, 7, 8	100	1174	206	85.07	1241	139	89.92
5	Table 4: 2, 7	100	1207	173	87.46	1227	153	88.91
6	Table 4: 6, 7	100	1147	233	83.11	1226	154	88.84

Objective of this research work was to achieve maximum CRR with minimum support of PAC. Less support in PAC shows maximum degradation as well as considers less area in the character image to reduces the amount of time and storage space require for recognition.

Table 7. Performance of heterogeneous zones (integrated vector & PAC is known)

Sr. No	Zone or Image	Support PAC in %	Zernike moments			Zernike Complex		
			Hit	Miss	CRR	Hit	Miss	CRR
1	Table 3: 6, 11, 16, 21, 23, 27, 31, 35, 37	94.30	991	389	71.81	1264	116	91.59
2	Table 5: 4, 6, 7, 8	100	1220	160	88.40	1267	113	91.81
3	Table 5: 3, 4, 6, 7, 8	100	1231	149	89.20	1267	113	91.81
4	Table 5: 6, 7, 8	100	1233	147	89.34	1272	108	92.17
5	Table 5: 2, 7	100	1296	84	93.91	1277	103	92.53
6	Table 5: 6, 7	100	1249	131	90.50	1284	96	93.04
7	Table 3: 25, 27	87.50	1256	124	91.01	1308	72	94.78
8	Table 3: 27, 31, 32	75.00	1261	119	91.37	1303	77	94.42
9	Table 3: 25, 31, 32	75.00	1229	151	89.05	1285	95	93.11
10	Table 3: 25, 27, 31	81.25	1187	193	86.01	1288	92	93.33
11	Table 3: 25, 27, 32	81.25	1202	178	87.10	1272	108	92.17
12	Table 3: 7, 11, 31, 32	62.50	1310	70	94.92	1285	95	93.11
13	Table 3: 10, 11, 31, 32	65.50	1290	90	93.47	1268	112	91.88
14	Table 3: 5, 11, 31, 32	50.00	958	422	69.42	1263	117	91.52

Further we assumes that middle part of each character is important for CRR as degradation occurs at the corner PAC with specially for MODI script. Considering importance of centerportion in character image, PAC was analyzed by eliminating corner PAC to recognize exact shape of the character. CRR for MODI handwritten basic characters indicates that highest 94.92% was achieved by Zernike moments using Euclidian classifier as shown in Table 7.

7.3 Classification and Recognition

Entire experiment was further applied to analyze improvements in CRR using different soft techniques with ensemble bagging, K-NN, Decision tree and SVM classifier for PCR. Comparative analysis of performance of features was illustrated in Fig. 16. Ensemble bagging with decision tree achieved better CRR as compare to other classification techniques for partial character recognition at each zone.

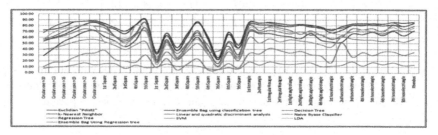

Fig. 16. Comparative analysis of performance of features with soft techniques.

Ensemble methods were learning algorithms that constructs set of classifiers to classify new data points by using a vote (weight) for predictions [43]. Data set used for experimental work was big in size which possesses significant noise in data. Ensemble bagging has been applied as it works well in the presence of noise. Detailed comparison of performance of features using ensemble bagging with decision tree was illustrated in Figs. 17. As shown in Fig. 17, Ensemble bagging with decision tree was produced better

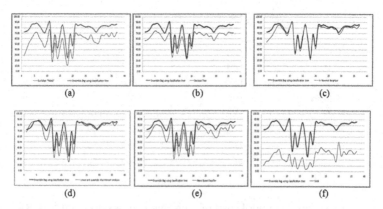

Fig. 17. Comparison of performance of features with ensemble bagging with decision tree.

results as compare to Euclidian classifier, Decision Tree, k-NN, LDA and QDA, Naïve Byase and SVM as shown in Fig. 17a, 17b, 17c, 17d, 17e and 17f respectively. Experimentation was followed in same criteria with distinct and integrated approach with homogeneous as well as heterogeneous zoning patterns. Partial character recognition of MODI handwritten character was increased using Ensemble bagging up to 97.68% with integrated approach as shown in Fig. 17f.

8   Conclusion

Research work was done to recognize handwritten partial characters of MODI script using extracted partial area of a character. To consider PAC we have extracted various zoning patterns and used with various combinations. Support of partial area in character was a measure of available part of the character which was used with zoning. Experimental results concludes that zoning was not only important for the recognition of a character but also give significant confidence in partial character recognition. This research work justifies new zoning patterns using planer geometrical shapes for HOCR. Effectiveness of these patterns was measured using Zernike and Zernike Complex moment with respect to find a zone of a PAC as well as analyzed using different soft techniques.

The overall recognition of MODI handwritten character using Zernike moments was 94.92% for integrated approach and the using Zernike Complex moments was 94.78% for integrated approach. This result clearly shows use of Zernike moments or Zernike Complex moments features which increases the recognition rate of system when used with zoning and integrated approach. CRR using Zernike complex moment is more important when we consider used sample set and support of PAC also in most the case Zernike complex moment shows improvement over Zernike moments. Partial character recognition of MODI handwritten character was increased using soft computing techniques. Ensemble bagging achieved 97.68% CRR with integrated approach for PCR.

Concluding this remark by stating that to recognize a handwritten character system does not require entire part of the character, 50% PAC focusing to the central portion of the character image was sufficient to produce considerable CRR to recognize complex and cursive type of handwritten MODI basic character when zone of the PAC was supervised and known to the system.

9   Scope for Further Study

Future scope was hidden in millions of MODI documents which were waiting to be explored and unfold the mysteries written on the pages of history. Segmentation of Text line, characters was emerged as a global problem for many historical script documents in automated HOCR. Character segmentation problem leads various difficulties in case of MODI script as it was ancient script and vanished from usual transaction as well as it does not have any concept of word and sentence. MODI script stands as a superset in extensive research for handwritten character recognition problem due to lot of uncommon hurdles that it includes even from character representations to the recognition. Figure 18 shows a sample of a historical document of MODI script.

Fig. 18. Sample of historical document of MODI Script.

References

1. Lalmalsawma, D.: India speaks 780 languages, 220 lost in last 50 years–survey (2013). https://blogs.reuters.com/india/2013/09/07/india-speaks-780-languages-220-lost-in-last-50-years-survey. India Insights, Reuters Edition US. Accessed 2 Aug 2014
2. Mahesh, R., Sinha, K.: A journey from Indian scripts processing to Indian language processing. IEEE Ann. Hist. Comput. **12**(27), 8–31 (2009)
3. Wikipedia: "Brahmic scripts" (2018). https://en.wikipedia.org/wiki/Brahmic_scripts. Accessed 7 Jan 2018
4. Pal, U., Chaudhuri, B.B.: Indian script character recognition: a survey. Pattern Recogn. **37**, 1887–1899 (2004)
5. Khobragade, R.N., Koli, N.A., Makesar, M.S.: A survey on recognition of Devnagari script. Int. J. Comput. Appl. Inf. Technol. **II**(I), 22–26 (2013)
6. Prabhanjan, S., Dinesh, R.: Handwritten devanagari characters and numeral recognition using multi-region uniform local binary pattern. Int. J. Multimed. Ubiquit. Eng. **11**(3), 387–398 (2016)
7. Dineshkumar, R., Suganthi, J.: A research survey on sanskrit offline handwritten character recognition. Int. J. Sci. Res. Publ. **3**(1), 1–7 (2013)
8. Singh, S.K., Sachan, M.K.: Opportunities and challenges of handwritten Sanskrit character recognition system. Int. J. Future Revolut. Comput. Sci. Commun. Eng. **3**(7), 18–22 (2017)
9. Dineshkumar, R., Suganthi, J.: Sanskrit character recognition system using neural network. Indian J. Sci. Technol. **8**(1), 65–69 (2015)
10. Magare, S.S., Deshmukh, R.R: Offline handwritten Sanskrit character recognition using hough transform and Euclidean distance. Int. J. Innov. Sci. Res. **10**(2), 295–302 (2014)
11. Ajmire, P.E., Dharaskar, R.V., Thakare, V.M.: A comparative study of handwritten Marathi character recognition. In: National Conference on Innovative Paradigms in Engineering & Technology, Proceedings published by IJCA, pp. 26–28 (2012)
12. Kamblea, P.M., Hegadi, R.S.: Handwritten Marathi character recognition using R-HOG feature. Proc. Comput. Sci. **45**, 266–274 (2015). In: International Conference on Advanced Computing Technologies and Applications (ICACTA 2015), Elsevier
13. Pal, U., Wakabayashi, T., Kimura, F.: Comparative study of Devanagari handwritten character recognition using different features and classifiers. In: Proceedings of the 10th Conference Document Analysis Recognition, pp. 1111–1115 (2009)
14. Kulkarni S.A., Borde, P.L., Manza, R.R., Yannawar, P.L.: Recognition of Handwritten MODI Numerals using Hu and Zernike features. arXiv preprint arXiv:1404.1151 (2014)
15. Kulkarni, S.A., Borde, P.L., Manza, R.R., Yannawar, P.L.: Offline Handwritten MODI Character Recognition Using HU, Zernike Moments and Zoning. arXiv preprint arXiv:1406.6140 (2014)

16. Kulkarni, S.A., Borde, P.L., Manza, R.R., Yannawar, P.L.: Review on recent advances in automatic handwritten MODI script recognition. Int. J. Comput. Appl. (0975–8887) **115**(19) (2015)
17. Kulkarni, S.A., Borde, P.L., Manza, R.R., Yannawar, P.L.: Analysis of orthogonal moments for recognition of handwritten MODI numerals. In: 2ND Natural language Processing and Data Mining (NLPDM), Veer Narmad South Gujarat University, Surat, SNLPDM04, pp. 1–6 (2015)
18. Sadanand, A.K., Prashant, L.B., Ramesh, R.M., Yannawar, P.L.: Offline MODI character recognition using complex moments. In: The Second International Symposium on Computer Vision and the Internet (VisionNet-2015), SCMS School of Engineering and Technology, Kochi (Ernakulam), Kerala, India, Sponsored by Elsevier, Procedia Computer Science, vol. 58(C), pp. 516–525, May 2015
19. Sadanand, A.K., Prashant, L.B., Ramesh, R.M., Yannawar, P.L.: Impact of zoning on Zernike moments for handwritten MODI character recognition. In: 2015 International Conference on Computer, Communication and Control (IC4), Indore, IEEE International Conference on Computer Communication and Control, pp. 1–6 (2015)
20. Sadanand, A.K., Prashant, L.B., Ramesh, R.M., Yannawar, P.L.: Text line segmentation of handwritten historical modi documents. Int. J. Inf. Commun. Comput. Technol. (JIMS8I) **5**(1), 285–291 (2017). https://doi.org/10.5958/2347-7202.2017.00008.1. ISSN 2347-7202.
21. Singh, S.K., Sachan, M.K.: Opportunities and challenges of handwritten Sanskrit character recognition system. Int. J. Future Revolut. CS CE **3**(7), 18–22 (2017). ISSN 2454-4248
22. Pal, U., Chanda, S., Wakabayashi, T. and Kimura, F.: Accuracy improvement of Devnagari character recognition combining SVM and MQDF
23. SonalKhare, J.S.: Handwritten Devanagari character recognition system: a review. IJCA **121**(9), 10–14 (2015)
24. Dongre, V.J., Mankar, V.H.: A review of research on Devnagari character recognition. IJCA **12**(2), 8–15 (2010)
25. Yetirajam, M., Nayak, M.R., Chattopadhyay, S.: Recognition and classification of broken characters using feed forward neural network to enhance an OCR solution. IJARCET **1**(8), pp. 11–15 (2012). 2278-1323
26. Prema, K.V., Subba Reddy, N.V.: Two-tier architecture for unconstrained handwritten character recognition. Sadhana **27**(Part 5), 585–594 (2002)
27. e Silva, G.P., Lins, R.D.: An automatic method for enhancing character recognition in degraded historical documents. In: International Conference on Document Analysis and Recognition, pp. 553–557. IEEE Computer Society (2011)
28. Basappa B. Kodada, Shivakumar K.M.: Unconstrained handwritten Kannada numeral recognition. Int. J. Inf. Electron. Eng. **3**(2), 230–232 (2013). https://doi.org/10.7763/IJIEE.2013.V3.305
29. Mukherji, P., Rege, P.P.: Fuzzy stroke analysis of Devnagari handwritten characters. WSEAS Trans. Comput. **7**(5), 351–362 (2008). ISSN 1109-2750
30. Dhandra, B.V., Mukarambi, G., Hangarge, M.: Zone based features for handwritten and printed mixed Kannada digits recognition. In: International Conference on VLSI, Communication & Instrumentation (ICVCI), Proceedings by IJCA, pp. 5–9 (2011)
31. Arora, S., Bhattacharjee, D., Nasipuri, M., Basu, D., Kundu, M.: Combining multiple feature extraction techniques for handwritten Devnagari character recognition. In: IEEE Region 10 Colloquium & The Third ICIIS, Kharagpur, pp. 1–6 (2008)
32. Shobha Rani, N., Vasudev, T.: A comparative study on efficiency of classification techniques with zone level Gabor features towards handwritten Telugu character recognition. IJCA (0975–8887), **148**(1), 28–38 (2016)

33. Tripathy, N., Chakraborti, T., Nasipuri, M., Pal, U.: A scale and rotation invariant scheme for multi-oriented character recognition. In: 2016 23rd International Conference on Pattern Recognition (ICPR) Cancún Center, Cancún, México, pp. 4030–4035. IEEE (2016). 978-1-5090-4846-5/16/$31.00 ©2016

34. Tripathy, J.: Reconstruction of oriya alphabets using Zernike moments. IJCA (0975– 8887) **8**(8) (2010). (ISBN 978-93-80746-07-5)

35. Khotanzad, A., Hongs, Y.H.: Invariant image recognition by Zernike moments. IEEE Pattern Anal. Mach. Intell. **12**, 489–497 (1990)

36. Amitabh Wahi, S., Sundaramurthy, P.P.: Handwritten Tamil character recognition using Zernike moments and Legendre polynomial. Adv. Intell. Syst. Comput. **325**, 595–603 (2014)

37. Oujaoura, M., El Ayachi, R., Fakir, M., Bouikhalene, B., Minaoui, B.: Zernike moments and neural networks for recognition of isolated Arabic characters. Int. J. Comput. Eng. Sci. (IJCES) **2**(3), 17–25 (2012). ISSN 2250:3439

38. Kale, K.V., Deshmukh, P.D., Chavan, S.V., Kazi, M.M., Rode, Y.S.: Zernike moment feature extraction for handwritten Devanagari (Marathi) compound character recognition. (IJARAI) Int. J. Adv. Res. Artif. Intell. **3**(1), 68–76 (2014)

39. Alavipouz, F., Broumandnia, A.: Farsi character recognition using new hybrid feature extraction methods. Int. J. Comput. Sci. Eng. Inf. Technol. (IJCSEIT) **4**(1), 15–25 (2014)

40. Zernike, F.: Beugungstheorie des Schneidenverfahrens und seiner verbesserten Form, der Phasenkontrastmethode (Diffraction theory of the cut procedure and its improved form, the phase contrast method). Physica **1**, 689–704 (1934)

41. Teh, C., Chin, R.T.: On image analysis by the method of moments. IEEE Trans. Pattern Anal. Mach. Intell. **10**(4), 496–513 (1988)

42. Hasan, S.Y.: Study of Zernike moments using analytical Zernike polynomials. Pelagia Res. Libr. Adv. Appl. Sci. Res. **3**(1), 583–590 (2012)

43. Dietterich, T.G.: Ensemble Methods in Machine Learning. https://web.engr.oregonstate.edu/~tgd/publications/mcs-ensembles.pdf. Accessed 2 Mar 2018

44. Halder, C., Obaidullah, S.M., Santosh, K.C., Roy, K.: Content independent writer identification on Bangla Script: a document level approach. Int. J. Pattern Recogn. Artif. Intell. **32**(09), 1856011 (2018)

45. Santosh, K.C., Nattee, C., Lamiroy, B.: Relative positioning of stroke-based clustering: a new approach to online handwritten Devanagari character recognition. Int. J. Image Graph. **12**(02), 1250016 (2012)

46. Santosh, K.C., Nattee, C., Lamiroy, B.: Spatial similarity based stroke number and order free clustering. In: 2010 12th International Conference on Frontiers in Handwriting Recognition, pp. 652–657. IEEE, November 2010

47. Santosh, K.C., Wendling, L.: Character recognition based on non-linear multi-projection profiles measure. Front. Comput. Sci. **9**(5), 678–690 (2015)

A Modified Approach for the Segmentation of Unconstrained Cursive Modi Touching Characters Cluster

Manisha S. Deshmukh$^{(\boxtimes)}$ and Satish R. Kolhe

School of Computer Sciences,
Kavayitri Bahinabai Chaudhari North Maharashtra University,
Jalgaon, Maharashtra, India
manisha_d7@rediffmail.com, srkolhe2000@gmail.com

Abstract. In this paper, a robust character segmentation approach for cursive handwritten Modi script touching character cluster is presented. Prior to segmentation, the middle text region of the touching character cluster is separated by examining the location of Shirorekha and baseline. The middle text region is scrutinized for the estimation of ligature between two characters. Two different strategies are employed to find the location of the ligature. The selection of the strategy is based on the degree of connected component overlapratio. The foreground pixel intensity and vertical projection profile is scrutinized to segment the touching characters. The performance of the system is tested using the touching character clusters of the original archaic handwritten Modi documents. The proposed approach yields efficient touching characters cluster segmentation output and it is feasible to tackle most of the challenges in touching character cluster segmentation.

Keywords: Modi script · Touching character cluster segmentation · Overlap ratio

1 Introduction

The segmentation of the touching character is more challenging task if the script is handwritten, unconstrained, stylish and cursive. The Brahmi base ancient cursive Modi script is derived from Nagari family. This script is originated during 17th century and used in Maharashtra as administrative script up to 1950. It was used to write Marathi language as well as other languages as Hindi, Guajarati, Persian and so on. Mainly, this script was used for the fast writing. The text is written using Boru (Wooden stick/bird feather) and link over the Shirorekha without lifting the pen. Shirorekha is drawn before to write a text. Modi script text is not separated in sentences and words. Similarly, no punctuation mark is used to indicate the end of words or sentences. Thus, number of challenges are exhibits all over the segmentation of the characters as touching characters; nonuniform Shirorekha and base line; skewed or curved text lines; nonuniform

© Springer Nature Singapore Pte Ltd. 2021
K. C. Santosh and B. Gawali (Eds.): RTIP2R 2020, CCIS 1380, pp. 431–444, 2021.
https://doi.org/10.1007/978-981-16-0507-9_36

Fig. 1. Samples of original archaic handwritten degraded Modi Script document images.

text size and so on. Figure 1 shows the sample images of archaic original Modi script documents [15–19].

The number of segmentation challenges is under perception of the touching handwritten Modi character clusters as depicted in Fig. 2.

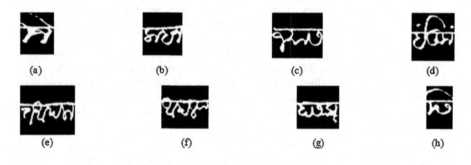

Fig. 2. Challenges in handwritten Modi touching character cluster segmentation. (a) Very dense touching character (b) Skewed Shirorekha (c) Entirely touching characters (d) Nonuniform base line (e) Nonuniform Shirorekha (f) Nonuniform size characters (g) Nonuniform touching characters (h) Looking like single character.

The accuracy of character recognition having one most important requisite aspect as the accuracy in character segmentation. However, the research work for touching Modi character cluster segmentation is not reported. Thus, there is essential to achieve the improvement in segmentation of touching handwritten Modi character cluster. The main objective of this research is to improve the accuracy of the freestyle, unconstrained, cursive and handwritten Modi touching character cluster segmentation. To improve the segmentation rate of the touching character cluster, a modified technique is proposed. The global and local zoning is employed with three types of analysis as: i) overlap ratio, ii) foreground pixel intensity and iii) vertical projection profile.

After giving the brief introduction, rest of the paper is clarified the proposed work as follows. Section 2 reviewed the related work. Section 3 discussed the framework of the handwritten Modi touching character cluster system. Details of the dataset which is used to check the performance of the proposed system is illustrated in Sect. 4. The experimental results are reported and discussed in Sect. 5. The conclusion is stated in the Sect. 6.

2 Literature Review

Generally, the character segmentation techniques are classified in two type explicit and implicit approach [2,5,6]. In the explicit approaches, segmentation point of the text part is finding out to separate the isolated characters. These approaches having the drawbacks given as follows [5].

- Over-segmentation or under-segmentation.
- Failed to segment the touching characters.
- Failed to segment overlapping characters.

In implicit approaches, to estimate the segmentation point intelligent system has been used. These techniques having two drawbacks given as follows [5].

- Failed to identify overlapping and touched text part.
- Requires huge training data and time which generates extensive overheads.

Handwritten character segmentation approaches found may vary significantly for the handwritten script like English, Chinese, Devanagari, Bengali, Guajarati etc. [1–9]. In the study of the handwritten character segmentation literature, it is found that the approaches are script specific and the number of issues are considered for character segmentation. It uses the prior knowledge about script's character structuring, writing style of script etc. [14]. The research presented in [13,16,18,19,21] proposes different types of strategies for the handwritten Devanagari script character segmentation. Graph distance theory-based approach for isolated, overlapping and touching Devanagari character segmentation is discussed in citech36ref10. This approach has two inefficiencies as: i) In locating accurate boundaries between characters through post-processing, and ii) Vertical cuts are gained for overlapped characters. The cursive handwritten touching English character segmentation techniques are presented in [10,12] and [23].

The research work presented in [13,16–21] proposes different types of strategies for the handwritten Devanagari script character segmentation. The work presented in [13,18] and [21] is the text-based approach used the structural properties to segments the touching Devanagari characters. This approach is script specific, parametric and having over-segmentation problem. It fails to segment the characters with broken left modifier and the vertical left modifier is too small. It also does not tackle with broken characters, touching characters. Graph distance theory-based approach for isolated, overlapping and touching Devanagari character segmentation is discussed in [16]. This approach has two inefficiencies as: i) In locating accurate boundaries between characters through post-processing, and ii) Vertical cuts are gained for overlapped characters. Morphological operation with minutiae detection algorithm is presented in [19] for the segmentation of Devanagari compound characters. A constrained based Devanagari touching character segmentation system is presented in [20] using analysis of bounding box with vertical bars technique. This system is failed to segment the broken and overlapping characters.

Kapoor S., & Verma V. [20] reported three opinions in the area of the character segmentation approaches as: i) The vertical projection profile-based character segmentation approaches are not suitable for free style, handwritten cursive, unconstrained overlapping characters; ii) The character segmentation approaches using Hidden Markov Model does not works well with overlapping characters; and iii) The water reservoir-based techniques are constrained based and are not able to segment the overlapping characters [22].

3   System Framework

A modified framework for Modi touching character segmentation system is illustrated in Fig. 3. The cluster of touching Modi characters is the input of this system. The proposed handwritten Modi touching character cluster segmentation procedure includes four stages, which are described as below.

3.1   Stage I

The initial stage of the character segmentation includes three processing sub steps. The input cluster images are in gray level. These images are converted into binary level by using Otsu's thresholding method [23]. The binarization of the images is desirable for the estimation of the location of the Shirorekha and text region. For the formation of the text region (Treg) the location of Shirorekha (Hline) and base line (Bline) is detected by calculating maximum and minimum peak of the horizontal projection profile using Eq. 1 and Eq. 2 respectively [2]. These locations are used for the separation of the text region of the Modi touching character cluster image as demonstrated in Fig. 4.

$$Hline = max_{(j=1:N)}\left(\sum_{i=1}^{M} C(i,j)\right) \tag{1}$$

$$Bline = min_{(j=1:N)}\left(\sum_{i=1}^{M} C(i,j)\right) \tag{2}$$

Here, C is the Modi touching characters cluster image of size M X N.

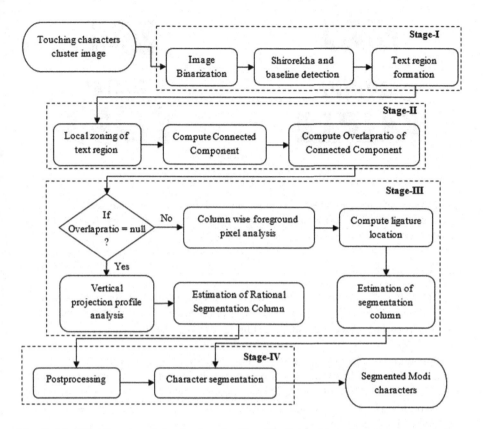

Fig. 3. Modified framework for the handwritten Modi touching character segmentation system.

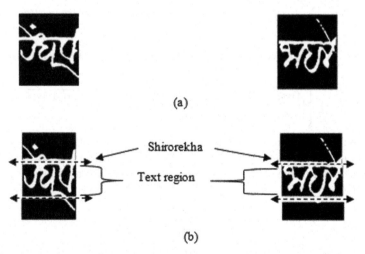

Fig. 4. The illustration of initial stage I of Modi character touching cluster segmentation (a) Input touching characters cluster (b) Shirorekha and base line detection and text region formation.

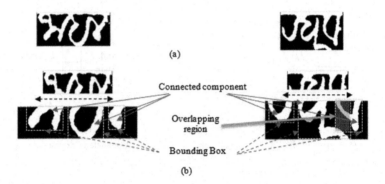

Fig. 5. Illustration of connected component and bounding box formation (a) Text region of the overlapping/touching characters cluster (b) Text region lower zone connected component and bounding box of the component.

3.2 Stage II

The next successive stage of the cluster segmentation includes local zoning of the text region (Treg). The text region is partitioned into two non-overlapping zones horizontally from the middle. The connected components (CC) from the lower region are intended as depicted in Fig. 5(b).

For each connected component the two elements are determined as its bounding box and area. The bounding box is rectangular region specified by a vector gives [X Y Width Height] of each component as shown in Fig. 5(b). Similarly, area (Areafig) is the actual number of pixels in the component computed which is calculated using Eq. 3.

$$Areafig(k) = \sum_{i=1}^{Height_k} \sum_{j=1}^{Width_k} CC_k(i,j) \qquad where\, k = 1..Number\, of\, connected\, component \tag{3}$$

Further, the operative connected components (CCfig) are discriminated using the Eq. 4.

$$CCfig = \begin{cases} Areafig_k & Areafig_k \geq \sqrt{\mu(Areafig) + \sigma(Areafig)}/2 \\ none & otherwise \end{cases} \tag{4}$$

Where function μ and σ are mean and standard deviation of the area of the all connected components respectively. The overlap ratio between the bounding boxes of each operative connected component pair is computed using union ratio type as given in Eq. 5.

$$Oratio = \frac{CCfig_A \cap CCfig_B}{CCfig_A \cup CCfig_B} \tag{5}$$

Let $CCfig_A$ and $CCfig_B$ be the two connected components with Box_A and Box_B bounding box respectively. The overlap ratio (Oratio) between these two bounding boxes is an $M_o X N_o$ matrix. Each element (r_1, r_2) of this matrix is corresponds to overlap ratio between row r_1 in Box_A and row r_2 in Box_B. The overlapratio is computed in the between 0 and 1 where 1 implies that a perfect overlap. This overlap ratio is exploited for the selection procedure of the touching cluster type. Clusters are classified in two classes as i) Partially touching clusters (Fig. 2 (b, d, e and g)) and iii) Entirely touching clustered (Fig. 2 (a, c and h)). The full process of this stage I and II is illustrated in Algorithm 1 from step1 to step8.

Algorithm1 SegTouch (Cfig)
Input: Cfig – Cluster of touching character's non-segmented text region
Output: Schar – Segmented characters

1: Cfig₁ ← img_Binarizarion (Cfig)   // Gray to binary image conversion.
2: [H, W] ← heightWidthOfImageOf (Cfig₁)   // Find height and width of image
3: [Lb , Ls] ← findSB (Cfig₁, H, W)   //Find location of Shirorekha and baseline.
4: [Left, Right, I₂] ← findLeftRightEnd(Cfig₁)   // Find left and right end location of the text line.
5: [Upartfig, Mpartfig, Lpartfig] ← separteUML(I₂, Lb, Ls)   // Find text zone region
6: HalfMpartfig ← extrLowerHalf(Mpartfig)   // Extract lower half part of Mpartfig
7: [CCfig, Areafig] ← calAreaCC(HalfMpartfig)   // Calculate connected component and area
                                                  of each component in HalfMpartfig
8: Oratio ← calOverlapRatio (CCfig)   // Compute the overlapping ratio of connected components which is operative
9: CntOratio ← countOratio(Oratio)   // Count the region whose Oratio is greater than zero
10: if isempty(CntOratio)   // Determine the cluster is touching
        Function2 (Mpartfig, fig, h, w)
    else
        Function1 (Mpartfig, fig, h, w)
    endIF
11: return

3.3 Stage III

The overlapping ratio (CntOratio) is counted for the all the connected components. And this overlapping ratio is applied for the selection of the criteria of the touching character cluster segmentation process using Eq. 6. This is depicted in Algorithm 1 from step 9 to step10.

$$Criteria = \begin{cases} Function2() & CntOratio = null \\ Function1() & otherwise \end{cases} \tag{6}$$

A] **Function1():** The partial touching character clusters are segmented using Function1 method. A window of size 3 X N_t is scanned through the text region. Related to each window first occurrence of the foreground pixels are searched from the bottom side. The ligature location (LocX) is finalized by scrutinized the location vector (Loc) with height of the text region M_t using Eq. 7.

$$LocX(s) = \begin{cases} Loc(i) & Loc(i) \leq M_t \wedge Loc \neq 0 \\ none & otherwise \end{cases} \tag{7}$$

Where $i = 1...\text{length(Loc)}$. The ligature location vector is used to finalize the segmentation column. This character segmentation method is described in Algorithm 2.

Algorithm2 Function1 (Mpartfig, fig, h, w)
Input: Mpartfig – The text region below to Shirorekha and upper to baseline of fig
    fig – Character cluster
    h – Height of Mpartfig
    w – Width of Mpartfig
Output: Schar – Segmented characters

1: for c ← each three successive columns of Mpartfig
    lc ← (Mpartfig(c))   // Extract the three successive columns region of Mpartfig
    for j ← each row from bottom side
      if isForegorundPixel(lc(j))   // Check for all foreground pixels
        Loc ← Loc U j+1
        break;
      endIf
    endFor
  endFor
2: for l ← each value of Loc   // Estimate the ligature location
    if Loc(l) ≤ h/2 and Loc(l) ≠ 0
      LocX ← LocX U Loc(l)
    endIf
  endFor
3: for l ← each value of LocX -1   // Calculate estimated character region locations
    if LocX(l+1) - LocX(l+1) ≠ 3
      SegLoc ← SegLoc U LocX(l)
    endIf
  endFor
4: if size(SegLoc) =1   / Check for the if character cluster is contain only two
characters
    SegLoc=1 U SegLoc;
  endIf
  if SegLoc(x) <= 2
    SegLoc= SegLoc U w;
  endIf
5: Schar ← segCharacter(fig,Fec)
6: return

B] **Function2():** The entirely touching characters clusters are segmented using vertical projection profile-based method. The vertical projection profile (Vpp) of the text region (Mpartfig) is calculated using Eq. 8.

$$Vpp = \sum_{i=1}^{M_t} Mpartfig(i,j) \qquad where \ 1 \leq j \geq N_t \tag{8}$$

The location vector (Loc) is formed by using the Eq. 9.

$$Loc(s) = \begin{cases} i & Vpp(i) \geq \mu(Vpp) + \sigma(Vpp) \\ none & otherwise \end{cases} \tag{9}$$

Where $i = 1..Nt$. Further, the estimated location vector (Loc) is analysed in the formation of the Rational segmentation column (SegLoc). The illustration of entirely touching characters cluster segmentation procedure is described in Algorithm 3.

Algorithm3 Function2 (Mpartfig, fig, h, w)
Input: Mpartfig – The text region below to Shirorekha and upper to baseline of fig
        fig – Character cluster
        h – Height of Mpartfig
        w – Width of Mpartfig
Output: Schar – Segmented characters

1: Vpp ← VerticalPP(Mpartfig)   // Compute horizontal projection profile
2: for c ← each column of Mpartfig
        if Vpp(c) ≥ mean(Vpp)+ std(Vpp)   // Check for ligature
            Loc ← Loc U c
        endIf
    endFor
3: for l ← each value of Loc   // Estimate Rational segmentation column
location
        if Loc(l) and Loc(l+1) are not consecutive
            SegLoc ← SegLoc U Loc(l)
        endIf
4: Fec ← postProcessing (SegLoc) // Compute the Finalize segmentation column location
5: Schar ← segCharacter(fig,Fec)   // Segment the character
6: return

3.4 Stage IV

The handwritten Modi script document are highly degraded due to number of reasons like aging, writing material and so on. Consequently, there may be under segmentation problem is occurred during the estimation of the Rational segmentation column. To reduce this problem, the Finalize Segmentation Columns (FSCs) is decided by analysing the Rational segmentation column (SegLoc) vector using the postprocessing method described in [2].

4 Dataset

The archaic original handwritten Modi script documents collected from the various archaeological places as Rajwade Sanshodhan Mandir, Dhule, Shri Samartha Vagdevta Mandir, Dhule etc., are used to test and evaluate the performance of the proposed system. The dataset contains 2540 document images. These document images already preprocessed means de-noised and globally de-skewed using the approaches presented in [25] and [1] respectively. The preprocessed document images are segmented in the text lines using the approach presented in [24]. The Modi text lines are segmented into the isolated Modi characters and touching characters clusters using the approach presented in [2]. These Modi touching characters clusters are the input of the proposed system.

5 Results and Discussions

The performance of the proposed handwritten Modi touching character cluster segmentation method is evaluated using a similar evaluation strategy that was illustrated in [2,28]. The evaluation method uses five evaluation factors as: Correct segmentation rate (CSR), Successful Segmentation Rate (SSR), precision, recall and F-measure illustrated in Eqs. 10–14 respectively. These aspects are calculated by counting the number of matches between the resultant segmented characters by the algorithm and ground truth characters in text line segments [2,28].

$$CSR = \frac{NC_R - (NC_c + NC_B)}{NC_G} \times 100 \tag{10}$$

$$SSR = \frac{NC_I}{NC_R} \times 100 \tag{11}$$

$$Precision = \frac{NC_I + NC_C}{NC_R} \tag{12}$$

$$Recall = \frac{NC_I + NC_C}{NC_G} \tag{13}$$

$$Precision = 2 \times \frac{Recall \times Precision}{Recall + Precision} \tag{14}$$

where,
NC_G: Number of ground truth characters.
NC_R: Number of resultant characters.
NC_I: Number of correctly segmented isolated characters.
NC_C: Number of overlapping or touching characters clusters.
NC_B: Number of incorrectly segmented characters.

Ground truth values are not available for the testing the performance of the handwritten Modi touching character cluster segmentation system. Thus, the numbers of 2249 Modi touching character clusters in 1072 text lines of ninety-two Modi documents are manually calculated and ground truth values are evaluated. Table 1 gives the result of touching Modi character cluster segmentation.

Table 1. The Modi touching character cluster segmentation result.

No. of clusters	NC$_G$	NC$_R$	NC$_C$	NC$_B$	NC$_I$	SSR(%)	CSR(%)	Precision	Recall	F-measure
1072	2249	2412	206	189	2017	89.68	83.62	0.9	0.9	0.9

The Successful Segmentation Rate (SSR) and Correct Segmentation Rate (CSR) are achieved using the proposed method for the Modi touching character cluster segmentation as 89.68% and 83.62% respectively. Partial touching Modi character clusters are segmented efficiently by proposed method. There are two issues are found about the bad segmentation. The first issue is with very tightly overlapping characters with touching characters exist in the same cluster. The second issue is the broken touching character as shown in Fig. 6(b). Still very tightly coupled character clusters and overlapping character clusters are not segmented properly. Figures 6, 7, 8 and 9 shows the examples of the segmented touching Modi character clusters.

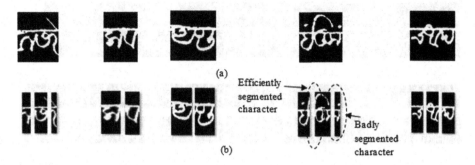

Fig. 6. Example of Modi script character segmentation of a Modi touching characters cluster (a) Modi touching character clusters (b) Segmented Modi touching character clusters.

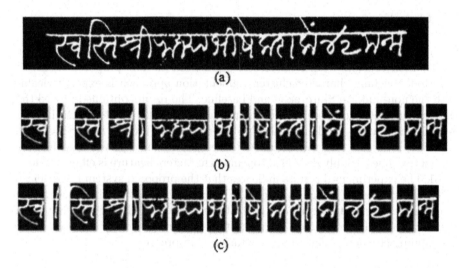

Fig. 7. Step wise example of Modi script character segmentation of a Modi document text line (a) Segmented text lines of a Modi Document (b) Segmented touching character clusters and isolated characters (c) Segmented characters of text lines.

Fig. 8. Example of Modi script character segmentation of a Modi document text line.

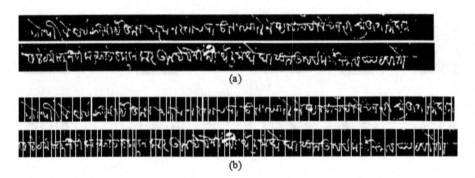

Fig. 9. Modi character segmentation (Broken characters and Shirorekha, non-uniform base line and Shirorekha) (a) Input Modi text lines (b) Segmented Modi characters.

6   Conclusions

The connected component overlapratio analysis effectively works on the different problems in touching character cluster segmentation. The proposed handwritten Modi touching character cluster segmentation approach is expertly dealing with the non-uniform Shirorekha and baseline. The results obtained proved that the presented character segmentation approach efficiently tackled with the character segmentation challenges like broken character, broken Shirorekha, variable size characters, variable distance between characters, skewed text lines and curved text lines. Highly degraded touching characters ligature is efficiently identified. The experimental results indicates that the proposed system is efficient to tackle the challenges in handwritten Modi touching character cluster segmentation. Hence, this system can be a part of the archaic handwritten freestyle and unconstrained Modi document segmentation system. Currently the work on the overlapping characters cluster segmentation is in progress.

References

1. Obaidullah, S.M., Halder, C., Santosh, K.C., Das, N., Roy, K.: PHDIndic_11: page-level handwritten document image dataset of 11 official Indic scripts for script identification. Multimed. Tools Appl. **77**(2), 1643–1678 (2017). https://doi.org/10.1007/s11042-017-4373-y
2. Obaidullah, S.M., Santosh, K.C., Halder, C., Das, N., Roy, K.: Automatic Indic script identification from handwritten documents: page, block, line and word-level approach. Int. J. Mach. Learn. Cybern. **10**(1), 87–106 (2017). https://doi.org/10.1007/s13042-017-0702-8
3. Obaidullah, S.M., Santosh, K.C., Das, N., Halder, C., Roy, K.: Handwritten Indic script identification in multi-script document images: a survey. Int. J. Pattern Recognit. Artif. Intell. **32**(10), 1856012 (2018)
4. Choudhary A., Rishi, R., Ahlawat, S: A new character segmentation approach for off-line cursive handwritten words. Proc. Comput. Sci. **17**, 88–95 (2013)

5. Kumar, M., Jindal, M.K., Sharma, R.K.: Segmentation of isolated and touching characters in offline handwritten Gurmukhi script recognition. Int. J. Inf. Technol. Comput. Sci. **6**(2), 58–63 (2014)
6. Kurniawan, F., Rahim, M.S.M., Daman, D., Rehman, A., Mohamad, D., Mariyam, S.: Region-based touched character segmentation in handwritten words. Int. J. Innov. Comput. Inf. Control **7**(6), 3107–3120 (2011)
7. Garg, N.K., Kaur, L., Jindal, M.K.: Segmentation of touching modifiers and consonants in middle region of handwritten Hindi text. Pattern Recognit. Image Anal. **25**(3), 413–417 (2015). https://doi.org/10.1134/S1054661815030050
8. Saba, T., Rehman, A., Elarbi-Boudihir, M.: Methods and strategies on off-line cursive touched characters segmentation: a directional review. Artif. Intell. Rev. **42**(4), 1047–1066 (2011). https://doi.org/10.1007/s10462-011-9271-5
9. Sharma, P., Sachan, M.K.: A review on character segmentation of touching and half character in handwritten Hindi text. Int. J. Adv. Res. Comput. Sci. **8**(3), 1078–1083 (2017)
10. Jindal, K., Kumar, R.: A novel shape-based character segmentation method for Devanagari script. Arabian J. Sci. Eng. **42**(8), 3221–3228 (2017). https://doi.org/10.1007/s13369-017-2420-7
11. Palakollu, S., Dhir, R., Rani, R.: Handwritten Hindi text segmentation techniques for lines and characters. In: Proceedings of the World Congress on Engineering and Computer Science, vol. 1, pp. 24–26 (2012)
12. Bag, S., Krishna, A.: Character segmentation of Hindi unconstrained handwritten words. In: Barneva, R.P., Bhattacharya, B.B., Brimkov, V.E. (eds.) IWCIA 2015. LNCS, vol. 9448, pp. 247–260. Springer, Cham (2015). https://doi.org/10.1007/978-3-319-26145-4_18
13. Golait Snehal S., Malik L.: Handwritten Marathi compound character segmentation using minutiae detection algorithm. Proc. Comput. Sci. **87**, 18–24 (2016)
14. Kapoor S.,Verma V.: Fragmentation of handwritten touching characters in Devanagari script. Int. J. Inf. Technol. Model. Comput. (IJITMC) **2** 11–21 (2014)
15. Behera, S., Pradhan, A., Majhi, B.: A novel clustering based fuzzy approach for character segmentation in handwritten Odia scripts. In: 2017 Fourth International Conference on Image Information Processing (ICIIP), pp. 1–6. IEEE, December 2017
16. Kavitha, A.S., Shivakumara, P., Kumar, G.H., Lu, T.: A new watershed model based system for character segmentation in degraded text lines. AEU-Int. J. Electron. Commun. **71**, 45–52 (2017)
17. Otsu, N.: A threshold selection method from gray level histogram. IEEE Trans. Syst. Man Cybern. **19**(1), 62–66 (1979)
18. Deshmukh, M.S., Patil, M.P., Kolhe, S.R.: A hybrid text line segmentation approach for the ancient handwritten unconstrained freestyle Modi script documents. Imaging Sci. J. **66**(7), 433–442 (2018)
19. Deshmukh M.S., Kolhe, S.R.: A hybrid character segmentation approach for cursive unconstrained handwritten historical Modi script documents. In: International Conference on Sustainable Computing in Science, Technology & Management (SUSCOM-2019). SSRN Elsevier Digital Library (2019)
20. Deshmukh, M.S., Patil, M.P., Kolhe, S.R.: The divide-and-conquer based algorithm to detect and correct the skew angle in the old age historical handwritten Modi Lipi documents. Int. J. Comput. Sci. Appl. **14**(2), 47–63 (2017)

21. Deshmukh, M.S., Patil, M.P., Kolhe, S.R.: A dynamic statistical nonparametric cleaning and enhancement system for highly degraded ancient handwritten Modi Lipi documents. In: 2017 International Conference on Advances in Computing, Communications and Informatics (ICACCI), pp. 1545–1551. IEEE, September 2017

22. Deshmukh, M.S., Manoj, P.P., Satish, R.K.: Offline handwritten Modi numerals recognition using chain code. In: Proceedings of the Third International Symposium on Women in Computing and Informatics. ACM (2015)

23. Kavallieratou E., Stamatatos E., Fakotakis N., Kokkinakis G.: Handwritten character segmentation using transformation-based learning. In: ICPR, p. 2634. IEEE, September 2000

24. Peng, G., Yu, P., Li, H., Li, H., Zhu, X.: A character segmentation algorithm for the palm leaf manuscripts. In: 2017 2nd IEEE International Conference on Computational Intelligence and Applications (ICCIA), pp. 354–358. IEEE, September 2017

25. Obaidullah, S.M., Santosh, K.C., Das, N., Halder, C., Roy, K.: Handwritten Indic script identification in multi-script document images: a survey. Int. J. Pattern Recognit. Artif. Intell. **32**(10), 1856012:1–1856012:26 (2018)

26. Halder, C., Obaidullah, S.M., Santosh, K.C., Roy, K.: Content independent writer identification on Bangla script: a document level approach. Int. J. Pattern Recognit. Artif. Intell. **32**(9), 1856011:1–1856011:24 (2018)

27. Mukherjee, H., Obaidullah, S.M., Santosh, K.C., Phadikar, S., Roy, K.: Line spectral frequency-based features and extreme learning machine for voice activity detection from audio signal. Int. J. Speech Technol. **21**(4), 753–760 (2018). https://doi.org/10.1007/s10772-018-9525-6

28. Santosh, K.C., Borra, S., Joshi, A., Dey, N.: Special section: advances in speech, music and audio signal processing (Articles 1–13). Int. J. Speech Technol. **22**(2), 293–294 (2019)

Resource Creation for Sentiment Analysis of Under-Resourced Language: Marathi

Rupali S. Patil[✉] and Satish R. Kolhe

School of Computer Sciences, Kavayitri Bahinabai Chaudhari North
Maharashtra University, Jalgaon, India
rupali.patil73@gmail.com, srkolhe2000@gmail.com

Abstract. With the hike of social networking sites like Facebook, Twitter, Instagram, the Marathi web data are increasing day by day. Mining these data towards the corporate and government has become a broad area of research under Natural Language Processing. Sentiment Analysis (SA), identification of the public's attitude, using machine learning or subjective lexicon, is easier for resource-rich languages like English. Still, for Marathi being poor resource language, it's a difficult task. In this research, the three approaches have experimented – Corpus-based, SentiWordNet3.0-based, and Hindi Senti-WordNet (HSWN)-based to create the Marathi sentiment lexicon (adjective, adverb). The first two approaches use Google Translator to make use of English resource-SWN3.0. The third approach uses HSWN and Marathi WordNet, which minimizes translation errors. The word coverage of the SWN3.0-based lexicon is noteworthy. This paper attempts the Marathi subjective lexicon creation for the first time, which would aid for SA chore precise to the Marathi data.

Keywords: Marathi subjective lexicon · SentiWordNet 3.0 · Hindi SentiWordNet (HSWN) · Marathi WordNet · Marathi sentiment analysis

1 Introduction

The evolutionary growth in social networking data has contributed massive data to the internet. These user-generated contents influence marketing strategies, government policies, and agendas, and individual's decision making. Social media platforms have endorsed people to express their opinions in their native languages, which results in an increase in Indian language data on the internet. There is a reasonable amount of work done for English, which has many resources for SA. The Hindi WordNet is the first resource among the Indian languages, which started to build in 2000 onwards [1] subsequently Marathi and Sanskrit WordNets at Indian Institute of Technology, Bombay.

To analyze the people's sentiments expressed in any language, a lexicon with polarity scores is essential. Two general approaches are used to build the lexicon. The first one is, train the machine learning algorithms [3, 4] using annotated data and test upon the new text which needs resources. Due to the limited or unavailable resources for non-English languages, and the creation of the resources is not feasible [18], the machine learning approach is hard to implement. The second approach is manual

K. C. Santosh and B. Gawali (Eds.): RTIP2R 2020, CCIS 1380, pp. 445–457, 2021.
https://doi.org/10.1007/978-981-16-0507-9_37

construction, using existing resources or Pointwise Mutual Information (PMI) [5]. This paper presents the Marathi subjective lexicon (Adjective and Adverb) using existing resources.

1. Corpus-based: This method uses the Google Translator [2] to translate the adjectives and adverbs fetched from a small Marathi corpus into English. Using Senti-WordNet 3.0, the polarity scores for these words are calculated.
2. SentiWordNet 3.0-based: The word-by-word adjectives and adverbs from Senti-WordNet 3.0 [6] are translated into Marathi using Google Translate, and polarity scores are assigned to corresponding Marathi words. The sentiment analysis based on subjective lexicon has the drawback that it does not cover adequate sentiment words [20]. This method is the solution to the problem due to its high word coverage, as compared with the rest of the two methods.
3. Using HSWN: The Indian language WordNets are linked to Hindi WordNet. With the help of this linkage, this module gets the polarity scores from HSWN and assigns it to the Marathi Adjectives/Adverbs, resulting in a Marathi subjective lexicon.

The first two approaches have some limitations, such as translation errors and change in part-of-speech of a word from one language to another as the language structure differs from one another.

The rest of the paper is designed as follows: Sect. 2 comprises the related work in this area. Section 3 discusses the methodology for the Marathi lexicon generation. The implementation details are given in Sect. 4. The results and discussion of the three approaches are discussed in Sect. 5. Lastly, the paper concludes in Sect. 6.

2 Related Work

The author [7] studied three main approaches in the Subjective lexicon construction: a manual, dictionary-based, and corpus-based. The manual method is the easiest, but a time-consuming procedure. The result of manual methods can be excellent in quality, but narrow in the scope [17]. The dictionary-based approach starts with a manually built small seed list with its polarity and then gets expanded through the dictionaries like WordNet by looking upon synonyms and antonyms of the words present in the seed list. However, the drawback is that this method creates the lexicon precisely for a domain [8]. For the generic domain lexicon of any language, a corpus-based approach is used in practice. The drawback of this method is that developing a corpus which comprises all the words of a language is not possible.

In [8], the sentiment lexicon is built for resource-poor Sinhala language using English SentiWordNet 3.0. They used an online English/Sinhala dictionary. The dictionary contains Sinhala word: it is an English translation and the synonym for the word. The polarity scores for the word are copied from SentiWordNet 3.0 to Sinhala word and its synonyms, resulting in the Sinhala sentiment lexicon. They worked on adjectives and adverbs only as these are the most significant components in any language [12]. The three classification algorithms Naïve Bayes, SVM, and J48, experimented for the positive, negative, and neutral classes, which lead to accuracies with 60%, 58%, and 56%, respectively.

The authors [9] constructed a subjective lexicon (adjective and adverb) using graph-based WordNet expansion. They used 45 adjectives and 75 adverbs as seedlist and expanded the list based on synonyms assumption made on by [10] and extended to antonyms. Hindi subjective lexicon is built with 8048 adjectives and 888 adverbs. They have used two additional methods – the use of a Bi-lingual dictionary using English SentiWordNet and English-Hindi WordNet Linking [11]. The lexicon contains 4335 adjectives and 1279 adverbs. The words generated by the system have evaluated with the help of 5 language experts on the voting basis. The average agreement of lexicon with annotators is 70.4%. This agreement is low due to the ambiguous Hindi words and the context in which they are used. The second method is using Google Translator; the Amazon product review dataset is translated from Hindi to English, which is authenticated by the judges. The Translated Dict contains 12086 adjectives and 1509 adverbs.

[13] proposed a method to create a SentiWordNet for Odia, the resource-poor language. They have used existing WordNets and SentiWordNets for other Indian dialects as a sound English-Odia machine translation system was not present. Word-Nets for four Indian languages Odia, Bengali, Telugu, and Tamil, are used to create the lexicon. These WordNets are linked through synset IDs, which are shared across the languages. The result contains 1839 positive and 2908 negative entries. The three-manual annotators evaluated with Cohen's Kappa agreement score 0.76 for Odia SentiWordNet.

The authors [14] proposed SentiWordNets for three Indian languages Hindi, Bengali, and Telugu using WordNets, dictionaries, corpus. They combined the English resources SentiWordNet and Subjectivity Word List, resulting in the source lexicon. To create a target lexicon, they have projected four different techniques. The first technique is based on Bilingual Dictionaries in which English-Hindi, English-Bengali, and English-Telugu are used. This technique resulted in 22,708 Hindi words, 34,117 Bengali words, and 30,889 Telugu entries. The second technique is WordNet-based, in which the available WordNets for Hindi and Bengali are used to expand the Senti-WordNets obtained from a dictionary-based approach. The third approach is corpus-based. They enlarged the developed SentiWordNets with the help of language-specific corpora. In the fourth approach, they involved the people on the internet through the game to produce and authenticate SentiWordNets. They validated Bengali Senti-WordNet using the subjectivity classifier and polarity identifier. For Hindi and Telugu, SentiWordNets are partially evaluated.

The authors [16] have performed sentiment analysis in Hindi. They developed the annotated corpus for the Hindi movie review domain. In the first approach, they trained the classifier for the corpus. The second approach involved the translation of the Hindi document to English and the use of standard English movie classifier. The third approach, Hindi SentiWordNet (HSWN), was developed using WordNet linking.

3   Methodology

The work aims to build the subjective lexicon for the Marathi language using three approaches.

3.1   Corpus-Based Approach

In this approach, the POS-Tagged monolingual corpus for the Marathi language collected by A. Kumaran, Microsoft Research, India, is used. It contains 1197 sentences (22,661 words) in the Devanagari script with UTF-8 format. The corpus-based approach is presented in Fig. 1.

3.2   SentiWordNet 3.0-Based Approach

In this research, the English lexical resource SentiWordNet (SWN) 3.0 [6] is used, which includes 117,659 words that come in various senses. The word from SWN has the part-of-speech (POS), unique id, polarity scores as positive and negative, synset terms, and glosses. For example, the word "active" appears with sense#3 as: "a 00038750 0.125 0 active#3" The objective score can be calculated as 1 − (positive score + negative score). The approach to generate a subjective lexicon based on SWN is presented in Fig. 2.

Algorithm 1: *Corpus-based Marathi Subjective Lexicon*

Input: Marathi annotated corpus
Output: Corpus-based Marathi Subjective Lexicon (adjective/adverb)
1. Extract all adjectives/adverbs from Marathi corpus
2. Translate adj/adv lists to English using Google Translator.
3. Get the first sense synset for all adj/adv
4. Assign the positive and negative score fetched from SentiWordNet 3.0 to the corresponding Marathi word and store to the final dictionary.

Fig. 1.   Algorithm to generate Corpus-based Subjective Lexicon

---

Algorithm 2: *SentiWordNet (SWN) 3.0-based Subjective Lexicon*

Input: SWN 3.0
Output: SWN-based Marathi Subjective Lexicon (adjective/adverb)
1. Extract adjective/adverb synsets with first sense from SWN.
2. Translate adj/adv lists to Marathi using Google Translator.
3. Project the positive and negative scores to the Marathi words.
4. Store the scores to the final dictionary.

Fig. 2.   Algorithm to generate SentiWordNet 3.0-based Subjective Lexicon

3.3   HSWN-Based Approach

In this approach, Marathi WordNet and Hindi SentiWordNet are used to produce the Marathi subjective lexicon. Marathi WordNet [15] is the lexical resource extended from Hindi WordNet in which 28,530 synsets are categorized under nouns, adjectives, adverbs, and verbs. These synsets are correlated through hypernymy, hyponymy, antonymy, and meronymy. HSWN [16] is the lexical resource formed by manipulating SentiWordNet and English-Hindi WordNet linking [11]. It contains more than 16,000 synsets with their polarity scores, part-of-speeches as noun, adjective, adverb or verb. These tokens have a common synset id linked to other Indian languages' WordNets. The linkage between HSWN and Marathi WordNet is shown in Fig. 3.

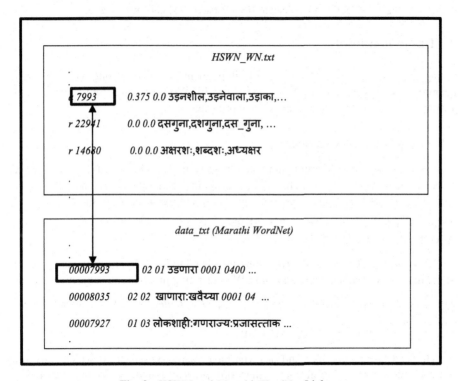

Fig. 3. HSWN and Marathi WordNet Linkage

The procedure to create the Marathi subjective lexicon using this approach is given in Fig. 4.

Algorithm 3: *Hindi SentiWordNet (HSWN) 3.0-based Subjective Lexicon*

Input: HSWN, Marathi WordNet
Output: HSWN-based Marathi Subjective Lexicon (adjective/adverb)
1. Get Marathi Adjective and Adverb lists from Marathi WN
2. Get Hindi Adjective and Adverb lists from HSWN
3. Get mar_id from Marathi adj/adv lists
4. Iterate mar_id through Hindi adj/adv lists and get corresponding pos/neg scores
5. Create a dictionary named Mar_Lexicon, update it with {mar_word: pos_score, neg_score}
6. Calculate obj_score and find the polarity of the word.

Fig. 4. Algorithm to generate HSWN-based Marathi subjective lexicon

4 Implementation

Python programming language is used to implement the system along with the lexical resources SentiWordNet, HSWN, and Marathi WordNet are used. The Google Translator tool is used for the first two approaches.

4.1 Corpus-Based Approach

This method requires Marathi annotated corpus in UTF-8 format and the lexical resource SentiWordNet 3.0. The corpus contained 561 adjectives and 73 adverbs tagged as 'JJ' and 'RB' tags, respectively. These are extracted from the corpus.

Adjective_list = ['हजर', 'इतर', 'यश', 'गंभीर',…].
Adverb_list = ['अखेर',…].

Using Google Translate, the words are translated to English, and the polarity scores of the first sense words are copied from SWN, resulting in a Marathi subjective lexicon.

Mar_Eng_Adj_list = *[('हजर', 'Present'), (इतर, 'Others'), (यश, 'Achievement'), (('गंभीर' 'serious'),…].*
Mar_Eng_Adv_list = [('अखेर', 'After all'),…].

The translated adjectives and adverbs have many synsets from which only first sense synset is chosen. For instance – the word *'present'* translated from the word हजर' has 18 synsets.

[Synset('present.a.01'), Synset('present.a.02') Synset('present.n.01'), Synset('present. n.02'), Synset('present.n.03'), Synset('show.v.01'), etc.….]

The polarity scores of first sense words with respect to adjectives or adverbs are copied for the Marathi word in the lexicon. Some translated words which do not have synsets at all are excluded from the final subjective lexicon. For example, the adjectives 'कायमस्वरूपी', and 'वेगळ्या' are translated to 'Permanently', and 'Differently', respectively. However, the translated words do not have the adjective synsets. So, the Marathi words are not included in the result.

4.2   SentiWordNet (SWN) 3.0-Based Approach

This approach is widely used in the generation of resources for the limited-resourced languages as the SWN is the rich and powerful English resource. From SWN, the adjectives and adverbs, along with their polarity scores, are extracted. For instance –

Adjective_list = *['concrete', 'adventurous',...].*
Adverb_list = *['blessedly', 'regrettably',...].*

The adjective and adverb lists are translated to the Marathi language using the Google Translate tool.

Eng_Mar_Adj_list = *[(' concrete', ठोस), (' adventurous ', साहसी),....]*

Eng_Mar_Adv_list = *[(' blessedly', आशीर्वादितपणे), (regrettably',' खेदजनकपणे),...]*

The Google translate tool serves the limited requests in a given period of time. The translation is achieved by translating the adjectives/adverbs file with size less than 10 KB at a time, which takes the significant amount of time. The polarity scores of English words extracted from SWN are assigned to corresponding translated Marathi words.

In SWN, the words have different senses depending on their contexts. However, the words with sense#1 are targeted as it is a primary sense.

4.3   HSWN-Based Approach

The pivot element of this approach is the linkage between WordNets through the common synset id. The adj/adv lists are created from HSWN and the Marathi WordNet.

From the Marathi WordNet, 7747 adjectives with their synsets are extracted, and the adj list is created.

Marathi adj list = [['भयरहित', '00002964'], ['अडाणी', '00000027','00002517'], ['सुव्यवस्थित', '00000854'] ...]

The word 'भयरहित' has the id '00002964'. The two ids are stored for the word 'अडाणी' out of which the first id '00000027' is the actual id, and '00002517' is its synset id. Similarly, the adv list is created from Marathi WordNet with 1059 adverbs and their synsets.

Marathi adv list = [['अकारण', '00002243', '00002244'], ['अक्षरशः', '00014680'], ['अखंड', '00002868'], ['अखेर', '00002093'], ...].

From HSWN, intermediate adj/adv list is created which contains ids and its corresponding polarity scores as below.

Hindi adj_list = [('10363', '0.0', '0.0'), ('2627', '0.0', '0.75'), ('11476', '0.125', '0.0') ...].

Hindi adv_list = [('28129', '0.125', '0.25'), ('23771', '0.0', '0.0') ...].

One by one the ids from Marathi WordNets are searched through the HSWN. If word id is present in the HSWN, then the polarity scores are assigned to the Marathi word and all its synsets. For example, the word 'असहाय' appears in Marathi WordNet as.

असहाय 02 01 0400 03 00000035 00000036 00003213.

The id 00000035 is searched in HSWN. In HSWN, it appears as a 35 0.0 0.625 अनाथ,यतीम,लावारिस,बेकस.

The polarity scores 0.0 and 0.625 are copied to all the three words with ids 00000035, 00000036, and 00003213 i.e. to the words 'असहाय', 'अगतिक' and 'हतबल'.

The main advantage of this method is that machine translation is not required.

5   Results

The results of the three approaches described in the methodology section are presented in this section.

5.1   Corpus-Based Approach

Table 1 gives the statistics of the lexicon-based on a corpus-based approach. One of the major concerns of this approach is the unavailability of the large annotated corpus for the Marathi language.

Table 1. Statistics for Corpus-based subjective lexicon

	POS	NEG	NEU	No Synsets
Adjectives	43	28	286	204
Adverbs	0	1	39	33

The resulting lexicon contains the words with their polarity scores, excluding 204 adjectives and 33 adverbs as the first sense synsets are not available for them. Some examples of Marathi words from the lexicon are shown in Table 2.

Table 2. Marathi words in Corpus-based subjective lexicon

Word	Translation	Polarity		
वेगळा	Different	0.625	0.0	0.375 (Positive)
चांगली	Good	0.75	0.0	0.25 (Positive)
भयानक	Scary	0.0	0.75	0.25 (Negative)
मानसिक	Mental	0.125	0.0	0.875 (Neutral)
धार्मिक	Religious	0.0	0.0	1.0 (Neutral)

5.2   SWN-Based Approach

Table 3 gives the statistics of the SWN-based method.

Table 3. Statistics for SWN-based subjective lexicon

	POS	NEG	NEU
Adjectives	784	1017	6571
Adverbs	76	52	1753

The coverage of the words is increased significantly as compared to corpus-based. One of the two main disadvantages of this method is that the translation from English to Marathi changes the part-of-speech of the words. The second drawback is due to the structure of the languages varies from one another; the exact word translation is not possible. For example-

1. superabundant - superabundant.
2. maltreated - maltreated.
3. hypoactive - हायपोएक्टिव्ह.

The words 'superabundant' and 'maltreated' are not translated to Marathi. The word 'hypoactive' is transliterated to 'हायपोएक्टिव्ह" instead of translation. Some of the words are translated into phrases. For example 'उच्चस्तरीय- *High level*,' 'वातानुकूलित- *Air conditioned*', 'मागासलेल्यापेक्षा- *Than backward*' So, the result is manually refined by discarding such words from the lexicon. 8372 adjectives out of 14,909 and 1881 adverbs out of 2772 are included in the final result. Table 4 shows a few examples of the SWN-based lexicon.

Table 4. Marathi words in SWN-based subjective lexicon

Word	Translation	Polarity		
फायदेशीर	Advantageous	0.625	0.0	0.375 (Positive)
निःस्वार्थ	Selfless	0.875	0.0	0.125 (Positive)
अप्रसन्न	unimpressed	0.0	0.625	0.375 (Negative)
भयानक	frantic	0.25	0.5	0.25 (Negative)
नवजात	nascent	0.0	0.0	1.0 (Neutral)
जन्मपूर्व	prenatal	0.0	0.125	0.875 (Neutral)

5.3   HSWN-Based Approach

Table 5 gives the statistics of the HSWN-based method. Table 6 shows a few examples of the HSWN-based lexicon.

Table 5. Statistics for HSWN-based subjective lexicon

	POS	NEG	NEU
Adjectives	207	393	1609
Adverbs	13	4	149

Table 6. Marathi words in HSWN-based subjective lexicon

Word	Polarity		
आदर्श	0.825	0.0	0.175 (Positive)
भाग्यशाली	0.875	0.0	0.125 (Positive)
अकुशल	0.0	0.75	0.25 (Negative)
दुर्दैवी	0.0	1.0	0.0 (Negative)
अणिक	0.0	0.0	1.0 (Neutral)
राजकीय	0.0	0.0	1.0 (Neutral)

5.4 Resource Evaluation

To evaluate the reliability of the three different Marathi subjective lexicon generated, which are based on Marathi annotated corpus, Hindi SWN, and SWN, random sampling of words was created from the three target lexicons. The 60, 400, and 1400 random words from positive and negative polarity lists of corpus-based, HSWN-based, and SWN-based lexicons were selected, respectively. These sample sets were made available to two manual raters to annotate the samples as positive or negative independently. The raters were native Marathi speakers and spoke Marathi on a day-to-day basis. No rater had the prior information about the assigned polarity to a word that assured unbiased annotation of the words. The statistical measure Cohen's Kappa [20] scores are calculated for the three annotated sample sets in order to measure the interrater agreement on the categorical scales. The Kappa κ is calculated as:

$$\kappa = \frac{p_o - p_e}{1 - p_e} \tag{1}$$

p_o is the observed agreement between raters on the sample set, and p_e is the agreement by chance. Suppose PP and NN be the number of agreements, PN and NP be the number of disagreements by the two raters.

$$p_o = \frac{PP + NN}{PP + PN + NP + NN} \tag{2}$$

For c categories, N observations and n_{ci} the number of times rater i projected category c.

$$p_e = \frac{1}{N^2} \sum_c n_{c1} n_{c2} \tag{3}$$

$$p_e = \left[\left(\frac{PP + PN}{PP + PN + NP + NN} \right) \cdot \left(\frac{PP + NP}{PP + PN + NP + NN} \right) \right]$$
$$+ \left[\left(\frac{NP + NN}{PP + PN + NP + NN} \right) \cdot \left(\frac{PN + NN}{PP + PN + NP + NN} \right) \right] \tag{4}$$

The details of sample sets were provided to two raters for two categories - positive and negative. The overall obtained Kappa score κ is presented in Table 7.

Table 7. Assessment of interrater agreement for the Marathi subjective lexicon

Marathi Lexicon	PP	NN	PN	NP	p_o	p_e	Kappa score (κ)
Corpus-based	27	24	3	3	0.8947	0.5014	0.79
HSWN-based	198	169	12	21	0.9175	0.5023	0.84
SWN-based	685	551	72	92	0.8829	0.5044	0.76

It is observed that the substantial agreement score for Corpus-based and SWN-based. Almost perfect agreement score $\kappa = 0.84$ for HSWN-based Marathi lexicon. Though the interrater agreement for the lexicon using annotated corpus and HSWN is higher than that of the SWN-based lexicon, the coverage of the words is noteworthy in the SWN-based Marathi lexicon.

6 Conclusion

The work in this research is the first-ever attempt to create the Marathi subjective lexicon and assists as a baseline. It will assist as a powerful resource in the Sentiment Analysis of Marathi data. In this paper, the three approaches are experimented using the corpus-based method, SWN-based method, and HSWN-based method. The first approach covers the limited words into the subjective lexicon as the size of the annotated corpus is small. The Marathi lexicon contains 43 positive, 29 negative, and 325 neutral entities. If the corpus size is adequate, the coverage can be increased by capturing the language-specific progressions. In the SWN-based approach, the significant word coverage is possible as compared to a corpus-based and HSWN-based approach. The Marathi lexicon contains 860 positive, 1069 negative, and 8324 neutral entities. However, all the senses other than primary are lost. The HSWN-based method built the lexicon with 220 positive, 397 negative, and 1758 neutral entities. The machine translation is not required, which minimizes translation errors. The proposed approach can be used by any Indian language for which the WordNet exists.

In the future, this resource can be enriched by using other Indian languages' SentiWordNets. The adjectives and adverbs are investigated, which can be extended further for verbs and nouns.

References

1. Kashyap, L., Joshi, S.R., Bhattacharyya, P.: Insights on Hindi WordNet coming from the IndoWordNet. In: Dash, N.S., Bhattacharyya, P., Pawar, J.D. (eds.) The WordNet in Indian Languages, pp. 19–44. Springer, Singapore (2017). https://doi.org/10.1007/978-981-10-1909-8_2
2. Google Translate. https://translate.google.com

3. Al-Sallab, A., Baly, R., Hajj, H., Shaban, K.B., El-Hajj, W., Badaro, G.: AROMA: a recursive deep learning model for opinion mining in Arabic as a low resource language. ACM Trans. Asian Low-Resource Lang. Inf. Process. (TALLIP) **16**(4), 25:1–25:20 (2017)

4. Alomari, K.M., ElSherif, H.M., Shaalan, K.: Arabic tweets sentimental analysis using machine learning. In: Benferhat, S., Tabia, K., Ali, M. (eds.) IEA/AIE 2017. LNCS (LNAI), vol. 10350, pp. 602–610. Springer, Cham (2017). https://doi.org/10.1007/978-3-319-60042-0_66

5. Saif M., Salameh, M., Kiritchenko, S.: Sentiment lexicons for Arabic social media. In: Proceedings of the 10th Edition of the Language Resources and Evaluation Conference (LREC), pp. 33–37. Portoroz, Slovenia LREC (2016)

6. Baccianella, S., Esuli, A., Sebastiani, F.: SentiWordNet 3.0: an enhanced lexical resource for sentiment analysis and opinion mining. In: Proceedings of the Seventh Conference on International Language Resources and Evaluation (LREC 2010), pp. 2200–2204. European Languages Resources Association (ELRA), Valletta, Malta (2010)

7. Liu, B.: Handbook of Natural Language Processing, 2nd eds. CRC Press, Taylor and Francis Group, Boca Raton (2010)

8. Medagoda, N., Shanmuganathan, S., Whalley, J.: Sentiment lexicon construction using SentiWordNet 3.0. In: Proceedings of 11th International Conference on Natural Computation (ICNC), pp. 802–807. IEEE, Zhangjiajie (2015)

9. Bakliwal, A., Arora, P., Varma, V.: Hindi subjective lexicon: a lexical resource for Hindi polarity classification. In: Proceedings of the Eighth International Conference on Language Resources and Evaluation Conference (LREC), pp. 1189–1196. Istanbul, Turkey (2012)

10. Kim, S.M., Hovy, E.: Identifying and analyzing judgment opinions. In: Proceedings of HLT/NAACL-2006, pp. 200–207. ACL, NY (2006)

11. Karthikeyan, A.: Hindi English wordnet linkage (2010)

12. Benamara, F., Cesarano, C., Picariello, A., Reforgiato, D., Subrahmanian, V.: Sentiment analysis: adjectives and adverbs are better than adjectives alone. In: Proceedings of the International Conference on Weblogs and Social Media (ICWSM), pp. 1–7. ICWSM, Boulder, CO (2007)

13. Mahanty, G., Kannan, A., Mamidi, R.: Building a SentiWordNet for Odia. In: Proceedings of 8th Workshop on Computational Approaches to Subjectivity, Sentiment, and Social Media Analysis, pp. 143–148. Association for Computational Linguistics (ACL), Copenhagen, Denmark (2017)

14. Das, A., Bandyopadhyay, S.: SentiWordNet for Indian languages. In: Proceedings of the 8th Workshop on Asian Language Resources, pp. 56–63. Coling 2010 Organizing Committee, Beijing, China (2010)

15. Popale, L., Bhattacharyya, P.: Creating Marathi WordNet. In: Dash, N.S., Bhattacharyya, P., Pawar, J.D. (eds.) The WordNet in Indian Languages, pp. 147–166. Springer, Singapore (2017). https://doi.org/10.1007/978-981-10-1909-8_8

16. Joshi, A., Balamurali, A.R., Bhattacharyya, P.: A fall-back strategy for sentiment analysis in Hindi: a case study. In: Proceedings 8th International Conference on Natural Language Processing, ICON (2010)

17. El-Haj, M., Kruschwitz, U., Fox, C.: Creating language resources for under-resourced languages: methodologies, and experiments with Arabic. Lang. Resourc. Eval. **49**(3), 549–580 (2014). https://doi.org/10.1007/s10579-014-9274-3

18. Al-Thubaity, A., Alqahtani, Q., Alijandal, A.: Sentiment lexicon for sentiment analysis of Saudi dialect tweets. In: Proceedings of the Fourth International Conference on Arabic Computational Linguistics (ACLing 2018), pp. 301–307. Elsevier, Dubai, United Arab Emirates (2018)

19. Wikipedia contributors, "Cohen's kappa" Wikipedia, The Free Encyclopedia. https://en. wikipedia.org/w/index.php?title=Cohen%27s_kappa&oldid=928044732. Accessed 29 Nov 2019
20. Xu, G., Yu, Z., Yao, H., Li, F., Meng, Y., Xu, W.: Chinese text sentiment analysis based on extended sentiment dictionary. IEEE Access **7**, 43749–43762 (2019)

Review on Offline Signature Verification: Datasets, Methods and Challenges

Amruta B. Jagtap[1(✉)], Dattatray D. Sawat[1], and Ravindra S. Hegadi[2(✉)]

[1] Department of Computer Science,
Punyashlok Ahilyadevi Holkar Solapur University, Solapur 413255, Maharastra, India
`amrutaj88@gmail.com, sawat.datta@gmail.com`
[2] Department of Computer Science, Central University of Karnataka,
Kadaganchi, Kalaburagi 585367, India
`rshegadi@gmail.com`

Abstract. Signature verification is one of the major field of biometrics for authentication of human beings. Biometrics refers to the metrics related to human characteristics. From the last decade, the research on signature verification is going vigorously, but still, the research problem is being explored. Due to multiple challenges present in automated signature verification and identification, the study is open and inspiration for researchers. The major objective of the offline signature verification system is to discriminate between genuine(original) and forged signatures. There are many factors that make the processing of offline signature very complex. This paper describes what kind of approaches used in previous research attempts. In those attempts, some of the methodologies achieved a significant improvement. We will analyze how the problem is handled to improve the verification and identification task in the existing literature.

Keywords: Biometrics · Offline signature · Verification · Identification · Genuine · Forged

1 Introduction

The Biometric system is alienated into two types: Physiological and behavioral biometrics. Signature recognition falls under the behavioral biometric system. As it has a behavioral characteristic it gives statistically reliable data. In earlier times, the manual method was used which consist of confirmation of identity using its shape. However, now the Biometric system can recognize a lot more things to identify whether it is an authorized user or an impostor. Physiological biometrics is related to the measurement, dimension, and traits of the body such as the face, fingerprint, iris recognition, etc. [20].

In Biometrics, classification can be divided into two types of tasks:

1) Verification
2) Identification

© Springer Nature Singapore Pte Ltd. 2021
K. C. Santosh and B. Gawali (Eds.): RTIP2R 2020, CCIS 1380, pp. 458–468, 2021.
https://doi.org/10.1007/978-981-16-0507-9_38

Verification: It refers to the matching of two subjects in the particular biometric modality. The 1:1 matching takes place in the verification. For example, the signature of a person can be matched with another signature, and depending upon the matching outcome verification can result in a similar or dissimilar label.

Identification: It is a process to retrieve or match the query with reference to one of the subjects among multiple subjects present in the database of the particular biometric modality. It requires 1: N matching. For example, a signature can be matched against multiple signatures present in the database. Verification is less computationally intensive than identification due to fewer numbers of operations taking place during the process. The signature authentication system is also classified into identification and verification task. In signature identification, we verify who's signature it is and in the verification task, we verify whether two signature belongs to the same person and whether the provided signature is genuine or false. An approach of signature recognition system falls into two scenarios: Online and Offline [32]. Online signature are popularly called as dynamic signature since dynamic information is available at high resolution. In case of online signatures, the Online data records the various signals such as motion of the stylus, velocity, acceleration and pen pressure while the signature is in progress. These signals are captured as as function of time and this information is stored during the signature acquisition process. Offline signature is also called a static signature because during the acquisition process signatures are taken on paper and then they are scanned at high resolution. In offline signatures where dynamic information is unavailable, the processing of offline signature becomes difficult. The nature and variety of the writing pen, highly stylish and unconventional writing styles may also affect the nature of the signature obtained. The presence of variation in the signatures is due to age, illness, environment and perhaps to some extent, the emotional state of the person may accentuates the problem. A robust system has to be designed in such a way that it should not only be able to consider these factors but also detect various types of forgeries. Depending on the forgery done by the individual they can be classified as:

1. Random
2. Simple
3. Skilled

In the first case, i.e random forgery, forger don't have any information about the users signature. Forger sign in his own way without any knowledge. In the case of simple forgery, forger knows the shape of signature, but without much practice. In skilled forgery, the forger has knowledge about users signature very well with much practice. They try to sign much similar to a genuine signature, so it is difficult to detect skilled forgery. It is not so hard to detect random and simple forgery since these forged signature varies in shape, style, etc. from genuine signature. The offline signature verification system can be designed into two ways i.e Writer Independent (WI) and Writer Dependent (WD) [2]. In the first scenario, i.e WI one classifier is used to determine the authenticity of a user, means a single model is trained for all users. In the WD system, one model is trained for each new user.

For automatic Offline signature verification, many attempts were made by researchers to improve the performance of the system. We provide a systematic review of research attempts made recently regarding improvement in offline signature recognition. We discuss these attempts through the following sections. We have organized review in various sections: Sect. 2 represents major challenges for signature verification. Section 3 describes the most commonly available signature datasets. Section 4 presents the Pre-processing techniques used in these attempts. Section 5 discusses the features extraction methods. Section 6 provides a review of classifiers uses in those research attempts and results achieved by their methods. The last section concludes the paper.

2   Challenges

Following are some major challenges:

1. The similarity between genuine and skilled forger along with variation in Intra-class signature. Due to the nature of the handwriting process and circumstances present at the time of collecting signatures, there will be variation between signee's signatures. For better training of models both genuine and forged signatures are required. In forged signature skilled forgery is also required, but this present a new sub-challenge, i.e there will be less variation between genuine and skilled forgery of the same signee.
2. Non-availability of forged signature of actual signee: Datasets are well suited for research purpose and it is proven. But at the deployment of signature verification applications, it is better to train the models on actual data. The data for such training need to have skilfully forged signatures, which is a trivial task because it is not guaranteed that such skilled forgery of signatures will be available. Furthermore, the time taken to get skilled forgery for several thousand signatures is a very time-consuming task.
3. What makes genuine and skilled forgery different is still a point to look after: Genuine and skilled forged signature looks so similar that it is hard to differentiate them. In this context, it is still unknown that, what are those characteristics which make them different. Since it is unknown, implementing the Genuine and skilled forgery signature verification system has to depend upon the researcher's analogy or their point of view.
4. A common experimental setting for non-biased result comparison is needed. The common setting includes datasets, a number of training and testing samples from the particular dataset and hyperparameters like epochs, batch size, etc. The performance comparison of any two or more methods will be justified if it is done using a common experimental setting.

3   Datasets

The process of acquisition of data from users for all signature datasets is often similar. For a publicly available database, after collection of signatures, they are scanned under 300 or 600 dpi and preprocessed. We can create our own signature image database i.e private database, but while the comparison of result complexity occurs. Most commonly used public dataset is GPDS-960 which contain 24 genuine and 30 forged signature of 960 individuals, which has 23040 (24 × 960) genuine signatures and 28800 (30×960) forged signatures. Another public signature dataset GPDS Synthetic database contains signature data from 4000 individual, with 24 genuine and 30 forged signatures of each individual and these signatures were generated by different modeled pens. These datasets are huge and they have a large number of samples. MCYT-75 offline signature corpus is composed of 2250 signatures from 75 individuals. Each class has 15 genuine (totally 75 × 15 = 1125) and 15 forged (75 × 15 = 1125) signatures. CEDAR signature database is composed of 2640 signatures from 55 individual. Each class contain 24 genuine and 24 forged signatures. In CEDAR database, signature images are in gray scale mode. UTSig is a Persian offline signature database which contains distinct characteristic of persian signature. UTSig contains 8280 signatures from 115 classes where each class have 27 genuine signatures (totally 115 × 27 = 3105), 3 opposite hand signatures (115 × 3 = 345) and 42 skilled forgery (115 × 42 = 4830) signatures.

The following Table 1 presents most commonly used datasets (Fig. 1):

Table 1. Commonly used offline handwritten signature datasets

Datasets	Users	Total genuine signature	Total forged signature	Total number of samples
GPDS 960 [39]	960	23040	28800	51840
GPDS Synthetic [11]	4000	96000	120000	216000
MCYT-75 [29]	75	1125	1125	2250
CEDAR [21]	55	1320	1320	2640
UTSig [38]	115	3105 and opposite hand signature: 345	4830	8280

(a) GPDS Synthetic   (b) MCYT75   (c) CEDAR   (d) UTSig

Fig. 1. Signature samples from offline handwritten signature datasets mentioned in Table 1

4 Preprocessing Techniques

To obtain high quality of images preprocessing step plays a very important role in digital image processing and pattern recognition [33,34]. Signature obtained from users may contain variation in signature images like noise, the thickness of pen, difference in size, rotation, etc. For further processing of images, the quality of the digital image must be high so that the performance of the developed algorithm will be good.

1. Input image conversion: Input signatures can be in RGB format. These RGB images are then converted to grayscale and further to binary images [22].
2. Noise Removal: After scanning of images it may contain some noise. To remove this noise various noise removal technique are used like median filter, min, max or wiener filter [4]. Depending upon the type of noise it contains such as salt and pepper, Gaussian, etc., a particular technique can be used.
3. Morphological operation: To make signature single-pixel thin i.e to remove selected foreground pixels from binary images morphological thinning operation is performed [17].
4. Normalization: There will be variation in height and width of the signature differs for each person. Even the same person can sign the signature with different sizes. So there is a need for unique size for all input images. Many authors used bounding box, which contains coordinates of a rectangle that encloses the signature image [13,17]. Some of them used fixed frame size i.e height, width and center of the frame [15,30].

Recently deep learning-based approaches have been used by researchers and most of them do not require any preprocessing except resizing.

5 Feature Extraction

Feature extraction for recognition of signature is somewhat easier than verification between genuine and forged signature, where in the latter requires a complex set of features to be extracted. Broadly, feature extraction verification can be categorize into two scenarios: Handcrafted and Learned features.

I. Handcrafted Features:
Hand-designed features are extracted by using mathematical formulations. Features that are extracted may be Global, Local, Geometric, Texture, Interest point matching, Pixel matching, etc.

1. Global features: Global features describe an image as vector ie. signature image as a whole. Here features are extracted from the whole image such as height, width, slope, skewness, area, etc [31]. Area of signature is the number of pixels that belongs to the signature. Height is the distance between vertical projection of signature whereas Width is the distance between Horizontal projection of signature.

2. Local Features: Local features for an image patch is computed by considering multiple points on signature images by dividing the images in a grid [41]. They use the local feature based on gradient information (histogram of the oriented gradient) and pixel neighborhood pattern.
3. Geometric features: Geometric features represent the shape of the signature such as baseline slant angle, aspect ratio, area, the center of gravity, geometric centroid etc. If the signature is more complicated then it includes closed loops and endpoints [1]. Many authors used local geometric features by segmenting the signature into the grid and extracted features like pixel density within grids [1,8].
4. Texture features: Recently, authors used texture features such as Local binary pattern (LBP) and Gray level co-occurrence matrices (GLCM) [12,40]. In LBP grayscale image is processed and after processing binary code is generated for each pixel in an image and histogram is computed describing the common texture pattern [35,36,41].
5. Interest point matching: To detect interest points three approach are mostly used ie. SIFT (Scale Invariant Feature Transform), Binary Robust Invariant Scalable Keypoints (BRISK) [25] and SURF (Speeded-Up Robust Feature). They have been largely used in computer vision task. In SIFT, key points of the object are extracted from reference images and stored in the database. SIFT descriptor is complex than SURF and it requires more computational time [5]. To classify between genuine and forged signature, Malik [26] used SURF descriptor which extracts interest point from signature images and during classification only strong interest point was considered for matching purpose.

II. Learned Feature:

Nowadays instead of handcrafted features, most of the researchers focus on the deep learning models. In machine learning, Deep neural networks are superior algorithms which are composed of multiple layers. This network has the ability to learn features from input images and classify according to the target. Convolutional Neural network is one of the types of deep neural networks which are broadly researched and have superior performance in various vision-based tasks.

To learn the features from signature input images, The author Luiz G. Hafemann et al. [14] used deep convolutional neural network and this model was pre-trained on set of signatures signed by outsiders. As the input size of the neural network is same, they developed a model for the fixed-sized representation of signatures, however the size of signature varies from one user to other. By addressing this problem they customized the network architecture via Spatial Pyramid Pooling. Sounak Dey et al. [6] implemented different network structure called Siamese Network. This network is used to recognize similar and dissimilar images. They proposed a network called SigNet using the convolutional siamese network for offline signature verification which was designed to be writer independent. They minimized the Euclidean distance for a similar pair while maximized distance for dissimilar pair. Experiments were carried on different datasets such as GPDS 300, CEDAR, Bengali, Hindi, GPDS Synthetic and their performance was good as compared to state-of-the-art performance.

For Persian signature recognition, khalajzadeh et al. [23] used Convolutional neural network that is composed of nine layers and for classifying the output using CNN, multilayer perceptron network is used. For testing, only random forgeries were considered. Jagtap et al. [19] designed CNN architecture with 18 layer. The output of the layer is given as input to the next layer. The experiment was performed on GPDS, SVC20 and BME2 datasets and achieved less misclassification. Further, they implemented a Siamese neural network using medium sized CNN. In siamese architecture, two embedding vectors are generated by a common CNN for two inputs of signatures. To make this vector more robust, authors calculated statistical measures on embedding vector itself. The proposed network improved verification rate and accuracy compared to state-of-art-performance [18].

For offline signature verification, Soleimani et al. [37] proposed classification method called Deep Multitask Metric Learning (DMML) that can discriminate genuine and forged signature samples of other class. To learn distance metric they combined two approaches: Writer Independent and Writer Dependent. The proposed method is implemented on four different offline signature datasets UTSig, GPDS Synthetic, MCYT-75 and GPDS-960 and compared against SVM. Proposed DMML outperforms SVM model.

6   Trained Model and Performance on Different Datasets

A model can be trained for two approaches: Writer Independent and Writer Dependent. For WI only single classifier is trained for all users. Whereas for WD model is trained for each new user ie. specific classifier is designed for each individual. Eskander et al. [9] proposed hybrid WI-WD system in which for WI is used a selection of features WD set is used for training and evaluation purpose. Hafemann et al. [14] proposed two-phase approach: For feature learning, they used WI which is followed by WD classification. Support vector machine (SVM) is used for both writer independent and writer dependent approaches. Yilmaz et al. [41] performed classification using SVM, for training they used global and user-dependent SVM. Lastly, they combined both WI-WD classifier to obtain results. To improve the performance of automatic signature verification Manabu Okawa [27] proposed feature encoding method ie. bag-of-visual words and vector of locally aggregated descriptors and these feature vector are fed to SVM for classification. For signature verification task Jagtap et al. [16] used Neural network based pattern recognition classifier which is two-layer Feed-Forward network. To verify and classify offline signature Ali karouni et al. [22] used Artificial Neural network (ANN). In ANN output is compared with target values. Soleimani et al. [37] proposed classification method i.e Deep Multitask Metric Learning (DMML) that can discriminate genuine and forged signature sample of other class. To learn distance metric they combined two Writer Independent and Writer Dependent approaches. Most of the genuine and forgery verification methods use distance based technique to classify.

Evaluation Protocol used by many researchers for verification signature are FAR, FRR and EER is a point where FAR and FRR are equal. FAR and FRR are calculated as follows:

$$FAR = \frac{No. \; of forged \; Pairs \; accepted \; as \; a \; geniune \; pairs}{Total \; number \; of \; Forged \; Pairs \; submitted} \times 100 \qquad (1)$$

$$FRR = \frac{No. \; of \; Geniune \; Pairs \; rejected}{Total \; number \; of \; Geniune \; Pairs \; submitted} \times 100 \qquad (2)$$

Following Tables represent the State-of-the-art performance on standard databases using different feature extractors and classifiers. Table 2 shows results on MCYT-75 database. Table 3 demonstrates results on GPDS and results on CEDAR is represented in Table 4.

Table 2. Sate-of-the-art performance on MCYT-75 database

Reference	Methods (features and classifiers)	FRR	FAR	EER
[37]	HOG and DRT - (DMML)	6.13	12.71	9.86
[28]	DRT + PCA - (PNN)	–	–	9.87
[27]	VLAD with KAZE + PCA - (SVM)	–	–	6.4
[40]	LBP + Contour - (SVM)	8.69	6.54	7.08
[15]	Feature Learning - (SVM)	–	–	2.87

Table 3. Sate-of-the-art performance on GPDS database

Reference	Methods (features and classifiers)	FRR	FAR	EER
[41]	HOG and LBP - (SVM)	–	–	15.41
[40]	LBP and GLCM - (SVM)	9.66	8.64	9.02
[7]	HOG - (SVM)	27.62	28.34	27.98
[19]	Feature Learning - (SVM)	–	2.3	–
[10]	Geometric - (HMM, SVM and Euclidean Distance)	14.10	12.60	13.35
[15]	Feature Learning - (SVM)	3.94	3.53	1.69
[6]	Feature Learning - Euclidean Distance	22.24	22.24	22.24

Table 4. Sate-of-the-art performance on CEDAR database

Reference	Methods (features and classifiers)	FRR	FAR	EER
[24]	Surroundness - (NN)	–	8.33	8.33
[21]	GSC - (Bayes and KNN)	22.45	19.50	20.9
[15]	Feature Learning - (SVM)	–	–	4.63
[27]	VLAD with KAZE + PCA - (SVM)	–	–	1.0
[3]	Chain Code - (SVM)	9.36	7.84	–

7   Conclusion

The recent studies of offline signature verification intend to improve the performance of automated signature verification system. Several authors used different feature extraction and classification techniques to discriminate between Genuine and forged signature. But for skilled forgeries still system performance is low because their properties are similar to the genuine signature, so this research problem is open for further research. Through this survey it is found that, researchers try to extract strong features from signature though the signature is complicated and classify them by using different classifiers. We also noticed that the performance of methods based on learned features is better than hand-designed features. Recently, Deep Neural Network approaches dropped error rates of verification task. According to a survey, the performance of a signature verification system increases when the available training data is large in size. Future attempts should focus on optimizing the performance of deep neural network-based systems.

Acknowledgments. Authors thank the Ministry of Electronics and Information Technology (MeitY), New Delhi for granting Visvesvaraya Ph.D. fellowship through file no. PhD-MLA\4(34)\2015-16 Dated: 05/11/2015.

References

1. Baltzakis, H., Papamarkos, N.: A new signature verification technique based on a two-stage neural network classifier. Eng. Appl. Artif. Intell. **14**(1), 95–103 (2001)
2. Bertolini, D., Oliveira, L.S., Justino, E., Sabourin, R.: Reducing forgeries in writer-independent off-line signature verification through ensemble of classifiers. Pattern Recogn. **43**(1), 387–396 (2010)
3. Bharathi, R., Shekar, B.: Off-line signature verification based on chain code histogram and support vector machine. In: 2013 International Conference on Advances in Computing, Communications and Informatics (ICACCI), pp. 2063–2068 (2013)
4. Bhattacharya, I., Ghosh, P., Biswas, S.: Offline signature verification using pixel matching technique. Proc. Technol. **10**, 970–977 (2013)
5. Calonder, M., Lepetit, V., Fua, P., Konolige, K., Bowman, J., Mihelich, P.: Compact signatures for high-speed interest point description and matching. In: 2009 IEEE 12th International Conference on Computer Vision, pp. 357–364 (2009)

6. Dey, S., Dutta, A., Toledo, J.I., Ghosh, S.K., Lladós, J., Pal, U.: SigNet: convolutional siamese network for writer independent offline signature verification. arXiv preprint arXiv:1707.02131 (2017)
7. Dutta, A., Pal, U., Lladós, J.: Compact correlated features for writer independent signature verification. In: 2016 23rd International Conference on Pattern Recognition (ICPR), pp. 3422–3427 (2016)
8. El-Yacoubi, A., Justino, E., Sabourin, R., Bortolozzi, F.: Off-line signature verification using HMMs and cross-validation. In: Neural Networks for Signal Processing X. Proceedings of the 2000 IEEE Signal Processing Society Workshop (Cat. No. 00TH8501), vol. 2, pp. 859–868 (2000)
9. Eskander, G.S., Sabourin, R., Granger, E.: Hybrid writer-independent-writer-dependent offline signature verification system. IET Biometr. **2**(4), 169–181 (2013)
10. Ferrer, M.A., Alonso, J.B., Travieso, C.M.: Offline geometric parameters for automatic signature verification using fixed-point arithmetic. IEEE Trans. Pattern Anal. Mach. Intell. **27**(6), 993–997 (2005)
11. Ferrer, M.A., Diaz-Cabrera, M., Morales, A.: Static signature synthesis: a neuromotor inspired approach for biometrics. IEEE Trans. Pattern Anal. Mach. Intell. **37**(3), 667–680 (2014)
12. Ferrer, M.A., Vargas, J.F., Morales, A., Ordonez, A.: Robustness of offline signature verification based on gray level features. IEEE Trans. Inf. Forensics Secur. **7**(3), 966–977 (2012)
13. Ghandali, S., Moghaddam, M.E.: A method for off-line persian signature identification and verification using dwt and image fusion. In: IEEE International Symposium on Signal Processing and Information Technology, pp. 315–319 (2008)
14. Hafemann, L.G., Sabourin, R., Oliveira, L.S.: Writer-independent feature learning for offline signature verification using deep convolutional neural networks. In: 2016 International Joint Conference on Neural Networks (IJCNN), pp. 2576–2583 (2016)
15. Hafemann, L.G., Sabourin, R., Oliveira, L.S.: Learning features for offline handwritten signature verification using deep convolutional neural networks. Pattern Recogn. **70**, 163–176 (2017)
16. Jagtap, A.B., Hegadi, R.S.: Eigen value based features for offline handwritten signature verification using neural network approach. In: International Conference on Recent Trends in Image Processing and Pattern Recognition, pp. 39–48 (2016)
17. Jagtap, A.B., Hegadi, R.S.: Offline handwritten signature recognition based on upper and lower envelope using eigen values. In: 2017 World Congress on Computing and Communication Technologies (WCCCT), pp. 223–226 (2017)
18. Jagtap, A.B., Sawat, D.D., Hegadi, R.S., Hegadi, R.S.: Siamese network for learning genuine and forged offline signature verification. In: Santosh, K.C., Hegadi, R.S. (eds.) RTIP2R 2018. CCIS, vol. 1037, pp. 131–139. Springer, Singapore (2019). https://doi.org/10.1007/978-981-13-9187-3_12
19. Jagtap, A.B., Hegadi, R.S., Santosh, K.: Feature learning for offline handwritten signature verification using convolutional neural network. Int. J. Technol. Hum. Interact. (IJTHI) **15**(4), 54–62 (2019)
20. Jain, A., Hong, L., Pankanti, S.: Biometric identification. Commun. ACM **43**(2), 90–98 (2000)
21. Kalera, M.K., Srihari, S., Xu, A.: Offline signature verification and identification using distance statistics. Int. J. Pattern Recogn. Artif. Intell. **18**(07), 1339–1360 (2004)
22. Karouni, A., Daya, B., Bahlak, S.: Offline signature recognition using neural networks approach. Proc. Comput. Sci. **3**, 155–161 (2011)

23. Khalajzadeh, H., Mansouri, M., Teshnehlab, M.: Persian signature verification using convolutional neural networks. Int. J. Eng. Res. Technol. **1**(2), 7–12 (2012)
24. Kumar, R., Sharma, J., Chanda, B.: Writer-independent off-line signature verification using surroundedness feature. Pattern Recogn. Lett. **33**(3), 301–308 (2012)
25. Leutenegger, S., Chli, M., Siegwart, R.: BRISK: binary robust invariant scalable keypoints. In: 2011 IEEE International Conference on Computer Vision (ICCV), pp. 2548–2555 (2011)
26. Malik, M.I., Liwicki, M., Dengel, A., Uchida, S., Frinken, V.: Automatic signature stability analysis and verification using local features. In: 14th International Conference on Frontiers in Handwriting Recognition, pp. 621–626 (2014)
27. Okawa, M.: Offline signature verification based on bag-of-visual words model using kaze features and weighting schemes. In: Proceedings of the IEEE Conference on Computer Vision and Pattern Recognition Workshops, pp. 184–190 (2016)
28. Ooi, S.Y., Teoh, A.B.J., Pang, Y.H., Hiew, B.Y.: Image-based handwritten signature verification using hybrid methods of discrete radon transform, principal component analysis and probabilistic neural network. Appl. Soft Comput. **40**, 274–282 (2016)
29. Ortega-Garcia, J., et al.: MCYT baseline corpus: a bimodal biometric database. IEE Proc.-Vis. Image Signal Process. **150**(6), 395–401 (2003)
30. Pourshahabi, M.R., Sigari, M.H., Pourreza, H.R.: Offline handwritten signature identification and verification using contourlet transform. In: 2009 International Conference of Soft Computing and Pattern Recognition, pp. 670–673 (2009)
31. Qi, Y., Hunt, B.R.: Signature verification using global and grid features. Pattern Recogn. **27**(12), 1621–1629 (1994)
32. Radhika, K., Gopika, S.: Online and offline signature verification: a combined approach. Proc. Comput. Sci. **46**, 1593–1600 (2015)
33. Santosh, K.C., Lamiroy, B., Wendling, L.: DTW for matching radon features: a pattern recognition and retrieval method. In: Blanc-Talon, J., Kleihorst, R., Philips, W., Popescu, D., Scheunders, P. (eds.) ACIVS 2011. LNCS, vol. 6915, pp. 249–260. Springer, Heidelberg (2011). https://doi.org/10.1007/978-3-642-23687-7_23
34. Santosh, K., Lamiroy, B., Wendling, L.: DTW-radon-based shape descriptor for pattern recognition. Int. J. Pattern Recogn. Artif. Intell. **27**(03), 1350008 (2013)
35. Serdouk, Y., Nemmour, H., Chibani, Y.: Combination of OC-LBP and longest run features for off-line signature verification. In: 2014 Tenth International Conference on Signal-Image Technology and Internet-Based Systems, pp. 84–88 (2014)
36. Serdouk, Y., Nemmour, H., Chibani, Y.: Orthogonal combination and rotation invariant of local binary patterns for off-line handwritten signature verification. In: International Conference on Telecommunications and ICT (2015)
37. Soleimani, A., Araabi, B.N., Fouladi, K.: Deep multitask metric learning for offline signature verification. Pattern Recogn. Lett. **80**, 84–90 (2016)
38. Soleimani, A., Fouladi, K., Araabi, B.N.: UTSig: a persian offline signature dataset. IET Biometr. **6**(1), 1–8 (2016)
39. Vargas, F., Ferrer, M., Travieso, C., Alonso, J.: Off-line handwritten signature GPDS-960 corpus. In: Ninth International Conference on Document Analysis and Recognition (ICDAR 2007), vol. 2, pp. 764–768. IEEE (2007)
40. Vargas, J.F., Ferrer, M.A., Travieso, C., Alonso, J.B.: Off-line signature verification based on grey level information using texture features. Pattern Recogn. **44**(2), 375–385 (2011)
41. Yilmaz, M.B., Yanikoglu, B., Tirkaz, C., Kholmatov, A.: Offline signature verification using classifier combination of HOG and LBP features. In: 2011 International Joint Conference on Biometrics (IJCB), pp. 1–7 (2011)

Detection of Fraudulent Alteration of Bank Cheques Using Image Processing Techniques

S. P. Raghavendra[1(✉)], Shoieb Ahamed[2], Ajit Danti[3], and D. Rohit[4]

[1] Department of Computer Application, JNN College of Engineering,
Shimoga, Karnataka, India
raghusp.bdvt@gmail.com
[2] Department of Computer Science, GFGC, Sorab(T), Shimoga, Karnataka, India
shoiabahmed@gmail.com
[3] Department of Computer Science and Engineering,
Christ (Deemed to be University), Bangalore, Karnataka, India
ajitdanti@christuniversity.in
[4] NMIT, Bangalore, Karnataka, India
rohitdanti98@gmail.com

Abstract. In today's world illegal alteration and illegal modifications of authenticated financial documents is increasing rapidly as a fastest growing crimes around the world. The result of this kind of crimes may result in a huge financial loss. In this paper image processing and document image analysis techniques are used to examine such cases in order to identify the fraudulent bank cheques. However, it is very difficult to detect an alteration made on documents once the printing ink of alike color is employed. In this paper, alterations and modifications caused with handwritten ball point pen strokes are considered and proposed a technique for recognition of such types of corrections by employing standard techniques under Digital image processing and pattern recognition. The results are quite promising during the experiments conducted.

Keywords: Alteration detection · Fraudulent cheques · Trimmed mean function · Morphological thinning

Nomenclature: Forensic Document Examiners (FDEs) · Cheque Truncation System (CTS) · FAR (False Acceptance Ratio) · FRR (False Rejection Ratio)

1 Introduction

Bank documents, cheques, Demand Drafts, and over drafts may contain precious data present on them are frequently subjected to illegal alterations. Some of the most popular instances like forgery of signature is one among.

© Springer Nature Singapore Pte Ltd. 2021
K. C. Santosh and B. Gawali (Eds.): RTIP2R 2020, CCIS 1380, pp. 469–477, 2021.
https://doi.org/10.1007/978-981-16-0507-9_39

A fraudulent processing to bank cheques, death wills, business contracts, financial bonds and additional legal authorized documents may cause a severe financial damage stipulated to human suffering in addition to severe financial and monetary loss. As per the survey conducted by the American Bankers Association, the standard damage, caused by fraud and document alteration, per cheque in the U.S. is $1545 and is likely to grow by 2.5% annually in the coming years.

The various examinations and investigations conducted by the authorized agency so called Forensic Document Examiners (FDEs) in order to identify such malicious activities may contains some of the practices and techniques which involve manual examination of physical cheque, Chemical and die based investigations and microscopic observations. Some of the imaging tools can also be employed in recognition of these alterations but not giving the expected or desired results since the procedure is extremely complex in particularly forgery and deliberate alteration due to similar type of pen color might be used. The incidence and severity of such offences claim current contemporary computerized techniques of research for the detection of these types of illegal alterations and forgeries.

2 Related Work

Numerous efforts have been made to detect an alteration in a document starting from, Antima Singh [3] proposes a secure fragile watermarking Algorithm. This is an extension of an existing data hiding scheme with binary images. The given concept is implemented using MATLAB, and the performance of Algorithm is evaluated using the different performance parameters that are compression, encryption, detection, decryption, confidentiality and Integrity of data using secret key Authentication technique. Alsadig Bashir Hassan[2] investigates the current techniques for countering document forgery threats long with their achievements and limitations.

K Dhanva [4] proposed an approach for securing cheque image using SVD marking and AES encryption. M Rajender [5] proposes a method to tackle fraud cases occurred by taking advantage of inadequate security mechanisms of the system. Oloidi [6] focused on the causes, types, detection and prevention of frauds and forgeries [F&Fs] in the Nigerian banking sector. Prabhat Dansena [7] proposed novel a technique for extracting important regions from a cheque image based on identification of lines.

R. Jayadevan [10] proposed comprehensive bibliography of many references as support for researchers working in the field of automatic cheque processing. Vineeta Khemchandani [13] proposed to automate cheque issue and generation process that will replace paper cheque at payer end and digital signature is generated and embedded into the cheque using robust watermarking technique to prevent alteration. Raghavendra S P [9] proposed a novel technique for recognition of hand written signature using feed forward neural network and Euclidean distance as metric.

In this paper, detection of the alteration in the bank cheque image is addressed as a pattern recognition problem. In the first phase preprocessing will be conducted on image to denoise and highlight the potential alteration regions. In the second phase resembles to the events where strokes made by illegal alterations are highlighted using bounding box and trimmed mean. Since the mean value evaluated corresponding to an individual region of the cheque image, these values are then used for recognition of the alteration using threshold value based on thickness of the altered handwritten characters. The performance of the proposed system is assessed and comparison will be done to measure the durability of it.

The rest of the paper is organized as follows. Section 2 focuses on the importance of the problem dealt with in this paper, using some real life consequences. Section 3 depicts the acquisition of data and briefly explains the techniques explored. Division 4 exhibits the anticipated procedure. Investigation results and trials conducted are presented in division 5. Finally, Sect. 6 gives the conclusion part of the paper along with the future directions.

3   Alteration Examples

Document alteration is nothing but change or modification also by deletion or addition authentic and significant data written on a legal authenticated financial document. This section focuses on the various alteration done by the addition of handwritten strokes [14, 15].

In our daily life for making financial transactions and for other reasons application of paper documents is vital and essential. These financial documents are vulnerable and prone to alterations. Some of the real worlds instances like a financial agreement may be fabricated after the individuals or even companies have come to a settlement contract and signed it; a bank cheque may be altered higher denomination amount; the date on a document may be changed; These are some of the typical illustration form the real world scenario for document alterations, still there are many cases reported daily across the world and since all these data belongs to forensic agency more cases are under review and under investigation all details may not available due to legal constraints.

4   Proposed Methodology

In the proposed methodology cheque images are examined for illegal alterations and if so, to recognize them. For this purpose, manual cheque database has been constructed which stores altered cheque images. An alteration is illegal strokes, overwriting of numerals and characters on the legitimate fields of the bank cheque. The proposed methodology emphasizes on the regions which may be altered or may be overlapped and to decide the authenticity of the cheque ie either legal or illegal for carrying financial transaction. Moreover, the methodology is to locate the alteration made in the input image, obtaining the correct position and declare that the query image under consideration will be a legal or altered as given below.

Step1: Consider the test bank cheque image, apply suitable preprocessing and denoising mechanism by using morphological operations.

Step2: Horizontal projects are employed in order to segment the lines which share or overlap among neighboring pixels on another hand the lines which never make interference with neighboring pixels or share pixels are segmented using connected component regions.

• *Touching and overlapping lines and characters:*
In this context highlighting and segmentation of the altered line segments will begins by using preprocessed cheque image then applying horizontal projections in order to scan and detect core regions of altered cheque image, The region of interest ie the core region is detected by plotting a bounding box around it by using the created & structured contour as the component after the location spot somewhere pixel dissemination intensity or thickness is higher than the subjective bound or threshold of the connected component under consideration. In the proposed methodology the threshold value will be evaluated by using Trimmed mean T_m. Consider a given binary altered cheque image $f(x, y)$. For Each Connected component the trimmed mean is evaluated by using the following equation.

$$T_m = \frac{1}{width-2k} \sum_{m=k+1}^{n=width-k} f(m, n) \tag{1}$$

Where $f(m, n)$: Each connected component in the image $f(x, y)$, $k = \alpha * width$ and α is degree of freedom.

Moreover, for highlighting the altered regions of the bank cheque the following steps are accomplished.

Step 3: Morphological thinning operation is applied on each connected component along with overlapping regions, in order to describe the skeletal pattern and structural knowledge.

Step 4: By using run-length separation mechanism the thinned cheque image is separated into two separate constituents. The run-length transition is applied on both fore ground as well as on background pixels. However, there might be loss of some pixels due to the fact that if their value does not exceed the predefined threshold value. By using the technique of run length encoding mechanism conversion from forefront picture elements to contextual picture elements and conversely are summarized. There may be chances of skipping of some of forefront picture elements provided that their values will be within the predefined bound value as threshold. The threshold bound rate is estimated as inter quartile range for all the connected regions.

Step 5: The threshold value of each connected component of the thinned image is evaluated as a Trimmed mean will be compared with the average threshold value obtained from the Step3. Thus, the thinned connected component whose value still higher or closer than the trimmed threshold is highlighted.

5   Proposed Algorithm

Algorithm 1. Detection of Fraudulent Alterations

Input: Test bank cheque image.
Output: Recognize Fraudulent Alterations in the bank cheques

1: Input the test image and apply preprocessing to denoise.
2: After preprocessing label the binary cheque image and evaluate the Trimmed mean as threshold value for each connected component.
3: Apply Morphological thinning operation in order to skeletonize the connected regions.
4: Once again evaluate the trimmed mean of each thinned connected component and compare with average threshold value
5: Draw the Bounding box for each region whose trimmed mean value is still same or having higher than the threshold.

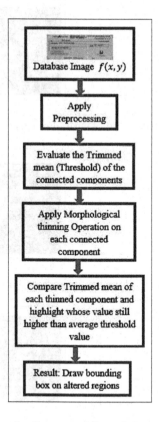

Fig. 1. Block Diagram for the recognition of alterations in bank cheque.

6   Experimental Results

In this work abnormally altered, overlapped and normal legal Digitally scanned copies of Indian bank cheques viz Canara, SBI, Kotak and UBI will taken into account for investigation purpose, as exhibited below: In the Fig. 2, 3, 4 and 5.

 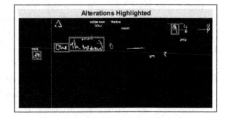

Fig. 2. Sample experimental results with alterations in Canara Bank cheque.

Fig. 3. Sample experimental results with alterations in Kotak bank cheque.

Fig. 4. Sample experimental results with alterations in SBI bank cheque.

Fig. 5. Sample experimental results Canara bank cheque without alterations.

For experiments around 150 different Indian bank cheques are collected in order to create a manual cheque database. Around 80 cheque samples of are illegally altered for four different bank classes under consideration with 20 samples for each with different handwritten strokes and tested using the trimmed mean function with altered cheque template which was created initially. Among which 73 illegally altered bank cheques are detected yielding the success rate of around 91.25% with different banks as shown in the following graph.

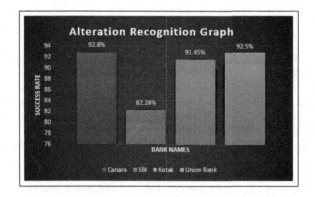

Fig. 6. Plot showing success rate comparison.

The accuracy is also analyzed by two factors viz Fault Acceptance Ratio (FAR) & False Rejection Ratio (FRR). FAR is defined as fraction of No of altered images recognized by overall incorrect images multiplied by hundred and FRR is defined as fraction of number of normal cheques rejected as altered by overall normal images multiplied by hundred.

Table 1 exhibiting the complete precision estimation of altogether altered cheques.

Table 1. Comparative analysis for accuracy.

BANK	Accuracy	FAR	FRR
4 Classes of Bank cheques	91.25%	0%	8.75%

Fig. 7. Sample misdetection results.

7   Conclusion

In this paper, an algorithm is proposed for the recognition of the illegal alterations made in the bank cheque image using trimmed mean as metric and recognition of illegally altered and legal bank cheques is presented. By considering the analysis of the proposed methodology is which is considerably superior in terms of accurate results & execution speed with the alteration detection rate of 91.25%.

References

1. Dongare, A.A., Ghongade, R.D.: Artificial intelligence based bank Cheque signature verification system. Int. Res. J. Eng. Technol. (IRJET) **03**(01) (2016). e-ISSN: 2395–0056
2. Hassan, A.B., Fadlalla, Y.A.: A survey on techniques of detecting identity documents forgery. In: Sudan Conference on Computer Science and Information Technology (SCCSIT). IEEE (2017). 978-1-5386-0667- 4/17/$31.00
3. Singh, A., Yadav, S.K.: An approach to detect alteration in text document. Int. J. Curr. Eng. Technol. **7**(2), 2347–5161 (2017). E-ISSN 2277–4106, P-ISSN 2347–5161
4. Dhanva, K., Ariskrishnan, M.H., Babu, P.U.: Cheque image security enhancement in online banking. In: Second International conference on Inventive Communication and Computational Technologies (ICICCT), pp. 1256–1260 (2018)
5. Rajender, M., Pal, R.: Detection of manipulated cheque images in Cheque truncation system using mismatch in pixels. In: 2nd International conference on Business and Information Management (ICBIM), Durgapur, pp. 30–35 (2014)
6. Oloidi, G.A., Ajinaja, O.T.: Bank frauds and forgeries in Nigeria: a study of the causes, types, detection and prevention. IOSR J. Econ. Financ. (IOSR-JEF) **4**(2) (2014). e-ISSN: 2321–5933, p-ISSN: 2321–5925
7. Dansena, P., Kumar, K.P., Pal, R.: Line based extraction of important regions from a cheque image. In: 2015 Eigth International Conference on Contemporary Computing (IC3), pp. 183–189 (2015)
8. Raghavendra, S.P., Danti, A.: A novel recognition if Indian bank Cheque names using binary pattern and feed forward neural network. IOSR J. Comput. Eng. **20**(3), 44–59 (2018). Ver I. UGC Approved Journal(Jr. No. 5019). e-ISSN:2278–0661, p-ISSN:2278–8727
9. Raghavendra, S.P., Danti, A.: Recognition of signature using neural network and Euclidean distance for bank Cheque automation. In: Santosh, K.C., Hegadi, R.S. (eds.) RTIP2R 2018. CCIS, vol. 1037, pp. 228–243. Springer, Singapore (2019). https://doi.org/10.1007/978-981-13-9187-3_21
10. Jayadevan, R., Kolhe, S.R., Patil, P.M., Pal, U.: Automatic processing of handwritten bank cheque images: a survey. IJDAR **15**, 267–296 (2011). https://doi.org/10.1007/s10032-011-0170-8
11. da Silva Barboza, R., Lins, R.D., De Lira, E.D.F., Camara, A.C.A.: Later added strokes or text fraud detection in documents written with ballpoint pens. In: 14th International Conference on Frontiers in Handwriting Recognition. IEEE (2014). 2167–6445/14 $31.00
12. Chhabra, S., Gupta, G., Gupta, M., Gupta, G.: Detecting fraudulent bank checks. In: Peterson, G., Shenoi, S. (eds.) DigitalForensics 2017. IAICT, vol. 511, pp. 245–266. Springer, Cham (2017). https://doi.org/10.1007/978-3-319-67208-3_14

13. Khemchandani, V., Devi, R.: A novel scheme for prevention of forgery and alteration in automated cheque payment system. In: Proceedings of the 4th National Conference; INDIACom-2010 Computing for Nation Development, 25–26 February 2010 (2010)
14. Belaïd, A., Santosh, K.C., D'Andecy, V.P.: Handwritten and printed text separation in real document. MVA, pp. 218–221 (2013)
15. Santosh, K.C.: g-DICE: graph mining-based document information content exploitation. Int. J. Doc. Anal. Recognit. **18**(4), 337–355 (2015)

Character Recognition of Offline Handwritten Marathi Documents Written in MODI Script Using Deep Learning Convolutional Neural Network Model

Parag A. Tamhankar[1]([✉]), Krishnat D. Masalkar[2], and Satish R. Kolhe[3]

[1] Department of Computer Science, MES Abasaheb Garware College, Pune, India
paragishere@gmail.com
[2] Department of Mathematics, MES Abasaheb Garware College, Pune, India
[3] School of Computer Sciences, Kavayitri Bahinabai Chaudhari North Maharashtra University, Jalgaon, India

Abstract. One of the major research areas in data science is deep learning. Convolutional Neural Networks play a huge role in the recent success of the artificial intelligence-based applications. Cursive character recognition is still an active research problem from many years. This paper deals with recognition of offline handwritten Marathi documents written in MODI script using deep learning convolutional neural network model. The algorithm explained in this paper makes use of Rectified Linear Unit neuron activation function in the convolutional layers as it gives better performance and computationally least expensive and softmax neuron activation function in its fully connected layer. The max pooling layer is used for feature detection. The model designed uses 32 convolutional filters of size $3 \times 3 \times 1$. The model developed is trained by using more than 40000-character samples belonging to 31 different class labels. The trained neural network is tested on more than 10000-character samples from 31 different class labels, giving an accuracy of more than 60%.

Keywords: MODI script · Deep learning · Convolutional Neural Network · Character recognition

1 Introduction

In the current era, one of the most popular tools used to perform character recognition is convolutional neural network (CNN) [1]. CNN takes a MODI script character image as an input, processes it, and classifies it correctly in the desired class label. It uses a series of convolutional layers with appropriate kernels, followed by a pooling layer (typically max pooling), and fully connected layer(s) to classify a character with a probability ranging in a real, closed interval 0 to 1.

© Springer Nature Singapore Pte Ltd. 2021
K. C. Santosh and B. Gawali (Eds.): RTIP2R 2020, CCIS 1380, pp. 478–487, 2021.
https://doi.org/10.1007/978-981-16-0507-9_40

This paper is organized as follows: Sect. 2 deals with state-of-the-art, essentially focusing on character recognition work performed using artificial neural networks. Previous research work carried out by authors' is given in Sect. 3. The crux of the paper is explained in Sect. 4. The results obtained are shown in Sect. 5. Section 6 gives an insight into conclusion and future prospects. Finally, the paper ends with acknowledgments and references.

2 State-of-the-Art

Analysis of structural features of MODI script characters from recognition perspective in [2]. It also discusses differences and similarities between MODI script and Devanagari script.

Stentiford algorithm is used for Morphological thinning of individual characters in [3, 4]. Salt-and-pepper noise removal is performed through the use of Median filter. The algorithm used for thresholding is not mentioned.

Structured similarity approach is used to figure out structural similarities between standard and handwritten MODI script charactersin [5]. Various types of classifiers are analyzed for the purpose of character recognition. It uses decision-tree based approach for the recognition of MODI script characters. Morphological operation is performed at every node of the decision tree.

An approach for the recognition of MODI script characters using chain code approach is presented in [6]. It uses normalized and binarized character image as input.

Pros and cons of using Zernike moments and Hu's 7 moments for MODI script character recognition by applying zoning method is discussed in [7]. For training purpose, 100 epochs were used.

Kohonen Neural Networkfor the recognition of MODI script handwritten characters is used in [8]. First, it obtains global threshold using Otsu's method for image binarization.

Superiority of Zernike complex moments over Zernike moments using various zoning patterns for handwritten MODI script characters is highlighted in [9].

Chain code and image centroid is used for the feature extraction purpose [10]. Classification of MODI script vowels are carried out using multilayered feedforward neural network with scaled conjugate gradient.

3 Previous Research Work

MODI script handwritten character images are obtained for the recognition purpose by scanning the handwritten MODI script character samples taken by asking various people to write them on a piece of paper.

In all, 31 different MODI script characters are considered. More than 1500 samples belonging to each character class are used and inputted to the algorithm presented in this paper.

4 The Proposed Method

4.1 Problem Statement

Let $C = C(x)$ be a MODI script character image obtained using authors' previous research work, where $x = [i, j]^T \in R^2$ with 'r' rows and 'c' columns. The goal is to correctly assign a class label from among 31 different class labels, i.e. to recognize the character accurately.

4.2 Mathematical Formulation

The proposed Algorithm uses Deep Learning Convolutional Neural Network Model for two-dimensional MODI script character images. The concept of convolution uses two-dimensional Euclidean inner-product space particularly, $\mathbb{R}^2$. The abstract and most general mathematical framework is explained as follows:

The vector space $<E, F = \mathbb{R} \, or \, \mathbb{C}, +, ., <> >$ is called as inner product space if the last map $<., .>$ from E x E to $\mathbb{R}$ is a.

bilinear, that is $<au + bv, w> = a<u, w> + b<v, w>$,

positive definite, that is $<u, u>$ is positive for all $u \neq 0$,

and conjugate symmetric, that is $<u, v> = \overline{<v, u>}$.

$<\mathbb{R}^{n+1}, F = \mathbb{R} \, or \, \mathbb{C}, +, ., <> >$ with the inner product given by the usual dot product $<u, v> = u^t v$ is called as Euclidean spaces. These spaces are most useful tools in the CNN.

Let V_1, V_2, V_3 be any three vector spaces.

Let $\mathcal{L}(V_1, V_2)$ denote as set of all linear maps from V_1 to V_2 and $\mathcal{L}(V_1, V_2; V_3)$ as set of all bilinear maps from $V_1 \times V_2$ to V_3. Also let denote $\mathcal{L}^*$ as adjoint of $\mathcal{L}$.

Hadamard product:

Let E denote the inner product space with orthonormal basis $\{e_i : i = 1, 2, \ldots n\}$. The $\odot$ is symmetric bilinear operator from in $\mathcal{L}(E, E : E)$ defined using relations $<e_k, e_l> = \delta_{kl} e_k$, where δ is called as kronecker delta function. If $E_1, E_2, \ldots .E_n$ are inner product spaces naturally extend the inner product on direct product $E_1 X E_2 X \ldots \ldots X E_n$ and tensor product $E_1 \otimes E_2 \otimes E_3 \cdots \otimes E_n$ as below:

$$<(e_1, e_2 \ldots e_n), (f_1, f_2 \ldots .f_n)> = \sum_i <e_i f_i> \tag{1}$$

$$<e_1 \otimes e_2 \cdots \otimes e_n, f_1 \otimes f_2 \ldots . \otimes f_n> = \prod_{i=1}^{n} <e_i, f_i> \tag{2}$$

One can represent a neural network with N layers as a composition F of N functions f_i from $E_i X H_i$ to E_{i+1}, where E_i, H_i, E_{i+1} are inner product spaces for all i = 1, 2, 3, …N.

One can write

$$F(x; \theta) = f_N \, of_{N-1} o \ldots \ldots of_2 of_1(x) \tag{3}$$

is   a   map   from $E_1 X H_1 X \ldots . X H_n$ to E_{N+1},   where
$x \in E_1, \theta \in H_1 X \, H_2 X \ldots \ldots . X H_N$, and $\theta = (\theta_1, \ldots \theta_N)$ is a parameter set.

Also one can write F as $F = w_{i+1} f_i \alpha_{i-1}$ with $\alpha_i = f_i of_{i-1} o \ldots of_2 of_1 : E_1 \to E_{i+1}$
and $w_i = f_N of_{N-1} o \ldots . of_i$ are head and tail maps at layer i.

Now the action of a generic layer of CNN is discussed below:

If input to the layer as m_1 channeled tensor with each channel matrix of size $n_1 \times l_1$
and output as m_2 channeled tensor with each channel matrix size $n_2 \times l_2$.

Hence each input x and wiegthts (parameters) W to the layer are represented as
below:

$$x = \sum_{j=1}^{m_1} x_j \otimes e_j$$

where *each x_j is matrix of size $n_1 \times l_1$ and e_j is j^{th} vector.*
in the standerd basis of $\mathbb{R}^{m_1}$.
$W = \sum_{j=1}^{m_2} W_j \otimes \overline{e_j}$ where *each W_j is matrix of size $p \times q$ and $\overline{e_j}$ is j^{th} vector.*
in the standerd basis of $\mathbb{R}^{m_2}$.
Here x_j are called as feature maps and W_j are called as filter used for convolution.
Here some nonlinearity is introduced through some activation map f.
from $(\mathbb{R}^{n_1 \times l_1} \otimes \mathbb{R}^{m_1}) \times (\mathbb{R}^{p \times q} \otimes \mathbb{R}^{m_2})$ to $\mathbb{R}^{n_2 \times l_2} \otimes \mathbb{R}^{m_2}$ defined as

$$f(x, W) = \Phi(\Psi(C(x, W))) \tag{4}$$

Where Φ *is* max *pooling function,* $\Psi : \mathbb{R}^{\widehat{n_1} \times \widehat{l_1}} \otimes \mathbb{R}^{\widehat{m_2}} \to \mathbb{R}^{\widehat{n_1} \times \widehat{l_1}} \otimes \mathbb{R}^{\widehat{m_2}}$ is ele-
mentwise nonlinear function and C is convolution operator. It can be seen that f first
convolves input x with the filters W and then applies nonlinearity and lastly it opartes
max pooling operator.

Now the convolution operator C can be written as $C(x, W) = \sum_{j=1}^{m_2} c_j(x, W) \otimes \overline{e_j}$.

Where c_j are defined as $c_j(x, W) = \sum_{k=1}^{\widehat{n_1}} \sum_{l=1}^{\widehat{l_1}} \langle W_j, \mathcal{K}_{\rho(k,l,\Delta)}(x) \rangle \, \overline{E}_{k,l}$
Here $\mathcal{K}$ is cropping operator and $\rho(k, l, \Delta) = (1 + (k - 1)\Delta, 1 + (l - 1)\Delta)$ is
index for cropping operator and $\Delta \in \mathbb{Z}_{>0}$ defines the stride of the convolution. The
cropping operator $\mathcal{K}$ at index $(k, l) \in [n_1 - p + 1] \times [l_1 - p + 1]$ is defined as.
$\mathcal{K}_{k,l}\left(\sum_{j=1}^{m_1} x_j \otimes e_j\right) = \sum_{j=1}^{m_1} k_{k,l}(x_j)$ with

$$k_{k,l}(x_j) = \sum_{s=1}^{p} \sum_{t=1}^{q} \langle x_j, E_{k+s-1,l+t-1} \rangle \widetilde{E}_{s,t}$$

Here $[n] = \{0, 1, 2, 3, \ldots n\}$ and $E_{i,j}$ and $\widetilde{E}_{i,j}$ are standard bases of respective spaces. Also, Max pooling Φ operator is defined as

$$\Phi(y) = \sum_{j=1}^{m_2} \phi(y_j) \otimes \bar{e}_j \tag{5}$$

with $\phi(y_j) = \sum_{k=1}^{n_2} \sum_{l=1}^{l_2} \max\left(k_{\rho(k,l,r)}(y_j)\right) \overline{E_{k,j}}$

Where $\max(z) = \max_{(k,l)\in[r]\times[r]} \langle z, E_{k,l} \rangle$.

Neural networks use the softmax function for classification purpose. It is given by. $\sigma(x) = \frac{1}{<1, e^x>} e^x$ for all $x \in E$, where 1 is vector of all 1's.

Now derivative of σ is given by $D\sigma(x).v = \sigma(x) \odot v - <\sigma(x), v>\sigma(x)$.

Also have $D^*(Log(\sigma))(x).v = D\sigma(x).D(Log(\sigma))(x).v = v - <1, v>\sigma(x)$.

In classification Neural networks, one can have $<1, v> = 1$, so one has

$$D\sigma(x).D(Log(\sigma))(x).v = v - \sigma(x) \tag{6}$$

Now in Neural Networks in case of regression the target variable $y \in E_{L+1}$ can be any generic vector of real numbers for single input vector $\in E_1$, the loss function is given by

$$J_R = \frac{1}{2}\|y - F(x, \theta)\|^2 = \frac{1}{2}<y - F(x, \theta), y - F(x, \theta)> \tag{7}$$

Now to optimize this, consider its gradients with respect to θ, which are.

$\nabla_{\theta_i} J_R(x, y, \theta) = \nabla_{\theta_i}^* f(x_i) D^* w_{i+1}(x_{i+1})(\widehat{y}_R - y)$, where $\widehat{y}_R = F(x, \theta)$.

If the Neural networks is of classification type then one can have $\widehat{y}_c = \sigma(F(x, \theta)$ instead of $\widehat{y}_R$.

Hence the loss is given by $J_c = -<y, (Log(\sigma))(F(x, \theta))>$

Now to optimize it, one has to consider its gradient with respect to θ which is.

$\nabla_{\theta_i} J_C(x, y, \theta) = \nabla_{\theta_i}^* f(x_i) D^* w_{i+1}(x_{i+1})(\widehat{y}_C - y)$.

Note that although J_C and J_R are different, but their gradients have same form as in both $D^*_{w_{i+1}}(x_{i+1})$ is applied on same error term. $D^*_{w_{i+1}}(x_{i+1})$ is called as Backpropagation operator. The relation for Backpropagation for layers as below.

$D^*_{w_i}(x_i) = D^*f(x_i) D^*_{w_{i+1}}(x_{i+1})$ for all $x \in E_1 i \in [L]$, where $x_{i+1} = f(x_i)$.

ReLU is defined as

$$f(x) = \max(0, x) \tag{8}$$

It is most popular in its use because, it is scale invariant $(ie. f(tx) = tf(x)$ for any scalar t).

It is simple to compute rather than other activation functions such as σ (sigmoid function), tanh (hyperbolic tan function). The ReLU is often used in Deep Neural Networks. Onecan find its gradient by taking its smooth approximation using Bezier-curve technique.

In case of stochastic neuralnetworks, one additional layer is used, which is called as sampling layer. The stochastic neural networks are obtained by making random variations either by giving stochastic transfer functions to output layer of neurons or by giving some stochastic weights to neurons in the neural networks.

For sampling, one can use some probabilitydistribution.Generally Gaussian distribution. For Gaussian stochastic neuron, one can use re-parameterization trick. It has low variance and hence one can train them efficiently. Hopfieldnetworks are used to find solution to combinatorial problems that are expressed as minimization of energy function.

In particular, Boltzmann's machine is used as Hopfield networks,which is defined as below

$$The\ states\ x_i\ =\ 1\ with\ probability\ p_i\ and\ x_i\ =\ 0\ with\ probability\ 1 - p_i$$

With $p_i = \dfrac{1}{1+e^{\left(\frac{\sum_{j=1}^{n} w_{ij}x_j - \theta_i}{T}\right)}}$, where T is positive temperature constant, w_{ij} are weights of the network and θ_i are bias units.

The energy function in case of Hopfield networks are given by

$$E = -\frac{1}{2} \sum_{i=1}^{n} \sum_{j=1}^{n} w_{ij}x_i x_j + \sum_{i=1}^{n} \int_{0}^{x_i} s^{-1}(x)dx \qquad (9)$$

Where w_{ij} are wiegths of learning and $x_i = s(u_i) = \frac{1}{1+e^{u_i}}$ leads to new state.

The change in E with respect to time is $\frac{dE}{dt} = -\sum_{i=1}^{n} \frac{dx_i}{dt}(\sum_{j=1}^{n} w_{ij} - u_i)$ assuming that $w_{ij} = w_{ji}$. Now one can have $\frac{du_i}{dt} = \gamma(-u_i + \sum_{j=1}^{n} w_{ij}s(u_j))$.

Hence $\frac{dE}{dt} = -\frac{1}{\gamma} \sum_{i=1}^{n} \frac{dx_i}{dt}\frac{du_i}{dt} = -\frac{1}{\gamma} \sum_{i=1}^{n} s'(u_i)\left(\frac{du_i}{dt}\right)^2 \leq 0$ because s is sigmoid function which is monotonically increasing and hence $s'(u_i) > 0$.

Note that gradient descent method requires lots of computations in classification of the big data. In that case,one has to apply the gradient descents method to single sample or some mini –batch sample of the data. And this mini-batch sample is selected according some probability distribution, inparticular, Gaussian distribution. In this case Boltzmann's Machines are used.

4.3 Proposed Algorithm

The outline of the algorithm is described as follows:

Step 1: All the character images belonging to 31 different class labels are stored in the input folder, say, 'input_data'.

Step 2: Each character image is resized to 32 × 32 × 1 pixels each and the result is stored in another folder, say, 'input_data_resized'.

Step 3: A matrix named 'DS' is created with 'm' rows and 'n' columns, where 'm' represents number of samples and column of each row represents feature vector of that sample. This process is called as "flattening" of the data set. This matrix is fed as an input into the CNN model described later in this section.

Step 4: A one dimensional array named 'label' of size 'm' is created, where 'm' represents total number of samples. Each entry in this array represents the class label number of the respective character sample. i.e. all samples representing the same character will all have common class label number.

Step 5: The matrix 'DS' created in step 3 and the array 'label' created in step 4 are shuffled. The shuffling of data set is a key step performed before the actual learning of the model can start. Shuffling of the data set improves CNN model quality, and it also increases the predictive performance of the CNN model.

Step 6: The parameters of the CNN model are defined as follows:

   i.   Batch size to train is 3.
   ii.   Number of classes are 31.
  iii.   Number of channels is 1.
  iv.   Size of a convolutional kernel is $3 \times 3 \times 1$.
   v.   Number of convolutional kernels are 32.
  vi.   Size of max pooling window is $2 \times 2 \times 1$.
 vii.   Number of Epochs used for training is 25.
viii.   'relu' neuron activation function is used at convolutional layers.
  ix.   'softmax' neuron activation function is used at fully connected layer.

Step 7: The entire data set is split into training and testing with 80% of the total samples are used for training the CNN model, whereas, remaining 20% of the samples are used for testing.

Step 8: Since CNN requires data set to be in 2-D format, and currently, all the training and testing samples are in flattened form, they are reshaped back into their original form i.e. $32 \times 32 \times 1$.

Step 9: Class vectors are converted binary class matrices so that they can be used in categorical cross entropy function.

Step 10: The CNN model is trained to fix the weights and by using these weights it is tested on the testing samples.

5 Experimental Results and Discussion

(See Tables 1 and 2, Fig. 1).

Table 1. Precision/Recall/f1-score

Class label #	Precision	Recall	f1-score
Class 0	0.89	0.84	0.87
Class 1	0.84	0.78	0.81
Class 2	0.63	0.78	0.70
Class 3	0.68	0.65	0.66
Class 4	0.64	0.66	0.65
Class 5	0.62	0.65	0.63
Class 6	0.59	0.63	0.61
Class 7	0.53	0.53	0.53
Class 8	0.64	0.51	0.57
Class 9	0.65	0.59	0.62
Class 10	0.69	0.70	0.70
Class 11	0.66	0.73	0.69
Class 12	0.60	0.46	0.52
Class 13	0.38	0.53	0.44
Class 14	0.47	0.48	0.47
Class 15	0.66	0.60	0.63
Class 16	0.70	0.82	0.76
Class 17	0.72	0.65	0.68
Class 18	0.75	0.66	0.70
Class 19	0.82	0.81	0.81
Class 20	0.57	0.69	0.62
Class 21	0.51	0.49	0.50
Class 22	0.49	0.48	0.48
Class 23	0.47	0.49	0.48
Class 24	0.52	0.55	0.54
Class 25	0.58	0.49	0.53
Class 26	0.66	0.63	0.64
Class 27	0.61	0.71	0.66
Class 28	0.73	0.63	0.68
Class 29	0.81	0.74	0.77
Class 30	0.87	0.86	0.86

Table 2. Average statistics

Type	Precision	Recall	f1-score
Micro average	0.64	0.64	0.64
Macro Average	0.64	0.64	0.64
Weighted Average	0.64	0.64	0.64

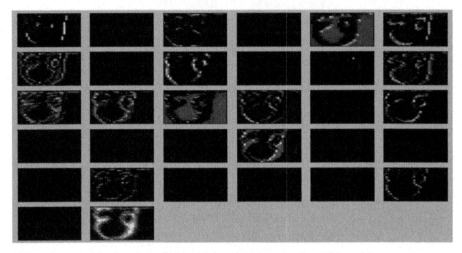

Fig. 1. Depicts 25 epochs used for learning the CNN model

6 Conclusion and Future Prospects

The results obtained using the algorithm presented in this paper are quite satisfying with an overall accuracy of 64%.

Future work involves building a better model to accommodate entire 'barakhadi' of MODI script with more accuracy. Fine tuning of hyper-parameters will also be tried to check if the current CNN model can provide even better accuracy than as of now. Once the accuracy goes above 75%, this trained CNN model shall be tested on the segmented MODI script characters for OCR/HOCR system.

Acknowledgments. The Authors would like to express their sincere gratitude towards Vice-Chancellor, Deccan College Deemed University, Pune, Maharashtra for permitting access to Marathi documents written in Modi script.

Especially, authors are immensely indebted to Dr. Girish Mandke, Curator, Maratha History Museum, Deccan College for providing access to the said documents.

The authors are grateful to the University Grants Commission, New Delhi for sustaining this work at School of Computer Sciences, North Maharashtra University, Jalgaon under the Special Assistance Programme (SAP) at the level of DRS-II.

References

1. Guha, R., Das, N., Kundu, M., Nasipuri, M., Santosh, K.C.: DevNet: an efficient CNN architecture for handwritten devanagari character recognition. Int. J. Pattern Recogn. Artif. Intell. **34**, 2052009 (2020)
2. Besekar, D.N., Ramteke, R.J.: Study for theoretical analysis of handwritten MODI script–a recognition perspective. Int. J. Comput. Appl. **64**(3), 45–49 (2013)
3. Rathi, S., Jadhav, R.H., Ambildhok, R.A.: Recognition and conversion of handwritten MODI characters. Int. J. Tech. Res. Appl. **111**(2), 28–34 (2015)
4. Ghosh, M., Obaidullah, S.M., Santosh, K.C., Das, N., Roy, K.: Artistic multi-character script identification using iterative isotropic dilation algorithm. In: Santosh, K.C., Hegadi, R.S. (eds.) RTIP2R 2018. CCIS, vol. 1037, pp. 49–62. Springer, Singapore (2019). https://doi.org/10.1007/978-981-13-9187-3_5
5. Ramteke, A.S., Katkar, G.S.: Recognition of off-line MODI script: a structure similarity approach. Int. J. ICT Manage. **1**(1), 12–15 (2013)
6. Besekar, D.N., Ramteke, R.J.: A chain code approach for recognising modi script numerals. Indian J. Appl. Res. **1**(3), 222–225 (2011)
7. Kulkarni, S.A., Borde, P.L., Manza, R.R., Yannawar, P.L.: Offline handwritten MODI character recognition using HU, Zernike moments and Zoning. arXiv preprint arXiv:1406.6140 (2014)
8. Anam, S., Gupta, S.: An approach for recognizing Modi Lipi using Ostu's Binarization algorithm and Kohenen neural network. Int. J. Comput. Appl. **111**(2), 28–34 (2015)
9. Sadanand, A.K., et al.: Offline MODI character recognition using complex moments. Proc. Comput. Sci. **58**, 516–523 (2015)
10. Besekar, D.N.: Special approach for recognition of handwritten MODI script's vowels. Int. J. Comput. Appl. (IJCA) **MEDHA**(1), 48–52 (2012)

Recognition of Handwritten Indian Trilingual City Names

Ramit Kumar Roy[1][(✉)], Himadri Mukherjee[2], Kaushik Roy[2], and Umapada Pal[3]

[1] St. Xavier's College (Autonomous), Kolkata, India
ramitkumar.roy@sxccal.edu
[2] West Bengal State University, Kolkata, India
himadrim027@gmail.com, kaushik.mrg@gmail.com
[3] CVPR Unit, Indian Statistical Institute, Kolkata, India
umapada_pal@yahoo.com

Abstract. For postal documents in India, irrespective of the fact that it bears a PIN or not, writing the destination city name is compulsory and without which a document will never be able to reach its desired location. Although in many countries like USA we find a fully automated system of postal services, lot of research works are still needed to be pursued for a multi lingual and a multi script country like India to develop such a postal system. Due to a large number of varieties in hand writings of individuals and applications of more than one language at the time of writing, recognition of the accurate destination city names written in Indian postal documents becomes a very challenging task. From our study on existing works on recognition of Indian city names we concluded that as on date research work on Indian city name recognition has been carried out for Indian city names written in English, Bangla, Hindi, Tamil and Gurumukhi languages out of the twenty three languages which officially exist in India and as a consequence there is definitely appreciable scope of research in this area. In this paper, we present our work dealing with recognition of handwritten trilingual Indian city names where we have considered a minimum of thirty samples in each case where the same city name is written in English, Bangla and Hindi. Bangla and Hindi are two of the most popular Indian languages and English though being a non Indian language is used very frequently in most of the postal documents in India even today. Our proposed work was carried on 2700 handwritten city names, each 900 of which were written in English, Bangla and Hindi respectively. Our proposed system was able to correctly recognize 2592 city names and thereby we achieved 96% accuracy using CNN.

Keywords: Indian postal documents · Postal automation · Handwritten trilingual city names

1 Introduction

Postal automation system is a mechanism which is capable of reading line by line each and every hand written address from the destination addresses of the various letters,

© Springer Nature Singapore Pte Ltd. 2021
K. C. Santosh and B. Gawali (Eds.): RTIP2R 2020, CCIS 1380, pp. 488–498, 2021.
https://doi.org/10.1007/978-981-16-0507-9_41

documents and parcels and in turn will automatically sort each of them so that accurate delivery of those materials can be ensured. Countries like USA, Canada, Germany, France and Japan have already implemented a totally automated postal service as on date. We find a good number of published research papers which deal with postal automation of foreign countries [1–6]. In India, the postal service which is more than one hundred and fifty years old acts as a key factor to ensure an efficient communication system all over the country, playing a major role towards the overall social and economic development of India. As on date more than 155,000 post offices are spread all over India which on an average covers more than 21 sq km thereby catering to approximately over 8000 people on an average. Even though the postal system that is implemented in India is regarded as the most widely distributed postal system all over the world, we still have very limited deployment of postal automation machines in Indian post offices even to day. Development of postal automation in India is a very challenging task for multiple reasons. Firstly, we have twenty three (23) languages and eleven (11) scripts in India. Those scripts are used in order to write any of the above mentioned twenty three languages. English inspite of being a foreign language is used in most of the postal documents of India. Next, a postal document in India is often written in combination of more than one language. As because the writing style of each individual is different, often at the time of writing, one character/numeral is found to touch its adjacent character/numeral and separation of the two touching characters/numerals for proper recognition obviously become a challenging task. In Fig. 4 as we have given below, touching of one character with another character for a Bangla city name is shown in red. Another very important parameter which we consider as a challenge in Indian city name recognition is the presence of compound characters. In English, there is no existence of compound characters but an appreciable degree of presence of compound characters are found in case of city names written in the other two languages i.e. Bangla and Hindi. A bangla city name with compound character which is marked in red shown in Fig. 5 below.

We have come to a conclusion that 12.37% of the documents are written in Bangla. 76.32% of the documents are written in English and 10.21% of the documents are written in Hindi and the detailed statistical information is available in [7]. We found that most of the postal documents of India are tri lingual as it comprises of English, Hindi and the official language of the state. In India we have large variations of documents, each of which is used for the postal communication purposes. Those documents include ordinary envelopes, parcels, specially printed envelopes and post cards. Out of all these documents specially printed envelopes and post cards are available from the post offices while ordinary envelopes are available in all the markets. With increase in on line purchases through Amazon, flip kart etc. delivery of products through parcels via postal service or through courier services has increased appreciably over the last decade. Irrespective of the fact that a postal document contain the PIN or the PIN is partially written or the PIN is not written at all, if the city name is not correctly written, the postal document will fail to reach its destination address. Therefore, correct identification of the city name is compulsory. In Fig. 1 as shown below we find an example of a monolingual postal document written in Bangla where the PIN is written partially. Similarly in Fig. 2. we find a bilingual postal document where the destination address is written as a combination of Hindi and English where the PIN is partially written in English. In case of Fig. 3. We have a postal document without any PIN.

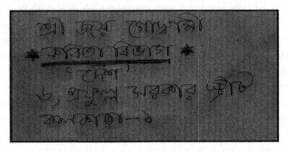

Fig. 1. A monolingual postal document where the PIN is partially written.

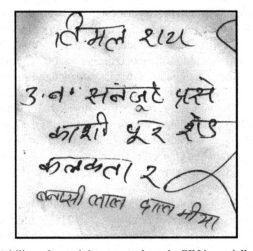

Fig. 2. A bilingual postal document where the PIN is partially written.

A block diagram (Fig. 6) is provided below which explains our entire process of city name recognition. At the very outset we take the scanned images of the city names as our input. The next step is the pre-processing of the input images.

Finally we use Convolutional Neural Network (CNN) to find out the rate of recognition of the input hand written city names. The remaining section of our paper is organized as below: - Sect. 2 deals with related works on hand written city name recognition. Section 3 deals with the database, Sect. 4 deals with CNN-based classification, Sect. 5 discusses the results and finally Sect. 6 concludes our paper.

Fig. 3. A postal document without PIN.

Fig. 4. A Bangla city name with touching of characters indicated in red. (Color figure online)

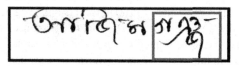

Fig. 5. A Bangla city name with compound characters indicated in red. (Color figure online)

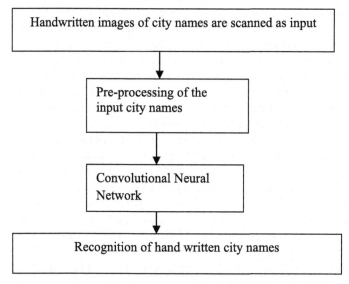

Fig. 6. Block diagram explaining our system of tri-lingual city name recognition using CNN

2   Related Works on City Name Recognition

In this section, we are going to discuss the existing works which deal with the hand written recognition of the Indian city names as on date. We would like to mention here that several works exist as on date which deal with recognition of PIN codes in the postal documents of India [14–18] though the number of works published towards recognition of handwritten Indian city names are very few. Pal et al. [8] had implemented a lexicon based scheme for recognition of handwritten Bangla city names. They had used dynamic programming matching techniques based on MQDF i.e. Modified Quadratic Discriminant Function. Directional features on the contour points of the components were used by them. The research work carried out on 84 Bangla city names achieved 94.08% accurate result. Thadchanamoorthy et al. [9] were able to achieve 96.89% of accuracy in case of handwritten Tamil city names when they had experimented on a hand written database comprising of 265 Tamil handwritten city names comprising of 26,500 samples. They had deployed dynamic programming matching techniques based on MQDF i.e. Modified Quadratic Discriminant Function in their research work. Roy et al. [10] proposed a water reservoir concept based technique for the automation of postal system in India which dealt with recognition of PIN and city names. A total of 2342 hand written words comprising of 1100 in Bangla and 1242 along with 650 printed words comprising of 400 in Bangla and 250 in English were used in this paper 98.42% accuracy was achieved in case of printed words and 89% accuracy was achieved in case of handwritten words. All the works we have referred till now dealt with the recognition of mono lingual hand written city names. Pal et al. in [11] had proposed a lexicon based method for recognition of bi lingual city names. 11875 city names of which 8625 were written in Bangla and 3250 were written in English were considered for their work. Here, the number of the total city name class was 173 out of which 84 were in Bangla and the remaining i.e. 89 were in English. In each of the above mentioned classes a minimum of 20 samples were present. 93.19% of accuracy was achieved by them. Since this was the first published work towards recognition of bilingual i.e. handwritten Bangla and English city names, their results could not be compared with other existing works. The only published work as on date dealing with tri- lingual hand written city name recognition was carried out by Pal et al. in [12]. 16312 samples of tri lingual hand written city names were taken into consideration comprising of 4257 samples of handwritten Hindi city names, 8625 samples of hand written Bangla city names and 3250 samples of hand written English city names. The number of the total city name class was 290 out of which 117 were in Hindi, 84 were in Bangla and the remaining i.e. 89 were in English. In each of the above mentioned classes a minimum of 20 samples were present. Overall 92.25% recognition accuracy was achieved by them through this experiment. From the above discussions we can conclude that as on date all the research works are done dealing with mono lingual Indian city names written in either Bangla or Tamil or English.Only one research paper published as on date deals with bi-lingual city names i.e. Indian city names written in Bangla and English and trilingual city names i.e. Bangla, English and Hindi respectively.

3 Dataset

We found that publicly available datasets which can be used as a benchmark in research on recognition of hand written city names are very few in number. To provide a platform where the researchers can compare in between the various techniques for hand written city name recognition, Kaur and Kumar [13] have published a publicly available dataset of 40000 samples of names of various cities written in Gurumukhi script. Since no such database is available for city names written in English, Bangla and Hindi,we had collected 7500 postal documents from West Bengal, a state of India and over and above that we had prepared and circulated specially designed forms exclusively for data procurement as shown in Fig. 7 below. For our present work, we have used a database which consisting of 2700 city name samples, each 900 of them where written in English, Bangla and Hindi respectively. We had a total of 30 city name classes having 90 instances each, where each of them where written in English, Bangla and Hindi respectively. English is a foreign language but even today in most of our Indian documents we find that English is used completely as in Fig. 3 or partially as in Fig. 2 respectively. Bangla is one of the most popular languages in India as well as it is the national language of Bangladesh. Hindi is the national language of India and is often used as a medium of oral communication in between the people living in different parts of India.

4 CNN Based Classification

Since, it is very difficult to get desirable results by individually segmenting the city names properly, we have not considered any segmentation framework in our proposed work [20, 21]. CNN [19, 22] which is the acronym for Convolutional Neural Network is actually a network where the mathematical operation named convolution which is one kind of linear operation is implemented. The convolution operation is used for extraction of different features from an input image. The first convolution layer is used to extract low-level features such as edges, lines and corners. Higher-level layers are deployed to extract higher-level features. The name Convolutional Neural Network is given because at least in one of their layers, convolution operation is used instead of ordinary multiplication of matrices. The constituents of Convolutional Neural Network are as under:- 1. Input layer. 2. Output layer. 3. More than one hidden layers in between the two input and output layers. The hidden layers comprises of a series of Convolutional layers in case of CNN. The greatest advantage behind the deployment of Convolutional Neural Networks over other existing neural networks is hierarchical treatment of features. A Convolutional layer has three components; An input tensor which can be visualized as a two dimensional matrix such as the pixels present in any image; A filter tensor alternatively known as a kernel. This kernel is responsible to capture the patterns present in an image; An output tensor. Pooling layer is another component of a CNN. The pooling layer progressively reduces the spatial size of the representation to reduce the amount of parameters and computation in the network. Pooling layer operates on each feature map independently. Max pooling is the most common approach used in pooling. The final layer of a CNN is a fully connected layer, often termed as dense layer. In this experiment we used a 32 connected layer, often termed as dense layer. In this experiment we used a 32 dimensional convolutional layer working with images of 5×5 dimension. This output was max pooled followed by another 16 dimensional convolution layer of 3×3 dimensional images. This output was again max pooled and finally fed to a 256 dimensional dense layer. The convolution layers had ReLU activation while the final layer used Softmax activation. The used CNN architecture is illustrated in Fig. 8.

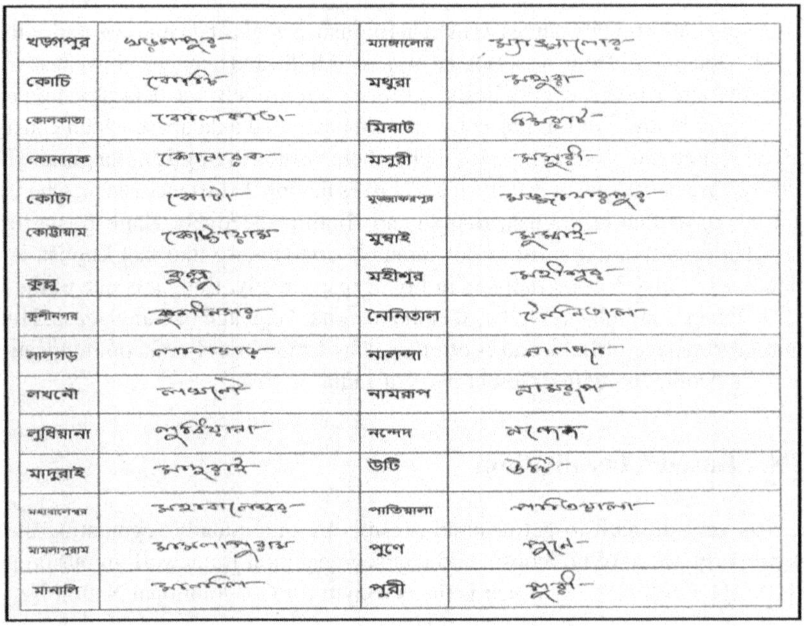

খড়গপুর		ম্যাঙ্গালোর	
কোচি		মথুরা	
কোলকাতা		মিরাট	
কোনারক		মসুরী	
কোটা		মুজাফরপুর	
কোট্টায়াম		মুম্বাই	
কুলু		মহীশূর	
কুশীনগর		নৈনিতাল	
লালগড়		নালন্দা	
লখনৌ		নামরূপ	
লুধিয়ানা		নন্দেদ	
মাদুরাই		উটি	
মহাবালেশ্বর		পাতিয়ালা	
মামল্লাপুরাম		পুণে	
মানালি		পুরী	

Fig. 7. A form exclusively prepared for procurement of data.

5 Result and Discussion

In this section we are going to discuss the results of our experiment. We have used CNN (Convolutional Neural Network) on our datasets to determine the different levels of accuracy on different batch sizes as well as on different fold techniques. We initially experimented with 5 fold cross validation and 100 fold cross validation on a batch size of 100 whose results are reflected in the following Table 1 as furnished below. From our experiments we found that 10 fold cross validation had produced best results and as a consequence we further continued our experiment with the same by varying the sizes of the batch and our results are reflected in Table 2 below. The results show that the minimum level of accuracy we have obtained is 95.11% where the size of our batch is 50. The maximum accuracy we have achieved is 96% when we had carried on our experiment on a batch size of 150. Table 3 as furnished below deals with the individual city names and the accuracy and errors obtained by us in each case as an outcome of our experiment. We had 90 samples against each and every city name, 30 of them were written in English, 30 in Bangla and the remaining 30 in Hindi. The total number of city names was 2700 and our system could accurately recognize 2592 city names, thereby yielding an accuracy of 96% on the whole.

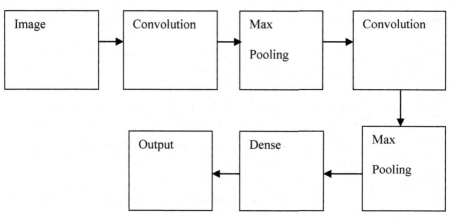

Fig. 8. Block diagram explaining the architecture of used Convolutional Neural Network (CNN).

Table 1. Obtained accuracies for different folds of cross validation.

Fold	Accuracy (%)
5	90.07
10	95.56

Table 2. Obtained accuracies for different batch sizes with 10 fold cross validation.

Batch size	Accuracy (%)
50	95.11
100	95.56
150	96.00
200	95.48

5.1   Error Analysis and Comparison

From Table 3 we find that 100% accuracy in case of individual city name has been achieved by us in case of two city names viz. Gwalior and Kanyakumari.

Table 3. Class wise accuracies for 10 fold cross validation with batch size of 150 (best result).

City	Agartala	Agra	Ahmednagar	Barasat	Barelly
Accuracy (%)	95.55	94.44	98.88	94.44	97.77
City	Barmer	Belur	Chennai	Chitorgarh	Cuttack
Accuracy (%)	94.44	97.77	93.33	94.44	98.88
City	Delhi	Dhanbad	Dharamsala	Dibrugarh	Goa
Accuracy (%)	98.88	96.66	97.77	95.55	94.44
City	Gwalior	Hassan	Howrah	Hyderabad	Jaipur
Accuracy (%)	100	97.77	94.44	91.11	92.22
City	Jaisalmer	Jalandhar	Kanchipuram	Kanyakumari	Kargil
Accuracy (%)	94.44	94.44	95.55	100	92.22
City	Kathgodam	Kolkata	Ludhiana	Mumbai	Ooti
Accuracy (%)	97.77	96.66	98.88	95.55	95.55

The lowest percentage of accuracy achieved in case of individual city name is 91.11% and 8.88% is the rate of error in case of city named Hyderabad. Our findings reveal that 75% of the wrongly recognized samples i.e. 6 out of 8 wrongly recognized samples are because of the fact that they are confused with the city Ahmednagar. The second lowest percentage of accuracy achieved in case of individual city name is in for the city Jaipur i.e. 92.22% where the percentage of error is 7.8%. Here we present a tabular comparison (Table 4) of the results where we have taken into consideration the size of the dataset, the classifier deployed and the level of accuracy obtained in each case among the different published works which deal with recognition of Indian city names. This Table is also a summary of all the works till today published towards recognition of Indian city names either mono-lingual or bi-lingual or tri-lingual. From Table 4 we find that the maximum level of accuracy has been achieved in case of 96.89% where 26500 monolingual (Tamil) city names were taken into consideration. As far as trilingual (Bangla, English and Hindi) city names are concerned, the maximum level of accuracy till date is 92.25% when tested on 16312 samples. Our work has achieved 96% accurate results on 2700 samples which is fairly encouraging as till date it is the highest level of accuracy in comparison to other existing works. In all other earlier works MQDF i.e. Modified Quadrant Discriminant Function was used. We have used Convolutional Neural Network in our present work. It is expected that if we perform our future work on larger tri lingual city name data set, it will also yield results which will outperform the performance of the other existing works.

Table 4. Comparative study of existing works on Indian city name recognition.

Reference	Dataset	Classifier deployed	Accuracy (%)
[8]	8625 Bangla City Names (Monolingual)	MQDF	94.08
[9]	26500 Tamil City Names (Monolingual)	MQDF	96.89
[11]	11875 Bi-lingual city names where 8625 written in Bangla and 3250 written in English	MQDF	93.19
[12]	16312 Tri-lingual city names where 8625 written in Bangla and 3250 written in English and 4257 written in Hindi	MQDF	92.25
Our proposed work	2700 Tri-lingual city names where 900 written in Bangla and 900 written in English and 900 written in Hindi	CNN	96

6 Conclusion

At present though postal automation system is available in a few states of India, they deal with sorting of postal documents written in English only. Our paper has dealt with recognizing of city names of India written in English, Bangla and Hindi. From the results obtained by us, we conclude that the results of our existing works on tri lingual city name recognition for hand written Indian city names are appreciably ahead of existing works dealing with both the recognition of bi-lingual and tri-lingual Indian city names. Till now research work has been carried only on four Bangla, Hindi, Tamil and Gurmukhi languages out of the twenty three Indian languages. In future, our plan is to develop a publicly available dataset of the city names written in the above four languages i.e. Bangla, Hindi, Tamil and English. We also plan to perform our research on a much larger tri lingual city name data base in the days to follow.

References

1. Liu, L., Koga, M., Fujisawa, H.: Lexicon driven segmentation and recognition of handwritten character strings for Japanese address reading. IEEE Trans. PAMI **24**, 1425–1437 (2002)
2. Plamondon, R., Srihari, S.N.: On-Line and off line handwritten recognition: a comprehensive survey. IEEE Trans. PAMI **22**, 62–84 (2000)
3. Mahadevan, U., Srihari, S.N.: Parsing and recognition of City, State, and ZIP Codes in handwritten addresses. In: Proceedings of 5th ICDAR, pp. 325–328 (1999)
4. Wang, X., Tsutsumida, T.: A new method of character line extraction from mixed-unformatted document image for Japanese mail address recognition. In: Proceedings of 5th ICDAR, pp. 769–772 (1999)
5. Srihari, S.N., Keubert, E.J.: Integration of hand-written address interpretation technology into the United States postal service remote computer reader system. In: Proceedings of 4th ICDAR, pp. 892–896 (1997)

6. Kornai, A.: An experimental HMM-based postal OCR system. Proceedings of ICASSP **1997**, 3177–3180 (1997)
7. Vajda, S., Roy, K., Pal, U., Chaudhuri, B.B., Belaid, A.: Automation of Indian postal documents written in Bangla and English. Int. J. PRAI **23**(8), 1599–1632 (2009)
8. Pal, U., Roy, K., Kimura, F.: A lexicon-driven handwritten city-name recognition scheme for Indian postal automation. IEICE Trans. Inf. Syst. **E92.D**(5), 1146–1158 (2009)
9. Thadchanamoorthy, S., Kodikara, N.D., Premaretne, H.L., Pal, U., Kimura, F.: Tamil handwritten city name database development and recognition for postal automation. In: Proceedings of 12th International Conference on Document Analysis and Recognition, pp. 793–797 (2013)
10. Roy, K., Vajda, S., Pal, U., Chaudhuri, B.B., Belaid, A.: A system for Indian postal automation. In: Eighth International Conference on Document Analysis and Recognition (ICDAR 2005) (2005)
11. Pal, U., Roy, R.K., Kimura, F.: Bangla and English city name recognition for Indian postal automation. In: Proceedings of International Conference on Pattern Recognition, pp. 1985–1988 (2010)
12. Pal, U., Roy, R.K., Kimura, F.: Multi-lingual city name recognition for Indian postal automation. In: Proceedings of International Conference on Frontiers in Handwriting Recognition, pp. 169–173 (2012)
13. Kaur, H., Kumar, M.: Benchmark dataset: offline handwritten Gurmukhi city names for postal automation. In: Sundaram, S., Harit, G. (eds.) Document Analysis and Recognition. DAR 2018 (2019)
14. Basu, S., Das, N., Sarkar, R., Kundu, M., Nasipuri, M., Kumar Basu, D.: A novel framework for automatic sorting of postal documents with multi-script address blocks. Pattern Recogn. **43**(10), 3507–3521 (2010)
15. Wen, Y., Lu, Y., Shi, P.: Handwritten Bangla numeral recognition system and its application to postal automation. Pattern Recogn. **40**(1), 99–107 (2007)
16. Basu, S., Das, N., Sarkar, R., Kundu, M., Nasipuri, M., Basu, D.K.: Recognition of numeric postal codes from multi-script postal address blocks. In: Chaudhury, S., Mitra, S., Murthy, C.A., Sastry, P.S., Pal, S.K. (eds.) PReMI 2009. LNCS, vol. 5909, pp. 381–386. Springer, Heidelberg (2009). https://doi.org/10.1007/978-3-642-11164-8_62
17. Pal, U., Roy, R.K., Roy, K., Kimura, F.: Indian multi-script full pin-code string recognition for postal automation. In: Proceedings of 10th International Conference on Document Analysis and Recognition (ICDAR), pp. 456–460 (2009)
18. Basu, S., Seth, S.S., Sarkar, P., Das, B., Dey, S., Ghosh, S.: Recognition of Pincodes from Indian Postal Documents, Soft Computing. Allied Publishers, 817764632-X, 9788177646320, pp. 239–245
19. Krizhevsky, A., Sutskever, I., Hinton, G.E.: Imagenet classification with deep convolutional neural networks. In: Advances in Neural Information Processing Systems, pp. 1097–1105 (2012)
20. Rakshit, P., Halder, C., Ghosh, S., Roy, K.: Line, Word, and character segmentation from Bangla handwritten text—a precursor toward Bangla HOCR. In: Chaki, R., Cortesi, A., Saeed, K., Chaki, N. (eds.) Advanced Computing and Systems for Security. AISC, vol. 666, pp. 109–120. Springer, Singapore (2018). https://doi.org/10.1007/978-981-10-8180-4_7
21. Pal, U., Jayadevan, R., Sharma, N.: Handwriting recognition in Indian regional scripts: a survey of offline techniques. ACM Trans. Asian Lang. Inf. Process. (TALIP) **11**(1), 1–35 (2012)
22. Hijam, D., Saharia, S., Nirmal, Y.: Towards a complete character set Meitei Mayek handwritten character recognition. In: Fourth International Conference on Computing Communication Control and Automation (ICCUBEA) (2018)

Deep Learning for Word-Level Handwritten Indic Script Identification

Soumya Ukil[1], Swarnendu Ghosh[1], Sk Md Obaidullah[2], K. C. Santosh[3], Kaushik Roy[4], and Nibaran Das[1(✉)]

[1] Department of CSE, Jadavpur University, Kolkata 700032, WB, India
soumyaukil60@gmail.com, swarbir@gmail.com, nibaranju@gmail.com
[2] Department of CSE, Aliah University, Kolkata 700156, WB, India
sk.obaidullah@gmail.com
[3] Department of CS, University of South Dakota, Vermillion, SD 57069, USA
santosh.kc@usd.edu
[4] Department of CSE, West Bengal State University, Kolkata 700126, WB, India
kaushik.mrg@gmail.com

Abstract. In this work, we present a novel method that uses convolutional neural networks (CNNs) for multi scale and multi spectral feature extraction. The model is not only limited to conventional spatial domain representation but also multilevel two dimensional discrete Haar wavelet transform, where image representations are scaled to a variety of different sizes. These are then used to train different CNNs to select features. To be precise, we use 10 different CNNs that select a set of 10240 features, i.e. 1024/CNN. With this, 11 different handwritten scripts are identified, where 1000 words per script are used. In our test, we have achieved a maximum script identification accuracy of 94.73% using multi-layer perceptron (MLP). Our results outperform several state of the art techniques.

Keywords: Convolutional neural network · Deep learning · Multi-layer perceptron · Discrete wavelet transform · Indic script identification

1 Introduction

Document image processing or Optical character recognition (OCR) has always been some of the challenging fields in pattern recognition. OCR techniques are used to convert handwritten or machine printed scanned document images to machine-encoded texts. These OCR techniques are script dependent. Therefore, script identification is considered as a precursor to OCR. In particular, for a country like India with several languages, script identification is an important task for processing documents such as postal documents and business forms which contains different scripts simultaneously (see Fig. 1).

Indic handwritten script identification has a rich literature [2,3,8,13]. More often, earlier approaches works have been carried out focusing on word-level

© Springer Nature Singapore Pte Ltd. 2021
K. C. Santosh and B. Gawali (Eds.): RTIP2R 2020, CCIS 1380, pp. 499–510, 2021.
https://doi.org/10.1007/978-981-16-0507-9_42

script recognition [7,10]. Not stopping there, in a recent work [7], authors introduced page-level script identification performance to see whether we can expedite the processing time. In general, in their works, hand-crafted features that are based on structural and/or visual appearances (morphology-based) were used. The question is, are we just relying on what we see and use apply features accordingly or can we just let machine to select features that are required for optimal identification rate? This inspires to use deep learning, where CNNs can be used for extracting and/or selecting features for identification task(s).

Needless to say, CNNs have stood well with their immense contribution in the field of OCR. Their onset has been marked by the ground-breaking performance of CNNs on MNIST dataset [6]. Very recently, the use CNN for Indic script (Bangla character recognition) has been reported [11]. Not to be confused, the primary of goal of this paper is to use deep learning concept to identify eleven handwritten Indic scripts, namely, Devnagari, Gurumukhi, Gujarati, Kannada, Oriya, Malayalam, Roman, Telugu, Tamil, Urdu and Bangla. Inspired from deep learning-based concept, we use CNNs to select features from handwritten document images (scanned), where we use multilevel 2D discrete Haar wavelet transform (in addition to conventional spatial domain representation) and image representations are scaled to a variety of different sizes. With these representation, several different CNNs are used to select features. In short, the primary idea behind this is to avoid using hand-crafted features for identification. Using *multi-layer perceptron* (MLP), 11 different handwritten scripts (as mentioned earlier) are identified with satisfactory performance.

Fig. 1. Two multi-script postal document images, where Bangla, Roman and Devanagari scripts are used.

The rest of the paper can be summarized as follows. In Sect. 2 a quick overview of our contribution has been provided, where it includes CNN architecture and the feature extraction protocol. In Sect. 3, experimental results are provided. It also includes a quick comparison study. Section 4 concludes our paper.

2   Contribution Outline

As mentioned earlier, in stead of using hand-crafted features for document image representation, our goal is to let deep learning to select distinguishing features for optimal script identification. For a few but recent works, where CNNs have used with successful classification, we refer to [5, 6, 12]. We observe that CNNs work especially when we have sufficient data to train. This means, data redundancies will be helpful. In general, CNN takes raw pixel data (image) and as training proceeds, the model learns distinguishing features that can successfully contribute to identification/classification. Such a training process produces a feature vector that summarize the important aspects of the studied image(s).

More precisely, our approach is twofold: first, we use a two- and three-layered CNNs with three different sizes of the input; Secondly, we use CNNs for two different scales of the input transformed bu wavelet transform. We then merge those features and make ready for script identification. In what follows, we explain our CNN architecture including definitions, parameters for wavelet transform and the way we produce features.

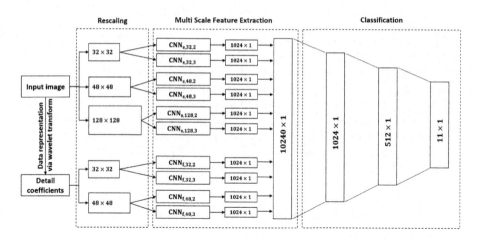

Fig. 2. Schematic block diagram of handwritten Indic script identification showing different modules: feature selection/extraction and classifier.

2.1   CNN Architecture

In general, a CNN has a layered architecture consisting of 3 basic types of layers, that is, *convolution layer* (CL), *max pooling layer* (PL) and *fully connected layers* (FCL) for classification. CLs consist of a set of kernels that produce parameters and help in convolution operation. In CL, every kernel generates a feature map as an output. PLs do not have parameters but, their major role is to avoid possible data redundancies (still preserving their significance). In our approach, all CNNs have max-pooling operation at their corresponding PLs. In addition to these two different types of layers, FCL is used, where MLP has been in place.

In Fig. 2, a complete schematic block diagram of handwritten Indic script identification has been provided, showing different modules such as feature extraction/selection and identification. In our work, 10 separate CNNs are implemented to select features from a variety of representations of the studied image and we label each of them as $CNN_{d,x,y}$. In every $CNN_{d,x,y}$, d and x respectively refer to domain representation and dimension of the processed image, and y refers to the number of convolution and pooling layers in that particular CNN. For example, domain representation can be expressed as $d = \{s, f\}$, where s refers to spatial domain and f, frequency. In our case, either of these is taken into consideration. It is to be noted that, with the use of the *Haar wavelet transform* (HWT) (see Sect. 2.2), certain frequencies are removed. In case of dimension (x), we have $x = \{[32 \times 32], [48 \times 48], [128 \times 128]\}$, and for simplicity, $x = \{32, 48, 128\}$ is used. All of these dimensions signify resolution to which the input images are scaled. In case of CL and PL, $y = \{2, 3\}$: one of the two is taken in CNN, and $y = 2$ means that there are two pairs of convolutional and pooling layers in the CNNs. In our model, two broad CNN architectures: $CNN_{d,x,2}$ and $CNN_{d,x,3}$ are used and can be summarized as in Table 1.

1. $CNN_{d,x,2}$: We have six different layers, i.e. two CLs, two PLs and two FCLs. The first two CLs are followed by PLs. In FCLs, the first layer takes image representation that has been generated by CLs and PLs and reshapes them in the form of a vector, and the second FCL produces a set of 1024 features.
2. $CNN_{d,x,3}$: Every CNN has eight different layers: three CLs, three PLs and two FCLs. In general, such an architecture is very much similar to previously mentioned $CNN_{d,x,2}$. The difference lies in additional pair of CL and PL that follows second pair of the same. Like the $CNN_{d,x,2}$, these CNNs produce a set of 1024 features for any studied image.

Table 1. Architecture: $CNN_{d,x,y}$, where $y = \{2, 3\}$.

Architecture	Parameter	Layer								
		CL1	PL1	CL2	PL2	CL3	PL3	FCL1	FCL1	Softmax
$CNN_{d,x,2}$	Scale	32	32	64	64	–	–	1024	512	11
	Filter size	5×5	2 × 2	5 × 5	2 × 2	–	–	–	–	–
	Pad size	2	–	2	–	–	–	–	–	–
$CNN_{d,x,3}$	Scale	32	32	64	64	128	128	1024	512	11
	Filter size	7 × 7	2×2	5 × 5	2 × 2	3 × 3	2 × 2	–	–	–
	Pad size	3	–	2	–	1	–	–	–	–

Index
CL = convolutional layer, PL = pooling layer, FCL = fully connected layer

Once again, the architectural details of aforementioned CNNs are summarized in Table 1 that follows schematic block diagram of the system (see Fig. 2). For more understanding, in Fig. 3, we provide the activation maps for $CNN_{s,128,3}$.

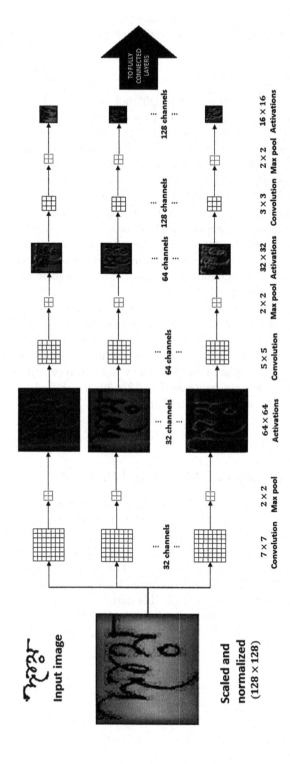

Fig. 3. Illustrating the activation maps for $CNN_{s,128,3}$: spatial domain image representation with the dimensionality of 128 and three-layered convolutional and pooling layers.

This means that it uses spatial domain image representation with the dimensionality of 128 and three pairs of convolutional and pooling layers in the CNNs.

2.2 Data Representation

In general, since Fourier transform [14] might not be appropriate for successful information extraction about what frequencies are present at which time, short time Fourier transform [9] and wavelet transform (WT) [1] are used to address this. Both of these help identify the frequency components present in any signal at any given time. WT, on the other hand, can provide dynamic resolution.

We consider an image a 2D time signal that can be resized. We then use multilevel 2D discrete WT on a scaled/resized image (128 × 128) to generate frequency domain representation. To be precise, we use the *Haar wavelet* [15] with seven different level decomposition that can generate approximated and detailed coefficients. Since the approximated coefficients are equivalent to zero, we use the detailed coefficients in addition to modified approximated coefficients to reconstruct the image. In the modified approximated coefficients, we consider only high frequency components.

In our method, using a variety of different WTs, such as the Daubechies [16] and several decomposition levels, the best results were observed with the Haar wavelet and a decomposition level of 7. This reconstructed image is further resized to 32 × 32 (x = 32) and 48 × 48 (x = 48), and are fed into multiple CNNs as mentioned in Sect. 2.1. Like in the frequency domain representation, spatial domain representations are resized/scaled to 32 × 32 (x = 32), 48 × 48 (x = 48) and 128 × 128 (x = 128) are fed into multiple CNNs.

3   Experiments

3.1   Dataset, and Evaluation Metrics and Protocol

To measure the robustness of our proposed method for word-level handwritten script recognition, we have considered the dataset named PHD_Indic_11 [7]. It is composed 11K scanned word images (grayscale) from 11 different Indic script, i.e. 1K per script. A few samples are shown in Fig. 4. For more information about dataset, we refer to recently reported work [7]. The primary reason behind considering PHD_Indic_11 dataset in our test is, no big size data has been reported in the literature for research purpose, till this date.

Using the exact same CNN representation as before, $C_{d,x,y}[i][j]$ represents the count where an instance with label i is classified as j. Accuracy of the particular CNN can then be computed as

$$\mathrm{acc}_{d,x,y} = \frac{\sum_{i=1}^{11} C_{d,x,y}[i][i]}{\sum_{i=1}^{11} \sum_{j=1}^{11} C_{d,x,y}[j][i]}.$$

Precision can be computed as

$$\text{prec}_{d,x,y} = \frac{\sum_{i=1}^{11} \text{prec}_{d,x,y}^i}{11} \text{ and } \text{prec}_{d,x,y}^i = \frac{C_{d,x,y}[i][i]}{\sum_{j=1}^{11} C_{d,x,y}[i][j]},$$

where $\text{prec}_{d,x,y}^i$ refers to precision for any i-th label. In a similar fashion, recall can be computed as

$$\text{rec}_{d,x,y} = \frac{\sum_{i=1}^{11} \text{rec}_{d,x,y}^i}{11} \text{ and } \text{rec}_{d,x,y}^i = \frac{C_{d,x,y}[i][i]}{\sum_{j=1}^{11} C_{d,x,y}[i][j]},$$

where $\text{rec.}_{d,x,y}^i$ refers to recall for any i-th label. Having both precision and recall, f-score can be computed as

$$\text{f-score}_{d,x,y} = \frac{\sum_{i=1}^{11} \text{f-score}_{d,x,y}^i}{11} \text{ and } \text{f-score}_{d,x,y}^i = 2 \times \frac{\text{prec}_{d,x,y}^i \times \text{rec}_{d,x,y}^i}{\text{prec}_{d,x,y}^i + \text{rec}_{d,x,y}^i}.$$

Following conventional 4:1, i.e. train:test evaluation protocol, we have 8.8K images for training and the 2.2K images for testing. We ran our experiments by using a machine: GTX 730 with 384 CUDA cores and 4 GB GPU RAM. Besides, it has Intel Pentium Core2Quad Q6600 and 4GB RAM.

3.2 Experimental Set up

As mentioned earlier, are are required to train the CNNs first before testing. In other words, it is important to see how training and testing have been performed.

Our CNNs in this study represented by $\text{CNN}_{d,x,y}$ are trained independently using the training dataset (as mentioned earlier). To clarify once again, these CNNs has either two or three pairs of consecutive convolutional and pooling layers. Besides, each of them has three fully connected layers. The first of these three layers function as an input layer with number of neurons that depends on the scale of the image specified by x. The next layer in CNNs has 1024 neurons, and during training, we apply a dropout probability of 0.5. The final layer has 11 neurons, whose outputs are used as input to an 11-way soft-max classifier that provides us with classification/identification probabilities for each of 11 possible classes. Our training set 8.8K word images are split into multiple batches of 50 word images and the CNNs are trained accordingly. For optimization, Adam optimizer [4] was used with learning rate of 1×10^{-3} having default parameters: $\beta_1 = 0.9$ and $\beta_2 = 0.999$. This helps apply gradients for loss to the weight parameters during back propagation. We computed the accuracy of the CNN as training proceeds by taking ratio of the of images successfully classified in the batch to the total number of input images in the processed batch.

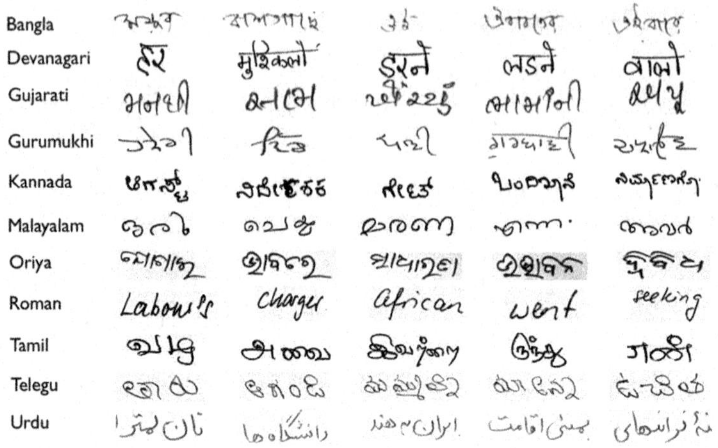

Fig. 4. Illustrating few samples from dataset named PHDIndic_11 used in our experiment.

After training CNNs 8.8K word images, we evaluated/tested each of them independently with the test set that is composed 2.2K word images.

More specifically, for each input size specification, we have two CNNs, i.e. for domain (d) and input size $(x \times x)$: $CNN_{d,x,2}$ and $CNN_{d,x,3}$. Altogether, we have 10 different CNNs since we have three different input sizes ($x = \{32, 48, 128\}$) for raw image and two different input sizes ($x = \{32, 48\}$) for wavelet transformed image/data. For better understanding, we refer readers to Fig. 2. Note that we have trained the CNNs to extract 1024 features from each one. Then, each of the 1024×1 dimensional CNN features are concatenated to form a single 10240×1 vector. Like in the conventional machine learning classification, these features are used for training and testing purpose using MLP classifier.

3.3 Our Results and Comparative Study

In this section, using dataset, and evaluation metrics (see Sect. 3.1), and experimental setup (see Sect. 3.2), we summarize our results and comparative study as follows:

1. We provide results that have been produced from different architectures (CNNs), and select the highest script identification rate from them; and
2. We then take highest script identification for a comparative study, where previous relevant works are considered.

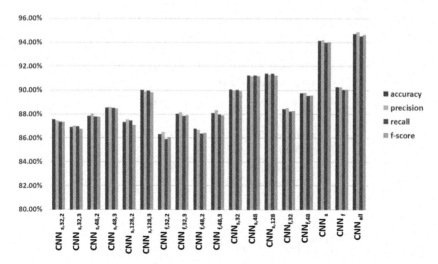

Fig. 5. Our results (in terms of accuracy, precision, recall and f-score) for all networks: CNNs and their possible combinations.

Our Results: Fig. 5 shows the comparison of the individual CNNs along with the effect of combining them. The individual $CNN_{d,x,y}$ produced the maximum script identification rate of 90% for $CNN_{s,128,3}$. As we ensemble two- and three-layered networks of corresponding domain (d) and input size (x), we observe a positive correlation between input size and accuracy. $CNN_{s,128}$ provides the maximum script identification rate of 91.41% in this category. The primary reason behind the increase in accuracy is that the ensemble of two- and three-layered networks suggests that these networks complement each other. Further, to study an effect of the spatial (s) and frequency (f) domain representation in $CNN_{d,x,y}$, we ensemble networks across all input sizes and depth of network. The spatial representation, CNN_s, have produced script identification rate of 94.14% and the frequency domain representation, CNN_f, have escalated up to 90.27%. However, the frequency domain representations learning can be complimented and it has been clearly seen when we combined them. In their combination, we have achieved the highest script identification rate of 94.73%. Since we have not received 100% script identification rate, it is wise to provide a few samples where our system failed to identify correctly (see Fig. 6).

Table 2. Comparative study.

Method	Accuracy
Obaidullah et al. [7] (Hand-crafted features)	91.00%
LeNet [6] (CNN)	82.00%
AlexNet [5] (CNN)	92.14%
Our method (Multiscale CNN + WT)	94.73%

Gurumukhi (Bangla)	Tamil (Devanagari)	Gurumukhi (Gujarati)
Bangla (Gurumukhi)	Bangla (Oriya)	Kannada (Tamil)

Fig. 6. Misclassified samples, where script names in the bracket are the actual scripts but, our system identified them incorrectly. For example, in the first case, word image has been identified as Gurumukhi and it actually is Bangla.

Like we have mentioned in Sect. 3.1, we also provide precision, recall and f-score for all architectures in Fig. 5. In what follows, the highest script identification rate, i.e. 94.73% will be taken for a comparison.

Comparative Study: For a fair comparison, widely used deep learning methods, such as LeNet [6] and AlexNet [5] were taken. In addition, recently reported work on 11 handwritten Indic script dataset [7] (including their baseline results) was considered. In Table 2, we summarize the results. Our comparative study is focused on accuracy (not, precision, recall and f-score), since other methods reported accuracy. Of course, in Fig. 5, we are not just limited to accuracy.

In Table 2, our method outperforms all other methods. Precisely, it outperforms Obaidullah et al. [7] by 4.7%, LeNet [6] by 2.73% and AlexNet [5] by 2.61%. We also observed that AlexNet requires higher hardware configuration (like GTX 1080).

4 Conclusion

In this paper, we have proposed a robust method that uses convolutional neural networks (CNNs) for multi scale feature extraction. In our method, in addition, to conventional spatial domain representation, we have used multilevel two dimensional discrete Haar wavelet transformation, where image representations have been interpolated to a variety of different sizes. Having these, several different CNNs have been used to select features. With this, eleven handwritten scripts, namely, Devnagari, Gurumukhi, Gujarati, Kannada, Oriya, Malayalam, Roman, Telugu, Tamil, Urdu, and Bangla, have been identified, where 1000 words per script are used. In our test, we have achieved the highest script identification accuracy of 94.73% using multi-layer perceptrons (MLP). To the best of our knowledge, this is the biggest data for Indic script identification work. Considering the size and complexity of the dataset, our method outperforms the previously reported techniques.

References

1. Daubechies, I.: The wavelet transform, time-frequency localization and signal analysis. IEEE Trans. Inf. Theory **36**(5), 961–1005 (1990)
2. Ghosh, D., Dube, T., Shivaprasad, A.: Script recognition – a review. IEEE Trans. Pattern Anal. Mach. Intell. **32**(12), 2142–2161 (2010)
3. Hangarge, M., Santosh, K., Pardeshi, R.: Directional discrete cosine transform for handwritten script identification. In: 2013 12th International Conference on Document Analysis and Recognition (ICDAR), pp. 344–348. IEEE (2013)
4. Kingma, D., Ba, J.: Adam: a method for stochastic optimization. arXiv preprint arXiv:1412.6980 (2014)
5. Krizhevsky, A., Sutskever, I., Hinton, G.E.: ImageNet classification with deep convolutional neural networks. In: Advances in Neural Information Processing Systems, pp. 1097–1105 (2012)
6. LeCun, Y., Bottou, L., Bengio, Y., Haffner, P.: Gradient-based learning applied to document recognition. Proc. IEEE **86**(11), 2278–2324 (1998)
7. Obaidullah, S.M., Halder, C., Santosh, K., Das, N., Roy, K.: Phdindic_11: page-level handwritten document image dataset of 11 official indic scripts for script identification. Multimed. Tools Appl. 1–36 (2017)
8. Pal, U., Jayadevan, R., Sharma, N.: Handwriting recognition in Indian regional scripts: a survey of offline techniques. ACM Trans. Asian Lang. Inf. Process. (TALIP) **11**(1), 1 (2012)
9. Portnoff, M.: Time-frequency representation of digital signals and systems based on short-time fourier analysis. IEEE Trans. Acoust. Speech Signal Process. **28**(1), 55–69 (1980)
10. Rani, R., Dhir, R., Lehal, G.S.: Script identification of pre-segmented multi-font characters and digits. In: 2013 12th International Conference on Document Analysis and Recognition (ICDAR), pp. 1150–1154. IEEE (2013)
11. Roy, S., Das, N., Kundu, M., Nasipuri, M.: Handwritten isolated Bangla compound character recognition: a new benchmark using a novel deep learning approach. Pattern Recogn. Lett. **90**, 15–21 (2017)

12. Sarkhel, R., Das, N., Das, A., Kundu, M., Nasipuri, M.: A multi-scale deep quadtree based feature extraction method for the recognition of isolated handwritten characters of popular indic scripts. Pattern Recogn. (2017)
13. Singh, P.K., Sarkar, R., Nasipuri, M., Doermann, D.: Word-level script identification for handwritten indic scripts. In: 2015 13th International Conference on Document Analysis and Recognition (ICDAR), pp. 1106–1110. IEEE (2015)
14. Smith, S.W., et al.: The scientist and engineer's guide to digital signal processing (1997)
15. Sundararajan, D.: Fundamentals of the discrete Haar wavelet transform (2011)
16. Vonesch, C., Blu, T., Unser, M.: Generalized Daubechies wavelet families. IEEE Trans. Signal Process. **55**(9), 4415–4429 (2007)

A Survey on Line Segmentation Techniques for Indic Scripts

Payel Rakshit[1]([⊠]), Chayan Halder[2], Sk. Md. Obaidullah[3], and Kaushik Roy[4]

[1] Department of Computer Science, Maheshtala College, B.B.T Road,
Kolkata 141, India
prmylife20@gmail.com
[2] Department of Computer Science and Engineering, University of Engineering
and Management, Kolkata 160, India
chayan.halderz@gmail.com
[3] Department of Computer Science and Engineering, Aliah University,
Kolkata 156, India
sk.obaidullah@gmail.com
[4] Department of Computer Science, West Bengal State University,
Kolkata 126, India
kaushik.mrg@gmail.com

Abstract. Optical Character Recognition (OCR) from handwritten documents is a very challenging task of document image processing (DIP). It composed of various crucial pre-processing steps, out of those, text line segmentation is the most essential which not only helps the process of character recognition but also non-trivial for tasks like word recognition, alignment of texts or images, authentication of specific fields and then extraction of those which are very useful application nowadays. In this paper, a short survey of the available methods on text line segmentation of handwritten documents is presented. Comparative study of different state-of-the-art methods is presented to provide a broad view of the current scenario of line segmentation in the area of DIP. It is our belief that potential researchers in this field will be benefited immensely by this survey.

Keywords: Line segmentation · Projection profile · Hough transform · Morphological · Smearing

1 Introduction

Line segmentation is generally considered as one of the prerequisite of OCR. Text line segmentation (TLS) techniques can be categorised into some certain number of categories based on their main methodologies. Mostly, horizontal projection and top-down projection based methods are used for their implementation simplicity but whenever the variation of skew angle is very high in document images, horizontal or top-down projection based methods are not suitable to segment the text lines [1]. Hough-based methods can handle only the documents where skew

© Springer Nature Singapore Pte Ltd. 2021
K. C. Santosh and B. Gawali (Eds.): RTIP2R 2020, CCIS 1380, pp. 511–522, 2021.
https://doi.org/10.1007/978-981-16-0507-9_43

angles varry between text lines, but whenever the skew varies along the width of the same text line, this method become failure. Piece-wise projections are suitable for both types of skew angle variations but has some limitations also. They are sensitive to the character size and successive word gaps [1]. These drawbacks influence the usefulness of smearing methods but smearing also not successful for every scenario which leads to use of hybrid methods [2].

The complexity of some scripts and limited availability of benchmark datasets are among the prime hindrances in this area of research. According to best of our knowledge there is scarcity of survey on line segmentation which covers Indic scripts, so, currently there is a pressing need for a survey in this area. As far as our knowledge there are very limited significant works of line segmentation are attempted by the researchers for scripts like Telugu, Tamil, etc.; but only one instance of TLS on handwritten historical MODI documents is available in literature [23]. Due to these reasons, in this paper a survey covering some of the line segmentation methods for Eastern (Bangla, Bangla-English mixed, Devanagari, and Oriya) and Southern Indic (Kannada, Gujarati) scripts are presented [27].

1.1 Challenges of Line Segmentation

TLS is one of the challenging aspects of building an OCR. The variability of interline distance and baseline skew of unconstrained handwritten text makes the line segmentation task more difficult than the printed one. Some challenging difficulties like variable character size, skew angle variation between text lines, skew angle along the same text lines, the existence of touching or overlapping text lines, variation of inter-line and inter-word distances, etc. one has to face for handwritten text-line segmentation [1]. In the case of Indic scripts, the scenario is more difficult as they contain several modified and compound characters. This paper presents a short survey of the existing line segmentation and extraction techniques that are proposed during the last decades and dedicated to handwritten text documents of Indic scripts. As the writing style of different writers highly varies from each other, various line segmentation techniques are developed for different scripts and languages depending on the writing properties.

2 Databases

Performance validation of any proposed line segmentation approach is very important as it will represent the robustness of that approach where publicly available standard databases play a crucial role. Some popular datasets with their ground truth data were already used for various line segmentation tasks directly. In this section some publicly available and widely used standard databases are given namely CMATERdb 1.1.1 [4], CMATERdb 1.2.1 [4], ICDAR2013 Handwriting Segmentation Contest Bangla database [3], and Kannada handwritten text database [5]. Details of these databases are provided in Table 1. Some samples of these databases are given in Fig. 1.

Table 1. Popular standard Indic Script datasets used for line segmentation

#	Dataset	Year	Images	Writers	Script/language
1	CMATERdb1.1.1 [4]	2012	100	40	Bangla
2	CMATERdb1.2.1 [4]	2012	50	40	Bangla-English mixed
3	ICDAR2013 Handwriting Segmentation Contest Bangla database [3]	2013	50	-	Bangla
4	Kannada handwritten text database (KHTD) [5]	2011	51	51	Kannada

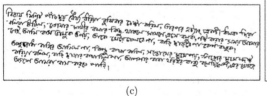

(a)	(b)
(c)	(d)

Fig. 1. Sample images of different standard databases (a) CMATERdb1.1.1, (b) CMA-TERdb1.2.1, (c) ICDAR2013 Handwriting Segmentation Contest Bangla database, (d) Kannada handwritten text database

3   Overview of Some State-of-the-Art Line Segmentation Techniques

Different heterogeneous TLS techniques for Indic Scripts are already reported in literature. Depending on the segmentation strategy the existing methods can be grouped into some categories namely (i) Projection profile based methods (ii) Hough transform based methods (iii) Smearing based methods (iv) Morphology based methods and (v) Hybrid approaches. In the following sections, brief descriptions of these types of existing methods on Indic scripts are discussed.

3.1   Projection Profile Based Methods

Projection Profiles are the simplest and most commonly used methods in the field of line segmentation. This method is broadly used for skew estimation, line segmentation and in many more applications. For line segmentation purpose this technique is especially used for printed documents and can be applied to handwritten documents with small overlapping. In case of handwritten documents this method gives a good result only for well separated text lines [8]. In the scenario of skew or medium variation of the text lines, the image may be segmented into vertical bands and profiles sought inside each band which is called piece-wise projection profile method [8].

In [6] Pal and Dutta presented a modified piece wise projection profile based method called Piece-wise Separating Lines (PSL) for Bangla unconstrained handwritten TLS. Here, they assumed the text documents in portrait mode and divided the documents into vertical stripes of a certain width. Depending on the text width and number of stripes, they calculated the width of the last stripe of the text. Then they computed PSL from each of these stripes and row-wise addition of all object pixels of a stripe. The row where the addition is 0 is a PSL. By identifying and joining the potential PSLs they obtained the text lines. In [7], Tripathy et al. developed a scheme for unconstrained Oriya text segmentation using water reservoir based concept and PSL. Sample PSLs and potential PSLs used in [6] are shown in Fig. 2.

3.2   Hough Transform Based Methods

In case of automated analysis of digital images, detection of the simple shapes like straight line, circle or ellipse, is a frequently arising problem. The Hough transform works by voting method of feature points in polar co-ordinate space of all potential lines going through it [10]. A line can be represented in an alternative way also. In case of vertical lines both m and c may be infinite. To eliminate this type of problem a line is represented using Cartesian coordinate form. The Hough transform performs the line to point transformation of Cartesian to polar coordinate space [9]. In [10], Saha et al. developed a Hough transform based technique for handwritten text line segmentation, especially for Bangla and English scripts. They applied Hough transform on the binarized edge map to generate the Hough image of it. Lines were extracted as a set of connected words of the image and then CCL algorithm was applied to segment the lines.

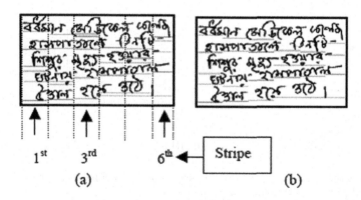

Fig. 2. (a) PSLs for Bangla text, (b) Potential PSLs for the same [6]

3.3 Smearing Based Methods

Alaei et al. [12] proposed a smearing based method called piece-wise painting algorithm (PPA) for unconstrained text line segmentation. A number of operations like dilation, trimming and thinning are also applied to segment the lines. Similarly, Malakar et al. [11] came up with a new idea of spiral run length smoothing algorithm (SRLSA) for multi script documents. Sometimes standard RLSA fails when the neighbouring data pixels do not lie along a particular horizontal or vertical line. Such pixels are spatially very near to each other and most of the cases may be a part of a single component. Due to high variation of different individuals this is a common scenario in handwritten documents. To overcome such limitations of traditional horizontal RLSA (HRLSA) (Fig. 3a) and vertical RLSA (VRLSA) (Fig. 3b) a new method is introduced called SRLSA (Fig. 3c). Each digitized document is partitioned into vertical fragments and SRLSA is used to identify the text line segments (TLSs) in each fragment. Finally the identified TLSs are merged in order to form the text lines.

3.4 Morphology Based Methods

Morphology based operations are a collection of non-linear operations that are dependent on the shape of an image. It is not dependent on their numerical values but only on comparative ordering of pixel values. For this reason, these operations are especially well suited for binary images. Generally morphological techniques explore an image with a small structure or template called a structuring element. There exist a lot of techniques of line segmentation based on morphological operations. In case of document image processing, morphological operations are mostly useful for line and multiple column detection, bold and italic words recognition in documents, images extraction, rule detection etc.

Roy et al. [13] came up with an idea using morphological operations especially erosion to extract background and foreground information of the images. After that they generated separator line (SL) between two consecutive lines and

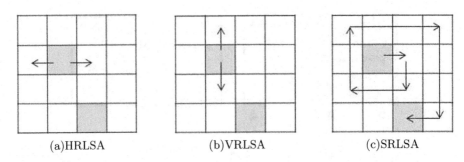

(a)HRLSA   (b)VRLSA   (c)SRLSA

Fig. 3. Different RLSAs for smearing of neighbouring pixel pairs (color shade indicates foreground pixels) [11] (Color figure online)

applied a smoothing operation to have the foreground seed components (FSC). SLs guide FSC joining to have the actual segmentation. In [14] Sarkar et al. proposed an idea of line extraction for multi scripts based on line contour estimation. At first the images are partitioned into vertical fragments and then the neighbouring line segments are analysed to place them inside the computed line boundary.

3.5   Hybrid and Other Methods

The hybrid schemes use the combination of bottom-up and top-down approaches to get better result [15]. The above mentioned methods are some of the most popularly and commonly used text line segmentation methods. Except all of these there exists a huge list of line segmentation methods based on some distinct way of implementation or some specific algorithms. Some of them may give a poor result but show some new ideas to do something creative in the field of line segmentation.

Basu et al. [16] came up with an idea for line extraction of multi-skewed handwritten documents for English and Bangla languages. The idea is based on hypothetical water flows, from both right and left sides of the image frame based on block covering. After that a set of morphological operations are applied for line segmentation. This approach is specially designed for overlapping and multi-touching components of handwritten documents. Kumar et al. [17] proposed a simple TLS for multi-script handwritten documents based on different intensity values whereas in [18], Dixit et al. [18] presented a TLS method for Kannada handwritings. The method is mainly based on computation of the standard error of the sampling distribution for the components in the image and used weighted bucketing algorithm to form a line segment. Mamatha et al. [19] came up with a segmentation approach for unconstrained handwritten Kannada scripts and for line segmentation they used Morphological operations and projection profile based approach. Oh et al. [20] proposed a handwritten documents TLS method based on baseline estimation and watershed. In [21], Zhang and Tan gave an idea of multi-language (including Bangla) handwritten

Table 2. An overview of all the discussed methods on Indic scripts

An overview of Projection profile based methods					
SI. No.	Author and year	Script / Language	Database used / volume of database	Methods applied	Result claimed
1	Pal and Datta (2003) [6]	Bangla language	1560 text lines	Vertical projection profile	35% of total lines=100%, 37% of total lines=99-100%, 19% of total lines=98-99%, 9% of total lines≤97%
2	Tripathy et al. (2004) [7]	Oriya Script	1627 text lines	Water reservoir concept-based scheme	60% of total lines=100%, 18% of total lines=97-99%, 22% of total lines < 97%
An overview of Hough transform based methods					
1	Saha et al. (2010) [10]	Bangla, English and mixed-script	Bangla documents(15) + English documents(15) + mixed-script documents(15) = 45 documents(812 lines)	Hough transform	Surveillance camera images (88%), business cards (94.6%) and document images (85.7%)
An overview of Smearing based methods					
1	Alaei et al. (2011) [12]	Bangla, Oriya, Persian, Greek, German, French, and English	Three databases: i) English + German + French + Greek = 152 handwritten text documents (3382 lines); ii) ICDAR2009 handwriting segmentation contest database of 200 images (4034 lines); iii) Bangla + Oriya + Persian = 78 handwritten text documents (1044 lines)	Piece-wise painting algorithm (PPA)	For 152 text pages: i) DR=95.70%, RA=95.17%, TLDM =95.43% ii) DR =98.35%, RA=98.76%, TLDM =98.55% iii) DR=95.87%, RA=94.34%, TLDM =95.10%

(*continued*)

Table 2. (*continued*)

SI. No.	Author and year	Script / Language	Database used / volume of database	Methods applied	Result claimed
2	Malakar et al.(2012) [11]	Multi-scripts	CMATERdb 1.1.1 (written in Bangla script and contains 2207 text lines) CMATERdb 1.2.1 (Bangla + English mixed contains 1240 lines)	Spiral run length smearing algorithm	87.09% and 89.35% respectively for two databases
An overview of Morphology based methods					
1	Roy et al.(2008) [13]	Multiscripts (Bangla, Devanagari, English, Oriya and Gujarati)	125 document images (Bangla text lines 520, Devanagari(195 lines), English text lines 406, Oriya text lines 210 and Gujrati text lines 115)	Morphological operation and run-length smearing algorithm (RLSA)	Overall 92.68%, Bangla 94.23%, Devanagari 93.33%, English 96.06%, Oriya 94.76% and Gujrati 93.04%
2	Sarkar et al. (2012) [14]	Multiscripts	CMATERdb 1.2.1 (1240 lines)	Based on line contour estimation	88.44%
An overview of Hybrid and Other Methods					
1	Basu et al. (2008) [16]	English and Bangla	printed text(360 lines), handwritten text(1191 lines)	Morphological operation and Hypothetical water flow	Bangla 90.34% and English 91.44%
2	D. Brodic (2011) [25]	Multiscript (Latin, Serbian Cyrillic, Glagolitic, and Bangla)	Various multiscript text samples	extended binary classification	Algo1: precision= 33%, recall= 100% , f-measure= 49% Algo2: precision= 33%, recall= 100%, f-measure= 49%,

(*continued*)

Table 2. (*continued*)

SI. No.	Author and year	Script / Language	Database used / volume of database	Methods applied	Result claimed
3	Kumar et al. (2012) [17]	Kannada, English, Devanagari and Arabic scripts	500 documents (Kannada-150, English-200, Hindi-100 and Arabic-50)	Hybrid Approach	98%
4	Dixit et al. (2012) [18]	handwritten script document images for Kannada language	80 Kannada handwritten scripts	Hybrid Approach	98.12%
5	Oh et al. (2014) [20]	Different handwritten text images	ICDAR database 2009 (100 documents)	Baseline estimation and watershed	97%
6	Zhang and Tan (2014) [21]	Greek, English and Bangla	ICDAR2013 Handwritten Segmentation Contest dataset	Seam carving	DR(%)= 98.34, RA(%)= 98.49, FM(%)= 98.41
7	Mamatha et al. (2012)[19]	Kannada	100 document pages	Morphological operations and projection profile based approach	94.50%
8	Biswas et al. (2017) [24]	Bangla	ICDAR 2013 Handwriting Segmentation Contest dataset	Strip based	97.99%
9	Mullick et al. (2015) [22]	Bangla	ICDAR 2013 Handwriting Segmentation Contest dataset	Hybrid Approach	DR=93.16%, RA=92.32%, FM=92.74%
10	Rakshit et al. (2018) [26]	Bangla	50 document images	Hybrid Approach	90.46%

** DR=Detection Rate, RA=Recognition Accuracy, FM=F-Measure, TLDM=Text Line Detection Metric

TLS based on constrained seam carving. Mullick et al. [22] presented a hybrid approach for line segmentation of handwritten document images. The proposed method combined smudging, blurring, shredding, thinning etc. to obtain the line segmentation output. Biswas et al. [24] proposed a strip based TLS method for handwritten Bangla text. This method also performs efficiently for English and Devanagari handwritten documents. Brodic [25] gave an idea on evaluation of algorithms for TLS based on extended binary classification. In the following Table 2, a summarization of all the discussed methods of line segmentation on Indic scripts is provided.

4   Conclusion and Future Scopes

In this paper, summarised state-of-the-art methodologies of line segmentation on different Indic scripts are described. The studied taxonomy contains four major types listed as: projection-based, Hough-based, smearing based and morphology based. Analysing these methods, it is found that only a single approach sometimes fails to deliver the expected line segmentation accuracy for which recent study shows researchers are more interested to combine two or more techniques to form Hybrid methods which are more capable in this respect. The study also shows that, quality researches on Devanagari, Gurumukhi, Southern Indic scripts like Tamil, Telugu, Malayalam, etc. are very thin. So, there is a pressing need to work on line, word and character segmentation on these Indic scripts. The lack of standard databases with proper ground truth data of Indic scripts is one of the prime bottlenecks for quality research in this area. In future, we plan to present a complete literature study of the line segmentation methods available on Indic and non-Indic scripts along with the available standard databases which will help the research community to understand the potential area of research in this respect. Also, in future, we will make the database of Halder et al. [28] publicly available to the research community with the ground truth data for this kind of research.

References

1. Yin, F., Liu, C.L.: A variational Bayes method for handwritten text line segmentation. In: Proceedings of 10th International Conference on Document Analysis and Recognition, pp. 436–440 (2009)
2. Yin, F., Liu, C.L.: Handwritten text line segmentation by clustering with distance metric learning. In: Proceedings of International Conference Frontiers in Handwriting Recognition (ICFHR), pp. 229–234 (2008)
3. Stamatopoulos, N., Gatos, B., Louloudis, G., Pal, U., Alaei, A.: ICDAR 2013 handwriting segmentation contest. In: International Conference on Document Analysis and Recognition (ICDAR), pp. 1402–1406 (2013)
4. Sarkar, R., Das, N., Basu, S., Kundu, M., Nasipuri, M., Basu, D.K.: CMATERdb1: a database of unconstrained handwritten Bangla and Bangla-English mixed script document image. Int. J. Doc. Anal. Recognit. 15(1), 71–83 (2012)

5. Alaei, A., Nagabhushan, P., Pal, U.: A benchmark Kannada handwritten document dataset and its segmentation, pp. 141–145 (2011)
6. Pal, U., Datta, S.: Segmentation of Bangla unconstrained handwritten text. In: Proceedings of the 7th International Conference on Document Analysis and Recognition, pp. 1128–1132 (2003)
7. Tripathy, N., Pal, U.: Handwriting segmentation of unconstrained Oriya text. In: International Workshop on Frontiers in Handwriting Recognition, pp. 306–311 (2004)
8. Arivazhagan, M., Srinivasan, H., Srihari, S.: A statistical approach to line segmentation in handwritten documents. In: Proceedings of Document Recognition and Retrieval XIV, pp. 1–11. SPIE (2007)
9. Sulem, L.L., Hanimyan, A., Faure, C.: A hough based algorithm for extracting text lines in handwritten document. In: Proceedings of International Conference on Document Analysis and Recognition (ICDAR), pp. 774–777 (1995)
10. Saha, S., Basu, S., Nasipuri, M., Basu, D.K.: A Hough transform based technique for text segmentation. J. Comput. **2**(2), 134–141 (2010)
11. Malakar, S., Halder, S., Sarkar, R., Das, N., Basu, S., Nasipuri, M.: Text line extraction from handwritten document pages using spiral run length smearing algorithm. In: Proceedings of Communications, Devices and Intelligent Systems (CODIS), pp. 616–619 (2012)
12. Alireza, A., Pal, U., Nagabhushan, P.: A new scheme for unconstrained handwritten text-line segmentation. Pattern Recognit. **44**(4), 917–928 (2011)
13. Roy, P.P., Pal, U., Llados, J.: Morphology based handwritten line segmentation using foreground and background information. In: Proceedings of International Conference on Frontiers in Handwriting Recognition (ICFHR 2008), pp. 241–246 (2008)
14. Sarkar, R., Halder, S., Malakar, S., Das, N., Basu, S., Nasipuri, M.: Text line extraction from handwritten document pages based on line contour estimation. In: Proceedings of the 3rd ICCCNT, pp. 26–28 (2012)
15. Ouwayed, N., Belaïd, A.: A general approach for multioriented text line extraction of handwritten documents. Int. J. Doc. Anal. Recognit. **15**(4), 297–314 (2012)
16. Basu, S., Chaudhuri, C., Kundu, M., Nasipuri, M., Basu, D.K.: Text line extraction from multi-skewed handwritten documents. Pattern Recognit. **40**(6), 1825–1839 (2007)
17. Ravi Kumar, M., Pradeep, R., Puneeth Kumar, B.S., Babu, P.: A simple text-line segmentation method for handwritten documents. In: IJCA Proceedings on National Conference on Advanced Computing and Communications (NCACC), pp. 46–61 (2012)
18. Dixit, A.S., Ranjitha, B.S., Suresh, C.H.N.: Segmentation of handwritten Kannada text document through computation of standard error and weighted bucket algorithm. Int. J. Adv. Comput. Technol. (IJACT) **3**(2), 55–62 (2012)
19. Mamatha, H.R., Srikantamurthy, K.: Morphological operations and projection profiles based segmentation of handwritten Kannada document. Int. J. Appl. Inf. Syst. (IJAIS) **4**(5), 13–19 (2013)
20. Oh, K., Kim, S.H., Na, I., Kim, G.: Text line segmentation using AHTC and watershed algorithm for handwritten document images. Int. J. Contents **10**, 35–40 (2014)
21. Zhang, X., Tan, C.L.: Text line segmentation for handwritten documents using constrained seam carving. In: Proceedings of 14th International Conference on Frontless in Handwriting Recognition (ICFHR), pp. 98–103 (2014)

22. Mullick, K., Banerjee, S., Bhattecharya, U.: An efficient line segmentation approach for handwritten Bangla document image. In: Eighth International Conference on Advances in Pattern Recognition (ICAPR), pp. 1–6 (2015)
23. Kulkarni, S., Prashant, L., Manza, R., Yannawar, P.: Text line segmentation of handwritten historical MODI documents. Int. J. Inf. Commun. Comput. Technol. **5**, 285 (2017)
24. Biswas, B., Bhattacharya, U., Chaudhuri, B.B.: A robust scheme for extraction of text lines from handwritten documents. In: Proceedings of International Conference on Computer Vision and Image Processing, CVIP 2016, pp. 107–116 (2017)
25. Brodic, D.: Methodology for the evaluation of the algorithms for text line segmentation based on extended binary classification. Meas. Sci. Rev. **11**(3), 71–78 (2011)
26. Rakshit, P., Halder, C., Ghosh, S., Roy, K.: Line, word, and character segmentation from Bangla handwritten text—a precursor toward Bangla HOCR. In: Chaki, R., Cortesi, A., Saeed, K., Chaki, N. (eds.) Advanced Computing and Systems for Security. AISC, vol. 666, pp. 109–120. Springer, Singapore (2018). https://doi.org/10.1007/978-981-10-8180-4_7
27. Obaidullah, S.M., Halder, C., Santosh, K.C., Das, N., Roy, K.: PHDIndic_11: page-level handwritten document image dataset of 11 official Indic scripts for script identification. Multimed. Tools Appl. **77**(2), 1643–1678 (2018)
28. Halder, C., Obaidullah, S.M., Santosh, K.C., Roy, K.: Content independent writer identification on Bangla script: a document level approach. Int. J. Pattern Recognit. Artif. Intell. **32**(9), 1856011 (2018)

Peruse and Recognition of Old Kannada Stone Inscription Characters

C. M. Nrupatunga[1](✉) and K. L. Arunkumar[2]

[1] Department of CIE, Jawaharlal Nehru National College of Engineering,
Shimoga, Karnataka, India
nrupatunga@jnnce.ac.in
[2] Department of MCA, Jawaharlal Nehru National College of Engineering,
Shimoga, Karnataka, India
arunkumarkl@jnnce.ac.in

Abstract. Karnataka is known for its tradition, culture, literature and ritual knowledge abundant in our historical documents in the form of inscription. Identify and recognizing the ancient Kannada inscription characters allows archaeologists made to disclose the historical events done in ancient Karnataka history and literature work done by Kannada ancient poets. The wastefulness of this manual procedure will unfavourably influence on the future research in the field of archaeological office. To overcome from all these negative impact, an venture made by utilizing the computerized version technique and procedure system to perceive and peruse the stone engravings having old Kannada words. Regular methodologies of manual procedure requires enormous amount of time and energy. This research method has easy way to digitalization of stone engraving characters using normal camera of our mobile phone. System utilized in this research is straightforward and viable in expelling the noise and perceive the words present in inscription in various condition disorder as follows, blurred, destroyed, shaded with dust and unprotected old stone inscriptions.

Keywords: Kannada stone inscription · Digitalization · Faster R-CNN · Stone engraving characters

1 Introduction

The name Shivamogga is gotten from the word 'Shiva-mukha'. Another historical underpinnings is the 'sweet-mogge' (sweet bud), which progressed toward becoming 'Shimoga'. Samrat was the southernmost purpose of Asoka's Mauryan domain in the seventh century. The locale was administered by a few administrations in the next hundreds of years: the Kadambas in the fifth century, the Chalukyas in the fifth century and the Gangas in their fifth century, the Rashtrakutas in the sixth century, the Hoysalas in the sixth century, and the Vijayanagara rulers in the ninth century. Shimoga was a free town during the

© Springer Nature Singapore Pte Ltd. 2021
K. C. Santosh and B. Gawali (Eds.): RTIP2R 2020, CCIS 1380, pp. 523–529, 2021.
https://doi.org/10.1007/978-981-16-0507-9_44

seventh century under the standard of the lower heads. Shimoga was a piece of Mysore State until the autonomy of India after the seventh century.

Many inscriptions are found in Shimoga Districts having lot of information's about the ancient literature, history of kingdom, administration details of kingdom and so on. Exhibiting the contents present in these inscriptions will be exceptionally valuable significant to make research about the historical scenery of Shivamogga. Right now the contents present in these inscriptions lines are changed over into current kannada language manually by an archaeological exploration masters. This physically technique would be more tedious.

In spite of the way that the old Kannada Inscriptions are utilized as a one of the collection of data which act as a prestigious resources to study the development in our kannada language, perceiving the substance present in all the engraving turns into an immense test because of different reasons. They might be harmed or potentially in part eradicated. Absence of specific information and absence of accessible assets for engraving perusing are additionally another serious issue. As of now, the current pale history specialists need to end over to peruse engravings. Further they additionally need to perceive the characters of all these inscriptions characters engravings physically. The fundamental point of this research involves recognize and perceive the each remote outlying character set of all these kannada inscriptions by utilizing the accepted way of character recognition process and perceive process then plot them into current universal words of kannada language.

1.1 Research Objectives

The mentioned below points contains our research destinations:

1. Database creation of Kannada inscriptions found in and around Shivamogga.
2. Primarily capture the stone inscriptions images using normal camera or mobile camera.
3. Recognize the old individual characters of inscriptions and computerize them.
4. Converting the old character recognized with current words of Kannada character.
5. Fetch the Kannada language inscriptions through character recognition features.

2   Related Work

As indicated by the report prepared at Root Web. Ancestry.com regarding Alternative Unconventional Gravestones Studying Method (2015) Hand Rubbing takes conceivable to consistently shaded stone exterior. Particular one needs broom engravings outside layer delicately engraving through hand, particularly elevate light residue, leaves recessed engraving dull shading. Further technique through utilizing mirroring to coordinate brilliant daylight corner to corner over the essence of a tombstone with the goal that it can without much of a stretch cast shadow endanger in spaces. Particular flow engravings significantly additional obvious allows simple peruse. Further methodology includes utilizing a review tube arranged opposite stone to anticipate light entering afterward finish of the cylinder contacting stone marginally in this manner, compact brightness enters afterward sees engraving far side cylinder. Anyway right now scientists give a lot of consideration on modernizing the character acknowledgment undertaking to accomplish more proficiency and accommodation.

Publications focus on OCR are Niranjan P (2015), Nikhi P, Jayakumar, kolkure (2015) Yasser Alginahi (2004) discussed about optical character recognition procedure altogether advanced technologies in their artful research papers. Hubert Maraa, Jann Hering and Susanne Kromoker (2014) utilize procedure involved Optical Character Recognition (OCR) in their experimental examination peruse the old traditional chinese writings includes cut into stones. A computerized framework created purpose handling old chinese engravings. Luke V Rasmussenn, Peggy L Peissing, Catharine A MccCarty, Justina Starren (2012) conducted experimental activities create optical character acknowledgment channel handles manually written structure sphere referred electronic wellbeing record (EHR). Examination process done under two fundamental stages. Initial centred around planning structures to catch hand-printed information explicitly for OCR handling. Second one has used specially created OCR motors to play out the penmanship acknowledgment.

3 Proposed Algorithm

The proposed algorithm flow will be as follows:

1. Ganga's and Hoysala's period Kannada words database creation.
2. Input image: Capturing the Kannada Stone inscriptions pictures by utilizing normal digitalized camera.
3. Letter identification: Four letters are identified from the input image.
4. Extracted letters: Features of the extracted letters are identified and stored in the database.
5. Root mean square deviation and sum of absolute difference algorithm.

Step 1. Here, Hoysalas and Ganga periods stone inscriptions are captured around Thirthahalli which takes 60 KM from Shivamogga are captured Part of pictures of old Kannada engravings are caught and chose just 2 critical Hoysalas, Gangas stone engravings to get better acknowledgment. Chosen caught Hoysalas and Gangas period engravings demonstrated as follows:

Step 2. Pre-processing

1. To unclear the and to move out the pictures has been done using Gaussian filtering methodology. Through single measurement, the Gaussian's capacity [1,2] is as (Figs. 1 and 2)

$$G(x) = (1/(Sqrt(2pie * sigma)))e(x^2/sigma^2) \tag{1}$$

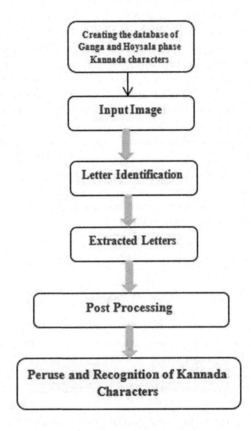

Fig. 1. Showing proposed methodology.

Fig. 2. 12th century inscription

2. Picture Edge identification: Sobel's edge identification system utilized also Sobel's ascertains most extreme angle of picture and it perform smoothing of picture, in the event that picture is smooth, at that point the data found in that can without much of a stretch concentrate [3,4].

3. Morphological operations: The edge recognized picture is extremely dainty so widening pursued by disintegration having performance called opening [5,6], which builds edge thickness recognized picture, expansion joins between listed comparable pixels along with disintegration execute ABB.

4. Words Rebuilding: Picture opened hold particular disturbed outskirt afterwards fringe recreated through filling gaps [7,8]. Recreation procedure to building a picture through pixel filling into splintered outskirt, all these reproduction significant to words acknowledgment [9,10].

4 Results

1. Database created of Hoysala and Ganga period. 2. Test the picture captured Catch some Hoysala's and Ganga's old stone engravings characters have a place with utilizing 16 MP customary computerized camera appeared in below Fig. 3:

Fig. 3. Trial out the picture.

3. Characters selection: In this step character selection is done based on the requirement.

Current proposed work few characters of the 12th century stone inscription is selected. 4. Pre-processing: The pre-processing is performed on the selected characters for segmentation of the character. Shown in Figs. 4 and 5.

Fig. 4. Particular word recognition in stone engravings

Fig. 5. Picture pre-processed.

5   Conclusion

Current work novel strategy for old ancient kannada words acknowledgment created. The method contains simple helpful identification strategy to recognize ancient kannada words. Digitalization of ancient Kannada engravings performed causes typical client to know about current Kannada literature work done. Created product tried alongwith picked words alongwith informational indexes. Outcome accomplished productive alongwith 98.75% exactness.

References

1. Lowe, D.G.: Distinctive image features from scale-invariant keypoints. Int. J. Comput. Vis. **60**, 91–110 (2004). Computer Science Department University of British Columbia Vancouver, B.C., Canada
2. Kumar, V.D.A., Ramakrishnan, M.: A comparative study of fuzzy evolutionary techniques for footprint recognition and performance improvement using wavelet-based fuzzy neural network. Int. J. Comput. Appl. Technol. **48**, 95–105 (2013)
3. Root Web: Alternative Gravestone Reading Methods (2015). http://www.rootsweb.ancestry.com
4. Niranjan, P.: Literature review of segmentation problems in nepali optical character recognition. Project Report, Masters of Technology in Information Technology, Department of Computer Science and Engineering, Kathmandu University (2015)

5. Nikhi, P., Jayakumar, V., Kolkure, S.: Optical character recognition: an encompassing review (2015). http://esatjournals.net/ijret/2015v04/i01/IJRET20150401062.pdf

6. Yasser, A.: Preprocessing techniques in character recognition (2015). http://cdn.intechopen.com/pdfs/11405.pdf

7. Hubert, M., Hering, J., Kromker, S.: GPU based optical character transcription for ancient inscription recognition (2014). https://www.researchgate.net/publication/224610728

8. Rasmussen, L.V., Peissig, P.L., McCarty, C.A., Starren, J.: Development of an optical character recognition pipeline for handwritten form fields from an electronic health record (2012). http://www.ncbi.nlm.nih.gov/pmc/articles/PMC3392858/

9. Safronov, K., et al.: Optical character recognition using optimisation algorithms. In: Proceedings of the 9th International Workshop on Computer Science and Information Technologies, CSIT 2007, Ufa, Russia (2007)

10. Kala, R.: Offline handwriting recognition using genetic algorithm. IJCSI Int. J. Comput. Sci. Issues **7**,(2), No I (2010)

Emotion Recognition Using Standard Deviation and Pitch as a Feature in a Marathi Emotional Utterances

Ashok R. Shinde[1]([⊠]), Shriram D. Raut[1], Prashant P. Agnihotri[2],
and Prakash B. Khanale[3]

[1] Punyashlok Ahilyadevi Holkar Solapur University, Solapur, India
arshinde@sus.ac.in
[2] Sub-Centre Latur, Swami Ramanand Teerth University, Peth, India
[3] Dnyanopasak College, Parbhani, India

Abstract. Emotion recognition plays a very important role to make the human-computer interaction more natural. Basically two approaches were used by various researchers i.e. by using facial expression and tone of the voice. In this proposed work speech utterances in Marathi language are used. Seven basic emotions of human beings like angry, happy, disgust, surprise, sad, neutral, and fear have been used in the experimental work. The Marathi emotional words like Gap re (गपरे), Are wa (अरेवा!), Are Deva (अरेदेवा) are used as speech samples for feature extraction. The standard deviation and pitch of voice were determined using PRAAT software. Three speech samples have been used angry and neutral emotion. The Four speech samples have been used for remaining emotions i.e. happy, disgust, surprise, sad and fear. By analysing the feature value of standard deviation 100% recognition accuracy rate obtained for happy, disgust and surprise emotion. 75% accuracy rate for sad & fear and 66.66% accuracy rate for angry and & neutral emotion. The average recognition accuracy rate of seven emotions is 90%.

Keywords: Emotion recognition · SER · HCI

1 Introduction

Emotion recognition is very important research domain to make more natural communication between human and computer. Speech Emotion Recognition (SER) is also very growing research topic in the Human Computer Interaction (HCI). To make human-computer interaction more natural, it would be beneficial to give computers the ability to recognize emotional state the same way as human does. Speech or tone of the voice is considered as a powerful approach to communicate with intention and emotion. Many researchers have proposed important speech features which contain emotion information, such as energy, pitch, formant frequency, Linear Prediction Cepstrum Coefficients (LPCC) [1]. The experimental results specifies that the feature combination of MFCC and MS has the highest accuracy rate on both Spanish emotional database using RNN classifier 90.05% and Berlin emotional database using MLR 82.41% [2, 3]. Speech is one of the most natural communications between human beings. Humans

© Springer Nature Singapore Pte Ltd. 2021
K. C. Santosh and B. Gawali (Eds.): RTIP2R 2020, CCIS 1380, pp. 530–539, 2021.
https://doi.org/10.1007/978-981-16-0507-9_45

also express their emotion via written or spoken languages. Speech emotion is an important role to express the feeling of one's expression [4].

2 Literature Review

Oh-Wook Kwon et al. 2003 [5], author has discussed the motions recognition by speech in one of the broad research area for Human Computer Interaction (HCI) or affective computing. The major problem in emotion recognition is that there is no common database for it. So that researchers cannot take the previous results for future work. Performance of emotion recognition depends on how we can extract the relevant features invariant to speaker, language and contents.

Author extracted the base features for each frame and formal feature streams by adding velocity acceleration components. For emotion recognition log energy, formant coefficients used as base features. The pitch and energy plays an important role in recognition of emotions.

S. Lalitha et al. 2014 [6], in this paper author has considered 7 emotions for his experiment. He has used pitch and prosody as features. SVM Classifier has been used for classifying the emotions. Berlin emotional database is chosen for the task. He got 81% recognition rate for emotions.

Nobuo Sato et al. 2007 [7], in this paper author discussed that emotion recognition algorithms using prosodic features are not sufficiently accurate. Hence they focused on the phonetic features of speech for emotion recognition. They focus on the classification of MFCC feature vectors, rather than their dynamic nature over an utterance. In the experimental work they got 66.4% recognition accuracy in speaker-independent emotion recognition experiments for specific emotions. This recognition accuracy is higher than the accuracy obtained by the conventional prosody-based and MFCC-based emotion recognition algorithms. In the experiment only four emotions have been considered i.e. anger, neutral, sadness and happiness.

3 Speech Database Used for Emotion Recognition

Two emotional speech databases are available as a standard for emotion recognition i.e. Berlin and Spanish database. The Berlin speech database is frequently used in emotion recognition. These databases contain total 535 utterances spoken by 10 actors (5 female and 5 males) in 7 simulated emotions (anger, fear, boredom, sadness, joy and neutral).

The second speech database is Spanish emotional database which contains utterances from two professional actors (one male and one female). These databases recorded for six emotions i.e. anger, joy, fear, sadness, surprise, disgust and normal. This database contains total 4528 utterances [1].

4 About Marathi Emotional Speech Database

We have developed a speech database in Marathi language. This is the regional language (Mother tongue) of Maharashtra state. To express different emotions by using Marathi words (Verbal communication i.e. speech), we have considered most common Marathi words which is strongly used to express the exact emotion of human being. For development of these database total 50 speakers we have considered (age between 20 to 45 years). Total 25 Male speaker and 25 Female speakers has recorded their Marathi speech samples in closed computer Lab to reduce noise, for noise free recording.

In the proposed paper, we have developed s speech database in Marathi language. In Marathi language there are various words and phrases are available which can be useful for recognizing human emotions. The emotions such as happy, angry, sad, surprise, fear, disgust and neutral are the basic emotions. The words in Marathi such as "Aare Deva" (Oh God!), "Kiti Chan" (How Good!) are used to express human emotions. While developing this database, we have considered four words/phrases of each emotion as shown in Tables 1 and 2.

Table 1. Four Marathi emotional words/phrases (for **Happy** emotion)

Sr_No	Words/phrases in Marathi	Meaning in English	Written in Devanagari Word-net
1	Are Wa	Great!	अरेवा!
2	Kitti Chan	How good!	कितीछान
3	Kitti God	How nice!	कितीगोड!
4	Mast	Superb!	मसत!

Table 2. Four Marathi emotional words/phrases (for **Angry** emotion)

Sr_No	Words/phrases in Marathi	Meaning in English	Written in Devanagari Word-net
1	Gap Re	Don't talk	• गपरे
2	Hat	Shut up	हट!
3	Nakoch mala	Don't need!	नकोचमला!
4	Chal Nigh	Gate out	चलनिघ!

5 Feature Extraction

The prosodic features are known as the primary indicator of the speakers emotional states. Speech indicates that pitch, energy, duration, formant, Melfrequeny cepstrum coefficient (MFCC), and Linear prediction cepstrum coefficient (LPCC) are the important features. With the different emotional state, corresponding changes occurs in the speak rate, pitch, energy, and spectrum. Typically anger has a higher mean value and variance of pitch and mean value of energy [9]. Therefore statistical features like mean and standard deviation these values plays very important role in finding specific emotion.

The basic features of speech like standard deviations and pitch are extracted in this proposed work. The standard deviation is similar to the average deviation, except the averaging is done with power instead of amplitude. This can be done by squaring each of the deviations before taking the average. To finish, the square root is taken to compensate for the initial squaring. Mathematically standard deviation is calculated as:

$$\sigma^2 = \frac{1}{N-1} \sum_{i=0}^{N-1} (x_i - \mu)^2 \tag{1}$$

The calculation of the standard deviation of a signal. The signal is stored in x_i, μ is the mean found from the mean equation, N is the number of samples, and σ is the standard deviation.

In the different notation:

$$\sigma = sqrt((x_0 - \mu)^2 + \ldots + (x_{N-1} - \mu)^2 / (N-1))^2 \tag{2}$$

Notice that the average is carried out by dividing by $N - 1$ instead of N. The tearm σ^2 occurs frequently in statistics and s given the name variance. The standard deviation is a measure of how far the signal fluctuates from the mean. The variance represents the power of this fluctuation. The second term is rms (root-mean-square) value, frequenctly used in electronics. By definition, the standard deviation only measures the AC portion of a signal, while the rms value measures both the AC and DC components. If a signal has no DC component, its rms value is identical to its standard deviation. Following figure shows the relationships between the standard deviation and the peak-to-peak value of several common waveforms (Fig. 1).

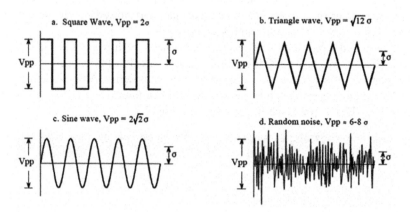

Fig. 1. Ratio of the peak-to-peak amplitude to the standard deviation for several common waveforms

On the other hand pitch as a feature of speech is considered. Speech signal can be divided into voiced, unvoiced and silence regions. The near periodic vibration of vocal folds is excitation for the production of voiced speech. The random region like excitation is present for unvoiced speech. There is no excitation during silence region. Mainly of speech regions are voiced in nature that includes vowels, semivowels and other voiced components. The voiced regions appear like a near periodic signal in the time domain representation. In a short term, we may consider the voiced speech segments to be periodic for all practical analysis and processing. The periodicity related with such regions is defined as 'pitch period T_0' in the time domain and 'Pitch frequency or Fundamental Frequency F_0' in the frequency domain. Unless specified, the term 'pitch' refers to the fundamental frequency 'F_0'. Pitch is an main attribute of voiced speech. It contains speaker-specific information. It is also necessary for speech coding task. Thus evaluation of pitch is one of the important issues in speech processing.

There are a great set of methods that have been developed in the speech processing part for the estimation of pitch. Among them the three mostly used methods include, autocorrelation of speech, cepstrum pitch determination and single inverse technique (SIFT) pitch estimation. One success of these methods is due to the participation of simple steps for the estimation of pitch. Even though autocorrelation method is of hypothetical interest, it create a frame work for SIFT methods.

6 Methodology

In this proposed work Marathi emotional database are used for experimental purpose. Total 26 utterances are considered for feature extraction. Mainly in this work standard deviation is taken as a major feature and pitch of the tone is taken as a supportive feature where some of the values of standard deviation are mixed or matches with more than one emotion while classification or comparison.

The proposed work starts with reading emotional speech words like Gap re (गापरे), Are wa (अरेवा!), Are Deva (अरेदेवा) etc. In Praat software. Praat is an open-software tool for the analysis of speech in phonetics. Firstly by considering Analyse periodicity in which by selecting to pitch option we have to set Pitch floor (Hz) as 75.0 and 600.0 as Pitch ceiling (Hz) as per given in the following Fig. 2.

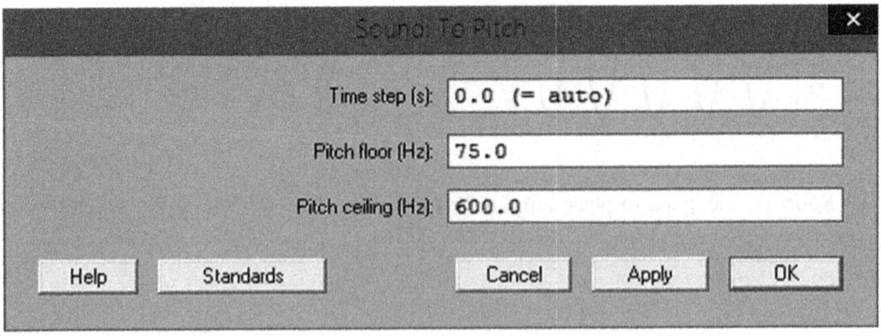

Fig. 2. Shows pitch for given speech sample

After setting these values by using query option we can get the standard deviation and pitch of selected speech file. To get standard deviation and pitch of speech, select only voice portion of speech as per shown in the following figure in pink color shade. Then use pitch info from query menu to get standard deviation and pitch of the speech which is given in the following figure in highlighted portion (Figs. 3 and 4).

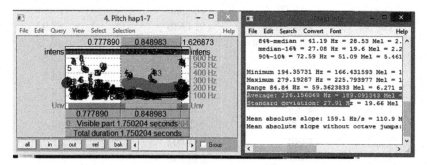

Fig. 3. Shows the standard deviation and pitch of hap1-7 (अरेवा!) (Color figure online)

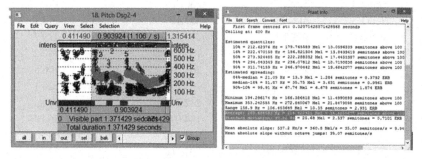

Fig. 4. Shows the standard deviation and pitch of Dsg2-4 (हेशक्यनाही)

The standard deviation and pitch of 26 Marathi speech samples are calculated and are given in the following Table 3.

Table 3. The values of standard deviation and pitch of speech

Sr. No.	Speech file name	Marathi emotional words	Mean f0 in speech/pitch of speech	Standard deviation
1	Ang1-4	गपरे	268.513	12.05
2	Ang2-4	हट!	323.595	16.62
3	Ang1-5	गपरे	211.499	30.03
4	Dsg1-5	जाऊदेरे!	263.686	37.92
5	Dsg2-4	हेशकुयनाही	214.686	37.92
6	Dsg4-4	कितीकंटाळवाणे	245.639	40.22
7	Dsg3-4	नेहमीचच!	243.819	47.21
8	Fear2-4	अरेदेवा	252.315	14.5
9	Fear4-5	कितीभयानक	169.188	14.57
10	Fear3-4	आईगं	250.864	17.2
11	Fear4-4	कितीभयानक	257.832	34.67
12	Hap3-6	मसृत!	224.802	25.73
13	Hap1-7	अरेवा!	226.156	27.91
14	Hap2-7	कितीछान	249.137	32.84
15	Hap2-8	कितीगोड!	238.178	34.79
16	Neut3-5	कायचाललय	215.551	106.4
17	Neut4-4	ठीकआहे	260.327	146
18	Neut4-5	ठीकआहे	253.12	174.1
19	Sad3-6	आईगं!	244.882	47.57
20	Sad1-5	अरेदेवा!	195.606	84.32
21	Sad3-5	आईगं!	207.011	106.5
22	Sad4-5	किती वाईट	207.271	124.1
23	Sur1-6	अबब!	232.765	61.8
24	Sur1-5	अबब!	184.072	66.74
25	Sur2-6	अरेबापरे!	331.199	68.2
26	Sur3-5	कितीवलिक्षण!	201.986	79.13

7 Result

The results are obtained for happy emotion within range between 25–35 (Hz), similarly for disgust and surprise emotion, the standard deviation is obtained within range between 37–48 (Hz), and 61–80 (Hz) respectively. Total 4 speech samples of each emotion are used and recognition accuracy is 100% for happy, disgust and surprise emotions. The recognition accuracy for sad and fear emotions is 75%. The average recognition accuracy rate of these five emotions we got i.e. 90%. These observations are given in the following Table 4:

Table 4. Feature classification by standard deviation and pitch of speech sample

Sr_No	Emotion	Marathi utterances	Range of std. deviation/pitch	Total speech samples	Correct identifier	Mismatch	Accuracy rate
1	Angry	गपरे, हट!	12–17 Hz	3	2	1	66.66%
2	**Happy**	मस्त!,अरेवा!	25–35 Hz	4	4	0	**100%**
3	**Disgust**	जाऊदेरे!, हेशक्यनाही	37–48 Hz	4	4	0	**100%**
4	**Surprise**	अबब!, अरेबापरे!	61–80 Hz	4	4	0	**100%**
5	Sad	अरेदेवा!, कतीवाईट	81–125 Hz	4	3	1	75%
6	Neutral	कायचाललय, ठीकआहे	145–177 Hz	3	2	1	66.66%
7	Fear	अरेदेवा, कतीभयानक	Pitch value 250–257 Hz	4	3	1	75%

There is overlapping the values of fear and angry, therefore the second feature i.e. pitch of the speech is considered for classification. The value of pitch ranges between 250 to 270 (Hz) for fear emotion (Fig. 5).

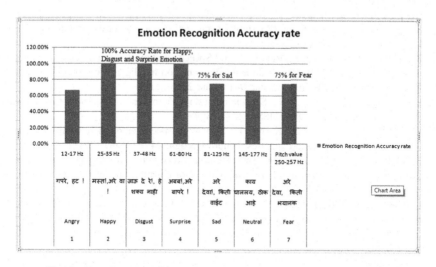

Fig. 5. Emotion recognition accuracy rate represented in graphical form

8 Conclusion

The standard deviation and pitch determination of speech utterances recorded in Marathi language gives better performance in emotion recognition of basic seven emotions.

References

1. Vaishnav, S., Mitra, S.: Speech emotion recognition: a review. Int. J. Eng. Technol. (IRJET) **03**(04) (2016)
2. Kerkeni, L., Serrestou, Y., Mbarki, M., Roof, K., Mahjoub, M.A.: Speech emotion recognition: methods and cases study. In: Proceedings of the 10th International Conference on Agents and Artificial Intelligence (ICAART 2018), vol. 2, pp. 175–182 (2018)
3. Santosh, K.C., Borra, S., Joshi, A., Dey, N.: Preface: special section: advances in speech, music and audio signal processing (articles 1–13). Int. J. Speech Technol. **22**(2), 293–294 (2019)
4. Desai, D.: Emotion recognition using speech signal: a review. Int. Res. J. Eng. Technol. (IRJET) **05**(04) (2016)
5. Kwon, O.-W., Chan, K., Hao, J., Lee, T.-W.: Emotion recognition by speech signals. In: EUROSPEECH 2003 - INTERSPEECH 2003 8th European Conference on Speech Communication and Technology Geneva, Switzerland, 1–4 September 2003 (2003)
6. Lalitha, S., Madhavan, S., Bhushan, B., Saketh, S.: Speech emotion recognition. In: International Conference on Advances in Electronics, Computers and Communications (IJAECC) (2014)
7. Sato, N., Obuchi, Y.: Emotion recognition using mel-frequency cepstral coefficients. J. Nat. Lang. Process. **2**, 835–848 (2007)
8. Zhang, Q., An, N., Wang, K., Ren, F., Li, L.: Speech emotion recognition using combination of features. In: 2013 Fourth International Conference on Intelligent Control and Information Processing (ICICIP), Beijing, China, 9–11 June 2013 (2013)
9. Ingale, A.B., Chaudhari, D.S.: Speech emotion recognition. Int. J. Soft Comput. Eng. (IJSCE) **2**(1), 235–238 (2012). ISSN 2231-2307
10. El Ayadi, M., Kamel, M.S., Karray, F.: Survey on speech emotion recognition: features, classification schemes, and databases. Pattern Recogn. **44**, 572–587 (2011)
11. Schuller, B., Rigoll, G., Lang, M.: Speech emotion recognition combining acoustic features and linguistic information in a hybrid support vector machine - belief network architecture. 0-7803-8484-©2004 IEEE
12. Mukherjee, H., Obaidullah, S.M., Santosh, K.C., Phadikar, S., Roy, K.: Line spectral frequency-based features and extreme learning machine for voice activity detection from audio signal. Int. J. Speech Technol. **21**(4), 753–760 (2018). https://doi.org/10.1007/s10772-018-9525-6
13. Gaikwad, S.K., Gawali, B.W., Yannawar, P.: A review on speech recognition technique. Int. J. Comput. Appl. **10**(3), 16–24 (2010)
14. Yannawar, P.L., Manza, G.R., Gawali, B.W., Mehrotra, S.C.: Detection of redundant frame in audio visual speech recognition using low level analysis. In: 2010 IEEE International Conference on Computational Intelligence and Computing Research, Coimbatore, pp. 1–5 (2010). https://doi.org/10.1109/ICCIC.2010.5705746

15. Gawali, B.W., et al.: Marathi isolated word recognition system using MFCC and DTW features. In: Proceedings of the International Conference on Advances in Computer Science, vol. 1 (2010)
16. Borde, P., Varpe, A., Manza, R., Yannawar, P.: Recognition of isolated words using Zernike and MFCC features for audio visual speech recognition. Int. J. Speech Technol. **18**(2), 167–175 (2014). https://doi.org/10.1007/s10772-014-9257-1
17. Bordea, P., Varpeb, A., Manzac, R., Yannawara, P.: Recognition of isolated words using Zernike and MFCC features for audio visual speech recognition (2014). arXiv preprint arXiv:1407.1165
18 Satonkar Suhas, S., Kurhe Ajay, B., Prakash Khanale, B.: Face recognition using principal component analysis and linear discriminant analysis on holistic approach in facial images database. Int. Organ. Sci. Res. **2**(12), 15–23 (2012)

Citation Classification Prediction Implying Text Features Using Natural Language Processing and Supervised Machine Learning Algorithms

Priya Porwal[(⊠)] [ID] and Manoj H. Devare[ID]

Amity University, Mumbai 410206, India
priya.porwal20@gmail.com, mhdevare@mum.amity.edu

Abstract. Citation count of any research paper published is valuable to researcher's career. Millions of research papers are available and it keeps growing fast. These published articles referred by upcoming research, but not all papers having same impact because of huge depository of research papers, only few publications reach researchers. So it will be interesting to study which articles are getting more citation, so in this paper citation count are considered as quantification parameter. To bring quality literature, it is important to analyze text in the research paper. With this motivation, this paper focuses on different technology to predict citation count considering text and structure features from research articles. For implementation purpose, title, abstract and conclusion fields are abstracted from research papers as the main content to analyze. The linguistic analysis of the corpus of research papers having high and low citation count is done using Natural Language Processing and Machine Learning. A system is implemented using supervised classification model, which takes input few features of a particular publication and gives output as it belongs to either high or low citation category after 9 to 10 years of its publication. There are few classification models considered to evolve learning process and appraise its performance using few performance measures. Experimental results on dataset shows performance accuracy of 60.67% by Random Forest model. The comprehensive experiments on dataset exhibits that proposed models outperform and achieve convincing results.

Keywords: Citation count · KNN · LDA · Logistic regression · Machine learning · Natural language processing

1 Introduction

In the present era the research creating a very high volume of publications every year. This will keep on increasing as day by day more people are involving in research for example the number of publications in 2009 almost triples than that of 10 year before [10]. For accomplishing research, referring existing literature is must but to reach all existing publications is difficult due to large volume of existing literature. Therefore, researchers cite small proportion of publications in which they find relevancy of their research area. In this circumstance few research papers attracts more readers hence

© Springer Nature Singapore Pte Ltd. 2021
K. C. Santosh and B. Gawali (Eds.): RTIP2R 2020, CCIS 1380, pp. 540–552, 2021.
https://doi.org/10.1007/978-981-16-0507-9_46

get more citation count compare to others. If citation count considered as popularity measure, it is important to analyze the text attracting the reader and making its citation count higher than others.

From this burgeoning collection of papers, it will be interesting to know which literature will get more citation over a period. There are many factors influencing the citation count of the particular article. Such as author impact factor, venue impact factor [18], author's affiliation, the author(s) background, the social media activities by the author, the Journal impact factor, number of authors [15], content (topic rank, diversity) [10], the timely importance of the issue addressed in the paper. One of the important factor which influences the citation is the quality of the text wrote by the author. The quality index of the particular published document can be calculated using text mining. The Text Mining subcategory Natural Language Processing is good at content analysis. In text mining when you are more focus on words instead of document and try to understand the meaning or structure of the text then NLP is helpful [12].

In this paper, citation count considered as measurement of impact among researchers. The literature divided into two categories one is high citation and other is low citation articles. As this paper focuses on the features taken from the text in the published paper, it is important to identify which section from research paper is meaningful to analyze. To decide on this, while selecting any paper for reading, generally before going into details of paper researcher first study the title, abstract, keywords and conclusion and then decide whether to cite the paper or not.

Considering this for experiment purpose, title, abstract and conclusion are extracted from published articles and a corpus is prepared. The complete data is preprocessed using NLP techniques and set of features are decided. This study addressed why few papers are getting more citations compare to others within same duration. To predict the citation category, there exist several challenges: The first challenge is to build a dataset, as it is not available. Secondly, to decide effective features from text to predict future citation count such as title length, number of words in abstract. Selected classification models used to predict whether the publication belongs to either high or low citation category.

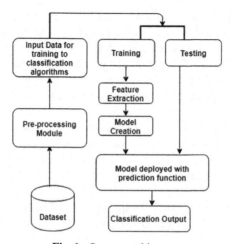

Fig. 1. System architecture

Usually the paragraphs contain some repetitive words and stop words like 'the', 'is', 'are' which are of less importance for analysis purpose. The first step is preprocessing the data, after which Random forest, Logistic regression, Decision tree, K-Nearest Neighbor (KNN) and Linear discriminant analysis (LDA) are implemented. Fig. 1. Shows the system architecture:

The organization of the Paper is as follows. The next section discusses existing literature (Sect. 2), Sect. 3 presents methodology including preprocessing steps and Predictive Models description. Section 4 details experiments performed, evaluations methodologies, and the experiments results. Final section includes conclusion and future work.

2 Related Work

First Scientists document their research output and proclaim knowledge. These published articles are referred and applied in different research domains. Therefore to analyze the scientific articles's content in terms of citing behavior is helpful to identify how knowledge is emerging. To extract the key concepts from citation context, NLP is used. It is challenging to identify correct section in citing paper and window size for proper citation context. Content-based citation analysis interprets citation values based on its context at both syntactic and semantic value [7]. Diversity in the literature is very high, nowadays large-scale research papers are available. Someway the quality is degrading day-by-day compare to papers publishing with good quality text.

The importance of citation count sometimes related to allocation of research fund and the position assignment. It is also considered for recruiting junior faculty positions and post-doctoral fellowships. In one of the research by Amin Mazloumian it is stated that h-index very well predict the future citations of published as well as future papers. From the results it is concluded that at the time of predictions the annual citations is the best predictor of future citations and shows that existing citation indices are not helpful in predicting future work. Even test with multiple citation indicators are not helpful in predicting future work. The Ambiguity problem in the name of researchers was identified [1].

Text Mining is very helpful to extract meaning from unstructured data and to analyze that data. For better result, this was the first attempt by the author to combine text mining with bibliometric and network analysis. The data source was web of science;publication period taken from 2004 to 2015. Total 20,218 publications taken. Data divided into two parts, one is base data and other is citation data. The techniques used are word segmentation, Latent dirichlet allocation (LDA) to extract features and k-means algorithm is used [2].

In academia, some decisions related to personnel or committees funding based on research by faculty, even some colleges do tenure analysis based on the research paper published by the faculty. It is observe that volume of research paper is became more important rather than the quality research paper. So those who are working on quality lagging behind in quantity.

In one of the experiments, 198,310 papers published in duration 1975–2012 in the field of Operations Research considered as database. The Data is collected from Thomson

Reuters Web of Science. The name ambiguity problem is resolved by considering either first initial with last name or first and last name for each author.The process is done in two steps: first, the author predicts the chances that two-person sharing the same first initial and last name are same persons and then used agglomerative clustering to assign each paper to an author cluster. Secondly, network analysis is performed.To predict if the scholar is performing well on some success metrics using statistical models trained on scholar's publications of the first five years of publication. Afterward to evaluate whether the statistical models can be used to improve future publication metrics. The improvements can be done by increasing total scholars in the analysis set, by considering different subject areas other than OR and for making tenure decisions [3].

One of the paper examined methods used by Altmetrics to predict research paper citation in public policy and tested the receiver operating characteristic curve (ROC) on different features. Then trained classifiers and calculate various classification metrics. At the end calculate the coefficient of determination (R^2) value to determine the relationship between feature set and citations.In future clustering methods can be checked for accuracy [4].

This paper examined that the scores of altmetric.com reliably indicates future impact. On basis of regression analysis from Nov. 2015 data and citation count from Oct. 2017 from 30 fields from altmetrics.com, it is observed that only Mendeley reader counts are reliable predictors of future citation impact [5].

Altmetrics measure the research impact in days instead of years, which shows that it is not effective tool to predict future citation count [6]. It is evident that highly influential papers have more citations but no clue exists that all high cited papers will be highly influential [8].

In Twitter sentiment analysis, sentiment classifier is able to determine positive, negative and neutral sentiments from corpus. To train sentiments, feature extraction is done includes filtering, Tokenization, Removing stop words and constructing n-grams. Best analysis result obtained by using bigram. For filtering salience and entropy are used [9].

The citations count are good measurement parameter to examine any research paper popularity. The author studied the citation count prediction to test popularity features. Several challenges exist to this study includes the paper content quality, venue impact and author expertise. The second challenge is to collectively identify interesting papers in a unified predictive model. Author used regression models to count future citations. The performance was measured for 10 years citation count prediction. The results shown, the paper quality is affected by author/venue [10].To measure productivity and impact of published research paper h-index is effective index [11].

The author focused on predicting citation count for individual publication. Some evaluation criteria existed for authors i.e. h-index. In this paper the input, learning and prediction is used. The proposed prediction model is implemented using recurrent neural network (RNN) along with long short-term memory (LSTM) by considering four parameters named as long term scientific impact quantification, the recency effect,intrinsic quality, the aging effect and the Matthew effect. The results shown that longer the duration of training set better performance of long-term prediction. Two evaluating Matrices are used i.e. Mean absolute percentage error (MAPE) and Accuracy (ACC) [13].

Wikipedia articles, which is a knowledge-sharing platform. Huge population access it, so author worked on to develop an automatic quality classier for Wikipedia articles using deep learning approach. Author proposed two methods; one is Doc2Vec to learn features from textual data and second is Deep Neural Network with four hidden layers. For six quality classes it achieved 55% accuracy [14].

The Author used binomial regression analysis. Total ten years citation windows considered. Cumulative citation and annual citation considered as dependent variable and Journal Impact Factor (JIF), statistical citedness of references, the number of authors and pages as independent variable. The impact of paper belongs to cognitive content and secondly through publication medium of paper [15]. To measure citation count for newly published paper, frequent graph pattern mining so-called citation network designed for available dataset [16]. The method introduced to predict individual citations over a particular period of time. it explored the aging effect, recent citations role by which papers are achieving or losing popularity [17].

3   Methodology

3.1   Dataset

The dataset consists of 1000 full text articles of top 1000 scientists listed on https://www.guide2research.com/scientists/. The scientists listed here having H-Index>=40 for computer science and electronics. The most publications are from IEEE, elsevier and springer. Remaining few papers taken from the dataset available at https://www.openacademic.ai/oag/. The existing datasets like dblp, Aminer, Arnetminer, MAG are observed. In these datasets the important issue to notice is incompletion or loss of data which can affects prediction results [20] and secondly it consists of metadata features like author, journal, institution etc. which is not enough to fulfill my implementation requirement. So a fresh dataset is prepared. My metadata consists of title, abstract, conclusion and citation count. The time window well-chosen 9–10 years for dataset. The Publications considered for 3 years from 2008 to 2010 year. The impact prediction observed considering papers having high citations and low citations category. To classify in the category of high and low, randomly it is considered that the citation count 1000+

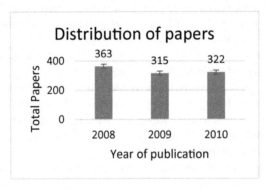

Fig. 2. Number of publications per 3 years.

as high citation papers and below 1000 as low citation papers. The total distribution of papers among given years is shown in Fig. 2.

As this research is based on the text analysis, the text features extracted from textual content from research papers. The major advantage of using text features is that these are less demanding to obtain. Considering this, length and structure features are measured from extracted text. Length features represents article size and structure features represents article organization [18].

Length Features: Length of title, No. of words in abstract, No. of words in conclusion,

Structure Features: unique words in abstract, unique words n title, unique words in conclusion, number of tables, number of references, number of diagrams and graphs and total number of pages.

3.2 Pre-processing

Data Pre-processing is very important part to be performed while implementing Machine algorithms. It helps in improving the quality of data and helps model to do better predictions. The pre-processing steps involved as below:

- Tokenization
- To lower case
- Removal of punctuation and removal of tokens that are not alphabets.
- Removing Stop words
- Stemming
- Lemmatization

The pre-processing steps have performed in pycharm software. The above steps implemented using regular expression. Python libraries used are nltk, pandas, os, numpy, argparse etc. After applying all pre-processing steps, the paragraphs converted into tokens and all noise removed. For example:

Input: Inferring friendship network structure by using mobile phone data.
Output: infer friendship network structure use mobile phone data.

Using python pandas library feature values are calculated. Hence prepared the dataset.

3.3 Predictive Models

The goal of this study is to predict where the particular paper belongs to which citation category. There are many classification algorithms exists out of which it is decided to implement few based on the dataset and results required.

Random Forest: it is a supervised learning algorithm. It can be used for both classification and Regression. It consists of many decision trees. To build individual tree, it uses bagging (bootstrap aggregation) and feature randomness to generate uncorrelated forest of trees whose prediction accuracy is more than that of individual tree [19].

Logistic Regression: it is a supervised classification algorithm. It can be binomial, multinomial or ordinal. It uses a complex cost function known as 'sigmoid function', which limits the cost function between 0 and 1. This takes one or more independent variables from dataset to determine the output and measure output with two possible outcomes [19].

Decision Tree: It uses a tree like model. Dividing efficiently based on maximum information gain is key to decision tree classifier [19]. The data split with respect to certain parameter. The tree having two entities: one is decision nodes and other is leaves. The leaves indicate outcomes and nodes indicate data split.

K-Nearest Neighbor (KNN): The KNN is used in pattern recognition and statistical estimation for classifying objects based on closest training examples in feature set [10]. KNN is a non-parametric i.e. there is no assumption for data distribution. The algorithm does not require any training data for model generation.

Linear Discriminant Analysis (LDA): LDA is dimensionality reduction technique commonly used for supervised classification problems. It is used to project the features in higher dimension space into a lower dimension space [19].

Below Fig. 3. Represents experimental setup:

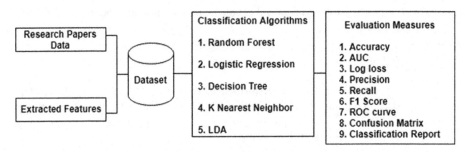

Fig. 3. Experimental setup

3.4 Evaluation Metrices

To measure Performances of ML algorithms applied in the experiments, Accuracy, confusion matrix, ROC curve (AUC), Log loss, Precision, Recall, F1 score and classification report. These are widely used in classification supervised ML algorithms. The description of all metrics are defines below.

- Classification Accuracy: Total number of correct predictions/Total predictions
- Confusion Matrix: It describes total performance of model. The x-axis represents predictions and y-axis represents accuracy. Each cell represents the number of predictions made by a ML algorithm.

- ROC (AUC): AUC gives a single number as performance measure and ROC form a graph shows performance of binary classifier.
- Log loss: In Log Loss, probability assigned to each class for all available samples. If there are N samples and M classes then Log Loss calculated as below:

$$\text{logarithmic loss} = -\frac{1}{N}\sum_{i=1}^{N}\sum_{j=1}^{M} y_{ij} * \log(p_{ij}) \tag{1}$$

Where y_{ij} = whether sample i belongs to class j or not.
P_{ij} = the probability of sample i belonging to class j.
Its range is $[0, \infty]$. The value nearer to 0 has high accuracy.

$$\text{Precision : True positive/(False positive + True positive)} \tag{2}$$

$$\text{Recall : True positive/(False negative + True positive)} \tag{3}$$

$$\text{F1score : } 2*\frac{\text{Precision} * \text{Recall}}{\text{Precision} + \text{Recall}} \tag{4}$$

Its range is $[0, 1]$. The higher the F1 score the better performance of model.

4 Results and Discussion

4.1 Evaluation Results

The proposed Models discussed in previous section are implemented and appraised on the dataset. The dataset used as training and testing in 70:30 ratios. All features examined together considering citation count as dependent feature and all other as independent features. The Table 1 shows the results of various performance metrics on given dataset. The highest accuracy is given by Random Forest as 60.67% compare to other models. RF handles classification model with numerical features very well and it handles unbalanced data sets [21]. The F1-score is high and Log loss value is less in Random forest compare to other models. So over all, Random Forest is doing better from rest of algorithms.

Table 1. Evaluation measures results of different algorithms

Performance metrices	Algorithms				
	Random forest	Logistic regression	Decision tree	KNN	LDA
Accuracy (%)	60.67	54.33	56.34	53	54
AUC	0.64	0.57	0.56	0.55	0.57
Log Loss	0.67	0.68	3.65	1.84	0.68
Precision	0.64	0.56	0.57	0.53	0.56
Recall	0.61	0.54	0.56	0.53	0.54
F1 Score	0.59	0.53	0.56	0.53	0.52

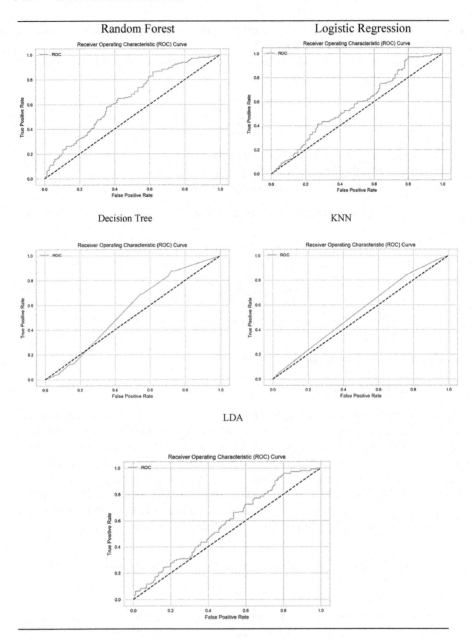

Fig. 4. ROC curves (Color figure online)

- ROC Curves

The ROC curve which lies at upper left corner of the plot will be a great model to fit to classification. While observing ROC curves in Fig. 4 of different models, the ROC of Random forest is far from blue line towards upper left shows the best result. Others are very close to blue line shows poor job separating classifier.

- **Confusion Metrics**

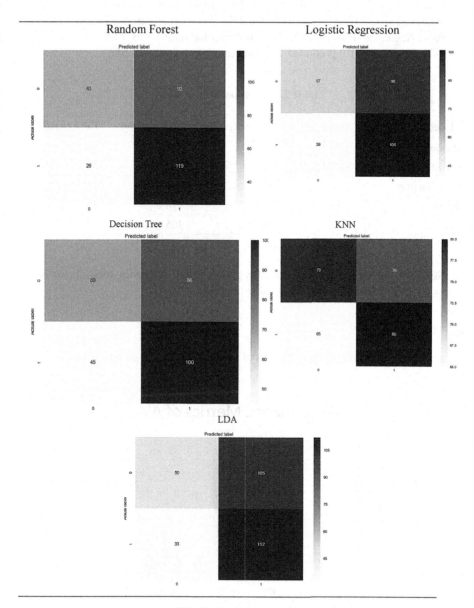

Fig. 5. Confusion matrix

Our problem is binary classification model. The Model tested on 300 samples. Confusion matrix consists of 4 terms:

True Positives (TP): predicted YES and the final output was also YES.
True Negatives (TN): predicted NO and the final output was NO.
False Negatives (FN): predicted NO and the final output was YES.
False Positives (FP): predicted YES and the final output was NO.

Table 2. Confusion matrix values

Model	True positive	True negative	False positive	False negative
Random forest	119	63	92	26
Logistic regression	106	57	98	39
Decision tree	100	69	86	45
KNN	80	79	76	65
LDA	112	50	105	33

So observing Table 2 Random forest is giving best result having total TP = 119 and TN = 63, other all models have less value than RF.

4.2 Discussion

Figure 6 shows the performance metrics of all 5 algorithms on given dataset.

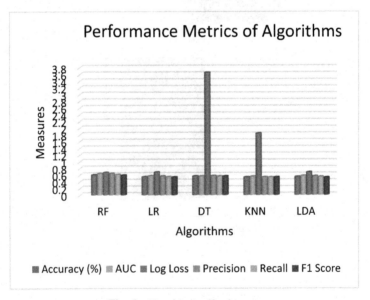

Fig. 6. Algorithms effectiveness

Figure 6 clearly indicates that DT and KNN are giving very high value for log loss, which is not acceptable. The RF is better choice than other algorithms.

5 Conclusion and Future Work

Citation count of particular research paper helps a researcher in tenure analytics. To analyze citation count of any research paper based on quality of text written in it is very important. The challenging part will be to find good quality text papers having high citation count and to define window size. This research is important as many researchers get research fund, other faces tenure analytics based on citation count. So these things related to someone's career. So genuine analysis is required. The evaluation results of different algorithms are presented. To predict the citation category, few algorithms were tested for giving effective results and it is found that Random Forest is showing the best performance for prediction on a given dataset. Still, there is a scope to predict more good results. New classification models can be tested to give improved results.

There are few challenges exists on basis of which these algorithms may be evaluated (a) scalability of dataset (b) change and increase in the feature set. In this paper, text and structure features are considered. Total 5 algorithms implemented on dataset having 10 features. In future, more features like venue impact, author impact can be explored with text features having large dataset. More advanced ML algorithms like deep learning, clustering can be used. Time series analysis can be performed. It will be interesting to try on few Regression and hybrid Models.

References

1. Mazloumian, A.: Predicting scholars' scientific impact. PloS one **7**(11), e49246 (2012)
2. Nie, B., Sun, S.: Using text mining techniques to identify research trends: a case study of design research. Appl. Sci. **7**(4), 401 (2017)
3. Bertsimas, D.: OR forum—tenure analytics: Models for predicting research impact. Oper. Res. **63**(6), 1246–1261 (2015)
4. Bailey, C.: Exploring features for predicting policy citations. In: ACM/IEEE Joint Conference on Digital libraries (JCDL), pp. 1–2 (2017)
5. Thelwall, M., Nevill, T.: Could scientists use Altmetric.com scores to predict longer term citation counts? J. Inf. **12**(1), 237–248 (2018)
6. Barnes, C.: The use of altmetrics as a tool for measuring research impact. Aust. Acad. Res. Libr. **46**(2), 121–134 (2015)
7. Ding, Y.: Content-based citation analysis: the next generation of citation analysis. J. Assoc. Inf. Sci. Technol. **65**(9), 1820–1833 (2014)
8. Zhang, G., Ding, Y., Milojevi, S.: Citation content analysis (CCA): a framework for syntactic and semantic analysis of citation content. J. Am. Soc. Inf. Sci. Technol. **64**(7), 1490–1503 (2013)
9. Pak, A., Paroubek, P.: Twitter as a corpus for sentiment analysis and opinion mining. In: LREc, vol. 10, no. 2010, pp. 13201326 (2010)
10. Yan, R., et al.: Citation count prediction: learning to estimate future citations for literature. In: Proceedings of the 20th ACM International Conference on Information and Knowledge Management, pp. 1247–1252. ACM (2011)

11. Hirsch, J.: An index to quantify an individual's scientific research output. Proc. Natl. Acad. Sci. U.S.A. **102**(46), 16569–16572 (2005)

12. Fast, A., Elder, J.F.: Text mining versus text analytics. International Institute for Analytics, August 2014

13. Yuan, S., et al.: Modeling and predicting citation count via recurrent neural network with long short-term memory. arXiv preprint arXiv:1811.02129 (2018)

14. Dang, Q.V., Ignat, C.-L.: Quality assessment of wikipedia articles: a deep learning approach by Quang Vinh Dang and Claudia-Lavinia Ignat with Martin Vesely as coordinator. ACM SIGWEB Newsl. Autumn **5** (2016).

15. Bornmann, L., Leydesdorff, L.: Does quality and content matter for citedness? A comparison with para-textual factors and over time. J. Inf. **9**(3), 419–429 (2015)

16. Pobiedina, N., Ichise, R.: Predicting citation counts for academic literature using graph pattern mining. In: Ali, Moonis, Pan, Jeng-Shyang., Chen, Shyi-Ming., Horng, Mong-Fong. (eds.) IEA/AIE 2014. LNCS (LNAI), vol. 8482, pp. 109–119. Springer, Cham (2014). https://doi.org/10.1007/978-3-319-07467-2_12

17. Xiao, S., et al.: On modeling and predicting individual paper citation count over time. In: IJCAI, pp. 2676–2682 (2016).

18. Hasan Dalip, D., et al.: Automatic quality assessment of content created collaboratively by web communities: a case study of wikipedia. In: Proceedings of the 9th ACM/IEEE-CS Joint Conference on Digital Libraries (ACM), pp. 295–304 (2009)

19. https://towardsdatascience.com. Accessed 10 Nov 2019

20. Bai, X., et al.: An overview on evaluating and predicting scholarly article impact. Information **8**(3), 73 (2017)

21. https://towardsdatascience.com/why-random-forest-is-my-favorite-machine-learning-model-b97651fa3706. Accessed 9 Dec 2019

Author Index

Printed in the United States
By Bookmasters